THE COMPLETE REPORTER

THE COMPLETE

REPORTER

Fundamentals of
News Gathering,
Writing, and Editing

SIXTH EDITION

Julian Harriss

Kelly Leiter
The University of Tennessee

Stanley Johnson

MACMILLAN PUBLISHING COMPANY
New York

Editor: David Chodoff
Production Supervisor: Linda Greenberg
Production Manager: Nick Sklitsis
Text and Cover Designer: Natasha Sylvester
Cover photograph: J. Blaustein/Woodfin Camp & Associates, Inc.
This book was set in Century Book by TCSystems, Inc.
and was printed and bound by Hamilton Printing Company.
The cover was printed by Phoenix Color Corp.

Macmillan Publishing Company
866 Third Avenue, New York, New York 10022

Macmillan Publishing Company is part of
the Maxwell Communication Group of Companies.

Library of Congress Cataloging-in-Publication Data

Harriss, Julian.
    The complete reporter: fundamentals of news gathering, writing,
and editing   /   Julian Harriss, Kelly Leiter, Stanley Johnson.—6th
ed.
        p.   cm.
    Includes bibliographical references and index.
    ISBN 0-02-350640-7 (paper)
    1. Reporters and reporting.   2. Journalism—Handbooks, manuals,
etc.   I. Leiter, Kelly.   II. Johnson, Stanley P., 1892–1946.
III. Title
PN4781.H34   1992   91-18553
070.4′3—dc20   CIP

Printing: 3 4 5 6 7   Year: 3 4 5 6 7 8

Dedicated to
JULIAN HARRISS
1914–1989

A quiet, gentle man whose intellect
and immense writing talents could never
be hidden behind his shy demeanor.

PREFACE

The sixth edition of *The Complete Reporter* contains much that is new. But it has preserved the basic concept and organization that has served students and teachers well in the first five editions.

All chapters have been rewritten to reflect changes in the newspaper profession. In addition, the chapters have been edited to strengthen them. Many new examples and illustrations are included to help students visualize the principles discussed.

The exercises in all chapters are largely new. They are taken from daily and weekly newspapers and were carefully selected to give students experience writing the kinds of stories they will have to handle when they become professional journalists. The exercises are practical and their range is broad. Many of them can be used as feature or human-interest stories as well as straight news stories.

As in all earlier editions, the exercises are written in incomplete sentences to resemble a reporter's notes. This gives the student examples of note taking and practice in composing complete sentences from brief notes. The exercises are designed to challenge the student's ability to think carefully before writing. They often include examples of libelous and unethical statements as well as trivia to help the instructor make the point that careful reporters should avoid using such material in their stories.

Many of the suggestions offered by teachers who have used the textbook over the years have been incorporated into this edition. All the features of previous editions that have been so effective as teaching tools have, of course, been retained.

The Complete Reporter is a practical, basic textbook designed to teach students how to gather, write and edit news stories. Its broad scope makes it an excellent text for beginning and advanced reporting classes.

Acknowledgments

Dozens of editors and reporters have generously provided help with this edition. I am indebted to them as I am to the teaching colleagues and students whose valuable suggestions I have incorporated into the text. I also owe a debt of gratitude to the late Bill Golliher and Andrew R. Pizarek who have given me their unstinting support and encouragement. Thank you all.

K.L.

CONTENTS

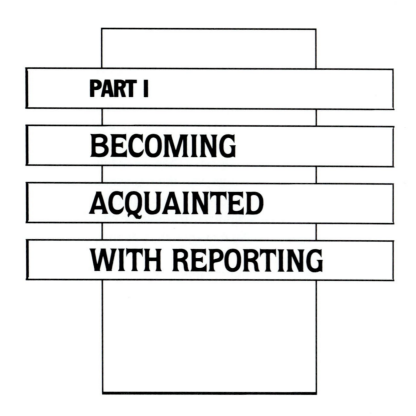

PART I

BECOMING

ACQUAINTED

WITH REPORTING

Journalists today are faced with a greater challenge than any they have faced in history. Change has invaded the newsroom just as it has society. Perhaps the biggest change of all for newspapers is that writing and editing for a "typical reader" have become obsolete.

Newspapers now have to try to reach a vastly segmented and rapidly changing audience that has a wide choice of alternative sources of news, information and entertainment. The growing role of women as a consumer group as well as their changing role in the workplace, the rise of single-family households and the mobility of the American family are just a few changes that are challenging editors and reporters to produce newspapers relevant to the needs and demands of readers.

In addition to demographic changes, declining newspaper readership among younger adults, rising television viewing, high occasional readership and low scores on satisfaction with the news media in general have caused the nation's editors to seek innovative ways to hold on to their customers while adding new and younger subscribers.

For a reporter, this means not only knowing the demographics of the newspaper's readers as well as its circulation area, but also understanding the changing patterns of consumer behavior. Today's reporter has to have a far broader perspective than ever before. No longer can a reporter simply tell the reader, "Here's what happened." Readers want to know "What does this mean to me?" and "What, if anything, can I do about it?" They want news that is useful to them.

The Orange County Register, Santa Ana, California, assigned a full-time reporter to cover shopping malls. A story on how to find rest rooms in a mall got tremendous response, N. Christian Anderson, editor and vice president, told Editor & Publisher. It is one example of "news you can use," which, studies show, has great appeal to readers.

There is far more to being a reporter than knowing how to write a basic story. News does not exist in a vacuum, and the reporter shouldn't either. Every reporter should learn as much about the complete operation of the newspaper as possible. It is also important for a reporter to know the characteristics of journalism as practiced today and to be flexible enough to change as the profession and society change.

A reporter needs to understand the unique role of a newspaper in society. It is basically a business, but it is a very special business. After all, the press is the only private business singled out in the Bill of Rights. The First Amendment to the Constitution thrusts a tremendous responsibility on journalists. The true professional will always be aware of that.

WHAT IS NEWS?

There are almost as many answers to that question as there are editors and reporters. In fact, no uniformly satisfactory definition has been found. The question will be thoroughly explored in Chapter 3. However, it is a given in most city rooms that news is what the editor says it is.

While there may be no definitive definition of news, there is a body of knowledge dealing with writing and presenting news that every reporter should master. To be effective, a reporter simply has to understand the theories and concepts of how news is gathered and written as well as the particular role a newspaper plays in a community.

DEVELOPING NEWS STYLE

News writing follows all the accepted rules of English grammar, sentence structure, spelling and punctuation. Yet it differs in many ways from other forms of writing. It strives for certain qualities of style: simplicity, conciseness, vividness, directness, clarity, brevity and accuracy. News style is discussed in Chapter 4.

RESPONSIBILITIES AND RESTRICTIONS

A reporter's first obligation is to tell a story as accurately, clearly and fairly as possible. However, this task is not always as easy as it may sound. A variety of restrictions can make writing a news story difficult. Some may be the reporter's own, based on how thoroughly he or she has gathered the information needed to make the story complete. Some restrictions may result from a particular newspaper policy. And still others are imposed by the laws regarding libel and invasion of privacy. It should be noted that while legal restrictions are somewhat limited, violation of them could cost a reporter a fine or a term in prison.

Most restrictions, however, come under the voluntary classification, recognized in journalism as codes of ethics that are observed for the welfare of both the press and society. (See Chapter 5.)

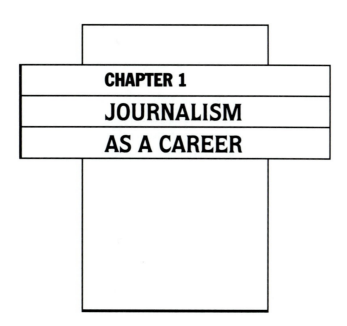

CHAPTER 1
JOURNALISM
AS A CAREER

Once, when Robert Casey, a legendary Chicago newsman, was introduced to a woman at a social event, she expressed her delight at meeting a newspaper reporter and added, "You must meet the most interesting people."

"Yes, I do," Casey is said to have replied. "And they all are newspaper people."

Casey, who was a star reporter for The Daily News during the rough and tumble days of Chicago journalism, may have been overstating the case slightly. But it is true that the nation's newsrooms today, as in the 1920s when Casey was reporting, often are populated with bright, talented and interesting young men and women who say they are attracted to journalism because it gives them an opportunity to write and because they find journalism exciting and challenging.

The authors of the report on human resources by the American Society of Newspaper Editors (ASNE), "The Changing Face of the Newsroom," wrote in 1989:

> There are probably more talented, engaging and creative workers per square foot in the newspaper newsroom than in most other companies or fields of work. Each day starts and ends with a fresh product, generally accompanied by a good deal of hooting and hollering and fast-paced decision making. Challenging, exhilarating and an interesting mix of co-workers are almost guaranteed. Unlike some businesses or fields, the newsroom rocket goes off every day, giving editors, reporters and photographers an exciting edge in worker motivation.

The ASNE report, based on 1,200 valid responses to 1,345 questionnaires, showed that most reporters and editors love their work, if not their bosses. Eighty-one percent of those surveyed said they like their present jobs better than previous positions they had held. Three out of four said their present jobs meet or exceed expectations.

Today, some reporters, especially those on major television stations and networks, may become more famous than many of the men and women they cover. But most never become quite so famous, nor can they command million-dollar salaries, as some television journalists do. Yet they play important roles in their communities and enjoy exciting and rewarding careers.

There is far more hard work than glamor and glory involved in being a journalist. Even those who gain some measure of fame and fortune do so because they are talented and work hard. There is no escaping it—the journalist's work often is so routine and exacting that it is boring. But it is this very routine, boring—and extremely vital—groundwork that often leads to interesting and exciting news breaks that can turn a journalist into a public personality.

In their daily work, most American journalists write more news stories about city council meetings than they do about the rich and famous. They spend more time reporting activities of the police and fire departments and local schools than they do writing about sensational scandals in high office. And if they do their work with care and accuracy, they perform a far more vital function daily for their readers and their communities than the reporter who does major investigations or who writes only about the stars of stage, screen and television.

In a democracy, information is vital, and in the information explosion that has marked the last half of the twentieth century, the role of the journalist is not only to report this information but also to analyze and interpret it for the public. Through the journalist and the mass media, most Americans gain most of the information that has an impact on their daily lives. That makes the journalist a vital cog in the democratic system.

A WRITER ON CURRENT EVENTS

Journalists are writers who deal chiefly in current events. As contrasted with some other types of writers who employ imagination in their quest for reader appeal, reporters must deal with facts. Their chief role is to record what has happened and sometimes to analyze or interpret what has happened or will happen. Occasionally reporters give their own opinions on events they have reported, but opinion traditionally is not included in news stories. Opinions are expressed on the editorial pages.

Vitality and drive are important assets for journalists, but even more important are the passion for facts and the ability to write well. The two distinctive functions of journalists are gathering facts—more information than can be used—and composing accurate and interesting stories with that information.

The term "journalist" as used above is interchangeable with "newspaper reporter," for reporting the news is fundamental to virtually all journalistic occupations. Although television has challenged newspapers as a principle channel through which news is widely disseminated (studies show that the public turns to it for national and international news), newspapers still are the major source of local news for most persons. With few exceptions, most television stations provide little more than a headline summary of local news. This is particularly true in the non-metropolitan areas. The typewritten script of most television news shows would fill less than three-fourths of a single page of standard-sized newspaper.

And, despite the rapidly increasing technology in the field of electronic communications, data banks and other information storage systems, newspapers remain the chief permanent record of current events. This does not imply, however, that careers in journalism are largely limited to reporting and editing. Many journalism school graduates find successful and fulfilling careers in newspaper design and production as well as various business functions in the advertising and circulation departments of newspapers. Other communications media offer as many or more journalistic opportunities. But, historically, newspaper reporting is the grandfather of all modern journalistic careers.

REPORTING, DOORWAY TO MANY VOCATIONS

Experience as a newspaper reporter often is the foundation for a variety of other careers. A hurried check of the backgrounds of public persons both living and dead will produce an impressive list of former newspaper reporters who became mayors, governors, representatives and senators, ambassadors, actors, corporation presidents, college professors, and even a U.S. president and a president's wife.

The history of American literature, for example, is laced with names of authors who were former newspaper reporters—Walt Whitman and Ernest Hemingway among them. In its long and illustrious life, The Chicago Daily News was the training ground for poets, playwrights, humorists, biographers, novelists, screenwriters, critics and historians. The list of former news reporters includes Carl Sandburg, poet and Lincoln's biographer; Ben Hecht, novelist, playwright and screenwriter; and Meyer Levin, novelist.

And some of the most widely read popular authors of the past several decades, such as Tom Wolfe, author of "The Right Stuff" and other books, began their careers as newspaper reporters.

Intangible Benefits

The common reward for all newspaper men and women is being where the action is. They have a front seat at most public events. They are ex officio members of public organizations and committees. Even beginning reporters carry with them the influence of the newspaper, and doors are opened that often remain closed to persons in other professions. Reporters observe events in the making, and in the words of Philip Graham, late editor of The Washington Post, they write "the first rough draft of history." Especially for a beginner, this can be a heady ego trip. In fact, some reporters never get over it.

But exposure to the reality of a reporter's life tends to bring the truly dedicated person back down to earth. Practical experience ripens a reporter's character as perhaps no other schooling can. Reporters soon learn that not everyone loves newspapers and that people—often those in high places—will try to use newspapers for their own gain. They also learn quickly that not everyone is cooperative, and some are hostile, if not violent, when reporters arrive. Nevertheless, the conscientious reporter never stops growing as a reporter, a writer and a judge of others. And through it all, the serious reporter will develop and maintain a sense of personal and professional integrity.

The movie and novel stereotype of the reporter who takes periodic breaks from the party circuit to turn the scoundrels out of office and to rescue and uplift the downtrodden is more fiction than fact. To be sure, some reporters lack manners, morals and integrity. Some, in fact, abuse their rights and privileges. Others succumb to the temptations thrown into their paths. But most reporters, like other professionals with jobs to do, develop a code of conduct and personal integrity in keeping with the responsible positions they hold in the community.

Opportunities on Newspapers

The future of most reporters is limited only by their talents and their ambition. A talented, self-disciplined ambitious reporter can become a "big name" news writer whose by-line is readily recognized and respected or a columnist or commentator who analyzes current events. News writing opportunities are available on thousands of daily and weekly newspapers or with the wire services (The Associated Press (AP) and United Press International (UPI)), syndicated newspaper services, news magazines and a variety of other organizations dealing in news.

Another newspaper career open to the reporter is the field of editing. In general, editors supervise the news-gathering activities of reporters, review and copyread their stories, write headlines and plan the design of the pages using their stories and pictures. These responsibilities generally do not include gathering and writing news, but some persons carrying the title of editor may have fewer or more duties than those mentioned here.

The science editor, sports editor, education editor and other staff members with similar titles are generally by-lined reporters who specialize in one area of journalism, but some of these editors may also edit copy and write headlines. The editor of a small daily or weekly newspaper usually combines news writing and editing and sometimes is responsible for business management as well. The duties of the principal editor (editor in chief) of a metropolitan daily may be limited to writing editorials, supervising the entire staff and making policy decisions.

The editor is sometimes (but not necessarily) the owner or part owner of the newspaper, and as such he or she is the publisher—another newspaper opportunity open to reporters. The publisher is the chief officer of the newspaper, responsible for its entire operation—editorial, business and mechanical. To be successful as a publisher, one obviously needs management ability in addition to a knowledge of printing processes and a capital investment to purchase or lease either an existing newspaper or the plant and equipment needed to start one. Ayer's Directory of Publications and the Editor & Publisher Yearbook list more than 10,000 weekly, semiweekly, small and medium-sized dailies and large metropolitan daily newspapers in the United States. Publications serving the newspaper industry frequently have a number of smaller newspapers listed in the "For Sale" columns. Often they may be bought on the installment plan with a reasonable down payment and the balance in periodic payments.

Opportunities in Other Fields

Although the editorial departments of newspapers do not like to be considered as training grounds for other professions, the truth is that some reporters leave after several years of experience to take positions in a variety of other fields. Reporting is an invaluable introduction to life at many points. Because reporters go everywhere and meet hundreds of people, they can make excellent contacts and learn of other opportunities that might be available to them. Often the skills developed in gathering facts, interviewing people and writing news will increase a reporter's chances for success. The worlds of business and public service are well populated with men and women who got their start on newspapers.

But by far most of the reporters leaving newspaper work find employment in related journalistic areas—press associations; general circulation magazines; trade journals and industrial publications; radio and television stations; publicity and public relations agencies; and publications of business firms, industries, institutions and associations. Advertising is another large field that frequently absorbs individuals with newspaper experience, for journalistic techniques are applied in its various communications efforts.

Finally, the newspaper is a splendid training ground for creative writers. Many successful authors and playwrights of yesterday and today acquired their basic training as newspaper writers. The list is long, but a few excellent examples are Ernest Hemingway and Charles MacArthur, and more recently Bruce Catton, Tom Wicker, David Halberstam and Gay Talese. The varied experience and constant practice in the careful and precise use of the English language provide an excellent basis for literary achievement.

QUALIFICATIONS OF A REPORTER

What makes a good reporter? There probably are as many answers to that question as there are reporters, for few agree completely on what makes a good reporter. However, most do acknowledge that, although some persons are better fitted than others to become reporters, it is not true that reporters are born and not made. Given reasonable intelligence, most of the attributes of a successful reporter are acquired, not inherited. Perhaps the best qualifications for a reporter—aside from desire and ability to write for print—are insatiable curiosity (which surely will express itself in part through a strong habit of reading), a flexible and social personality, a nature that relishes a variety of experiences, a temperament to work under the pressure of deadlines and a tolerance permitting objective observations of people and events. A successful reporter also needs ambition, drive, determination and, most certainly, self-discipline.

Richard J. Cattani, editor of The Christian Science Monitor, listed the attributes needed by professional journalists as self-operating, productive, caring, exemplary, versatile, authoritative, expansive, supportive, visionary, sensitive, considerate, confident, distinctive, intuitive, teachable, selfless, responsible, active, paced and, finally, impelled: "If you don't wake up writing, try a different trade."

Attributes Needed for Success in Reporting

A broad knowledge of the English language and the ability to use words with style and grace are the essential tools of a good reporter. Journalism is not a logical career choice for anyone who does not enjoy writing.

In a career guide published by The Newspaper Fund, Paul McKalip, editor of the Tucson (Ariz.) Citizen, said the following is what he looks for in an applicant for a reporting position: "Intelligence, wide range of interests, ambition to advance, skills, thoroughness, accuracy, ability to meet deadlines, excellence in spelling and grammar."

Other editors added such attributes as "insatiably curious," "patient but persistent," and "the ability to write a clear, carefully constructed sentence." These attributes may seem unrealistic in a profession not known for its unusually high salaries. Nevertheless, they are the qualities and abilities that editors of good newspapers expect. Without them, the staff would produce a dull, routine, lackluster newspaper.

Anyone seeking a career in journalism should be aware that although much of a reporter's work is routine, it is essential never to fall into the trap of treating a story routinely. Each story, whether it is about a local rose festival or an interview with the president, should be the best possible story the reporter can write at that time. There really are no dull stories, only unimaginative, lazy reporters.

Most of the routine a reporter faces is part of a daily kaleidoscope of events. Assignments may change rapidly from the commonplace to the exciting. A reporter must be alert and fast-thinking to move smoothly from one assignment to another when stories vary greatly in news value.

Reporters work under a great deal of pressure much of the time. They constantly race against the clock to meet deadlines, so another important attribute is the ability to work calmly under pressure.

Perhaps the most difficult challenge facing every reporter is the ability to separate personal beliefs and biases from what is being written. A good reporter simply must take a position as an unbiased witness in reporting the news and accurately interpreting the facts.

Educational Needs of a Reporter

Although educational training for journalists dates back to the turn of the century, college-educated journalists were not common on most newspapers until well into the 1930s. Today it is often difficult to obtain a position on a newspaper without a college degree and, in many cases, a degree in journalism. Accredited colleges and schools of journalism require students to get a broad liberal arts education with a concentration of journalism courses. Because of the vast amount of knowledge needed by a journalist, students in accredited journalism programs take only one-fourth of their work in specific journalism courses; the other three-fourths of their college work is in the arts, sciences and humanities. Those students who hope to specialize in a particular area—politics, science, foreign relations, home economics, agriculture and other fields—are encouraged to bolster their education with additional courses in these specialized areas.

Journalism students generally are required to take courses in English composition and literature, history, political science, economics, psychology, one or more of the natural sciences and one or more foreign languages. A foreign language—Spanish, for example—would be a tremendous asset to a reporter working in an area where there is a large Latin American population, such as southern Florida, the southwestern states or southern California. A course in public speaking often is required. It can prove helpful when covering a speech or when asked to give one, as many reporters and editors are asked to do.

The ability to type with speed and accuracy is absolutely essential. Even the smallest newspapers are now converting their newsrooms to electronic, computerized operations. Reporters must use electric typewriters or compose their stories on the keyboard of a video-display terminal (VDT). In fact, technology is advancing so rapidly that many newspapers are already installing newer, more highly developed automatic systems that require even greater typing skills.

Education is tremendously important for a reporter. However, some persons without a college education have become successful as reporters. Many newspapers in the past have employed high school graduates and "brought them up" in the editorial department. A few still do. But most employers are aware that, in comparison with high school graduates, college-trained reporters generally have a greater capacity for success and thus are worth considerably more to the newspaper.

A college-trained reporter brings to the job not only knowledge of history, psychology, political science and the like but also the ability to use that knowledge to help interpret the events of the day, to put them in their proper perspective so the reader can understand them. Journalism courses are designed to show how to use the knowledge obtained in other courses for the benefit of the readers.

Advantages of Journalistic Training

Journalistic training is another phase of college education that at first was ridiculed by some newspaper editors (and still is by a few) but is today widely recognized as valuable for the beginning reporter. Many editors, because they were not college graduates, argued that the best education for a reporter was practical experience in the newsroom.

In more recent years the same editors admitted, somewhat reluctantly, that while the newsroom is good experience, it is also limiting. They discovered that college training in journalism not only affords a shortcut to learning the basic journalistic techniques and skills but also gives the beginning reporter a broader understanding of his or her work. In short, city editors and other staff supervisors have not been as successful in teaching journalistic fundamentals with the trial-and-error method as have instructors using formal classroom procedures. Hour for hour, the student in the classroom learns those fundamentals in less than one-third the time spent by the beginning reporter taught by the trial-and-error process.

A CRAFT OR A PROFESSION?

The 1980s have been labeled "The Information Decade." Never before has so much information been available in so short a time. And never before has so much attention been focused on the men and women who deliver that information.

Many journalists have become glamor figures or immediate public personalities, especially those reporting from Washington, D.C. In fact, in the view of several social critics, journalists have become part of a new society dubbed "mediacracy," described as a public aristocracy of people important in the media and people who gain power through the media.

Enrollments in journalism schools continue to rise. Some say it is because of the glamor surrounding the profession as a result of the Watergate scandals in the administration of President Richard M. Nixon. Others insist the increase is caused by the lure of fame and fortune offered by journalism, especially to those who become network television anchors. Still others say young men and women, aware of the declining popularity of the traditional liberal arts degree, are simply seeking an education that will make them more hirable.

But as Watergate faded into the past, enrollments continued to increase. By the mid-1980s enrollments were near the 70,000 mark (this includes all programs—journalism, broadcasting, advertising and public relations). Now some journalists and educators are suggesting that enrollments be limited and that more rigid entrance requirements be established.

All this debate has done little to settle the long-standing dispute: Is journalism a craft or a profession? Despite the advancements in education and training and the sophistication in reporting and writing techniques, some insist that news writers and commentators have no right to place themselves among the professionals with such time-honored groups as lawyers, physicians, teachers, ministers and engineers.

The Press and Society

The press, including the spoken and the written words of journalists, is an important institution in modern society. It is recognized as the principal medium of mass communication and has become increasingly important because scientific and technological advancements make it more essential than ever to keep people informed of day-to-day developments. The task of sorting this information and presenting it to the public in a clear, coherent manner has placed an increased burden on the press. Most news professionals realize this, just as they are aware that without an independent and often aggressive press, a democracy such as ours might not survive.

Particularly in a democracy, the role of the press is of vital importance, as the events surrounding the Watergate scandals attest. The success of a democratic government depends on the wise decisions of an informed citizenry, for a democracy is ruled by people at the polls. Therefore, the press must be utilized to give the people the information they should have in casting votes on candidates and issues. In this respect the press is a great educational institution. Its responsibilities in informing the public fairly, accurately and objectively in all matters of public concern are paramount. A responsible newspaper must remove itself from partisan politics in its news columns.

The press as an institution serving the people of a democracy was identified when journalists were designated as the "Fourth Estate." This unofficial title was given to members of the press near the turn of the nineteenth century by the British Parliament in recognition of the fact that the press represents the people and has strong influence on public opinion. The other three recognized "estates" or classes representing the British people were the clergy, the nobility and the commons. The "Fourth Estate" title is just as applicable today as it was then, for as government grows larger and more complex by the day, it is not humanly possible for a single individual to understand even a small amount of what it does without the aid of the mass media as sources of information and interpretation.

Just as it is used to enlighten the people, the press, under the thumb of dictatorial control, can be used to enslave a nation. The media of mass communications can be employed to disseminate either truths or falsehoods. Hitler, like other dictators before and after him, gave the world a tragic lesson on a controlled press. The efforts of several presidential administrations in the past 30 years to control or intimidate the American press (such as the Nixon administration's efforts to prevent the publication of the Pentagon Papers and the Reagan administration's ban on journalists going ashore with the troops during the invasion of Grenada) demonstrate just how fragile the constitutional guarantee of freedom of the press really is. Fortunately, the press has successfully resisted most overt attempts at control with the aid of some enlightened public officials. Yet this is a battle the press must continue to fight.

Equally important for the press in a free society is its relationship with the people, because they keep the press in business. Readers and subscribers are the life blood of the press. As a member of a free enterprise system open to anyone who cares to venture into competition, a newspaper must maintain the confidence and respect of its readers or its competitors will take over.

The press can be described as a quasipublic agency. It has the responsibility of keeping the public informed, and it is given freedom to do so by the U.S. Constitution. But because the press operates under the private enterprise system, it is divorced from governmental control and its economic fate is placed directly into the hands of the people.

Journalism and the Professions

Although the press is accorded a special place in a democratic society, whether this warrants professional status for journalists can still be debated. Many of the attributes of journalists give them strong claim to this distinction. Compared to members of the accepted professions, journalists also have great responsibilities of public service that demand respect. Journalists are to a large degree educators. They influence public opinion, which, in turn, can influence the enactment or repeal of laws. They serve as guardians of the public by constantly monitoring and reporting on the actions of public officials and bodies. They have the power to bring credit or discredit to the names and reputations of everyone they write about. What other occupation provides so many important public services and carries so many responsibilities?

Yet journalism is unlike other professions in that it is not—and should never be—a licensed profession. Physicians, lawyers, teachers and others must be licensed (or certified) to practice, and to obtain a license they must complete specific educational programs and in some cases must pass examinations. Further, some of these professional people can lose their licenses if they are found guilty of unethical practices. Such requirements are designed to help maintain standards and to protect the public from damage that could be done by unqualified persons in the professions. (In reality, the licensing and examination system is far from perfect, and the enforcement of standards is highly erratic, resulting often in totally irresponsible delays in the revocation of licenses.)

Licensing journalists, however, would be a form of governmental control of the press. Through license laws, a dictatorial or spiteful government, by handpicking those who issue the licenses or those who are licensed to write for newspapers and other media, could nullify the constitutional guarantee of a free press. (Some members of the broadcasting industry charge that licensing radio and television stations, which has led to efforts to control content, is indeed a violation of the U.S. Constitution.)

Professional status for journalism cannot be attained by imposing high standards through license laws, but it can be achieved through voluntary efforts of journalists. Although no law should require beginning journalists to have a college education, this is a prerequisite that more and more employers are finding much to their advantage. Although no law can require that journalists abide by a professional code of ethics, journalists themselves, through organizations such as the Society of Professional Journalists (formerly Sigma Delta Chi), and the American Society of Newspaper Editors (ASNE), have established voluntary codes. Although journalists with a genuine respect for their responsibilities generally accept those voluntary standards, there are and will continue to be men and women in journalism who violate them for personal gain, without any feeling of guilt or fear of prosecution.

As a result of criticism leveled at the press from both inside and out, during the period of the war in Vietnam in particular, a number of watchdog publications came into being. They repeatedly called into question the actions and policies of individual newspapers, publishers, and the entire mass communications industry. Among the more notable of these were Columbia Journalism Review, the Chicago Journalism Review, More and the St. Louis Journalism Review. There have been several other journalism reviews as well, and occasionally a new one will appear. However, most of them have ceased publication, and the Columbia Journalism Review continues as the chief and most vigorous source of criticism of the media. Several national publications—The Atlantic, Harper's, and The Wall Street Journal—report regularly and often critically on the media. And there is an increasing number of books critical of the media published each year by journalists as well as others.

It was during this period of turmoil, also, that a number of press councils were established in several cities and states, and the National Press Council was created by the Twentieth Century Fund in the early 1970s. The councils generally investigate complaints against the media but at the same time work to defend freedom of the press. The councils have not had the overwhelming support of some of the nation's newspapers or the broadcasting industry, and most of them have ceased to function. The National Press Council ceased operation in 1984.

Several so-called independent organizations were founded to serve as watchdogs for the media. The most active has been Accuracy in Media (AIM). In addition, some newspapers have named ombudsmen—in-house critics—to review and critique the performance of the newspaper staff. The Louisville Courier-Journal and The Washington Post have used this technique for a number of years. In addition to reporting, as it were, their views to the senior editors, they often write a column critical of the way in which a particular story or issue was handled. This in-house-critic idea has been praised by many outside the profession but is generally not popular among newspaper staffs.

Even with these watchdogs, the press has its unethical journalists just as medicine still has its quacks, law its shysters and education its tenure-protected, inept teachers. Those who faithfully serve the profession of journalism, like those serving other professions, can only hope that the unethical encroachment on their privileged profession can be kept at a minimum and prosecuted as far as possible through regular legal channels.

EXERCISES

1. Invite the editor of the local newspaper and the news director of the leading radio or television station in the area to class to discuss journalism careers. Each member of the class should prepare a list of at least 10 questions to ask, such as "What attributes do you look for when interviewing an applicant for a position as a reporter?" Write a report on the class discussion.

2. Invite a local by-lined reporter or newspaper columnist to class to be interviewed about her or his career as a journalist. Write a brief report of the discussion.

3. Interview at least 10 persons in your community (not your fellow students) and ask them their views of the quality of the press in your community. Write a brief paper on the results of your interviews.

4. The press is the subject of constant review and criticism in a variety of national magazines and specialized publications such as Columbia Journalism Review and the Washington Journalism Review. Study those reviews and such other publications as The Atlantic, Harper's, The Wall Street Journal and the press sections of the national news weeklies. Write a report on the articles you find in them in which the press is criticized.

5. Interview the editors of your campus newspaper, yearbook and literary magazine about the restrictions, if any, that have been placed on them by university officials. Using those interviews and material collected from articles in journalism reviews in your library, write a report comparing press freedom on your campus to the national trends in student press freedom.

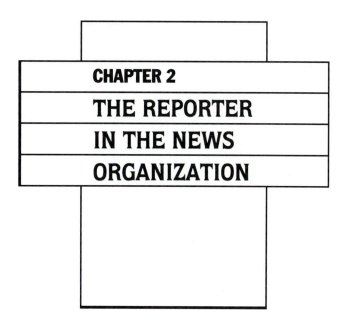

CHAPTER 2
THE REPORTER
IN THE NEWS
ORGANIZATION

Everyone who works for a newspaper is there to make it possible for a reporter's stories to get into print and be delivered to the readers.

Although reporters play a key role in any news organization, their stories would never be printed and seen by readers without the important work of dozens—often hundreds—of men and women in the other departments of the newspaper.

Most of the public's attention is focused on reporters chiefly because they are the "point" men and women of the news business. More people know reporters by name or reputation than they do press operators. Yet both are essential to a newspaper.

A newspaper's reputation often is based on the public's perception of its reporters. They usually are blamed by the public for all the perceived sins of the press simply because they are the most visible members of the staff.

Despite the prominent role of the reporter, increasing attention has been given in recent years to the dramatic advances in the technology of printing and the speed with which news can be delivered to the public. At times, in the trade press in particular, it has appeared that the technology of the industry was more important than the human beings involved in the news process.

Like printing technology, however, the American reporter is better than ever. At the same time, reporters cannot afford to be arrogant about their importance, because without the important work performed by all the others in the organization, business and technical as well as editorial personnel, their work would be useless. Each of the three major departments of a typical newspaper plays a significant role in the delivery of news to readers.

Editorial Department. The function of the newspaper's editorial department is to gather news from various sources and to write it into readable, interesting stories, edit them and plan how they will be displayed on the printed plates. Other functions of the editorial department are to instruct or influence the public through editorials, commentary and analysis, as well as to entertain the public through its by-lined columns, comics and other features. All the editorial content of the newspaper is processed by the editorial department.

Mechanical Department.   The complicated and highly technical process of transforming the reporter's stories into type and reproducing them on thousands of pages of newsprint is done by the mechanical department, which includes the composing room and the pressroom. In the past decade the printing process has become highly computerized.

Business Department.   To finance the two other departments, advertising space must be sold, subscriptions must be solicited and the finished product must be delivered to the readers. To handle these important duties, most newspapers have separate advertising and circulation departments under the business department.

A third division handles problems of management, personnel and business administration at many newspapers. Advertising, circulation and management may be combined into one unit at small newspapers. But at larger ones, they generally operate as separate units and report to a business or general manager.

DETAILS OF ORGANIZATION

The organization of a newspaper will vary considerably, depending on its size. Metropolitan newspapers frequently have highly developed organization charts similar to that in Figure 2–1. At smaller newspapers some of the duties of various departments may overlap. And in rare cases, there may be no formal organization chart at all; everyone does what has to be done to get the paper out.

All papers have a publisher. The title often is assumed by the owner or the majority stockholder in the corporation or it can be given to someone hired to serve in that position. The latter is particularly true at newspapers owned by both large and small chains. The men and women hired as publishers may have no direct ownership in the publication, although some companies do offer opportunities to buy stock in the firm.

The degree of involvement by the publisher in the daily operation of the newspaper varies greatly. On smaller newspapers a publisher may also be the editor and general manager. On larger newspapers he or she may serve as the chief executive officer of the company and delegate authority for daily operation to a general manager.

Although a publisher technically has the power to dictate all policies, editorial as well as business, it usually does not work that way. Policies are generally worked out among the publisher—or owners, if the publisher is hired—the editors and often members of the business staff. The publisher is ultimately, and legally, responsible for everything that appears in the newspaper.

On smaller dailies and weeklies, the publisher may be the owner, editor and even one of the reporters. Nancy Petrey, co-publisher of The Newport Plain Talk,

Sample Newspaper Organization

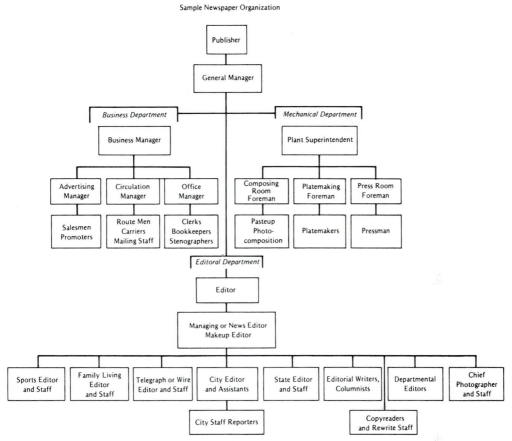

FIGURE 2–1. This chart shows the organization of the three major departments of a typical daily newspaper.

Newport, Tennessee, the largest non-daily in the state, sells advertisements, takes photographs, writes stories, sells subscriptions and delivers her prize-winning newspaper. She has been known to put on a pair of coveralls and crawl up on the press when a mechanical problem develops.

The business manager generally has authority over advertising, circulation and the office manager, if the newspaper is large enough to need an office manager. In many instances the business manager also fills that position. In that type of organization, the advertising and circulation managers report to the business manager, who then reports to the general manager or publisher. On smaller newspapers it is not uncommon for the publisher also to act as the business manager and an advertising sales representative.

In the past two decades, the process of getting a story into print has changed dramatically. The Age of the Computer is in full flower at newspapers all over the nation. Reporters write their stories on a video-display terminal (VDT). Copy editors use VDTs to edit stories and write headlines. Graphic artists use personal computers, often the Apple Macintosh®, for designs, charts, graphs and maps and at some papers to design the pages.

Computers drive the photocomposition machines that produce the finished stories and headlines on smooth, flexible photographic paper that is glued to page-forms and photographed. The image from those negatives is burned onto thin sensitized plates that are then attached to the press. The image is produced on newsprint by the offset method. In that process the ink adheres only to the image that has been burned onto the plate; it is then imposed on a rubber roller on the press that transfers the image to the newsprint. The result is generally a much sharper, cleaner-appearing newspaper. The most modern newspaper presses are computer driven.

Major benefits of computerization have been increased speed and the reduction of personnel, particularly in the composition and printing operations. However, there is still considerable debate in newsrooms over whether the end product is as good. A number worry that the editing is not as carefully done, although a number of studies show that there is little or no difference in the quality of editing whether it is done on the VDT or by hand. Some reporters complain that the VDT turns them into typesetters and proofreaders. And other studies have been conducted on the possible health hazards that could be caused by working on VDTs for extended periods. The city of San Francisco was the first to establish safety guidelines for persons who use VDTs in their daily work.

While the editor of a newspaper works in concert with the publisher and often the business manager, he or she is primarily responsible for the editorial content. At larger papers, the editor generally delegates the responsibility for running the daily operation to a managing editor who, in turn, directs the activities of the city editor and the various department editors.

All local news stories are written by staff reporters who work under the city editor. Stories received from the national wire services are handled by the wire editor. Correspondents (out-of-town reporters) work through the state editor. Editors in charge of lifestyles, sports, entertainment, business and other editorial departments handle all the stories for their pages. However, they work closely with the managing editor, the city editor and the graphics editor in an effort to coordinate their efforts.

Editorials are written by editors and editorial writers. Usually, if an editor has administrative duties, he or she may write few editorials. Newspapers that are owned by chains may receive some of their editorials from the corporate editorial offices. And some newspapers may even buy editorials from syndicated services. In addition, the public relations offices of a number of the state and national business and professional organizations and other special-interest groups send materials for editorials to newspapers. Some newspapers use them, but others consider their use unethical and will not print them.

Stories written by staff reporters are carefully read by copy editors not only for errors in spelling, grammar and punctuation but also for errors in facts and in style. Staff members also serve on the rewrite desk. They may take stories by phone from out-of-the-office reporters working their beats or covering a breaking news event, or they may be given press releases to rewrite.

On larger newspapers most headlines are written by the copy editors. On smaller ones much of the copyreading and headline writing may be done by the city, wire and state editors. And on very small publications, a reporter may write the headline on the story he or she has just composed.

Photographers may serve under a chief photographer, but their assignments generally come from a photo editor or one of the departmental editors. They may accompany a reporter on an assignment, or they may cover an event alone. On smaller newspapers reporters often serve as their own photographers.

Department editors are in charge of special sections devoted to such topics as business; sports; and entertainment, including radio, television, motion pictures, the arts, music and books. Department editors also are responsible for the special Sunday sections of most newspapers. However, on smaller newspapers coverage of those areas may be assigned to various staff reporters in addition to their regular duties. The book page editor may be an editorial writer, for example. Or a beat reporter may also do movie reviews.

The availability of personal computers and the growing use of computers to collect data and sort vast collections of government records introduced a new term to the journalism lexicon at the start of the decade: "computer-assisted reporting." Reporters quickly learned to make good use of Nexis, Lexis, Vu/Tex and other commercial data bases and many have moved on to using computer software programs to analyze government data bases.

The Atlanta Journal-Constitution analyzed bank records with a common Lotus software program for its Pulitzer Prize-winning series on racial bias in bank lending practices, for example. Two reporters for the Washington bureau of Cox Newspapers used government records to develop a data base on the ownership of assault weapons. Then they analyzed it to see if assault rifles or their ilk really were serious problems in American society. Their analysis allowed them to determine how often assault guns, as opposed to more conventional firearms, were used in crimes. They also were able to determine the preferred gun of drug traffickers and terrorists and to compare the numbers of foreign and domestically manufactured assault weapons that had been traced to crimes.

Investigative reporters say computer analysis of data bases can cut months or years of legwork. To promote the use of personal computers as reporting tools, the National Institute for Computer-Assisted Reporting was established at the University of Missouri.

THE LIBRARY/MORGUE

An important tool for all reporters and editors is the newspaper's reference file, traditionally called the "morgue" but more often the "library." Most libraries keep rather complete clippings of all previously reported major news stories and photographs that have been printed. In many cases, they also keep extensive background material gathered by reporters on various subjects and persons as well as clippings from competing newspapers and other sources. Pictures, both used and unused, generally are kept in the library also. In addition, most libraries keep a wide variety of reference books, from world almanacs to the various

Who's Who publications, along with social, political and economic data on the city and state.

A complete library also has on hand biographies of prominent persons— city, state, national and international—ready for instant use. In fact, many newspapers have these biographies written as news stories and stored in their computer memory bank. They are updated regularly. A newspaper the size of the Chicago Tribune or The Los Angeles Times will have hundreds of them already prepared, and when a famous person is thrust into the news, the staff has only to write a brief new lead on the story and it is ready for instant printing.

Depending on the size of the newspaper, the library may range from a few files to a large reference collection. Some newspapers keep their files on microfilm, but more and more are computerizing their libraries. Large newspapers, such as The New York Times, have established data banks for the complete storage of all information that has been printed in the publications. Some of them sell the information to other newspapers. In fact, today's newspapers have a choice among a number of data banks and information retrieval services that can be used by reporters conducting research for stories.

NEWS CHANNELS

The editorial department of a newspaper receives news through a variety of sources and channels.

1. From local sources through the newspaper's own reporters, who gather news from regular beats, flesh it out with background from the newspaper's library, and do most of the writing in the newspaper office under the direction of the city editor or one of the departmental editors.

2. From national and foreign sources through the wire services and syndicates such as The Associated Press (AP), United Press International (UPI), Reuters, The New York Times, The Los Angeles Times and The Washington Post news services. In addition, commercial syndicates provide many of the features and columns used. Some of this material is received by wire and, except for copyreading, is ready for publication. Many feature services send material to their client newspapers by mail if it does not fit into the immediate-news category. The wire editor or a department editor is responsible for handling this material, although the task may be assigned to a copy editor. Credit is given by use of the name or initials of the press service that provided the material on each story used. The press service or syndicate may be credited in a by-line, or the initials may be included in the dateline, which is the line at the beginning of a story giving its place of origin: WASHINGTON (AP). A local story needs no dateline, although some papers—The New York Times, for example—use them. Some papers reserve the right to combine stories from various press services to which they subscribe. In those cases the story usually carries a by-line saying "Compiled from press services."

3. From state and regional sources through correspondents. Much of this material is written and ready for publication, although many state editors either rewrite the stories or heavily edit them. Occasionally a correspondent simply dictates his notes to a state desk reporter who will write the story. Such stories often have "Special to the (name of newspaper)" preceding or in the dateline. In addition, some state editors gather stories by telephone from news sources such as police and city officials in communities in the newspaper's circulation area.

4. From various individuals and organizations, such as chambers of commerce; public information offices of various social, fraternal and educational organizations; public relations agencies through the mail, by telephone or during personal visits. Most of this material is rewritten by the city staff under the direction of the city editor.

SOURCES AND BEATS

At most newspapers, as much as 90 percent of all local news comes from regular beats and sources. They are the same at almost every newspaper. Reporters are assigned to them by the city editor to cover daily. They are:

1. The city police station, county jail, sheriff's office, state police, fire department and local hospitals.

2. The city hall, which houses the offices of the mayor and the city manager, most of the city department offices and the meeting room for the city council or aldermen.

3. The county courthouse, which houses the offices of the county's chief executive officer, the county departmental offices, meeting room for the county commissioners and the county courts.

4. The state capitol or state offices, which house the governor, members of the governor's cabinet and various state departmental offices. State government departments usually maintain satellite offices in many cities and towns.

5. The federal building or offices, which house the post office, federal law enforcement agencies and other federal operations such as the Internal Revenue Service and the Immigration and Naturalization Service. The federal courts also are housed in the federal building. However, some agencies maintain offices outside the federal building.

6. City, county and private schools; colleges; universities; trade schools; and associated organizations.

7. Chambers of commerce, business firms, industries and labor organizations.

8. Civic, fraternal and professional organizations such as the local medical society.

9. Churches and associated organizations.

10. Organizations and welfare agencies associated with the local Community Chest or United Fund, as well as health organizations in such fields as medicine, mental health, and alcohol and drug counseling, which might be financed independently or through public fund drives.

11. Motion picture theaters, radio and television stations, and all organizations offering theatrical or musical productions, such as the local symphony orchestra, amateur and professional theater groups, athletic events, or performances by nationally and internationally known music groups and individual performers.

12. Funeral homes.

13. Convention centers, hotels, airlines and other firms engaging in tourism or accommodating meetings and visitors, such as the local tourist bureau.

14. Businesses and industries important to the local community, such as shipping and mining.

Many newspapers also have specialized beats dealing with the environment, agriculture, science news and other areas of public concern. Some have even experimented with doing away with beats altogether.

It should be apparent from this list of beats that most news is gathered in a regular, formalized, systematic way. A reporter does not stroll about the streets looking for news to happen. Every day, the beat reporter is responsible for covering the specific offices and organizations in which most news originates. Even news of murders, fires, accidents and disasters generally comes from regular sources—police and fire departments, hospitals and the local weather service.

The number of beats often is determined by the organization of the newsroom. For example, some newspapers in larger cities have a metropolitan editor who attempts to coordinate all the news in the city and the area immediately surrounding the city. In others, everything beyond the immediate city limits may be the responsibility of the state editor or zone section editors. The physical location and other conditions may cause a reporter to cover parts of several beats.

In addition to beat reporters, every newspaper has general assignment reporters who cover a wide range of stories, depending on the particular need on any given day.

THE STORY PROCESS

Although the process will vary from paper to paper, generally speaking, a story will follow this path from the event itself, into print and then into the hands of the reader.

1. A reporter is sent to cover a newsworthy event. He or she gathers the facts by interviewing the participants and others and makes careful

notes for the story. A beat reporter may interview an official, cover a meeting or search public records to gather information for a story.

2. Most reporters return to the office to write the story. In some cases, because of deadlines a reporter may write the story on the spot and dictate it over the phone to another staff member in the office. Or the reporter may use a portable VDT terminal to send the story back to the office. At some newspapers the reporter may give only the basic facts of the story over the phone to a staff member in the office who will write the complete story. Some metropolitan dailies have installed VDTs in the pressrooms at city hall and the courthouse; the reporter writes the story on the VDT and feeds it directly into the computer at the newspaper by telephone.

3. After a reporter writes the story on a VDT and files it in the computer, the city editor (or department editor) calls up the story on another VDT screen and reads it. Changes may be made at that point by the editor, or the story may be sent back to the reporter for rewriting. Once the story meets the city editor's approval, it is filed in the computer again until called up by a copy editor who completes the editing process and writes the headline. When ready for publication, the story can be sent directly to the photocomposition machine, which sets it in type, or it can be stored for later use.

4. During a news meeting involving the managing editors and all department editors (or during the editing process), where the story will appear in the newspaper is decided. The person responsible for designing the pages works closely with the editors. At some newspapers all the page layouts are done by the same designers. But at larger papers, one group of designers handles the news sections while others do the layouts for the special sections such as business and sports.

5. Wire copy generally is fed directly into a newspaper's computer and called up on the VDT screen by the wire editor or a copy editor for editing and headline writing.

6. Once the stories have been set in type in the composing room, they are pasted on a page-form by staff members who use the page dummy drawn by the designer as a guide. The completed pages generally are checked by someone from the newsroom before they are released.

7. From the page-forms a photographic negative is made. The image from the negative is burned onto a thin, sensitized plate, which is then fitted on the presses in the pressroom where the newspaper is printed, cut and folded in one operation.

8. The printed newspapers are delivered to the circulation department for home delivery, street sales and mailing.

Although there are a number of complaints about the impact of computerization on the quality of newspapers and the health of the staff, it is apparant that advancing computer technology will continue to have a significant influence on the gathering of news and the printing of newspapers.

EXERCISES

1. Arrange a tour of the newspaper in your community. Before the visit, study the newspaper organization chart and the steps in the story process in this chapter and the newspaper terminology in the appendix.

   a. In the editorial department, ask how many reporters work for the paper and what their beats are. Do the same for the departmental staffs and the copy desk. Ask for a demonstration of the equipment they use.

   b. In each of the other departments—advertising, circulation and mechanical—ask the supervisor to explain the department's role in the newspaper and how it relates to all other departments.

   c. In all departments identify the original source of material that is printed in the newspaper and ask the supervisors to explain the steps the material must go through before reaching the public.

2. After your visit to the local newspaper, assume that you are starting a newspaper to compete with the established newspaper. Draw up a plan of news coverage for your newspaper. Indicate what you would offer the readers and advertisers that the established newspaper does not provide. Include the kinds of news, information and entertainment you would include in your newspaper and describe how your paper would look.

3. Select a single issue of a daily newspaper published in your city or a nearby city. Using the list of sources in this chapter, indicate the source or sources of each front page story.

4. With that same issue of the newspaper in hand, watch both a local television newscast and a national newscast the same evening. List the stories covered by both. Compare the differences in the amount of coverage given each story and the emphasis given that story as well as the method of presenting the facts; for example, was the story illustrated?

5. Select an issue of a daily newspaper published in your city or a nearby city on the same day the local weekly or semiweekly newspaper in your community is published. Compare the stories used in both publications. Make a list of every story on the front page of both and indicate their source or sources.

6. Using newspapers available in your college or university library, select a major state, national or international news event that has been reported for several consecutive days—perhaps a natural disaster like a major flood, tornado or hurricane—and compare the way several newspapers covered it. Look for similarities as well as significant differences. Use a newspaper that is published at or near the site of the event and at least one from another state.

7. Arrange through the city editor of your local newspaper to spend the day with a beat reporter. Write a report on your day "in the field" with the reporter.

8. Arrange to spend a day observing the staff of one of the departments at your local newspaper, such as business, sports or lifestyle. Write a report on your observations.

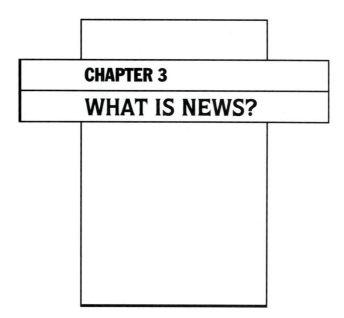

CHAPTER 3

WHAT IS NEWS?

Is news "the first rough draft of history"? Or is it "something you learn today that you didn't know yesterday"? Or could it simply be "what the editor decides it is" on any given day?

Actually, it is all of the above and more. There is no single acceptable definition of news because the elements that constitute news are constantly changing, and so are the women and men who select it for print and broadcast. The dramatic social, economic, political and technological changes sweeping the world have had a profound impact on what is considered news today just as they have had on the readers of newspapers.

What may be news in one community may not be in another. For example, a newspaper in California's Silicone Valley may devote a regular section to computers and technology, while one in Texas may focus special attention on the oil industry and another on tourism.

Reader interest varies greatly. That is why an event that would rate the front page in a community of 10,000 may not make the calendar of events in a newspaper in a city of 500,000.

Despite the complexity of trying to pin down just what news is, there is general agreement in the nation's newsrooms about the kinds of events and individuals that are newsworthy.

NEWS VALUES

The qualifications or characteristics of news generally recognized by editors and reporters are known as news values. They include:

Conflict. Most conflicts are newsworthy to some degree because they disrupt the status quo. Physical conflict is considered newsworthy because it may lead to injury and damage. Violence arouses emotions, not only in the participants, but also in the spectators, and can be of enormous and immediate importance.

War is a classic example of conflict. It will dominate the news. However, a fist fight between two partisans at a championship football game may rate no more than a single line of type, if that, in a game story. But let the partisan fans riot after the game, damaging cars, blocking traffic, breaking windows in stores and looting, and the story probably will be spread all over page one because of the magnitude of the "conflict."

Wars, murders and violent strikes—conflicts of a more disruptive nature— always receive space on the front page, which leads critics to complain that newspapers devote too much space to violence. Until recently, other conflicts— political, economic, social, scientific—did not always receive similar attention. However, that has changed, and today the often impassioned debates over the safety of nuclear energy, global warming, protection of the environment and other less violent clashes often are played out on the front pages of newspapers, too.

Progress and Disaster.   In conflict, one side usually wins and the other loses. For the routine struggles of life, not generally newsworthy in themselves, shining successes frequently emerge. For example, from quiet laboratories come new inventions, new advances in science and medicine and new devices to improve the quality of life that genuinely represent progress.

Sometimes progress can lead to disaster. Such was the case with DDT, hailed as a major breakthrough in the control of crop-destroying insects. But after twenty years, it became the subject of major news stories when the federal government finally banned its use after it was linked to cancer in humans. Saccharin was for years a seemingly harmless substitute for sugar welcomed by diabetics and persons with weight problems. But it, too, became the subject of major news stories when it was linked, in some scientific studies, to cancer. Congress even debated banning it. The great promise of nuclear power after the splitting of the atom lost some of its luster more than thirty years later due to the accident at the Three Mile Island nuclear plant in Pennsylvania.

Disasters, both natural and man-made, often dominate the news in a community. Figure 3–1 is an example of how The Detroit News covered the story of a passenger jet that crashed on takeoff from that city's airport, killing 158 persons.

Tornados and earthquakes strike suddenly. Lives are lost and millions of dollars' worth of property is damaged. Hundreds, sometimes thousands, of persons are displaced. Businesses are closed. The recovery from such a disaster often becomes a story of progress.

Progress can be a new industry that provides jobs and brings millions of dollars into the local community. But it also can be the recovery of a child severely burned in a house fire.

Consequence.   Any event that causes or is capable of causing a sequence of activities that affect many persons is newsworthy. Obviously, certain events are of more consequence than others, and they will receive more space and larger

FIGURE 3–1. Disasters are news. The crash of Northwest Flight 255 at Detroit's Metropolitan Airpoirt, in which more than 150 persons died, dominated the news for days in that city and across the nation. This front page of The Detroit News is an excellent example of how newspapers cover major disasters. (Reprinted with the permission of The Detroit News, a Gannett newspaper, copyright 1987.)

headlines. For example, the newspapers in Knoxville, Tenn., gave extensive coverage to consequences of a U.S. Department of Education order to desegrate the local public school system. The desegration plan called for the closing of a number of elementary and high schools: parents who did not want their children to attend schools outside their neighborhoods bitterly opposed the plan.

It should be noted that all newsworthy events, for whatever other reason they are newsworthy, have some consequence. Conflicts have consequence. For example, one consequence of the war in the Persian Gulf was the problem of caring for the thousands of Kurdish people who were fleeing Iraq to avoid further repression by the Iraqi army.

Disaster and progress also have consequences, as noted earlier in this chapter. (Figure 3–2 illustrates a consequence of progress—the new Toyota plant will bring 1,500 new jobs to that city.)

Prominence.   It is a given in the news business that names make news and big names make bigger news. The "name" must do something or have something done to her or him to be newsworthy. A prominent person may do no more than stop over in the city en route to a national conference to rate a story in the local paper, for example.

What a prominent person says or does often makes news because of its consequences. A nationally known economist's predictions could influence the stock market. A national political leader might enhance a local political candidate's chances for election by joining the local campaign for a dinner or speech. State-level politicians have been known to fly great distances at enormous costs and considerable inconvenience just to be seen and photographed with a president or a leading candidate for the presidency. They know it is almost certain to rate space in the state's newspapers or on local television. Prominent individuals are newsworthy for the same reason a political conference or a summit meeting of world leaders is newsworthy. The potential is there for significant change that makes news. The decision of a U.S. Supreme Court justice to step down, for example, could lead to a shift in the balance between conservatives and liberals on the court and influence the court's rulings on such issues as abortion for decades.

Timeliness and Proximity.   Two other news values commonly recognized are timeliness and proximity. Both are important measures of news. Although they alone do not make an event or individual automatically newsworthy, in combination with events that have other news values they can help determine newsworthiness. An accident today that tied up local rush-hour traffic for two hours is more timely than one that happened even 24 hours before and will rate more attention in a newspaper. That same accident is more newsworthy because it happened locally than a similar one that tied up rush-hour traffic in the state capital 200 miles away.

Novelty.   Readers and editors alike are attracted by novelties in the news. They are a staple in all newspapers: the two-headed calf, the 350-pound pumpkin, the

FIGURE 3–2. A new Toyota assembly plant that would add 1,500 jobs was the major news story in Louisville the day the plan to build the plant was announced. This front page of The Courier-Journal is an excellent example of how a major local economic story is handled. (Courtesy of The Courier-Journal.)

cat that walks 200 miles to find its owner who moved to another city, the whale that keeps getting stranded in San Francisco Bay. Novel ways of making a living, unusual habits and hobbies, superstitions—anything different—all have strong reader appeal. The common element is simply that the event or the individual is unusual.

Human Interest.   Many stories that appear in newspapers at first glance do not seem to be news because they do not meet the tests of conflict, consequence, progress and disaster, or any other specific news value. Generally they are called "human-interest" or "feature" stories. Although they may border on being novelties, they frequently have considerably more substance. They may be about the desperate efforts of a lifeguard to save the life of a stranded dolphin, a famous author's battle with depression, a 78-year-old man who returns to high school to work for his diploma; there are hundreds of such stories in newspapers every day. They have broad reader appeal.

Some events and individuals lend themselves more readily than others to human-interest treatment. They may lack the basic values that would make them a news story, yet they have special qualities that have reader appeal.

Often major news events spawn a variety of human-interest stories. One such story grew out of the crash of a Northwest Airlines jet at Detroit's Metropolitan Airport in which 158 people were killed. Four-year-old Cecilia Cichan was the only survivor. The child's recovery from injuries she suffered in the crash and her adjustment to the death of her parents and brother captured the attention of millions of readers who flooded her hospital room with gifts.

Sex.   Most editors consider sex a news value. This is especially true when it is coupled with prominence. The marital problems of millionaire-developer Donald Trump rated almost as much space in the press as his financial wheeling and dealing. The multiple marriages of movie star Elizabeth Taylor have been reported in detail and read avidly. Each new alliance between actress-singer Cher and a younger man grabs an inordinate amount of space. The on-again-off-again romances, marriages and casual housekeeping arrangements of many major rock stars have lasting reader appeal, especially when they contain such other elements as conflict or, perhaps, disaster.

Miscellaneous Values.   Stories of animals often are well read, even by people who do not like animals. Write a story critical of cats and hundreds, perhaps even thousands, of cat owners will respond with vehemence if not violence. Tell the story of a singing dog and you'll be swamped with requests to do stories about other clever canines. Some editors believe the only story better than an animal story is one that involves an animal and a baby, especially if the animal rescues the baby.

Many other types of stories used in newspapers are not news from the standpoint of such news values as conflict, progress and timeliness. But they are used because they inform or entertain the reader. Stories about current fashions, trends in leisure time activities and unconventional health care fit this category.

Summary: Nature of News and News Values

Newspapers deal in a commodity—news. It can be defined this way:

1. News is an account of man's changing relationships.
2. News is an account of events that disrupt the status quo or have the potential to cause disruption.
3. News is an event of community consequence.

Items of news have intrinsic characteristics known as news values. The presence or absence of these values determines the newsworthiness and reader appeal that in turn establish an event's worth to the newspaper. The intrinsic characteristics of news values are

1. Conflict (tension, surprise)
2. Progress (triumph, achievement)
3. Disaster (defeat, destruction)
4. Consequence (effect on individuals or community)
5. Prominence (the well-known or famous)
6. Novelty (the unusual, even the bizarre)
7. Human interest (unusual or emotional)

Desirable Qualifications
8. Timeliness (freshness and newness)
9. Proximity (local appeal)

General Interest
10. Sex
11. Animals.

MEASURING THE IMPORTANCE OF NEWS

Reporters quickly learn, by intuition or applying news values, to recognize news. They also quickly become aware that not everything that happens in a city in a day can be printed, even if it meets all the standard categories of news. From the mass of material gathered daily, only the most important, significant and interesting is offered to the reader.

To know what is the most important, significant and interesting, reporters must know their community and the readers of the newspaper. One of the greatest handicaps a reporter can have is to not know his community and the people who live in it.

News always must be measured for its comparative importance to the reader. Stories must be compared to determine their relative reader appeal, which will influence not only their length, but also where and how they are displayed in the paper. The following factors are generally considered by editors in measuring the relative importance of stories:

1. The extent of disruption of the status quo
2. The number of persons affected by the event
3. The nearness of the event
4. The timeliness of the event
5. The extent of the results of the event—its consequence or significance
6. The variety of news values in the event.

STORY TYPES

Generally, reporters and editors do not discuss news values or the relative importance of most stories, although in some cases they may. They merely apply these values instinctively in writing and editing the news. They do, however, recognize and discuss stories in other terms. They talk of "fire stories" or "accident stories," perhaps, or a "meeting," a "speech" or a "murder story" and, always, the "weather" story.

Most newspaper stories fall into well-defined types. Here are the types of stories newspapers generally recognize:

General Types

1. Personals and briefs
2. Speeches, publications, interviews
3. Meetings and events

Stories that are classified by a "package" in which they are "wrapped" rather than the content or subject matter

Simple Types

4. Illnesses, deaths, funerals
5. Fires and accidents
6. Seasons and weather
7. Crime

Stories that generally require little interpretive writing by the reporter

Complex Types

8. Courts, trials, lawsuits
9. Government and politics
10. Business, industry, agriculture, labor
11. Education, research, science
12. Religion, philanthropy, promotion

Stories that generally require interpretation from the reporter's background of specialized information

Special Types

13. Lifestyles (including social events and consumer news)
14. Sports
15. Entertainment (films, television, popular music, art, theater, criticism)
16. Editorials and editorial columns
17. Interpretative and investigative

Stories and articles that encompass a variety of subjects often requiring a high degree of specialized knowledge on the part of the writer

Some story types are more clearly defined than others. Many of the classifications overlap. For example, accidents frequently figure into weather stories, or a trial may also be a political story; a major sporting event could be an economics story. Because the lines of distinction between types of stories are not always clear, the reporter who masters each type will have no trouble writing a story in which several types merge.

NEWS SOURCES

Newspaper stories obviously come from many sources. The main beats covered regularly by reporters were noted in the preceding chapter. They include all available offices of the state, county, city and federal government; the headquarters of all civic and professional organizations; churches, schools and charities; and many individuals, public and private, who occupy key positions in business, industry, transportation utilities and other major fields. A number of "events" are purposely staged for the news media by public relations people to promote an opening or gain space in a newspaper about a new product, for example. Editors and reporters should be skeptical of being "used" by the sponsors of such pseudo-news events. However, they should also remember that public relations people can be important sources of legitimate news.

Many stories come from a single source. The public relations chairman of a national convention, for example, may provide all the necessary information for a story on the event in a press kit. On the other hand, information will have to be pieced together from several sources to ensure a balanced final story.

A careful reporter will always double-check the facts with at least a second source. In the case of the national convention, it might be the manager of the hotel where the convention is headquartered. Many reporters have been told by public relations representatives that 1,000 persons were expected, when only a couple of hundred actually registered.

Many stories will have to be pieced together from a half-dozen or more sources. To write a complete story about a major labor strike, a reporter should talk to the strikers; their labor union representatives; the employers; the police;

the mayor; the governor; hospitals if there is violence; charities if it is a protracted strike; and others, including the president, if the strike is of nationwide significance.

Because all details in a news story are facts gathered by the reporter, the information in every story should be traceable to its source. The source should be named, and statements should be attributed to the person who made them. Here is an analysis of a news story showing how the facts in the story were drawn from various sources:

Source of News	News Type: Crime	News Content
Police	An Eastside man knocked down two police officers with his car during a dramatic chase after they tried to arrest him on drug charges Thursday.	What took place
Police	Lamont Jones, 32, of 1009 Granada Ct., was jailed under $250,000 bond. He was charged with two counts of aggravated assault on a police officer, one count of evading arrest and one count of soliciting to purchase drugs.	Identification of man arrested and charges
Police	Metro Police had raided a known drug house at 504 Vernon Ave. and arrested four other people on drug charges when the incident occurred about 8 p.m.	Specific details
Police	Jones allegedly purchased what he believed to be cocaine from undercover officers, then ran to his Buick when they attempted to arrest him, Homicide Detective E.J. Bernad said.	More details
Police	Officer Jim K. Reed opened the passenger door just as Jones slammed the car into reverse. He was dragged 10 to 15 feet before he fell to the ground.	More details
Police	The car struck Officer Ron D. Riddle, who was behind the vehicle, "a glancing blow and knocked him down," Bernad said.	More details
Police	Jones wrecked his car about a half-block away, then tried to escape on foot before he was caught by police.	More details
Hospital officials and police	Reed and Riddle of the West Central Sector crime suppression units were treated at Metro General Hospital and released.	Details of injuries
Correction Department	State Corrections Department officials said Lamont C. Jones was sentenced to a maximum of eight years in prison in Hamilton County in 1987 for receiving and concealing stolen property, and simple robbery.	Background details

Correction Department Police	He was paroled last July. Others who were arrested and charged with soliciting to purchase a controlled substance were: —Timothy E. Pratt, 21, 2926 Old Buena Vista Rd. —Robert Lee McCormack, 40, 1100 Hemlock Ave. —Kevin Wilson, 23, 1515 Seymore Ave. —Gwenevere A. Gross, 31, 1100 Hemlock Ave.	More details Other police action

The outstanding news value of this story is conflict—a police raid, an attempted escape, two police officers injured. It also is timely because it happened the day of publication. It was given more length and displayed prominently because of the unusual aspect of the man's attempting to flee and the injury to the police officers. In addition, the on-going "war on drugs" by police had strong reader appeal.

EXERCISES

1. Invite the city or managing editor of the daily newspaper in your city to class to discuss news values. Bring a copy of the newspaper to class and ask him or her to explain the news values in each of the stories appearing on the front page and why each of the stories was displayed as it was. Look through the paper carefully, locating stories that are not on the front page but have a strong appeal to you, and ask her or him why those particular stories were not used on the front page.

2. Most daily newspapers are a combination of local, state, national and international news. However, many newspapers, especially smaller dailies, tend to emphasize local news. With that in mind, apply the test of news values to the following items and determine which are worth publishing in a non-metropolitan daily. Indicate which items deserve to be placed on the front page along with significant state, national or international news that may be selected that day. Indicate the sources from which you would expect to obtain enough information to write a complete story:
   a. Mayor leaves on trade mission to Tokyo, Japan.
   b. Five thousand demonstrate against abortion.
   c. State university refuses to open student crime records.
   d. Organizers seek $2,500 to help build bicentennial playground.
   e. Local malls boost security after sex assaults.
   f. Former head of bar association faces cocaine charges.
   g. Telethon raises $322,000 for United Negro College Fund.
   h. Officer suspended for writing phony traffic tickets.
   i. Local biology teacher elected president of national teachers' group.
   j. John Lain, former U.S. senator, reports he has 350-pound watermelon in his garden.
   k. Nine women, six men jailed in prostitution sweep.
   l. Boy, 12, dies after being hit by car; driver charged.
   m. Man pleads guilty to shooting out fire hall windows.
   n. Former newswoman Paula Casey elected president of State Women's Political Caucus.
   o. Fire lieutenant demoted for using marijuana.

   p. New $70 million runway at airport completed, opens today.

   q. Maj. Bill Britt, assistant chief, has been appointed to chief's post by mayor.

   r. Local physician sentenced to 30 months in federal prison for conspiracy to possess and distribute steroids and cocaine.

   s. School board president says tax boost inevitable.

   t. Police seek "gentleman robber" in connection with three bank robberies this week.

   u. Man sentenced to six months, fined $1,000 on a charge of baiting bears in national forest.

   v. Audit shows utilities board chief owes utility $4,500 for water lines extended into his subdivision.

   w. Pocket radio stops bullet fired at man's chest during holdup.

   x. Two police officers suspended for using undue force.

   y. Fire in college dorm displaces 250 students.

   z. City Council considers plan to aid homeless and street people.

3. Using daily newspapers available in your college or university library, compare the coverage of a major national or international news event in at least three papers, one from your state and the others from different sections of the country. Check the stories carefully for the use of sources, and compare their use of anonymous sources. Write a brief paper on which story you found most believable, and explain why.

4. Here are rough notes from stories or story leads taken from community newspapers. They are typical of stories you will find in most non-metropolitan newspapers. Classify each story under one or more of the story types described in this chapter. Examine each for the importance of its news values—consequence, conflict, human interest, and so on—and indicate the news values in each one. What additional information is needed to expand each story? What sources would you ask for additional information?

   a. Three women and a baby were found dead in a small frame house at 1011 Fifth St. that was destroyed by an early morning fire today. A man in the house was flown to a burn center in Chattanooga.

   b. A 26-year-old woman was shot Thursday while trying to chase drug traffickers from in front of her apartment in an Eastside housing project. She is in critical condition at Memorial Medical Center.

   c. A circuit court jury awarded $11,500 Thursday to a woman who filed suit after an auto accident caused one of her breast implants to burst.

   d. West High School will be completely redesigned and be almost doubled in size in the next two years, George Wheeler, school facilities administrator for the County School Board, said today.

   e. A 39-year-old woman was struck on the head with a baseball bat during a fight at the Woodlawn Cafe last night. She was treated at the emergency room at County Hospital.

   f. A 92-year-old woman used the loaded .22-calibre pistol she keeps under her mattress to chase an intruder from her home.

   g. City School Superintendent Wayne Matusiak said today the local high schools will begin offering classes in English as a second language, citizenship, literacy and remedial education this spring.

   h. A wind-whipped fire believed to be caused by arson raged through a residential area near the center of the Old City early today, destroying at least seven apartments before firefighters brought it under control.

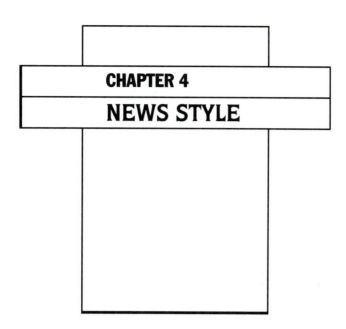

CHAPTER 4

NEWS STYLE

"Words are sacred. They deserve respect. If you get the right ones, in the right order, you can nudge the world a little. . . ." Tom Stoppard wrote in "The Real Thing."

Unfortunately, many individuals writing for American newspapers are simply not getting their words in the right order. In fact, they aren't even selecting the right ones in the first place. There is not a whole lot of "nudging" going on in their writing.

A quick review of a dozen American newspapers will turn up embarrassing examples of misused words, poorly constructed sentences, bad grammar, misspellings, incorrect punctuation, mixed metaphors, non sequiturs, cliches, redundancies, circumlocutions, imprecision and jargon. For years, James J. Kilpatrick has collected these assaults on the language for his excellent syndicated column, "The Writer's Art." He has never been at a loss for examples from newspapers large and small, daily and weekly.

The "good newspaper writing" movement of the 1980s had lost some of its steam by the start of the 1990s, but a number of newspapers continued to put a premium on good writing. Critics, however, claim it is simply not enough. And some writers blame the basic news style for everything from their bad grammar to their dull, unimaginative stories.

Basic news style is short words, short sentences, short paragraphs and active verbs. It is writing that is clear, precise, succinct and expressive. This lead from a story by Frank J. Murray in The Washington Times is a good example of news style:

> President Bush's policy on new taxes changed yesterday from "read my lips" to "read my mind."
> Eight senators and nine House members from both parties came to the White House yesterday and told the president that new taxes will be needed for the second Bush budget in fiscal 1991.

For the first time the President didn't say "no."
He did not say anything.

That lead gives readers of the newspaper what they want—news written in a way that won't confuse them, bore them or waste their time. The remainder of the story went on to help clarify the complex economic as well as political issues of the national budget.

Readers also want writing that illuminates people, places and things with the subtle light of well-used language, as James P. Gannon wrote in a special report on better writing for "The Bulletin of the American Society of Newspaper Editors." Here is an example of writing that illuminates, Ira Berkow's story on Cus D'Amato's Gym, written for The New York Times:

> Nighttime, and the walk up the poorly lit, steep, narrow wooden staircase to the shadowed area on the third floor seemed long. The street noises grew muffled and the creak of the stairs became louder.
> The climb Tuesday night in this old building at 116 East 14th Street to the Gramercy Gymnasium at the top of the stairs—quiet now, because it is just past closing time, 8 o'clock, and the punching, skipping, snorting fighters have gone home—brought to mind the words of Cus D'Amato.
> "Any kid coming here for the first time who thinks he wants to be a fighter, and who makes the climb up those dark stairs," said Cus, "has it 50 percent licked, because he's licking fear."
> Cus D'Amato, the sometimes strange, usually sweet, often suspicious, invariably generous teacher and philosopher and boxing manager and trainer, owned this gym for some 30 years. . . .

The best thing a newspaper has to offer the reader is good stories, well told. That is why good newspapers put so much emphasis on good writing, which begins with a mastery of the language. It is difficult to write with clarity, precision and accuracy if you do not know the accepted rules of punctuation and grammar and the principles of rhetoric.

No newspaper intentionally permits its writers to misuse the English language. Most spend countless hours and amounts of money attempting to make certain that the language is used properly, but errors still slip through the editorial safety net.

Newspapers follow accepted rules of English grammar and sentence structure. But they also strive for certain qualities of style: simplicity, clarity, brevity, accuracy, precision and originality. These qualities cannot be sharply defined. However, they can be developed by every writer who cares about using the right words in the right order.

Most newspapers have their own style book or use the "Associated Press Stylebook" as a basic guide for reporters when they write their stories. Style books not only deal with such fundamentals as grammar, punctuation and spelling, they also set the standards for the use of titles, addresses and numbers in an effort to bring a uniformity to those aspects of writing that are common to all stories. Many of them also offer suggestions and examples of clear, precise, succinct and expressive writing of stories and headlines.

Here are some general principles of news style. Most of them conform to the "AP Stylebook."

NEWSPAPER ENGLISH

---

1. Eliminate Unnecessary Words

1. Eliminate Unnecessary Words
   a. Unnecessary articles
      Weak: The Club members attended the meeting.
      Strong: Club members attended the meeting.
      Weak: He returned a part of the money.
      Strong   He returned part of the money.
(However, only unnecessary articles should be eliminated. For example, the article in "Club members attended the meeting" cannot be eliminated. The same applies to "a" and "an.")
   b. Circuitous verb forms
      Weak: The group will hold a meeting.
      Strong: The group will meet.
      Weak: The judge arrived at a decision.
      Strong: The judge decided.
   c. Adjectives, adverbs, prepositions
      Weak: Both cars were completely destroyed.
      Strong: Both cars were destroyed.
      Weak: A tall 18-story building
      Strong: An 18-story building
      Weak: He stepped off of the train.
      Strong: He stepped off the train.
      Weak: The club will meet on Friday.
      Strong: The club will meet Friday.
   d. Connectives
      Weak: He said that he would go.
      Strong: He said he would go.
(However, when two or more "that" clauses follow a verb, the conjunction should be used with all clauses for purposes of clarity.)
   e. Well-known place names
      Weak: He came from Chicago, Ill.
      Strong: He came from Chicago.
   f. Phrases
      Weak: The accident occurred at the corner of Vine and Maple streets.
      Strong: The accident occurred at Vine and Maple.
      Weak: The debate lasted for a period of two hours.
      Strong: The debate lasted two hours.

g. Clauses
   Weak: All who are interested can vote.
   Strong: All can vote.
   Weak: The drought that occurred last summer.
   Strong: Last summer's drought.
h. Redundancies
   Weak: Past experience had taught him the way.
   Strong: Experience had taught him the way.

2. Use Simple, Accurate, and Vivid Words

a. Short, common words are usually best. The newspaper is written to be read hurriedly by persons of all levels of intellect.

Use	*Rather Than*
fire	holocaust, conflagration
died	passed away, deceased
man	gentleman
woman	lady
left	departed
body	remains
buried	interred
cancer	carcinoma

b. Superlatives are usually inaccurate. There are few "catastrophes," "panics" and "fiascos."

More Accurate	*Less Accurate*
a beautiful woman	the most beautiful woman
an exciting game	the most exciting game
seldom	never
frequently	always
probably true	absolutely true
escape	miraculous escape

c. Caution must be taken in the accurate use of the present tense.
   Wrong: The policeman grabs the prisoner and pushes him into the cell.
   Right: The policemen grabbed the prisoner and pushed him into the cell.
   Wrong: Smith says he favors the proposal.
   Right: Smith said he favors the proposal.
   Right: Smith favors the proposal.
d. Tarnished word ornaments (figures of speech) are not vivid; avoid

charming hostess	blushing bride
tastefully decorated	host of friends
watery grave	received an ovation
busy as bees	dance divinely

view with alarm	brutally murdered
point with pride	Joe College
stormy session	Mother Earth

e. The active voice is usually more forceful than the passive.

Weak: The man was seen by the students.

Strong: Students saw the man.

Weak: The accident was witnessed by many persons.

Strong: Many persons saw the accident.

Stronger: Eleven persons saw the accident.

But in order to emphasize the proper element, the passive voice must frequently be used.

Weak: The County Election Committee elected W.P. Jones chairman.

Strong: W.P. Jones was elected chairman of the county Election Committee.

Weak: An automobile killed John Brown, county attorney, today.

Strong: John Brown, county attorney, was killed in an automobile accident today.

3. Do Not Editorialize (Express Opinion) in New Stories

News stories should be written from an objective point of view. They should not render verdicts or pass judgment. Such words as "I," "me," "my," "we," "us," or "ours" are not used in news stories unless the reporter is quoting another person directly. (Certain types of by-lined stories are also exceptions to this rule.) Favorable or unfavorable phrases in a news story about a person, place or thing must be facts, not the opinion of the reporter.

Improper: He is well qualified for the position.

Proper: He is a graduate of Michigan and has 10 years of experience.

Improper: An interesting program has been prepared.

Proper: The program follows.
(Let the "interesting" things speak for themselves.)

Improper: The decision was unjust.

Proper: The attorney general said the decision was unjust.

Improper: The prisoner lost his temper.

Proper: The prisoner kicked the chair over.

Improper: The witness lied.

Proper: The prosecuting attorney said the witness lied.

Improper: He committed suicide by jumping from the window.

Proper: He was killed in a fall from the window, and the coroner ruled it a suicide.

Improper:	Little Johnny Black, 6-year-old darling son of Mr. and Mrs. W.R. Black, died today.
Proper:	Johnny Black, 6, died today. He was the son of Mr. and Mrs. W.R. Black.
Improper:	The young lady will win the hearts of all visitors when she begins serving as hostess at the chamber of commerce next week.
Proper:	The young woman will begin serving as hostess at the chamber of commerce next week. ("Attractive young woman" is permissible in some newspapers if she is attractive and young, but many newspapers consider such phrases puff.)
Improper:	The judge told me (told this reporter) the case was dismissed.
Proper:	The judge said the case was dismissed.

4. Sentences and Paragraphs Should Be Short

The news paragraph rarely should exceed 50 words and should be broken up into two or more sentences, if possible. Thirty to forty words often makes a well-proportioned paragraph, although at some newspapers paragraphs often are considerably longer.

The object of the paragraph is not only to provide facts and information for the reader but also to present it in an easy, readable fashion. Although newspaper paragraphs should be short, they should not sacrifice standard qualities such as unity and coherence.

News style calls for short sentences. They are easier to read than long involved ones. But the writer should avoid overusing short sentences exclusively. A blend of short and slightly longer sentences generally makes a news story read more smoothly.

Here is an example of a long, one-sentence paragraph that tries to tell too much at once:

> One man died and another was critically injured about 6 p.m. Tuesday when their Mercury Cougar crossed the median on Interstate 24, just past the Old Hickory Boulevard exit, and struck a Cadillac headed in the opposite direction, then was "totally destroyed" by a tractor-trailer rig loaded with steel bars, State Highway Patrolman Frank Biggs said.

That lead is more than 50 words. It is just too long and too involved. This rewritten version shortens it considerably. The details omitted from the first lead can be used later in the story:

> One man died and another was critically injured Tuesday when their car crossed the median on Interstate 24, struck another car and ran under a tractor-trailer rig.
> State Highway Patrolman Frank Biggs said the Mercury Cougar, driven by Michael Pritzl, 27, Gallatin, was dragged nearly 150 feet by the semi. Pritzl is in critical condition at Vanderbilt Hospital.

His passenger, Edwin L. Roberts, 27, also of Gallatin, died of massive internal injuries at 8:30 p.m. Tuesday at HCA Southern Hills Hospital.

The remainder of the story gave the time of the accident, the exact location on the interstate, the names of the drivers of the other two vehicles involved and other pertinent facts about the accident.

5. Persons Named in News Stories Should Be Identified

When using the name of a public official, it is sufficient simply to use a title. For example: Mayor Paula Casey or Senator Frank Gibson. However, if a person named in a story is not well known, the reporter should find another way to identify him or her.

Numerous types of descriptive facts are used to identify persons named in news stories. The most common include age, home address and occupation. But reporters also can use well-known nicknames as well as affiliations with social or religious organizations if the person holds or has held a prominent post in them. For example: former president of the Chamber of Commerce or former director of the YMCA. It is also possible to use the relationship of a person to local or prominent individuals such as "nephew of Congressman Tom Jones." Or a person's achievements ("city golf champion") or infamy ("ex-convict") may be used. The most commonly used identification for anyone who is not well known is the home address. Some newspapers use both age and home address as a general rule. But the reporter should use other identification if it leads to a clearer understanding of who the person is. For example, in a story about the manager of a local motel being robbed, more persons would know the person by his occupation than by his street address. In that case the identification should be "Richard Bodkin, manager of the Downtown Holiday Inn, was robbed" rather than "Richard Bodkin, 52, 1109 Bennet St., was robbed." More people will know Bodkin by his occupation than by his residence.

6. Every News Story Should Name or Clearly Imply Its Source

"Attribution" means naming the source of the facts used in the story. Unless a reporter is an eyewitness to an event, the facts will have to come from another source. And that source should be identified. The facts in a news story should be attributed to a person, a group, or a document or report.

The reporter usually has three options in attributing facts:

a. To state the source explicitly

Senator Mark Pizarek said the United States will have to impose a tax increase to pay for a long-term Middle East presence if we don't get more financial help from our allies.

The California Independent told the Exchange Club . . .

or

> The state Supreme Court today ordered a new trial for convicted drug dealer Paul Pullen.
>
> Pullen, serving two life sentences for the murder of his partner in a 10-state drug distribution ring, did not get a fair trial, the Supreme Court ruled.

b. To leave the source implied

> Five more Mid-state National Guard units have been put on alert for possible deployment to the Middle East as part of Operation Desert Shield.
>
> They are: . . .

The implied source in the lead is the National Guard itself. Later in the story a direct quote from the commander makes that plain.

c. To conceal the source purposely to protect some individual or to maintain a news advantage

> Gov. Betty Bradley is expected to seek a 5-cent hike in gasoline taxes this year, a high-ranking member of central administration said today.
>
> The official, who asked that his name not be used, said the money would be used to support the governor's educational reform package.

These are common options reporters face daily. The use of unnamed sources continues to be debated, sometimes hotly, by reporters, editors and publishers. Some studies show the readers are skeptical when a source is not named in a story. Critics, and some reporters and editors, agree that not using a name gives the source an unfair advantage. Sources cannot be held responsible for what they say since their names are not made public. But others argue that without the guarantee of anonymity, some sources will not speak and reporters will miss excellent stories. In one of the more celebrated legal cases involving the press, a source who had been assured anonymity sued a major daily after his name was printed as the source of a derogatory story about a political candidate and won on the trial-court level.

Except in unusual cases, editors always insist that the reporter give the source of all opinionated statements:

> Community activist Nancy DeCosta today accused the Solid Waste Authority of "playing politics" with the lives of Eastside residents.
>
> "None of you want a rat-filled cesspool of garbage in your section of the city," DeCosta told the stony-faced members of the board, "but you are willing to ruin property values and threaten the lives of the poor people who live on the Eastside because they are poor."

It is essential to be fair. Every derogatory statement or accusation in a news story should be attributed to a source. The reporter must make an exceptional effort to seek out the person or persons subjected to the attack or allegation and allow him or her a chance to reply in the same news story.

The best way to attribute facts in a story is to state the source explicitly. However, to avoid the monotony of repeating "DeCosta said" throughout the story, a reporter should use direct and indirect quotations and other devices.

In news stories, the authoritative expression commonly is placed at the end of the sentence. The word "said" may be replaced with other words such as "declared," "insisted," "stated," "pointed out" and others, if they are applicable. But remember: "Said" is still the strongest choice.

Variety can also be achieved by presenting the authoritative phrase within the sentence rather than at the end.

> "I can't recall," Tucker told the Council, "when I have seen a worse proposal."

instead of

> "I can't recall when I have seen a worse proposal," Tucker said.

Words used to replace "said" should be chosen with care. Reporters often use words like "asserted," "stated" and "declared" to avoid repeating "said." But they really aren't the same. In fact, they are stronger and more formal words. "Pointed out" implies an indisputable fact. "Admitted" implies guilt. "Claim" casts doubt on the statement. Descriptive words such as "whispered," "screamed," "thundered," "declared," "insisted" and others should be used for the sake of accuracy only, not for the sake of variety.

7. The Story Itself Should Be Well Organized

The incidents of a story may actually occur in great chaos and confusion. The written story must analyze and relate these incidents one to another and to the central story theme. A speaker may actually ramble in this fashion:

> Gentlemen, this is a bad bill and ought not to pass. I was talking to Senator Williams last night, and he said the state can't afford all these welfare payments. I'm just as anxious to help the unfortunate as the next man, but I know down in my section we've got more people on welfare than we have people working. Some of them make more money off welfare than they did when they were working. That's why we shouldn't increase payments. This state's practically bankrupt. This bill might just push it over the edge. All we're doing if we pass this bill is paying people to rip off the taxpayer some more. You know it's true.

But the news story would probably read:

> Senator Jones opposed the bill. He argued that the state is nearly broke and cannot afford to increase welfare payments. He warned that this bill might push the state over the edge into bankruptcy.

THE STYLEBOOK

Before attempting to write news stories, the reporter should study thoroughly the stylebook of the publication for which he or she works. This guide, which usually is handed to a new reporter on the first day, explains the newspaper's style in preparing copy, spelling, punctuating, capitalizing, abbreviating and other such details. The common style is observed by all staff members.

The stylebook does not pretend to be an English grammar or a guide to composition and rhetoric. A reporter is expected to know common grammatical rules before beginning a newspaper career. Also, the careful reporter should make constant use of a standard handbook of English composition. The stylebook is designed to clarify certain disputed or difficult points and to explain certain accepted usages. One newspaper capitalizes "street" and "avenue" when they are used in place names ("Fourth Street"), which is called the "up style." Another newspaper uses a lowercase letter (Fourth street), the "down style." Some newspapers use a short form for a word such as "through," making it "thru." Obviously, not all stylebooks are alike, but the following style specifications can be studied as typical.

SPELLING

Any standard dictionary is the reference for spelling. Also, a city directory, telephone directory, almanac and Bible are useful in checking on the spelling of proper names. The "Associated Press Stylebook" and others also have sections on spelling.

PUNCTUATING

Use of the Period
1. Omit the periods in abbreviations of well-known governmental and other agencies.

   FBI   ROTC   AAA   FCC   ICC   PTA   USDA

2. Use three periods (. . .) to indicate quoted matter that has been omitted (four periods if at the end of a sentence and another sentence follows).
3. Use a period to indicate cents only when the figure is more than one dollar and when the dollar mark is used. Otherwise, write the word "cents."

   $1.01   43 cents   nine cents

4. Omit periods in headlines, subheadings, captions, and with Roman numerals and letters used in formulas.

Use of the Comma
1. Avoid superfluous use of commas, but do not violate accepted rules as set out in a standard handbook of English composition.
2. Use commas to set off the identification of a person, unless the identification is preceded by "of."

   John Smith, 1012 Towne St.
   John Smith of 1012 Towne St.

3. Use commas in listing a series (see Semicolon, 1).
4. Do not use a comma between a man's name and "Jr.," "Sr." or "II."

John Jones Sr.   James Smith Jr.   George VI

Use of the Colon

1. Use a colon to introduce a formal series of names or statements.

The following officers were elected: John Smith, president . . . (but "Officers elected are John Smith, president . . .").

2. Use a colon before minutes in writing the time of day, as in "3:30 p.m." (but "3 p.m.").
3. Use a colon between chapter and verse in referring to the Bible.

Luke 1:3–5

Use of the Semicolon

1. Semicolons should be used to separate a series of names and addresses or similar series containing commas.

Those attending were John Jones, 405 Trace St,; James Smith, 910 Drew Ave.; . . .

2. Semicolons should be used instead of periods in headlines.

Six Convicts Escape; Prison Guard Wounded

Use of the Dash

1. Use dashes to indicate unfinished sentences or broken sentence structure.
2. Use dashes to set off highly parenthetical elements and to enclose appositives containing commas.

A crowd assembled in front of the building, but the sheriff—the man for whom they called—was not to be found.

The six students selected—three seniors, two juniors and one sophomore—will receive . . .

3. Use dashes to indicate omitted letters.
4. Use a dash to separate a dateline from the first word of the lead.
5. Form the dash with two hyphens (--) on the typewriter.

Use of the Hyphen

1. Use the hyphen in compound adjectives.

coal-black chimney	well-known man
old-fashioned dress	so-called enemy
10-year-old girl	10-yard gain

2. Use a hyphen with prefixes to proper names.

un-American   pre-Christian   anti-Wing

3. Use a hyphen in writing figures or fractions.

   sixty-five   two-thirds

4. Use a hyphen between two figures to indicate the inclusion of all intervening figures, as "May 1-5."
5. Use a hyphen instead of "to" in giving scores, as "13-6."

Use of Parentheses

1. Use parentheses to insert a word within a title.

   The Bridgetown (Conn.) Fire Department

2. Use parentheses in a direct quotation to insert words that are not the speaker's.

   "They (the strikebreakers) shall not pass," said the foreman.

3. Use parentheses to enclose figures or letters that indicate subject divisions within a sentence.

   The committee decided (1) to refuse permission. . . .
   The board voted (a) to build a new athletic field. . . .

4. Parentheses are no longer used to indicate the political party or state, or both, of a government official, in abbreviated form. Current style is "Sen. John Smith, D-R.I."

Use of Quotation Marks

1. Use quotations marks to set off direct quotations.
   Special Note: While most sentences can be written as either direct or indirect quotations, the use of direct quotations in newspaper stories is reserved largely for statements that are best displayed within quotation marks. Examples are highly controversial statements, ironic expressions, facts rendered inaccurate by rewording, ideas rendered ineffective by paraphrasing, and unusual combinations of words.
2. Use quotation marks to set off titles of speeches, articles, books, poems, plays, operas, paintings, television programs.

   "Pride and Prejudice"   "Hamlet"   "Mona Lisa"   "Aida"

   (Note: Newspapers generally do not use italic body type, and quotation marks are employed as a substitute. However, quotation marks are not used in naming newspapers and magazines.)

3. Use quotation marks to set off coined words, slang and unusual words or expressions the first time such words are used in a story. Do not use quotation marks if the same words are used again.
4. Use quotation marks to set off nicknames when the full name is used but not when the nickname is used instead of the full name.

   John "Bud" Smith   Bud Smith

5. In a series of quoted paragraphs, use quotation marks at the beginning of each of these paragraphs and at the end of the last paragraph only.

6. Use single marks for a quotation within a quotation.
7. In headlines use the single quotation mark.
8. Quotation marks should always follow adjoining periods and commas.

"Here," she said.
His style recalled "Leaves of Grass."

If the punctuation belongs to the quotation, the question mark, the exclamation point, the colon, the semicolon and the dash also are followed by quotation marks.

"What do you want?" she asked.

Otherwise, quotation marks precede these punctuation marks.

Have you seen the new motion picture "May Queen"?

9. Do not use quotation marks in Q-and-A quotations.

Q: How old are you? A: Fifty-four

Use of the Apostrophe

1. Use the apostrophe to form the plural of letters but not the plural of figures, as "A's," "70s."
2. Use the apostrophe to indicate the possessive case.

New Year's Day   master's degree   children's home

3. Omit the apostrophe in such names as Blank County Farmers League and City Lawyers Association.

CAPITALIZING

Capitalize

1. Religious denominations and orders:

Protestant   Baptist   Jesuit   Franciscan

2. Nationalities, races:

Germans   Afro-American   Chinese

3. Names of animals, as Fido or Rover (no quotation marks).
4. Names of political organizations:

Democrat   Republican   Communist Party

5. National, state and local subdivisions:

North   South   West Montana   East Blankville

6. Political divisions:

Blank Counts   First District   Fifth Ward

7. Words used with numerals to form a proper name:

   Operator 7   Room 32   Lot 21   Journalism 301

8. Titles preceding proper names but not "former" or "ex" preceding such titles:

   President K.L. Burns   Prof. T.M. Smith   former President K.L. Burns

9. Nicknames, including those of states, cities, schools.
10. Complete titles of all public or private organizations:

General Assembly	City High School
City School Board	First Baptist Church
City Council	City Department Store
First National Bank	Jones and Company
Southmoor Hotel	Center Country Club

11. Place names:

Lake Michigan	Ohio River	Vatican City
First Creek	Atlantic Ocean	Great Smoky Mountains National Park

12. The first and all principal words in titles of speeches, plays, books, poems:

    "An Answer to Questions on War"   "The Way of the World"

13. Complete titles of streets, avenues, boulevards, roads:

    King Street   Elm Lane   Queen's Way

14. Holidays:

    Fourth of July   Labor Day   Lincoln's Birthday

15. The "Union," in referring to the United States.
16. Abbreviations of college degrees, as "B.A."
17. Abbreviations of "junior" and "senior" to "Jr." and "Sr."
18. Names of legislative acts or sections of documents, as Smith Law, Title D. (A final reminder: If in doubt about capitalizing a word, make it lowercase.)

Do not capitalize

1. Seasons of the year, as "spring" or "summer."
2. Points of the compass, as "northeast."
3. The abbreviations "a.m." and "p.m."
4. Titles that follow proper names, as "K.L. Burns, president."
5. Names of studies, except languages, as "mathematics," "French," "literature."

6. Scientific names of plants and animals, except names derived from proper nouns ("Hereford cattle").
7. "National," "government," "state," "federal," except in titles.
8. "Association," "club," "society," except in titles.
9. "Alma mater."

ABBREVIATING

Abbreviate

1. Months of the year of more than five letters when the day of the month is given:

    Nov. 24   the last week in January   March 21

2. Times of the day, as "6 p.m."
3. Familiar college degrees, as B.A., Ph.D., M.D.
4. Names of states only when they follow names of cities or countries:

    Blankville, Ark.   a town in Arkansas

5. "Mr.," "Mrs.," "Dr.," "the Rev.," "Prof.," "Gov.," "Gen.," etc., when they precede the name of a person.
6. "Saint" and "mount" only when preceding names:

    St. Louis   Mt. McKinley   "Sermon on the Mount"

7. "Sr.," "Jr.," "III" following proper names.
8. Titles of public and private organizations that are well-known by the readers after such titles have been used once in spelled-out form:

    FBI   SEC   CIO   YMCA   UCLA

Do not abbreviate

1. "Christmas."
2. "Percent" as " %," except in tabulation.
3. Names of persons.
4. Points of the compass.
5. Names of cities or countries.
6. Days of the week.
7. "Street," "avenue," "boulevard," etc., when not preceded by both the house number and the name.
8. "Company," except when a part of the official name.
9. "Association," "fraternity," "university."
10. "Department" or "building."
11. "And" as "&," unless it is part of a formal name of a firm.
12. Weights or measures, as "pound" and "foot."

TITLES

1. Always give a person's first name or initials with the surname the first time any name is used. Use the first name of unmarried women, not their initials, unless they are known by those initials. For example: M.F.K. Fisher, the California writer of a series of classic books with food as their central theme, is known to her legions of fans, editors and readers as M.F.K. Fisher. No one calls her "Mary," her first name.

2. On second reference and thereafter, most newspapers use just the last name. However, some still use so-called courtesy titles such as:

   Ms. Fisher   Miss Fisher   Mrs. Fisher

   Or in the case of a man:

   Mr. Smith   Dr. Smith   Prof. Smith

3. For most religious denominations, it is correct to refer to a minister first as "the Rev. John Smith," and thereafter in the story as "Mr. Smith." "Dr. Smith" should be used only if the minister holds a doctor of philosophy degree. There are exceptions: For Roman Catholic clergy, "the Rev. Patrick O'Malley" becomes "Father O'Malley" or whatever his rank in the priesthood may be. Jewish clergy should always be referred to as "Rabbi," "Rabbi Samuel Brown" on first reference and "Rabbi Brown" in the rest of the story. Latter Day Saints (Mormons) refer to their leader as "President John Smith," following which it should be "Mr. Smith." Christian Scientists have official titles such as "Practitioner," "Lecturer" and "Reader" instead of "the Reverend."

4. Do not use long and cumbersome titles before a name. Instead of "Director of Public Parks John Smith," make it "John Smith, director of public parks."

5. Do not refer to a woman as "Mrs. Dr. John Smith" or "Mrs. Prof. John Smith." A wife has no claim to her husband's title, and a husband has no claim to his wife's title.

6. Instead of "Mesdames" or "Messrs.," use titles singly.

7. Write "Mr. and Mrs. John Smith" instead of "John Smith and wife."

8. Do not use "honorable" in a title unless quoting someone else.

9. Do not use double titles such as "President Dr. John Smith." Choose the higher title or the one of greater relevance to the story.

10. Give exact titles of faculty members, public officials, business executives. "Professor" and "Instructor," for example, are not synonymous.

FIGURES

1. Spell out numbers from one through nine and use digits for all numbers above nine, except for the following:
   a. Spell out any number that begins a sentence.

b. Spell out numbers referring to centuries, as "tenth century."

c. Spell out ordinal street names, as "Fourth Street" up to "twenty-first."

d. Instead of "thirty-fifth" and "fiftieth," use "35th" and "50th," except in referring to centuries.

e. Spell out numbers in such phrases as "one in a hundred."

f. Use figures for all sums of money: "$5," "$6.01," "$23."

g. Use figures for the time of day, as "3 p.m.," "8 o'clock."

h. Use figures in tabulations.

i. Use figures for any whole and fractional number, as "91 1/2" and "4.1."

2. Spell out fractions, except after whole numbers, as "one-third."

3. Do not use "st," "nd," "rd," or "the" after dates. Write "Aug. 10, 1984."

MISCELLANEOUS RULES

Use the following style:

all right	cheerleader	homecoming	re-elect
all-state	cooperate	Joneses (plural)	somebody
anti-Catholic	everybody	line up	someone
anybody	everyone	newspaper	statewide
anyone	ex officio	nobody	text book
attorney general	governor-elect	no one	two-thirds
baseball	half-dollar	Old Glory	upstate
basketball	half-dozen	Post Office	

PREPARING COPY

For the convenience of those who may not yet write their stories on a video-display terminal (VDT), instructions for preparing copy on a typewriter and correcting copy with a pencil are included in Appendix A.

EXERCISES

1. The following sentences have errors in style, language use and spelling. Retype them on your VDT screen and correct them or copy them on a separate sheet of paper and correct the errors. There is at least one error in each sentence.

   a. Jones told police he had been laying around the house all day and didn't go near the bar.

   b. The faculty senate voted to censor the President for his failure to support academic freedom.

   c. Nearly fifteen hundred students walked out of classes today to protest the firing of the Women's Basketball coach.

    d. In spite of shortage of funds, Dean of Admissions and Records John W. Ragsdale IV said the university would be able to accommodate the overflow freshman class.

    e. The satellite was placed in stationery orbit over the equator.

    f. "Showboat," based on Edna Ferber's masterpiece, opens at 7:30 p.m., tonight in the Riverside amphitheater.

    g. The contractors said the new basketball arena will be completed by summer.

    h. Eighteen cars and trucks were completely demolished in the early morning pile up on fog shrouded Interstate 10.

    i. An FBI spokeswoman said Bailey's wife convinced him to surrender.

    j. The coroner said she was strangled to death in her bed.

2. Using any daily or weekly newspapers available to you, select five news stories in which the opening sentences are more than 40 words long. Rewrite them, using no more than 25 or 30 words.

3. Select five news stories from any daily or weekly newspaper available to you. Read them carefully, and mark each place in them where you think attribution should have been used but was not.

4. Compile a list of 25 synonyms for the word "said."

5. Compare the words on your list to the synonyms used in the stories on the front pages of any five newspapers available to you.

6. Analyze the following sentences and select the correct word of the choices given in parentheses:

    a. "What the team needs is (fewer, less) critics," Coach Paul Ashdown told newsmen today at his weekly press conference.

    b. Officials said the budget cuts will have a disastrous (affect, effect) on social programs.

    c. The 89-year-old man was (eager, anxious) to take his first plane ride.

    d. The parade was delayed (because of, due to) a thunderstorm.

    e. The state Supreme Court's ruling will have an (adverse, averse) impact on freedom of the press.

7. Some writers unconsciously pad their sentences with extra words. Copy these examples onto a separate sheet of paper, then delete the unneeded words and substitute shorter ones:

    a. Prior to the start of the season, he said he expected to win more games than he lost.

    b. The redesigned park will open in the near future, Mayor Victor Ashe said.

    c. Former Secretary of State George Schultz lectured on the subject of "A New World Order."

    d. Police said on a few occasions they had used force to quell student disturbances.

    e. Contestants will have to fill out a personality profile form in order to qualify for the competition.

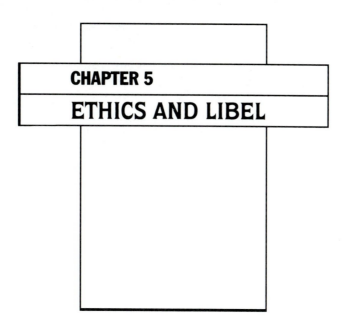

CHAPTER 5
ETHICS AND LIBEL

National surveys consistently show that large numbers of Americans harbor a deep resentment toward the media. The public says it feels overwhelmed by the media and that it finds the media aloof, arrogant, unaccountable and unresponsive to the needs of the readers and viewers.

Newspapers simply do not have a great deal of credibility with the public in general. One survey showed that only 13.7 percent of the respondents had "a great deal of confidence" in the American press. In another study, only 38 percent of the respondents told surveyors that they believed newspapers were usually fair and dedicated to telling both sides of the story.

Perhaps no other issue, except declining readership and advertising revenue, has been discussed as often by editors and reporters in the past decade as "credibility." There are almost as many explanations and excuses for why the public distrusts the press as there are individual speakers and panelists at professional press meetings.

Louis D. Boccardi of The Associated Press (AP) has said that newspapers need to re-examine attitudes and practices that alienate the readers. Newspapers must recognize an obligation not to do some of the things the First Amendment gives them a right to do, he said.

David Lawrence Jr., who was the first editor to head the American Society of Newspaper Editors' Credibility Committee, said readers and non-readers believe newspapers fail to revere either facts or fairness ". . . are scared of newspapers and are convinced newspaper editors and reporters are the sort of folks who always must have the last word."

Creed Black, now president of the Knight Foundation and former publisher of the Lexington (Ky.) Herald-Leader, said the credibility problem stems from the fact that the public lumps the printed press together in something called "the media" and makes little if any distinction between the printed press and television news. The result, he says, is that newspapers are blamed for the sins and shortcomings of what television, which remains basically an entertainment medium, calls news.

Loren Ghiglione, editor and publisher of the Southbridge (Mass.) News, says the press's unpopularity may have less to do with its performance, better or not, than with influential images from films, television shows, novels, and even rock and roll hits. The press of the popular imagination remains ". . . the amoral bearer of bad tidings, glorying in breaking the law to beat the competition to good gossip and gore."

Others blame the credibility problem on too many errors, a lack of understanding of what really concerns the public today, newspaper monopolies, superficial news coverage, poor writing and a host of other sins both real and imagined.

Michael G. Gartner, when he was president and editorial chairman of the Des Moines (Iowa) Register, said editors and publishers are "masochistic." He said they beat themselves up too much when what they should do is go home from their professional meetings and "keep trying to put out the very best newspaper we know how to produce—newspapers that are as fair, that are as accurate, that are as thorough, that are as newsy and as well-written as time will allow. If we do that, the public will trust us and buy us. We might not be loved, but we'll be respected."

While it is true that a few diehards in the news business will hold to the cherished hope that the First Amendment literally means that a newspaper has a right to print anything it wants to print, most responsible editors and reporters know better. A newspaper simply cannot and in a number of cases should not print anything it wants to, even if the courts permitted. There are numerous reasons—social, economic, ethical—that the First Amendment cannot be applied in its broadest, most literal sense to every story.

If the reporting staff is doing its job properly, every newspaper will have material that is both printable and unprintable. Deciding what should and what should not be printed is a constant moral and ethical dilemma for the editor and the reporter. Not all stories fit conveniently into a "print" or "do not print" category. In a moral and ethical sense, many fall somewhere in that gray area in between. In such cases, many reporters have considerable difficulty in knowing not only what to write but how to write it and when.

Stories such as the one about Senator Gary Hart's extramarital affair during the time he was seeking the presidential nomination often touch off as much debate inside the newspaper industry as they do with the public. However, the story involving Ohio Representative Donald Lukens' arrest and conviction for having sex with a juvenile generated little or no discussion of the ethical conduct of the press. The chief difference was the conduct of the reporters in the Hart case. While tracking down rumors about Hart's extramarital activities, reporters followed him in cars at night and hid in the hedge outside the house where he was meeting his model "friend." In the case of Lukens, the press simply covered his arrest and trial as it would in any other case involving a prominent person.

Was the conduct of the reporters in the Hart case unethical? Some journalists agreed with a lot of readers that it was. Others insist it was good "investigative" journalism. Did the public really need to know about Hart's private activities? Some critics of the press say no. Others insist his role as a prospective president made it essential that the public know everything about his character.

Debate over ethical issues goes on daily in every newspaper. Usually it does not involve individuals as prominent as Hart or Lukens, but the debate is just as intense. To help inform readers about these ethical problems, a number of newspapers, including the Charlotte (N.C.) Observer and News, invited readers to respond to hypothetical stories involving the names of rape victims, embezzlement by prominent businessmen, the criminal record of a prominent philanthropist, and others.

Generally, the readers participating in the exercise leaned more toward privacy and were more compassionate than the professionals in deciding how to handle such stories. However, they all agreed that it was difficult to come up with a consistent set of principles to apply to every story. Editors also reported that such exercises not only helped sensitize the public to their dilemma, but also helped attune the staff to questions of fairness.

Public interest frequently collides with special private interests in the news. And where these two are clearly conceived, the newspaper's policy (discussed in Chapter 14) may influence its decision and dictate its course of action. Normally, however, newspaper editors deal with each story of this nature on an individual basis.

Where certain larger issues of ethics and policy are concerned, newspapers frequently are influenced by what they consider to be acceptable community standards and by public opinion. For example, how graphic and detailed should a newspaper's description of a murder-rape case be? Should a newspaper publish more, or less, crime news? Under what condition, if any, should a newspaper report the name of a rape victim? Should the names of juveniles be printed if not forbidden by state law? Most newspapers attempt to be responsible to the opinions of their readers in these areas, although no newspaper can please every reader every day. Even the most well-meaning, carefully reasoned decision dealing with a moral or ethical issue may bring howls of protest, angry letters to the editor, and, on occasion, a cancelled subscription.

Members of a news staff can and sometimes do influence a newspaper's ethical or moral standards. In one instance, protests by the reporters forced an editor to reverse a decision to print the name of every woman who brought rape charges against a man. Every reporter wants to be proud of the newspaper's general moral or ethical standards. However, the reporter's principal concern should be for his or her own professional code of ethics.

Relations to the Public

Reporters cannot ignore the fact that the public welfare may be involved in much that they write. Newspapers are addressed to the general public. In many cases, what appears in a newspaper is the only, or chief, source that the public (individually or collectively) has for information. This responsibility makes careless, slipshod, inaccurate or biased reporting inexcusable.

One of the major criticisms of the press—one that creates a credibility problem—is "the press is biased." Often what is mistaken by the reader as bias is careless, inaccurate reporting by the writer of the story and the headline.

Ideally, a reporter would not make mistakes in judgment, but such mistakes are sometimes made. All reporters face situations in which they have to make decisions on what, how, when and how much information should be revealed in a story. Most reporters are guided by their conscience in these cases. A carefully trained, educated and enlightened reporter ordinarily should be able to make sound and unbiased judgments.

Relations to the Newspaper

Most newspapers are genuinely concerned about their reputation for fairness and accuracy. Editors want the respect of their readers and insist that reporters be fair and accurate. However, some publishers, in pursuit of a particular policy that may be social and economic as well as political, may expect much more or much less than the plain, unvarnished truth as the reporter sees it. In some instances, a change in ownership may cause a newspaper to reverse a policy, political or other.

A reporter faces a difficult choice if instructed by the editor or publisher to twist the truth in a story. Three possible courses seem to be open: Refuse to alter the story and resign; write a fair and accurate story and insist that it not carry a by-line if the editor inserts material that would make it misleading; and, finally, attempt to work out with the editor a change of assignments to avoid such conflicts in the future. There can be no doubt that the first and third of these choices are strictly ethical and should be satisfying in the long run, in terms of self-respect if not money.

The problem of ethics was one of the motivating forces behind the establishment of a number of journalism reviews. Perhaps the best known are the Columbia Journalism Review, published at Columbia University in New York City, and the Washington Journalism Review, established as an independent magazine and later given to the College of Journalism at the University of Maryland. Both evaluate the performance not only of newspapers but also of all the mass media.

The Chicago Journalism Review was among the first of the reviews established by staff members of local newspapers. Although it ceased publication after several years, it was a lively and often provocative publication that pointed out what its editors considered to be the shortcomings of the local media. Others were established in a number of cities, but most have disappeared.

Industry trade publications such as Presstime, published by the American Newspaper Publishers Association, and Editor & Publisher, the industry's oldest publication, do from time to time include press criticism. But generally they report current events and trends in the industry and are not known for biting critical analysis of the performance of newspapers.

In addition, several national organizations have been established by individuals or groups to monitor the performance of the mass media. The most prominent of these is AIM—Accuracy in Media—which represents a conservative point of view in its approach to the news.

Relations to News Sources

The reporter's access to news sources is a major professional asset. Sources must be carefully cultivated, honorably maintained and respected. On the other hand, reporters must not become the "captive" of their sources and work as their personal "press agents." Sources often attempt to use their close relationship with reporters to control the news in some fashion.

Good reporters know much more than they can get into print. And they do not divulge secrets or betray confidences. Of course, if ordered to do so by a judge, the reporter faces a dilemma: to reveal the source or go to jail. The U.S. Supreme Court has ruled that the First Amendment does not guarantee the right to protect the confidentiality of news sources. A number of states, however, do grant that right in cases tried in state courts. Sometimes it is wise for a reporter not to accept some so-called confidences, for the same information may be obtainable from other sources. Reporters who are intelligent and who work hard developing a network of sources should have little difficulty managing the ethics of this type of situation.

Reporters should have a clear understanding with every person they deal with. They should explain the role of the reporter as well as that of the editor so the source will know what to expect. They need to make it clear that reporters gather facts and write stories, whereas editors decide how much of a story goes into the paper and on which page. Reporters should be careful about making promises to sources and should not agree to let a source read a story in advance of publication. And they should be constantly aware that many sources, particularly in the area of politics, attempt to use reporters to personal advantage in an effort to color the news. On the other hand, they should respect confidences and release dates.

Increasing numbers of persons in public life are resorting to backgrounding sessions or informal conferences during which they will speak to reporters "off the record." Often they use these sessions to get information out to the public without being identified as the source. A number of reporters willingly cooperate, but the practice is criticized soundly by others. And some newspapers have a policy of not permitting their reporters to remain at such sessions if the source insists on not being identified in the news story that may grow out of the meeting.

Accuracy as a Protection

The best protection against bias in reporting is the indefatigable pursuit of fact and the careful checking of all facts. It has often been said that the three cardinal rules of journalism are accuracy, accuracy, accuracy. As long as reporters present the news as it actually occurs, without any ideological shading or emotional coloring, they are performing their duty professionally.

Of course, this will not make them or their newspapers immune to resentment or attack. A large proportion of the news will be injurious to someone or some cause or will be thought so by the individuals involved. The more important the revelation, the more resistance there is, usually, to the reporting of it. (Certain technical problems of privileged and non-privileged documents will be examined later on.) Every reporter should remember that in many cases, especially in the area of public affairs, even the most recalcitrant news source often is dependent on the media for his or her public image. But a reporter should never use that as a lever with a news source. In general, a reporter's reputation for accurate, professional reporting will often overcome resistance, solve problems and open many doors to the sources of news.

Importance of Authoritative News Sources

The careful use of authority in the news is an important means of solving certain ethical problems for reporters. The facts in every news story should be attributed to a reliable source. Reporters should know their sources well enough to know if they are trustworthy as well as authoritative. Even then, the careful reporter will seek verification of material with another source. Verification is especially critical if the reporter is dealing with an unfamiliar source. Despite precautions taken to cite authority and to confirm or verify information with additional sources, the reporter must occasionally face the fact that sources will lie.

CODES OF ETHICS

Although there are no concrete "rules of honor" for newspapers and their staffs that apply uniformly, an increasing number of publications are developing written codes in response to growing criticism by readers. There always is a danger in trying to put together an all-inclusive list of what the newspaper will and will not permit its staff to do because such restrictions can "handcuff" the staff, and there always will be someone who will find a way to circumvent the standard. Nevertheless, a written code does indicate what the newspaper considers ethical and can serve to raise the consciousness of the staff.

Whether they have a written code or not, most newspapers today attempt to follow a set of principles or a code of ethics established by such professional groups as the American Society of Newspaper Editors (ASNE) and the Society of Professional Journalists (SPJ). Here is a Statement of Principles adopted by the ASNE in 1975, which supplanted the organization's Code of Ethics, originally written in 1922:

PREAMBLE
The First Amendment, protecting freedom of expression from abridgement by any law, guarantees to the people through their press a constitutional right, and thereby places on newspaper people a particular responsibility.

Thus journalism demands of its practitioners not only industry and knowledge but also the pursuit of a standard of integrity proportionate to the journalist's singular obligation.

To this end the American Society of Newspaper Editors sets forth this Statement of Principles as a standard encouraging the highest ethical and professional performance.

ARTICLE I—RESPONSIBILITY

The primary purpose of gathering and distributing news and opinion is to serve the general welfare by informing the people and enabling them to make judgments on the issues of the time. Newspapermen and women who abuse the power of their professional role for selfish motives or unworthy purposes are faithless to that public trust.

The American press was made free not just to inform or just to serve as a forum for debate but also to bring an independent scrutiny to bear on the forces of power in the society, including the conduct of official power at all levels of government.

ARTICLE II—FREEDOM OF THE PRESS

Freedom of the press belongs to the people. It must be defended against encroachment or assault from any quarter, public or private.

Journalists must be constantly alert to see that the public's business is conducted in public. They must be vigilant against all who would exploit the press for selfish purposes.

ARTICLE III—INDEPENDENCE

Journalists must avoid impropriety and the appearance of impropriety, as well as any conflict of interest or the appearance of conflict. They should neither accept anything nor pursue any activity that might compromise or seem to compromise their integrity.

ARTICLE IV—TRUTH AND ACCURACY

Good faith with the reader is the foundation of good journalism. Every effort must be made to assure that the news content is accurate, free from bias and in context, and that all sides are presented fairly. Editorials, analytical articles and commentary should be held to the same standards of accuracy with respect to facts as news reports.

Significant errors of fact, as well as errors of omission, should be corrected promptly and prominently.

ARTICLE V—IMPARTIALITY

To be impartial does not require the press to be unquestioning or to refrain from editorial expression. Sound practice, however, demands a clear distinction for the reader between news reports and opinion. Articles that contain opinion or personal interpretation should be clearly identified.

ARTICLE VI—FAIR PLAY

Journalists should respect the rights of people involved in the news, observe the common standards of decency and stand accountable to the public for the fairness and accuracy of their news reports.

Persons publicly accused should be given the earliest opportunity to respond.

Pledges of confidentiality to news sources must be honored at all costs, and therefore should not be given lightly. Unless there is clear and pressing need to maintain confidences, sources of information should be identified.

These principles are intended to preserve, protect and strengthen the bond of trust and respect between American journalists and the American people, a bond that is essential to sustain the grant of freedom entrusted to both by the nation's founders.

THE PITFALLS OF LIBEL

Every reporter works with the specter of a libel suit nearby because there simply is no sure-fire method of preventing libelous material from getting into a newspaper story. In writing news it is not always easy to determine the exact point at which the public's right to know is greater than the individual's right to his or her good name. A reporter must never forget that every person is protected by law from the publication of libelous or slanderous statements. A person's name—reputation—is of tangible value. And if a reporter damages it, even unintentionally, he or she could do irreparable harm to a person's position in society or that person's means of earning a living.

Damage to a person's reputation, if it is beyond the bounds of what a newspaper is legally entitled to print, is called "defamation." As a general rule, defamation is divided into two categories—libel and slander. In the view of the courts, libel is written defamation; slander is spoken. Over the years, the courts have expanded the definition of libel, making it include all defamation that offers a greater possibility of harm than does slander because it is written (and is therefore more permanent than slander). Written materials, signs, cartoons, television, and even radio broadcasts that have been taped or presented from written scripts have been held by the courts to be libelous.

Libel Defined

Libel laws vary in each state. As a result, definitions of libel may be slightly different from state to state. However, they are all essentially the same. Libel can be defined as:

> A false statement printed or broadcast about a person that exposes that person to public hatred, ridicule, or contempt, lowers him in the esteem of the community, causes him to be shunned, or injures him in his business or profession.

It is important to remember that a person may libel another either by outright expressions or by insinuation or innuendo. A person also may be libeled even though he or she may not actually be named.

Elements of Libel

Anyone filing a libel suit, regardless of status, has to establish these elements:

- *Publication*—that the statement was published (communicated) in some form. In the case of the news media, the most common way is either a newspaper article or a radio or television broadcast.
- *Identification*—that the statement was generally understood to refer to the person suing by persons who knew him or her or members of the general public. The person suing does not have to be specifically named. And members of a group, such as a school board, can be libeled even though they are not individually named.
- *Injury*—that the statements caused actual damage in some tangible manner. This could mean actual loss of money as a result of a lost job or a business contract, for example, or damage to the person's reputation, humiliation, or mental anguish and suffering.
- *Fault*—the status of the person suing determines what must be proved. If the person suing is a public person or public figure and the alleged libelous statement concerns his or her public role, he or she must prove that the statement was made by the newspaper or broadcast station even though it was known in advance to be false or that there was serious doubt as to its truth. But if the person suing is a private individual, or a public official or figure suing about a statement concerning a purely private matter not affecting his or her public role, then all that has to be proved is that the publisher or broadcaster was negligent in failing to determine that the statement was false and that it defamed the person suing.

Who Can Be Defamed?

Any living person can be defamed. A dead person cannot be defamed; however, if the words reflect upon any living survivor of that person, he or she can bring an action. A corporation or a partnership can be defamed by language that casts aspersions on its honesty, credit, efficiency and other business character. Individual professionals such as doctors and lawyers can be defamed if the language casts aspersions on their honesty or ability to practice their professions. For example, to call a doctor a quack or a lawyer a shyster could be libelous.

Every person instrumental in the publication of a libelous statement is responsible. This usually includes the person making the statement, the reporter, the editor, and the newspaper itself, but the newspaper alone is made the defendant in many suits.

Interpretation of Defamatory Words

In all actions for libel and slander, the words alleged to be defamatory must be interpreted as such; they must be understood in the defamatory sense whether or not they are believed by the listeners or readers. It is not necessary that the defamatory meaning be apparent on the face of the communication; a communication may be defamatory as a result of circumstances known to the reader. For example, a false report that a woman had given birth to twins was held to be defamatory when the woman was able to prove that readers knew she had been married for only one month. A subject may be defamed even though the communication does not refer to that subject by name if the subject can show that the defamatory meaning referred to him or her. Such statements as "it is alleged," "it was reported," or "according to police" do not protect a reporter who writes a libelous statement.

Proof Needed

Formerly all libel was actionable without proof of some injury or harm to persons or property. Today, however, many jurisdictions treat libel like slander in that they require proof of damages incurred, except in the following cases:

1. The imputation of a serious crime involving moral turpitude
2. The imputation that the party is infected with a contagious disease
3. The imputation affecting the plaintiff in his or her business, trade, profession or office
4. The imputation reflecting upon the chastity of a woman.

However, all jurisdictions hold that words that are libelous per se are actionable without damage having to be shown. In most libel cases, however, an effort is made to show damage in order to increase the amount of the judgment.

Intent to Libel

The U.S. Supreme Court, under the late Chief Justice Earl Warren, changed the direction of libel law to favor the news media. In its landmark decision in 1964—New York Times vs. Sullivan—the Court ruled that the constitutional guarantees of a free press prohibit a public official from recovering damages for a libelous, false statement relating to official conduct unless the official could prove that the statement was made with actual malice. To prove actual malice, the court said, the public official must prove that the statement was made with deliberate knowledge that it was false or that it was made with reckless disregard of whether it was false or not. The burden of proof was on the public official.

The so-called New York Times rule was expanded in the Butts vs. Curtis Publishing Co. case in 1967 to apply not only to public officials but also to public figures. In 1971 it was expanded again in the Rosenbloom vs. Metromedia, Inc. case to include private individuals involved in matters of general and public interest.

The problem of determining who qualified as a public official frequently plagued the press after the Times ruling. Generally, the press gave the Times rule a broad interpretation. However, in 1974, the Court, under a new chief justice— Warren Burger—took another look at who was public and who was private and came up with a new interpretation in the case of Gertz vs. Robert Welch, Inc.

Gertz, a Chicago lawyer known for his trial work on behalf of civil rights and other causes and the author of several books, charged that he was libeled by the John Birch Society magazine American Opinion. Among other things, the magazine called him a Leninist and a communist fronter. The magazine article appeared while Gertz was representing a family that had sued the Chicago police department over the death of their son, who had been shot and killed by a policeman. The magazine alleged that the suit was part of a plot to destroy the Chicago police department. Throughout the trial against the police department, Gertz kept a low profile, refusing to be interviewed and rejecting efforts of the media to get him to discuss the case publicly.

When he sued the magazine for libel, Gertz was able to find twelve jurors who claimed they had never heard of him despite his local fame. It was a major factor in helping him prove that he was not as well known as the magazine would claim in defending the suit. A jury found that Gertz had been libeled and awarded him $50,000 in damages. In the legal maneuvering that followed, the trial judge threw out the jury's award and said that Gertz was a public figure under the Times rule. Gertz appealed and the District Appeals Court upheld the trial judge, ruling that, because the story concerned matters of public interest, Gertz should have to show actual malice on the magazine's part, even though he might be a private citizen. He had failed to do this, the Appeals Court ruled.

Gertz appealed to the Supreme Court, which reversed the Appeals Court. The Supreme Court ruled that Gertz was not a public figure in this case and did not have to prove actual malice. In this decision, the Court established that there are two kinds of public figures. One kind is the individual who achieves such pervasive fame or notoriety that he or she becomes a public figure for all purposes and all contexts or the individual who voluntarily injects himself or herself or is drawn into a particular public controversy and thereby becomes a public figure. Gertz did neither, the Court ruled. The second kind is the limited public figure. Under this concept, the Court said, the nature and extent of an individual's participation in a particular controversy giving rise to the defamation must be considered. In short, the Court was saying that an individual must play a prominent role in a particular controversy before being considered a full public figure.

In 1976 the Court further narrowed the definition of public figure in Time, Inc. vs. Firestone. That case involved a divorce suit and resulted from a blurb in Time magazine that said Russell Firestone had been granted a divorce from his wife, Mary Alice, on the grounds of adultery. He had not been. The wife sued Time, claiming she had been called an adulteress. Time claimed she was a prominent socialite and a public figure. It said the 17-month divorce case was well publicized and that she had held several press conferences during the trial. But the Court said a divorce suit was not the kind of public controversy referred to in the Gertz decision. It noted that while there was public interest in the case, it was not an important public question.

Under the Times rule, a public official seeking to prove actual malice was barred from inquiring into the state of mind of the reporter and editors when the alleged libelous story was being prepared for publication. Over the years, the Supreme Court has chipped away at that concept. Finally, in 1979, in the Herbert vs. Lando decision, the Court reversed the Times ruling on that point. In that case, Col. Anthony Herbert, an army officer who gained national recognition for his charges that he reported misconduct of troops and officers in Vietnam but was ignored by his superiors, sued Barry Lando, a television producer for the Columbia Broadcasting System. Herbert charged he had been libeled in a CBS program produced by Lando, which discredited him and his charges against the army. In preparing for the case, Herbert's lawyers sought to ask questions about Lando's state of mind when preparing the telecast. Lando refused to answer their questions. When the case reached the Supreme Court, it ruled that a libel plaintiff, obliged to prove actual malice because he is a public figure, has the right to inquire into a reporter's state of mind. The decision brought a warning from the Reporters Committee for Freedom of the Press that it "will encourage harassing libel suits and will discourage news about public events."

Late in 1979, the Court acted again to put additional restraints on who might be considered a public person. One case involved U.S. Senator William Proxmire and a scientist. The other involved a former State Department interpreter and Reader's Digest.

Proxmire, in a press release, had ridiculed the scientist, Ronald Hutchinson. He awarded Hutchinson his monthly "Golden Fleece" award for wasting taxpayer's dollars with his publicly funded research. Hutchinson had received more than $500,000 to study aggression in monkeys to help the Navy and the National Aeronautics and Space Administration better select crews for submarines and spaceflights. In his press release, Proxmire called the research "monkey business." Hutchinson sued for $8 million.

The other case involved Ilya Wolston, a former State Department interpreter, cited for contempt by a federal grand jury when he refused to appear during an investigation of Russian spying in the United States. Wolston later cooperated with federal officials and was never indicted for espionage. However, in 1974 he was listed as "among Soviet agents identified in the U.S." in a book called "KGB: The Secret Work of Soviet Agents." He sued the author, John Barron, and the publisher, Reader's Digest Association, Inc.

At the lower court trials, both Hutchinson and Wolston were ruled to be public figures and their libel suits dismissed. When the cases finally came before the U.S. Supreme Court, it reversed those decisions. In its decisions, the Court said that neither Hutchinson nor Wolston had "thrust" himself into a public controversy in order to affect its outcome. Mere involvement in a newsworthy event, the Court ruled, did not automatically make a person a public figure. (This is a reversal of the Rosenbloom decision and several others of the 1960s.) The Court also rejected Proxmire's defense that he was immune from libel suits by the Constitution, which states that "for any speech or debate in either House," members of Congress "shall not be questioned in any other place." Proxmire argued that congressmen cannot be held liable for what they say on the floor of Congress. The Court pointed out that what the senator had said was not said on the floor of Congress but in a press release. It ruled that congressional press releases and newsletters were not immune from libel suits.

The U.S. Supreme Court continued to consider libel cases during the 1980s and early 1990s. Several cases dealing specifically with the First Amendment protection of "opinion" led to what libel lawyer E. Eddie Wayland termed "a revolutionary turnabout in the judicial interpretation of the First Amendment."

In their libel manual, "The Media and the First Amendment in Tennessee," Wayland and his colleagues at King & Ballow, a Nashville law firm that has gained a reputation as one of the leading media law groups in the nation, say that was particularly true in Milkovich vs. Lorain Journal Co. In that case the Supreme Court concluded that a sports column implying that a high school wrestling coach had committed perjury during a court proceeding investigating a fight between two rival wrestling teams did not rate separate privilege in addition to existing First Amendment protection.

The coach had lost his original lawsuit largely because the Ohio court held that the article expressed the columnist's "opinion," which under the law at that time was fully protected by the First Amendment. But after 15 years of litigation in the Ohio courts, the U.S. Supreme Court decided that a separate privilege for opinion was unnecessary.

Wayland and his colleagues explained that before the Supreme Court's Milkovich decision in 1990, the lower courts had classified statements three ways: (1) pure fact, (2) pure opinion, and (3) mixed fact and opinion. Reporters used those classifications as guidelines. False statements of facts were actionable. Statements of opinion were not actionable. However, courts required that the facts underlying the opinion be presented. And if they were false and defamatory, the writer and the publication could be sued.

The mixed opinion category required that a court determine whether the opinion was based on undisclosed facts that could be considered defamatory. If the plaintiff could prove that the mixed opinion was reasonably understood as relying on defamatory, undisclosed facts, then the mixed opinion was actionable.

The significance of the Supreme Court decision in this case, Wayland said, is its rejection of the proposition that the First Amendment requires a separate privilege for opinion. He pointed out that the Court reiterated its earlier Philadelphia Newspapers vs. Hepps ruling that "a statement of opinion relating to matters of public concern which does not contain a provable false factual connotation will receive full constitutional protection." This means that a writer or speaker must fully disclose the injurious facts underlying the opinion or rely on non-defamatory undisclosed facts in order for the opinion to be protected.

The Philadelphia Newspapers vs. Hepps case, decided in 1986, is considered an important victory for the media. It deals with libel suits brought by private individuals against the media. The Court held that private figures must prove the falsity of the defamatory statements in order to recover damages if the article or broadcast covered is a "matter of public concern." The decision brought private figures under the same constraint as public officials and public figures who have been required to prove falsity in order to recover damages.

Television and Radio—Libel or Slander?

Defamation via television is generally considered libel because it is the type of defamation that can be detected by the sense of sight. The vast audience and the ensuing increase in the likelihood of harm are additional reasons given for this interpretation. Radio presents a different problem. Most courts have held that defamation through the medium of radio is slander unless the broadcast is made from a prepared script or from a tape or other recording.

Defenses of Libelous Statements

There are five basic defenses in a libel suit:

The statement is the truth.

The newspaper is "privileged" to print the statement.

The statement is fair comment or criticism.

The statement was made with the consent of the person who claims he or she was libeled.

The newspaper offered the person the right of reply to the alleged libelous statement.

In general, the first three are the most significant defenses. However, the last two could prove to be of extreme importance to the newspaper's defense in a libel suit. In defending itself against a libel suit, the newspaper has the responsibility to prove that one or more of the defenses existed when the story was published.

Truth as a Defense

A newspaper's strongest defense against libel is to be able to prove what it prints is true. A reporter must not rely on hearsay, opinions or rumors if a statement in any way borders on libel. A report that "Detective Smith said Tom Johns robbed the store" is libelous unless the reporter can prove Johns actually robbed the store (or unless the report is privileged, as explained in the following paragraphs). Calling a building an "alleged house of ill repute" libels every person living in that house unless the statement can be proved. Fortunately, it is not necessary to prove that a story is meticulously true. Slight inaccuracies of expression are immaterial provided the defamatory charge is true in substance.

If a statement is true, a libel suit probably will not arise, for truth is generally accepted as a "complete defense." In some states, however, the newspaper must show a good motive for publishing the statement even if it is true.

A common misconception is that a newspaper or a radio or television station is safe as long as it merely repeats or attributes the false and libelous statement to a particular person. This simply is not true. And a newspaper cannot base its defense on the fact that the person it has libeled is guilty of even worse conduct than that implied in the libelous statement. If a newspaper falsely publishes that a person is guilty of robbery, it is no defense to be able to prove that he or she committed a murder. Likewise, a newspaper cannot imply that a person is guilty of repeated misconduct and then offer as its defense that the person was guilty of such conduct at least one time.

Privilege as a Defense

The reporter is privileged to report derogatory statements that are taken from legislative, judicial, or other public and official proceedings and records without fear of successful libel or slander action. Because the meetings and records of such groups as city councils and state legislatures are generally open to the public, the newspaper has a right to step in and represent the public. If a person is defamed in those proceedings, he or she cannot recover damages. The public's interest in such cases outweighs the individual's right to reputation, even though he or she may suffer real harm. The immunity for the participant in official proceedings is called "absolute" privilege. As long as what is said is relevant to the business of the proceedings, it is privileged and therefore not actionable. Anyone reporting such proceedings is given an immunity from successful suit for defamation, also.

The protection granted the reporter, however, is somewhat more limited in that in most states it does not protect malice in reports. As a result, it is known as "qualified" privilege. There are other considerations that must be met by the reporter to enjoy this qualified privilege. The story must be a fair and accurate account of the proceedings. Great caution is necessary in quoting from official proceedings, public records, police reports and other public sources of information. Some states have laws that spell out in considerable detail the kinds of proceedings and records protected as privileged communications. The Proxmire case, cited earlier, is an example of how the concept of privileged material has been narrowed down by court decisions.

Fair Comment

Newspapers and other mass media have the right to comment on and criticize the acts of public persons who offer themselves or their particular talent for public approval. But the comment must be

Fair

Made without malice

Not unjustifiably extended to the private life of the person involved.

Actors, artists, authors, composers, speakers and others who offer themselves or their works for public acceptance are subject to comment or criticism by the press. The press also has the right to criticize the public performance of public officials. However, the defense of fair comment is lost in most cases when a newspaper invades the private lives of such persons. To say that an author is a poor writer because he or she knows nothing about plotting a novel could be fair comment. To say that the author is a poor writer because of his or her sexual proclivities could bring a libel suit. Writers should be careful to criticize only the substance of an author's book, the caliber of an artist's painting or the quality of an actress's performance.

A classic example on how far a publication can go in commenting on a matter submitted for public acceptance was illustrated by the Cherry Sisters case

(114 Iowa 298). The defendants had published an article in which a reviewer gave the following graphic description of a public performance by three sisters who danced and sang:

> Effie is an old jade of 50 summers, Jessie a frisky filly of 40, and Addie (the plaintiff in the case), the flower of the family, a capering monstrosity of 35. Their long skinny arms, equipped with talons at the extremities, swung mechanically, and anon waved frantically at the suffering audience. The mouths of their rancid features opened like caverns and sounds like the wailing of damned souls issued therefrom. They pranced around the stage with a motion that suggested a cross between the danse du ventre and fox trot—strange creatures with painted faces and hideous mien.

That style of criticism is still practiced by some critics today. John Simon, theater critic for New York magazine, gained considerable reputation for his biting, sometimes even savage, attacks on performers. In a review of a musical starring actress-singer-dancer Liza Minnelli, he wrote:

> I always thought Miss Minnelli's face deserving—of first prize in the beagle category. Less aphoristically speaking it is a face going off in three directions simultaneously: the nose always enroute to becoming a trunk, blubber lips unable to resist the pull of gravity, and a chin trying its damnedest to withdraw into the neck, apparently to avoid responsibility for what goes on above it. It is, like any face, one that could be redeemed by genuine talent, but Miss Minnelli has only brashness, pathos and energy.

Miss Minnelli did not sue despite the fact that Simon's attack was not directly related to her performance in this particular musical. He made no attempt to relate her physical appearance to the role she was playing or the plot of the musical, but the implication was clear.

In writing about public officials, a newspaper reporter has the right to comment on or criticize that official's performance on the job. The courts have even given the press more latitude in commenting on public officials than they have allowed in criticizing the work of creative artists. Some comment on the private life and personal conduct of the public official is allowed if the official's private conduct has an influence on the way he or she conducts the public's business. For example, the late Drew Pearson and Jack Anderson, syndicated columnists, were not sued for libel when they reported in a series of columns that a very influential senior member of the House of Representatives was an alcoholic. He was subject to fair comment, no matter how damaging it might have been, because he was unable to separate his alcoholism from the conduct of his public office.

However, every reporter should be aware that the Supreme Court has continued to narrow the definition of who is a public person or public official. Its recent decisions indicate a growing concern for the privacy of even the most public persons.

Consent

It is not uncommon for a person to give consent to the publication of material and then change his or her mind after it is in print. On occasion the person may even sue because the material is libelous. In most cases, the newspaper is privileged to publish libelous matter if the libeled person has consented to it. A person does have a right, however, to place restrictions on consent. The person may, for example, want to limit publication to a particular time or for a particular purpose. The newspaper loses the defense of consent if it breaks the agreement.

A person may consent to publication of material by either oral or written authorization, or consent may be implied from the person's words or other conduct. Implied consent may be obtained by requesting and receiving a voluntary acknowledgment and confirmation of the libelous material. But the mere denial of, or refusal to answer questions concerning, the libelous material does not qualify as consent. A newspaper is on much safer ground if it has written consent when potentially libelous statements are involved.

The Right of Reply

Right of reply is a much stronger defense than consent. "Right of reply" simply means that a newspaper gives the person who has been libeled an opportunity to answer the charges or attack. Generally newspapers, simply as a matter of good faith, will not print a libelous attack, even if privileged to do so, without giving the attacked person a right to reply in the same article. It is important to note that the reply cannot exceed the scope of the original attack. The reply must be limited to answering the original attack only. It cannot be expanded to include any other area of concern or to introduce any new material. The chief purpose the right of reply serves is to demonstrate that the newspaper is acting in good faith and is not simply being a party to the original libelous attack. It helps the newspaper prove that it was not acting maliciously.

Statute of Limitations

Most state libel laws set a specific time limit on the filing of libel suits. Generally this ranges from one to three years after the first publication of the libelous material. A newspaper that circulates in several states should take the precaution of learning about the statute of limitations in each of those states.

Criminal Libel

Most libel cases go to civil courts, with the plaintiff suing for damages. Some libel cases can be tried in criminal court and may be punishable by fine and imprisonment. A number of states have laws that criminal prosecution is possible if the statements tend to provoke the wrath of the person about whom they are printed; to expose that person to public hatred, contempt or ridicule; or to deprive him or her of the benefits of public confidence and social intercourse. However, the Garrison vs. Louisiana case has done away with this area as a serious threat to journalists.

Two other special circumstances can be involved. One is libel of the dead, which is presumed to provoke relatives and friends of the deceased to violence; the other is libel of groups when the libel provokes violence. Both are quite rare. Since criminal statutes vary on these points, it is advisable for the reporter to consult state laws for the exact rules to follow.

Retractions of Libelous Statements

Newspapers attempt to avoid libel suits by publishing retractions of statements that are unquestionably libelous. The retraction should point out and correct the newspaper's errors, and the newspaper should apologize to the person or persons concerned. The retraction notice, in order to be effective, must generally be given space or time that is equivalent to that of the defamatory matter. For instance, if the defamatory material was printed on the first page of a newspaper, the retraction notice should be published on the first page. (In several states, all retraction notices are required by law to be published on the front page no matter where the original story appeared in the paper.) The retraction does not nullify the claim for damages against the newspaper, although it satisfies many libeled persons and causes them to decide against filing suit. If a libel suit is filed, the retraction may help reduce the damages awarded by indicating lack of actual malice.

INVASION OF THE RIGHT TO PRIVACY

Although laws of libel date back almost to the dawn of civilization, the right of privacy—the right to be left alone—is relatively new. The concept was first introduced formally in the 1890s. Originally it related to the use of a person's consent. However, privacy law has been expanded over the years and has been recognized as a constitutional right by the U.S. Supreme Court. Simply stated, the right of privacy is the right of a person to be left alone. It guarantees all citizens that they can, under most circumstances, expect to be free from unwarranted publicity and to enjoy life without fear of waking up and finding their names, photographs or personal activities in print. Of course, they can waive that right. The right of privacy is personal, protecting the feelings and sensibilities of living persons only. A corporation or public institution such as a university has no right of privacy, unless granted by special law. A person's right to privacy ends at death and is generally not transferable to relatives.

A person's privacy can be invaded by newspapers, radio stations, television stations, photographers, motion pictures, books, advertisements and dozens of electronic means ranging from wiretapping to supersensitive microphones that can pick up conversations at great distances. However, the extent to which anyone is protected generally depends on his or her status as a public or private figure. Public officials and public figures are more legitimately open to public comment, criticism and scrutiny than are ordinary citizens. However, there are limits on the press even in the case of public officials and public persons.

A person's privacy can be invaded in four ways:

Wrongful Intrusion.   Wrongful intrusion generally involves the invasion of a person's solitude or private affairs without his or her knowledge or consent. It often involves the use of spying devices such as hidden microphones, wiretaps, hidden tape recorders and high-powered cameras, or illegal obtainment of a person's private documents. A reporter who gains access to a place or a person by misrepresentation, especially on private property, could be subject to an invasion of privacy suit.

Publishing Private Matters.   A newspaper may be guilty of invading privacy when it publishes facts about the private life of a person that would offend ordinary sensibilities and that may cause that person mental suffering or embarrassment. Publishing sensational private matters about a person's economic, social or sexual activities, for example, could lead to an invasion of privacy suit.

Placing a Person in a False Light.   Placing a person in a false light may be said to occur when a news story or photograph, for example, implies something other than the facts. The nature of the published material must not lead the public to assume or believe something that is not specifically mentioned or portrayed by the material. This commonly occurs when a writer embellishes facts for dramatic effect.

Appropriation.   A publication is guilty of invading a person's privacy if it uses that person's name, likeness or personality for advertising or other commercial use. This does not apply to news coverage. For example, a newspaper could photograph Burt Reynolds arriving at the local airport to begin filming a movie. That's news. That same publication could not reproduce Reynolds' photograph on a poster and sell it to make money without his permission.

Most states have laws that grant the mass media the right to use the name or a picture of a person without previous consent in connection with a current or even previous news event as long as there is genuine public interest. The Supreme Court has upheld that right in several important cases. On the other hand, the courts have granted entertainers, sports figures and other public persons the "right to publicity." That means they have a right to protect themselves for commercial exploitation. They can "sell" their names and likenesses and profit from so doing. The press cannot use a name except in connection with a legitimate news story.

Defenses

Truth is normally not a defense in invasion of privacy suits. However, there are three standard defenses:

1. *Newsworthiness.* The newsworthiness defense requires the publication to establish that the information revealed about the person who is suing was newsworthy or in the public interest.

a. *Public figures.* A publication can use the name or photograph or information about a public official; candidate for public office; or public figure such as a writer, actor or musician without prior consent as long as it is reporting matters of legitimate public concern about that person's life. Even such a person's private life can be made public without consent as long as the information relates legitimately to his or her role as a public official or person. The case involving Drew Pearson and Jack Anderson cited earlier is a good example. In addition, the courts have ruled that the public has a continuing interest in public figures even after they retire from public life.

b. *Private individuals.* Private persons generally cannot sue successfully for invasion of privacy if they become part of a public event, even unwillingly. A person who happens to be in a crowd watching while police raid a local pornographic bookstore has no legitimate cause for a suit if his or her picture appears in a newspaper report of that raid. Any private citizen may become the object of legitimate news interest to the public either as an individual or as part of a group event, even though the involvement was unexpected or involuntary.

2. *Consent.* A consent defense requires that the publication show it had the prior consent of the person who is suing. Consent is not needed for legitimate news events. However, an invasion of privacy suit might grow out of such an event if the reporter obtained information illegally or wrongfully intruded on the private property of a person in order to collect information for a news story. Consent, as noted under the section on libel, is not a strong defense.

3. *Constitutional Privilege.* The constitutional privilege provides that persons involved in matters of public concern cannot recover damages for a story that may place them in a "false light" unless they can prove the newspaper printed the material knowing it was false or had serious doubts about its truth.

Courts have held that public officials and public figures have virtually no right of privacy insofar as the facts relate, even remotely, to their public lives. And almost any logical connection between a private person and an event of public interest places them in the same category as a public official or figure. Disclosures of arrests, births, deaths, marriages, divorces, personal tragedies, civil suits and interesting accomplishments generally have been found to be protected.

In almost all cases, disclosed material that is a part of a public record has been held to be nonactionable. A publication generally cannot be held accountable for public disclosure of private facts when it simply further publicizes matters that are already public or that the plaintiff has left open to public scrutiny.

Wayland and his colleagues cite these examples of unsuccessful claims of invasion of privacy: the publication of a plaintiff's jail term and a discussion of his six marriages (information gathered from public records open to public scrutiny); a magazine article's estimation of an attorney's wealth (newsworthy);

property ownership and business ventures (public records); a newspaper's publication of confidential child abuse information that had been included in the prosecution's case file and lawfully obtained by the reporter (public records); a newspaper's publication of events surrounding a suicide attempt by a jail inmate who tested positive for AIDS (newsworthy); the unauthorized disclosure of a confidential report that a plaintiff had been found unqualified for judicial appointment (newsworthy and public figure); and publication of a plaintiff's homosexuality in a story dealing with his efforts to avert the attempted assassination of a U.S. president (newsworthy and already open to public scrutiny).

It should be noted that many persons—scholars, writers, lawyers, journalists and lawmakers—believe that the right of privacy is in great peril as a result of sophisticated electronic equipment that permits almost undetectable spying on individuals. There also is a great concern about the invasion of privacy as a result of law enforcement agencies, credit bureaus, insurance firms, governmental agencies and a host of others who are collecting dossiers on private citizens for a variety of reasons and storing them in computer data banks.

Major scandals have developed out of the practice of certain government agencies of spying on private citizens, and both the federal government and many state governments have passed laws seeking to control the collection of information about private citizens. Despite these efforts, collection of data continues and more and more computer data banks come on line each year containing all types of information, both true and false, and posing a threat to the right of privacy of millions of Americans.

NONTRADITIONAL CLAIMS AGAINST THE MEDIA

The past decade has seen an increase in the number of nontraditional claims against the media. Among them have been charges that the media inflicted emotional distress and that a newspaper violated a contract by disclosing the name of a source of derogatory remarks about a political candidate.

Most individuals who have sued over emotional stress have not been successful. To prove an emotional distress claim, the person suing has to prove that the publication or broadcast station's actions (1) were intentional or reckless, (2) offended generally accepted standards of decency or morality, (3) was causally connected with the plaintiff's emotional distress, and (4) caused severe emotional distress.

Here are several examples of emotional distress suits in which the newspapers were found not guilty of inflicting emotional distress: (1) a story that a family of the plaintiff in a highly publicized lawsuit had been in 13 lawsuits in 10 years; (2) a feature story about the murder of the plaintiff's daughter that quoted from the deceased's diary, obtained from the police department; and (3) a newspaper story based on trial testimony that identified the plaintiff as a victim of sexual assault.

The breach of contract suit was brought by Dan Cohen, who provided information to the Minneapolis Star Tribune and the St. Paul Pioneer Press

Dispatch. Cohen, who was working for a candidate for governor, provided damaging information about the criminal record of another politician. He had been promised he would not be identified in the story as the source. However, the newspapers used his name in the story and he was fired.

Cohen sued the newspapers for breach of contract because they did not give him the confidentiality they promised. Two courts in Minnesota agreed that the newspapers had violated their "contract" and awarded him $700,000. The U.S. Supreme Court agreed to hear the newspapers' appeal of the case.

The Supreme Court also agreed to review the $10 million libel suit in which the psychoanalyst, Dr. Jeffrey M. Masson, sued magazine writer Janet Malcolm. He charged that she fabricated quotations that he claims made him look ridiculous. The suit had been dismissed by two federal courts earlier. The current question for the Supreme Court is whether Dr. Masson is entitled to take his case to a jury.

OTHER LEGAL ASPECTS OF JOURNALISM

In addition to the laws of libel and invasion of privacy, which are the most important legal provisions that limit a reporter's freedom, there are other legal aspects of journalism that can restrain both the reporter and the newspaper.

Censorship

The Constitution of the United States guarantees freedom of the press as a fundamental right in a democracy, but the extraordinary power of the federal government during times of national stress (insurrections, wars, threats of war) has resulted in a body of law that encroaches upon this freedom. Throughout our history there have been repeated efforts to censor the press under a variety of disguises. Chief among them have been the various sedition acts that have been passed, restricting publication of information that would "aid and comfort an enemy." The nation does not have an official secrets act; however, official secrets are protected under a variety of other acts, especially since the onset of the atomic age in the mid-1940s. In addition, repeated attempts to revise the U.S. Criminal Code, to include provisions that would essentially be a secrets act, have been made. Official secrets also are protected by the classification system for documents established by presidential executive order. Since government officials and newspaper people have not always agreed on what should be censored, the press continues to fight a battle to protect its right to print.

The press's constitutional rights were upheld in the famous Pentagon Papers case. The "papers" were classified Department of Defense documents detailing the historical development of the war in Vietnam. They were given to The New York Times by Daniel Ellsberg, a former Pentagon official who was working for the RAND Corporation, a firm that did consulting work for the Department of Defense. The Times began printing excerpts from the papers on June 13, 1971, and four days later Attorney General John Mitchell asked the

Times to print no more of the documents "because they would do irreparable injury to the defense interests" of the nation. The newspaper refused, and the Department of Justice asked U.S. District Court Judge Murray I. Gurfein to halt publication of the stories. Judge Gurfein, serving his first day as a federal judge, issued a temporary injunction on June 15 preventing the Times from continuing the publication. The Washington Post and other publications began printing parts of the papers. The Justice Department also obtained a temporary injunction against the Post.

The case was rushed to the Supreme Court, and after two weeks the Court, in a 6-3 decision, ruled that the government had not shown sufficient justification for imposing prior restraint. Although the press won eventually, many journalists were gravely concerned that a precedent may have been set in which, for perhaps the first time in American history, federal court injunctions imposed prior restraint upon American newspapers.

The media are not free to print everything, of course. The U.S. Criminal Code and the statutes of all states carry numerous penalties for the publication of pornography and obscenity. Although those laws may not directly affect a newspaper of general circulation, many reporters have a genuine concern about them because there is no accepted definition of obscenity and pornography. As a result, the laws are subject to broad interpretation and certainly might cause difficulty for a newspaper, especially one that tends to print the more explicit types of material.

Reporters should also be aware of additional Supreme Court decisions that have a direct influence on their work. In 1972 the Court ruled in Brandzburg vs. Hayes that a reporter has no right to withhold information about his or her sources from a grand jury in criminal investigations. Because that case involved the federal courts, a number of states quickly passed laws to permit reporters to keep the names of their news sources confidential in state criminal cases. However, several later Supreme Court decisions have cast a cloud over the validity of the state confidential sources laws.

As a result of the Zurcher vs. Stanford Daily case in 1978, police, with a warrant, were permitted to make a surprise raid on a newsroom to search for evidence of crimes committed by others. In short, police could go into a newsroom and search through the newspaper's files. However, the power of police to conduct searches of newsroom files was curtailed when President Carter signed a federal law that limited such searches except where they would prevent a death or injury. In 1979 the Court refused to review an appeals court ruling that allowed government investigators access to the telephone company's records of phone numbers called by journalists.

In a series of three cases between 1974 and 1978, the Court ruled each time that the press has no more right of access to public institutions than does the general public. These rulings can successfully block reporters from investigating conditions in jails, prisons and mental hospitals, for example.

The Court handed the press another setback in 1979, when it refused to hear the appeal of New York Times reporter Myron Farber, who spent 40 days in jail for contempt for refusing to turn over to the defendants his notes at a murder trial. He had claimed protection under a New Jersey law protecting confidential sources.

A decision that created great concern about court control of the press came in the Gannett Co. vs. DePasquale case in 1979. The case dated back to 1976, when Judge Daniel DePasquale, at the request of defense lawyers in a murder case, barred the press and the public from a pretrial hearing. The lawyers argued that the adverse publicity would jeopardize their clients' chances for a fair trial. The prosecutor did not object. However, reporters for Gannett's Rochester (N.Y.) Democrat & Chronicle and Times Union challenged the judge's ruling on the basis of the Sixth Amendment's guarantee of a public trial. Judge DePasquale refused to open the pretrial hearing. His decision was first overturned on appeal and then upheld before it finally reached the Supreme Court in 1979.

In a 5-4 decision, the Supreme Court upheld Judge DePasquale. In the majority opinion, Justice Potter Stewart wrote that the Sixth Amendment's public-trial guarantee belongs only to the criminally accused, not to the public itself. He refused to concede that the press or the public possesses a constitutional right under the First Amendment to attend criminal trials. In a separate opinion, Chief Justice Burger stressed that the ruling applies only to pretrial hearings, not to trials themselves. Justice William Rehnquist, who concurred, wrote that defendants, prosecutors and judges should be free to bar press and public from any trial for any reason they choose. He wrote that the public had absolutely no right to attend any criminal proceedings. He said that the First Amendment was not some kind of "constitutional sunshine law."

The decision resulted in so much judicial confusion that Justice Burger and Justice Powell broke a long-standing court tradition and began discussing the case in public. Both of them gave a number of public speeches defending and explaining the decision. They insisted that the Court meant only pretrial hearings could be closed. But in the first five weeks after the decision, judges across the nation had closed their courts to the public and the press more than 30 times, and at least eight of them involved full trials. Several news organizations—Gannett among them—issued cards to reporters on which was printed a formal protest. The reporters were instructed to read the statement aloud in court if a judge decided to close the court to the public or the press.

The following year the Supreme Court handed down a decision that cleared up much of the confusion created by the Gannett case. In the case Richmond Newspapers Inc. vs. Commonwealth of Virginia, the Court ruled that both the public and the press have a constitutional right to attend trials. The case grew out of the murder of a Virginia motel manager in 1975. Three men were charged with the murder and were granted separate trials. One of the defendants was tried three times in secret before charges against him were finally dismissed. The Commonwealth attorney did not object when the judge closed the court to the public and the press. However, the Richmond Times-Dispatch and the Richmond News-Leader *did* object because their reporters were barred from covering the trials. Their appeal to the Virginia Supreme Court was turned down. That court said the judge had acted with legal authority when he ordered the secret trials. The newspapers pushed the case all the way to the U.S. Supreme Court. In its 7-1 decision, the Court said, "We hold that the right to attend criminal trial is implicit in the guarantees of the First Amendment: without freedom to attend such trials, which people have exercised for centuries, an important aspect of freedom of speech and of the press could be eviscerated." The decision was hailed as a victory for the public and the press by news executives and First Amendment attorneys.

The Court also recognized that the right of access is not absolute and that closing a trial may be justified under certain circumstances. Two years after the Richmond case, in the Globe Newspapers case, the Court reaffirmed the right of access and said that the press and the public can be barred from a criminal trial only in very limited circumstances where the justification for exclusion is substantial. Before closing a criminal trial, or a portion of a trial, the judge must have a hearing and must make findings supporting the closure.

In a later decision (Press-Enterprise I), the U.S. Supreme Court ruled that courts could not be closed during jury selection except in extreme circumstances. And in Press-Enterprise II, the Court ruled that preliminary hearings before a magistrate are presumptively open to the public and cannot be closed unless specific, on-the-record findings are made that "closure is essential to preserve higher values and is narrowly tailored to serve that interest."

In addition to censorship, there are other legal aspects of journalism that restrain the newspaper and reporter alike.

Copyrights

The U.S. Constitution provides for copyrights just as it does for freedom of the press, and newspapers must observe the copyright holdings of others. By the same laws, the newspaper can prevent unauthorized use of original material it publishes by obtaining copyright privileges.

Obtaining a copyright is a relatively simple procedure. Application forms are available from the Register of Copyrights, Library of Congress, Washington, D.C. An author or publisher may secure a copyright by submitting a completed application, a small fee and the required number of copies of the material, and by carrying a notice of copyright on all published copies.

Written materials may be protected by copyright in the form in which they appear. However, the news facts or the ideas stated in the materials cannot be copyrighted. Copyright is an interest in the way the story is organized and treated. In other words, newspaper cannot obtain exclusive use of the facts pertaining to a murder story, for example, by copyrighting the initial news break on that story, but it may obtain a copyright to the story as it is organized and presented.

Even though a newspaper cannot claim exclusive rights to the facts in a news story through the copyright procedure, it can employ other legal methods to protect itself from the wholesale use of its stories by competing news media. Several state courts have ruled that such unauthorized use of news items, taken from a newspaper and not independently gathered, is unfair competition and "violation of property right."

Reporters may quote copyrighted material verbatim without permission provided such quotations do not exceed a reasonable length and provided the quoted material is properly acknowledged. The privilege protects newspapers' use of quotations in book reviews and other types of stories. However, as a common practice, most newspapers do seek permission before printing copyrighted material other than news stories. In using copyrighted material from another newspaper, most papers give the other paper credit almost immediately in the story in this fashion: "The Miami Herald, in a copyrighted story today, said that . . ."

For a fuller understanding of copyrights and especially the fair use standards, reporters should read the current copyright law passed by Congress in 1976.

EXERCISES

1. Invite the editor of the local newspaper to class to discuss the efforts the newspaper makes to avoid libeling individuals in news stories. Encourage the editor to bring with him or her the lawyer who serves as the newspaper's libel adviser.

2. Look up your state's libel law in a copy of the annotated state code in your college library. Write a brief report on the law's major provisions, such as the definition of libel and the defenses permitted.

3. If your state has a privacy law, look it up in a copy of the annotated state code in your college library. Write a brief report on the law's major provisions, such as the definition of invasion of privacy and the defenses permitted.

4. Most states have laws providing for open public meetings and open public records. A number of states have laws that give reporters the right to protect the names of their confidential sources. Check with your state press association headquarters to obtain copies of the laws, or look them up in a copy of the annotated state code in your library. Invite a newspaper and a radio or television reporter who cover government in your community to class to discuss the problems they have obtaining public records from government officials. Write a story on their class discussions.

5. Using a standard reference book such as Media Law Reporter or Reader's Guide to Periodical Literature in your college library, look up a recent libel suit and an invasion of privacy suit and write a brief report on those cases. Most trade publications, such as Editor & Publisher and the Quill, also carry reports of significant legal cases.

6. Using any newspapers available to you, clip five stories containing several types of derogatory statements about individuals. Paste them on a blank sheet of paper and comment in the margins if you believe the statements to be libelous. In each case indicate what defense you would use if a libel suit resulted from the story.

7. Using those same stories or five others, look for statements that you might consider to be invasion of privacy. In each case explain why you believe the information invades the privacy of the individual. Indicate what defense you would use if a suit resulted from the story.

8. If there has been a libel suit involving a newspaper or broadcast station in your area in the past five years, invite the reporters and editors involved in it to class to discuss their experiences in court. Write a brief report on their discussion.

9. Critics accuse newspapers of violating good taste in reporting and use of photographs, especially when covering sensational events. Using any newspapers available

to you, look for examples of stories, parts of stories, and pictures you consider to be of questionable taste. Clip them and paste them on blank sheets of paper; in the margins explain why you think the material is objectionable and should not have been used.

10. In the following paragraphs some statements are libelous, invade the privacy of the subject or are in questionable taste. Rewrite those paragraphs to eliminate any libelous or questionable information. Following each rewritten paragraph, explain the changes, specifically pointing out the material you believe to be libelous or objectionable. Note that some of the statements are from news stories and others from editorials or by-lined reviews.

   a. James Garfield Howard Brewer III, president of Evergreen National Bank, announced his immediate resignation today. Neither he nor other bank officials would say why. Although the resignation was a surprise, a source in the financial community, who asked that his name not be used, said there have been rumors floating around for several months implying that Brewer was involved in a number of questionable transactions with Paul Pullen, recently indicted building contractor and developer.

   b. Most members of Reverend Tompkins' church expressed shock at his arrest on bank robbery charges. However, one elder said he "pegged that guy as a con man the first day he set foot in our church. I told everyone he was too slick, too crafty to be a true man of God."

   c. County Commissioner Bette Lively accused Sheriff Maurice Fisher of being a "compulsive liar" during a heated debate over the Sheriff Department's budget hearing last night.

   d. So many elements are necessary for a restaurant to be successful. Solicitous service, inviting surroundings, satisfying cuisine and good value are all essential elements in capturing the dining public's attention. Unfortunately, the Mother Jones, a new family-style restaurant, has none of these. In a word it is a "disaster." The decor is ugly, the staff surly and the food pure slop.

   e. About halfway through the first act of the world premiere run of the stage version of Frank Capra's "It's a Wonderful Life" at the Belasco last night, I wanted to stand up and shout: "Stop the world, I want to get off." I know bad, and this play is bad.

   f. Detective Michael Morrow said today he is trying to track down Floyd Geiger, former owner of the Best Bet Used Car Lot, for questioning in connection with a suspicious fire that destroyed the office and showroom of the car lot Monday night. "I've been told by some people I talked to that Geiger bore a grudge against the new owners because he thought they rooked him."

   g. Dear Editor: It's about time someone did something about the way that those left-wing professors at State College are corrupting the minds of innocent students, turning them away from Christian family values and toward Godless Communism.

   h. "The All Seeing Eye" has learned that outgoing Gov. Virginia Marmaduke is about to "take care of" her long-time personal aide, confidant and traveling companion and statehouse heartthrob, handsome Rudi Morales, by naming him to a six-year term on the state Waste Water Control Board at $98,000 a year. The word around the statehouse is he earned it the hard way.

11. Interview a local judge about the influence of pretrial publicity on major criminal cases. Then ask the editor of your local newspaper to respond. Write a news story presenting the views of both individuals.

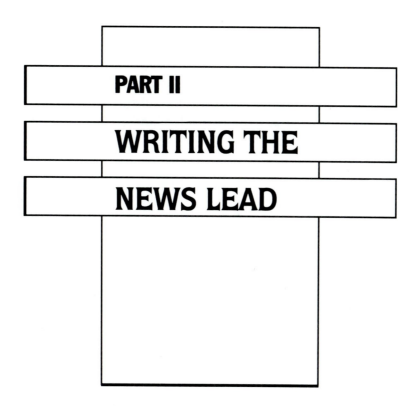

PART II

WRITING THE

NEWS LEAD

In the excellent book "On Writing Well," William Zinsser says: "The most important sentence in any article is the first one. If it doesn't induce the reader to proceed to the second sentence, your article is dead." That is why it is so important for a writer to think about what he or she is going to say before putting the first word on paper or a video display terminal (VDT) screen.

Thinking is the key to good writing. In fact, Saul Pett, the Pulitzer Prize-winning writer for The Associated Press (AP), says, "Writing begins and ends with thinking." Rene J. (Jack) Cappon, The Associated Press's (AP's) newsfeatures editor and writing coach, went even further in his book "The Word." He says, "Writing is the art of second thought. What first springs to mind is seldom good enough. . . . By good enough, I mean copy that's clear, precise, succinct and expressive."

Thinking doesn't stop with the lead. Good writers think constantly about how the story is being organized. But those first words are crucial. They require careful, sometimes prolonged, thought even under the pressure of deadlines. Those first words form the first sentence—the lead—of the story. They have to reach out and grasp the reader's attention and coax him or her to move on to the second and third sentences.

Lead writing may appear to be simple. It isn't. Although some reporters may be able to dash off a lead in a hurry, most cannot. The most difficult part of writing a complete news story for many reporters, the lead takes a lot of thought and a lot of practice.

The basic forms and principles of writing the news lead are presented in the following pages. However, every reporter should remember that while forms and principles are extremely helpful, they are not substitutes for the clarity and precision in writing needed to capture readers and compel them to continue reading a story.

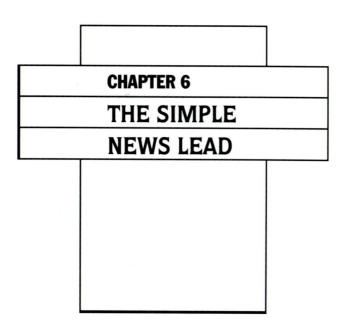

CHAPTER 6
THE SIMPLE
NEWS LEAD

News writing is narrative writing turned upside down. A narrative prose writer places the major emphasis on the end of the story, carefully building to a climax. The news writer does the exact opposite. In news stories, the most important fact is told first.

The two styles of writing also differ in other aspects. News writing style calls for short words, short sentences, short paragraphs and a generous use of quotes. Sentences and paragraphs in narrative writing tend to be longer, and the choice of words often is more expansive. (Both, however, adhere to the standard rules of grammar, punctuation and sentence structure.)

This example will illustrate the difference in the two writing styles:

Ordinary Narrative Style

Andrew R. Pizarek, senior partner in Golden State Auditors, an accounting firm with 16 offices across the state, left his office in the Franklin Building at 917 Market Street about 7:30 last night. He took the elevator to the second level in the building's underground garage where he had parked his car when he arrived at his office in the morning. As he approached his silver-blue 1990 Jaguar, two men came rushing out of the shadows and attempted to grab his briefcase and car keys. In the struggle that followed, Pizarek was struck in the face, but he kicked one of his assailants in the groin. The other one pulled a small revolver from his jacket pocket and fired three shots at the accountant. One bullet struck Pizarek in the left forearm and the other two went through the car's windshield. Both men fled on foot when they heard the elevator open. Several other occupants of the building rushed to Pizarek's aid. One alerted the building safety office on his cellular telephone and all exits to the building and garage were sealed off. Five police cars were dispatched to the scene in response to a call from the building security staff. Police and guards searched all five floors of the building but were unable to find the two men. Pizarek was taken to St. Mary's hospital where he underwent a two-hour operation to remove the bullet and repair damage to the muscle in his left forearm. He is resting comfortably, a hospital spokesman said. Police Sgt. George Brown said robbery and car theft appearently were the motives for the attack. Pizarek said he had never seen either of his assailants before. And the only thing he had in his briefcase, besides some unfinished tax forms, was half a sandwich left over from his lunch.

The News Story

A Santa Clara accountant was shot in the arm last night by two men who attempted to rob him and steal his car from a downtown parking garage, police said.

Andrew R. Pizarek, senior partner in Golden State Auditors, 917 Market St., was wounded when he struggled with his assailants on the second floor of the underground parking garage of the Franklin Building.

The assailants fled on foot when several other occupants of the building got off the elevator on the second floor of the garage.

Pizarek underwent a two-hour operation at St. Mary's Medical Center to remove the bullet and repair damages to the muscles in his left forearm. He is in stable condition.

Pizarek told police the two men jumped him as he was opening the door to his car at about 7:30 p.m. In the struggle, he kicked one of the assailants in the groin. The other one fired three shots, one hit Pizarek in the left forearm and the other two went through the windshield of his silver-blue 1990 Jaguar.

Police sealed off all entrances to the garage and made a floor-by-floor search but were unable to locate the assailants.

Pizarek said he had never seen either of the men before. He told police he thought they were trying to steal his car and his briefcase.

The briefcase, he said, contained some unfinished federal income tax forms and half a chicken sandwich left over from lunch.

The difference between the two stories is immediately apparent. The events in the prose story are recounted in chronological order. In the news story they are arranged, from beginning to end, in order of their newsworthiness. The shooting of Pizarek and the escape of his assailants are the two most newsworthy events of the story. They are the first things told in the news story. In the narrative version they are presented well into the story.

In ordinary narrative, the entire story becomes clear gradually, building to a climax. In the news story the most newsworthy fact is flashed before the reader in the opening sentence—the lead. The object of the lead is to tell the reader as quickly as possible what the story is about. This generally is done in a single sentence or two that form a single paragraph.

The narrative story will include all the minute details. The news story generally omits details or includes them in a final paragraph. This style of writing is usually called the "inverted pyramid" because the "bottom," or end or climax, of a story told in chronological order is inverted and placed at the top of the news story.

The style is an outgrowth of the Civil War, when correspondents were restricted from sending long stories by telegraph. To make certain all the essential information was sent, writers gave the most important facts first. Although the style has been refined considerably since then, most basic news stories still follow that pattern.

Logical Order

The order in which newsworthy facts are organized in a news story will be referred to as the "logical order." This term is used to distinguish this order from the arrangement of events as they actually occur (chronological order). "Logical" implies that the events will not be rearranged haphazardly but will be rationally ordered according to their importance. The order of importance is measured by reader appeal and the lead in the "showcase" of all or of the most newsworthy materials contained in the story. Since the lead reveals either the whole story or its most newsworthy aspects, the subsequent parts of the story should develop in logical order to support the lead. That is, the second most important fact comes second, then the third and so on. This order makes the relationship of a lead to a news story similar to that of a topic sentence to a paragraph.

If news is so written that the story is fully summarized in the lead, what constitutes a "whole story"? What is it that people want to know about a news event? How can one know when he or she has presented all the essential information? Are there not, for example, many more essential facts in a bank robbery than there are in an automobile collision? Does not every story differ from every other in the kind of information presented in its lead summary? These questions may be puzzling, but the fact is that, although stories differ in their content, the story lead has a fixed and limited purpose to perform.

All good news writing is based on careful and accurate reporting. Ideally, a reporter will collect much more information about an event than that actually needed to write a clear, accurate and fair story. No amount of flashy writing will cover up the fact that the reporter did not follow Saul Pett's advice to "think" about the story before trying to write it. Good writers listen, watch and absorb first; then they write.

THE FIVE W'S

Every news story should answer the questions: Who? What? When? Where? Why? and, for good measure, How? They should be answered as quickly as possible for the reader. Some writers still attempt to cram answers to all those questions into the opening sentence, which frequently results in 60 to 70 words of almost incomprehensible prose. For example, a lead containing answer to all those questions might come out like this:

> Andrew R. Pizarek, a Santa Clara accountant, is in stable condition at St. Mary's Medical Center today, recovering from a gunshot wound in his left forearm which he suffered while struggling with two assailants who tried to rob him and steal his car from an underground parking garage at 719 Market St. at about 7:30 last night as he was leaving the building where his offices are located.

That certainly answered all the questions:

Who?:   Andrew R. Pizarek, a Santa Clara accountant
What?:   Was shot in the left forearm
When?:   About 7:30 last night
Where?: The second floor of the underground garage at the Franklin Building
Why?:   Two men were trying to rob him and steal his car and he resisted
How?:   With a small revolver

But it also is 68 words and it is ponderous. It would have been even longer if the fact that the assailants fled or the source—in this case, the police—had been included.

Countless readership studies show that shorter sentences are more understandable and are easier to read. As a result, most news writers now do not attempt to cram all of the traditional five W's into the lead sentence or even the first paragraph of a story. Generally, newspapers strive to keep the lead sentence to 30 or so words, depending, of course, on the story. Some even try for shorter leads.

PLAYING UP A W

Simpler, shorter leads can be written that feature the single W that is more important than the others. Occasionally, it may be difficult to select a single W as the most important, especially if a news event is complex. However, here are some examples of how one news element can be featured effectively:

The "Who" Lead. If the "Who" is a prominent person or place or thing, it is usually the feature of the lead. The name alone attracts the reader's attention. Unless one of the other elements is particularly outstanding, the "big name" comes first, as in these examples:

> President Bush Wednesday offered to help the Soviet Union overcome its "difficult times" by extending a $1 billion line of credit to buy U.S. food.

> Israeli Prime Minister Yitzhak Shamir today urged the immediate opening of diplomatic relations with the Soviet Union—and backed "in principle" the idea of a nuclear-free Middle East zone.

> LOS ANGELES—Frank Sinatra is going home for his 75th birthday.
> Ol' Blue Eyes returns on Tuesday, the eve of his birthday, to an area near his New Jersey hometown of Hoboken to begin a yearlong world tour. He plans to fulfill a lifetime dream of performing in the Soviet Union and possibly China.

A "Who" lead frequently is used even when a person is not widely known. In such cases, it is usually the person's occupation, sex, age or other distinguishing characteristics that are featured.

A former high school guidance counselor went on trial on drug charges in Criminal Court today and immediately was given the bad news that his supplier had pleaded guilty and agreed to testify against him.

A Columbia teen-ager freed on bond on first-degree murder charges was arrested Friday on charges of armed robbery in the holdup of a market earlier this month.

A Dickson County farmer was sentenced to six years in prison today for shooting a woman he allegedly pursued for 37 years and claimed to love.

The "What" Lead.   If an event or action is more important than the persons involved, that element should be featured.

A new law requiring colleges and universities to reveal their crime statistics will give students and parents a look at just how safe the nation's campuses really are.

A three-year investigation into reports of public corruption and illegal gambling on high school sporting events in northern Alabama turned up "no credible evidence" to support the charges, authorities said today.

SYRACUSE, Sicily (AP)—A moderate earthquake shook eastern Sicily early yesterday, killing 19 people and injuring about 300, panicking thousands and destroying part of a small town, officials said.

Although the following example starts with a "Who," the "What" circumstances probably would be considerably more significant than the persons involved.

A 75-year-old Smithville man, who told police he "accidentally took a wrong turn," almost crashed into a twin-engine plane that was landing at Downtown Island Airport Monday.

The "Where" Lead.   On occasion, the "Where" is significant enough to overshadow the other W's. Often it is used by writers trying to establish a mood or recreate a scene. Here are several examples:

FRANKFURT, Germany—The band in the big hall at the Frankfort fairgrounds strikes up a stirring march, and suddenly 8,000 people are on their feet, all eyes turned to the back of the hall as the massive figure of Chancellor Helmut Kohl materializes.

(Ray Moseley, Chicago Tribune)

KANSAS CITY, Mo.—After its day in the glare of national publicity, New Madrid, across the state, is settling comfortably back into its role as a small Mississippi River town, enjoying the sudden return to peace and quiet, but mulling its new memories and counting yesterday's profits.

For many there, a newly penned country song heard on a local radio station summed up the sentiment:

"Thank you, Mr. Browing, for putting New Madrid on the map. Now the whole country knows where New Madrid's at."

The reference was to Iben Browing, the New Mexico climatologist who made the projection that gave New Madrid its day in the sun. Dr.

Browing, a private consultant, said there was a 50-50 chance that a major earthquake would strike the New Madrid Fault Zone on Dec. 3, plus or minus 48 hours.

The earthquake did not strike and William Robbins of The New York Times visited the town and described how the town and its residents were handling the readjustment to a normal life after days of media attention.

George Curry of the Chicago Tribune filed this report on Love Canal, a neighborhood in upstate New York that he called the nation's most famous toxic waste dump.

NIAGARA FALLS, N.Y.—The neighborhood is about as close to a modern ghost town as there is.

Most of the modest homes that sold for less than $10,000 when they were built in the 1950s are vacant, thick boards covering their windows. The 99th Street School has no pupils. The Church of God has not held a service in more than a decade. And it's rare to see automobiles moving or people walking the streets. . . .

Over the decades, more than 22,000 tons of PCBs and other toxic waste were buried in the abandoned canal, and then the neighborhood was built around it.

In 1978, more than 2,500 residents were evacuated from a 350-acre area, and, inspired largely by the emergency, the federal government created the so-called Superfund program for cleaning up hazardous waste across the country.

The "When" Lead.   "When" is automatically included in most leads, but it is not often the most important feature. There are some instances when the writer elects to emphasize "When" in the lead, as in these examples:

FOLKSTONE, England—At 11:21 a.m., Saturday, Robert Graham Fagg of Dover climbed through a 3-foot by 4-foot hole in the wall of chalk marl 130 feet below the seabed of the English Channel, shook the hand of Phillippe Cozette of Calais and shouted: ''Vive la France.''

The English and French construction workers then hugged each other as a crowd of 100 onlookers cheered, celebrating the breakthrough of the channel tunnel—known as the Chunnel—which rejoined Great Britain to the European continent after 8,000 years of isolation.

(The New York Times)

ASHLAND CITY—An April 29 trial date has been set for a Graham County couple charged with manufacturing one of the largest marijuana crops in the county and running an illegal bulldog fighting operation.

(The Tennessean, Nashville)

The "When" element can be used effectively in feature stories. Here is an example of a feature lead by Laura Pappano of the Quincy (Mass.) Patriot Ledger, cited in the "Write Stuff" column in The Bulletin of the American Society of Newspaper Editors:

It is 9:30 in the morning, and 3-year-old Carolyn Cutler has reported to work.

Sitting on the floor mat, she gingerly removes the top of a wooden cube box and is delighted when the sides collapse, revealing a cache of brightly painted wooden blocks inside.

She takes the blocks out one at a time, turns them in her hand and contemplates the task ahead. Tightening her lips, she struggles to fit the blocks back in, knowing there is only one way to do it.

The Montessori way.

The "Why" Lead.   The motive or cause of an event sometimes can be the most important element of a story to feature in the lead. Writers may avoid it because it could make for a long lead. Here are a couple of examples of strong, direct, "Why" leads:

WARSAW—(AP)—Saying cigarettes kill hundreds of thousands of East European men each year, an international group of doctors have declared war on smoking in a region where the Marlboro man still rides proudly.

BATON ROUGE, La.—Prodded by lawsuits over pollution and damage claims from a number of explosions, several of the nation's largest oil and chemical companies are spending millions of dollars to create safety zones by buying up the homes around their plants.

(The New York Times)

To meet the 5 percent impoundment of state funds ordered by the governor, State University officials here said they would have to eliminate all travel, freeze hiring and cut back on maintenance of buildings and grounds.

The "How" Lead.   Although it can be an effective device, the "How" lead is not used as often as the others. Some reporters shy away from it because it can become too wordy. Here are several examples:

Using fraudulent applications and identification papers, thousands of people from Central and South America who entered the United States illegally are seeking amnesty.

Immigration and Naturalization Service officials said they have been overwhelmed by fraudulent applications listing phony addresses and employment data.

More than a dozen false driver's licenses and Social Security cards helped escaped convict Peter Dukakis and his girlfriend, Mary Edith Thomas, elude capture for nearly six months.

FBI Agent George Orwell said Dukakis and Thomas each had six fake driver's licenses and four Social Security cards when they were arrested yesterday.

Crowding the Lead

The lead of a simple news story should not say too much or too little. In this type of story the best leads generally are those that emphasize a single W. If other W's deserve attention, they can be emphasized in the second paragraph.

The shorter the lead, the better, as long as it tells the reader the most important details. Newsworthy details not included in the lead will fall properly into the body of the story. If no single element in the story seems to stand out above the others, reporters generally write a "Who" lead:

> A 32-year-old transient who murdered a car salesman during a test drive was sentenced to 27 years to life in the state prison Friday.
> Yale Booskas was convicted Aug. 6 of one count each of first-degree murder, robbery, larceny of a motor vehicle and driving a car without the owner's consent.

> A Virginia woman has filed a $200,000 lawsuit in Circuit Court after her former fiance refused to buy her an engagement ring and then withdrew his proposal of marriage.
> Edith J. Salling, who now lives in Gate City, Va., said in the suit that James V. Cunningham's decision to withdraw his proposal of marriage left her "disappointed in her reasonable expectations of the social, domestic and material advantage to be derived from the promised marriage."

Although the "Who" lead certainly is adequate, it also tends to be dull. Reporters should always examine the facts of a story carefully before writing to find an angle that will make the story more interesting. Both examples cited above have the potential of being more interesting if the writer had not treated them as routine "Who" leads.

Often reporters are faced with determining who is the "Who" in a story, especially when two or more individuals or groups are involved. For example, if the police chief and a city council member have a heated verbal exchange during the council's budget hearings, the reporter has to determine which of the two is to be the "Who" in the lead. In this case, of course, the reporter might evade the issue and use both by writing: "Two public officials clashed today. . . ." However, the reporter could have focused on the person who apparently provoked the argument.

COMPLETE REPORTING

Reporters should remember to answer every question the reader might have about a story. The reader should not have to make a phone call after reading a story about an upcoming event to find out what it will cost, if the event is open to the public, if it will be telecast, and when and over what channel. The complete story should give all those details. It is not enough to identify a person by his or her address if other forms of identification are available. They all should be worked into the story at some point. It is not enough to say "Fire destroyed the Marvel Manufacturing Company" without telling what the firm manufactured and how many persons worked for it. Incomplete reporting can produce lackluster leads such as:

> The state's citrus producers today asked the Environmental Protection Agency to lift its ban on the pesticides Aldren and Dieldrin to help fight an invasion of the Apopka bug.

Although that lead is adequate, it really doesn't give the reader any indication of the seriousness of the problem and what it could mean to the state's economy.

The following is another version that provides the reader with a clear picture of the impact the bug could have on the citrus crop:

> Florida's billion-dollar citrus crop will be destroyed if the Environmental Protection Agency doesn't lift its ban on two pesticides that control the Apopka bug, citrus producers predicted today.
> The beetlelike insect has already infested 30,000 acres of fruit trees, causing an estimated loss of $100 million to producers.
> "The bug is eating its way across the groves of Central Florida leaving behind a trail of bankrupt grove owners," Thomas Ballard told EPA officials.

The second lead gives the reader a more dramatic picture of what the insect is doing to an important industry in the state. The first gives the reader only a minimum amount of information.

Obviously, there are limits to how much material can be crowded into a lead. But there should be no limit on the quality of the material. In his excellent book on writing, "The Word," Rene (Jack) Cappon said writers should think of leads "as though they cost you 10 bucks per word, each word to be engraved on stainless steel while you're sitting on a hot stove. . . ." That is good advice.

TESTING THE LEAD

There is no single formula for writing leads. Every reporter has to develop his or her own way to measure how adequate the lead is after it is written. No matter what device is used, reporters must never forget that a good lead makes a direct statement of the essential facts of the story. In addition, it must say something to readers in such a way that a reader is hooked on that story and will continue to read beyond the opening sentence.

This lead from The Christian Science Monitor, written at a time when the miniseries "The Winds of War" was dominating television, is a classic example of one that hooks the reader:

> If you think "The Winds of War" is hard to follow, take a look at "The Winds of Waste"—a Washington mini-drama starring EPA administrator Anne Gorsuch, ex-deputy administrator Rita Lavell, Congress, and a California sludge pit.
> The story so far: Congress is threatening to throw Mrs. Gorsuch in jail. . . .

Note: Few reporters write complete sentences while gathering information for a story. In keeping with that practice, some of the notes and exercises in this chapter and the following chapters are deliberately written in incomplete sentences.

At the end of each set of notes the source of the information is given in parentheses unless the source is otherwise included or obvious. Remember, in many stories it is absolutely essential to credit the source of information in a very specific way, often in the lead. However, if the source is obvious, it is not necessary to attribute the information.

This is an example of a story in which the source should be credited specifically:

> Seven members of an elite Lincoln County Sheriff's Department narcotics unit have been charged with stealing $1.4 million in cash seized during drug raids, District Attorney Donald Scroggins said today.

A reporter would have no way of knowing that the police officers had been charged with the crime unless the district attorney announced it. In the following example, however, the source is obvious:

> NORTH POLE, Alaska—Santa Claus is getting a gift from the U.S. Postal Service: a bar code to help sort the tens of thousands of letters sent to him at the North Pole.

In that story, it is apparent that the announcement came from the Postal Service. It is not absolutely essential to say "Postal Service officials said" in the lead.

Students should use good judgment in the use of direct quotations in completing these assignments. The notes within quotation marks indicate direct quotations. If they are used, additional words may have to be added to make them complete sentences. But only obvious additions should be made.

Because these are reporter's notes, they should be viewed as accurate statements from the sources of information. If the instructor permits, the students may convert an unquote note into a direct quotation. For example: A note reading "Thomas refused to comment on the council's action" may be written " 'I have no comment to make,' Mayor Thomas said." However, in converting an indirect quotation into a direct quotation, the student should not embellish it with imaginary facts.

Students also should be aware that the exercises may contain some material that, if used as given and sometimes if used at all, will constitute errors. These notes contain trivia, editorialized matter, statements violating newspaper ethics, libelous statements and misspelled words.

Some instructors may require students to hand in all completed and corrected assignments at the end of each quarter or semester. Students should keep a folder of all their work as a means of tracking their progress in the writing assignments.

EXERCISES

1. Using the front page of any newspaper available to you, identify the W's in the lead on each of the stories.

2. Using newspapers available in the library, compare the leads on five stories in both a morning and an afternoon newspaper in the same city or the same stories appearing in the local newspaper in a neighboring city. Write a brief report on the differences in the leads.

3. Identify the five W's in each of the following sets of notes for story leads and then write a lead on each one:

   a. Willa Cook, 88, 1107 Avenue A
      Crossing the 3900 block of Fern Street
      Pushing shopping cart
      Filled with empty cardboard boxes
      Hit by car driven by
      Glenda M. Lemon, Louisville
      Police officer Carlene Campbell
      Said Lemon could not see Cook
      Because her view was
      Blocked by other cars
      Cook was crossing against light
      Accident happened about 6:40 p.m.
      Cook in critical condition
      At University Medical Center
      Suffered fractured skull
         (Source: Officer Campbell, Hospital spokesperson)

   b. Police Lt. Walter Hall
      Answered call to home
      At 104 Ashwood Drive
      Found Carl T. Vaughn, 34
      Lying on floor in kitchen
      He had been shot to death
      He arrested Edith S. Gibson, 34
      Who lives at the home
      She was crying and hysterical
      Told Hall that Vaughn
      Had come home to beat her
      She said he was her former husband
      She said she was tired
      Of Vaughn coming around hitting her
      She said she still loved him
      He had been shot once
      With a .38-calibre pistol
      She is being held without bond
      She will be arraigned today
         (Source: Police Lt. Hall)

   c. Police Officer Steve Tinder
      Reported two persons were killed
      In head-on collision on
      Neyland Drive near Cumberland Avenue
      Just after 1 a.m. today
      Tinder said a car
      Driven by Robert L. Carr, 21
      Who gave a Barton Street address
      Veered into westbound lane
      Struck other car driven by
      Damon McGhee, 25, Townsend

    McGhee and passenger
    Glenda H. Polk, 40, Fountain City
    Were killed in the accident
    Carter suffered facial injuries
    Taken to Regional Medical Center
    Tinder said Carter believed
    To be driving 85 mph or more
    When accident occurred
    No one was wearing seat belts
       (Source: Officer Tinder)

d. Albert Frazier, secretary
    Calvary Baptist Church
    In suburban Beech Grove
    Reported to Beech Grove police
    That $10,500 was stolen
    From the church's staff
    Money was stolen sometime
    During first two weeks of month
    Police said there are no suspects
    In the theft of the money
    Safe normally unlocked
    During work hours
    Frazier told police
    Office left unmanned occasionally
       (Source: Det. Joe Johnson, Frazier)

e. Fire chief Leonard Basler
    Said Broadway Cafe
    Longtime Main Street business *where*
    Badly damaged by fire
    About 3:30 a.m. today *when*
    Building engulfed in flames
    When firefighters arrived *when*
    Took 3 hours to control fire
    Damages estimated at $45,000
    Owner Buddy Berkowitz said
    Arson investigators investigating
    Cause of the fire, Basler said
       (Sources: Fire Chief Basler, owner Berkowitz)

4. In the following notes for story leads, identify the fact or facts ("Who," "What," "When" and so on) you think deserve the most conspicuous play in each lead. Then write the lead.

    a. A 23-year-old woman
    Walking to her car
    In Garden Green Mall
    About 5:30 p.m. Friday
    Grabbed from behind by large man
    He tried to force her into
    A gray, two-door Chevrolet
    She said she struck the man
    With her fist and ran back

Inside mall and called police
She described man as 200 pounds,
Medium brown hair in his 50s
She said there was
A second man in the car
    (Source: Det. Margaret Cook)

b. Knox County Sheriff's Office
Reported two armed gunmen
Robbed Balck's convenience store
11013 Northshore Drive
Men entered store about 10:30 p.m. Friday
One wore werewolf face mask
Other wore Phantom of the Opera mask
Went behind counter, pointed gun
At clerk Brenda Moore's head
Order her to give them
Money out of cash register
One had long-barrel handgun
Other a blue-steel revolver
Owner declined to say
How much money was taken
    (Sources: Deputy Tom Clark, Moore and store owner)

c. Dr. James Shanksy
Arrested in February
On charges of possession
Of steriods and cocaine
Police found $53,000 in cash
2,400 doses of anabolic steroids
Valued at $36,000
Hidden under seat in car
After it was involved
In an accident in front
Of the Downtown Hilton Hotel
Sentenced to 30 months
In federal prison today
By U.S. District Judge Susan Wiandt
He must remain under supervision
For two years after he gets out of prison

d. State Wildlife Resources Agency officers
Arrested two men, seeking third
In alleged game poaching operation
Involving slaughter, sale
Of up to 1,200 doves
Arrest followed undercover probe
Man may have also killed
Deer and sold meat illegally
Charles Chester and Tommy Bartlet
Arrested after they sold
Undercover agents 500 doves
    (Source: Ed Carter, WRA Director)

e. Elbert J. Hooker
President of Hooker Industries
State's largest construction firm
Has given $1.3 million gift
To State University
For scholarships for
Minority students from
State's high schools
University President Gener Puett
Said gift will provide
Support for 250 students annually
Hooker, a self-made millionaire
Never attended college
Began working at 16 as a carpenter
Established his own firm at 25
　　　(Source: State University Press Release)

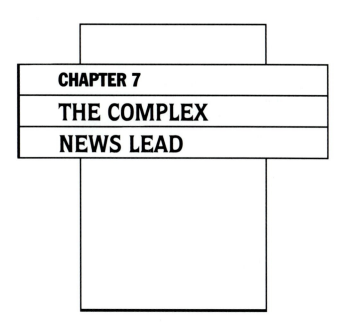

CHAPTER 7
THE COMPLEX
NEWS LEAD

Not all news events fall into the single-incident story category. Many stories are far more complex, and the reporter may be faced with having to juggle two or three important news elements in a lead. This complex type of story requires careful planning and organization to make certain that the separate parts come together clearly and coherently for the reader.

Suppose, for example, that the following happened during a heavy fog that shrouded the area early one morning:

- Dense fog blanketed the area for a 50-mile radius.
- Eighty-three cars and trucks were involved in chain-reaction wrecks on Interstate 75.
- Several dozen cars and trucks caught fire and burned.
- Thirteen persons were killed.
- At least 50 others were injured and required hospitalization.
- Southbound traffic on the interstate was blocked and motorists were rerouted.

The general rule in writing a story about a news event is to place the most noteworthy item first. This rule presents no serious problem as long as the story has only a single incident to be the focus of the lead. However, when the story has more than one significant incident, as in the above event, the reporter's job becomes more complicated. One of two basic methods generally is used in handling a more complex story:

1. Summarize all features—in order of importance—in the lead sentence or paragraph.
2. Emphasize the most important or significant of the features and then quickly summarize all the other important ones in logical order in succeeding paragraphs.

In either approach, all of the features should be clearly established in the reader's mind as quickly as possible before the reporter proceeds very far into developing any open feature.

Here is an example of how the details of the chain-reaction crashes might have been summarized in a lead:

> Thirteen persons were killed and at least 50 others injured and hospitalized when 83 cars and trucks smashed into each other and caught fire on a fog-shrouded section of Interstate 75 near the Calhoun exit in McMinn County early today, state police said.

That lead, like most summary leads, simply is too long. Most editors do not like summary leads because they often overwhelm the reader by saying too much.

Here is how that summary lead might have been developed. At the left is a diagram in which each geometrical shape represents a separate story feature. The diminishing size of the figures signifies the diminishing newsworthiness of the story material.

The Diagram
Summary of
Features

□ 1   ○ 2   △ 3

Details of Feature
No. 1, the dead

Details of Feature
No. 2, the injured

Details of Feature
No. 3, the fog
that caused the
accident

△ 3

Other Paragraphs
in Completed
Story

▽

The Written Story

Thirteen persons were killed and at least 50 others injured and hospitalized when 83 cars and trucks smashed into each other and caught fire on a fog-shrouded section of Interstate 75 near the Calhoun exit in McMinn County early today, state police said.

A complete list of the dead has not been compiled. And Henry Smithson, director of the County Emergency Agency, said some of the victims were so badly burned they may never be identified.

The injured were given emergency first aid at the scene and taken by ambulances to hospitals in five nearby communities. The hospitals called in off-duty nurses and doctors to help treat the injured.

"Visibility was no more than 10 to 15 feet in the two-mile stretch where the cars and trucks were piled up," Smithson said. "It was so thick drivers could not see the yellow fog warning lights."

Rescue vehicles had difficulty reaching some of the vehicles because of the fog and the burning and wrecked vehicles.

Hundreds of rescue workers responded to repeated calls and helped pull victims and survivors from the wreckage of the vehicles.

One rescue worker said the heat was so intense a compact car and a pickup were fused together by the melting metal. Another reported flames shooting 200 feet into the air from a tanker truck apparently loaded with a volatile liquid.

State Trooper Jordan Ragsdale said it appeared that traffic on the southbound side of the interstate slowed down when entering the fog bank and was run down by faster traffic.

(Further details on all the features would be developed in the rest of the story.)

EMPHASIZING AN OUTSTANDING FEATURE

To avoid a long summary lead, most editors would instruct the reporter to put the emphasis on the persons who had been killed and injured. Here is how that shortened lead might be written:

The Diagram

Outstanding
Features

Summary of
Other Features

The Written Story

Thirteen persons were killed and at least 50 injured early today in a series of chain-reaction crashes on a stretch of Interstate 75 that was blanketed by dense fog.

State Police said more than 83 cars and trucks plowed into each other in the fog that had cut visibility to 10 to 15 feet near the Calhoun exit of I-75 in McMinn County. Many caught fire and burned.

A complete list of the dead has not been compiled. And Henry Smithson, director of the County Emergency Agency, said some of the victims were so badly burned they may never be identified.

The injured were given emergency first aid at the scene and taken by ambulances to hospitals in five nearby communities. The hospitals called in off-duty nurses and doctors to help treat the injured.

(Further details of all the features would be developed in the rest of the story.)

In that example, all the emphasis is placed on the dead and injured. However, because of the unusually dense fog that caused the accidents, an editor may want to emphasize it in the lead. In that case, here is how the story might be written:

The Diagram

Outstanding
Feature

Details of Feature
Nos. 2 and 3

Other Paragraphs
in the Complete
Story

The Written Story

A fog-blanketed stretch of Interstate 75 became a murky inferno of broken and burning vehicles today in possibly the worst traffic accident in the state's history.

At least 13 people were killed and more than 50 others injured near the Calhoun Exit of I-75 in McMinn County when more than 80 vehicles were involved in chain-reaction collisions. The fog cut visibility to 10 to 15 feet at some points.

"The fog was so thick it was impossible for the drivers to see the yellow fog warning lights," Henry Smithson, director of the County Emergency Agency, said.

A complete list of the dead and injured has not been compiled. And Smithson said some of the victims were so badly burned they may never be identified.

(Further details would be included in the body of the story.)

Here is a more complicated story. A reporter covering a meeting of a county commission has the following facts, each worth considering for the lead, to work with:

1. County Commissioner Roy McKenzie introduced a list of major cuts totalling nearly $60 million in the proposed $968 million budget for next year.
2. McKenzie accused County Manager Charles Whitehead of "dragging his feet" in making cuts in the budget.
3. Whitehead accused McKenzie of a "personal vendetta" against him and resigned immediately.
4. A majority of the commission agreed that Whitehead's original budget was too high and approved McKenzie's cuts.
5. Approximately 250 persons will be cut from the Sheriff's Department, the staff of the County Hospital and the County Highway Department.
6. Whitehead said McKenzie's cuts were not made in the interest of efficient government or for financial reasons but "just as a means of getting rid of me." McKenzie and several other commissioners have tried to force Whitehead's resignation on three other occasions.

Each of these is worth considering as a separate lead. However, all are related, so the reporter has to weave most, if not all, of them into one lead. Here are several examples of how the story might be written:

The Diagram
Summary of
Features

1 2 3 4

The Written Story

The County Commission today slashed nearly $60 million from the $968 million budget next year and cut 250 County Hospital, Sheriff's and Highway Department jobs.

The action brought the immediate resignation of County Manager Charles Whitehead.

Here's what happened at the Commission meeting today.

Feature No. 1 1

—County Commissioner Roy McKenzie introduced a list of major budget cuts totalling nearly $60 million.

Feature No. 2 2

—McKenzie told his fellow commissioners he made the cuts because County Manager Whitehead had been "dragging his feet" about trimming the budget.

Feature No. 3 3

—The commissioners, by a 5-4 vote, approved McKenzie's cuts.

Feature No. 4 4

—Whitehead accused McKenzie of carrying on a "personal vendetta" against him and resigned immediately after the Commission approved the cuts.

—Whitehead said McKenzie's cuts weren't made in the interest of "efficient government" or for "financial reasons" but as a "means of getting me."

Feature No. 5

—The cuts will cost 250 persons in the County Hospital and Sheriff's and Highway Departments their jobs.

(Details of the cuts and Whitehead's resignation as well as other features would be presented in the body of the story.)

Listing the major points immediately helps the reader understand quickly what took place at the meeting. Some editors would prefer a short, direct lead focusing on the resignation of the county manager. Here is an example of how the story might have been written to emphasize that single element:

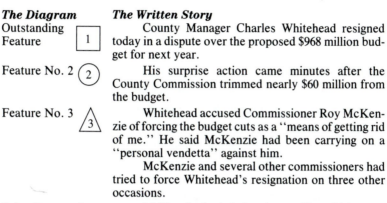

The Diagram	The Written Story
Outstanding Feature [1]	County Manager Charles Whitehead resigned today in a dispute over the proposed $968 million budget for next year.
Feature No. 2 (2)	His surprise action came minutes after the County Commission trimmed nearly $60 million from the budget.
Feature No. 3 /3\	Whitehead accused Commissioner Roy McKenzie of forcing the budget cuts as a "means of getting rid of me." He said McKenzie had been carrying on a "personal vendetta" against him.
	McKenzie and several other commissioners had tried to force Whitehead's resignation on three other occasions.
Other Paragraphs in the Complete Story ▽	McKenzie denied the charge. He said he proposed the cuts, which will cost 250 county workers their jobs, because Whitehead had been "dragging his feet" about trimming the budget.
	(Details of his resignation and all other features would be presented in the body of the story.)

The several-feature lead forms, as illustrated in the preceding examples, go beyond the lead sentence and the lead paragraph. Still they are leads in the sense that they summarize the various features of the story in showcase fashion before the reporter begins to develop the body of the story. In the long stories necessary to develop multiple features, several lead paragraphs are frequently needed and may be thought of as a "lead block."

OTHER LEADS

The Combination or Scrambled Lead

There are no hard and fast rules for writing the several-feature lead. The choice of the lead usually is determined by the facts of the story. Some of the features may be summarized, but not all. Or an outstanding feature may be singled out. It might also be combined with related features. And in some cases the reporter may want to take advantage of the drama of an event to depart completely from the hard news lead.

Suppose, for example, that the following took place during a local school board meeting:

1. The School Board rejected a plea from several hundred parents to ban a controversial reading book for sixth-grade students.
2. Voted not to appeal a federal court order prohibiting Bible classes as part of the public school curriculum
3. Hired The Survey Group, Inc., an engineering firm, for $9,900 to survey all school buildings in the system for asbestos-containing material

The first paragraph summarizes two of the features because they deal with academic issues in the system. The second paragraph adds other features that are related because they deal with the conditions of school buildings and the safety of the pupils. These features are equally important, but they are not as emotionally charged as the issues in the lead paragraph.

Tabulations

Many newspapers use tabulations either above or within the story as a way of summarizing for the reader the action reported in the body of the story. It is a way of letting the reader know a lot of information quickly. It permits the reporter to focus on a single fact. Some papers use numerals with tabulated items; others use dashes or dots. Here is an example:

A One-Column Box or a Boldfaced List Preceding the Story

HIGHLIGHTS OF YESTERDAY'S ELECTION
—Governor: Fred Farnsworth
—Lt. Governor: Lydia Mapes Williams
—Property Tax Referendum: Defeated 2-1
—Environmental Referendum: Defeated 3-1

Simplified Lead Made Possible by Preceding Tabulation

For the first time in 100 years Republican candidates have won the top offices in the state.

Fred Farnsworth, a former real estate developer who was running for public office for the first time, was elected governor yesterday.

His running mate, Lydia Mapes Williams, a long-time Republican party worker in the state, won the lieutenant-governor's post.

Governor-elect Farnsworth said . . .

Another type of lead is a variation of the summary. Instead of a single sentence including all the important features, this style briefly itemizes each feature, as in this example:

State Senator Betty Bradley today called for a constitutional convention to consider:
• A state income tax
• Educational reform, including the appointment of all school superintendents
• A state lottery
• The election of State Supreme Court justices
• The election of the State Attorney General

"If the state is going to have an income tax, it should be spelled out in the constitution," Bradley, a Republican from Blount County, said. "My motivation is not to come out with some tax scheme the people have no control over."

The senator's plan drew immediate criticism from the Democrats in both the House and Senate.

(Details on each of the items in the list would be developed fully in the body of the story.)

The leads discussed so far are the styles most commonly used in writing straight news stories. There are, however, some other variations that are acceptable at a number of newspapers. One of them is discussed in the following paragraph. Others are discussed in Chapter 8, "Devices to Polish the Lead," and Chapter 10, "Features and Human-Interest Stories."

The Interpretive Lead

Rather than using one of the news leads already discussed, a reporter may elect to write an interpretive lead. In this type of lead, the reporter attempts to tell readers what the facts mean. Interpretation should always be fair and objective. It should be based on the facts and the background knowledge of the event or situation, and it should be an accurate analysis of the facts. If the interpretation is simply the reporter's subjective view, then it becomes editorial opinion.

The standard straight news lead simply reports on an event, but the interpretive lead attempts to put the event into perspective for the reader. This type of lead is often used on a second-day story or by a newspaper whose competition got the story first. However, it is not uncommon for papers to use an interpretive lead when telling the story for the first time.

For example, if the governor sent a message to the state legislature asking for a one-cent increase in the state sales tax to finance his "Better Schools" proposal, a standard story might begin:

> Gov. Joseph Chavez today asked the state legislature for a one-cent increase in the state sales tax to finance his "Better Schools" program.

In the rest of the story, the reporter gives the details of the governor's proposal, citing the overall cost of the program to show why the governor is asking for an increase in the sales tax.

A reporter interpreting the governor's request for the reader might have written:

> Gov. Joseph Chavez yesterday ignored strong pressure from teachers, some legislators and consumer groups to push hard for a one-cent sales tax hike to finance his controversial "Better Schools" program.
>
> Teachers bitterly opposed the plan because it established a merit pay system. Legislators up for re-election this year are reluctant to vote for a tax increase. And consumer groups have charged that the sales tax hike would put an unfair burden on the poor and elderly.
>
> But the governor insists that a sales tax increase is the only way to finance the program now.
>
> "This school program is critical to our future," the governor said. "We can't wait for the courts to decide if an income tax is legal."
>
> The governor's "Better Schools" program would . . .

If such a lead is used, it is important to include as quickly as possible the facts and important details—in this case, the highlights of the "Better Schools" program. Some editors try to get those details into the second or third paragraph. Others include them in the third or fourth, depending on the circumstances of the

"In the period studied for the report, 29,011 people in the 15-24 age group committed suicide. That is a 41 percent increase in the suicide rate for the previous 10-year period.

"Strangely enough, the rate for the remainder of the population has remained stable.

"The methods used for suicide also changed during the period studied. Firearms and explosives were used more frequently than poisoning.

"The Center for Disease Control in Atlanta is reviewing the report and expanding its studies in an effort to identify the causes of suicide among the young. But better records and research providing socio-economic information on the victims are needed before health officials can attempt to reverse the trend."

c. Five Fire Department units responded to a call about 10 p.m. at Fifth Avenue Apartment Motel. Two apartments were found burning. More than 100 persons were evacuated. Firemen fought blazes for about 45 minutes. Both apartments were gutted, while others suffered water and smoke damage. Owner Joe Beasley said he would have to close up until he could have the building completely repaired. One resident told firemen a "former girlfriend" deliberately set the fires after he and the occupant of adjoining apartments had an argument with her over a six-pack of beer. Police arrested Vickie Sue Young, who gave a Virginia Avenue address, and charged her with arson. She is in jail in lieu of $40,000 bond. She will appear in court next Friday. Firemen said Young splashed lighter fluid on drapes and furniture in both apartments and tossed a lighted match at them. Police plan to question Young about fires in two other apartment buildings where she was a frequent guest.

(Source: Fire Captain Leonard Basler, Detective Bill Cory)

d. Freezing rain iced down all streets and highways in an eight-county area overnight, forcing the closing of schools, industrial plants and stores. More than 200 homes were without power. Police reported hundreds of "fender-bender" accidents and were unable to respond to all of them. The airport was closed and flights were delayed. Hospitals report treating scores of people for injuries suffered in accidents or from falls while trying to walk on icy streets. Morning temperatures dipped to 10 degrees above zero at the airport. It is not expected to be above freezing today. Police have urged everyone to stay at home, calling streets and highways treacherous. Some 250 bus passengers were stranded in the bus station when Greyhound buses stopped running before midnight. State Police said interstates were impassable. Weather forecasters said rain started turning to sleet and ice about 7 p.m. and continued through the night and may not stop before midafternoon.

(Sources: State Police, City Police, Sheriff's Department, Weather Service)

e. Two Jefferson High School students were questioned by fire officials about two telephone bomb threats that caused a 30-minute evacuation of the high school yesterday. Fire officials declined to identify the two male students, and also declined to say if they thought the bomb threats were connected with the suspension of the students over a protest at the school last week. The principal suspended the students because of their conduct in the hallways and cafeteria. Principal Mary Sanchez said she thought the two were connected. The bomb threat calls came within minutes of each other at about 9:45 a.m. Fire officials said they expect to file charges on the case within a week. Sanchez said she thinks most students "are tired of all this foolishness." Parents of the suspended students have protested to the school board.

(Sources: Fire Inspector Royce Hamilton, Principal Sanchez)

f. Here are highlights of a speech by Dr. Judith Dockery, a professor of psychology at State University and a specialist in youth behavior. The speech was given at the annual convention of the state's Clinical Psychology Association at the Civic Center. More than 500 people attended.

"Suicide is the third leading cause of death among people 15 to 24.

"Current statistics show that young Americans are killing themselves at a rate triple that of 25 years ago.

"Young men commit suicide four times as often as young women in the 15-24 age group, a federal study shows.

"The rate of male suicides during the time the study was conducted was twice as high among the 20-24 age group as it was in the 15-19 age group. About 88.8 percent of the male suicides are white.

"In the period studied for the report, 29,011 people in the 15-24 age group committed suicide. That is a 41 percent increase in the suicide rate for the previous 10-year period.

"Strangely enough, the rate for the remainder of the population has remained stable.

"The methods used for suicide also changed during the period studied. Firearms and explosives were used more frequently than poisoning.

"The Center for Disease Control in Atlanta is reviewing the report and expanding its studies in an effort to identify the causes of suicide among the young. But better records and research providing socio-economic information on the victims are needed before health officials can attempt to reverse the trend."

tendency to be long, and some editors prefer to group individual stories on the same page with separate headlines or group them under a single major headline. To avoid long stories, some reporters will write a lead story on the major action taken and separate shorter stories on secondary actions.

EXERCISES

1. Clip from any newspaper available to you leads that illustrate three different methods of writing a several-incident lead. Bring them to class and be prepared to discuss their strengths and weaknesses.

2. Here are rough notes for several-incident leads. Use them to complete the following tasks: First, list the various features in order of their newsworthiness; second, write a summary lead, another lead emphasizing an outstanding feature and a third lead in one of the forms explained in this chapter.

   a. City Council meeting last night:
      i. Approved internal transfer of $42,000 in Police Department funds to allow Chief Paul Page to give merit pay raises to officers.
      ii. Voted to create a new Trolly Board to oversee the operation of trolly shuttles through the downtown business district.
      iii. Voted not to support financially a project to bring the Christopher Columbus Celebration to the World's Fair Park.
      iv. Approved Councilwoman Elsie Emory's ordinance banning bed-and-breakfast inns from most residential neighborhoods. The city had no regulations governing bed-and-breakfast inns, but councilwoman Emory and others were responding to complaints from homeowners in several "high-rent" districts that several "inns" were being operated in their neighborhoods, which threatened property values.
      v. Voted to change next regular meeting from Monday at 7:30 p.m. to Thursday at 7:30 p.m. to avoid conflict with the observance of the birthday of the Rev. Martin Luther King Jr.

   b. Police arrested Dewayne W. Parton after a high-speed chase today. They charged the 37-year-old man with aggravated robbery in connection with the robbery of the First State Bank, 2121 Ellis Rd. About 9:30 a.m. today bank officials said Parton entered the bank and said he wanted to make a loan. Loan Officer Helen Davis took him to her office. He pulled a long-barrel gun and told her to fill a bag that he had with money. She explained she had no money. He demanded she get some from the teller's cages. She stalled him until customers left the counters. She placed the money, hidden with three red dye packs, in his bag. He insisted Davis leave the bank with him. When they got to his car, she bolted to a nearby car in the parking lot and hid. The dye packs exploded. A passing motorist saw the packs explode as Parton got into his car and drove away. He notified police that Parton was headed west on I-40. Police and Sheriff's deputies began chasing Parton's car at speeds up to 85 mph. Parton's car smacked into a guard rail as he tried to exit from I-40 at Webster Rd. Police and Sheriff's deputies surrounded the car with guns drawn. Parton got out of his car with his hands up. He apologized to police for causing so much trouble, and asked the police to pick up his wife and baby at a shopping center where he had left them before the robbery. He is held on $60,000 bond, pending a hearing in General Sessions Court.
      (Source: Police Chief Martin Mull, Sheriff Bart Simpson)

"Where" it happened; "Why" it happened; and "How" it happened. Obviously the news values discussed earlier in this chapter will influence the process. Reporters should always remember that the purpose of the lead is to give the reader an accurate and complete picture of what is to come later in the story.

Summarizing the Features

Once the features have been recognized, the reporter's job is to decide whether to try to summarize them or select one to emphasize in the lead. Here are several examples of leads in which the efforts to summarize all of the features produced leads that really are too vague:

> Four points in favor of consolidating city and county schools were given today by Mrs. Cyndi Tipton, president of Save Our Schools, Inc., in a speech to the . . .

> Problems of taxation and public health were debated today by the State House of Representatives.

> Four important pieces of consumer legislation were passed by Congress today.

Each of these leads recognizes the existence of several features, but the attempt to summarize them results in vague, dull and uninteresting leads. "Four points in favor" has little reader appeal and actually does not summarize those points. A brief summary of the points would make the lead more specific and catch the reader's attention.

> Mrs. Cyndi Tipton, president of Save Our Schools, Inc., told the Downtown Kiwanis Club that the consolidation of city and county schools would:
> —Sharply reduce the cost of public schools
> —Bring uniform educational standards to all students
> —Reduce teacher-pupil ratios
> —Reduce the number of students who would be bused

Another approach would be to emphasize one feature in the lead sentence and summarize the others in the next one, as in the following example:

> The cost of public schools would be reduced sharply by consolidating the city and county school systems, Mrs. Cyndi Tipton, president of Save Our Schools, Inc., told the Downtown Kiwanis Club.
> Consolidation would also bring about more uniform educational standards, reduce teacher-pupil ratios in the classrooms and greatly reduce the number of students who would have to be bused.

COMBINING STORIES

Separate stories about a single event naturally will differ in content, although there will be some overlapping of facts in each one. As a result, some newspapers will combine the stories into one. But combined stories have a

The leads discussed so far are the styles most commonly used in writing straight news stories. There are, however, some other variations that are acceptable at a number of newspapers. One of them is discussed in the following paragraph. Others are discussed in Chapter 8, "Devices to Polish the Lead," and Chapter 10, "Features and Human-Interest Stories."

The Interpretive Lead

Rather than using one of the news leads already discussed, a reporter may elect to write an interpretive lead. In this type of lead, the reporter attempts to tell readers what the facts mean. Interpretation should always be fair and objective. It should be based on the facts and the background knowledge of the event or situation, and it should be an accurate analysis of the facts. If the interpretation is simply the reporter's subjective view, then it becomes editorial opinion.

The standard straight news lead simply reports on an event, but the interpretive lead attempts to put the event into perspective for the reader. This type of lead is often used on a second-day story or by a newspaper whose competition got the story first. However, it is not uncommon for papers to use an interpretive lead when telling the story for the first time.

For example, if the governor sent a message to the state legislature asking for a one-cent increase in the state sales tax to finance his "Better Schools" proposal, a standard story might begin:

> Gov. Joseph Chavez today asked the state legislature for a one-cent increase in the state sales tax to finance his "Better Schools" program.

In the rest of the story, the reporter gives the details of the governor's proposal, citing the overall cost of the program to show why the governor is asking for an increase in the sales tax.

A reporter interpreting the governor's request for the reader might have written:

> Gov. Joseph Chavez yesterday ignored strong pressure from teachers, some legislators and consumer groups to push hard for a one-cent sales tax hike to finance his controversial "Better Schools" program.
>
> Teachers bitterly opposed the plan because it established a merit pay system. Legislators up for re-election this year are reluctant to vote for a tax increase. And consumer groups have charged that the sales tax hike would put an unfair burden on the poor and elderly.
>
> But the governor insists that a sales tax increase is the only way to finance the program now.
>
> "This school program is critical to our future," the governor said. "We can't wait for the courts to decide if an income tax is legal."
>
> The governor's "Better Schools" program would . . .

If such a lead is used, it is important to include as quickly as possible the facts and important details—in this case, the highlights of the "Better Schools" program. Some editors try to get those details into the second or third paragraph. Others include them in the third or fourth, depending on the circumstances of the story. In no case should they be ignored or placed much farther down in the story than the fourth or fifth paragraph. The reader needs those facts to understand why the governor has proposed the tax hike and why the various groups oppose it.

Considerable debate about interpretive reporting continues among journalists, and many newspapers still approach it with extreme caution. But it is being used increasingly in reporting government and politics, and it frequently brings cries from the persons whose action is being interpreted that the reporter is "biased" or, worse, "simply dead wrong." Nevertheless, the increasing complexity of modern society—not just government and politics—tends to require that newspapers explain facts as well as report them. Newspapers have a responsibility to make certain that the reporter who does the interpretation is careful and thorough and has the necessary background and maturity to present an accurate and fair analysis of the facts.

Separate Stories

Elections, storms, strikes, wars and frequently large fires and other major events may demand more than one story. For example, the story about the persons killed and injured in the chain-reaction crashes cited earlier in this chapter would require a main story about the crashes plus stories on the rescue efforts; stories on the survivors; interviews with officials about the causes; a story on similar crashes, especially if others occurred in the same area; and a story on what might be done to prevent similar crashes. In each one of these "sidebar" stories, the original event would need to be recapped in a brief paragraph early in the story.

Many of these stories lend themselves to strong dramatic feature leads. Often these stories are grouped in one section of the newspaper to make it easier for the reader to have immediate access to everything that is written about the event. It is not uncommon for a newspaper to collect all of its coverage of a major event such as an earthquake or major air crash in which lives are lost into a special section that is issued a week or so after the event.

IDENTIFYING THE FEATURES

It is difficult if not impossible to write a clear, coherent news story without identifying the features in the mass of story details the reporter has collected. Simply defined features are the highlights—the outstanding, most interesting and most significant items in any news event. The reporter has to determine which of these features are the most interesting and newsworthy.

For example, a reporter assigned to cover a speech should always look for the main arguments or contentions of the speaker to emphasize in the lead. However, the speaker's ad-libbing that the president should be impeached, a fist fight's starting in the audience, or hecklers' being ejected would be "features" that might rate even more attention than the highlights of the formal speech.

Perhaps the best guide in recognizing the worthwhile features is to look for these elements first: "Who" was involved; "What" happened; "When" it happened;

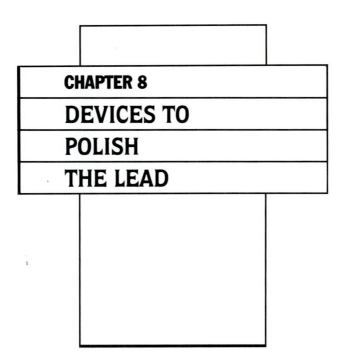

CHAPTER 8

DEVICES TO POLISH THE LEAD

News is repetitive. Unfortunately, so are a lot of leads on news stories. Although every reporter quickly learns that the chief purpose of a lead is to grab the reader's attention, hundreds of them write leads every day that begin the same way:

> The City Council voted 6-4 last night to . . .
> The County Commission voted unanimously last night to . . .
> City School Board members voted 9-1 last night to . . .
> The House of Representatives today passed a bill that will . . .
> The Senate today passed a bill that hikes taxes on . . .
> The governor signed into law today a bill creating a . . .
> The president signed into law today a bill that will . . .

The authors of such leads ignore the fact that the opening sentence of any story is crucial. The lead has to convince the reader to go on reading the rest of the story. If it doesn't, it has failed.

Reporters generally agree that the lead is the hardest part of a newspaper story to write. Some call it sheer agony, and that is often obvious in what they finally produce.

Frequently a lead will follow all the rules and principles discussed so far but still not be interesting enough to grab the reader's attention. It may contain all 5 W's, the proper identification and attribution, and it may emphasize a significant feature. In short, it may be adequate, but it may also be dull and uninteresting. It may lack originality, vividness, style, class, distinction and imagination.

A good lead is more than just adequate. It is clear, crisp and inviting. The Associated Press' Rene Jack Cappon says in his excellent book "The Word" that "A good lead makes a clear statement of the essential news point and when possible includes a detail that distinguishes the story from others of its kind."

Here is a well-written, imaginative lead from the AP:

WASHINGTON (AP)—If oil were liquor, the government would know where to find virtually every drop of it.

The remainder of the story detailed how the government had been far more successful in finding illegal moonshine stills than in finding new oil fields during the emergency crisis that gripped the nation at the time the story was written.

Here is an outstanding lead written by Camilla Warrick for The Cincinnati Enquirer:

On one side is a church with a mission.
On the other side is a city with a need.
In the middle is an aging, former elementary school.
These are the ingredients of a church-state confrontation that is pitting Northside Baptist Church against the North College Hill City Council.
It is a familiar story about one party coveting what the other has. In this case, it is the city hankering after what the church bought from under its nose.

Judy Holmes wrote this fine lead for the Neptune (N.J.) Asbury Park Press:

There's only one thing missing from the state's study commission into the most common women's surgery: a woman.

Her story went on to detail the appointment of an all-male task force to study Caesarean sections being performed on women in that state.

RHETORIC

Good writing demands the use of clear, crisp, colorful, precise language. When such language is combined with short sentences and short paragraphs, you have the essence of good news writing. But a reporter must always use variety in sentence and paragraph length as well as in sentence structure.

The most common sentence form is subject-predicate:

More than half of the people killed or maimed worldwide by terrorists are Americans, a U.S. diplomat said Friday.

It is favored by many reporters and editors, especially when dealing with straight news. But if all leads were written that way, they would fail in their basic goal to grab the reader's attention. While this type of lead sentence often is adequate, it just as often is dull. Focusing on one of the various W's gives variety to the lead.

Reporters often turn to other sentence forms to avoid writing all leads in the subject-predicate form. Here are some examples:

Phrases

Infinitive: To halt the flow of illegal drugs into South Florida, the U.S. Coast Guard today launched a . . .

Participial: Trying to shore up his crumbling political machine, Gov. Elbert Hooker called a secret meeting of . . .

Prepositional: In a slashing attack on the administration's treatment of the homeless, Senator Elise McMillan accused . . .

Gerund: Naming another so-called blue-ribbon panel of all-white males to investigate sexual and racial bias in hiring police and fire personnel is a joke, Councilwoman Marian Martin said. . . .

Clauses

Substantive: That congress will vote to support the President's plan to use force in the Middle East is a forgone conclusion in the minds of political observers.

Adverbial: If the public does not take a strong stand against drug dealers, pushers and users, the police won't push the "War on Drugs," Jeanne Barry, president of Mothers on the March. . . .

Although there is nothing wrong with these leads, many writers avoid them and many editors rewrite them simply because they have a tendency to be clumsy. They can, if not written with great care, sound stilted and often are quite long.

EMPHASIZING NEWS VALUES

It is important for the reporter to study all the features carefully to avoid overlooking a newsworthy feature or angle that might make the difference between a routine lead and a bright, imaginative one. While it is important not to bury the news, the reporter should always seek out that special angle that might make the lead reach out to the reader. There are a number of approaches, based on the traditional news values, available to a reporter. Here are several examples:

Timeliness

The words "today" and "tomorrow" characterize most newsworthy leads on straight news stories. Occasionally, however, a story concerns events that happened "last night," "last week" or even "last month" that result in a current story. In such cases the reporter should look for a "today" angle. It isn't always easy. Here are two versions of a "today" story that illustrate the point:

First Version
Mayor Rebecca Bromley's campaign promise last October to end her first year in office with a balanced city budget has cost 95 city employees their jobs.
Dismissal notices were mailed today to . . .

Second Version, Today Angle Emphasized
Ninety-five city employees got dismissal notices today. They were the victims of Mayor Rebecca Bromley's campaign promise in October to end her first year in office with a balanced city budget.

Other Today Angle Leads

Today marks that giddy, impression-making first day of school for the nation's high school class of 2003.

As self-effacing David Souter slips behind a red-felt-covered witness table again today, the vacant Supreme Court seat two blocks away is almost within reach.

Proximity

In addition to striving for a "today" angle, the reporter should also look for a "local" angle to the story.

A General Lead

Three Tennessee lawyers have been named to the board of directors of the American Trial Lawyers Association.

They are . . .

A Localized Lead

Richard Hollow, who served as U.S. Attorney here for four years, has been named to the board of directors of the American Trial Lawyers Association.

He is one of three state lawyers. . . .

Major national and international stories often have a local angle. The war in the Persian Gulf, for example, produced hundreds of stories with local angles. Here's an example:

Having five sons in the Persian Gulf is a source of pride for Minnie Pearl Jurnett.

But having all her sons—one of whom is a Metro police officer—in the military is also a cause for unspeakable fear for the resident of Maury City.

"My kids have been trying to tell me it's going to be OK, but . . . it's hard," she said. . . .

Prominence

Prominent names make eye-catching leads. Here are several examples:

A General Story

LOS ANGELES (AP)—More than 2,000 persons took the oath of U.S. citizenship today in a ceremony at the Shrine Auditorium.

U.S. District Judge . . .

Prominent Name Emphasized

LOS ANGELES (AP)—Actor and body-builder Arnold Schwarzenegger donned a pinstripe suit today and took the oath of U.S. citizenship in a ceremony at the Shrine Auditorium.

The star of "Conan, the Barbarian" and more than 2,000 others became naturalized citizens. . . .

Bill Cosby wears them. So does screen sex symbol Richard Gere.

Al Pacino doesn't want a tie or soap-on-a-rope this holiday season. "The best present would be to get back to the pure faith in other people I had as a child," Pacino says.

Pure faith might be hard to find in a store, but Patrick Swayze's wishes wouldn't be too difficult to grant—all he wants is a little time, a T-bone steak and maybe a new guitar.

What do celebrities want from Santa? The following is a short list, but some tall orders . . .

NOVELTY LEADS

Reporters today have considerable freedom in writing leads, although there are some editors who still prefer that every story have a straight news lead. "Novelty," as used here, simply means using any one of a number of devices from questions to quotations to attract the reader's attention.

There are as many approaches as there are imaginative writers and editors. Usually, the facts of the story will dictate the type of lead, and the reporter should not strain to write a novelty lead on a story that does not justify such treatment. Here are a few of the more common forms of novelty leads.

The Question Lead

A question lead works best when a problem with reader appeal or public interest is the central point of the story. Unfortunately, the question lead is used far too often as a crutch by a reporter who does not take the time to work on another more effective approach. Some editors put a limit on the number of question leads that can be used. Nevertheless, there have been some classic question leads, such as

O, say can you sing "The Star Spangled Banner" without mumbling the words and petering out on the high notes?

Here's an artful question lead from the Tennessean in Nashville:

Know anybody who needs 59 toilet seat covers? They come in all colors—blue, brown, pink, yellow.

How about 100 units of blood plasma? Or a good glue machine?

Today in East Nashville, you can get . . .

The rest of the story detailed the odd collection of items police collected during a sting operation.

Brad Kava, a reporter for the San Jose Mercury News, used a question lead effectively on his story about a new high-tech voice-controlled synthesizer:

So you sound great singing in the shower, but the only instrument you've mastered is the air guitar?

The wizards of SiliconValley have just introduced a product to turn your air guitar into a real one—all you have to do is hum, and you don't even have to do that very well.

The invention, called a Vocalizer 1000, is a voice-controlled synthesizer that works like an electric kazoo, translating phrases you sing or hum
into any one of more than 50 instruments. . . .

The Punch, Capsule or Cartridge Lead

This type of lead uses short, punchy statements to attract the reader's
attention. Here is an example from the Knight-Ridder Newspapers:

Big boys don't cry. Big boys are strong. Big boys bring home the big
bucks.
Big boys also suffer a higher rate of ulcers and heart attacks, not to
mention incidence of violence and sexual abuse.

The story went on to detail the efforts of the National Organization for
Changing Men to "liberate males from the traps of big-boy stereotypes."
Here is another written by Douglas Harbrecht for the Scripps-Howard
Newspapers:

WASHINGTON—Yuppies, take heart.
Reinforcements are on the way.
More than ever, today's college freshmen want money and status
when they get out of school.

The story went on to report the results of a national survey of the goals and
values of college freshmen.

The Direct-Quotation Lead

The direct-quotation lead can be extremely effective if the quote is a good
one and if it is not too long. Frequently, reporters use quotes that are too long and
involved. Several paragraphs may be needed to explain them to the reader. The
following is an interesting quote lead on Mongol herdsmen from The Christian
Science Monitor.

"A horse," says herdsman Davaasuren, "is the most precious thing a
Mongolian man can have."
Davaasuren, grizzled leader of a small group of nomadic herdsmen,
says he is happy these days. A gradual evolution of "perestroika"—
economic reform—in Mongolia has made it possible for him to resume the
life he loves, and to have as many horses as he wants.

In the next lead, Sally Quinn of The Washington Post not only used an
"eye-catching quote," she also captured the flavor of her subject's Southern
accent.

MONTGOMERY, Ala.—"Ah been lookin' for a husband for two
years now, ever since Dr. Austin died," said Ruby Golsom Ellis Austin.
"But ther's slim pickins in Montgomery. There ain't nothin' here."

"Ah got the only bachelor in Montgomery," said her daughter Cornelia Wallace. "And ah'm scared to death mama's gonna go after George."

"Shoooooooot honey," said Big Ruby, "he ain't even . . . "

The Contrast Lead

A contrast lead reaches for the reader's attention by comparing extremes—the big with the little, comedy with tragedy, age with youth, the past with the present.

Lance Cowan of the Nashville Banner used the contrast between a school with money troubles and one that had an excess.

> FRANKLIN—A local high school had a problem other schools would like to have—too much money.
> The Williamson County School board has agreed that Franklin High School's general fund balance of $180,000 is too high and the money should be spent to keep the balance more in line with other county schools.

The rest of the story explained how the money was raised for the fund and how a committee had been appointed to review ways to spend the money.

In this Associated Press (AP) lead, the contrast between birth and death during the poison gas disaster in Bhopal, India, adds a dramatic touch to the story updating that tragic event.

> BHOPAL, India—Six years ago, as Rani drew her first breath, hundreds of others nearby took their last. She was born as clouds of poison gas spewed from a Union Carbide plant and billowed deep into the city of 1 million people.
> The Bhopal accident was the world's deadliest industrial disaster, and its medical, legal and economic cost is still being reckoned. More than 3,800 people have died because they inhaled the gas that leaked from the plant at midnight on Dec. 2, 1984.

And there certainly is implied contrast in this unusual rape story by Edna Buchanan of The Miami Herald:

> A 39-year-old man, jogging in a Southwest Dade residential neighborhood, told police he was abducted by a gang of women and raped, Metro-Dade police said Thursday.
> "He's very hysterical, very traumatized," Rape Squad Lt. Linda Blue said.
> The victim, whose name is being withheld, is a professional man, with children, police said. . . .

The Direct-Address Lead

This lead speaks directly to the reader, often about a subject of broad interest or appeal. Consider this example, written by Craig Wilson for USA Today, which advises women where to find a single man:

Go west, young man.

The June issue of Playgirl magazine, out today, has compiled a list of places just crawling with men—and man-hunting women—in six states: Alaska, Hawaii, Nevada, North Dakota, Wyoming and Montana. . . .

Weather, taxes and other broad subjects lend themselves to the direct-address approach:

You'd better break out the blankets tonight.

The temperature is going to drop to zero, weather forecasters say.

You have less than 24 hours to file your federal income tax return!

And to help you meet that midnight deadline, the Post Office will set up a half-dozen outdoor drops outside the mail branch tonight.

"We'll take the return from anyone who is in line by midnight and make certain it has an April 15 postmark on it," Postmaster Irene Busse said.

Florence Fabricant of The New York Times used the direct-address approach effectively in this Thanksgiving food story:

It's the annual showdown: you versus the turkey. With the turkey trussed and the oven lighted, it hardly seems fair. But the outcome may still be in doubt.

The Descriptive Lead

In a descriptive lead, the reporter tries to paint a word picture of an interesting person, place or event. A descriptive lead also helps create the mood for the story and for that reason should match the subject carefully. In the next example, John M. Crewdson of The New York Times describes the scene as illegal aliens cross the border from Mexico into the United States:

WHY, Ariz.—It was the sweetest and gentlest of desert evenings, pitch-black except for a sliver of new moon and the light from a hundred thousand stars. Nearby, a coyote scampered among the stately organ pipe cactuses, its occasional mournful howl slicing the night like a jagged knife.

Presently the stillness was broken by a softer sound, a brief two-toned whistle. For half a minute there was nothing, then an identical whistle was heard from beyond the rise, followed by a flash of light and an answering flash, the signal that the way was clear. Within seconds, shadowy figures emerged from the desert. Smiling and talking softly, they gathered in a circle near the little-used highway.

This story by Mike Sager for The Washington Post describes the change of season in the Virginia countryside:

CULPEPER, Va.—The dawn is chilly inside the barn, and Greg Smith's breath hangs in the air like puffs from a hand-rolled smoke. A Holstein stands motionless before him, and he strokes the cow's black and white face with a rough, stained hand. A few steps away, the sun outlines the open barn door on the earth, and there summer lingers, warm to the skin.

It is autumn, harvest time at Ashland Farm. And while Smith still rises, with the certainty of the chime, at 5:30 sharp, the sun dawdles 60 seconds more each morning and moves imperceptibly to the south. Smith pulls a handful of brown corn silage from the trough, stirring the kernels and the chopped pieces of cob, stalk, and shuck with a finger. He closes his hand tightly. When it opens again, the coarse, fluffy matter springs back to size. Perfect. The right amount of moisture to last the winter.

It has been a good year at Smith's 1,112-acre dairy farm, so bountiful. . . .

The Christian Science Monitor used a descriptive lead in recounting the story of the first woman to drive a car across the United States:

It was pouring rain that gloomy June morning as a crowd gathered under umbrellas at curbside on a New York City street. The Maxwell, a forest green touring car with a leather-like pantasote top, was parked by the curb exactly at the place where Lincoln Center now stands. The year was 1909, the same year that Robert E. Peary set foot on the North Pole.

Next to the car stood a dimpled and impatient Alice Huyler Ramsey. She wore a bulky, ankle-length black poncho and rubber helmet with detachable goggles. Someone had given her a bouquet of carnations. Undaunted by rain or tradition she smiled for the photographers, as did the three women next to her.

But the dimples and smile were mere camouflage. This 21-year-old Alice H. Ramsey was half steel, half lightning rod in an era when nearly all women washed, ironed, changed diapers, and cleaned their houses instead of even thinking of driving a 2,100-pound car 4,000 miles from New York to San Francisco. Ramsey didn't toy with the idea; she was doing it. . . .

The Parody Lead

This lead attempts to play on words, using widely known proverbs, quotations, song titles, currently popular sayings, book titles and other expressions to help establish an immediate identification with the reader and bring a bit of sparkle to what otherwise might have been a routine story, as in these examples:

Waste not, want not, the chairman for the Senate Budget Committee warned the Pentagon today.

He had just learned that the Department of Defense is wallowing in more than $100 billion worth of spare parts, including $300 million of equipment the military doesn't need.

If winning isn't everything, why do they always fire the losing coach, sometimes even before the season ends?

Love may not be forever, but support is a different matter.

The Historical or Literary-Allusion Lead

This type of lead draws on some character or event in history or literature that is familiar to an average reader to attract and hold attention. The Bible and literary works often are used as reference points by writers. Here is an example of how one writer used a line from the Bible to begin a story on the demise of the World Football League's Chicago franchise:

> In the beginning, there was hope. And opulence. In the end? Well, in the end, really, there was nothing.
> It all started in a posh office building out in . . .

In his excellent feature on The New Yorker magazine, Phil Casey of The Washington Post used this classic literary line for his opening:

> Once upon a time, there was a unique and splendid magazine beautifully written, edited and produced, a little weekly work of art, perhaps the happiest blend of fact and fiction, reminiscence, humor, journalism, commentary and criticism there ever was.

And when Carl "The Truth" Williams was knocked out in 93 seconds by Mike Tyson in a championship fight, a number of writers tried a variety of ways to work the truth-and-consequences theme into their leads. Here's one example:

> "Truth" met consequences in the ring last night.
> And it took Mike Tyson just 93 seconds to convince Carl "The Truth" Williams that the truth of the matter was that Williams was simply out of his class.

The Staccato Lead

A staccato lead consists of short, clipped words, phrases and sentences, sometimes separated by dashes or dots or simply made into a list, to help create a certain mood for the story. Often this type of lead is descriptive in nature. Although it is not used as often as other types of leads, it can be effective, as in the following examples:

> DICKSON CITY, Pa. (AP)—A dress factory was damaged. A lumberyard and department store were burned. Vacant houses were torched.
> And authorities say the men who set some of the fires went back to fight the flames. Eight volunteer fire fighters were arrested. . . .

> The noise begins high. Up in the rafters. It gathers strength. Spills down the aisles. Building relentlessly. It cascades over the railing. It engulfs the expensive box seats. And spills out into the playing field. A raging torrent of sound. The eardrums vibrate painfully. The heart flutters.
> Pele, the world's greatest soccer player, has just received another message of love from his adoring fans.

Leon Alligood, senior staff writer at the Nashville Banner, used the technique effectively in this prize-winning feature about students with learning disabilities:

> TRACY CITY—Sam Baker has a learning disability.
> Lena Cox has a severe speech impediment.
> Frankie King is autistic.

They live in Grundy County, one of the poorest in Tennessee, where the number of students who quit high school almost equals the number who graduate.

But the county school system's special education students, like Sam, Lena, and Frankie, defy those numbers. Their dropout rate is far below the rate for the entire school system.

On Thursday, 29 special education students, those with the steepest path to academic success, will don cap and gown to receive their diplomas. . . .

Miscellaneous Leads

Occasionally a story lends itself to special treatment in sentence structure and display to catch the reader's attention. But a reporter must be careful not to try to be too clever or too cute. Although there are many examples of novelty leads, these examples are typical of those found in newspapers:

For Sale: One Town
Connie Carpenter, film and television actress who bought a remote hamlet in the Colorado Rockies, today put the town up for sale. Miss Carpenter said she plans to sell Echo Cross Roads and buy an island in the South Pacific. . . .

The Budget
By Mayor Norman Thomas
299 pp.
City of Jamestown
     Reviewed by Justin Smith
What can you say about a book that you can get a copy of for free, but it's going to cost you $3.76 for every $100 worth of property you own? Anyone who loves charts and tables and statistics will be fascinated. . . .

The flexibility of computer graphics makes it possible for newspapers to combine a reporter's story with charts, graphs, sketches and headline type to create a novelty presentation of a story. More and more newspapers are trying novelties, especially on their feature pages.

COMPLETE REPORTING

Good writers use words that tell the reader what he or she needs to know in as few words as possible. They use short words, strong words, colorful words and specific words. And they select details a reader can see. Good writers think about what they are going to write before they ever put a word on paper. Good writers have something to say and say it with style, grace and impact.

Most leads can be improved if the reporter stretches his or her imagination, knows what makes this particular story different and stresses that angle in clear and concise words. Here is an excellent example of a story by a writer who obviously thought about her lead before writing it. It was written by Lucette Lagnado of The Village Voice.

She was born in the maternity ward of Columbia-Presbyterian Hospital and that is also where she died.

Sharon Michelle Davis married her first love, flipped hamburgers at McDonald's, worked at a supermarket checkout counter. She was a working-class girl who saved her middle-class dreams for her unborn baby.

But early in the morning hours of Halloween, at perhaps the most prestigious medical center in the country, she suffered the most macabre trick of all. After enduring induced labor and surviving a difficult cesarean section, Sharon Michelle Davis, age 20, died in a maternity ward run by one of the nation's leading obstetrician-gynecologists. She died without being seen by any doctor—not even her attending physician—until it was too late.

Lucette Lagnado let the drama of the story speak for itself. She did not try to overdramatize the tragic situtation. Her choice of words set just the right tone for the story.

In a lighter vein but equally effective is this story written by Jim Laise for the Nashville Banner. When the University of Alabama's football team, traditionally a national powerhouse, ran out of steam, so to speak, Laise went south to talk to the Crimson Tide's loyal fans and filed this story:

TUSCALOOSA, Ala.—Good gawd ya'll, they've done raised the white flag in The Heart of Dixie.

That's right. Alabama football fans, faced with their team's worst start in 26 years, have just about conceded. Already.

"People are always saying, 'Wait till next week,'" said Bill Hogue, a Dothan resident dining Tuesday in Bessemer's Bright Star Restaurant. "Now, we might as well say, 'Wait till next year.'"

The reason is simple. The Tide is 1-2. That's right. The same Tide that some fortune-teller from one of them girlie magazines picked to finish No. 2 in the whole darn shootin' match can't even beat Georgia Tech, for Pete's sake.

Although Alabama fans may take the team's poor showing seriously, Laise used the right light-hearted tone in his story.

Tone has to ring true to the subject of the story. If it does not, the reader will know it immediately—and you will lose her or him. Both reporters struck the right tone in their stories.

EXERCISES

1. The following leads are quite long; rewrite them to be shorter and more direct.
   a. WASHINGTON—After five months of negotiations and partisan bickering, top Congressional leaders said today that they struck a compromise on taxes that they believe would have the support of the White House and a majority of the members of the Senate and House.
   b. WASHINGTON—The Department of Transportation issued new standards for automobile safety today that are intended to protect occupants when cars are struck from the side, saying the rule would prevent more than 500 deaths and 2,600 serious injuries a year.
   c. Responding to community outrage over the "absurdly low" bail set for two white teen-agers suspected of murdering a black pastor the Los Angeles County district

attorney's office apologized to the victim's family Friday and announced a new policy that will generally prohibit bail in murder cases.

d. Unauthorized charges to a telephone credit card number several months ago alerted the city recorder to keep a closer eye on the city's telephone bills, which led to discovering hundreds of dollars charged to a 900 sports service information number from the Police Department.

e. State auditors criticized the financial operations of the Cocke County Highway Department, reporting the department's spending exceeded appropriations last year by $205,001.

2. Newspapers are often faced with having to update stories that took place after the previous daily or weekly edition was published. What information would you seek, and from what sources, to make the following leads more "timely"?

   a. The American Civil Liberties Union is investigating a local coach in connection with a flier that urged students to attend the baptism of his football players.

   b. Three families were left homeless Friday after a fire destroyed the Southside apartment building in which they lived.

   c. A man was in critical condition Tuesday night after being shot in the head at an East Knoxville lounge, authorities said.

3. Explain in detail how you would "localize" the following stories

   a. The FBI today advised all airport managers to increase security measures following widespread rumors that a major terrorist act is imminent.

   b. Officials of the State Water Quality Control Department said acid rain poses a "major threat" to the state's streams, rivers and lakes and endangers the water supply to most towns and cities.

   c. FAYETTEVILLE—A disaster relief center will open here Tuesday to assist residents of Lincoln, Marion, Franklin, Grundy and Warren counties whose homes and businesses were damaged by last week's flooding.

4. Prominent names are not given immediate play in the following leads. Rewrite them to focus on the well-known individuals.

   a. A new task force has been established by the City School Board to find ways to make the schools safe. The group plans to draft a behavior code to discourage gang activities and to find ways to interest students who may want to join gangs in alternative activities, said Mark Della, who directs gang-prevention, conflict, and anti-drug and alcohol programs for the city school system. The task force will include teachers, parents, principals, social service workers and law-enforcement officials, as well as teen-agers, who have not been selected yet. Della said one of the first things the task force will do is seek several gang members to talk about gang activity and why it appeals to them.

   b. Dr. Wilbert Hooker, an Edwardsville dentist who grew up on a sheep ranch in the west, has developed false teeth for sheep, which he claims will lengthen their breeding lives. When sheep grow old their teeth break down, making it difficult for them to feed themselves. As a result their useful lives are cut short several seasons. Hooker claims that he has successfully fitted a half-dozen sheep with false teeth.

5. Using the following situations, write a question lead based on the notes and another one based on one of the other lead styles discussed in this chapter.

   a. Wayne D. Shelby received
   Notice from the State Department
   Of Economic Security ordering
   Him to sign up for job placement

Or lose his food stamp eligibility
He was given 10 days to report
To job placement offices
Wayne is only 13 months old
His family signed up for
Food stamps last week
But his father was not ordered
To report for job placement
Rev. Richard Williams
Wayne's grandfather said
"We thought it was cute"
Family said they will take
Wayne to job placement office
"To prove he's too young to work"
State Employment officials
Refuse to discuss the case.

b. Donald Scroggins, a graduate student
In communications at William & Mary
Woke up to find water pouring
From cupboards and electrical outlets
In his apartment at University Heights
Apparently from ruptured water pipe
In apartment directly above him
He called building manager
Who turned off the water and told
Scroggins to rent some cleaning equipment
To help clean up the apartment
Scroggins went to his car and
Discovered he had a flat tire
Returned to apartment to call a friend
To help with the cleanup
Picked up phone and was zapped by electric shock
When he jumped back the phone fell off the wall
He tried to leave the apartment
But water apparently caused wall to shift
He was unable to get the door open
Manager kicked it down
Scroggins went outside to discover
Side of his car had been hit and badly damaged
Returned to his apartment to assess damage
Discovered all his clothes, books, and food
Had been soaked by the water
He had taken refuge with a friend
"I think God had it in for me today,"
Scroggins said. "It must have been some kind of test."

6. Attend a campus event such as a parade, an art exhibit, a dance recital, a major athletic event, or a concert by a popular music group and write a descriptive lead of the event.

7. Visit the most scenic place you know on or off campus and write a descriptive lead for a story about that spot.

8. Write a parody or literary-allusion lead based on the following set of notes:

   a. Mary Ruth Emrick, 26, who lives
   In Christenberry Homes
   A public housing project
   Told police her neighbor
   Christine Chapman, 29, beat her up
   When she went to Chapman's apartment
   To borrow a cup of sugar
   To bake her son a birthday cake
   Emrick said she had loaned
   Chapman "all kinds of food, even money"
   But when she asked for a favor in return
   Chapman got mad and cussed her out
   And "beat up on me bad"
   She signed a warrant for Chapman's arrest
   On charges of assault and battery
   Detective Laura Ashley said Emrick
   Did not require medical attention
   "But she has a beauty of a shiner."

   b. Herman Leon Ford, 21, 1074 Second Ave.
   Arrested at his home
   Charged with robbing and kidnapping
   Harley Pierce, 2300 Seminole Ave
   A U.S. Marine Corps recruit
   About 9 p.m., Friday on LaFayette Street
   Police said Ford was dressed like a woman
   And pretended to be a female prostitute
   He flagged down Pierce and got in his car
   When Pierce asked Ford where he was headed
   Ford suggested having sex for $20
   Pierce refused and Ford pulled pistol
   From his handbag and robbed Pierce
   Of $150 and his credit cards
   And fled from the car
   Pierce called police who using
   The description Pierce provided
   Went to Ford's home and arrested him
   Vice Squad Dt. James Stovall said
   "We've been watching this guy for
   A couple of weeks now. He's not a
   Very convincing woman at all."
   Police said they found wigs, dresses,
   High heeled shoes and makeup in
   Closet in Ford's apartment
   They plan to question him
   About similar robberies

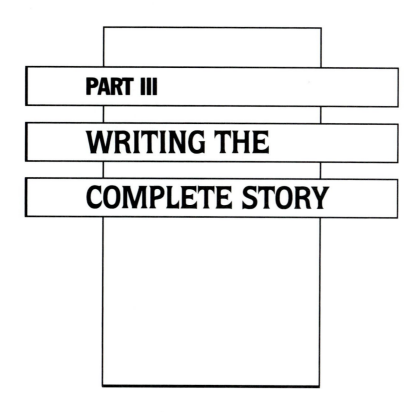

PART III

WRITING THE

COMPLETE STORY

A news story needs more than just a good lead.

It is true that the lead is what attracts a reader's attention in the first place, but it is the body of the story that holds it.

A news story comes together in the body and delivers to the reader what the lead has promised. If the body does not support the lead in a careful and lucid fashion, if it isn't as interesting as the lead, the reader may feel cheated. What is worse, the reader might not finish the story.

Organizing and developing the body of a news story is tremendously important. Often it can present even greater problems than writing the lead. Just as there are a number of styles or approaches to handling leads, the body of a news story can be developed in a variety of ways.

Part III presents organizational patterns for both straight news and feature stories. It also deals with four other areas that may present problems for which there are specific techniques to use in writing a complete story. These include the organization of (1) stories on events about which previous stories have been published; (2) cutlines to go with pictures, which are often important supplements to stories but which sometimes stand alone in the coverage of an event; (3) news stories for radio and television; and (4) stories requiring special treatment if a newspaper's policy is involved.

The chapters in this section form a basis for writing all of the types of newspaper stories considered throughout the book.

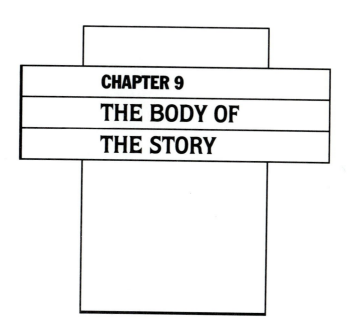

CHAPTER 9
THE BODY OF
THE STORY

An effective news story has to be more than just a loosely assembled collection of facts. It must have an interesting lead to grab the reader's attention. The lead should be followed by the main body of the story, which expands and elaborates—documents—the lead. Then the story should come to a logical end.

Each part should be carefully tied to the other so the story progresses in an interesting, informative and logical manner. Often a single fact seems to have great possibilities as a lead, but there is nothing to support it. That is why the reporter has to carefully sort and organize the facts, first in the mind and then on the video-display terminal (VDT) screen.

Like the lead, the body of the story should be clear and concise. It should take the reader through the details of the story in logical progression, emphasizing the facts in order of descending importance. Here is a long and convoluted lead that almost defies understanding:

> City Council members have been told that because of nearby potential hazards to children, it might be "inadvisable, perhaps even negligent" to site 46 units of public housing designed for low-income families on the so-called "Federal Office Building Tract" because of potential dangers from heavy equipment, plating solutions and radioactive material in that area.

The rest of the story was equally muddy and difficult to wade through. Among other problems, the writer did not tell the reader who gave the council this information until about the sixth paragraph. Obviously, the writer did not organize the material carefully before writing it, and the copy editor apparently made no effort to rewrite it into a clear, crisp report of a rather complicated event.

By contrast, here is a short lead playing off the lyric to a Christmas carol that gets right to the point and is quickly supported by the body of the story:

''Tis the season for fraud and robberies.'' That's what police are singing in these days before Christmas as the number of reported thefts, robberies and check cashing scams increase almost daily in the city.

''It's driving us crazy,'' Metro Robbery Sgt. Ron Parrish said. ''Everything gets pretty wild this time of year . . . we need some relief.''

The rest of the story gave the statistics showing the increase in crime and tied them to the fact that the period between Thanksgiving and Christmas is the prime shopping period of the year, and shoppers often have more money with them than they have at other times of the year.

The following is an example in which the lead and the first paragraph in the story are somewhat at odds, which damages the effectiveness of the lead:

MONTEREY, Calif.—Adorable quotient aside, sea lions these days are more a rank and nasty nuisance to Monterey city officials than the cuddly creatures gliding through the water that tourists love.

It's not cute, they say, when a dozen of the 800-pound mammals climb aboard a tugboat and sink it with their combined weight. It's not sweet when they take over entire boat slips, preventing even the proudest yacht owners from stepping out of their crafts.

The problem with this lead is that the writer calls an 800-pound sea lion cuddly and adorable. There are few things that weigh 800 pounds that are cuddly or adorable. Sea lions are very large and very ugly and often ill-tempered. It could be the writer has mistaken the sea lion for the sea otter. At any rate, the lead is certainly out of sync with the second paragraph of the story.

The reporter should use good judgment in writing the lead and in developing the body of the story. The object is to attract the reader's attention with the lead and then hold it by arranging all the significant facts and incidents of a story in their logical order of importance or newsworthiness. In telling the story in logical order—arranging facts in order of descending newsworthiness—the reporter should lead the reader carefully from one paragraph to the next. One weak paragraph preceding several interesting ones might mean that the latter paragraphs are not read.

Although editing techniques and the ability to match stories to available space are now more sophisticated than they were when the inverted pyramid style became common more than 60 years ago, the logical order is still an important aid to the mechanical process of the newspaper. If the copy editors or makeup editor must reduce the length of a story, he or she cuts paragraphs from the end of the story. The copy editor takes for granted that the final paragraphs contain the least important facts. The following rule is an excellent one to use when writing a standard news story: Write your story so that if it is terminated at any point, nothing below that point will be as newsworthy as anything above it, so that at the terminating point the story will be complete, intelligible and effective.

The body of the story serves one or both of two purposes: (1) it explains and elaborates the feature or features in the lead or lead block; (2) it adds and elaborates on minor features not summarized in the lead.

DEVELOPING THE SINGLE-FEATURE LEAD

If a story contains only one feature, the lead is built around it. The body of the story will elaborate and document the lead by adding the pertinent facts. In this case the task is to judge the newsworthiness of all facts so that they may be presented in logical order. Here's an example of this type of story.

The Diagram
Lead: Single Feature ⌐1⌐

Details of the Feature ⌐1⌐

Additional Details ⌐1⌐

Further Details ⌐1⌐

All Other Paragraphs in the Complete Story ▽

The Written Story

Creation of a non-political Civilian Review Board to investigate all cases of alleged police brutality was recommended in a report sent to Mayor Elizabeth Ragsdale today.

The report, from a special commission named three months ago by the mayor to study the Police Department, said:

"A Civilian Review Board is needed because the Police Department is hopelessly politicized and incapable of fairly and impartially investigating itself."

The report noted that the Police Department's internal security division had not taken disciplinary action against a single police officer although more than 30 persons have charged that they were beaten or manhandled by policemen during questioning and arrest in the past 18 months.

"In two cases where policemen were found guilty in court of assault and battery, the Police Department still failed to take any disciplinary action," the report said.

The proposed Civilian Review Board would be appointed by the mayor and confirmed by City Council. One member would be selected to represent each of the council districts. They would serve three-year terms.

Mayor Ragsdale named the special commission to study the Police Department in response to dozens of complaints about police brutality.

(Additional paragraphs would give more details and background.)

DEVELOPING THE SEVERAL-FEATURE LEAD

The several-feature story often presents problems for the reporter. Chief among them is the organization of the body of the story.

Since the body of the story should explain and elaborate on all the features presented in the lead or lead block, the reporter is faced with the problem of giving each of the features the proper amount of attention without burying important facts deep within the story.

Too often reporters get carried away and load the body of the story with insignificant facts about one or more of the features, delaying the explanation of the other features. If a feature has enough reader appeal to deserve a place in the lead or lead block, it deserves to be supported high in the body of the story.

Reporters also frequently have problems with minor features not summarized in the lead. Minor features should not be introduced into the body of the story until all the features in the lead have been explained fully. When they are introduced, they should be summarized before their details are presented.

Summary Development

If more than one feature is summarized in the lead, each feature should be elaborated in the order it was presented (logical order) as in this example:

The Diagram

Lead: Summary of All Features

1 ② △3

Details Common to All Features

Details Common to All Features

Details of First Feature

1

Details of Second Feature

②

Details of Third Feature

△3

More Details on First Feature

1

All Other Paragraphs in the Complete Story

The Written Story

Creation of a non-political civilian board to investigate cases of alleged police brutality, special human relations training for all police officers and reorganization of the Police Department's Internal Security Bureau were recommended in a report sent to Mayor Elizabeth Ragsdale.

The report was prepared by the special commission named by the mayor three months ago to study the city's trouble-plagued Police Department.

The proposed review board would investigate all cases of alleged police brutality because the Police Department is "hopelessly politicized and incapable of fairly and impartially investigating itself," the report said.

Asserting that most instances of alleged manhandling of citizens are unnecessary, members of the commission urged that all police officers be required to take special training in human relations.

"Police are given no courses in human relations during their training period, and they obviously do not get any training in it after they are placed on active duty," the report said.

Public dissatisfaction with the department stems chiefly from the work of the Internal Security Bureau, which is responsible for investigating civilian complaints against police officers.

"The Internal Security Bureau has not recommended disciplinary action against a single police officer, although more than 30 persons in the last 18 months have charged that they were beaten or manhandled by police officers during questioning or while being arrested.

"In two cases where police officers were found guilty in court of assault and battery, the Police Department did not take any disciplinary action," the report said.

In recommending a Civilian Review Board, the report suggested that members be named by the mayor and confirmed by the City Council. Each member would represent one of the city's council districts and would serve for three years.

(Additional paragraphs would give further details and background.)

Outstanding Feature Development

One feature may be so significant that the reporter may elect to emphasize it in the first paragraph and then summarize all the other features in the second paragraph. The third paragraph then should elaborate and explain the feature emphasized in the lead. The remainder of the body of the story should consider each of the features given in the second paragraph in their logical order, as in this version of the story:

The Diagram
Lead: Outstand-
ing Feature

Summary of
Other Features

Details Common
to All Features

Details Common to
All Features

Details of Out-
standing Feature

[1]

Details of First
Minor Feature

(2)

Details of Second
Minor Feature

/3\

More Details of
Outstanding
Feature

[1]

The Written Story

Creation of a non-political Civilian Review Board to investigate all cases of alleged police brutality was recommended in a report sent to Mayor Elizabeth Ragsdale today.

The report also urged that all police officers be given intensive training in human relations, and that the Police Department's Internal Security Bureau be reorganized. The report requested a special allocation of $150,000 to begin the training within 30 days.

The mayor received the report for the special commission she appointed three months ago to study the Police Department. She took the action after a rash of reports of alleged police brutality over the past 18 months.

The Civilian Review Board is needed, the report said, because the Police Department is "hopelessly politicized and incapable of fairly and impartially investigating itself."

Asserting that most instances of alleged man-handling of citizens are unnecessary, the report urged that all police officers be required to take intensive training in human relations.

"Police are given no courses in human relations during their training period, and they obviously do not get any training in it after they are placed on active duty," the report said.

Much of the public's dissatisfaction with the Police Department stems from the work of the Internal Security Bureau, which is responsible for investigating civilian complaints against individual officers, the report said.

"The Internal Security Bureau has not recommended disciplinary action against a single police officer, although more than 30 persons in the last 18 months have charged that they were beaten or man-handled by police officers during questioning or while being arrested.

"In two cases where policemen were found guilty in court of assault and battery, the Police Department still failed to take any disciplinary action," the report said.

In recommending a Civilian Review Board, the report suggested that members be named by the mayor and confirmed by City Council. One member would represent each of the city's council districts and would serve for three years.

All Other Paragraphs in the Complete Story	(Additional paragraphs would give further details and background.)

If the minor or secondary features are not as important as some of the details of the outstanding feature, they need not be introduced until the details of the outstanding feature have been spelled out. This organization still observes the logical order of presenting the information.

The Diagram

The Written Story

Lead: Outstanding Feature

1

Creation of a non-political Civilian Review Board to investigate all cases of alleged police brutality was recommended in a report sent to Mayor Elizabeth Ragsdale today.

The report, made by a special commission appointed by the mayor three months ago to study the trouble-plagued Police Department, said:

"A Civilian Review Board is needed because the Police Department is hopelessly politicized and incapable of fairly and impartially investigating itself."

It pointed out the failure of the Department to take any steps to prevent "the kind of action on the part of police officers that has led to 30 citizens charging that they had been manhandled or beaten."

"An apparent lack of concern for the public welfare pervades the entire Department," the report said.

Additional Details

1

A Civilian Review Board would ensure the citizens that all complaints against police officers would be fairly and objectively investigated because the board would be non-political and not affiliated with the Department in any way, it added.

Members of the board would be appointed by the mayor and confirmed by City Council. One member would be selected to represent each of the council districts in the city. They would serve three-year terms.

Summary of Other Secondary Features Associated With Outstanding Feature

② ⁄3\

The report also recommended that a special staff be hired for the review board, and it asked for an emergency appropriation of $150,000 to begin the board's operation as soon as possible.

More Details

②

"A separate staff of investigators and special assistants is absolutely essential to the operation of the proposed board," the report said. "Without its own staff the committee will have to rely on the Police Department for its investigative work. This obviously would create a serious problem for the board."

More Details

The need for an independent office staff and team of investigators makes it essential that approximately $150,000 be appropriated on an emergency basis to get the board into operation, the report said.

It points out that a regular budget for the board would have to be included in the city's annual budget in future years, if the board is to operate as an effective independent, non-political agent.

Summary of Other Features

The report also urged that all police officers be given intensive training in human relations and that the

Police Department's Internal Security Board be reorganized.

Details of Other Features

(Additional paragraphs would elaborate and explain these two other recommendations of the special committee named by the mayor.)

It should be noted that some editors would consider this too far down into the story to introduce the recommendations for human relations training and the reorganization of the Internal Security Bureau. Some editors would have the reporter write separate stories to avoid making the lead story long. Some studies have shown that unless a story is compelling, readers begin to lose interest if it runs more than 15 inches.

The Combination Development

The Diagram
Lead: Summary or Two-Lead Features

Summary of Other Features

Details Common to All Features

Details of First Lead Feature

Details of Second Lead Feature

Details of First Minor Feature

The Written Story
Creation of a non-political Civilian Review Board to consider cases of alleged police brutality and special training in human relations for all police officers were recommended in a report sent to Mayor Elizabeth Ragsdale today.

The report also recommended that the Police Department's Internal Security Bureau be reorganized. And it requested an emergency allocation of $150,000 to begin the human relations training within 30 days.

The report was made by a special commission appointed by Mayor Ragsdale three months ago to study the Police Department. The mayor took the action after a rash of reports of alleged police brutality over the past 18 months.

In recommending a Civilian Review Board, the report said it is needed because the Police Department is "hopelessly politicized and incapable of fairly and impartially investigating itself."

Board members would be appointed by the mayor and confirmed by the City Council. One would be selected from each of the city's council districts. They would serve three-year terms.

Asserting that most instances of alleged police manhandling of citizens are unnecessary, the report urged that all police officers be required to take intensive training in human relations.

"Police are given no courses in human relations during their training, and they obviously do not get any training in it after they are placed on active duty," the report said.

Calling the Internal Security Bureau "ineffective" in its present form, the report said the bureau took months to conduct the most routine investigation. And then it rarely came up with any recommendations that "would help relieve some of the intolerable conduct on the part of some police officers."

It noted that the bureau had not recommended disciplinary action against a single police officer, although more than 30 persons in the past 18 months had

Details of Second
Minor Feature

All Other Para-
graphs in the
Complete Story

charged that they were beaten and manhandled by police during questioning and arrest.

The $150,000 emergency allocation would allow the department to begin an intensive course in human relations on a crash basis within 30 days, the report said. Additional money would have to be allocated in the department's budget to include this kind of training for all new officers in the future and to provide periodic review courses for veterans of the force.

In advocating the Civilian Review Board, the report suggested . . .

(other details in logical order)

A combination development with some features buried deep in the story (note the following example) is a common form. This is much like the outstanding-feature form illustrated previously in this chapter. In long stories, minor features may be introduced in summary paragraphs at several points in the body of the story.

The Diagram
Lead: Summary
of Two Main
Features

Details of First
Lead Feature

Details of Second
Lead Feature

Summary of
Other Features

Details of First
Lead Feature

Details of Second
Lead Feature

The Written Story
Creation of a non-political Civilian Review Board and special training in human relations for all police officers were recommended in a report sent to Mayor Elizabeth Ragsdale today.

The mayor received the report from the special commission she appointed three months ago to study the Police Department. She took the action after a rash of reports of alleged police brutality over the past 18 months.

The Civilian Review Board is needed to investigate all cases of alleged police brutality because the Police Department is "hopelessly politicized and incapable of fairly and impartially investigating itself," the report said.

Asserting that most instances of alleged manhandling of citizens are unnecessary, the report urged that all police officers be required to take intensive training in human relations immediately.

The report also recommended that the Police Department's Internal Security Bureau be reorganized. And it requested an emergency allocation of $150,000 to begin the human relations training within 30 days.

"The Civilian Review Board would reassure the citizens that all complaints against police officers would be fairly and objectively investigated because it would be non-political," the report said. Members would be appointed by the mayor and confirmed by City Council. One would represent each of the city's council districts. They would serve three-year terms.

The report noted that "Police are given no courses in human relations during their training period, and they obviously do not get any training in it after they are placed on active duty."

"It is obvious that some police officers prefer to restrain rather than reason with persons they are questioning or arresting," it added.

Details of First
Minor Feature

The report stated that much of the public dissatisfaction with the Police Department stems from the work of the Internal Security Bureau, which is responsible for investigating civilian complaints against police officers.

It pointed out that the Internal Security Bureau "has not recommended disciplinary action against a single police officer, although more than 30 persons in the last 18 months have charged that they were beaten or manhandled by police officers during questioning or while being arrested."

All Other Paragraphs in Complete Story

(other details in logical order)

As noted earlier, some newspapers attempt to keep stories reasonably short and, when confronted with handling a report such as the one cited in these examples, elect to make it into a series of stories. The major story might be a general review of the report, emphasizing the major point and highlighting the minor ones. The secondary stories would be devoted to each of the other recommendations made in the report. Often, in a story of this importance to a community, the main story would be used on page one and perhaps continue to an inside page where the secondary stories would be displayed. A number of newspapers use the same technique when handling city council and school board stories in which a lot of action takes place. This is a graphic device used to attract readers who would read the shorter stories but would be unwilling to wade through one very long story.

Multiple-Casualty Story Development

Many newspapers have a standard form for stories involving several casualties. Here is an example of how an accident resulting in several deaths might be handled:

The Diagram
Summary Lead

The Written Story

Three members of a Southside family were burned to death early today in a fire that destroyed their two-story home at 1165 Roswell Blvd.

Two others were hospitalized in critical condition. They suffered burns over most of their bodies, fire officials said.

The Dead

Jose Chavez, 31, his wife, Rosa, 29, and their six-month-old son, Luis, were trapped in an upstairs bedroom and unable to escape.

The Injured

Two other sons, Jamie, 3, and Roberto, 6, who were sleeping downstairs, were rescued by firemen. They are in critical condition at St. Mary's Medical Center.

Summary of
Other Features or
Details on Lead

Fire Chief Leonard Basler said the fire apparently started about 5 a.m., and spread quickly to the upper floor. . . .

(Details of the fire would follow in chronological order.)

Newspapers generally group the names of casualties into a single paragraph when they are related. However, if the casualties are not related and the list is long, the names are given on separate lines immediately following the leads, as in this example:

The Diagram	*The Written Story*
Summary Lead	Five officials of the Rainbow Manufacturing Co. were killed today when the company's jet crashed on takeoff from McGee Tyson Airport. They are:
The Dead	Michael Connely, company president Thomas Lewis, vice president for sales Gregory Thompson, vice president for manufacturing George Ramos, treasurer Darlene Yhieme, personnel manager
The Injured	The pilot, Brian Prentice, and copilot, Gail Palmer, were critically injured in the crash.
Summary of Details of Other Features	Airport officials said the plane . . . (Details of the accident would follow in chronological order.)

The object in using a list here is to make it easy for the reader to see the names of the dead quickly. Some newspapers even set the names of the victims in boldface type.

CHRONOLOGICAL ORDER

Stories with strong narrative elements may sometimes best be told in chronological order, rather than logical order, in the body of the story. After the lead has summarized the outstanding feature or features, the body of the story may be developed as a narrative. In most cases, however, the narrative paragraphs are interrupted by paragraphs adding additional facts, as in the following example:

The Diagram	*The Written Story*
Lead: Summary	A gunman demanding $1 million and a plane to fly him to Mexico held two employees of the First National Bank hostage for three hours yesterday before surrendering to FBI agents and city police. The hostages were not injured. FBI Agent Joseph Westfall identified the gunman as Bobby Mack Cable, 41, a former mental patient.
Non-narrative Details	Becky Barnette, secretary, and Jackson McDonald, vice president and comptroller of the bank, said Cable walked into her second-floor office in the bank building about 12:45 p.m.

Narrative

"When I asked him if I could help him, he pulled a gun out of his windbreaker pocket," Mrs. Barnette said. "I guess I screamed because Mr. McDonald came running out of his office. We were the only two there. All the others were out to lunch."

McDonald said Cable told them: "OK! Keep calm. Just do what I tell you and nothing will happen to you."

Cable ordered McDonald to lock the door from the inside and made the banker push a desk and file cabinet against it as a barricade.

Narrative Details

"Now, get on that phone and call the president of this bank and tell him I want $1 million in small bills and an airplane to fly me to Mexico," Cable said. "If I don't get them and get them soon he'll be shopping for two new employees tomorrow."

McDonald said he called Harry Jameson, bank president, whose office is on the fourth floor. "He wasn't sure that I wasn't just kidding at first, but Cable yanked the phone out of my hand and repeated the demand. He also warned Mr. Jameson not to call the police. He wanted Mr. Jameson to drive us to the airport in his personal car and then, he said, he would release us just before boarding the plane."

James said he talked to the bank security chief and they decided to call the FBI and the police.

Within 15 minutes, more than 50 city policemen and FBI agents had surrounded the bank. They cleared patrons from the first floor of the building and the parking lot. Police rerouted traffic in the downtown area so no cars passed the bank building at 911 Jefferson St.

Mrs. Barnette said Cable seemed calm and sure of himself. "He talked about the weather and how nice it is in Mexico at this time of the year for about 20 minutes. Then he forced Mr. McDonald to call Mr. Jameson again."

Cable grabbed the phone from McDonald and told Jameson: "Listen, turkey, I know you called the cops. You just bought yourself two dead ones," Mrs. Barnette said.

"He was very nervous then and when I started to cry, he told me to 'shut up, them tears ain't gonna do you any good where you're going.' "

Non-narrative Details

Westfall said he called McDonald's office in an effort to speak to Cable. At first Cable refused to talk to the FBI agent, but then he repeated his demands. He agreed to give Westfall three hours to arrange for the money, the safe trip to the airport and the plane to Mexico.

Narrative

"That was the longest three hours of my life," McDonald said. "We sat there not knowing what was going to happen next."

Non-narrative Details

Westfall, Jameson and Dr. Robert Marcetti, a psychiatrist, each talked to Cable on the phone during the three hours he held the two hostages.

Narrative

"When he would talk to Mr. Westfall or Mr. Jameson, he would get angry and scream his demands at them repeatedly," Mrs. Barnette said. "But when he talked to Dr. Marcetti he was just like a little boy who was ashamed of himself."

McDonald said Cable kept repeating, "Yeah, I know, Doc. They ain't harmed me. Yeah, I know, Doc. But I gotta do it."

"I think my hopes finally began to rise when I heard him talking to the doctor," McDonald said. "Before that I was just plain scared I'd never see sundown."

Non-narrative Details | Dr. Marcetti said he talked to Cable four times, for a total of 45 minutes, before Cable agreed to release the hostages and give himself up.

Narrative | Westfall said Cable "agreed to send Mrs. Barnette and McDonald out with his gun, if we would agree to take him out the back way and not parade him in front of spectators who had gathered in the area."

Non-narrative Details | Mrs. Barnette and McDonald were released about 3:45 p.m. McDonald handed Cable's gun to Westfall. Cable waited inside the office for Westfall and Dr. Marcetti. He was led down a flight of stairs and out a rear door to a waiting FBI car.

Cable will be arraigned before U.S. Magistrate Carlos Wilson today.

(Personal details about Cable follow.)

The chronological order in the body of the story is a popular form for many types of stories—accidents, fires, crimes, debates, trials, sports, even weddings. Most of these stories have strong narrative elements such as fast-moving action that lend themselves to being told in chronological order after the lead has summarized the major news elements.

Use of the chronological order does not relieve the reporter of the responsibility for adequate summarizations in the lead and throughout the story when they are appropriate. Care must be taken to avoid jumping into telling the story chronologically too quickly. Sometimes only one paragraph of summary is needed, sometimes more than one. A story written in chronological order may be either a single-feature or a several-feature story.

DIRECT QUOTATIONS

To overcome the problem of monotony in the body of the story, the reporter should use well-attributed indirect and direct quotations. The story should not be simply a series of direct quotations, just as it should not be wholly indirect quotations or summary statements. A "happy medium" is most effective.

Direct quotations aid a story if they are used carefully. Woven in between indirect quotations and summary statements, they breathe life into a story while helping to emphasize certain points. They also add authority to the story. Readers believe direct quotes. They often are skeptical of material summarized by the reporter. Direct quotations also help make the story look more attractive because they break up long blocks of type.

Some editors frown on a lead that begins with a direct quotation. This is largely a matter of personal choice. Direct quote leads work best if the quote is short and interesting. Unfortunately, too many reporters start stories with very long and very dull quotes. In most cases, a weak summary lead is better than a poor direct-quotation lead.

Most editors prefer that the reporter keep the quote to a single paragraph. However, an exceptional quote may be worthy of several consecutive paragraphs.

TRANSITIONAL DEVICES

A news story must have unity, and to achieve it the reporter has to weave together the various parts of the story by using connective words and phrases. Unless the sentences within a paragraph or the paragraphs within a story are obviously related, the reporter must indicate their relationship. Sometimes such common connectives or transitions as "also," "on the other hand" or "meanwhile" may be sufficient. But in many cases the transition must be clarified by reference to the material that preceded it. In the previous example of combined development (page 137) the reporter needed to connect the material in the first three paragraphs with what was to follow, so this line was used:

In recommending a civilian board, the report said it is needed. . . .

The transition refers to "Creation of a nonpolitical Civilian Review Board . . ." The transition is essential to clarify the relationship of the two parts of the story.

In making a transition, the reporter should avoid the verbatim repetition of previous wording in the story. The transition should be as short as possible.

Transitional words or phrases provide a minor problem for copy editors who may want to change the order of paragraphs in a story during the editing process. A paragraph cannot be shifted without editing if a transitional phrase directly connects it with a paragraph that precedes or follows it. That is why reporters should keep the transitional words and phrases as short as possible.

Clutter

Every reporter is faced with the question: How much detail should be included in a story? Some reporters never like to waste a fact. If it is in the notes, it will be in the story whether it adds anything or not. Others seem to horde the facts and don't include enough of them to make a complete story. They leave the reader wondering. The problem of how much detail to include is a real one because newspaper style calls for generally shorter stories, and news space in any edition is limited. There is no general rule to guide a reporter on what to put in and what to leave out. But once a story is completed, the reporter should read it over carefully and ask: "What have I left out that needs to be in here?" and "What have I included that really doesn't serve any useful purpose, no matter how interesting it may be?"

COMPLETE REPORTING

Quantity is not the object in a news story. Quality is. The effectiveness of the body of the story doesn't depend on how much is included but on what is included. Details alone do not make for good reading. Every reporter should be something of a human vacuum cleaner, sucking up every tidbit of information available about a news event or individual. But he or she doesn't have to dump all of that into the story as if emptying the dust bag. Reporters have to be selective. They have to use only those facts that are needed to make the story complete and understandable.

Complete reporting requires that a reporter develop the skills of a researcher. Reporters have to know how to gather facts. The best writers on a newspaper cannot produce a clear, crisp, informative news story if there are no facts to work with.

EXERCISES

1. Invite a well-known reporter from your local newspaper to class to discuss reporting techniques. Suggest he or she bring some examples of stories in which a great deal of fact gathering was involved.

2. Using the following notes, write a story illustrating the single-feature story form.

   Parents Against Porn
   Held organizational meeting
   At West High School auditorium
   Approximately 350 persons
   Attended last night's meeting
   Organization is result of
   Campaign by two mothers
   Mrs. Mary Corbett and
   Mrs. Myrtle Manning whose
   Sons attended West High School
   Mrs. Corbett said "pornographers
   Have invaded public schools
   And are destroying the minds
   Of our sons and daughters"
   Mrs. Manning said "there is
   A direct link between pornography,
   The Mafia and organized crime"
   She told the audience that
   "Pornography is responsible for
   Rapists and child molesters
   And we must rid our community
   Of this scourge immediately"
   Both women told the audience
   That police were hampered
   Weak laws and liberal judges

Mrs. Corbett urged mothers to
"Go home and search your kids'
Bedrooms. You'll be surprised
What you find under the mattresses"
They passed out a pamphlet
Describing in graphic details
The kinds of pornographic material
Available to high school students
And the kinds of crimes
That type of material is
Alleged to cause among
High school-aged individuals
Both women urged the audience
To pressure City Council,
The County Commission and
The State Legislature to pass
"The toughest anti-porn
Laws in this nation" and
They urged the audience to
"Take aim at those video
Stores who sell and rent
Pornographic movies to
Our sons and daughters"
Mrs. Corbett was asked by
The audience to serve as
President of Parents Against Porn
Mrs. Manning was asked to be
The group's secretary-treasurer
They agreed to take the positions

3. Adding the following notes to those in Exercise 2, write a story illustrating the several-feature summary story form.

Group took up collection
And agreed to pay regular dues
To hire a lawyer
That would provide
Tougher fines and jail terms
For anyone possessing
Pornographic material for sale
Including mandatory jail sentences
With no parole or time off
For good behavior
Group also voted to
Launch petition drive
To get signatures of
Every parent in the county
To endorse proposed legislation
"This is a fight for the hearts
And minds of our children. It
Is a fight for the American

Family and family values,"
Mrs. Corbett told the
Cheering audience at
The end of the meeting

4. Adding the following notes to those in Exercises 2 and 3, write a story illustrating the first outstanding-feature story form.

Group also voted to
Commission a study
Of arrests made in
The county last five years
Of people selling or distributing
Pornographic materials and
The outcome of those cases
"We want to prove that the
Judges in this community are
Soft on pornography,"
Mrs. Corbett said. "They pay
A fine and are back in business
Before the sun goes down."
Mrs. Manning said they
Will ask Dr. Jack Haskins,
Professor of Sociology at
State University, to supervise
The study of pornographic cases
He is a specialist in deviant behavior

5. Adding the next set of notes to those in Exercises 2 and 4, write a story illustrating the second outstanding-feature story form.

Group also voted
To organize lobbying group
To put pressure on
Police, prosecutors, judges
To launch a "War on Porn"
Also agreed to organize into
Groups of five to call on
Merchants who sell magazines
Book stores and other outlets
That carry what Mrs. Corbett said is
"Filthy and obscene material that
Is destroying the very fabric
Of family life in our community"

6. Using the notes in Exercises 2, 3 and 5, write a story illustrating the combined form described earlier in this chapter.

7. Using the multiple-casualty form described in this chapter, write a story using the following notes:

Forty-five students from
John F. Kennedy High School
On a botany field trip

To Fall Creek Falls State Park
In the Chilhowee Mountains
Bus overturned on narrow road
As it was coming down
The mountain about 3 p.m.
Five students were killed
Twenty others had minor injuries
Police and Park Officials
Listed the dead students as
Fred Baxter, 17, 110 Green St.
Marty Robertson, 18, 3276 N.W. 38th St.
Maria Montez, 17, 896 Palm Ave.
Sunny Tuffs, 18, 1801 Chestfield Dr.
Gloria Jean Dubchek, 17, 8731 Northshore Dr.
Complete list of injured
Not immediately available
They were taken to
Cumberland County Hospital
For treatment before
Being brought back to city
Bus driver Dale Burton said
Brakes on the school bus failed
He was unable to control speed
As bus headed down hill
On narrow, winding road
School Superintendent John Alvarez
Said brakes would be checked
Immediately on all school buses
Jamesetta Johnson, botany teacher
Who supervised the trip, said
"This was a tragic accident
And I will never get over it
They were such lovely young people
I feel so sorry for their parents"
She suffered a broken right arm
And cuts and bruises in the accident
    (Sources: Miss Johnson, Park Superintendent
    James Davis, Superintendent Alvarez, bus
    driver Burton and Park Police Chief Jimmy
    (Buster) McGhee)

8. Write a story using the chronological order from the following notes:

Eugene Michael McCoy, 19
Freshman at State University
Who lives in Reese Hall
High-rise male dormitory
Told police that Sunday night
He began receiving phone calls
In his room about 10:30
Callers kept asking for

His roommate or would just hang up
McCoy said he got the last call
About 1:22 a.m., then fell asleep
About 2 a.m. he heard knock at door
He looked out peephole but
He couldn't see anyone in the hall
He said he cracked the door
And when he did about eight men
Came charging through door
One had red bandanna covering
Part of his face and black hood
Covering his head while others
Had white sheets over their faces
McCoy said they threw him
On his roommate's bed
Began kicking and hitting him
Tried to tie his feet and
Hands with bedsheets
He said they put pillow
Over his head and kicked
Him in the back and stomach
A noise outside interrupted
And the men fled
McCoy tried to call police
But his phone had been ripped apart
He said his class ring and
Twenty-three dollars missing
He said he waited a few minutes
To get up enough nerve to leave
Went to home of friend
Who lives off campus
Friend called police
City and University police
Investigating the attack
McCoy said he will move out of dorm
And drop out of college
He told police he had never
Had trouble before and
Had never been threatened
He said he would stay here
And look for a full-time job
He said when he saved money
He would enroll in another
College or university in area
McCoy is from Oak Ridge

9. Write a story based on each of the following sets of notes. In each case explain at the end of the story your choice of lead and story form.

   a. David Friend, owner of
      Speedy's Auto Parts

1200 North Ave.
Told police he was at his
Store about 6 a.m. today
Young man in green fatigue jacket
Blue jeans, stocking cap
Tapped on front window
He opened the door and let man in
When he turned about
Young man stuck gun in his back
Told Friend he would
"Blow his head off"
If he didn't turn over his money.
Friend said he opened
File cabinet drawer and
Handed robber "several thousand"
Friend said man fired
Two shots at him but missed
He said he ducked behind counter
Robber fled out the door
Friend called 911
He told police the robber
Had one gold upper tooth
    (Sources: Friend, Detective Tom McNamara)
b. William Kinser, manager
Of Human Resources for
City Utilities Board
Proposed a drug testing policy
For employees who drive large trucks
The policy is the minimum
Required by federal law
For municipal utilities
Policy includes postaccident
Testing and requires
Supervisors be trained
To notice indications of drug abuse
Federal regulations require
Drug testing for anyone
Who drives a vehicle
Weighing 26,001 pounds or more
Board approved the policy
To begin within 30 days
J.D. (Buster) Brown,
Board member, recommended
Requiring drug test as
Pre-employment condition
He also recommended a
Drug testing policy for
All Utilities Board employees
Board agreed to consider
Brown's recommendations

Board also approved
Purchase of 65-foot
Bucket truck for $99,400
Lowest bid received
It was made by Aztec Equipment

c. Rock band "In and Out"
Playing for dance at
Holiday Inn on the Ocean
Uses electronically detonated
Device for pyrotechnic effects
During its show
Late Saturday night
The "flash pot" exploded
Shrapnel sprayed the room
Twenty-four persons, including
One band member, taken
To three Punta Gorda hospitals
All but seven were treated
One man listed in critical condition
Following surgery for leg injuries
Three of the injured reported
In serious condition
Detective Gary Depaulo said
Band's homemade device
Set in middle of dance floor
Sent debris flying into crowd
When it exploded about 11:30 p.m.
The device consisted of a pipe
Screwed into piece of wood
Smokeless powder packed in cylinder
Detonated electronically to
Create flash of light
Witness Tracye Catania said
"It was unreal. I was pulling
Pieces of floor tile out of my hair"
Explosion damaged part of stage
And some floor and ceiling tiles.
    (Sources: Depaulo, Sara Baily, hotel manager)

CHAPTER 10
FEATURES AND HUMAN-INTEREST STORIES

Readers want to know how it feels to be held captive by a gunman for six hours. They wonder what goes on in the mind of a mother who has just lost a son to AIDS. They are eager to share the rush of excitement with the housewife who has just won $50 million in a state lottery.

Details, numbers, statistics are important. But more than that, the reader wants to be right there—to feel, to share, the whole mosaic of human emotions. The reader wants the drama and excitement, the joy and despair. Those emotions are the real story to the reader.

Carefully reported and well-written feature and human-interest stories will provide those emotions for the reader. Good feature writing is simply good storytelling. And good storytelling, says Rene J. Cappon, a long-time editor and writing coach for The Associated Press (AP), "thrives on color, nuance, wit, fancy, emotive words, dialogue and character."

A good feature engages the reader emotionally. Here is the lead from an award-winning feature about the return to society of a five-year-old girl who had been burned beyond recognition. The emotionally charged story was written by Julie Klein of the Albuquerque Tribune:

> Denise Volkman cradled a daughter she didn't recognize and carried her through a house she didn't know.
> She wrapped the tiny naked frame in a towel, and the two of them sat in front of a full-length mirror. It would be the first time her daughter would see herself since the fire.
> The mirror reflected an incomplete face. "You're looking great, Sage," Denise told her 5-year-old daughter. "When I first saw you, you looked like a pumpkin." She hesitated. "You know, you don't have a nose."
> "Yeah, I guess you're right. I don't have a nose," said Sage, studying her face in the mirror. "I don't have an ear either. Oh well."
> Denise opened the towel. Sage's missing body parts could have composed a shopping list. A nose, a left ear, both eyelids, all her fingers. The fire

that exploded the family camper also melted the skin on her face, chest, arms and legs. . . .

While the word "feature" has many meanings in the lexicon of reporters, in this chapter it is applied to a story that is based wholly on human interest—the story that does not quite conform to the rigid standards of hard news.

At the heart of a feature or human-interest story are facts representing solid reporting techniques, just as in a straight news story. But the stories differ in style. The news story is timely and written in a straightforward, concise, unemotional style. The feature, on the other hand, may not be particularly timely (though it could be), and it is marked by a blending of imaginative and creative use of the language that can touch readers' curiosity, amaze them, arouse their skepticism, or make them laugh or cry. To complicate matters, in the relationship between features and straight news is the fact that it is a rare reporter who can handle human-interest or feature stories well until he or she knows how to write a compact, coherent, straight news story that is packed with names, facts and details.

An example of a feature lead on a hard news event follows. It was written by Richard Seven for The Seattle Times.

> RENTON—Police Chief Allen Wallis stood outside the immaculate home that Walter and Frances Sneedon had tended for more than 30 years and tried to piece together King County's sixth murder in a week.
> An intruder, apparently trying to burglarize the house at 12:15 yesterday morning, slashed elderly Frances Sneedon's hand when she walked into her kitchen. When she ran for help, the intruder fatally stabbed 70-year-old Walter Sneedon several times and left him to die on the dining room floor.
> Amid recounting the details, Wallis shook his head.
> "This kind of crime shouldn't happen here, not in this city, let alone this type of neighborhood," Wallis said. "It stuns you. People should be safe in their beds at 12:15 in the morning. . . ."

The rest of the story recounted the details of the murder but included a description of the neighborhood and a number of additional quotes from the police chief, as well as the neighbors, about the couple.

Human-Interest Stories

One writer summed it up accurately when he said that there is no sharp line of division that runs between straight news and human-interest stories any more than there is an abrupt line between the colors of the rainbow. One hue may shade into the total rainbow and be lost to view, just as certain elements of a story that might make it a feature (or straight news) can be lost from the view of a not-too-perceptive writer. Frequently the straight news account contains strong feature elements, whereas the human-interest story may owe its very existence to a news event and in such cases has to be printed along with the news story or lose its impact. But it should be obvious that as the human-interest values are increased—as the dramatic, emotional and human background materials of the story are played up—they will become, at some point, more important than the news incident itself. When this point is reached, the story becomes primarily a human-interest (feature) story rather than a straight news story.

Consider the lead in this dramatic story by Charles Bowden of the Tucson Citizen about the plight of illegal aliens from Mexico and Central America trying to cross the western Arizona desert to seek entry into the United States:

> TACNA—They play a game but there are no spectators.
> The players are called wets by those who hunt them. They cross one of the hottest, most deadly deserts in North America with a gallon of water. They are looking for work. The walk is 30, 40, 50, 60 miles.
> Here are the rules:
> Get caught and you go back to Mexico.
> Make it and you get a job in the fields or the backroom.
> Don't make it and you die.
> Each month during the summer, about 250 people try the game in this section of western Arizona, a 3,600-square-mile stretch that lies roughly between Yuma and the Maricopa County line.
> Half get caught—mainly because the heat and thirst and miles grind them down. . . .
> Some die.
> Nobody pays much attention to this summer sport. . . .

The remainder of the story details the writer's own trek across the relentless desert describing just how it feels to walk some 30 miles in the searing heat with little water.

The writer used his powers of observation and his command of the language to describe just what the illegal aliens experienced in their desperate effort to slip into the United States. Hundreds of stories have been written about the plight of illegal aliens, so the news value of the story was not great. What made it so special was that the writer, through his own experience, was able to take the readers right into the desert and let them share the painful journey with the aliens.

Any given incident or situation can be handled within the following degrees of human-interest appeal:

1. As straight news with little or no human interest
2. As straight news plus some or much human-interest treatment
3. As human interest with little or no hard-news value.

Although there is a tendency now, probably as a result of competition from television, to give hard-news stories the feature treatment, the incident itself, if properly evaluated, will usually determine what treatment it deserves. In general, human-interest treatment of the kind listed as item 3 is selected for those incidents that have slight or nonexistent news value or values but that suggest a rich background of human interest. The human-interest treatment is applied to numerous stories every day that might not otherwise be reported. They have become an important part of what every newspaper offers its subscribers daily because of the broad appeal that human-interest stories have for readers. In this sense the human-interest story is considered as a separate story type, and it is one form of the more general feature stories.

Here's an example of a feature on a retired plasterer who publishes and markets his own collection of down-home stories. It was written by Leo W. Banks for the Los Angeles Times:

> Retired plasterer Walter Swan doesn't fit the image of a hot author. He wears denim coveralls and a black cowboy hat. At 15, he dropped out of the eighth grade after spending so much time there he had carved his initials in almost every desk in the school.
>
> By his own admission he can't write or spell. In his Bisbee, Ariz., bookstore, he proudly displays one of his report cards from 1932—straight Fs in spelling and straight Ds in English.
>
> "I don't know nothin' about writing," says the gregarious 73-year-old. "I don't even know what adjectives and vowels and things like that are. But I know plastering. I could plaster your house up one side and down the other."
>
> But his book, "Me 'n Henry," a collection of down-home stories about Swan and his brother, growing up in Cochise County, is gaining widespread attention. He got a brief mention in Erma Bombeck's column, and he's been interviewed on radio talk shows in Salt Lake City and Boston. Several newspapers and TV stations in Arizona have sent reporters to tell his story.
>
> Now the publicity is going national. "CBS This Morning" traveled to Bisbee to tape a spot on Swan and the "Tonight Show" is also trying to line him up for an appearance. And a man strolled into Swan's store and announced, "I'm with Walt Disney Co. Have you sold the movie rights to that book yet?" Swan keeps the Disney fellow's phone number on a crumpled slip of paper in his wallet.
>
> "It's going all over the country and I can't stop it," Swan says, amazed at his brush with fame. "But it ain't my fault. I just wrote the book."

The remainder of the story described how Swan's book was rejected by publishers, so he and his wife produced the book on a computer, paid to have it printed and set up a bookstore selling just his book. More than 6,000 copies had been sold at $21 a copy when the Los Angeles Times' story appeared.

In the typical newspaper office both the human-interest story and the feature article are loosely termed "features" or "feature stories." (Some other newspaper features include columns, cartoons, comic strips and virtually all materials other than advertisements and editorials.) The story could also be a news feature, sometimes called a "sidebar," that depends on a timely news event for its peg. For example, the reaction of the survivors of an airplane crash might be printed beside the main story about the accident. Other examples include a color story, such as a description of the crowd the night before the Kentucky Derby or Indianapolis 500; an interpretative piece on the impact of the new tax hike passed by Congress; or an informational piece on the new industries in the city. Whatever the terminology, the human-interest story and the feature article are usually distinct and distinguishable in form, content and purpose. The former is usually a dramatic story proposing to touch the readers' emotions in some way. The latter is usually an expository article, such as the kind used by magazines, and its major purpose is to inform.

SOURCES OF FEATURES

Today's straight news stories on the appointment of a new cabinet officer, the firebombing of a public building, or the signing of a contract for construction of a new library could be tomorrow's feature presenting a personality sketch of the new official; the history of revolutionary activity in the nation; or the growth in book publishing, the use of libraries or the entire library system of a city. Much feature material is related to the news, as pointed out earlier, and many newspapers, as a result of television and radio's ability to "get there first," are turning more and more to feature treatment of the news. But giving news the feature treatment takes time and an inclination to do the necessary research.

Of the regular sources, the police beat yields a wealth of tragedy, humor and pathos from which many features may be developed. The most important news stories—murders, airplane crashes, spectacular fires, space shots and hundreds of others—can be highlighted and sidelighted by features: the murderer's life story or the impact of a murder on the victim's family; an eyewitness account of the crash; heroic rescues by firemen; life aboard a spacecraft. Much of the content of material in magazines or documentaries on television is feature material suggested by the news. In most cases the reporter has to do little research beyond going to regular news sources to develop features. A reporter must be willing to take the time to dig deeper and to be curious enough to ask questions that go far beyond the obvious.

Many features are developed independently of the news, however. The following general classifications of situations and incidents suggest the varied fields in which features may be found:

1. *The unusual.* Oddities, freaks, coincidences, unusual personalities.
2. *The usual.* Familiar persons, places, things, landmarks. For example, the handicapped young man who sells newspapers outside city hall, the street-corner minister. The feature writer evokes the reader's "I've always wanted to know about that" response.
3. *Dramatic situations.* Sudden riches, the prize winner, the abandoned baby, the heroic rescue or nerve-shattering peril, hard luck, animal heroes, the underdog.
4. *Guidance.* Advice to the troubled, recipes, health, etiquette, stamp collecting, flower arranging, woodcraft, advice on how to vote and a host of others.
5. *Information.* Statistics, studies, records, historical sketches, analogies, comparisons and contrasts of then and now, biographies.

WRITING FEATURE ARTICLES

No standard form or style is used for feature articles. They follow no set rules for leads or for the body or end of the story as news stories generally do. Some conform to the straight-news style with a five W's summary lead, but use of the novelty lead (see Chapter 8) is more common. Feature articles may be narrative, descriptive or expository. They tell stories, paint pictures, explain conditions—but are fact, not fiction. Features may differ radically from news stories in style of writing and arrangement of material, but the incidents, facts and persons involved are real, not created. The feature article is generally designed to convey information and not, as in the case of the human-interest story, to dramatize events for the sake of an emotional impact on the reader.

Because the feature article cannot rely on news values for reader appeal, it must deal with otherwise interesting and vital subject matter. The feature story must be written with a flair for words that will turn a somewhat pedestrian topic into an interesting story with high reader appeal. In brief, the chief rule in writing features is "make them interesting from beginning to end."

Features can be used to provide the reader with a variety of information. Here is the lead from a Wall Street Journal feature marking the anniversary of the volcanic eruption at Mount St. Helens in Washington:

> TOUTLE, Wash.—How do you commemorate an eruption? That's easy; you let off steam.
> This tiny logging town, 25 miles west of Mount St. Helens, will pull out all the stops as it holds its traditional Volcano Daze festival this weekend to mark today's 10th anniversary of the eruption that caused wide-spread destruction and about 60 deaths.
> Initially staged by local residents as a way of fighting their post-disaster depression, the annual festival has itself been a disaster of sorts in recent years, because of apathy, high liability insurance rates and laissez-faire planning.
> Moreover, purists believe that sales of souvenirs—ashtrays and vials of volcanic ash, among others—have commercialized the event.
> "The last one was sort of an eyesore," recalls local newspaper editor Terri Lee Grell.
> So this year, besides the chili cook-off, chain-saw-carving contest and tacky souvenirs, organizers have gone highbrow, bringing in five "logger-poets" to read poems of the Northwest woods.
> "I guess sailors like poetry, so why not loggers," says festival volunteer Ben Benjamin.

The remainder of the story provides additional information about the "logger-poets" and excerpts from some of their poems along with additional information about the festival.

The Los Angeles Times gave its readers a close-up look at the role of an arson investigator in this feature by Sebastian Botella:

> Dan Watters has gotten used to the smell.
> At the end of the day it sticks to you—the stench of ashes, sodden wood and sometimes death.
> For five years, Deputy Watters has been the only full-time investigator in the Santa Clarita and Antelope valleys for the Los Angeles County Sheriff's Arson/Explosives Unit. With more than 2,100 square miles to cover, he has the biggest and perhaps the toughest arson beat in the county.
> In his territory, the number of fire investigations increased 43 percent this year, from 350 in the first six months of last year to 500 during the same period this year. Countywide, the increase was 28 percent.

> "June and July were the busiest months in my career," said Watters, 46, a 23-year Sheriff's Department veteran who previously worked as a narcotics investigator. "I thought it was never going to end. I have never seen anything like that."

The story goes on to describe Watters' work and provides the reader with a detailed picture of the serious arson problem in the county.

The Nashville Banner brought its readers up to date on the ongoing debate over vitamins with this feature by Whitney Clay:

> Cher does it. Martina Navratilova and Victoria Principal do it, too. Even Ronald Reagan is rumored to do it.
>
> In fact, nearly 50 percent of Americans take vitamin and mineral supplements, estimates James Scheer, coordinator for nutrition services at Baptist Hospital.
>
> But are they good for you?
>
> The debate over vitamin supplements has never been hotter. One side remains cautious, while the other accuses it of cowardice.
>
> And while both sides agree extreme megadoses can be dangerous, whether or not ingesting lesser amounts of individual vitamins is helpful, harmful or simply wasteful is still in question.
>
> "In general, I don't support supplementation," says Faye Wong, a nutritionist with the Center for Disease Control in Atlanta. "And that view is substantiated by many, many health and medical groups."
>
> But Patricia Housman, a nutritionist and author of seven books on nutrition, including *The Right Dose: How to Take Vitamins and Minerals Safely*, says groups that advise against supplements base their decisions on fear rather than fact.
>
> And she says she's upset by the widespread "hypocrisy."

The story goes on to present both sides of the argument, explains what vitamins do and quotes extensively from both national and local authorities on the advantages and disadvantages of vitamins. The story was accompanied by a graphic listing of each vitamin and its benefits as well as its risks.

Writers often use a descriptive lead. In the following story from The Wall Street Journal, the description of the subject was key to the theme of the story, which was written by Kathryn Graven:

> TOKYO—For Testsuro Ozawa, daily life in Japan can be a real pain. Mr. Ozawa is forever bumping his head. He also has trouble scrunching his legs under dinner tables while sitting on the floor. He is more than six feet tall, 6-feet-1 in fact.
>
> Not only is he particularly tall, as Japanese men go, he has big feet, which are hard to squeeze into the smallish slippers people provide guests to wear indoors.
>
> The 31-year-old lawyer dreads business trips. The beds in Japan's compact business hotels are too compact for him. "My feet are always dangling over the edge," he complains. Ryokans, the traditional Japanese inns, aren't much better. The futons are too short. So are the bathrobes. "I always have to call the desk and ask for an extra-large," he says.
>
> For centuries, the Japanese have thought of themselves as short people, and that is part of the stereotype foreigners have of them. They have always built houses with low ceilings and doorways that Westerners tend to knock their heads on. But truth to tell, the shape of this little island nation is changing: The Japanese are getting bigger. By turning small things into

something big (from Hondas to Sony Walkman to semiconductors), the Japanese earned fame and fortune. The latter was afforded more protein in the diet.

Today's average 17-year-old boy is 5-feet-8-inches tall, some four inches taller than a fellow of that age was in 1926, and only an inch shorter than the average American male (according to insurance company statistics). Japanese girls, too, are topping the charts, at 5-feet-3, up three inches from 1926, according to the Ministry of Education which measures every school-child every year through high school. How much taller they get after that isn't tracked.

The remainder of the story describes the impact the increase in size has had on not only individuals but also schools, business, industry, and even social and cultural life.

The following is an example of how Wells Twombly used another type of description to set the scene for his personality piece on baseball's great Cookie Lavagetto:

The autumn days slip past in silent splendor with no tongues of their own to tell you the story of old men who once were young heroes so very long ago.

Hairlines retreat and then surrender. Stomachs push forward and collapse entirely. All that remains are misty memories and newspaper clippings turned to soft powder in crypt-cold library files.

Some athletes litter the record book with their accomplishments. They own a hundred-agate line of dry statistics. A few explode for one glorious moment and then disappear into oblivion.

Harry (Cookie) Lavagetto, whose father was a trash collector, whose mother immigrated from Genoa, is the sole owner of one precious moment in history. Always it will belong to him. It cannot be bartered, sold or bequeathed.

It is Oct. 4, 1947 and the New York Yankees are playing the Brooklyn Dodgers in the fourth game of the World Series. . . .

The similarity of feature articles and magazine articles has been pointed out, as has the writer's freedom in selecting the form used in composing the story. Although the reporter may abandon the regular news story organization and apply a narrative or expository form in feature articles, he or she is bound by other general rules of news writing: using short paragraphs, observing the newspaper's style, avoiding monotony in the use of direct quotations and unquoted summary, using transitional phrases to bridge paragraphs and achieve smooth reading, and so on. The logical order is used to the extent that the reporter attempts to hold the reader by introducing new features and details in the order of interest or by an interesting narrative. But the general rule of logical order, which permits cutting a story from the end, may be ignored, as it is in the surprise-climax story form (illustrated later in this chapter). Many if not most feature articles end with a summary or conclusions, a characteristic of expository writing. This style of writing makes editing a feature story to cut its length a painstaking task.

WRITING HUMAN-INTEREST STORIES

Because most human-interest stories are designed to evoke a certain response in the reader, they must rely heavily on the human background of the event, not just the plain, unvarnished facts. Even where a newsworthy event is lacking, there exist here and there predicaments and entanglements of human beings—stresses and strains and dramatic situations with which the human-interest story weaves its patterns. The thoughts, emotions, ambitions—the varied psychological and social data of humanity—are all part of the human background so essential to this type of story. They help dramatize the person, place or thing and create an emotional response in the reader.

Saul Pett, one of the AP's top feature writers for many years, put it this way:

> We can no longer give the reader the fast brush. We can no longer whiz through the files for 20 minutes, grab a cab, spend 30 minutes interviewing our subject, come back to the office, concoct a clever lead that goes nowhere, drag in 15 or 20 more paragraphs like tired sausage, sprinkle them with four quotes, pepper them with 14 scintillating adjectives, all synonymns, and then draw back and call that an incisive portrait of a human being.
>
> Today the reader wants more . . . he wants to be drawn by substance. He wants meat on his bones and leaves on his trees. He wants dimension and depth and perspective and completeness and insight and, of course, honesty.
>
> After 500 or 1,500 or 2,500 words, the reader wants to know more about a man's personality than that he is ''mild-mannered'' or ''quiet'' or ''unassuming'' . . . Willie Sutton, the bank robber, was mild-mannered, quiet, unassuming. So was Dr. Albert Schweitzer.
>
> How can you write about a man without knowing what others have written about him? How can you write about a man without knowing what others think and know of him? How can you write about a man without interviewing him at great length and in great detail and in such a way that he begins to reveal something of himself? How can you interview him that way without planning a good part of your questioning beforehand?
>
> How, when you've collected all you're going to collect, how can you write about a man without thinking long and hard about what you've learned? How can you write about a man without writing about the man, not merely grabbing one thin angle simply because it makes a socko anecdotal lead and leaves the essence a vague blur?
>
> How can you write about a man simply by telling me what he says without telling me how he says it? How can you write about a man simply by telling me what he is without telling me what he is like or what he'd like to be? How can you write about a man without telling me what he is afraid of, what he wishes he could do over again, what pleases him most, what pleases him least, what illusions were broken, what vague yearning remains? How can you write about a successful man without telling me his failures or about any man without somehow indicating his own view of himself?
>
> Give me the extraordinary and give me the ordinary. Does the richest man in the world have everything he wants? Does he bother to look at the prices on a menu at all? That strange, remote, isolated little village way up in the Canadian bush. Don't just tell me about the polar bear and the deer. Tell me, buster, how do they get a suit cleaned there?
>
> Tell me the large by telling me the small. Tell me the small by telling me the large. Identify with me, plug into my circuit, come in loud and clear . . . don't give me high-sounding abstractions. . . .

Don't tease me unless you can deliver, baby. Don't tell me the situation was dramatic and expect me to take your word for it. Show me how it was dramatic and I'll supply the adjectives. You say this character is unpredictable? When, where, how? Give me the evidence, not just the chapter headings. . . .

Pett's comments help point out an important difference between the art of human-interest writing and the art of writing a play, novel or short story, although the purpose and materials of the reporter are much the same as those of other writers. The reporter must present life as it is; the dramatist may present it as it ought to be. In the similarity and difference between the two forms of writing, a few principles guiding the reporter may be found.

The temptation of the reporter is to improve on reality in order to make a better story. Pett's warning that the reader wants honesty should be ingrained in every human-interest writer's mind. Of course, the writer has some leeway, but it is not easy to define. He or she is justified in some rearrangement of events as long as the essential truth of the story is presented. But a writer certainly should not distort for dramatic effect. He or she should not force a quote on his or her subject any more than make up a quote out of whole cloth and put it in the subject's mouth. A writer who repeatedly asks a striking miner, "You suffered greatly after the mines closed down, did you not?" to get the striker to repeat the phrase in those words is presenting a false picture.

The reporter also may be tempted to adopt emotionalized language to achieve an emotional impact. To do so, however, is to defeat the purpose. The drama and its impact must be inherent in the facts of the story. Simple language is the best medium for transmitting those facts to the reader. Ernie Pyle's famous story on Captain Waskow, which was reprinted in a collection of his war dispatches under the title of "Brave Men," is an excellent example of how a writer can achieve dramatic impact through the use of simple language.

The human-interest story takes no standard form. Almost any of the rhetorical devices and suspended-interest forms may be appropriate. A novelty lead with the body in logical order is a popular form. The summary lead with the body in chronological order is often used. Animal stories are extremely popular features. Here are two examples:

DUNSMUIR, Cal. (AP)—They call him Rudy the bungling Beagle. In his five years, he's been to the veterinarian 12 times. His master, Francis Lamere Jr., says Rudy is a good hunting dog but:
Once he leaped high as ducks flew over and caught part of the blast from Lamere's shot gun.
Another time, while tethered to a pickup truck on a hunting trip, Rudy jumped or fell off and ran the pads off his feet trying to keep up.
He has broken his tail twice, once falling off an ironing board on which he was sleeping.
He's been shot twice and caught once in a trap. He had eye surgery after one fight. Another fight cost him 28 stitches in one leg. He's had an emergency tonsillectomy and intravenous feeding for distemper.
Rudy now is recovering from an abdominal operation. He ate too much of a too-long-dead squirrel.
"We keep him for two reasons," says Mrs. Lamere.
"We love him—and he represents quite an investment."

DAWN, Va.—Snorts, grunts and squeals from the hog pen: How sweet it is to a Virginia Commonwealth University professor who electronically transforms hog small talk into music.

"I think it is important that we humans try to go to the stars, but I think it is important, too, that we try to know more about the other species with which we share this planet," says Loran Carrier.

He says he sees his work as aiding the understanding of communications between species.

The essence of the oinks he's recording from up to 40 hogs is going into a musical collection called "Swine Lake." Already on tape, scrambled, dissected and elongated, are "High on the Hog," "Thou Swill," "Roadhog," "Swine Song," "Scaredly Pig," "Overalls" and "Porkchop Sticks."

"I hope to make an LP someday," says Carrier, who holds a doctorate in music and is on sabbatical from VCU while he studies Greek and Latin at Hampden-Sydney College.

"This hog study," as he calls it, began last spring when he started taking a tape recorder into the hog pen at his six-acre Caroline County farm. But its roots lie in his childhood more than 40 years ago on a farm in northern Montana.

The remainder of the story tells how he grew up on a farm and went to a prep school in the East and taught at VCU for 14 years. It also explains how he transformed the hog sounds into music and tells of his remorse when the hogs he has recorded are shipped to market.

Surprise Climax Form

Still another form often used for human-interest stories is called the surprise climax, or "O. Henry ending." The following example is by Eldon Barrett of United Press International (UPI):

The Diagram	*The Written Story*
Narrative of Details	SEATTLE, Wash.—Based on a premise expounded by a psychiatrist, Seattle has just gone through one of the glummest summers on record. It hardly rained at all.
	Dr. S. Harvard Kaufman, a resident for 28 years, is convinced that nice weather in Seattle makes most of its residents gloomy.
	Why?
	"Because they figure it's going to get worse," said Kaufman. "People carry around a lot of guilt. When they are happy, they wonder when the knife is going to fall.
	"Good weather in Seattle activates a deep-seated sense of guilt in most of the residents.
	"From birth they are taught that the weather here is rainy," he said. "They also are taught that because of this the air is clear and the grass is green."
	The fact is, there is less annual rainfall in Seattle than in New York, Philadelphia, Washington, Trenton, N.J., and Atlanta, Ga.
	But the myth persists that Seattle is the sponge of the United States and Seattleites visiting elsewhere have found it usually expedient to let the legend linger on.

> "We are not exactly promoting rain," said Bill Sears, publicist for the Seattle-King County Convention and Visitors Bureau. "But we are promoting its by-products—fresh air, cleanliness and greenery!
>
> "If we can't scrub out the legend that Seattle is in a constant deluge, we might as well put the myth to work," Sears said.
>
> As he spoke, the first downpour of fall was bathing the region, where the worst drought in 33 years had turned the evergreen state into a dusty brown.
>
> And peering out from under umbrellas and foul weather hats were the smiling faces of passersby, obviously delighted that the ordeal of the long, pleasant summer was over.

Surprise Climax

The object of the surprise climax technique is to hold the reader's attention for an O. Henry type of story ending—a climax with a twist. No rules regarding the logical order or the five W's lead apply here; on the contrary, the story builds up as it continues. But the beginning must have an element of suspended interest to attract readers, and its narrative qualities must be strong enough to hold readers to the end.

Many newspapers use the feature story to tell the readers of very dramatic human events. One of the truly outstanding uses of this approach was made by Steve Sternberg to tell about the life and death of a young man from Atlanta who suffered from AIDS. The Atlanta Journal and Constitution devoted a 16-page special section to Sternberg's stories and the photographs taken by Michael A. Schwarz. Here is the lead on Sternberg's story:

> Tom Fox sat up as best he could and put his arms up for his mother's kiss. They kissed and hugged until he was exhausted and fell back weakly into the hospital bed.
>
> "Are you afraid?" Mrs. Fox asked.
>
> Tom shook his head. No.
>
> "This is horrible," Mrs. Fox said outside her son's hospital room. "This is so horrible I can't believe it's happening." Inside, a chaplain was exhorting Tom to "go towards the light."
>
> On this morning in July, family members were gathered in an intensive care hospital room in Eugene, Ore., to help Tom die. He had made the decision to go off the ventilator that forced pure oxygen into his AIDS-ravaged lungs. He knew he would never recover enough to go home to Atlanta, that even force-fed oxygen could not sustain him much longer.
>
> "He's ready to see us all now," Robert Fox Sr. said to his two other sons, Bob Jr. and John.
>
> It was 8:30 a.m. Tom was lying on his bed, wearing his glasses, his clipboard on his chest. With the oxygen tube threaded through his vocal cords, writing was the only way he could communicate. His skin was sallow.
>
> The nurse was ready to start the morphine that would deaden the pain, minimize the struggle.
>
> "It's going to be all right when they take the tube out of you," Doris Fox said to her son. "I'm going to give you the biggest hug you've had since you've been here. We're all going to give you hugs.

"I love you all very much, each one of you. You're all my favorite sons," she said to Bob Jr. "I love you," she said, hugging her husband. "We've done very well, haven't we?"

"Three wonderful sons," Bob Sr. said to his wife. He was crying openly, unashamedly, as the nurse busied herself with disconnecting Tom's heart monitor.

Tom appeared unruffled by the activity, and the unbridled grief. He asked for a cup of ice and, with difficulty, spooned some beneath the hose of the ventilator into his mouth.

Bob Jr. stood by the bed, stroking his brother's hair without looking at him. Eyes rimmed with red, he looked out the window at Spencer's Butte and the forest of fir trees outside the city.

"Do you need some relief, Bob?" Bob Sr. asked his son.

At 8:45, the doctor entered. He looked perfectly composed, powder-blue jacket, dark-blue tie, dark slacks. He unknotted the ribbon of tape holding the ventilator tube securely in Tom's nostril.

"Here we go, Tom," the doctor said.

He smoothly withdrew the corrugated ventilator tube.

For an instant, it appeared to be a relief. "He may be feeling fine for a while and can even talk to you," Dr. Matthew Purvis said.

"Handerkerchief," Tom said. He noisily blew his nose.

Doris, who was tearfully watching her son, broke her silence and laughed sympathetically for an instant. Over the past week Tom had asked repeatedly whether he could blow his nose.

"It must be a relief to blow your nose," his mother said.

"Beats that long catheter," the respiratory therapist said.

"It's a big 'un," Tom said. Then, "I can't breathe."

His chest heaved again and again, but weakly. He had no strength. "I can't breathe," he said again. It was as he had predicted all along: a fish out of water, no fight left in him.

"He's asleep," Doris Fox said, leaning over and stroking his forehead. "He's asleep now. I love you. I love you so much, son."

"Just relax and let it go. Slip on out, Tom, slip on out. We're all with you."

"He's letting go," his father said through his tears.

Tom gasped for breath. His eyes were open, but he could not speak.

"Good night, Tom," Bob Jr. said, his head thrown back, his mouth open, his voice a tortured sob.

"It's almost over," Dr. Purvis said.

"Almost there, Tom," Doris said.

The figure on the bed was motionless.

"It's over," she said.

It was 8:55. The dying had taken barely 10 minutes.

One by one, everyone passed by the head of the bed, kissing Tom on the forehead.

"I could never be so brave," John said.

"It's hard to leave him," Doris said. "I want to look at his lesions. He wouldn't let us look near the end."

She uncovered his legs. "They're like leather."

"So hard," his father said. "There'll be a cure someday."

"Not soon enough," Doris said.

The section included three other major stories by Sternberg about various aspects of Tom Fox's life and AIDS, along with nearly three dozen photographs by Schwarz. The section was the result of more than 1,000 hours the reporter and photographer spent with Fox during a 16-month period to chronicle the life of a person with AIDS.

EXERCISES

1. Invite a feature writer from a local or area newspaper to class to discuss his or her work. Based on the class presentation and questions asked, write a feature story on what it's like to be a feature writer on a newspaper.

2. Using any newspaper available to you, clip two human-interest stories and rewrite them as straight news stories.

3. From any newspaper available to you clip two major hard-news stories and rewrite them with a feature angle.

4. Write a human-interest story based on the following information collected from Jesse Johnson Sr., who lives in a rural area about 10 miles out of the city on Manus Road.

> Johnson describes himself as an "animal lover." He has on his two-acre home-site: a boar hog named Rusty; a sow named Lucy; a flock of what he calls "scurrying" chickens because they run all over the place; two frisky Saint Bernards; and an undetermined number of cats who, he says, spend most of their days "snoozing."
>
> Johnson said he raised Lucy and Rusty from the time they were three or four weeks old. "Actually, I rescued them. They were the litter runts and were soon gonna be knocked in the head. I'm an animal lover and I just couldn't see that, so here they are."
>
> Rusty has become more than just a pet. He is, as Johnson said, "a drinking buddy." Rusty loves beer.
>
> Johnson said it all started with an "innocent sip," which turned into a gulp, which turned into a "sloppy guzzle."
>
> "He prefers Coors Light and would drink it by the case if I'd let him," Johnson said. He added that he sees nothing wrong with a pig having a brew or two to quench a thirst.
>
> "Besides, he asked for a beer," Johnson said, looking serious. "That's right . . . pig Latin, you know. I can understand it."
>
> Rusty likes a good chew of tobacco, too, Johnson said. He prefers Granger Select.
>
> Johnson demonstrated by ordering the 300-pound red-haired hog to "sit." The animal did. Johnson then gave the hog a plug of tobacco, which it chewed a couple of times and then swallowed.
>
> Johnson ordered Rusty to get up. The hog stood up and walked over to a shady spot and stretched out to take a nap.
>
> Johnson said he hopes to find Rusty work in television commercials, using contacts from his 12 years as a movie stunt man and bit-part actor. He appeared in several Burt Reynolds movies.
>
> "The other day he told me he wanted a swimming pool," Johnson said, grinning. "I told him he's going to have to earn some money first."

5. Using the college or university library as your main source, research a little-known holiday or special event, either in the United States or abroad, and write a short feature about it.

6. Call a number of department heads or deans on your campus and ask for a list of research projects faculty members are conducting. Interview one of the researchers and write a feature story about the project.

7. Attend a major campus event, a concert by a popular musical group, a football game

between your team and an arch rival, or a campus fair or carnival, and write a descriptive feature story about it.

8. Write a short four- or five-paragraph feature story from these notes:

a. Taxi driver William T. Hampton
Filed $500 suit in City Court
Against Elizabeth Anne Batty
Couple had been lovers for 20 years
But relationship has been stormy
Hampton claims Batty still angry
Because 20 years ago
He hung her naked outside
A second floor window
During one of their spats
Until she gave the password
In the suit he wrote himself
Hampton claims Batty
Put a curse on his sex life
And on his dog "Fidel Castro"
He said he found a dead chicken
A voodoo doll and written curse
On his front porch one day
It read: "A curse upon your
Dog Fidel Castro. A curse upon
Your emotional and sexual relationships
With every woman you are presently
Involved with or ever will be. May
The Gods of Voo Doo curse you."
He claims the curse hasn't been effective
But he wants the court to fine Batty
$500 to cover his mental anguish

b. Dentist Fred Schultz
Working with faculty at
State Veterinarian College
Plans to conduct experiments
In fitting false teeth to sheep
To lengthen their breeding lives
Dr. Schultz said he has devised
Technique for fitting teeth
Attached to a metal plate
To bottom jaw of ewes
He said he has done it
Successfully a half-dozen times
Veterinarians say as
Sheep grow old their teeth break down
Making it difficult for them
To feed themselves
As a result their useful lives
Are cut short by several seasons
Experiment expected to last four years

    c. Allen and Annette Clausen
      Purchased vacant two-story house
      From U.S. Department of Veterans Affairs
      Paid $78,000 for three-bedroom house
      Planned to put in new carpets
      Tile and baseboards before moving in
      House had been vacant two years
      Clausens discovered honey
      Dripping down walls inside
      Dropping onto floors
      Fumigators found 300-pound
      Beehive between fireplace and wall
      They killed hundreds of bees
      Behind fireplace and under kitchen stove
      Some live ones returned
      Estimated several thousand bees
      In walls of the house
      Plans for moving in on hold
      "It's a nightmare," Clausen said
      "This has been the worst thing
      We've run up against," said
      Bruce Manning, vice president of
      Land Ho, company that managed
      Property for Veterans Department

  9. Select the most historic building on your campus or in your community and write a feature story about it. Use reference material from the college and community libraries as well as interviews with long-time faculty members, university employees and community leaders as your sources.

10. Arrange an interview with a prominent campus visitor—a nationally known concert performer, popular music performer or distinguished visiting professor—and write a human-interest story based on the interview.

11. Interview the person who plans the half-time show for the college or university band and write a feature story on her or him. Make certain you interview band members for their reactions to the maneuvers they have to execute during the show.

12. Select an interesting historical site, city, vacation resort or tourist attraction within driving distance of the campus and write a descriptive feature about it.

13. Visit a local senior citizen center and do a human-interest story on the women and men who visit it regularly. Focus on the individuals and how they use the center, not the center officials.

14. Write a feature story on your campus after dark. Interview the individuals whose jobs begin late in the day on campus and run through the night—the custodial staff, the steam plant operator, the cooks and bakers who work at night for the campus food service, and so on.

CHAPTER 11

REWRITES AND FOLLOW-UPS

To survive in this age of increasing competition, a newspaper has to be perceived as being indispensable to its readers and its advertisers. Even in one-newspaper cities there still is competition from national publications such as USA TODAY and the national edition of The New York Times as well as area newspapers, radio and television stations, and a host of new "information delivery systems."

A good editor, whether faced with head-to-head competition or not, will know exactly what the competitors are doing and will make every effort to do better. Stories will be clipped from area newspapers, and local radio and television news programs will be monitored. National newspapers and news magazines and television news programs and documentaries will be checked for stories that may have a local angle. After all, if a local citizen appears on national television, that's news.

In using a story from another source that has not been covered by the newspaper's own staff, an editor generally will order the facts checked and the story rewritten. Follow-up stories may be ordered on others. And ideas from radio, television and national publications may be developed into local stories.

Editors frequently send reporters clippings of their own stories with suggestions and instructions for follow-up in an effort to make certain that every possible angle of a story is developed. And dozens of press releases are turned over to staff members to be rewritten after the facts have been verified. Rewriting a story or press release requires good reporting instincts as well as an ability to write clear, accurate and interesting copy, often under the pressure of a deadline.

REWRITES

In most newsrooms, the word "rewrite" has a variety of applications. On metropolitan dailies it usually refers to a group of writers whose chief role is to take information over the phone from reporters on regular beats and then prepare a news story, often with the reporter's by-line on it.

These same writers work with one or more reporters who may be covering the scene of a major fire, bridge collapse or other disaster. The reporters on the scene phone the information in to the rewrite desk, where the facts are woven into an accurate and interesting story. Papers in smaller cities use this system of rewrite only occasionally, usually for last-minute stories gathered right on deadline.

"Rewriting" can also mean producing a new story from a clipping taken from another publication or a press release. It can also mean rewriting a story because the editor did not like the way it was written originally. Most editors will give the story back to the reporter who wrote it for rewriting. However, if the reporter is not available, a rewrite person may handle it.

Often the persons assigned to rewrite on larger newspapers are among the best writers and most capable members of the staff. They usually work with reporters on the beats. The job of rewriting less significant stories from clippings and press releases frequently goes to the newest reporter on the staff.

In rewriting a story from another newspaper or other source, the reporter must first verify the facts in the clipping and then attempt to get additional facts to use in the rewrite. The object is to have the story appear to be a new one, not simply a repeat of the original story. To accomplish this, a reporter may start the rewrite by (1) playing up an additional newsworthy fact or facts, or (2) reorganizing the story if no new facts are available. In the second case, the story often is shortened unless it is about a very important news event. Obviously, the first method is preferred, but sometimes there simply are no new facts to add to a story. In any event, the rewritten story, especially the lead, should be as different as possible from the original one.

Here are two leads for the same story. The first one appeared in a morning newspaper:

> WASHINGTON—Jordan's King Hussein appealed to the United States in a live televised message Saturday to withdraw its troops from Saudi Arabia as soon as possible and avert "death, destruction and misery."

Because there were no new facts to add, an afternoon newspaper used a slightly different approach to the story:

> AMMAN—In an address aimed at the American people this evening, King Hussein of Jordan pleaded for understanding of his country's increasingly difficult position in the Persian Gulf crisis; but he repeated his call for the removal of American troops from the Middle East.

To accommodate its subscribers, The Associated Press (AP) sent out this lead for the morning newspapers:

> WASHINGTON—The House on Wednesday OK'd a $283 billion defense bill that would make wholesale cuts in President Bush's fiscal 1991 budget request for the Strategic Defense Initiative and the B-2 stealth bomber.

And for the afternoon newspapers, the story carried this lead:

> WASHINGTON—The House is on a collision course with the Senate over the B-2 stealth bomber and other vast differences in their versions of the fiscal 1991 defense bill.
>
> By a party-line vote of 256-115, the House approved a $283 billion defense bill that stops production of the B-2 bomber at 15 planes in development and slashes $2.4 billion from President Bush's request for the Strategic Defense Initiative, commonly known as Star Wars.

Meetings of city councils and county commissions frequently overlap a newspaper's deadline. In such a case, a reporter will have to base his or her lead on action taken early in the meeting, whereas a competitor from another paper can focus on action taken much later in the meeting. The following is an example of a lead on a story about a county commission meeting written for an afternoon newspaper. It was written to meet a deadline that came more than an hour before the morning meeting was over:

> County Commissioner James V.H. Brewer today accused the county school system of mismanagement and misstatement concerning budgetary matters.
>
> Brewer distributed his charges in a printed report at the regular meeting of the County Commission. Chairman Vernon Bradshaw said he will ask for a written response from County School Superintendent Mary Cimino and report back to the commission.

The rest of the story detailed Brewer's charges against the school system.

The morning newspaper's reporter was not on deadline, so he was able to stay through the entire meeting. His lead focused on other action taken by the commission.

> Members of the County Commission failed yesterday to override County Executive John Ragsdale's veto of an extra allotment of $46,450 for the sheriff to continue a drunken driving educational program to the end of the year. The vote was 9 to override and 10 against.

The story gave additional details on the veto action as well as other action taken by the commission. The morning newspaper also carried a much shorter, separate story on the commissioner's charges and focused on the response of the school board.

> County School Board Chairman Joyce Marshall labeled charges of mismanagement against the board by County Commissioner James V.H. Brewer "a self-serving, one-sided, perverse view of the county school system."
>
> She called the charges made yesterday at the commission meeting a mixture of "half-truths and innuendoes. . . ."

The rest of the story briefly summarized the charges and reported that the commission chairman had asked for a written reply from the school board.

Often the angle featured in the rewritten lead is taken from the body of the original story, as the next examples show. The morning newspaper used this lead on its city council story:

> A request to rezone 9.6 acres of land south of Northshore Drive and east of Willman Lane to permit construction of a $3.5 million apartment complex was delayed by the City Council last night.
>
> Councilwoman Brenda Frazier asked for the delay to give the developer and residents of the area, who oppose the development, an "opportunity to work out a compromise."
>
> Earlier the Metropolitan Planning Commission ignored the opposition from the homeowners and recommended rezoning the property from single-family to multi-family to permit construction of the apartments.
>
> If the Council gives final approval Tuesday, residents of the area say they will file a suit in Circuit Court to block the rezoning.

The story went on to give details of the apartment complex and the dispute between the homeowners and the developer, as well as other action taken by the council at the meeting. The afternoon newspaper's coverage of the same meeting used the following lead:

> If you park illegally and your car is towed in, you'll have to pay $40 instead of $20 to get it out.
>
> The City Council voted last night to double the towing and impoundment fee after police said the problem with illegally parked cars has become "epidemic."

The afternoon newspaper's story did not get to the rezoning until about the eighth paragraph. The morning newspaper's story did not introduce the hike in towing fees until the sixth paragraph.

Facts omitted purposely or otherwise by the reporter of the original story are often featured in the rewrite because they give the story a fresh aspect. In striving for a fresh angle, however, a reporter must guard against distorting the essential facts and significance of the story. Sometimes new events occur and give the rewrite man a feature that was not available to the reporter of the original story. In that case, the story is a combination rewrite and follow-up.

PRESS RELEASES

Hundreds of press releases are received each week by most newspapers. They come from private industry, civic groups, religious organizations, educational institutions, and just about anyone else who has some information they want to get before the public. Many of them are extremely well written by very talented public relations writers. Others are, quite frankly, badly written. In many cases, the press release contains no news or information that is of any value to the newspaper's readers. The careful editor has them checked by a staff member and then rewritten for publication. However, at some newspapers, both large and small, press releases often find their way into print as originally written.

Often the task of rewriting a press release can be easy because the real news may be buried down in the third or fourth paragraph after the public relations writer has plugged his or her client shamelessly in the lead. However, a number of press releases are very well written, and the task of rewriting them can be tough. A person on rewrite handling a well-written press release needs all the skills and imagination at his or her command to improve what is basically a good story to start with.

Here is an example of how a press release was rewritten to emphasize the most important news element. The original lead on the press release read:

> The Tennessee Valley Authority said today that in order to meet quality standards established by the State of Tennessee and approved by the Environmental Protection Agency, TVA will of necessity be forced to add a $42 million cooling tower system to Sequoyah Nuclear Plant, now under construction northeast of Chattanooga.

That lead has 51 words in it and backs into the story. Here is how it was rewritten without damaging the integrity of the agency and its wordy board:

> A $42 million water cooling tower system will be added to the Tennessee Valley Authority's Sequoyah Nuclear Plant, under construction northeast of Chattanooga.
>
> Members of the TVA Board of Directors said the cooling system is being added to meet water quality standards established by the state of Tennessee and approved by the Environmental Protection Agency.
>
> However, they said they "doubt the tower will add any environmental benefits." And they called the system a "dubious expenditure" that will add millions to consumers' electric bills in the region.

In the following example, an awkward direct quote lead was rewritten to take the emphasis off the president of the company and focus on the news element. The original lead on the press release was

> "For the first time in 19 months, the company's earnings have risen above the annual dividend rate of $1.54 a share," Alvin W. Vogel Jr., president of The Southern Company, announced today.

The rewritten lead put the company's name at the start of the sentence rather than at the end and told what the actual earnings were for an average share of common stock:

> The Southern Company today reported that the average earnings of its common stock rose to $1.54 a share for the 12 months ending January 31—an increase of 17 cents a share over last year.
>
> Consolidated net income for the electric utility totaled $231 million for the period—up nearly $33 million, Alvin W. Vogel Jr., company president, said.

Although many reporters object strongly to being assigned rewrites, it can provide excellent experience in handling a wide variety of news as well as human-interest and feature stories.

FOLLOW-UPS

A follow-up is usually an updating of an earlier news story in which the latest developments are reported. A follow-up story naturally features the new developments, but the reporter must summarize enough of the background of the original story for the benefit of readers who did not see it and to refresh the memories of those who did. Because this summary refers to an earlier story, it is called a "tie-back."

The tie-back of one or two short paragraphs follows the lead or second paragraph, but no set rules govern its length or position in the story. One sentence or phrase within a paragraph or within the lead itself may be sufficient to make new developments clear. If the story remains prominent for several days, the tie-back becomes shorter and shorter because chances decrease daily that a reader has missed all the earlier stories. However, in some stories, several paragraphs may be necessary, particularly when the follow-up is published some time after the original story appeared.

Here is an example of a major new development nearly a year after the original story was printed. The tie-back comes in the third paragraph:

> For almost a year the family of Ellen Maples has pressed for answers to her death following a fight with her boy friend.
> At their request, her body will be exhumed Wednesday for study by two forensic anthropologists. They cited in court documents "suspicious circumstances" surrounding her death last October.
> The 18-year-old Carbondale woman died in St. Mary's Medical Center following an evening of partying at a local dance hall during which she was beaten by her boy friend, witnesses said, and later jumped from his speeding pickup truck.
> In issuing the order allowing her body to be exhumed, Circuit Court Judge Tom Barry cited a "partial and inconclusive autopsy" done last October as another reason for further study by forensic anthropologists.

The follow-up is handled in the same manner as the rewrite; the reporter uses the facts already in hand and diligently seeks new developments. Except for the tie-backs, follow-ups are written in the same form as a news story.

Most rewrites are brief and about rather insignificant items, as a general rule. The pressure to conserve space is so heavy that information previously seen by a large number of readers must be condensed as much as possible. However, if a big story—a natural disaster such as a flood or earthquake, for example—breaks on the competitor's time, the story is not rewritten, in the usual sense of the term. In fact, reporters are sent to cover the story along with the competition, only they have longer to write it. Subsequent stories will be follow-ups, just as they are when the newspaper's own first account deserves later development. Most stories of importance are pursued through later developments for days or weeks and, on rare occasions, even years. Reporting of the Watergate scandals in the federal government covered more than two years. A fire or a storm is followed by accounts of relief and reconstruction. Crime is followed through the trial and sentencing. Gradually, the force of the first explosive event plays out, and the follow-ups dwindle away.

Sometimes the follow-up can develop into a much larger story than the original one. A short story may be followed by a longer, more detailed account over several days or weeks until a major story develops. Bank failures, embezzlements of public funds or congressional investigations may be the bases for stories that will build slowly. That is what happened in the Federal Bureau of Investigation's Abscam investigation, in which congressmen and one senator were eventually convicted of accepting bribes from a phony oil sheik.

THE DEVELOPING STORY

Another type of follow-up that offers problems of rewriting is the story requiring "latest developments" changes in several editions of one day's newspaper. If a major court trial is in progress, for instance, the newspaper may want an up-to-the-deadline report of the trial in every edition. A newspaper with three editions (early mail, out-of-city and early street sales; home distribution; and late street sales) will have a different deadline for each edition, and it may require the rewriting of one story (or parts of it) three different times to include the latest newsworthy features in each edition. This type of story is called the "developing story," or running story.

It is also a follow-up because it includes developments later than those in the previous story. Moreover, it is something of a rewrite, although it usually does not entail rewriting the bulk of the previous story. A new lead, including latest developments properly linked with previous developments, may be all that is required. Inserts, or "adds," for the original story may fill the need. As much of the original story as possible is left undisturbed.

Although not as common as it was when metropolitan newspapers had seven or eight editions a day (now most metros are down to two or three), this procedure is still used from time to time when a story develops over several editions. For example, a fire is reported at the city jail just before deadline for the first edition and the facts are sketchy. The first-edition story might say:

> A fire swept through the jail on the second floor of City Hall shortly before 9 a.m. today, and at least three inmates are known to be dead.
> "It could be a lot worse," Police Chief Bill Joe Biggs said. "I just can't tell you anything for sure until the fire is out and we can get in there."
> He said he did not know how many prisoners were in the jail, because he had not received the daily head count before the fire started.
> "Things have been quiet this week. I think maybe we had 12 or 15 locked up. But I can't really be sure," Biggs said.
> He added that he did not have time to identify the dead men.
> Heavy black smoke billowed through the 156-year-old building and inmates could be heard screaming for help as fireman pumped thousands of gallons of water through the second-floor windows.
> Dozens of policemen joined firemen in trying to reach the prisoners. But most rescue efforts failed because of the intense heat and the heavy black smoke.

''You can't get anywhere near the cell block,'' Patrolman Ira Bevins
said. ''If the flames and heat don't stop you, the smoke will.''

To round out the story for the first edition, the writer should include information
about evacuating city employees from other offices in the building. The story may
include some information about the building and the jail, especially if a check of
the clipping file at the newspaper shows there have been previous reports about
safety conditions at the jail.

Examples of how the story might be changed to include up-to-deadline
developments in later editions follow:

New Lead

At least eight prisoners were killed today when fire swept through the
jail on the second floor of City Hall.

The dead were trapped in a large holding cell in the jail. Other prisoners may have died in their locked cells at the rear of the second floor.

Insert After Fifth Paragraph of the Original Story

Two officers and a trustee who were downstairs smelled smoke and
ran to the second floor. They opened one of two doors to the large holding
cell, but were unable to open the other door, which may have been blocked
by the body of an unconscious inmate, Biggs said.

Add to End of Story

Three firemen were hospitalized from smoke inhalation.

Biggs said it was too early to determine how the fire started. He added,
however, that it was not uncommon for prisoners to start fires in their cells.

''They set fire to a half-dozen mattresses a month,'' he said.

Of course, if a final death toll is available by the final edition of the day, a
new lead should be written. Additional details of the fire may be inserted or
added at the end of the story. Because "patching" a story together in this fashion
can result in mistakes, many papers will have the story for the final edition
completely rewritten.

If time does not permit the revision of a story in an earlier edition, a short
(usually one-paragraph) "bulletin" is written to precede the lead of the earlier
story. However, this is usually done for the lead story on the front page and only
in the event the latest developments are significant enough to warrant this
special treatment.

EXERCISES

1. Using only the facts given, rewrite the following story, which appeared in the morning
   newspaper, for the competing afternoon daily:

   An apparently deranged gunman died in a barrage of bullets at the Montclair
   police station Thursday after allegedly taking a secretary hostage and firing a shot at a
   plainclothes sergeant.

He had demanded to talk to the police chief and the U.S. Marines.

The gunman was identified as Adrian Mark Vasquez, 27. He was a resident of Montclair, 35 miles east of Los Angeles.

Vasquez was killed when six policemen opened fire on him just inside the front door of the station after he had fired a shot from a .38-calibre revolver that missed the plainclothes officer and smashed through a window, Police Lt. Terry Gibson said.

"He was dead when he hit the floor," Gibson said.

Members of the man's family said he had "mental problems from . . . drugs" and that he had told a nephew on Wednesday that he was "going to kill a cop," Gibson said.

Vasquez had previously been in trouble with the law for drug and traffic violations, Gibson said. But he gave no details.

Police said they did not know why he demanded to talk to Police Chief Gregory Caldwell or the Marines.

"He was acting incoherent," Gibson said.

The short drama in the neat, white, one-story station on a quiet street began about 8 a.m. when a police secretary, who was not identified, arrived at work and was followed by Vasquez through a security door for authorized personnel.

Lt. Gibson said Vasquez took the secretary hostage at gunpoint and accompanied her to Caldwell's office, which was vacant. He then demanded that she phone the chief, as well as the U.S. Marines.

The secretary instead called the police dispatcher, who alerted other officers. After a brief telephone conversation with Caldwell, who was in a conference room in another part of the building, Vasquez stepped into the hall, saw a plainclothes officer and fired a shot at him.

Vasquez then walked through the security door, saw more officers, raised his revolver and was cut down in the lobby by police gunfire, Gibson said.

2. Rewrite the following story, which appeared in the afternoon newspaper, for the competing morning daily:

The naked body of a young woman was found in Antioch today, not far from an abandoned house that had satanic symbols scrawled on the walls.

But police said they are not drawing connections between the death of the woman and satanic rituals.

The victim was an East Nashville resident who lived in a trailer on Dickerson Road, but police were withholding her name pending notification of her family.

The body was found in a wooded area behind a large apartment complex on Rural Hill Road near Murfreesboro Road. The cause of death was unverified, but detectives said her body showed signs of a beating.

Loggers who had worked in the wooded area most of Thursday found the body late in the afternoon.

"They had been there all day and just happened to see the body as they passed by," Homicide Capt. Mickey Miller said. "She was lying off a dirt road. You could see her from the road if you looked real close."

Police believe the woman had been there several hours. Miller said the woman may have been sexually assaulted.

"We think she may have been because she was not clothed, but we won't know for sure until the autopsy."

An empty house at the end of the dirt road where the body was found had pentagrams—satanic symbols—painted on the walls. But detectives said they have no reason to believe there was any connection between them and the woman's death.

3. Rewrite the story in Exercise 2 using the following additional information:

Police identified the murdered woman as Mary Ann Potts, 44, who has a long criminal record for prostitution dating back to 1974. An autopsy revealed she had been beaten to death. Homicide Detective Mickey Miller said Friday night that police believe she probably was beaten to death elsewhere and her body dumped in the remote, wooded area off Rural Hill Road. She had been dead about 24 hours. "I believe the suspect is probably someone who knows the area," Miller said. "You would have to know the area pretty well to drive back there." Police have ruled out any connection between the murder and the symbols painted on an empty house near the site where the body was found. Similar signs were found painted on trees at a nearby pre-Civil War cemetery that had been vandalized.

4. Here is a press release that was distributed to the news media. It is reproduced here as it actually appeared. Nothing has been changed. Read it carefully and evaluate its news potential. Is it of any news value as written? If you believe it has no news value, list all the reasons why. Then make a list of everything you would need to know to be able to turn it into a news story.

UNITED FUND   TELEPHONE
48 O'Donnell Street   Thomas-2-1346

RELEASE: Tuesday, Oct. 12

"Every dollar spent today for character-building programs saves hundreds later on" was a statement made recently at a meeting of the Recreation Division of the Community Chest and Planning Council.

In elaborating on that statement, it was pointed out that it was much cheaper to train a boy or girl to cooperate with others, and to respect the rights and property of other people, than it is to punish them later for wrong-doing. Every problem child that is not properly considered today will be a problem later, it was stated.

Daniel Curley, chairman of the committee, presided over the meeting, which was attended by representatives of recreational-educational groups, many of which are financial participants in the United Fund. It was pointed out that most of these organizations make use of recreation as a basis for group-work character-building services.

Representatives of these agencies were urged to consider means whereby those participating in the programs could more fully meet the financial requirements of the agency. It was pointed out that many of these groups had their beginnings as religious organizations, while others were started through the philanthropies of wealthy individuals. These antecedents have "for the most part been outgrown, and the organizations are dependent upon publicly contributed funds and membership fees for their support."

The need for more, rather than less, character-building services exists, and it is expected that even more will be required as the full effects of the population explosion are felt.

In addition to the discussion on the role and future of these agencies, there was a discussion of the Junior Hostess Program. Samuel Leventhal, chairman of the Service Club Council, described the Junior Hostess Program as a community project organized to help servicemen enjoy wholesome activities during their leisure hours. He reported that there are 43 area girls registered at the present time, and that others between the ages of 18 and 30, who are single, are welcome to apply.

He pointed out that applications may be secured from the Jewish Community Center, the Y.W.C.A., the Catholic Womens Club and the Community Chest office.

5. Obtain a press release from the college or university's public relations office or sports information office. Call the persons named in it for additional details and then rewrite the press release as a news story.

6. Clip from any daily newspaper available to you three locally written stories you believe will result in follow-up stories. List the possible future developments that should warrant a follow-up for each one.

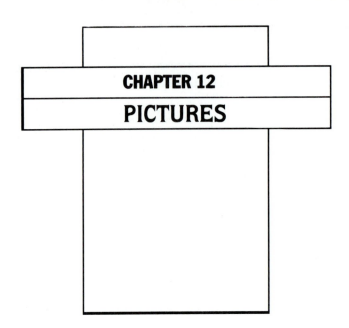

CHAPTER 12

PICTURES

Pictures are a universal language, easily understood by everyone. That is why they are a vital part of every modern newspaper. They not only document the news, but also serve as a permanent visual record of history. John Faber made that point well in his book "Great News Photos and the Stories Behind Them" when he recounted this incident during the chaos immediately after the shooting of Sen. Robert Kennedy following a speech in a Los Angeles hotel:

> As the senator lay dying, Los Angeles Times photographer Boris Yaro readied his camera. Before he could shoot, a woman with a camera around her neck screamed, "Don't take pictures! Don't take pictures! I'm a photographer and I'm not taking pictures!" Yaro pulled away. "Goddammit, lady," he said, "this is history." He took the picture.

A good news picture can take the place of many words in portraying a day's events. It can speak quickly, vividly and simply, and it can give a newspaper a more colorful and readable appearance. Pictures are a major element of design.

In our visually oriented society, pictures are increasingly important. As a result, it is essential that the reporter develop a keen sense of visual perception. Knowing good pictures and appreciating their importance will enhance a reporter's value to the newspaper.

A reporter does not have to be able to take pictures, but the ability to do so is an extremely useful talent, especially on smaller newspapers, where reporters often double as photographers. Nancy Petrey, co-publisher of The Newport Plain Talk, Newport, Tenn., hands every new reporter a camera along with a stack of reporter's notebooks and pencils. If the new staff member doesn't know how to use the camera, she gives him or her a short course right there on the spot. "In a paper our size, everyone has to be able to take pictures as well as report, write and edit," she says.

In general, pictures are used in connection with news and feature stories, usually on the same page with the story. Sometimes a picture may be used on page 1, for example, and the story will appear on an inside page. A number of editors, however, will not separate the picture from the story.

Frequently, a picture may tell its own story and stand alone, supported merely by cutlines. This type of picture usually features some vivid action that may not require a story. Often newspapers will use feature pictures of interesting faces or scenery with only a caption.

Newspapers generally prefer pictures that show action. Unfortunately, this often results in contrived and posed bits of action such as someone pointing at two persons shaking hands or one person handing a check to another. A formal head-and-shoulders photograph of an individual taken by a staff photographer or retrieved from the newspaper's files may be just as effective as the obviously posed action shot. More and more newspapers are using such photographs when action shots are not available. Today's flexible production methods have resulted in a number of newspapers combining head-and-shoulder photos with maps, charts and sketches to create a large visual to accompany a story whenever an action photograph is not available.

A creative photographer can make even the oldest situation seem new, just as an outstanding reporter can make the most routine story interesting. It is a matter of thinking innovatively, caring about the quality of the photograph and taking pride in one's work. Except for head-and-shoulder photographs (called "mug shots"), the gifted photographer avoids the stiff "facing the camera" pose and will have the subjects looking toward a focal point for the picture rather than "mugging" or looking straight into the camera.

A good photographer will avoid cliches—the handshakes, the ribbon cutters, the pointers, the check passers—whenever possible. If such assignments can't be avoided—most cannot—a good photographer will at least shoot them from a different angle.

Here are some general guidelines issued for photographers by Landmark Community Newspapers, Inc.:

- Avoid more than five people in a photo (except for crowd shots); ideally, three is enough.
- Insist that posing be tight. Space between heads is almost always wasted.
- Crop ruthlessly. Slash; don't slice.
- Full-length figures of adults should normally be cropped at the bottom of the rib cage.
- Enlarge generously. A good picture should always be one column wider than you first think it should be.
- Heads of people in photos should be at least the size of a dime.

Ideally, the photographer should always seek drama, human interest, conflict and other news values when taking a picture. All of this is important to a reporter who has to double as the photographer. In fact, to see creatively is just as essential for a reporter as it is for a photographer.

Picture Process.   The reporter should be familiar with the picture process:

1. The city editor, or photo editor if the newspaper has one, makes the assignment, which should be as specific as possible. The photographer should be given some idea of the type of picture the editor wants.
2. The picture is taken by a photographer; the film is developed and printed. (Some smaller newspapers use Polaroid cameras to eliminate the developing and printing process.) The glossy print is handed to the proper editor, usually the city editor for local pictures. The city editor as well as the Sunday, entertainment, sports or women's news editor will receive many pictures along with the press releases provided by other sources such as public relations persons.
3. The editor determines the news value of the picture, marks the picture where it should be cropped and indicates the size of the cut (or negative, in offset printing) that should be made of it. If the picture has flaws that can be corrected, the editor may give it to a staff artist, who may "retouch" it to strengthen weak lines or "paint out" objectionable features. The artist may also make a layout showing the arrangement of pictures to be used in a picture story.
4. The retouched print goes to the backshop. If the paper is printed by the offset method, a screened negative is made with the offset camera. If the newspaper is still printed by hot metal, an engraver makes a metal "cut" of it.
5. A proof (copy) of the cut is returned to the editor, who may mark it for a special place in the paper.
6. The editor gives the original print or proof to a reporter or copy editor for writing of cutlines. Often, however, the cutlines are written before the picture is sent to the backshop.
7. The print and its cutlines (checked by the editor or a copy editor) are returned to the composing room, where the cutlines are set and assembled with the negative or cut into the page where they will appear.

The introduction of highly sophisticated, computerized equipment in the late 1980s that permits a photo editor to rearrange the composition of a photograph has touched off a debate within the profession over the ethics of so-called "doctored" pictures. Several major magazines were criticized because they moved major elements in a picture to create a better visual impact shortly after the equipment became available. Critics of the new equipment argue that no longer will the public be able to "trust" photographs as an accurate historical record. As more and more newspapers and magazines begin to use the equipment, the debate is certain to continue.

Color Pictures.   Improved technology has brought about the increased use of color photography in many daily newspapers and a few weeklies. No doubt, the use of color on the front page of USA TODAY spurred many newspapers to use color news photos on their front pages, too. Sandy White, graphics editor of the

Detroit Free Press, said in an article in The Bulletin of the American Society of Newspaper Editors that

> with one exception, a commitment to Page One color news photography is a lot like getting married:
> —You don't really know what's involved before you get into it.
> —When you find out, it's too late to turn back gracefully and without considerable expense.
> —To succeed, you have to keep working on it.
> —You make a lot of mistakes along the way.
>   The exception is: With Page One color, your mistakes are public.

"A commitment to Page One color news photography," White said, "requires three things that cost money—more equipment, people and supplies—and two things everyone wishes money alone could buy—more communications and better planning." Despite the headaches front page color often causes the editorial and production staffs, it is, in the view of many editors and graphic designers, worth the trouble.

Richard Curtis, managing editor for graphics and photography for USA TODAY and co-founder of The Society of Newspaper Designers, points out the importance of good photographs and art work. "You must design a page that effectively displays the right photgraphs/artwork because they carry a tremendous burden," he said. "Photographs and their captions and artwork are almost always 'read' before the text."

He recommends that they be treated "as news." And he urged editors and graphic designers to resist the urge to use "a beautiful photograph of a pelican backlit by a beautiful sunset, a photograph with absolutely no news value." He says to use them is a waste of a newspaper's time and resources and a lot of the reader's time, too.

WRITING CUTLINES

Writing cutlines (captions) is one of the most difficult assignments at a newspaper. It takes practice, patience and a command of the language. Not everyone writes cutlines well. In fact, they often are the most poorly written parts of a newspaper. Many cutlines lack grace and style.

In a study of cutlines used with Associated Press Laserphotos during a single month, 60 percent had punctuation, spelling, sentence construction and word-use errors. In addition, writing errors such as cliches, pejorative adjectives, incorrect verb tenses, incorrect noun-pronoun or subject-verb agreement, and sentence fragments were found. One of the most common errors in captions is the use of "shown above" and "pictured here." They are unnecessary and are an insult to the reader. It is obvious that the subject is in the picture and that the picture is above the cutline.

Cutline styles vary greatly in newspapers. Most cutlines are placed underneath pictures. Some newspapers, however, place them at the side. This is commonly called "magazine style." Some newspapers make use of overlines placed above the picture. However, tests show that readers tend to miss or ignore them. Here are examples of various commonly used cutline styles:

Rescue workers dig through the wreckage of a collapsed house in the town of Carlentini after a quake struck eastern Sicily, killing at least 19 people and injuring 200.

EXAMINER/KURT ROGERS

Lee the Famous Reindeer Man: *"It's been really slow the last day or two."*

Morning stretch

Jack Kirkland/News-Sentinel staff

Second-seeded Buck Archer of Shelby, N.C., reaches to return a shot during his match Thursday morning in the National Senior 55 & 65 Clay Court Championship at Knoxville Racquet Club.

ASSOCIATED PRESS

BATTERED BILL: Houston's Al Smith (left) grabbed the Buffalo Bills' Thurman Thomas as he tripped over the Oilers' Bubba McDowell (25). The Oilers won Monday night's game in Houston 27-24. Story, Page D 3.

Tommy Bartlett National Player Of Year

Tommy Bartlett, standing in front of his numerous plaques and awards filling one of the walls at UT-Chattanooga's Racquet Center, now has to find room for another. Bartlett, the Lady Mocs' head coach and the head

Melissa Poe
Wrote President, Barbara Bush

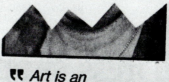

ʼʼ *Art is an opportunity to touch time in a bottle.* ʼʼ

Lois Riggins Ezzell
Tennessee State Museum director

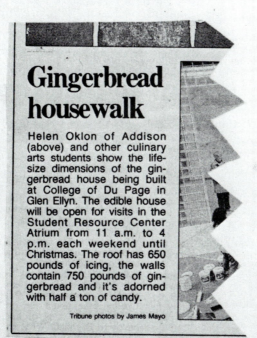

Gingerbread housewalk

Helen Oklon of Addison (above) and other culinary arts students show the life-size dimensions of the gingerbread house being built at College of Du Page in Glen Ellyn. The edible house will be open for visits in the Student Resource Center Atrium from 11 a.m. to 4 p.m. each weekend until Christmas. The roof has 650 pounds of icing, the walls contain 750 pounds of gingerbread and it's adorned with half a ton of candy.

Tribune photos by James Mayo

The most effective cutlines are brief and clear. They should tell what the picture is about and identify the people in it. An Associated Press Managing Editors Continuing Study Committee put together "Ten Tests of a Good Cutline." They are:

1. Is it complete?
2. Does it identify, fully and clearly?
3. Does it tell when?
4. Does it tell where?
5. Does it tell what's in the picture?

6. Does it have the names spelled correctly, with the proper name on the right person?
7. Is it specific?
8. Is it ready to read?
9. Have as many adjectives as possible been removed?
10. Does it suggest another picture?

The committee added what is called the Cardinal Rule, which should never, never be violated: Never write a cutline without seeing the picture.

Although cutlines are much like a story lead because they should include the five W's of the picture, they should not repeat the lead of an accompanying story word for word. In the case of a straight news picture, a cutline should emphasize the most important fact first. Cutlines similar to feature leads are appropriate with pictures that are not straight news.

When writing a cutline, the reporter should study the picture carefully first and know what is in it. Obvious features should not be described; after all, the reader will know if the person is laughing or crying. Everything a reader might misinterpret at first glance should be explained. Cutlines should be written in the present tense when describing the action taking place in the picture, but past tense should be used when giving additional details. Reporters should not mix tenses in the same sentence in a cutline any more than they would in a news story. And the cutline writer should never speculate on what the persons in the picture are thinking.

Remember that cutlines should not be loaded with excessive details. When a picture accompanies a story, many newspapers use the briefest possible cutline because the details are adequately covered in the lead or are high in the story. Under a photgraph of voters in Haiti participating in that country's first democratic national elections, one newspaper used this brief cutline on a picture accompanying a detailed story on the elections:

Haitians lining up in Port-au-Prince to vote yesterday

Under a picture of a shelter for the homeless that was burning, one newspaper used this short cutline because the picture accompanied a lengthy story on the fire:

Fire engulfs a vacant homeless shelter in Elkins

Here are other examples of the use of pictures:

Straight-News Picture Accompanied by a Story.   Not all W's are introduced in the picture, and the cutlines do not repeat the exact wording of the lead. (See Figures 12–1, 12–2, 12–3.)

Feature Picture Accompanied by a Story.   Cutlines are written in a more colloquial tone and contain few details. They generally emphasize something not mentioned in the lead of the story. (See Figure 12–4.)

Picture Not Accompanied by a Story. Frequently a picture is used without a story because it is interesting in itself or it is used in place of a story. In this case all five W's are presented in the caption, which substitutes for a story. (See Figure 12–5.)

Picture Stories. Newspapers use picture stories to present dramatic or unusual events. Occasionally they are used because they include beautiful pictures that convey a certain mood or idea. To be effective, a picture story must be a well-planned "essay" built around a strong central theme or idea. Everything should be worked out carefully before the photographer starts shooting. Every photo essay should have at least one dominant picture that can be used to establish the theme. There also should be a combination of action and reaction photos as well as closeups and general shots so the page will offer some contrast. A page of nothing but action shots on the football field or basketball court can be deadly dull. A good sports photo essay will include shots of coaches, the players on the bench and the audience. Similarly, a photo essay on a spectacular fire should include shots of the burning buildings, firemen at work, dramatic rescues, individuals who were evacuated and the crowd that has gathered at the scene.

When preparing cutlines (captions) for a photo story, the writer should remember to describe the action in the picture and provide some continuity from picture to picture on the page. Cutlines should be kept to a minimum, and they should be uniform in style.

Many picture pages use a central copy block rather than a complete story. On some picture pages the copy block, a brief summary of the event or action, is set in larger type than the cutlines and may supplant cutlines. The text of the copy block, in that case, relates specifically to all of the pictures. On others, the copy block is used to tie the pictures together, and each picture has a more detailed cutline. Information in the copy block should not be repeated in the cutlines.

Here are some examples of story leads and the cutlines on the accompanying picturers:

Story Lead, Figure 12–1
    Two men were injured today—one critically—in a two-car collision on Morristown Highway.
    Arnold Davis, 59, of Newport, was trapped in his 1971 Mercury for about a half-hour before being freed by the Newport Rescue Squad. He was flown to the University of Tennessee Medical Center by medical helicopter where he remains in critical condition.
    The other driver, Windell B. Ford, 18, of Route 1, Cosby, was taken to East Tennessee Baptist Hospital in Knoxville where he is in stable condition. . . .

Caption, Figure 12–1
William Arnold Davis Jr., pinned behind the steering wheel and dash of his 1971 Mercury, waits for members of the Newport Rescue Squad to free him.

Story Lead, Figure 12–2
    A man going to get his morning coffee saved the lives of several people in a burning apartment building today, but firefighters fear one resident may have died in the blaze.

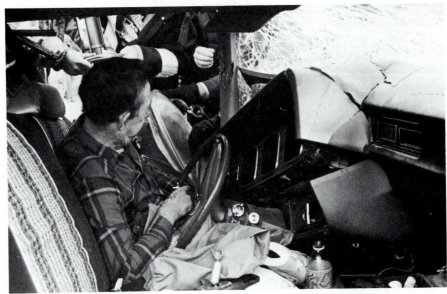

FIGURE 12–1. (Photo courtesy of The Newport Plain Talk, Newport, Tenn.)

Caption, Figure 12–2
Janet Pollack scampers away from the Hedrick Place Apartments with a friend's cat after today's fire in the three-story building at 116 31st Ave. N. Photo by Turner Hutchinson.

Story Lead, Figure 12–3
A suspected bank robber held police at bay for several hours today, wounding one police officer, before surrendering.

Caption, Figure 12–3
A Knoxville police officer draws a bead on a suspected bank robber who had held police at bay for several hours following high-speed chase. Photo by Jack Kirkland.

Story Lead, Figure 12–4
More than 200 Cub Scouts huffed and puffed their way through the annual Cub Scouts Regional Rainboat Regatta today at the Civic Coliseum.
And when all the wind died down, Tommy Johnson, Cub Pack 320, was the winner. His fragile craft, propelled by his lung power, made it down a 30-foot rain gutter in a record time. . . .

Caption, Figure 12–4
THEY'RE OFF
Cub Scouts Tommy Johnson (left) and Janson Manchester fill the sails of their boats with wind at the start of the Rainboat Regatta. Tommy powered his craft down the 30-foot rain gutter in a record time to win the annual competition. Photo by Don Campbell.

FIGURE 12–2. (Photo courtesy of the Nashville Banner.)

Caption for Feature Picture Without a Story, Figure 12–5
SNOW FORT

When the snow finally stopped falling yesterday, John Ragsdale IV and his younger brother, Jordan Lee, donned their camouflage outfits and set out to build a snow fort in the backyard. But it may not last long enough for more than a single snowball fight. The weather forecasters are predicting a warming trend starting tomorrow when temperatures are expected to reach the high 40s.

sentences. (One newspaper sentence will sometimes be divided into two newscast sentences, as in item 2.)

4. Verbs and their subjects are kept reasonably close together. This rules out the use of long "interrupters" between the verb and subject. Broadcast writers generally avoid introducing a second proper name between the subject and the verb. For example: "Mary Ross, secretary of Mayor Jackson Turner, died this morning." A listener may not hear the opening words and might believe that the mayor died.

5. Identification of the person quoted is shortened as much as possible and placed before instead of after the names. Sometimes the identification only is used in one sentence and the name in another to break up extraordinarily long combinations of the two.

6. Incompleted sentences, if used only from time to time, are generally permissible in newscasts.

7. Although broadcast news is written in a conversational style, it still follows all the standard rules of English grammar.

Language

1. The question of tense is often debated by radio and television news writers. Many stations insist that, to give news a sense of immediacy, the present tense rather than the past should be used at all times. Others consistently use the past tense. Some have adopted a practice of dealing with each story separately, using the most logical tense for that story. However, the present tense is most commonly used.

2. To prevent awkward pronunciations by the announcer, such combinations as alliteration in the sequence of words should be avoided (example: "The professor protested provisions. . . ."). Also, too many words starting with "s" will result in noticeable hissing (example: "Sister should send some . . .").

3. The overworked "quote" and "unquote" are not used by most newscast writers today. They frequently break down long direct quotes into a combination of direct and indirect quotes. They use such phrases as "He said—and we quote him. . . ."). If a long quote is used, newscast writers frequently insert a qualifier to let the listener know it is a direct quote. They use such terms as "he continued," "he went on to say" and "he concluded."

4. If possible, numbers should be rounded off, especially large and detailed numbers. The city budget may be $20,568,987, but the broadcast news writer will make it "20 million 569 thousand dollars." However, if the number must be specific, for example, "a new tax rate of 3 dollars and 24 cents," it is not rounded off. Newscasters generally try to use figures sparingly and avoid lists of numbers altogether. They never start a sentence with a figure if they can avoid it.

5. Contractions are acceptable in newscasts but should not be used to extremes. Contractions should not be used if they sound awkward on the

news writers know that listeners cannot "rehear" a word, phrase or sentence they do not fully understand, so every word has to count. On the other hand, a newspaper reader can go over a sentence as many times as desired, although the ideal newspaper sentence is as easy to comprehend as a well-written broadcast news sentence.

WRITING NEWSCASTS

Two important writing techniques mark the differences between news for radio and television and news for newspapers. One is the construction of sentences; the other is the casual, informal language. These and other differences are discussed in the sections that follow:

Sentence Structure

1. The inverted sentence structure used in newspaper writing generally is not used in newscasts. Often newspaper stories give the source at the end of the lead sentence unless the source is a major public figure such as the president or governor. Newcast writers generally start with the source or some other introductory phrase and place the important facts later in the lead sentence. For example, a newspaper reporter might write:

   > Fifteen elderly patients died today in a fire that destroyed the Resthaven Nursing Home in surburban West Hills, Fire Chief Leonard Basler said.

   The broadcast writer might use this approach:

   > Fire Chief Leonard Basler said 15 elderly patients died in a fire that destroyed the Resthaven Nursing Home shortly before dawn today. All were trapped in their rooms in the two-story building in surburban West Hills.

2. Sentences are shorter than those generally used in newspaper stories, but variety in sentence length is still preferred. For example, a newspaper reporter might write:

   > Pan American World Airways, responding to skyrocketing insurance rates caused by the Persian Gulf Crisis, said Thursday that it was suspending flights to Israel and Saudi Arabia.

   The broadcast news writer might use this approach:

   > Pan American World Airways said Thursday it was suspending all flights to Israel and Saudi Arabia. It took the action because of skyrocketing insurance rates caused by the Persian Gulf Crisis.

3. Only one principal thought is used in each newscast sentence. If longer sentences are used, they tend to be compound rather than complex

sentences. (One newspaper sentence will sometimes be divided into two newscast sentences, as in item 2.)

4. Verbs and their subjects are kept reasonably close together. This rules out the use of long "interrupters" between the verb and subject. Broadcast writers generally avoid introducing a second proper name between the subject and the verb. For example: "Mary Ross, secretary of Mayor Jackson Turner, died this morning." A listener may not hear the opening words and might believe that the mayor died.

5. Identification of the person quoted is shortened as much as possible and placed before instead of after the names. Sometimes the identification only is used in one sentence and the name in another to break up extraordinarily long combinations of the two.

6. Incompleted sentences, if used only from time to time, are generally permissible in newscasts.

7. Although broadcast news is written in a conversational style, it still follows all the standard rules of English grammar.

Language

1. The question of tense is often debated by radio and television news writers. Many stations insist that, to give news a sense of immediacy, the present tense rather than the past should be used at all times. Others consistently use the past tense. Some have adopted a practice of dealing with each story separately, using the most logical tense for that story. However, the present tense is most commonly used.

2. To prevent awkward pronunciations by the announcer, such combinations as alliteration in the sequence of words should be avoided (example: "The professor protested provisions. . . ."). Also, too many words starting with "s" will result in noticeable hissing (example: "Sister should send some . . .").

3. The overworked "quote" and "unquote" are not used by most newscast writers today. They frequently break down long direct quotes into a combination of direct and indirect quotes. They use such phrases as "He said—and we quote him. . . ."). If a long quote is used, newscast writers frequently insert a qualifier to let the listerner know it is a direct quote. They use such terms as "he continued," "he went on to say" and "he concluded."

4. If possible, numbers should be rounded off, especially large and detailed numbers. The city budget may be $20,568,987, but the broadcast news writer will make it "20 million 569 thousand dollars." However, if the number must be specific, for example, "a new tax rate of 3 dollars and 24 cents," it is not rounded off. Newscasters generally try to use figures sparingly and avoid lists of numbers altogether. They never start a sentence with a figure if they can avoid it.

5. Contractions are acceptable in newscasts but should not be used to extremes. Contractions should not be used if they sound awkward on the

The basic role of every reporter, no matter what the medium, is to tell the news. How it is told is largely a matter of style, dictated in large measure by technology. Writing is designed for readers who expect greater detail along with explanations and analysis. Radio and television newscasts are generally aimed at listeners and viewers who are seeking information rather than a detailed explanation. That is why broadcast news stories are condensed into a few sentences similar to the lead paragraph of a newspaper story.

News is a basic commodity. For the most part, no real differences exist in the elements that make something news for print or news for broadcast. All the news values used in selecting stories for newspapers apply to selecting stories for broadcast. Where the mediums differ is in the way those stories are told, and that often is affected by the audience.

Newspaper and broadcast audiences differ considerably in age and education. Newspaper readers tend to be older and have more education. Broadcast audiences tend to be younger—a lot of children—and generally are not as well educated. In fact, broadcast audiences include many persons who do not read because of lack of education or inclination.

In addition, the technology for delivering news for broadcast in many ways confines the writer of a newscast. Because air time devoted to news is so limited, many stories have to be told in 30 to 45 seconds. Two minutes devoted to a single news item on a newscast is considered a long story.

Stories in newspapers often run 15 or more inches long. A 15-inch story would amount to about 600 words. By contrast, one minute of news read aloud amounts to about 150 words. A typical 30-minute newscast on television actually amounts to about 22 minutes after time for commercials and opening and closing credits is subtracted. The total number of words used in those 22 minutes would amount to little more than half of the words printed on the front page of a standard-size American newspaper.

So the newscast writer has to make every single word count. He or she has to emphasize the who, what and where first and then if there is time include the why or how. But most of the time, the why and how are left out of most broadcast news stories.

There are other differences in writing news for print and broadcast caused by time constraints and technology. The writer of a television newscast, for example, must coordinate the words with film, still photos, graphics and other available visuals. Some stories, in fact, are selected for television because there are dramatic pictures to illustrate them.

Newspaper reporters pay particular attention to the accurate spelling of names of persons, places and things. The newscast writer, however, is more concerned with the proper pronunciation of names. In broadcast news copy, correct pronunciation often is inserted in parentheses immediately following unusual names, in this manner: Buehler (BEE-ler), Spivey (SPY-vee), Inglehart (EYE-gull-hart) and Smythe (SMEYE-th).

News for broadcast is written in a conversational style because it is heard, not read. Simple, short sentences are used. Adjectives and adverbs are kept to a minimum. Strong, active verbs are used rather than passive ones. Broadcast

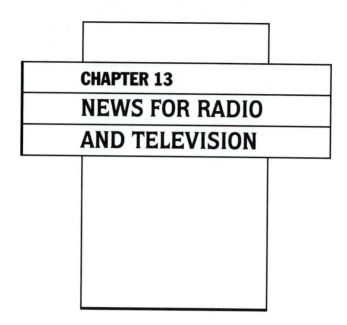

CHAPTER 13
NEWS FOR RADIO
AND TELEVISION

After months of waiting, war finally came to the Middle East, and the public first learned of it from television and radio. For the first several days after American forces and their allies began the campaign to drive Iraq out of Kuwait, the entire nation, it seemed, "watched television's anchormen and correspondents, caught in history's ambush, struggling to tell the story without yet knowing what it was," Time magazine said.

"Everywhere, the reports could not come fast enough. There was a national craving for news, despite the saturation coverage and frustration at the thinness of reports," Time added.

Much of that thinness, it should be noted, came as a result of American military censors who literally controlled the news out of the war zone. Some, however, came from the nature of the war itself in its early stages. It was essentially an air war at first, and the targets being hit were behind Iraqi lines. There were no American reporters in Iraq, and only a handful of television journalists from Cable News Network (CNN) were allowed to remain in Kuwait. All their stories had to pass through Iraqi censors.

Yet there were some outstanding reporting and dramatic photographs being sent back to the United States by satellite from the television journalists in the field. Once again, the nation was reminded of the greatest strength of broadcasting—timeliness.

That does not mean that timeliness is not as significant to print journalists. It certainly is. However, television and radio have a unique ability to bring the news to viewers and listeners almost instantly. It takes longer to get the news set in type and run off on presses.

Immediacy is the chief difference between print and broadcast journalism. They both deal in the same product—news. And what makes an event news for the print journalists generally makes it news for television and radio journalists.

3. Clip from any newspaper available to you three local news stories that might have greater impact if they had been accompanied by pictures. Explain what types of pictures you would have used with each story. Write cutlines to go with the suggested pictures. Hand in clippings with your cutlines.

4. Select cutlines from five pictures in any newspaper available to you. Rewrite the cutlines, using the styles illustrated in this chapter. Use a different style for each cutline. Turn in the original cutlines with your written versions.

5. Suggest five ideas for picture stories involving people, events or places on your campus or the surrounding area. Write a brief explanation of why you think each would make an excellent photo story and suggest the various pictures you would use in the story.

6. Analyze the cutline style in one issue of three newspapers available to you. Write a brief report on how the captions compare with the 10 tests of a good caption listed on pages 183–184.

Old bands removed from legs –
New bands attached
Wildlife agency says
More than 1,000 geese
Rounded up this year
About 175 more
Than last year

b. Tractor-trailer drivers
Begin state-wide protest
Over proposed ban
On mobile radar detectors
State police report
Protest started during
Afternoon rush hour traffic
On all interstates
Leading in and out of city
Traffic backed up on I-75
About five miles through city
Helicopter traffic reporter
Says she counted
Nearly 100 trucks
Bunched up on I-40
South of city
Traffic out of city
"Barely creeping along"
State Police Trooper Joyce Redden says
State legislature scheduled
To debate the bill
Early next week

c. Robin, 14-year-old
Siberian bear, takes
Practice ride on her
Motorbike at fairgrounds
During preparations for
Circus performance
This weekend
Rene Turciso, owner and trainer
Has been working with bears
More than 20 years
He says Robin likes
To ride so much
He has to lure her
Off the bike
With special treats
Circus performances
Will be at 3 and 7 p.m. Saturday
Sponsored by local
Chapter of Good Guys
Club that raises funds
To help needy children

FIGURE 12—6. Photographer Patrick Murphy-Racey created this impressive picture page with a story on the football team at the Tennessee School for the Deaf in Knoxville. (Courtesy of The Knoxville News-Sentinel.)

FIGURE 12–5. (Photo courtesy of Nancy Petrey.)

EXERCISES

1. Interview the chief photographer and photo or graphics editor of your local newspaper. If possible, accompany one of the paper's photographers on an assignment to observe him or her at work.

2. Here are brief notes to be used in writing cutlines for pictures that will not be accompanied by stories. Explain specifically what kind of picture you would suggest for use in connection with each exercise. Then write the cutlines for each of the suggested pictures.

    a. Rodney Blass, state waterfowl biologist
       Supervises annual roundup
       Of Canada geese
       On banks of Old Hickory Lake
       Roundup occurs each year
       At this time
       While geese are flightless
       Birds are herded into pens

FIGURE 12–2. (Photo courtesy of the Nashville Banner.)

Caption for Feature Picture Without a Story, Figure 12–5
SNOW FORT

When the snow finally stopped falling yesterday, John Ragsdale IV and his younger brother, Jordan Lee, donned their camouflage outfits and set out to build a snow fort in the backyard. But it may not last long enough for more than a single snowball fight. The weather forecasters are predicting a warming trend starting tomorrow when temperatures are expected to reach the high 40s.

FIGURE 12—3. (Photo courtesy of Jack Kirkland, The Knoxville News-Sentinel, Knoxville, Tenn.)

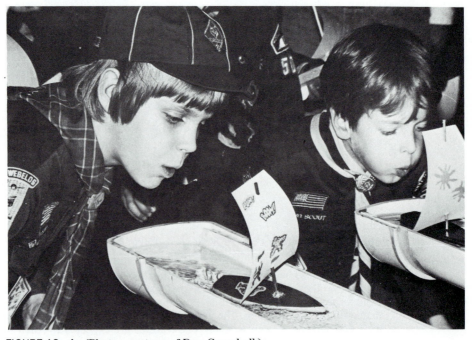

FIGURE 12—4. (Photo courtesy of Don Campbell.)

air. The use of slang should be avoided unless it is in a direct quote or is germane to the story.

6. Newscasters use adjectives sparingly. Nouns are much stronger words. In newscasts that are going to be augmented by film or still photos, adjectives should be avoided if they are relative words. The pretty blonde to the news writer may not be pretty to many of the viewers, for example, and the use of such a description may be considered sexist by others.

One of the best illustrations of the difference between newspaper and news broadcast writing can be found in stories written by the wire services.

The Newspaper Version

KNOXVILLE, Tenn. (UPI)— Cancer-stricken Pamela Hamilton was returned to a hospital Monday to resume court-ordered chemotherapy against her religious beliefs after a restful 11 days at home, officials said.

Officials said the 12-year-old daughter of a preacher weighed 89 pounds upon her return—three pounds more than when she left East Tennessee Children's Hospital Oct. 27 for her first trip home since she entered the hospital Sept. 17.

Pamela's treatment violates her family's fundamentalist Christian beliefs. But Dennis Prewitt, director of the Campbell County Human Services Department, said the family did not interfere with Pamela's return to the hospital.

Pamela stopped by a fast-food restaurant for tacos before she entered the hospital. From home she brought along two stuffed dolls and a stuffed dog named Russ, hospital spokeswoman Pat Kelly said.

"She wanted to know why she was not being put in the same hospital room. We told her somebody else was in it and she said, 'I don't like that.' But she'll get used to it," Ms. Kelly said.

Pamela's father, Larry Hamilton, a pastor for the Church of God of Union Assembly, LaFollette, Tenn., was upset when he was not allowed to drive his daughter home 11 days ago but gave officials no problems Monday when she was driven back to Knoxville by Human Services officials, Prewitt said.

The Broadcast Version

(KNOXVILLE)—Pamela Hamilton is back in the hospital today to resume court-ordered chemotherapy against her religious beliefs.

A spokeswoman at East Tennessee Children's Hospital said the 12-year-old cancer victim stopped at a fast-food restaurant for tacos before she was delivered to the hospital by state officials.

Pamela ended 11 days of rest at her LaFollette home with her parents . . . who are against her cancer treatment because it violates their fundamentalist Christian beliefs.

Pamela is in the custody of the state Department of Human Services . . . and Human Services officials said her parents did not interfere with her return to the hospital.

Pamela is to undergo a fourth round of chemotherapy tomorrow. Hospital spokeswoman Pat Kelly said if all goes well . . . Pamela may be allowed to go home November 16th for another 11-day rest.

Ms. Kelly said doctors should know later this month when to begin treating a cancerous tumor in Pamela's leg with radiation. Pamela suffers from a rare bone cancer known as Ewing's sarcoma.

Doctors previously gave her only a 25 percent chance of surviving . . . But they say the odds have increased because chemotherapy has reduced considerably the size of the tumor.

"We hope this (rest period) has been helpful for her and I hope it's something we're able to continue," Prewitt said. "I think we've gotten cooperation from her parents and I'm optimistic we can do this again."

Pamela, a shy seventh-grader, suffers from a rare bone cancer known as Ewing's sarcoma that produced a large tumor on her left thigh. The tumor has reduced in size considerably after three rounds of chemotherapy drugs and the fourth round begins today, Ms. Kelly said.

Once five rounds of chemotherapy are completed, doctors will decide when to begin treating the tumor with radiation, Ms. Kelly said. That could begin early in December, she said.

Ms. Kelly said Pamela had a low white blood count last week but apparently the count had returned to normal by Monday. Ms. Kelly said a low white blood count is typical of cancer patients undergoing chemotherapy because the drugs reduce the body's ability to resist infection.

After Pamela completes the fourth round of chemotherapy she will probably be allowed to return to her home 40 miles north in LaFollette for another 11-day rest starting Nov. 16, Ms. Kelly said.

Pamela was ordered hospitalized by a juvenile court judge who rejected the family's argument that they have a constitutional right of religious freedom to refuse cancer treatment.

The state Court of Appeals turned down the family's argument and Hamilton has been considering whether to appeal the case to the U.S. Supreme Court.

SPECIAL DEVICES IN NEWSCASTS

Because a newscast is made up of a number of short stories, the newscast writer often has to provide a "bridge" between them, particularly when the two have something in common. A variety of transitional phrases is used. Some examples are "Meanwhile, at City Hall, Mayor Jack Corn took action to . . ." (used between two stories dealing with city government in some way) and "Today's hazardous weather conditions did not keep Mayor Jack Corn from showing up at . . ." (used as a bridge from a weather story to a story on the Mayor).

The best rule for the use of transitions is: Use them when they seem helpful or logical; do not use them if they seem forced. Newscast writers should avoid using such editorialized transitions as "Here's an interesting item" or "You will like this story." Datelines, however, which are often used to identify where an item orginates, can serve as good transitions from one story to another, as in the example: "And from Washington comes a report that . . ."

As a teaser to attract listeners, a newscast often begins with a series of three or four rapid-fire, headline-style phrases from the leading stories of the day. Frequently they are flashed on the television screen at the same time the anchor is reading them. The "headlines" generally are followed by a commercial break, and then the regular newscast begins. Here are several examples of a television newscast headline:

COMING UP NEXT ON NEWS AT NOON . . .

    FIRE DESTROYS RESORT HOTEL
IN THE SMOKY MOUNTAINS . . . WE'LL
HAVE AN EYE-WITNESS REPORT FROM
COSBY.

    SEARCHERS FIND BODY OF MISSING
WOMAN FLOATING IN NORRIS LAKE . . .

    AND AN OUTBREAK OF FLU HAS
CLOSED THE CHRISTIAN ACADEMY FOR
THE REST OF THE WEEK . . .

    THOSE STORIES PLUS—
HOW TO BEAT THE WINTER BLAHS . . .
NEXT—ON NEWS AT NOON!

Stories told in chronological order are used from time to time on newscasts just as they are in newspapers. However, on newscasts they are generally extremely short, and they end with a surprise or a punch line.

THE EXTRA JOB OF TELEVISION WRITERS

The television newscast writer has to make certain that the words selected for the anchors to read blend smoothly with the action films, videotape, still photographs, electronic graphics or other visual material selected to illustrate the story. The words and pictures have to complement each other. That's why it is important that a writer never attempt to prepare a script for a piece in which videotape or film is to be used without having seen the visuals. If the mood of the words does not match the action on the film, the viewer will notice it quickly.

Planning and selecting the visuals may be part of the responsibilities of the newscast writer. At some small-market stations, the writer may even do the filming. However, at most television stations there is a news director and an assignment editor who assigns reporters and camera operators to specific stories.

News operations at television stations are similar in a number of ways to the city room of a newspaper. The news director and assignment editor keep abreast of news developments in the city and schedule reporters and camera crews to regular events such as meetings of governmental bodies. Many stations have reporters regularly assigned to major beats just as newspapers do. Coverage of fires, accidents and natural disasters often becomes a team effort with all available hands contributing.

The overriding concern is to get excellent visuals to help tell the story. What the visuals don't tell, the writer should. At a fire, the film may show flames and smoke engulfing a building, but there may be no immediate identification of the building. That means the writer has to tell the viewer what is burning and where it is. For example, say a fire destroys the main building at a knitting mill where workers have been on strike for two months. The film will show the burning building, but the writer has to tell the reader that

> A four-alarm fire destroyed the main building at the strike-bound Riverside Knitting Mill in suburban Rockwood today.

When the scene switches, the writer has to reestablish the scene for the viewer. If the film shows the fire chief talking to company executives, the writer has to explain for the viewer:

> Meanwhile, Company President George Everett urged Fire Chief Leonard Basler to begin an immediate arson investigation.

The viewer would then see and hear Everett making his request and explaining why he suspects arson. The writer follows this up with other details of the fire and gives some background on the labor troubles at the knitting mill while additional footage of the fire is being shown.

BROADCAST COPY

Although each news operation will have its own particular format for preparing the news copy that is read on the air, generally radio newscasters prefer triple-spaced copy with each line of type averaging about 10 words. Newscasters usually speak about 125 to 150 words a minute, so 12 to 15 lines will take about one minute of air time. At some stations, each story is prepared on a separate sheet of paper to allow for last-minute changes in the order the stories are presented. At others, the script simply runs from one page to the next. Some stations prepare their scripts in all capital letters. However, both capital and lowercase letters are easier to read than all uppercase and are more universally used in broadcast writing.

Television newscasts are generally written on the right half of the page with each line averaging five or six words. The left side of the page of a television script is used for the audio and video information so the anchors will know what pictures and audio material is being used. Of course, this material, usually in all caps, is not read aloud.

Here is part of a script for the 6 o'clock news at WBIR-TV, Channel 10, the NBC affiliate that dominates the news ratings in the Knoxville, Tenn., market:

HEADLINES
30/VP/6wed/01-09-91

(EDYE) COMING UP NEXT ON ACTION TEN NEWS . . .

TAKE VO ------------------------------- BAKER AND AZIZ COME FACE TO FACE—FOR THE LAST CHANCE TO AVERT WAR IN THE MIDDLE EAST . . . WE'LL HAVE A SKYLINK RE-PORT FROM WASHINGTON, D.C.

TAKE VO ------------------------------- (BILL) POLICE EVACU-ATE AN EAST KNOXVILLE BOARDING HOUSE AFTER FINDING A BODY—AND DI-LAPIDATED CONDITIONS . . .

ON CAMERA ------------------------- (EDYE) AND A PRIVATE CLUB IN LENOIR CITY MAY BE SERVING LIQUOR—BUT NOT WITHOUT A FIGHT . . .

(BILL) THOSE STORIES PLUS—IMPROVING THE LIVES OF CANCER PATIENTS . . . NEXT—ON ACTION TEN NEWS!

Page 2
BAKER-AZIZ TALKS
43/JMM/6wed/01-09-91

(BILL) THE FEAR OF WAR IS ON THE MINDS OF MOST AMERICANS TONIGHT AFTER PEACE TALKS FAILED TODAY IN GENEVA.

ACCORDING TO SECRE-TARY OF STATE JAMES BAKER, IRAQ IS UNWILLING TO WITHDRAW FROM KUWAIT AND PRESIDENT BUSH SAYS SADDAM HUSSEIN IS UP AGAINST A SITUATION WHERE THERE IS NO COM-PROMISE.

AS THE SITUATION WORSENS, WE HAVE TWO

STORIES ON EFFORTS TO
KEEP MORALE UP AMONG
THE SOLDIERS IN THE MID-
DLE EAST.

TOPPING OUR COVER-
AGE, SKIP LOESCHER RE-
PORTS ON TODAY'S DEVELOP-
MENTS IN GENEVA.

TAKE PKG
MIDDLE EAST CRISIS

JAMES BAKER/
SECRETARY OF STATE

TARIQ AZIZ/IRAQI
FOREIGN MINISTER

TIME: 1:42

(skip loescher) Hopes for a
peaceful solution were raised
this morning . . . as the Geneva
talks between Secretary of State
Baker and Iraqi Foreign
Minister Aziz continued for hours
. . . more than six-and-a-half hours.

But hopes were dashed this
afternoon when the talks ended in
failure.

(james baker . . .)

(skip loescher) President Bush
is said to be disappointed, discour-
aged and somber as a result of the
failure.

(president bush) This was a total stiffarm . . . this was a total
rebuff.

(skip loescher) But he is said
to be resolute in his determination to
force Iraq out of Kuwait, if it doesn't
withdraw by January 15th.

(president bush . . .)

(skip loescher) Iraqi Foreign Minister Aziz says his nation hasn't mis-
calculated the will of the United
States.

But he says Iraq is ready to
fight if the U.S. attacks.

And he made this threat.

(tariq aziz . . .)

(skip loescher) Today in Baghdad, Saddam Hussein is quoted as
saying: "Americans will swim in
their own blood" if war erupts.

And if that happens, will
Saddam Hussein be killed?

When asked that question a
short time ago, President Bush said
"I don't know."

Skip Loescher in Washington
for Action 10 News.

The script continued with a reference to the Secretary General of the
United Nations going to Baghdad. It then went into a story on a local national
guard unit serving in Saudi Arabia and the local efforts to keep up the morale of

the men and women, accompanied with interviews with family members and a local group that sends packages to the troops. The script then switched to a local story:

| | (EDYE) THE VICTIM OF AN AFTERNOON CAR WRECK ON INTERSTATE 75 IS IN SURGERY AND LISTED IN CRITICAL CONDITION AT THIS HOUR |
| TAKE VO ------------------------------ ##I-75/NORTH KNOX COUNTY | THE HIGHWAY PATROL SAYS THE MAN HAD STOPPED HIS TRUCK ALONG THE INTERSTATE NEAR THE EMORY ROAD EXIT TO FIX A CHAIN. HIS NAME HASN'T BEEN RELEASED YET. |

The script—41 pages in all—covered additional local stories, the weather and sports and ended with a promo for the 11 o'clock news:

TONIGHT ON NIGHTBEAT 41/MM/6wed/01-09-91	(EE) COMING UP TONIGHT ON THE NIGHTBEAT . . .
TAKE VO ------------------------------ ## TONIGHT AT 11	THEY ESCAPED RELIGIOUS AND POLITICAL PERSECUTION IN EASTERN EUROPE AND FOUND REFUGE IN EAST TENNESSEE . . . AND TONIGHT, FOR THE FIRST TIME IN YEARS, AN ENTIRE FAMILY WILL BE REUNITED . . .
BACK ON CAMERA	WE'LL TALK TO A LOCAL MIDDLE EAST EXPERT ABOUT THE INCREASED CHANCES FOR WAR IN THE MIDDLE EAST . . . AND A REMINDER THAT COMING UP NEXT ON N-B-C NIGHTLY NEWS, NEW EVIDENCE THAT THE ELDERLY CAN PROLONG AND IMPROVE THEIR LIVES WITH EXERCISE . . .
AND FINALLY 80/BW/6wed/01-09-91	TAL: BW PG: 26 SEQ: 36— (BILL)— AND FINALLY, THERE'S BAD NEWS FOR US EAST TENNESSEANS. NASHVILLE HAS BEEN CHOSEN THE MOST LIVABLE OF TENNESSEE'S FOUR MAJOR CITIES. BUT THE GOOD NEWS IS, KNOXVILLE RANKED SECOND IN THE SURVEY.

	THE STUDY WAS BASED ON ECONOMICS, EDUCATION, CRIME, HEALTH CARE, TRANSPORTATION, CLIMATE, CULTURE AND RECREATION.
	"TENNESSEE ILLUS-TRATED" MAGAZINE CON-DUCTED THE SURVEY, BUT FOLDED BEFORE IT COULD PUBLISH THE RESULTS.
	MEMPHIS WAS THIRD, AND CHATTANOOGA FOURTH IN THE SURVEY.
CAM (2-SHOT)	NOBODY ASKED ME . . . DID THEY ASK YOU, EDYE?

The cameras then pulled back from the anchor desk while the credits were superimposed on the scene. The entire newscast had 27 individual items, including news and weather, and used some 14 separate visuals to illustrate them.

EXERCISES

1. Invite the news directors of the leading local radio and television stations to class for a discussion of their broadcast news operations.

2. Buy a copy of the daily newspaper that circulates in your city, and with it in hand, watch a local television newscast that same evening. Compare the stories on the front page of the newspaper with the stories used on the television news program. Write a brief report comparing the two.

3. If there is a major radio station in your city that broadcasts a news program late in the day or early evening, make a similar comparison between the front page of the newspaper and the radio news broadcast. Write a brief report comparing the two.

4. Write a newscast version of each of the following opening paragraphs of newspaper stories.

   a. The body of a woman missing since Saturday, January 19, was found early today in a wrecked car down an embankment along Rankin Road.

      Police said the body of Beverly Jean Edwards, 28, of Newport was seated behind the wheel of her 1983 Oldsmobile Cutlass. She was last seen eight days ago when she left the VFW on Old Knoxville Highway.

   b. The Metropolitan Airport Authority Wednesday approved two construction projects for McGhee Tyson Airport—the rebuilding of two taxiways and improvement of the airport security system.

      The preliminary cost estimate for the projects is $1,500,000, Terry Cooke, airport authority director, said.

   c. A 26-year-old construction worker was in stable condition today after being repeatedly shot at a McCalla Avenue nightspot.

      Police said Mark Anthony Rogers of Grable Drive was shot by another patron after they "fought over a woman" about 10:30 last night in the El Rocco Lounge.

      He was taken to University Medical Center for surgery.

   d. A badly decomposed body, believed to be that of a woman, was found Saturday afternoon in some brush 50 yards west of South Dixie Highway at 218th Street.

A man taking a shortcut home spotted the body about 4:45 p.m., Metro-Dade Homicide Detective Pat Diaz said.

The body is believed to be that of a black woman.

e. About 40 members of the AIDS Coalition to Unleash Power (ACT-UP) staged a "die-in" Saturday afternoon to quietly demonstrate the numbers of people dying from AIDS.

"We want to indicate to people how tragic, how horrible, how needless these deaths are," said Joe Rapoport, a spokesman for the newly formed Miami chapter. ACT-UP, which is critical of the way the U.S. government has handled the epidemic, often uses loud and large demonstrations.

"This is a very visual thing, a very silent thing," said Rapoport. Members of the group also chalked body outlines on the sidewalk outside Bayside Marketplace.

5. Write a one-minute newscast (roughly 150 words) summarizing the following newspaper stories:

a. Red Bank police are trying to find out who killed 18 ducks in the pond at Memorial Cemetery over the last three weeks.

Police said someone had used a pellet gun to kill the ducks that had been donated by people who had relatives buried in the cemetery.

Employees are rounding up the other ducks and will keep them in pens for a while to prevent them from being killed too, Susan Smith, a cemetery spokeswoman said.

b. A 20-year-old man who collapsed while playing basketball at the Westside Recreation Center last night died of a heart attack, a hospital spokesman said Thursday.

Marcus L. Johnson, 2120 Pine Ridge Rd., was dead on arrival at Fort Sanders Medical Center, hospital public relations director Jerry Spurling said.

c. Williamson County now has its first female deputy sheriff.

Sharon D. Hughes Lambert, 23, was sworn in today by Sheriff Lance Taylor. She will be assigned to patrol duty and will work with a field-training officer until she attends the state's Law Enforcement Training Academy in March.

She had worked as a dispatcher with the Sheriff's Department for two years before qualifying as a deputy.

d. Jury selection was scheduled to begin today for a La Vergne man accused of killing his wife and then shoving her body off a cliff in her car.

The trial of Joseph Dick, 29, was expected to take all week, District Attorney General Tommy Thompson said.

Roxanne Dick disappeared Nov. 20 while selling insurance in Macon and Sumner counties. Her husband reported her missing the next day.

A rural letter carrier spotted her car off state Highway 52 Nov. 25 and discovered the body. Police said she had been stabbed and beaten. Her body was then placed in the car, which was set on fire.

Dick claims he was out of the city when his wife disappeared.

6. Using the following stories, write a three-minute newscast (roughly 450 words) organized according to international, national and local news.

a. A Spring City woman has filed a $750,000 lawsuit against the city Police Department and several of its officers, claiming they mishandled the incident last October when her 13-month-old son's throat was cut.

In her Circuit Court suit, Betty Jean Day claims that had Officer Sandy Peterson and five other unidentified officers used "due diligence and reasonable care," her infant son, Mitchell, would not have been killed.

The suit stems from an October 6 incident in which her boyfriend slashed the child's throat during a "rampage in her apartment" after she told him she didn't want to see him again.

Richard Tate, 25, has been charged with murder and aggravated assault in the case.

The suit claims police responded to a call for help but refused to force Tate to leave her apartment because they thought it was just another lovers' quarrel.

b. Two 19-year-old men were charged with two counts of aggravated robbery Monday of a Southside motel and a fast-food restaurant.

Walter Lee Williams and James Ray Roundtree were charged with robbing the Family Inn on Chapman Highway and Long John Silvers on Magnolia Avenue.

Police said they recovered evidence from the robberies at Roundtree's home on Richmond Avenue.

Both men are being held in the Police Intake Center in lieu of $100,000 bond.

c. A multimillionaire businessman has left $3.5 million in his will to Our Lady of Lourdes Medical Center, hospital officials said today.

Ralph Waldo Emerson Nelson, founder of Nelson Drugs, a retail chain with stores in 10 western states, died Oct. 15 at age 89 at his home in San Diego.

Nelson, known for frugality, left more than $80 million to colleges, universities and churches in a dozen states, including his gift to the Lourdes Medical Center here.

Hospital officials said he had been a patient at the Center for three months about five years ago after he suffered a heart attack during a visit to his drug stores in the area.

Frederick J. Turner, chairman of the Medical Center board of directors, expressed his gratitude for the "generous gift which took us by surprise." He said the board would consider ways in which to honor Nelson's memory "in a visible and permanent fashion."

d. Kenneth Church and Clifford Hensley went fishing and caught $50,000, but it got away. And that's no fish story.

The Greene County Sheriff's Department took the money because it was counterfeit.

Detective Bill Solomon said the men found the money Sunday floating on Douglas Lake.

Church and Hensley said they were drifting on the lake, casting for fish, when they noticed the money. They jumped into the water and picked up the money—50- and 20-dollar bills.

They said they realized the money wasn't real when they noticed the bills didn't have serial numbers.

Solomon said the money has been turned over to the U.S. Secret Service.

e. Former Monroe County Sheriff's Chief Deputy Garland Wilson was sentenced to two years in prison Thursday on drug charges.

Wilson, 44, was arrested in a federal roundup of drug suspects last August. In addition to the prison term, he will be on probation for two years and must perform 500 hours of community service.

He was charged with drug conspiracy and distribution of marijuana.

f. WEST PALM BEACH, Fla.—A woman protesting a ban on skimpy bathing suits was arrested Saturday when she stripped down to a copy of the Bill of Rights.

Tonianne Wyner, 43, was charged with disorderly conduct by Florida Park

Police officers after she refused to get dressed. She urged on-lookers to disrobe too, said Randy Lewis, a Department of Natural Resources spokesman.

Wyner was leading about a dozen nudists' rights demonstrators at John D. McArthur State Park, who were protesting a ban on thong-style swimsuits, when she stripped.

She had a parchment Bill of Rights under her clothes which, Lewis said, barely covered her chest and abdomen.

"I expected that they would acknowledge that there is a First Amendment and that the First Amendment is my permit to express myself the way that I choose," she said.

g. CHICAGO, Ill.—Freezing rain iced roadways and forced the closing of schools in at least seven states, while flooding left as many as 200 families homeless in Mississippi and threatened communities in Kentucky and Indiana.

Snow, ice and fog shut roadways and delayed flights at airports and even stalled trains.

Treacherous travel conditions caused numerous fender-benders and closed schools in some parts of Washington state, Illinois, Missouri, Mississippi, Maryland, Delaware and New Jersey.

Hospitals across the nation treated scores of people for injuries suffered in falls while trying to walk on icy pavements. It got so bad in parts of St. Louis that postal service to homes and businesses was delayed several days.

National weather forecasters predicted a warming trend would begin by the week's end.

h. ATLANTA—AIDS in the United States is rising faster among women than men, scientists say.

The U.S. Centers for Disease Control projected that by next year AIDS would be the nation's fifth leading cause of death among American women of childbearing age. It is now seventh, according to the CDC.

i. NEWARK, N.J.—A former U.S. soldier born in Kuwait was behind bars today on charges of plotting to kill President Bush and attack military bases.

Jamal Mohamed Warrayat, 32, allegedly discussed with an undercover FBI agent plans to kill the president, as well as the Secretary of State and members of Congress.

Court papers said he also conspired, as the leader of a group of seven people, to attack unspecified military installations in North Carolina and Texas.

j. BOSTON—Children with life-threatening illnesses may be forced to undergo treatments that conflict with their family's religious beliefs, but adults can refuse medical care, the state's highest court ruled Tuesday.

The state Supreme Judicial Court ruled in separate cases involving Jehovah's Witnesses, whose religious beliefs forbid them from receiving blood transfusions.

k. SINGAPORE—Judges no longer will wear wigs while presiding in the Supreme Court and need not be called "my lord" or "your lordship."

The change in judicial etiquette took effect Sunday at the opening of the legal year. Traditional white wigs as part of court dress and formal terms of address were a holdover from British colonial days.

Judges are to be addressed simply as "your honor" in court. Chief Justice Yong Pung How said the old terms "are considered inappropriate in the context of a sovereign republic and our egalitarian society."

l. NEW DELHI, India—A remote village in the Himalayan foothills was buried under landslides and at least 170 people were killed, according to news reports Saturday.

Press Trust of India said Talai was hit by landslides after a heavy rainstorm last Monday.

At least eight bodies had been found and soldiers were helping remove boulders and other debris from the village, 140 miles northeast of New Delhi.

m. GUATEMALA CITY—A well exploded at an unfinished geothermal power station in western Guatemala, spewing rocks and earth and killing at least 21 people, officials said Sunday.

Another 30 people were reported missing under the debris of shanty homes smashed by the hail of hot stones.

n. LIMA, PERU—Police stormed a jetliner Monday night and killed an armed rebel who had hijacked the plane with 125 people aboard and held them hostage, officials said.

At least two passengers were reported injured by gunfire during the seizure of the plane, police said. It was unclear if the shots were fired by the hijacker or police.

Police identified the hijacker as Jose Soto, about 25. Passengers said he had identified himself as a rebel fighter and had demanded $125,000 in ransom.

o. KAMPALA, Uganda—Uganda's elephant population has doubled within a decade due to an intensified war against poachers and other conservation measures, according to a news report Thursday.

The New Vision newspaper quoted Eric Edroma, director of Uganda National Parks, as saying that the number of elephants has risen from 1,350 in 1980 to an estimated 3,000.

7. If you were limited to four of the stories in Exercise 6, select the four you would use and write pre-newscast teaser headlines for them. Explain why you selected them.

8. Complete the following assignments:
   a. List the television visuals you would suggest for the local stories in Exercise 4.
   b. List the visuals you would suggest for the national and international stories in Exercise 6.

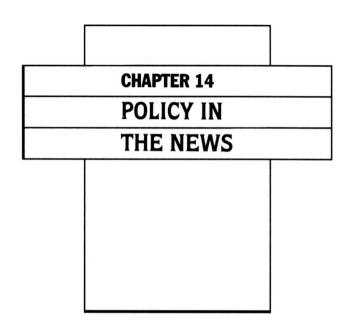

CHAPTER 14
POLICY IN
THE NEWS

"It is a significant fact that public interest in newspaper ethics and the conduct of the press was never so widespread in this country as it is today."

That quote might have been picked from the welter of criticism being leveled at American newspapers—and the press, in general—by countless and relentless critics today.

But it actually was written by Frederick Lewis Allen, social historian and editor, as the opening sentence of an essay for The Atlantic magazine in 1922.

Criticism of newspapers certainly hasn't changed much over the past six decades. There are large numbers of individuals who believe that newspapers are still unduly influenced by the whims—political, economic, ethical, social—of their owners.

Equally vocal are the critics who insist that newspapers are biased, unfair, insensitive, inaccurate and unethical, among a host of other sins both real and imaginary.

Although there is justification for some of those charges, the situation is not as diabolical as press critics would have the public believe. No newspaper would survive if it did not present a fair, accurate and balanced account of the day's events most of the time.

Few issues dominated programs at meetings of newspaper editors, publishers and reporters during the last decade as much as the issue of newspaper ethics. There was little general agreement among speakers on just what course newspapers could take to regain the confidence of readers.

One issue of The Bulletin of the American Society of Newspaper Editors reprinted a speech by Louis D. Boccardi, executive vice president of The Associated Press (AP), in which he said: "It is time for us to re-examine some of the basic assumptions we make about what we do." And he asked: "Have we reached a point where we must recognize an obligation 'not' to do some of the things the First Amendment gives us every right to do?"

On the opposite page, the Bulletin carried an article by Michael G. Gartner, then president and editorial chairman of the Des Moines Register, who countered with: "The sky isn't falling . . . what we must do is to go home and keep trying to put out the very best newspapers we know how to produce—newspapers that are fair, that are as accurate, that are as thorough, that are as newsy and as well-written as time will allow. If we do that, the public will trust us and buy us. We might not be loved, but we'll be respected."

While it is true that owners can and do influence the contents of their newspapers directly and indirectly from time to time, the same can be said for hired publishers, editors, managing editors or any person in authority at a newspaper. So it is essential that a reporter realize at the outset that most newspaper writers do not have total freedom to "do their own thing."

Every newspaper has specific policies that guide what news is reported and how it is presented to the public. Sometimes those policies are very specific and are included in the newspaper's stylebook. Some newspapers even carry the policy in their mastheads. The St. Petersburg Times, for example, states its ethical policies simply and directly: "The policy of our paper is very simple— merely to tell the truth."

Most often, however, a newspaper's policies are unwritten, and the reporter learns them through conversations with fellow reporters and editors, usually after he or she has violated one of them. Sometimes those policies are vague and may change with the circumstances of a story; other times they are blatantly obvious. For example, one newspaper may have a policy never to report divorce cases. Another may list divorces in its public record log. A third may even write news stories about divorces, especially those of prominent local persons. One newspaper may automatically support all candidates of a particular political party; another may mix its endorsements.

If a newspaper doesn't have a written policy guide for its staff, an astute reporter will learn the "policies" as quickly as possible. That does not mean a reporter should not work to change a policy, especially if it may be detrimental to the credibility of the newspaper. At one southern newspaper, for example, reporters worked for months to convince the editor to stop using the names of rape victims in news stories because they were aware the practice was resented by many readers.

But reporters should remember a newspaper is a business enterprise and can be operated as the owners see fit, no matter what the purpose, including personal, financial, political or social gain. A newspaper can promote political or other fortunes of the individual owner; the newspaper chain, if it is a part of one; or any special interests. Unfortunately, some newspapers do just that. However, responsible owners and editors will avoid any blatant misuse of the newspaper for personal reasons.

The newspaper is also—whether it wishes to be or not—a social instrument. It enters thousands of homes and is read by, or indirectly influences, every member of the family. It offers not merely news but information and entertainment. It promotes—whether it intends to or not—social, economic and political philosophies. The newspaper creates the atmosphere in which its character is nourished. Powerful and influential, it colors and infuses the character, ideals and institutions of the individual, the family and the community.

Because of its power and influence, the first duty of a newspaper is to keep its readers fully, accurately and truthfully informed. As long as it does this, a newspaper can promote its own policies without being accused of perverting the news.

In cities and towns served by only one newspaper, editors have a special responsibility to make certain they publish a wide range of opinion, not just their own. Unfortunately, it does not always work that way. Some editors take advantage of their position to force only their views on the public and exclude all others—especially opposing views. In other cases, editors are reluctant to adopt an outspoken editorial policy on controversial issues or political candidates. An editor may not want to face up to the pressure from various individuals and groups in the community, including some big advertisers. It may be that an editor sincerely believes the publication should be non-partisan and independent because it is the city's only newspaper. Rather than taking a stand, the editor may try to remain neutral by printing all the facts on all sides of public issues or campaigns for public office. However, this general policy should not prevent the editor from making certain exceptions.

When the public welfare of the community is at stake, every editor has an obligation to present and comment on the pros and cons of an issue. In such cases, the columns of the newspaper should be open to those who disagree with the newspaper's views. Even newspapers with admittedly strong partisan or other un-neutral general policies should be willing to print news and public statements that disagree with their policies. To do less would destroy the credibility of the paper.

DEVICES TO PROMOTE POLICIES

Editorials

The editorial section is generally recognized and accepted as the editor's (owner's) platform or soapbox. The editor has the same liberty to voice an opinion as the reader has to reject it.

Whether a newspaper should adopt strong policies or pursue a middle-of-the-road course—whether to attempt to shape public opinion or merely to reflect it—is an open question. Some newspapers take pride in their fighting qualities, but others boast of detached judgment. The answer is largely to be found in the personality of the editor (or owner if he or she is active as editor or publisher) and in the newspaper's circulation and advertising accounts. Some editors revel in a good fight. It wins them friends as well as enemies and perhaps a number of journalism awards for courage. Some even crusade at the risk of physical and financial danger. But, for the most part, a newspaper's editorial policy usually is determined on the basis of profitable reader appeal.

On smaller newspapers, most policy decisions are made by the owner, publisher or editor, who may be the same person. Larger newspapers may have an editorial board made up of the publisher, the editor, all the editorial writers and selected departmental editors. Some newspapers even have an advisory board of influential community leaders who regularly discuss the publication's policies with the editorial staff. Occasionally, they are called on to write columns for the editorial page as well.

Some larger newspapers also have an ombudsman, an in-house critic, who responds to letters of criticism from readers by investigating the complaints to determine their validity. Often, the ombudsman writes a column on the editorial page discussing a particular complaint. Sometimes ombudsmen are not popular with the editorial staff, especially when they are critical of how a particular story was handled by the reporter and editors. Staff members see this public discussion of their work as just another way of undermining their credibility.

One of the most difficult concepts for the public to accept is that a newspaper has the legal right to pursue any policy it pleases as long as it does not violate libel laws. In expressing editorial opinions, responsible newspapers will label them as such and confine them to the editorial page. In addition, they will publish opposing opinion.

Although some newspapers still present only their own views and opinions, many seek to balance their editorial pages by selecting columns that reflect a broad range of views. Several newspapers have selected local leaders or experts in a particular field and have asked them to express their views, which may or may not agree with the editor's stand on an issue.

On major local issues, the St. Petersburg Times, for example, often publishes its own editorial and in the next column an opposing point of view on an issue. The New York Times actively solicits diverse points of view for its "Op-Ed" page. Frequently its editors will take a particular stand on an issue in an editorial and print, on the opposite page, an article by someone diametrically opposed to the editor's view. Many other newspapers across the nation follow a similar policy. When the Gatlinburg (Tenn.) Press opposed a plan by the city council to purchase a defunct private golf course, it said so in an editorial. On the same page it permitted members of the council to tell its readers why they should vote in favor of the purchase at an upcoming city referendum.

Several newspapers have invited readers to participate in an exercise in editorial decision making by presenting a set of hypothetical situations involving the possible publication of private matters about the subject of a story. In most cases the readers tended to opt for privacy and compassion more often than the professionals. But they also tended to agree that it is difficult to produce simple, consistent, clear-cut resolutions of the ethical questions of journalism.

Other newspapers seek to accomplish the same goals through regular focus group sessions with readers. The focus groups usually are made up of a wide range of readers of the newspaper who meet regularly with an outside moderator to discuss the content of the newspaper. The moderator then reports the comments and opinions of the focus group members to the editorial staff.

The Front-Page Editorial

Occasionally, to reinforce the importance of an issue, a newspaper will print an editorial on the front page. The practice is generally accepted despite the criticism that it may be a confession of editorial-page weakness. The editorial should always be labeled as an editorial to let the reader know that he is reading an opinion, not news.

Other Policy Devices

A newspaper's policy is frequently reflected in cartoons as well as editorials. These "visual editorials" play an important part in political campaigns in particular, but they also are used most effectively to support other editorial points of view. A cartoon makes no pretense of being unbiased, as a general rule. It is frequently a frank and open criticism of an antagonist and in support of a definite policy. Patrick Oliphant, the Pulitzer Prize-winning cartoonist, told an interviewer that for him there "are no sacred cows . . . no forbidden areas. . . . If you are going to be in favor of something, you might as well not be a cartoonist."

Of course, not all editorial cartoons automatically support a particular point of view of the newspaper. Jim Borgman, editorial cartoonist for The Cincinnati Enquirer, wrote in The Bulletin of the American Society of Newspaper Editors that "at the Enquirer, to the everlasting credit of my publisher and editors, my cartoon has been allowed to roam, chancing upon the Official Editorial Stance only by coincidence. We get almost no letters that suggest readers are confused about the paper's position on issues by a contrary cartoon here and there. The signed cartoon is recognized as its own voice. What my editor may lose in control over the space, he gains in freshness, vigor and spontaneity, the stuff of debate."

Political cartoons were introduced in the American press by Thomas Nast in the mid-1800s and have since developed into a fine-art form. Many newspapers that cannot afford their own cartoonists regularly buy the work of major cartoonists, such as Oliphant, from feature syndicates. Lack of a cartoonist to support editorials of a purely local nature can sometimes handicap an editorial campaign. However, many editors employ photographs to help support editorials dealing with numerous local problems ranging from hazardous traffic conditions to slum housing.

In addition, columnists and other by-line writers may freely express opinions, and local citizens may be invited to contribute letters or articles to strengthen a campaign or crusade. Sometimes a newspaper adopts a slogan that promotes a policy.

The Newspaper Platform

Some of a newspaper's policies may be long-range programs. Others have immediate objectives. The policies of a Democratic, Republican or labor newspaper at election time may be predictable, but its responses to other issues will

FIGURE 14—1. Mike Ramirez, editorial cartoonist for The Commercial Appeal, Memphis, Tenn., turned to history for his inspiration for this biting cartoon about the rising price of oil and gas in the United States during one of the periodic oil crises that plague the nation. (Courtesy of The Commercial Appeal.)

not be. In fact, newspapers that oppose each other politically often may support the same local programs on new schools, more city recreation areas, improved street lights, higher salaries for city policemen and a host of other issues dealing with civic improvement. Many newspapers begin each year with a list of civic goals at the top of the editorial page and then campaign all year long to bring them about. All of its policies taken together, including its more permanent attitudes toward such issues as politics, constitute the newspaper's platform. It has a right to work to achieve that platform. As long as it is a constructive platform, the newspaper's policy is a powerful influence for the common good. In promoting such policy, the editorial, the cartoon, the signed article and the slogan are legitimate devices beyond question. However, a newspaper that permits its policies to influence the writing and display of the news fails in its responsibility to its community and to the journalism profession as a whole.

SLANTING THE POLICY STORY

The temptation is always present for a newspaper engaged in vigorous promotion of a policy to utilize other resources at its command. Its most potent other resource, of course, is the news column. Several methods have been used to promote a policy through the news:

1. Featuring (and somewhat overplaying) an event in line with the newspaper's policy. This may be done with a large headline, a prominent position in the newspaper and a detailed account of the event. For example, a newspaper campaigning for safe driving may put every accident—major or minor—on the front page with large headlines, saying in substance, "I told you so."

2. Ignoring or "playing down" events opposed to the newspaper's objectives. If mentioned at all, such events may be hidden under small headlines on an inside page or buried at the end of a story. If a newspaper opposes a candidate for sheriff, for example, it may give comparatively little space in which to present his or her side of the issues. If the candidate is an incumbent, the newspaper may suddenly discover, about two weeks before election time, that the county is riddled with vice and corruption. Apparently it does not expect its readers to ask why the vice and corruption had not been exposed months or even years earlier. Such transparent attempts to support a candidate by misleading readers can badly damage a newspaper's credibility.

3. Deliberately writing the news to emphasize certain points in a story while omitting others, thus interpreting an event so that it will best suit the newspaper's policy. Sometimes, unfortunately, facts themselves may be distorted or falsified. For example, suppose a speaker should say: "The working man does not deserve unemployment insurance. He deserves employment insurance, and it is the duty of the employer to see that he gets it." If, to make the speaker look bad, a reporter should play up the first sentence and purposely ignore the second, one would conclude that the speaker is against labor. Good reporting and honest newspaper policy would condemn such a purposely colored account.

4. Editorializing in the news. For example, if a newspaper favors a reduction in the tax rate, it may always refer to the existing *high* tax rate, taking for granted that everyone agrees the rate is high. The newspaper's opinions may be injected throughout the story in this manner. A review of some of the newspaper stories written about the increases in second-class postal rates would serve to illustrate this point extremely well.

5. Writing special stories deliberately designed to support the newspaper's policy. For example, the newspaper can always find prominent local persons or special-interest groups who agree with a given policy. These persons are interviewed, and their statements are prominently displayed in the newspapers. Persons against the policy are not usually interviewed, or their opposition is played down. Another example: If a newspaper wants to force an investigation of conditions at the jail, a local mental hospital or a nursing home, it might arrange to have a reporter locked up in the jail, committed to the hospital or hired at the nursing home to expose the "disgraceful" conditions that exist. Some editors consider such devices unethical.

Reporters should remember that under the law people who gather news have no more rights than ordinary citizens. They cannot break a law in pursuit of a story even if the person or institution they are investigating may be breaking the law.

JUSTIFICATION OF POLICIES IN NEWS STORIES

What are the justifications, if any, for promoting a policy by means of the news? Are all of the devices mentioned in the preceding section to be condemned? Obviously so, if their intent is to deceive. Obviously so, if their use prevents the complete, accurate and truthful presentation of the news. Under certain circumstances, however, there is some excuse—if not justification—for the influence of policy on the news.

Subjectivity

Few readers, but all editors, know that the process of gathering and writing news is subjective, despite all efforts to make it objective. The selection of assignments, the reporters picked to cover them and their approaches to handling stories are based on a series of value judgments. It is a cliche in the news business that seven reporters sent to cover the same speech probably will produce seven entirely different interpretations of that speech.

Although this may be an overstatement, it is based on sound observation. Theoretically, a speech has but one interpretation and that is the meaning that the speaker intends to convey. Actually, each person in the audience, including the reporter, may get a different impression of a speaker's message. A careful reporter will focus on the most significant point or points the speaker makes, using quotations from the speaker to support the reporter's interpretation. Despite vast experience in covering speeches, a reporter may give a speech story a slant quite different from what the speaker had intended. Yet the reporter is reporting the facts as seen and heard.

The complete objectivity necessary to perfect reporting has yet to be achieved by any reporter. All facts reported to newspaper readers must pass through the mind of the reporter. Every reporter observes events and understands facts against the screen of experience and through the film of human emotions. This human frailty plagues every reporter and all newspapers, but a reporter must not use this as an excuse for faulty or dishonest work.

Self-Censorship

Most newspapers practice self-censorship. Often this is dictated by what the editor considers good taste as well as by contemporary community standards. Although it is true that standards tend to grow more liberal, most editors make a serious effort not to offend the sensibilities of their readers. Obscene language used during a trial, the gruesome details of a brutal murder, the "inside" story behind a politician's downfall, or the "real dope" about the divorce of a prominent citizen may be censored from the story. The reader may not be given all the information about reported events or reports on all events. The newspaper to this extent fails to report the news fully.

Just how far this censorship on behalf of "decency" should go is debatable. Often, it may not be the public's taste as much as the editor's that generates the censorship. An Ohio editor was dismissed for allowing an infamous four-letter word to remain in a quote by a man known for the use of that type of language, despite the fact that only a handful of readers complained. The publisher, however, felt the use of the word was bad for the image of the paper and dismissed the editor. In practicing self-censorship, a newspaper must take care that it does not use this power on behalf of a special interest or a special cause. If it does, its policy reporting will be indefensible.

The Moral Purpose

Another excuse for faulty reporting and for allowing policy to influence the news may be the intention to do good. A story may purposely be warped to emphasize a moral—to teach a lesson. Many feature stories become nearly fiction in the process of passing from the scene of action through the reporter's mind, aglow with an honest (or possibly dishonest) emotion, to reach the printed page. Literary license is taken with the facts in many stories to stir readers. Sometimes it may be as "innocent" as the ever-recurring faithful dog story in which a dog allegedly saves its young master from drowning. In actual fact, the dog may have plunged in only when its master staggered into shallow water. Yet many reporters cannot resist the temptation to make a hero of the dog. Photographers rush to the home for the traditional boy-dog picture. Is no harm done? Does it make a good story? Maybe. But is it true? After all, the function of the newspaper is to present the news fully, accurately and truthfully, and this type of story is neither accurate nor truthful.

There is another hazard in stretching fact for a so-called moral purpose. Sometimes the well-meaning story can backfire. In one case out of the books on libel, a newspaper was found guilty of libeling a family it had tried to help. The father was out of work and the family without much food when the youngest child died. In an effort to help the family, the newspaper printed a sad and touching story of the family's misfortunes, including a statement that the child would have to be buried in a pauper's grave alongside the remains of drunks and derelicts. In the rush of emotion and a desire to move the readers to help the family, the reporter overstated the family's plight. The family sued, charging that it had been held up to ridicule through no fault of its own. The jury agreed and found the paper guilty of libel.

Dilemma in Weighing Stories

Another excuse for playing up a story on behalf of a policy may be found in an occasional dilemma. When two stories are of approximately equal value, it is almost too much to expect a city editor to bury the policy story. For example, if the newspaper is campaigning for a bond issue, the whole editorial staff might value the policy stories more highly than competing stories. Every item bearing on the need for the bond issue may appear to be important. In weighing stories that have a bearing on newspaper policies, the newspaper cannot excuse itself like a judge whose son is to be tried for murder. Must it not either favor its own child or commit the equal error of "leaning over backward"? Here again the reporter and the staff need almost superhuman objectivity to present the news fully, accurately and truthfully.

A problem sometimes arises when an editor, seeking to please the owner or publisher, gives special treatment to certain stories he or she thinks will please the publisher. Such a story may not have any real news value that given day, yet it may be prominently displayed, perhaps even on page 1. Often organizations deliberately name publishers to their boards in an attempt to gain favorable treatment in the newspaper. And they are quite successful, because many editors would not risk playing down a story they believe might be a "sacred cow" of the publisher.

In pursuing a policy, the newspaper and the reporter have an opportunity to serve the community by placing emphasis on fullness, accuracy and honesty in reporting. A policy to promote worthy causes may indeed be noble. But a newspaper that vigorously promotes the local community chest fund drive year after year but never carefully checks how much of that money goes for campaign overhead compared to how much is used to really help the people of the community is not reporting fully, accurately and honestly.

The issues reported in the press are too commonly the plain and unvarnished facts. They lack the intelligible background that an enterprising reporter would gather from library investigations, from studies of experiences of other communities, and from other sources of information. Reporters should never forget that not all newsworthy material is collected on the regular beats. The encyclopedia, librarian, schoolteacher and scientific laboratories are rich in background material outside the established boundaries of news beats. The reporter can offer a service to the community of a rare order of usefulness if he or she will utilize the cultural tools the community offers. In many cases the average citizen lacks the time and ability to use those tools, but in the hands of an enterprising reporter they can help report not only accurately and truthfully but also with the fullness needed by people trying to manage their own processes of government.

EXERCISES

1. Invite the publisher of the local newspaper to class for a dicsussion on the newspaper's policies about such important local issues as local property and sales taxes as opposed to an income tax, bond issues for public building projects, school consolidation and other significant issues. Write a news story on that class discussion.

2. After that visit, examine the newspaper carefully for a month to find examples of stories that might promote one of the policies the publisher discussed. Clip the

examples and paste them on a separate sheet of paper. Make marginal notes and point out material in them that specifically supports the newspaper's policy as you understand it from the publisher's class visit.

3. Examine the newspaper carefully for a month to find any stories or editorial columns or comment that might be critical of action by public officials who disagree with the newspaper's policy or editorial stand. Clip the examples and paste them on separate sheets of paper. Make marginal notes and point out material in them that shows that the newspaper disagrees with the action under consideration by public officials.

4. Study the locally written editorials in any newspaper available to you, but preferably a local paper. Clip at least six of them, paste them on separate sheets and in the margins point out the statements that indicate what the paper's policy is.

5. On those same editorial pages count the number of letters to the editor and guest columns that are printed opposing the editorial stand of the newspaper.

6. In every community there are many rumors that the editor does or does not allow to be printed in the newspaper. Collect as many of those rumors as you can. Then interview the local editor about them. Ask why some rumors are printed and others are not. Write a report on that interview.

7. Organize your own focus group of about six persons. Make it as balanced as possible, perhaps an undergraduate and a graduate student, a faculty member, a non-academic staff person, an hourly employee and so on. Ask them to read the daily paper critically for a week. Then meet with them and examine the paper, page by page, story by story, to elicit their comments, praise, criticisms and suggestions. Write a report detailing their likes and dislikes and suggestions for improving the paper.

8. Invite two or three persons who have been the subjects of articles in the local or campus newspaper to class to discuss their views on how fair and accurate the stories about them were.

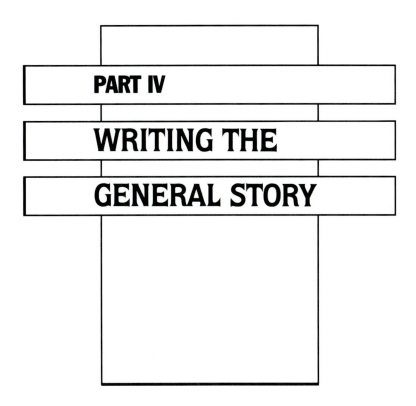

PART IV

WRITING THE

GENERAL STORY

Newspaper reporters and editors tend to label stories by subject—crime, politics, religion, sports, business, education, entertainment and so on. The label is a convenient way for the staff to classify stories. It also is a quick indicator of what department will handle a particular story and where it probably will appear in the newspaper.

Three types of stories, however, are most general in nature because they are not confined to a particular subject. They are personals and briefs; speeches, publications and interviews; and meetings and occasions. All are different types from the standpoint of categories. But all are used in connection with every subject covered by a newspaper. A personal item may grow out of a court story just as a speech story could feature a coach or a prominent businessman, for example.

It is important that these general types of stories be considered before the reporter studies the various "simple" and "complex" stories dealing with specific subjects.

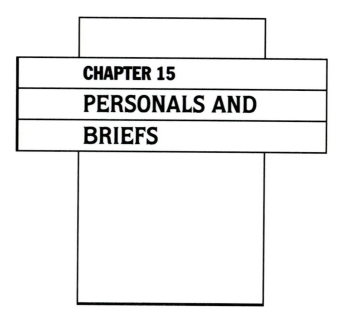

CHAPTER 15
PERSONALS AND BRIEFS

When the Charlotte (N.C.) Observer sought to gain circulation outside its core market, its editors talked to readers in those areas where suburban newspapers were pushing "hometown" news. They asked what the Observer should offer them to compete successfully with the community newspapers. Among their suggestions were one-year birthdays, anniversaries, Little League, obituaries and wedding announcements. In short, more personal news.

The readers were reminding the editors that it is important for them to know who got married, who came to visit, who won the trophies in the recreation league baseball playoffs and who made the dean's list. They were stating one of the ancient truths of the newspaper profession: Names make news.

Most newspapers, especially community newspapers, carry numerous short stories, often no more than a sentence or two, that are generally called "personals" or "briefs." Some collect them in "People" columns. Others use them as individual stories with their own headlines.

As a general rule, metropolitan newspapers carry briefs or personal items about only the most prominent persons. Frequently those items are collected in a column. However, community newspapers usually carry briefs and personals about practically everyone in town.

Many community newspaper editors say that personals are the best-read stories in their newspapers. Personals may be grouped into a column with a single headline in the family living or lifestyle section, or they may be scattered through the regular news sections. Occasionally an editor or one of the staff may write a personal column and use brief items about citizens in the community. The use and placement of briefs or personals is unlimited.

Briefs and personals serve several important purposes: They provide information on activities of various citizens as well as social, civic and religious groups in the community, and they can be used to facilitate makeup by filling in small spaces left after longer stories are placed on pages. Even when serving this last purpose, they should be written with the same care and effort that go into the main story each day. A mistake in a name, an address or a fact in a personal item is just as serious as a similar mistake in any page-1 story.

Personals and briefs are arbitrarily classified here as a separate story type. Actually, they are a type only in the sense that they emphasize personalities and are short. Otherwise they are relatively unimportant in news value in relation to the news value of the page-1 stories. In subject matter, personals and briefs range the entire spectrum of human activity. All of the subject-matter story types discussed more fully in later chapters are represented among them. At some newspapers they are considered to be merely elementary stories that the beginning reporters is often assigned to write. However, every seasoned reporter knows their value and regularly collects them.

PERSONALS

Names make news. This is a newspaper cliche, but it is also true. And they do not always have to be prominent names. Newspapers have always recognized the news value of names of quite ordinary persons. The names of visitors; guests; committee members; and those sponsoring or attending dinners, banquets, conventions and so on are usually listed by newspapers as fully as space permits. Lack of space, not failure to recognize the essential news value of names, excludes many of these smaller items from newspapers in larger cities. However, a number of metropolitan newspapers use such items as fillers in place of buying filler material from the news syndicates.

Announcements of trips, visitors, parties, newcomers and a large assortment of relatively minor events that take place in any community are considered to be personals. The lifestyle pages or family pages (discussed in Chapter 27) often use many such items, but other personals are used throughout the paper as one-, two- and three-paragraph stories with headlines.

News Value

It is often difficult to classify personal items by the standard tests for news value—disaster, progress, conflict and so forth—although a careful study of them will show that in a minor way they may fall into those categories. Mrs. Nancy Parker goes to the hospital, and that might border on disaster for her family. David Thomas is made a first-class petty officer in the Navy, and that suggests progress. If these items were of greater consequence, they would be expanded into longer stories, stories to be classified as illness, death or business. They are very seldom novelties. They contain little human interest of an emotional or dramatic nature. They might represent borderline eminence—that is, if they were about a reasonably well-known local person.

Why run them? Personals, as a class of story, would seem to be a composite of all the news values. Individually, they may be of little consequence except to the persons immediately involved; yet collectively they record life in any community on a very fundamental level. They contain virtually all human interests—gossip, birth, death, illness, conflict and the rest. They give the readers of any newspaper a daily look at the activities of their fellow citizens, not just the prominent ones. And they are extremely well read.

The most common characteristic of most personals is that they are quite local in nature. If a member of a local social club is planning an event—plant sale, card party or fashion show—it is local news of a personal type. A similar event in a community 50 miles away would mean nothing. The personal, then, is a standard item in the columns of newspapers in smaller communities. It is usually unnecessary to belong to an organization or take part in a major news event to be mentioned in the news columns of a small-town newspaper—daily or weekly. A shopping trip to a nearby city or the purchase of a new tractor may be sufficient for one to get his or her name in the local newspaper in many small communities. In the large city dailies the personal is somewhat confined to the more or less prominent persons, the activities of local groups and clubs, and the personalities of so-called high society. Rural or urban newspapers, however, consider the personal items as an important reader-interest and circulation builder.

Sources of Personals

Most personals are telephoned, mailed or brought to the newspaper office by interested persons. Hostesses report their party plans, themes and guest lists. Mothers announce schools or vacation plans for their children. Families report on out-of-town visitors. Dinners, parties and other social events are similarly brought to the family editor of the paper. The mail brings a steady stream of press releases from vacation hotels, convention centers and other tourist attractions reporting the local persons who visited there recently. Every regular beat yields personals and briefs to the alert reporter. Public officials and employees go on business trips and vacations. They have children going off to school, babies at home. Behind the public front of every person on every beat are many personal items of interest. Hobbies, along with other recreation and sports activities, are fertile fields for personals. On a rare occasion a personal item can lead to an even bigger story. The social activities and travels of a midwestern state official some years ago piqued the interest of a beat reporter who eventually discovered that the official had stolen $14 million from the state.

One community editor reports that she takes a notepad with her everywhere, even to church, and records items about individuals that later appear in the "Personals" column in her paper. Her reporters are required to bring personals in from their beats, and many readers phone or mail in items for the column. "It's one of our most popular features," she said.

Writing Personals

The personal should be written as a straight news story. It should have a well-written lead and contain all the necessary information to make the story complete. The lead requires:

1. The five W's. These are essential in all stories, of course, though some of them may be implied in the lead.
2. Identification of the person or persons mentioned. If a long list of persons is given (for example, the names of new club members), do not try to use them all in the lead. Write a more general lead and include the names in the second paragraph along with their identification. But if the item reports the activities of only one or two individuals, each should be identified. Wherever possible, a descriptive identity should be included to intensify reader interest. The descriptive identity, lacking in the first of the following personals, is underlined in the second item.

> Mrs. Gaylord Hampton, 1202 Briarcliff Ave., is making a month-long auto trip through the Southwest.

> Mrs. Gaylord Hampton, 1202 Briarcliff Ave., whose Southern cookbook was published in June, is making a month-long motor trip through the Southwest. She will collect recipes for a Chicano cookbook.

> Evelyn Biggs, 2412 Bradford Ln., is touring southern Louisiana for two weeks with her granddaughter, Shannon.

> Evelyn Biggs, 2412 Bradford Ln., whose photographs of life in the Smoky Mountains have been reproduced in national newspapers and magazines, is touring southern Louisiana for two weeks with her granddaughter, Shannon. She plans to photograph a day in the life of a Cajun family that will be used in a book on ethnic Americans to be published next fall.

Here is how to handle a personal with a long list of names:

> Eight members of the Clay County Garden Club will exhibit floral arrangements in the Piedmont Flower Show in Raleigh next month.
> They are: (List the club members and their addresses. If descriptions of the floral arrangements are available, include them. But do not include any if you cannot include all of them.)

> Ten members of the Recreation Department's Ceramics Club will enter their work in a juried crafts show sponsored by the Southern Guild of Folk Artists in Asheville next month.
> They are: (List the club members and their addresses. If descriptions of their ceramic pieces are available, include them. Do not include descriptions of some pieces and not others.)

Stressing an Interesting Feature

Reporters should always look for interesting features when writing personals and not be satisfied to use only the basic five W's. To say that "The Rev. Thomas O'Neal will leave for Rome Friday" is interesting to friends and members of his church. But what is he planning to do in Rome? Is he just on vacation? Is he attending a church meeting? Will he be going to school there? The minister probably would be willing to answer a few questions, and the reporter may find an interesting feature somewhere.

The following is an example of how a personal item might be improved by adding a few details:

> Bobby Mason, daughter of Mr. and Mrs. Jackson Mason, 117 Maplewood St., has been named to the dean's list at the University of the Pacific, Stockton, Calif.

> Bobby Mason, 117 Maplewood, a senior accounting major at the University of the Pacific, Stockton, Calif., has been named to the dean's list for the seventh quarter in a row. She is the daughter of Mr. and Mrs. Jackson Mason.

In writing a personal, every effort should be made to avoid referring to persons by such terms as "widely known," "popular" and "beloved." (In newspaper offices, such words are called "puffs.") This is not only poor writing, but also editorializing and should not be permitted in personals or briefs, just as it should not be permitted in any straight news story.

BRIEFS

It is often difficult to distinguish between a personal and a brief. Perhaps the best distinction between them is that briefs generally do not pertain to persons. The change in city library hours, the post office's holiday schedule, dates for obtaining new auto licenses, announcements of minor fund-raising events and dozens of other short but newsworthy items would be classified as briefs.

Briefs are usually one- or two-paragraph stories dealing with incidents or occasions having broad or limited appeal. Naturally, the wider the appeal—perhaps the closing of public buildings for a holiday—the more prominently they will be displayed in a newspaper. Briefs may be rewrites from other papers or new stories picked up by beat reporters or phoned in by interested persons. They are used because they are news, and they may be grouped together in a "News Briefs" column or used as fillers throughout the paper.

It is difficult to establish a dividing line between a brief and a longer, more important story. An event worthy of no more than two paragraphs in some newspapers may be "blown up," with the inclusion of more details, to five or six paragraphs in other newspapers. The size of the community and its newspaper, the availability of local news and the interest of the readers are factors to be considered by the reporter. A story's relative significance—the proportion of readers it will interest—is the major space-measuring device for the reporter.

Here is an example of a brief from a community newspaper:

> The Twentieth Century Club will hold a rummage sale Oct. 4, 5 and 6 at its clubhouse, 1722 Washington Ave.
> Sale hours Oct. 4 and 5 will be from 9 a.m. to 5 p.m. Oct. 6 the hours will be from 9 to 11:30 a.m.

Like a personal, a brief is obviously a single-feature story—and hardly more than a lead at that. The five W's, with the proper play given to the most important

W, usually compose the whole story. Further explanation of one or more of the W's may call for a second paragraph.

Careless reporting, notably the lack of an inquiring attitude, sometimes makes potentially long stories into briefs. If the beginning reporter becomes too "brief"-conscious, feeling that every story should be told in two paragraphs, he or she may fail to ask the kinds of questions that could develop a possible page-1 story. On the other hand, insignificant news events should not purposely be blown up or overplayed.

FILLERS

The standardization of advertising format in recent years and the trend toward six-column makeup throughout newspapers has reduced some of the need for fillers. However, many editors still are faced with awkward and often tiny spaces to be filled, especially above advertisements.

Some newspapers use briefs and personals to fill those spaces. Others keep on hand a supply of very short items to "plug" those holes. Such fillers are usually inserted without headlines. They usually contain information, perhaps trivia, rather than news in its classic sense.

Fillers come from a variety of sources, but the most common source is a news feature service (syndicate). A number of organizations, such as the National Geographic Society or the American Cancer Society, distribute fillers free to newspapers. Other special-interest groups include them in their press kits or publicity releases.

A number of newspapers develop their own fillers from almanacs, government reports, census data, history books and encyclopedias. They are selected with some care to present unusual facts, "fascinating" information or descriptive items highlighting the local community. Many newspapers coordinate fillers with the general subject of the page or section of the newspaper in which they are used. Fillers about food are placed on the food pages, and so on. Humor and quotes from famous people also are used as fillers.

Here are some examples:

> Be a reading tutor:
> Call 623-1336

> "A little learning is not a dangerous thing to one who does not mistake it for a great deal." —William Allen White

> Marion County has 117 churches representing every major religious denomination.

> Life has its disappointments but there is no reason to be one of them.

> State Park Information: 8 a.m. to 5 p.m., Mon.-Fri., 753-2027.

> To prevent food from sticking to a new fry pan, boil a little vinegar in it before using it the first time.

CONTRIBUTE TO THE COMMUNITY CHEST

BUY U.S. SAVINGS BONDS

Other newspapers use the space at the end of columns and above advertisements to promote the paper and some of its services. Here are several examples:

What's Sunday without The Daily News?

The New York Times Magazine
Illuminates the news.

The Plain Talk's Classifieds
Work for you—619-3354

EXERCISES

1. Using at least three large daily newspapers and three community newspapers available in your college library, compare their use of briefs and personals. Write a 250-word report on your findings.

2. Clip from any daily or weekly newspaper available to you six personals or briefs and make a sample news analysis of each.

3. Many community dailies and weekly newspapers employ country or rural correspondents who are paid by the inch for their contributions. Clip from several newspapers two or three examples of such columns. Paste them on a separate sheet of paper and circle each example of overwriting resulting from the use of cliches such as "beloved" and "a good time was had by all" and others discussed in this chapter.

4. There are flaws in each of the briefs and personals that follow. On a separate sheet of paper answer the following questions about each: What additional questions would you ask in an attempt to get an adequate, interesting story? Which statements would you eliminate from each as it is now written, and why?

   a. Friends will be sorry to learn of the death of Jackson (Big Jack) Driskill, husband of Addie Allen Driskill, and brother of Mrs. Barton (Effie) Hicks, Summerville. Mr. Driskill had resided in Sparta for several years.

   b. Rhoda and Mike Scuggs are the new parents of a beautiful little daughter, who arrived just 10 minutes after midnight Friday in Memorial Hospital. She weighed in at eight pounds and nine ounces and has been named Traci Marie. She reportedly has a very healthy set of lungs, according to grandma, Mrs. Willie V. Presnell.

   c. There will be a planning meeting at Stanley Memorial Library, Friday, at 2 p.m., for the classes of 1929, 30, 31 and 32 for a reunion set for October 20.

   d. The Town and Country Home Extension Club will have their monthly meeting Wednesday, Sept. 26, at 1:30 p.m. at the home of Mrs. Dorothy Ricks, Sweetwater. The members will meet at Cora Brown's at 1 p.m. Hostesses will be Ruth Emrick and Anna Belle Chapman.

   e. Tommy Cureton and Janie Lunsford have returned from a week's vacation in the Bahamas, where they were guests at the Princess Towers Hotel. They flew to Fort Lauderdale, Fla., where they boarded the ship Discover One. On their return they were guests at the Sheraton Resort in Fort Lauderdale.

5. Write personals or briefs from the following notes:
   a. The General Federation of Women's Clubs
      East Mound City chapter
      Will meet at Noon, Friday
      At the Holiday Inn-West
      Speakers will be Robert Nease,
      Executive director of the Chamber of Commerce
      Sherri Turner, Mound City recycling coordinator
      Program leader and hostesses are
      Sarah Brown, Hope Henderson, Nell Colzales
         (Source: Sarah Brown, secretary of club)
   b. Descendants of Gen. John Logan
      Civil War general and political leader
      Will have a family reunion
      At Southern Illinois University
      On October 25
      In Morris Fieldhouse
      A new photo book highlighting
      The general's military career
      Will be published in
      Conjunction with the reunion
      Call 623-8262 for more information
         (Source: Andrew Logan, Carbondale lawyer)
   c. William Blount Chapter
      Daughters of American Revolution
      Will sponsor annual bake sale
      Western Plaza Shopping Center
      9 a.m. to 3 p.m. Saturday
      To raise funds for chapter's
      Annual High School Essay Contest
      On "What Freedom Means to Me"
      Contest sponsored in conjunction
      With County Historical Society
      More than 300 high school seniors
      Submitted essays last year
         (Source: Etta Layman, chapter president)
   d. Dr. Nelson Ridley and
      Iva Jean Ridley, retired
      Franklin College faculty
      To present slide show
      Documenting the civil rights
      Movement in the city during
      The 1960s and early 1970s
      At annual meeting of
      Cumberland County chapter
      Of National Conference of
      Christians and Jews
      At 7 p.m., Saturday
      At the Hyatt Regency

They will also discuss
Personalities and politicians
Who shaped events
During that period
>(Source: NCCJ public relations chair, Bradley Whitman)

e. Alice Hoffman, retired
First-grade teacher
Will sign copies of her book
"May I Be Excused"
From 2 to 4 p.m. Saturday
At Dickens Book Store
Franklin Square Shopping Center
Book is a collection of
Stories and anecdotes of
Her 42 years as a teacher
Of first graders in
Cocke County Schools
>(Source: Grady Cantrell, bookstore owner)

6. Using material available to you in the college or city library or from the local chamber of commerce, write at least six fillers containing information about your city.

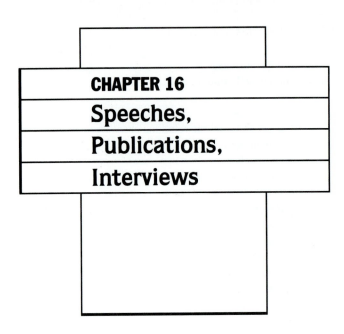

CHAPTER 16
Speeches, Publications, Interviews

News stories generated by speeches, press conferences, interviews and articles in professional journals or magazines add reader interest and often excitement to every newspaper. These stories may be vastly different in subject matter, but they all have something in common.

Basically, they are one-source stories that are a collection of direct and indirect quotations from the source. In most, only a minimum of material is provided by the writer through research. Rarely do they include any interpretation on the part of the writer. These stories require skillful handling to keep them from being dull.

Too many times, a reporter will settle for writing a straight news story on a speech, press conference or interview when a feature story might be more lively and interesting. This is especially true if the subject is not very articulate (and many subjects aren't). But they are legitimate sources because of their public position or personality.

SPEECHES

While speech stories are a staple in American newspapers, they often are neglected as "just another routine story" unless they are speeches given by major public figures. Many of these stories are poorly written because the reporter lacks interest in the assignment.

Covering a speech and writing a story about it can be exacting. It takes considerable skill to report a 7,500-word speech in 300 words and still give the reader an accurate report of what was said. It takes time, thought, hard work and writing talent.

For example, a reporter assigned to cover a meeting in Washington, where the speaker was to review the book "The Spanish Armada," took the assignment on with dread. But it was a "must" assignment. The meeting, sponsored by a Washington women's group made up of the wives of prominent federal officials, congressional leaders and military commanders, drew a stellar crowd of senators, representatives, cabinet officials and admirals and generals to a church hall across the street from the White House. The speaker didn't like the book and said so pointedly. The reporter, casting around for a way to handle what was basically a rather dull event, decided to use a feature lead. Here it is:

> The Spanish Armada was sunk again today—across the street from the White House.
> While two generals of the army, several four-star admirals, a marine commandant and what appeared to be a platoon of highly decorated Air Force brass looked on, Spain's glorious fleet was sent to the bottom in 35 minutes, with time for questions and answers. . . .

The remainder of the relatively short story focused on direct quotes from the reviewer as he told why the book was, for him at least, dreadful. The final paragraph gave some details of the club and its membership to help the reader understand why there were so many prominent individuals in the audience at a program sponsored by a social club. A basically dull assignment was turned into a lively short feature because the reporter used his imagination.

Some reporters dislike being assigned to cover speeches because speakers often are not very good and what they have to say is not very interesting. Yet every speech, no matter who is giving it or what is said, offers a chance for a reporter to show his or her resourcefulness and talent as a writer.

All speeches, whether formal addresses on special occasions or impromptu remarks during an unstructured gathering, are handled very much alike. The reporter must consider the following three elements:

1. The speaker
2. The audience
3. The speech.

A fourth consideration is the possible interpretation that any of the three elements may need. The proportion of the story to be devoted to each element varies with the comparative importance of each, but no speech story is complete without all three. Generally, in speech stories the emphasis should be put on what is said.

The speaker should be properly identified in the lead. Sometimes this can be done with a title or a short sentence. If more identification is needed, it can be in the body of the story. This is an amplification of the basic principle of identifying persons named in the news. The reader needs to know who the speaker is and why his or her statements are worth quoting. Even a description of the speaker's distinctive characteristics and manner of emphasizing certain points is sometimes woven into the story to give it more color. But this type of material should not be used in an attempt to hold the speaker up to ridicule.

The audience also should be described. How many people were there? Who were they? Why did they meet? The reporter looks over the crowd, talks with the leaders, and reads any available program carefully to help answer those questions. The names of persons in the audience need not be given unless it would be of interest to the reader to know the names of a few of the more prominent ones, but the reporter should tell whether they are bankers, teachers, taxpayers or miners. These facts are implied, of course, at regular meetings of civic clubs and similar organizations, when nothing more than the name of the organization is required. Audience reaction is also frequently worth noting.

The speech—what the speaker had to say—is the most important of the three elements. "What is the most important thing the speaker said?" is the first question that a reporter should ask when starting to write the story. Two reporters covering the same speech may not agree on what the most important thing is. Here are leads on two stories covering the same speech by former U.S. Secretary of Agriculture Earl Butz:

> The profit motive is responsible for Americans ''only having to spend 17 percent of their take-home pay for food,'' former U.S. Secretary of Agriculture Earl Butz said here Tuesday.
>
> ''Think of it. Food is still a bargain. Less than 17 percent of take-home pay. That's less than any other place in the world,'' Butz told about 500 agriculture equipment dealers meeting at the Opryland Hotel.
>
> ''You've got to stand up and say it is the greatest bargain we've got in America and do it now before we start coming under political attacks this summer,'' Butz urged the group.

> Earl Butz, the former U.S. agriculture secretary who toppled from his post after telling racist and ethnic jokes, called here last night for more profit incentives in the agriculture industry.
>
> In addition, Butz attacked Sen. Edward Kennedy, food price controls, policies on food stamps, and the Environmental Protection Agency—and he interrupted his speech to tell a sexist joke about kindergarten boys regarding their female teacher's anatomy.
>
> He compared the windfall profits tax on oil companies to ''penalties'' placed on the agriculture industry, saying that like the oil companies, farmers as well as middle men in the food business need more profit incentives.

Some interpretation of one or more of the three necessary elements may be needed. Perhaps the audience is not as representative as it appears to be for the occasion. Applause may be staged by partisan supporters of the speaker. Perhaps the speaker has affiliations or a record that should be presented to clarify his or her significance. Perhaps the speech content should be related to larger national movements, editorial campaigns or other programs. Frequently the speech will have significance in local issues. For example, if the speech concerns public reaction and if the community is campaigning for a national park, a story ignoring this relationship would be inadequate and noninterpretative. Interpretation, however, must avoid editorializing. The interpretative reporter is not authorized to express an opinion. Interpretation must be merely the presentation of pertinent facts to give the reader a clearer picture.

Getting the Speaker's Words

Ideally, a reporter should obtain an advance copy of a speech. However, many speakers do not provide advance copies, so the reporter has to attend the speech and make extensive notes. Most reporters do not take stenographic notes of everything the speaker says. Usually they make notes only on the important statements and arguments or points made by the speaker.

A careful reporter will make every effort to place only the speaker's exact words within quotation marks, particularly in matters that may be controversial. Many reporters like to tape a speech while taking notes to make certain the quotes are exact. Because direct quotations tend to add emphasis, the reporter should avoid quoting routine, obvious or minor points from speeches. Accurate paraphrasing is usually sufficient to convey the less important elements of a speech.

However, a reporter should not paraphrase too much. Direct quotes should be used liberally throughout a speech story. Under no circumstances should a reporter turn in a speech story with few or no direct quotes.

A speech may have one or several features just as any other type of story. In organizing the material, the reporter should look for the central theme, the logical division and unusual or provocative quotes. A good speech will have all of those elements. However, the reporter does not have to play up the central theme if some other aspect of the speech may have more reader appeal.

THE SPEECH STORY LEAD

On most speech stories, the lead should feature the most important point the speaker made. That is the whole point—to focus on the most newsworthy element of the speech. It can be done by using direct quotations, indirect quotations or interpretation. Summarizing the entire speech in the lead is acceptable; however, it can result in a long and dull lead. Summary leads should be used sparingly on speech stories. Here are several examples of speech leads:

> Former House Speaker Jim Wright told a Nashville audience Wednesday the budget crisis will not be resolved until the nation's leaders come to terms with taxes and their constituents.
> People in political life have been mesmerized into an inordinate fear of facing the American people squarely and saying, "This is what it's going to take," Wright told the audience of about 400 at Vanderbilt University's Langford Auditorium.
> Wright, who resigned under a cloud of ethics allegations last year, said the legacy of Walter Mondale's failed 1984 presidential bid created a myth in Washington, D.C., that the American people would not support any candidate who told them tax increases were necessary to reduce the national debt.
> "I don't believe that," he said. "That sells the American people short. . . ."

"Racism is a disease that infiltrates everyone's life," Nathan Rutstein, author of "To Be One: A Battle Against Racism," told a symposium of civil rights activists here today.

"Almost everybody is infected or affected by the disease," he said. "We are fooling ourselves if we think we are not."

Both the North and the South botched their chances to transform Southern society after the Civil War, historian Shelby Foote said Friday as the Southern Festival of Books got underway.

"The North missed its chance to be gallant, and the South had a chance to make things work legally, but instead, it instituted a system of peonage that in many ways was worse than slavery," Foote told a noontime crowd in the War Memorial Auditorium.

Secretary of State James Baker warned Iraq Monday the United States may attack if it continues to occupy Kuwait.

"Saddam Hussein must realize there is a limit to the international community's patience," Baker said in a tough talk to the World Affairs Council in Los Angeles. "Let no one doubt we will not rule out a possible use of force."

ORLANDO, Fla.—Supreme Court nominee David Souter did the right thing by "throwing off more fog than San Francisco Bay" during his Senate confirmation hearings, said Robert Bork, whose outspoken views cost him a seat on the high court three years ago.

Bork, speaking Friday to the Economics Club of Orlando, said the best way for potential justices to survive the confirmation process is to be vague on key issues on which they might rule.

"Liberals would have generated a storm over nobody knowing what he thinks," Bork said.

Here are some exceptions to the rule of featuring the most important point the speaker made in the lead: (1) If the speaker is very prominent, his or her name may be featured in the lead without focusing on the most important thing said; (2) if the occasion itself is important or embraces several speeches; (3) if the entire program is keynoted or has a central theme. The following examples illustrate the exceptions:

Mother Teresa, Calcutta's "Saint of the Gutters," opened the United Nations' Conference on World Hunger today.

The Nobel Peace Prize winner told delegates from 130 nations that . . .

Delegates to the United Nations' Conference on World Hunger today heard Mother Teresa, Calcutta's "Saint of the Gutters," describe how millions of people are starving each year.

The Nobel Peace Prize winner spoke at the opening session of the conference, which was attended by representatives from 130 nations.

The responsibility of rich nations to help feed the world's starving masses was the theme of the speakers who took part in the opening of the United Nations' Conference on World Hunger today.

These exceptions, however, are not strictly speech leads. They are leads for meetings and conventions. They bracket several speeches and lay the groundwork for speeches to follow. They should be used sparingly because they tend to be more general than specific.

THE BODY OF THE SPEECH STORY

The body of the speech story should be direct quotations, indirect quotations and interpretative summaries of the speech. They should be fairly well balanced, but the writer should remember that direct quotes often carry more impact than indirect quotes or summaries. Readers respond more favorably to direct quotes because they give a story more authority.

Quote-Summary-Quote Story

Newspaper reporters have over the years developed a popular form for stories containing a large number of direct quotes. Commonly referred to as a "quote-summary-quote" story, it can best be described in this example and accompanying diagram:

The Diagram	The Written Story
Lead summarizes all or emphasizes a major feature of the speech as this example does.	Changes in society are creating strains on family relations that could eventually threaten the existence of the family unit, one of the nation's psychiatrists said here today.

Quote on Feature or Features in Lead

"I think there have been a lot of subtle changes such as the effect of affluence on young people," Dr. Walter Menninger said.

"Those who don't have to work to help support the family have more free time, become bored more easily and may be more likely to use drugs or look for other artificial highs."

Dr. Menninger spoke at a workshop on "Parenting in a Changing Society" at Lakeshore Mental Health Institute. He is a senior faculty member at the Menninger School of Psychiatry and director of the division of law and psychiatry at the Menninger Foundation in Topeka, Kan.

Summary of Other Features or Details

Quote: Details

Other important changes in society include the changing role of women and the rapid advances in technology, he told the 250 persons at the workshop, which was sponsored by Child and Family Services, Inc.

"One of the biggest problems facing families today is the loss of a clear definition of roles," he said. "Instead of staying home to raise the family as their mothers did, many women today have to work full-time. And the number of single mothers who have to work has increased dramatically over the last decade."

Summary: Details

Quote: Details

These changes have had a major impact on the family as a unit, he said.

"In fact, sometimes it means not having a family at all," he explained. "When a couple meets in college and they each have an agenda that often precludes having a family, their relationship tends to be viewed with less of a commitment to permanence."

Most people have conflicting ideas and feelings about such issues as commitment to work and family, he said. ''And it is important for them to sort out these ambivalent feelings so they can more easily resolve conflicts with others,'' he added.

Summary: Details
(or new feature)

Menninger said he was concerned about the impact of our rapidly changing technology on the family as well.

(Remainder of story deals with Menninger's views on how technology has changed the way we live and as a result has changed the family.)

Take note of how the writer attributed all statements to the speaker. Attribution (the source or authority) is always a problem for news writers. Some tend to overuse it, others don't use it often enough. In this example, the writer was careful to use attribution throughout the story to remind the reader that the speaker, not the reporter, made the statements. Obviously, attribution is not needed in every sentence if the story is carefully organized so there can be no doubt who is being quoted. Attribution can be omitted with a quoted statement if the source of the quote is clear. Generally speaking, however, every paragraph containing indirect quotations should include some attribution.

Complete Reporting

The example of the quote-summary-quote story is straight news reporting. Some speech stories, however, require additional information to give the reader the full background. Here is an example of information added by a reporter to give the reader a more complete picture of the issue discussed in the speech:

Gov. Frank G. Munger told members of the state Press Association today he would ask the State Legislature again for a one-cent increase in the sales tax to fund his Better Schools program.
''We cannot compete for new high-technology industries in the future if we cannot provide a highly trained and educated work force,'' he said.
''The time is now. It is critical. We must start improving the education of our young people or they won't stand a chance in the high-technology future facing them.''
The governor introduced his Better Schools program last year. It includes increased math and science requirements as well as computer training for all students. The program was bitterly opposed by the state Education Association and the State Legislature refused to raise the sales tax to fund it.
''I think we have worked out our differences with the state Education Association over this program and I am confident the Legislature will not let the people of this state down this year,'' Governor Munger said.

The rest of the story follows the quote-summary-quote approach.

The importance of such interpretative reporting—if the occasion requires it—is apparent. Without editorializing, the third paragraph assembles additional pertinent facts to help the reader evaluate the speaker's comments, giving the whole story an altered significance and enabling the reader to understand the possible motivation involved.

Story Contents

A speech story should include:

Facts

1. Speaker
   a. Present position
   b. Experience
   c. Description (if apropos)
   d. Unusual speaking characteristics
2. Audience
   a. Name and type of organization
   b. Number present
   c. Purpose of meeting
   d. Reaction to speech
   e. Description
   f. Important persons present
3. Speech
   a. Theme
   b. Divisions
   c. Title
   d. Quotations

Sources

1. Speaker, various Who's Who publications, members of group before whom speaker speaks, observations of reporter

2. Officials of organization, observations of reporter

3. Speech

PUBLICATIONS

The New England Journal of Medicine may be the most quoted publication in the nation. Each issue produces at least one if not more news stories about important advancements in medicine, medical research and human behavior. Those stories often make the front pages of the daily newspapers.

Dozens of other national magazines also are a source for news stories. Celebrity interviews in People, Vanity Fair and other magazines often result in news stories carried by the national wire services. News and opinion magazines such as Time, Newsweek and The National Review publish articles that frequently are the source of important news stories. Even newspapers with national circulation such as USA TODAY, The New York Times and The Wall Street Journal are sources of stories picked up by the wire services and used by other newspapers. Many newspapers try to localize those stories if there is a logical tie-in.

In addition, thousands of issues of specialized publications, trade journals, academic journals and regional and local magazines are checked regularly by reporters searching for news and feature story ideas. In some cases, a story may have only local news value. However, in many cases the story may have state, regional or even national significance.

Here are some examples of stories published in USA TODAY that are based on stories in other publications:

> We should live so long. Or should we?
> Today's "Science" says 85 is about as high as we can expect to push the average U.S. lifespan. Average now: 75.
> But is living longer something to look forward to?

> Hard work and long hours do not, by themselves, hurt a woman's chances of a normal pregnancy and delivery, new research suggests.
>
> The study of more than 8,000 women—which focused on female medical residents working about 70 hours a week—casts doubts on previous studies suggesting long hours, night work and prolonged standing might lead to premature delivery and other problems.
>
> Finding women "who work longer hours, suffer more sleep deprivation and are under more stress than residents" would be hard, says the report in today's New England Journal of Medicine.

Here is an example from the business publication, Forbes:

> The USA's rich lost money this year, but they're still a long way from penniless.
>
> "The rich have been getting poorer," hit by declining stock prices and other asset values, Forbes says.
>
> One whose wealth grew: communications baron John Kluge, who added $400 million to his fortune.
>
> Now worth about $5.6 billion, Kluge won the No. 1 spot on the Forbes list of the USA's 400 richest people for the second year.

Reporting articles such as these should not be confused with a book review or with a critical analysis. The news story based on an article is not an evaluation of the ideas in the article. It is simply a news story based on what the article says, nothing more. The reporter should follow the same general principles and form that are used in reporting a speech.

There is very little difference between a story on a speech and a story on a published article. As in a speech story, the content of the article and not the fact that the article has been written is usually the substance of the lead. The remainder of the story can be handled effectively as a quote-summary-quote story. And, of course, a description of the publication in which the article appeared (name, type of publication, frequency of publication) may be necessary, just as a description of the occasion (audience, time of presentation) is necessary in reporting a speech.

PERSONAL INTERVIEWS

Virtually all stories in a newspaper are the result of interviews, which is why a reporter has to know what to ask, whom to ask and how to ask to be effective. Even reporters who witness events must ask questions of persons involved and others to obtain additional facts and quotations for a story. Police, hospital officials, witnesses and others are questioned for facts about an automobile accident or a fire, for example. A club president is interviewed about a program featuring a prominent speaker or unusual events. A public official is asked to reply to charges made by a political opponent.

Reporters should never stop asking questions—interviewing. Without asking the right questions, a reporter simply cannot write a complete story.

Interviews directly related to a news event or a public issue are done to collect facts rather than to draw out the personalities of the persons involved.

Here is an example of a major news story developed out of an interview:

> RIYADH, Saudi Arabia, Nov. 1—The commander of the American forces facing Iraq said today that his troops could obliterate Iraq, but cautioned that total destruction of that country might not be ''in the interest of the long-term balance of power in this region.''
>
> ''President Bush has stated again and again, our argument is not with the Iraqi people, and that would cause thousands and thousands of innocent casualties,'' the commander, Gen. H. Norman Schwarzkopf, said in an interview.
>
> ''I do not think there are other alternatives to having to drive on to Baghdad and literally dig out the entire Baathist regime and destroy them all in order to have peace and stability in the area. . . .''
>
> (The New York Times)

However, many interviews are conducted specifically to develop a profile or intimate closeup of a famous or infamous, or at least interesting, person. The subject of the interview may be a prominent scientist, nationally known novelist, professional athlete, or popular television or movie performer. Or it may be an interesting local person, someone with an unusual hobby or someone who is thrust into the news—perhaps a bank clerk who made news by refusing a holdup man's demand for money or a lottery winner or loser.

Here are two examples from USA TODAY:

> Richard Hovis, a warehouse manager who won the biggest lottery jackpot in Ohio history, won't fritter away his $50 million.
>
> ''I've always wanted one of them eight-slice toasters,'' Hovis, 37, of Erie, Pa., said Thursday.
>
> His annual salary was $14,000; after taxes, he'll get $1,471,154 for 26 years.
>
> Hovis says he'll take care of his parents and girlfriend and ''maybe Bondo my Pinto.'' Bondo is used to fill dents. . . .

> NASHVILLE—On stage she's Minnie Pearl, a picture of human frailty and pluck, wearing battered shoes and a dime-store hat from which she's forgotten to remove the price tag.
>
> The character is so real that hardly anyone outside Nashville can tell you the name of its creator. But at the Country Music Association Awards, Sarah Ophelia Cannon is among her own, a tastefully dressed, soft-spoken blueblood. . . .

In the personal interview story the reporter is trying to make the subject come alive on paper. In addition to basic biographical information, the reporter tries to capture for the reader the subject's mannerisms and personality as well as to elicit answers to questions that will give the reader additional insight into that person. To do that successfully, the reporter has to be able to ask good, often provocative, questions and to observe the subject carefully. Additional information often is collected from the subject's family, friends, co-workers, admirers and even detractors, if there are any.

Throughout the history of American journalism, a number of writers have made names for themselves as excellent interviewers. They range from Horace Greeley and his interview with Brigham Young to some of the brightest "stars" of the 1960s. Rex Reed became almost as prominent as some of the famous Hollywood stars he interviewed. Tom Wolfe and Gay Talese developed the basic interview story into an art form, helping to create the so-called New Journalism of the 1960s. Although it is true that Wolfe and Talese frequently wrote about the famous or infamous, they did not start out interviewing only that type of person. Each did his share of interviews with persons who were, at best, notable only on a local scale. Yet their interviews—even the ones written early in their careers—show that they went into their assignments prepared.

Advance preparation is essential to any successful interview. Without it, a reporter will be hopelessly over his or her head. One of the famous stories of interviewing illustrates that point beautifully. Mary Martin, a major star of the American musical theater, was making one of her rare American tours in the 1960s. At a press conference on one of the first stops on the tour an unprepared young reporter asked: "Who are you?" The fact that a reporter did not know the first lady of the American musical theater made a nationwide story and caused the reporter's publication—and surely the reporter—considerable embarrassment.

Every reporter must know at least some important bits of information about the person he or she is going to interview if the story is to be a major personality interview. Various Who's Who publications may provide a brief biography. The newspaper's library or morgue may contain photographs and biographical data in news clippings or press bureau material. Countless other reference books covering major personalities in practically every field are available at most libraries. Often only one or two reference books may be of help. A World Almanac and Book of Facts and a handy one-volume desk encyclopedia should be a part of every reporter's personal reference library. If no standard reference material includes information on the person the reporter has to interview, a telephone call to someone in the city may supply the needed background. With even a slim amount of information, the reporter can begin to formulate a few questions that can be asked in an interview.

Planning Questions

In general, questions should pertain to the work, life or personal interests of the person interviewed, but the questions should be planned to bring answers that will interest the general newspaper reader. Questions should be timely and, to whatever extent possible, local. Comments of a prominent person on a current national event in the person's field are timely. If there is a local angle to the national event, then questions about the local situation should also be asked. Of course, if the subject has absolutely no knowledge of what is happening locally, his or her time should not be wasted by asking questions about such subjects. Obviously, visitors to the city would not feel competent to comment on a strictly local issue.

Questions should be tailor-made for the subject's profession or background. If a television star is not particularly known as a political activist, do not spend a great deal of time asking him or her political questions. Most readers are not interested in how their favorite star votes. They usually want to know what the stars are really like. Are they as nice as they appear on television? Are they as tough? Are they like the characters they play?

In preparing questions, the reporter should keep in mind that one question should lead to another. The interview should move along in a conversational, informal manner while the reporter jots down on paper, tape-records or commits to memory the answers and attitudes revealed. Constantly taking notes is inadvisable except for dates, figures and the like, although in some cases it may be permissible to keep a pencil busy throughout the interview. If a reporter wants to use a tape recorder during a private interview, he or she should ask the subject for permission (some persons do object). However, in the case of a mass interview with the electronic media represented, no special permission is needed because radio and television reporters will be recording the interview on tape. The reporter should always be aware of whether note-taking or recording makes the interviewed person self-conscious and "quote timid"; if so, the use of pencil or tape recorder should be limited. As soon as possible after the interview, however, the reporter should type up the interview notes because the exact responses of the interviewee are then still fresh in the reporter's mind.

The reporter should watch as well as listen. The interviewee's mannerisms, dress, distinctive features and other personal characteristics make copy for the personal interview story. No matter how important the interviewee's statements, there is always room for a few phrases describing the subject. In this lead, Henry Mitchell of the Washington Post captures the language of his subject as well as the speech patterns of the region she lives in and writes about:

> JACKSON, Miss.—Some say Eudora Welty writes best of all, in all Hinds County, but she has never taken on prideful airs. Others say she's the best in all central Mississippi or all America.
>
> "Shoot!" she says, or "Foot!" when the paid-for, or you might say, store-bought critics start up their steady song of praise.
>
> "Now, Eudora," a friend once said to her, " how come you read those reviews? Lots of writers don't read reviews at all."
>
> "I know a lot of writers that don't," she said, "but I do. I've got too much curiosity not to."
>
> Which is, as the Lord knows, true. Miss Welty has more curiosity than a tiger cat. Besides, though she won't exactly say so, it's fairly nice to pick up a paper or magazine and see them having consistent and urgent fits about both your last two books. She writes them for hours off and on in her bedroom right here in Jackson and they are, as some would say, a wonder to behold.
>
> One fellow in the Washington Post (writer Reynolds Price) just flung up his arms in print and said there's no point comparing "Losing Battles" to other American novels. He suggested, for starters, you might compare it with "The Tempest" by the late W. Shakespeare, and then just took it on from there.
>
> "Yes, I know he did," said Miss Welty when I had the pleasure of her company and her cooking for two days recently, "and I am really going to speak to him about it. Shakespeare is a bit much."

The rest of the story was written in much the same tone, giving the reader the "flavor" of this unusual writer and the way people in Jackson respond to her.

Some reporters bring themselves into the personal interview far more than Henry Mitchell did in his story on Eudora Welty. However, the circumstances of the story rarely justify extensive personal references about the reporter. The reader wants to know about the subject of the interview, not the reporter.

Because of the increasing role of science and technology in our lives, reporters may find themselves having to interview persons in highly technical fields. Faced with such an assignment, a reporter has to make advance preparation. A reporter has an obligation to the interview subject to do some homework. The library usually is the best place to start. A speech the subject gave may have been reprinted in Vital Speeches. Articles the subject has written may be listed in the library catalog. General or special magazines may have carried earlier interviews with the subject. Reporters frequently are criticized by interview subjects for not being prepared or for pretending to know about a topic or issue when they do not.

John Jamison, director of corporate communications for the North Carolina National Bank, developed this "Interview Bill of Rights" as a guide for the reporter and the subject:

Rights of the Interviewee
- The right to an objective listening to the facts presented.
- The right to an accurate representation of his or her position.
- The right to a fair and balanced context for all statements.
- The right to know in advance the general area of questioning and to have reasonable time for preparation.
- The right to reasonable flexibility as to when to have the interview. (Just as there are times when a reporter cannot be interrupted near a deadline, there are times when others cannot be interrupted.)
- The right to expect the interviewer to have done some homework.
- The right to withhold comment when there is good reason without having this translated as evading or "stonewalling," for example, information governed by the Securities and Exchange Commission regulations, competitive secrets, matters in litigation or negotiation, information that could damage innocent persons.
- The right to an assumption of innocence until guilt is proven.
- The right to offer feedback to the reporter, especially to call attention to instances in which the story, in the honest opinion of the interviewee, missed the point or was in error—and to have this feedback received in good faith.
- The right to appropriate correction of substantial errors without further damage to the credibility or reputation of the interviewee's organization.

Rights of the Interviewer
- The right to access to an authoritative source of information on a timely basis.
- The right to candor, within the limits of propriety.

- The right to access to information and assistance on adverse stories as well as favorable ones.
- The right to preparation on a story the reporter has developed exclusively, until it has been published or until another reporter asks independently for the same information.
- The right not to be used by businesses for "free advertising" on a purely commercial story.
- The right not to be reminded that advertising pays the reporter's salary.
- The right not to be held accountable for ill treatment by another reporter or another medium at another time.
- The right to publish a story without showing it to the interviewee in advance.
- The right not to be asked to suppress legitimate news purely on the grounds that it would be embarrassing or damaging.
- The right not to be summoned to a news conference when a simple phone call, written statement, news release or interview would do just as well.

Jamison's "Bill of Rights" was originally published in the May 28, 1977, issue of Editor & Publisher and is just as valid today as it was then.

Conducting the Interview

Most reporters begin personal interviews with a brief period of small talk to establish rapport with the subject of the interview. This often is the most critical part of the interview. It gives the subject a chance to size up the reporter. Those first few minutes often determine the tone of the interview.

A good reporter will move quickly into the questions prepared for the interview. The questions should be arranged in order of their importance. The general questions should come first. The tough, intimidating or offensive questions should be asked near the end of the interview. If the tough questions are asked at the outset of the interview, the subject may refuse to answer and terminate the interview immediately.

A reporter should listen carefully to everything the subject says and be prepared at any point in the interview to ask the subject to clarify an answer. When in doubt, ask for the correct spelling of all names mentioned in the interview and for verification of important times, dates, places, addresses and statistics. A subject's memory may be hazy, and the reporter must not be too timid to ask for verification of the facts presented.

Interview Problems

Special problems can arise during interviews. The most common are off-the-record comments by the subject, sources who do not want to be identified in print, and requests by the interviewee to read the story before it is printed. Before agreeing to any of these requests, a reporter should know the newspaper's policy on each. It also would be helpful to the reporter to know the state's law on the protection of confidential sources. Some states give reporters total freedom to protect confidential sources. However, the U.S. Supreme Court has ruled that the First Amendment does not provide for protecting confidential sources in federal criminal cases.

In addition, there often is a credibility problem when unnamed sources are used in stories. Several readership studies show that readers often do not believe stories in which the source of information is not identified. Some readers have told researchers they suspect the reporter may have made up the information when a source is not identified.

The problems created when sources demand to read a story before it is printed seem to grow annually. Most newspapers refuse to allow sources to read stories in advance. However, it is common practice among reporters to check quotes, especially those dealing with highly technical or scientific subjects, with the source. A reporter should never agree to let a source read the story in advance without checking with the editor first.

Telephone Inteviews

Many interviews are conducted by telephone. It saves time for the subject of the interview and the reporter. However, many reporters consider the telephone to be ineffective for conducting personality interviews because they are unable to observe the subject's reactions to the questions. Reporters also say they are unable to observe the subject's mannerisms, dress, distinctive features and other personal characteristics that add a special dimension to personality profiles.

A reporter should prepare for a telephone interview the same way he or she prepares for an in-person interview. When conducting a telephone interview, the reporter should observe all the simple courtesies used during in-person interviews. The reporter should give his or her name and make certain the subject knows the information being collected will be used in print. The reporter also should (1) speak clearly and calmly and avoid long, rambling questions; (2) avoid irrelevant or obvious questions; (3) save the tough or embarrassing questions for the last; and (4) try not to obtain so much information in the telephone interview that the subject of the interview grows impatient.

Interview Story Forms

In the personal interview, the reporter finds that a variety of approaches will apply, depending on the person interviewed and what is said. But all interview stories have one thing in common: many direct quotes. A reporter can make use of the quote-summary-quote form in the body of the story, and in that regard the interview story is somewhat similar to the speech story. The lead can be a summary, an outstanding feature, a quote or an anecdote, or, to set the scene, it can be descriptive. The lead, of course, can contain the substance of the interview, but often a striking word picture of the speaker is more desirable if his or her personal characteristics are particularly impressive. By all means, somewhere early in the story, the importance of the interview must be established, although it does not have to be in the lead or first paragraph.

Another story form that has gained considerable popularity in interviews, especially in some magazines, is the "question-and-answer" structure. Newspapers, however, use this form sparingly because it generally requires large amounts of space. In this form, the reporter simply writes a short introduction similar to an editor's note, giving a brief biographical sketch of the interviewee, and then reproduces the questions and the interviewee's answers. Often these interviews are done on tape recorders and are simply transcribed and perhaps edited for style and length. Some of the best examples of question-and-answer interviews can be found on the opinion page of USA TODAY. The newspaper has effectively adapted the question-and-answer form to limited space.

EXERCISES

1. Using any newspaper available to you, clip five stories, paste them on separate sheets of paper and analyze them. Indicate in the margins that information in them came from questions obviously asked by the reporter.

2. Clip a speech story, a story taken from a publication and an interview story from any newspaper or publication available to you. Analyze each one on a separate sheet. Pay particular attention to the lead, story organization, and the use of full and partial quotes.

3. Using an issue of Vital Speeches in your college or community library, make a copy of one of the speeches. Write a news story based on the speech. Turn in the speech with your story.

4. Using a morning and an afternoon newspaper published in your area, compare the speech stories published in each or any speech given recently by a major figure such as the president, secretary of state or governor.

5. Check radio and television listings in your city for coverage of a speech by a major public figure. Listen to the speech on radio or watch it on television. Take careful notes and then write a news story based on your notes. Do not copy the version that appears in the local newspaper. Hand in your notes with the story.

6. Write a story on the following excerpts from a speech by Dr. Tara Vaughn, chief economist with the state's Bureau of Business Research. She spoke at the annual state labor-management conference in the state capital:

   Citizens of the state face some tough decisions about taxes if they want an adequately trained adult labor force to attract new industry which is the only way to ensure economic growth at the turn of the century.

   Taxes are low in the state and most of the available dollars are going to corrections and Medicaid, rather than education. Spending for education in 116 of the state's 138 school systems is below regional averages.

   The state needs to have a productive, better-trained labor force to attract new industry if it is going to show the kind of growth in the next decade it has shown in the last several.

   That is going to take money.

The state has four options for raising more tax revenues with which to train its labor force. They are:

a state lottery
raising the state sales tax rate
broadening the state sales tax base
adopting an income tax.

A state lottery does not raise enough money and it is not good public policy because it aggressively markets a dream that is by and large bought by low-income people. It is not a good way to do government.

Raising the sales tax rate doesn't solve any basic problem. It would get the state through the next five years but we'd end up where we are today.

An increase in the sales tax rate would encourage people to shop in other states because their rates would be lower. A sales tax hike would continue to take a larger percentage of income from low-income families.

Broadening the sales tax base to items not presently taxed is not necessarily a bad idea, but it still does not solve the tax structure problem. It leaves us with a structure that doesn't grow as the economy grows.

A state income tax is a major political issue although it would raise plenty of revenue and give the state a proportional to progressive tax structure. But there are political problems in getting an income tax enacted and signed into law.

Businesses and industries planning to move to the state or to expand existing operations will require better-trained workers than the state traditionally has available.

Because educational levels are much below other parts of the nation, the state has to question its ability to deliver that work force.

We've got a problem with our adult, already-educated, out-in-the-work-force population. We simply are going to have to solve that problem by converting our adults into lifetime learners, by providing the kind of technology that lets them learn where they live and work, and by dealing with illiteracy in our state.

We probably are going to have to rethink the way we do vocational versus academic education to help adults be ready to compete in the future.

7. Write a news story based on these excerpts from an article that appeared in The New England Journal of Medicine. Dr. Greg Brown is the lead author of the report on a study of 120 men with heart diease. The men in the study were all 62 or younger and had an average total cholesterol level of 270. The study was conducted at the University of Washington, Seattle. It found that:

Intensive treatment with cholesterol-lowering drugs can shrink fatty deposits in coronary arteries and cut the risk of a second heart attack.

Intensive drug therapy also:

Reduced by half the narrowing of the arteries.

Reduced by 73 percent the recurrence of angina, stroke and sudden death or heart attack.

After 2-1/2 years, those with drug therapy had decreased bad cholesterol (LDL), which clogs arteries, and increased good cholesterol (HDL) thought to protect against heart disease.

Side effects, including constipation and gout, were minor.

Dr. Brown said cholesterol-reducing drugs have shown promise in previous studies with heart disease patients. The findings in this study offer more evidence of the relationship between cholesterol and coronary disease. It shows that everything fits together, he said.

Men in the study were split into three groups: One took the cholesterol-reducing drugs lovastatin and colestipol; another, niacin and colestipol; the third got placebos.

Dr. Brown said lovastatin cost $1,500 a year, but he is hopeful drug manufacturers will fill the market with cheaper, more easily tolerated drugs.

Dr. James L. Cleeman of the National Cholesterol Education Program at the National Heart, Lung and Blood Institute said: "We may well be reaching a point where aggressive cholesterol-lowering will be common among people with coronary disease."

More than one in four in the United States have cholesterol levels of 240 and above, putting them at risk for coronary disease.

8. Attend an event on your campus or in the community featuring a prominent speaker. Take notes and write a news story on it. Many local service clubs both on campus and in the community usually have speakers at their weekly lunches. Do not use a copy of the speech, even if one is available. Hand in your notes with the story.

9. Review a number of professional journals and publications in your college library such as your state's historical journal or any professional publication for doctors, teachers or political scientists. Select a by-lined article dealing with an interesting event or study, and write a news story based on it.

10. Using any newspaper available to you, clip two interview stories with well-known stage, television or sports personalities written by the wire services. Compare the interviews with those in the books Fame and Obscurity by Gay Talese or Writing in Style, a collection of interviews from the "Style" section of the Washington Post. If those books aren't available, ask your librarian to help you locate any other collection of interviews in the collection.

11. Interview the most interesting person you know and write a story on her or him. Do not use the star athlete, head coach or campus beauty queen for this assignment.

12. Assume you have been assigned to interview your favorite television, movie or sports personality, who is visiting your city. Make a list of the questions you would ask during the interview.

13. Write an interview story from the following notes:

Ed Lawler is an 81-year-old local lawyer. For the past seven years he has been working on a book about his experiences as a member of the Office of Strategic Services, the forerunner of the Central Intelligence Agency, during World War II. Among his experiences, he cultivated one of the most valuable German "moles" the Allies ever had; frequently dealt with Kim Philby, the infamous British double agent; worked closely with the legendary OSS director, "Wild Bill Donovan," and CIA directors-to-be Allen Dulles and William Casey; and made several trips to Ireland to swap sensitive information with top government officials there late in the war. Here are quotes from the interview:

Weeks after the Japanese attack on Pearl Harbor, I was in the Navy. They assigned me to a Navy intelligence unit in New Orleans but I was bored with that work. I wanted to go overseas, so I signed on with the OSS.

They sent me to a school outside Washington where they taught me how to blow up trains and bridges and kill people with everything from a 45-caliber pistol to a folded newspaper. One course in lock-picking and safe-cracking was taught by convicts.

I'll admit that some of my fellow students were dismayed at learning such unsavory practices, but I hadn't led a sheltered life. In high school I worked in Texas stockyards and Idaho lead mines. And I was used to finding my way around the back streets of Chicago. Chicago has always been a rough place. It's a fine training ground for a spy.

I was ordered to China in 1944, but got a temporary assignment in London first that turned more permanent.

It was there that I was assigned to the case of Fritz Kolbe, a German who worked in his nation's foreign office. He had volunteered twice to supply information to British intelligence, but they rudely dismissed him because they didn't believe his story. Some American intelligence experts did, and I was assigned to his case. He said he wanted to rid his country of Adolf Hitler and he didn't want pay for his services.

I began putting together reams of documents Kolbe had provided and found the information they contained and the events they predicted were accurate.

Kolbe was assigned the code name, "George Wood," and he began providing information on impending attacks on England by German V1 and V2 rockets and filed reports on the effectiveness of Allied bombing missions against German military and industrial targets.

To us, George Wood was a hero, a man who put his life on the line every day and provided invaluable information at tremendous personal risk. I met him after the war and he was the most unimpressive man you could possibly imagine. He was a short, heavy-set, bald man who wore glasses. Nothing like the James Bond you might imagine.

But he was the best spy I ever met. An invaluable resource who has been largely overlooked by history.

By comparison, I never did like Kim Philby, mostly because he asked too darn many questions. He never gave any indication he was an alcoholic or that his allegiance was divided.

London was an adventure in itself those days and I got to work with a tremendously varied and fascinating group of characters. But I never had to use the skills I learned in spy school, although knowing how to pick a lock has come in handy when I locked myself out of the house or car.

To be a good spy you have to be independent, analytical, imaginative and ruthless. I think I was all of that but I came out with a clean conscience. When the lights go out I sleep like a baby.

Lawler is a native of Chicago and was graduated from Harvard Law School. He has practiced tax law here since 1946.

CHAPTER 17
MEETINGS AND
SPECIAL EVENTS

Dozens of meetings are held every day in smaller communities and hundreds in larger cities, often producing important news stories. The public's business is conducted at meetings of governmental bodies. Civic, religious, social, scholastic, business and professional and fraternal organizations meet and frequently generate news, which is why meeting stories are a staple in every newspaper.

There are so many meetings, they simply cannot all be covered, so editors have to decide which ones to cover and how to cover them in ways that would be both informative and interesting for readers. Editors consider such questions as:

- Do we write an extensive advance story about what is expected to happen, and then a brief follow-up after the meeting?
- Will a brief advance story do, with a detailed report on what actually happened?
- Do we rely on a press release for our advance, and in some cases, the follow-up?
- Do we assign a reporter and perhaps a photographer?

There are almost as many answers to those questions as there are editors and meetings. But, as a general rule, editors consider meetings of nongovernmental organizations particularly newsworthy if:

1. There is a prominent speaker or significant program that would interest readers.
2. There will be a large number in attendance.

Meetings about real issues often make important news. But significant stories can and do come from what may appear to be just another routine meeting. For example: A routine talk at a service club luncheon by the new director of a medium-sized southern city's art museum became the lead story in the "Local" section of the morning newspaper when the speaker used a very gamey reference to the male anatomy to explain how a person could determine if a photograph was obscene. It generated follow-up stories because the head of the museum's board of trustees hastily issued an apology to the service club while praising the director for his excellent work on behalf of the artistic community and art-loving public.

Obviously, not all speeches at service clubs generate that kind of coverage. But it is important for reporters to keep in mind that when reporting on a meeting, the most important aspect is to tell the reader what took place and why she or he should care.

Once an event has occurred, there is no news value in the simple fact that it happened. Even at meetings where little or nothing goes on, the reporter should look for a news peg or interesting fact for the lead. Far too many stories begin "The Downtown Business Circle met for lunch yesterday in Morrison's Cafeteria and heard an interesting talk by Superintendent Margaret Lopez." Tell what she said. That's the news. Even when writing an advance story about a meeting, the reporter should look for something interesting to put in the lead. Never settle for "A meeting will be held. . . ."

TYPES OF MEETING STORIES

The Advance

Most groups rely on newspapers to publicize their meeting through a story or stories printed in advance. Some groups mail or phone in announcements of upcoming meetings. Often the information they provide is incomplete, and the reporter has to call a representative of the group to obtain additional details to write a full and accurate story that will interest many readers—not just members of the organization.

Information needed for a meeting story includes the correct, formal name of the organization (and local chapter name if it is part of a national group); the exact time, date and place; and details on the program such as speakers, entertainment, election or installation of officers. The more the reporter knows about the organization, the easier it will be to write an interesting and informative story. Compare these two meeting leads:

> *Weak:*
>   Parents Without Partners will meet in the auditorium of Westwood Elementary School at 7 p.m. Wednesday to hear a talk by narcotics officer Patsy Hammontree on drug abuse by pre-teens.

> *Better:*
>   Patsy Hammontree, a 10-year veteran of the police narcotics squad, will speak on drug abuse by pre-teens at a meeting of Parents Without Partners Wednesday. The meeting, at 7 p.m. in the Westwood Elementary School auditorium, is open to the public.

Avoid starting meeting stories in the following ways:

> There will be a meeting of the Cocke County Senior Citizens Club at noon. . . .

> At 7:30 p.m. Wednesday, members of the Del Rio Rescue Squad will . . .

> An evening of fun awaits members of the Cosby Kiwanis Club when country comic Buster Curry . . .

The first example is not written in news style; the second one focuses on the time element, which rarely is the most important fact in the story; and the third one is editorial in nature. How can the writer be sure everyone will have fun? Maybe Buster will be a bust in the opinion of some members of the Cosby Kiwanis Club.

In the body of the story, the reporter should avoid editorial comment on the caliber of the program, such as "an excellent talk was given by" and a "thrilling presentation of operatic excerpts." Such expressions as "All members are urged to attend" and "The public is cordially invited" should be omitted. If the meeting features a speaker and the club or organization would like others to attend, include that the "meeting is open to the public."

The Follow-up

Most meetings worthy of more than a bare announcement will have produced something of substance on which the reporter can build the story, including

1. A definite action—passage of a law, adoption of resolutions, announcement of plans, endorsement of candidates or issues
2. One or more speeches
3. Discussion and debate—conflict, difference of opinion, voicing of views, criticism
4. Personnel—election of officers, nominations, new members, resignations, membership drives, visitors, prominent members or guests, interesting personalities
5. Miscellaneous features—music or other entertainment, unexpected interruptions.

The lead on the follow-up story can vary greatly from a summary of the entire meeting to a single outgoing feature followed by a summary of other features. In many cases, reporters attempt to develop a general theme for the entire story if there seems to be a central theme to the meeting:

> An urgent appeal for $2 billion in emergency federal aid to fight recession in the nation's big cities was made at the U.S. Conference of Mayors in Boston yesterday.

The remainder of the story would be built around the central theme of the recession and its effect on the cities and their need for more federal help.

A reporter should not try to develop a theme, however, if one does not logically exist. Often some feature that is far from the main purpose of a meeting will be the most logical lead because it has stronger reader appeal. The reporter's responsibility is to the reader, not the sponsors of the meeting. The story should be written with that in mind. At the same time, the story should not present a distorted view of the meeting.

It is important that the story be told in a logical order, with the most important thing that happened at the meeting being told first. The story should not be written in chronological fashion, and it should never sound like the minutes taken by the club secretary.

Here is an example of a story coming out of a meeting on public health issues. The USA TODAY writer treated the serious subject in a way that was certain to attract reader attention:

> Getting a move on could be the key to staying out of a nursing home for people over 70—the USA's fastest-growing age group.
> Just two 40-minute exercise sessions each week—emphasizing flexibility and stretching—will spur major health improvements within three months, a University of Michigan researcher reported at a meeting of the American Public Health Association Wednesday in New York City.
> "Most research on exercise and the elderly looks at people under 70. But they tend to be fairly healthy," says Tom Hickman, of the University of Michigan School of Public Health.
> "It's the over-70s that get the chronic conditions, and will become a real public health concern as their numbers continue to grow."
> Hickey gathered 100 Cleveland men and women, 75 to 98 years old. . . .

CONVENTIONS

Conventions have always provided newspapers with a wide variety of stories and, increasingly, they are becoming the focal point for major news breaks. Planners often schedule a particularly newsworthy speaker to attract the attention of newspeople as well as delegates. Speakers frequently use the convention platform to announce new scientific discoveries, plans for world peace, or formation of a new political party or pressure group.

Handling the stories generated by a large convention can be a major undertaking for any reporter. A big-scale convention is in reality a series of meetings that offer the reporter a wide variety of features and frequently requires the writing of multiple news stories. It is not uncommon for several staff members to be assigned to a large convention. If the convention is a major event—a political party convention or the national meeting of an organization that might attract several thousand delegates—a special convention staff of a dozen or more reporters and photographers under the direction of a special editor may be assigned.

Many newspapers make special efforts to "cover all angles" of a large local convention, frequently devoting more space to it than that warranted by its appeal to local readers. This type of treatment can be justified on several counts: Each of the many delegates is interested in the coverage and is a potential buyer of the newspaper and, furthermore, newspapers generally give broad coverage to such meetings as a matter of civic spirit. Conventions are important to the economy of any city, and the newspaper joins other organizations of the city in welcoming the visitors and promoting the city as a convention center.

Of course, a large convention also has many angles of local interest. Although it may attract little attention in the largest cities, several hundred visitors in the average city will create news in itself. Even the smallest of conventions might attract prominent visitors, newsworthy speeches and discussions, resolutions on important issues, unusual persons or incidents, and participation of local persons. Any of these should generate considerable local reader interest and make the convention worthy of coverage.

Preliminaries

If the editors of a newspaper decide to give maximum attention to a convention, a reporter may have weeks—perhaps even months—to begin preparing for the event. Long before the opening of the convention, the reporter may write stories almost daily to feature all phases of the upcoming event.

Most organizations planning a convention will have a publicity committee or manager to work with reporters, providing them much of the information needed to write stories. Often complete press kits are given to reporters to help them cover the event. A kit usually includes the complete program, pictures and biographical sketches of the speakers and officials of the organization, a history of the group, an explanation of important subjects on the program and a variety of other material that could be used for stories.

Some publicity managers also provide copies of speeches in advance. But they insist that a story on the speech not be printed until after it has been given. A copy of the speech can be extremely helpful because it gives the reporter time to read and digest the speech completely before writing the story.

Even with a copy of the speech in advance, a reporter should attend the meeting to make certain the speech actually was given and to record any material the speaker might add. On some occasions, often with permission of the speaker, a newspaper will publish an advance speech story in its editions on the day the speech is to be delivered. In those cases the lead usually contains the phrase "in a speech prepared for delivery at the (name) convention today." . . .

All this help from publicity representatives does not relieve the reporter of the responsibility for gathering material for stories on the convention. If a publicity manager is not available to help, it is the reporter's job to get as much material as possible about the convention in advance by writing or phoning officials of the organization and the speakers. Reporters should also work with the local convention bureau or the hotel or office serving as convention headquarters to gather information about the convention.

Sometimes the number of speakers and the variety of sectional meetings of a convention are so large that the newspaper must omit details of the less important ones. As in every other story, it is important for the reporter to develop a keen sense of what really is news when gathering and writing convention stories.

Presenting Convention Features

In preparing a number of advance reports on a convention, the reporter must plan stories to avoid repetition of the same features. Each story should have something new in its lead, but the time, date and place of the convention should be repeated somewhere (not necessarily in the lead) every time.

The first story lead generally announces that the convention will be held in the city. Often it emphasizes the approximate number of persons who will attend along with the time, date and place of the convention. Story leads of follow-up stories will highlight different phases of the program (speakers, discussion, officers, entertainment). A summary of other features (minus details) will be included in the body of the story. If a summary of all other features runs the story length beyond the space allotted for it, some of the less important features usually are omitted. It is also acceptable to play up—in the lead—features that have been summarized in the body of the preceding stories even though they are not new developments.

From the day before a convention opens—especially if it is a major one—until the day after it closes, there is a real rush. Often photographers and other reporters team with the reporter in charge to gather speeches, conduct interviews and search out other significant information that was unavailable in advance. In addition to reports on business and the speeches of the convention, many newspapers seek out human-interest stories on interesting delegates, unusual events in connection with the meeting, comments from delegates on the convention and the city, or other material.

All aspects of a convention may be put together in one long story, or they may be divided into a number of stories. The larger the convention, the more stories, generally speaking. If the stories are divided, one main story will be devoted to the major—most newsworthy—event of the convention and include such essential information as number of delegates and other general information. Other stories will present reports from sectional meetings within the convention, interviews and other sidelights. The exact manner in which the convention is covered depends on its size, overall newsworthiness in relation to all other news that day and the amount of space available in the newspaper.

SPECIAL EVENTS

Fairs, festivals, dedications, exhibitions and other large events that attract a great number of persons offer much the same sort of problems as do convention stories. Each presents the possibility of some significant straight-news reports as well as dozens of features. Advance preparation is necessary to obtain details.

Several stories, each playing up a different feature, are required before the event takes place, and adequate coverage of all features is necessary while the event is in progress. If the program of the special event is simply substituted for the convention program, the whole assignment involves the same procedure.

FIGURE 17–1. Often a special event, such as the visit to California by Pope John Paul II, creates so much public interest a newspaper will produce a special section of stories and photographs to commemorate the event. (Courtesy of the San Jose (Calif.) Mercury News.)

EXERCISES

1. Using a copy of any local or area daily newspaper available to you, make an inventory of all the stories in a single issue that pertain to meetings. Include both advance and follow-up stories. Make a list of the various kinds of meetings that are the subject of stories, such as church, civic, social and service groups as well as business and professional organizations.

2. Buy a copy of a local newspaper and clip five meeting stories, including an advance meeting story, a follow-up meeting story and a convention story, and analyze them. If local newspapers do not carry such stories at the time of the assignment, locate a newspaper from a larger city in your college library, copy five meeting and convention stories, and analyze each one.

3. Check the calendar of events for your campus for an upcoming meeting. Most university centers or student unions post a list of coming events. Call the sponsors of an upcoming meeting to obtain information for an advance story. Write the story and turn in your notes as well as the name of your source.

4. Check the local newspaper for an upcoming meeting of a community club or professional organization. Attend the meeting and write a news story about it. Hand in the notes taken at the meeting along with your story.

5. Check your campus calender of events for an upcoming special event such as a holiday festival or other campuswide activity. Contact the sponsors and obtain enough information to write an advance story. When the event takes place, attend it and write a news story.

6. Attend a special event in your community such as a crafts show, art exhibit, fair, flower show or river festival, and write a human-interest story about it. Try to capture the color and excitement of the event for the reader. Turn in your notes with your story.

7. A regional conference sponsored by the Union of Psychology & Astrology will be held in your city tomorrow and the next day. Write a story using the following information: About 200 persons are expected to attend the sessions at the civic convention center. The organization is made up of psychologists and astrologers who practice holistic counseling. The conference is designed to instruct therapeutic professionals as well as other interested individuals in ways to use psychology and astrology to broaden their professional skills and enhance personal experience.

8:30 to 9:30 a.m.	Registration in civic convention center lobby.
9:45 a.m.	Opening ceremony and welcome by Mayor W. Manion Rice. Introduced by regional president of the Union of Psychology & Astrology.
10:00 a.m.	"Exploring the Fear of Astrology Among the Educated." Michael Anne Conley, M.A., Lafayette, Calif., therapist and astrologer.
11:00 a.m.	"The Western Mind at the Threshold." Elbert Hooker, Ph.D., psychotherapist, researcher and teacher for 25 years. Co-founder and president of International Self-Actualization Foundation.

12:15 p.m.	Lunch with Hindu Astrologer Jamie Dasas presenting "Eastern and Western Perspectives on Issues of Fate and Free Will."
1:45 p.m.	"Blending Astrology and Contemporary Psychotherapies." Gail Palmer, Ph.D., teacher, author and therapist, who recently was commissioned by Macmillan Publishing Co. to write a book on the growing use of astrology by psychologists.
3:00 p.m.	A series of concurrent workshops on: "The Psychology of Place"; "The Use of Birth Charts in Psychotherapy"; and "Astrological Metaphor in the Counseling Arts."
7:00 p.m.	Dinner session "The Sun, The Earth and The Person." A talk by Zina Belle Chapman, M.A., and award-winning author of six books including "I See Me in the Sun," a national bestseller, who has been in private practice as an astrological counselor for more than 25 years.
The next day	
8:30 a.m.	"Symbolic Counseling in Chronic or Catastrophic Illness." Headly Davidson, a professional counselor who has been working in the fields of humanistic psychology and astrology for more than 30 years.
9:45 a.m.	"Healing the Past: Reconstructing Client Self-Concepts." Francoise Montebellow, Ph.D., internationally recognized consciousness researcher and teacher.
11:00 a.m.	Open Forum featuring all the speakers in a discussion and question-and-answer session.
Noon	Adjourn.

8. Write a news story on the final session of a state meeting of Rehabilitation Services workers sponsored by the state Department of Human Services. The convention was held in the state's Performing Arts Center in the state capital. Approximately 600 attended. Shirley Vaughn Pizarek, who works for the National Rehabilitation Hospital in Washington, D.C., and who is an expert in "rehab engineering," was the speaker. Here are some of the highlights of her speech.

"The landmark Americans with Disabilities Act prohibits discrimination against the disabled in the private sector and requires most businesses to accommodate disabled employees in the workplace.

"Many companies are having to make structural changes in their facilities—such as installing wheelchair ramps and widening doorways—so disabled workers can perform their jobs.

"Although companies, depending on their size, have between two and four years to comply, there are a large number who obviously will attempt to circumvent the law because it will cost them to make the necessary changes.

"There are millions of businesses around the country that have never had to come under such federal regulations before. As a result many employers do not know about the law and it will be extremely difficult to enforce it.

"There also is a strong possibility that some employers with disabled employees may attempt to eliminate everyone with a disability to avoid meeting the requirements of the law.

"There also is a danger of a lot of con artists and sharpies trying to cash in on the law and make a fast buck off businesses by offering to serve as consultants on the law—for a stiff price, of course.

"One company official called me and said: 'A consulting firm told me it would cost me $15,000 to lower all my drinking fountains.' I suggested he go down to the local supermarket and buy a Dixie-cup dispenser for $1.98 and hang it on the wall.

"Accommodations under the law need not be expensive. They can be made easily without making the workplace look like it has been specially designed.

"In one study of a California company's experience in modifying its facilities, there was no additional cost whatsoever for making the necessary changes to accommodate 458 workers. For 169 others, the extra cost totaled between $1 and $99. The most expensive changes—for 15 employees—ran to $20,000."

She urged the Rehabilitation Services workers to talk to business owners about the new law and encourage them to seek help from the Disability Rights Educational and Defense Fund in Washington, D.C., if they do not understand the law or if they are seeking the help of a professional rehabilitation engineer.

Rehabilitation engineers design homes and work sites to make them easier for the disabled to use. There are fewer than 500 people in the field in the United States, she said.

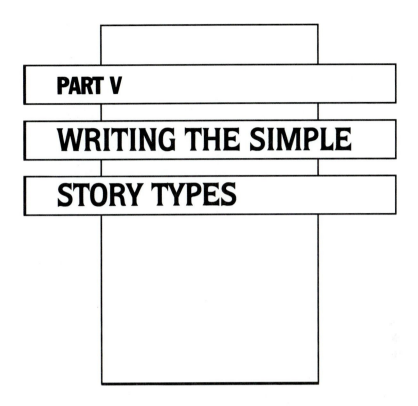

PART V

WRITING THE SIMPLE

STORY TYPES

Few beginning reporters start out writing major stories for a newspaper. Even on small community newspapers, the page-1 story generally goes to the experienced reporter and the beginner gets the simpler stories.

The classification of stories as simple or complex is a convenient and arbitrary division that most editors use when making assignments, even though there is no real technical significance in this classification. To most editors, single-incident stories—automobile accidents, deaths, illnesses, funerals, minor crimes—would fall into the "simple" classification. Those stories requiring little interpretative writing and little background might be added to the editor's list—an award or public appointment, for example.

However, it should be noted that any single story may turn out to be either simple or complex, depending on the facts and their news values. For purposes of proceeding from the less difficult to the more difficult stories, the "simple" or "complex" classification has proved useful.

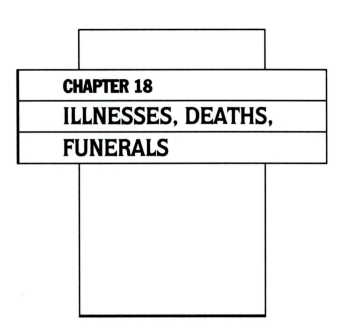

CHAPTER 18

ILLNESSES, DEATHS, FUNERALS

The obituary is one of the most important stories in any newspaper. It is read and reread, clipped, bound in plastic and often pasted in the back of the family Bible. It has the potential of making more enemies or friends for a newspaper than almost any other kind of story.

To a reporter, the obituary may be routine. But not to the family. The newspaper will be remembered for the careful, accurate way it reported even the smallest details during the family's time of sorrow.

Let the obituary be inaccurate—a name misspelled, facts incorrectly reported, survivors omitted—and the family will never forget it and never forgive the offending newspaper. Everything in the newspaper will be suspect in the eyes of that family whose members constantly will remind relatives and friends that the newspaper had Grandpa in the wrong lodge, left out the name of his beloved baby sister in the list of survivors, or made some other grievous error and cannot be trusted.

Writing obituaries requires a special sensitivity. That is why many newspapers, even small ones, use experienced reporters to write all obituaries. However, some still give the new reporter the job of writing them, even those of very prominent residents, as a test. How a new reporter handles obits often determines how rapidly he or she will be given other writing assignments. Sloppy and careless work soon marks a reporter as someone not to be trusted with important stories. Careful, thoughtful and dignified work results in attention from editors and often in more rewarding assignments.

News Values

Why are obituaries and stories about illnesses and funerals so important? Evaluating their news value shows they all fall on the disaster side of human experience. They are disruptions of the status quo, and they are of consequence in the community. The removal of almost any human being from the local scene requires social and economic readjustments among relatives and friends. His or her place must be taken; his or her job must be filled by another. The home may be offered for sale; the widow or widower may move to another city; the daughter or son may withdraw from college. All such changes touch the lives of others.

Factors of Magnitude

The importance of the news story is determined by several factors. Illness is measured by its gravity, approaching death as its climax. And both illness and death are measured by the number of persons affected in the community. Thus the prominence of the person and the nature of the illness may determine story importance. A rare disease or accident, even one involving someone who is comparatively unknown, is interesting because it is unusual.

Even more important may be stories about the threat of epidemics of quite common diseases. Since prominence usually means being well known, in addition to holding a position of importance, the community is more generally affected by matters involving prominent persons. Multiple deaths or cases of illness extend importance of the news. Although the story of illness or death (and of the funeral) may frequently stand stripped of its disaster appeal, its news importance may sometimes be heightened by prominence, novelty, consequence, human interest and even conflict.

ILLNESSES

Illness—grave illness—is reported less frequently than its news importance justifies. Patient, family, physician and hospital are often unwilling to have the illness known. Physicians and hospitals usually tend to avoid publicity even in the case of very prominent persons. Family and patient may wish to avoid unnecessary alarm to friends, employer or employees, and sometimes the family wants to hide information from the patient. Often if the person is very prominent—a public official or a major entertainment figure, for example—the illness may not be disclosed in order to assure the person's privacy.

Illness can affect business matters, contracts, perhaps even diplomatic negotiations, as well as various other obligations. Always in the background is the thought that tomorrow or the next day the patient may be well and the less uproar about the matter the better. If the patient's family, physician and hospital all refuse to give a statement on the illness, the reporter should use whatever information is available with extreme caution.

Illness is not easy to report properly. Highly technical or tenuous conditions may characterize the illness itself. The physician might not know the exact nature of the illness. The nature of the illness itself might be so technical that it is extremely difficult to translate into language the average reader can understand. Some medical schools, however, now have special courses to teach medical students how to write and speak in non-technical language.

The reporter should always keep in mind the emotions and the sensitivities of the patient as well as the family. Once the brief bulletin on the patient's condition is announced, little substance is left for the reporter to take hold of and expand, as a general rule. However, if the person is prominent—a major entertainer or perhaps the governor of the state—the attending physicians sometimes will hold a press conference and explain the nature of the illness and the patient's condition.

In the prolonged illness of such a prominent person, regular medical bulletins will be issued and the comings and goings of delegations, friends, relatives and others as well as their public statements may provide copy. The illness stories of lesser persons will usually be brief, however, unless they suffer from a rare or unusual ailment.

Although a list of patients admitted to and dismissed from hospitals often is published each day in newspapers in many smaller communities, the reporter gives individual attention to only a few. In addition, "tips" sometimes will lead the reporter to interesting stories about illnesses.

Story Content

Many accounts of illness contain only one, two or three paragraphs and are usually handled similarly to a personal. The following information is usually given:

1. Name and identification of the person who is ill
2. Cause of illness
3. Condition (fair, serious, critical—an accurate quotation from the doctor or hospital)
4. Name of hospital (sometimes "at a local hospital" if person is in a private institution such as a mental hospital)
5. Duration of illness
6. Members of family at bedside
7. Effect of illness on person's public position (especially in the case of an elected official) or business.

The "Who" is the most important "W" in most illness stories and should be in the lead. For variety, or if the disease or operation is unusual, the cause of the illness or the condition of the patient may be featured. However, if the story is a follow-up, the condition of the patient is usually the feature. Note these examples:

Who
      Dr. James Witherspoon, president of State Technology University, was taken to Widner Memorial Hospital today for observation after suffering several dizzy spells while working in his office at home.

Cause
      A severe ear infection caused Dr. James Witherspoon, president of State Technology University, to suffer several dizzy spells while working in

his office at home, doctors at Widner Memorial Hospital said today. He will remain in the hospital for several days.

Condition (a follow-up)

Dr. James Witherspoon, president of State Technology University, is in good condition at Widner Memorial Hospital, recovering from a severe ear infection. He was taken to the hospital Wednesday after he suffered several dizzy spells while working in his office at home.

Hospital Notes

Some newspapers regularly carry a hospital column. It may be merely a list of "Admitted" and "Discharged" with no details given. Some hospitals refuse to make such lists available; others have a more liberal policy on publicity. It is common practice at many hospitals to ask a patient or the family if there is any objection to being listed as a patient in the daily report to the press. But with or without the cooperation of the hospitals, many personals deal with hospitalization. The following are some common examples:

Gilbert Rader, Parrottsville, underwent hip surgery Wednesday at Tokamoa Hospital, Greenville. He expects to be released in six days.

Alicia Alfredo, former Hendry County School superintendent, has returned home from New Orleans, where she underwent heart bypass surgery seven days ago at Oschner Clinic.

Jim McMillan, 6, son of Mr. and Mrs. Tom McMillan, 1831 Newberry St., suffered a broken left arm today when he fell off a swing in the playground of West Hills Elementary School. He was admitted to Methodist Hospital, where he is reported in "good" condition.

DEATHS

Death is an important item of news. It may contain all the news values discussed previously. Regardless of news values, death is reported as a public record. No person ever becomes so unimportant that he or she is not valuable as a vital statistic. The public health records chart all deaths, and state laws fix standard forms of physician's reports. Even the nameless drifter found frozen to death under a superhighway overpass is not overlooked. The drifter fits somewhere in a chain of persons and events. Although practice will vary from paper to paper in the treatment of death stories, all newspapers report deaths.

One of the best descriptions of an obituary was given by Arthur Gelb, deputy managing editor of The New York Times. He said:

An obit is the summing up of a person's life, the last statement about him for the record. It has to have fairness, balance, accuracy, substantiation of fact. We see obits as short biographies, an analysis of the man and his time. What did his life mean? What was his impact on civilization? What was his paper? . . . We try to put him in the context of history and of his field and what he meant to the people in that field.

Obituaries

Just as the practice of reporting deaths varies, so the terms used to describe this type of news story will also vary. At some newspapers, the word "obituary" means a news story written about the death of a person that is published with an individual headline. At others the obituary is the black, agate-type alphabetical listing of everyone who has died and has not yet been buried. This list is also called "Death Notices" at some newspapers. All newspapers publish stories of deaths free if they use them as separate stories. Many newspapers, however, make a per-word charge for death-column notices just as they do for classified advertisements, and such charges become part of the funeral costs. Whether the obituary is a paid item or not, the form used by the newspaper is standardized to get all essential information. Many newspapers and funeral homes use a standard form such as the one illustrated on page 268.

From a report of this kind a rather standard notice is printed in the alphabetical listing in the newspaper. Funeral arrangements usually are included when they are available. Here are two examples of death notices written by family members or funeral home officials:

LELAH H. DIETZ—Age 93. Born June 17, 1897, in Page, N.D., died Friday. She moved to Spokane in 1920 and taught high school science for several years at Central Valley High School and other schools in Idaho and Washington. She was a member of the Catholic Daughters of America. She is survived by a niece, Betty D. Westin, of Seattle, and a nephew, Edward J. Dietz, of Arlington, Va., and grandnieces and nephews. Mass of Christian Burial will be celebrated Wednesday at 9:30 a.m. at St. Joseph's Church, Spokane. Burial will be at Holy Cross Cemetery, Spokane. Evergreen Funeral Home is in charge of services.

RUSSELL, MARY EDITH (JONES)—Age 80, was funeralized Oct. 22, in Indianapolis, Ind., at Bethel Faith Tabernacle. The Rev. Merritt Taliaferro officiated. She was a graduate of Anderson College and taught public school for 45 years. Attending the obsequies were: nieces, Mrs. Mattie S. Smith; Mrs. Joyce Williams; and Miss Theodosia Perrin.

The amount of information in a death notice will vary. Because it is paid for by the family, it can include such information as the names of the pallbearers, the name of the officiating minister and other material. At some newspapers, these notices are handled by a clerk or a secretary using information provided by the funeral homes. Others have reporters write the notices from the funeral home reports.

Death Stories

Reporters are called on to write death stories (or obituaries) that are handled in regular news style. Some newspapers publish these on the same page as the paid notices. Others have separate pages for them. The Indianapolis News, for example, has for years done an excellent job of reporting deaths in that city and its surrounding area. Each death is handled as a separate news item, and the stories vary in length depending on the person and the amount of available

```
                            OBITUARY

Name_____Age_____

Address_____

Place of death_____Date_____Time_____

Cause of death_____

Date of birth_____Place of birth_____

Parents_____

Education_____

Occupation_____

Husband or wife (maiden name)_____

Date of marriage_____Place_____

Residence here since_____

Previous residences_____

Name of present employer_____

Previous employers_____

Military record_____

Church affiliation_____

Clubs, fraternal organizations, other affiliations_____

_____

Special interests or hobbies_____

Survivors with relationships and addresses_____

_____

_____

Body at_____

Funeral arrangements_____
```

information. Other newspapers limit these stories to persons who are news-worthy enough to justify extra attention. In most large cities, the death of a person who has gained no prominence and who died of natural causes would be reported only in the paid notices column.

Although the information in the paid notice or the funeral home's report provides the basic facts for the news story, the reporter often must seek additional information by telephoning or visiting relatives or others mentioned in the notice. If the person is prominent, the reporter frequently checks the newspaper's morgue or library for additional information and calls friends, business associates and others for material on the deceased. If the person is exceptionally prominent, a reporter should refer to several standard reference books, such as Who's Who in America, for additional material.

The wire services and most large newspapers maintain rather complete files of hold-for-release obituaries on most big names—national and international leaders, for example. Many smaller newspapers maintain similar stories, ready for print, on the most prominent citizens in their communities. These usually are brought up to date at regular intervals.

Story Content

If a newspaper does carry individual stories on deaths, any reporter assigned to write them should keep in mind that the story must provide the following information:

1. Name and identification (address, occupation and affiliations) of the deceased
2. Age
3. Day and time of death
4. Place of death
5. Cause of death
6. Duration of illness
7. Names of members of the immediate family (survivors)
8. Effects of death on the person's public position (if applicable).

Although this information is routine, there should be nothing routine about the writing of the story. The reporter should use every journalistic device to show what manner of person the deceased was. This, of course, depends on details. The reporter should look for colorful incidents, anecdotes, personal traits, and personal remembrances of friends and family to convey exactly why this particular death is news.

The first paragraph should sum up the circumstances of the death with name, age, identification by position or profession, and time and place of death. The remainder of the story should be a carefully constructed biographical sketch of the person in an effort to picture for the reader what he or she really was like. It should not be a mere routine summation of the facts of his or her life and career. Although it should contain colorful highlights of the deceased's life history, it should not be light or frivolous. For example, when the Italian novelist Alberto Moravia died in 1990, most newspapers reported his death on an inside page. However, The New York Times featured the story prominently in the lower left-hand corner of the front page with a photograph and continued the story inside for about another 20 inches. The story began:

> ROME, Sept. 26—Alberto Moravia, whose many novels explored alienation and other social traumas while focusing almost obsessively on human sexuality, died today at his apartment overlooking the Tiber River. He was 82 years old.
> He had either a stroke or a heart attack, his doctors said in a preliminary report.

> Mr. Moravia was Italy's most widely read author of this century, his works having been translated into 30 languages and selling in the millions around the world.
>
> Movie versions of several novels further enhanced his popularity, perhaps none more than the 1961 film, "Two Women," directed by Victorio DeSica. . . .

The story continued for several more paragraphs on the front page before being moved inside.

When Gen. Curtis LeMay, World War II Air Force commander of the bombing of Japan and a builder of U.S. strategic forces, died, The New York Times announced it on page 1 with a one-column photo. The complete obituary covered nearly half a page inside and was accompanied by a photograph of the general and several of his staff officers during World War II. The story began:

> Gen. Curtis E. LeMay, the former Air Force chief of staff who was the architect of strategic air power and insisted that the nation be willing to use nuclear weapons when necessary, died yesterday in a California military hospital. He was 83 years old and lived in Morento Valley, Calif.
>
> The retired four-star general died of a heart attack at the 22d Strategic Hospital at March Air Force Base, an Air Force spokesman said. . . .

Often newspapers will solicit comments from friends, co-workers and admirers when a prominent citizen or public figure dies. Those comments are worked into a separate story that accompanies the story of the person's death. The more prominent the individual, the longer and more detailed the obituary. In some cases, several stories focusing on various aspects of the person's career also are used.

When composer-conductor Leonard Bernstein died, The New York Times story of his death began at the top of the front page accompanied by a photograph. It was jumped inside, where a full page was devoted to the remainder of the story detailing his long, colorful and occasionally controversial career. The story included numerous quotes from friends, colleagues and others evaluating his career and his contributions to music.

Later, when Mary Martin, often referred to as the "First Lady of the Broadway stage," died, the Times' story, accompanied by a picture, began in the lower center of the front page and was continued inside, where it covered three-quarters of the page. The story was an extensive review of her long and distinguished career in Broadway musicals.

Similar treatment is given by other papers to prominent citizens in their community. When Milton Roberts, a prominent businessman and city council member for more than 40 years, died, The Knoxville (Tenn.) News-Sentinel carried the story across the top of its front page and continued it to an inside page. The story reviewed his long public career and included quotes from current and former public officials who had served with him.

Obviously not every newspaper has the staff or the space to treat the death of a prominent citizen in the community in the same manner as the major dailies. However, a number of them often seek ways to present an additional tribute to someone who touched the lives of many. Here is an example of that type of story. It was written by Sam Venable, columnist for The Knoxville News-Sentinel:

> You don't have to read Miss Manners' column to know letters must be written in black or blue-black ink.
>
> Not if you were a student of Miss Geneva Anderson of Maryville, who died Friday at age 79 and will be buried today at Grandview Cemetery.
>
> Nor did you split your infinitives nor dangle your participles, splice complete sentences with commas nor (sin of sins) chew gum in class.
>
> "Now cherubs," she would say, "someone in this room is chewing gum. We will stop our lesson until this matter is resolved."
>
> That's when silence would fall upon her class—like an anvil. And tiny slivers of contraband Juicy Fruit in your mouth would balloon into a pumpkin.
>
> But if you were lucky enough to be assigned to Geneva Anderson for a year of senior English, you came away with more than the basics of letter-writing and etiquette. Just ask the thousands of pupils who studied under her at Robertville, Everett, Walland, Porter, Hixon and Young schools. Many students kept in contact with her until late this summer, when she suffered a debilitating stroke.
>
> In nearly two decades of formal education, I came in contact with countless dozens of teachers. Most were good, a few excellent . . . and, alas, a handful so poor they give "tenure" a bad reputation. Geneva Anderson was the bluest chip of them all.
>
> We met in the fall of 1964, the start of my final year at Young. English had never been a particularly difficult subject for me; but for three years, I had heard upperclassmen warn about nine months of enslavement if your name was included on her roster.
>
> Mine, gulp, was . . . and with fear and trembling, I entered her room.
>
> What I happily discovered was not a female Simon Legree but an utterly charming, humorous, knowledgeable and challenging tutor.
>
> Whenever Miss Anderson was particularly pleased with your work, she would write "sheer delight" at the top. I am here to tell you she was sheer delight from that first class in September until graduation in June.
>
> Geneva Anderson could read "Macbeth" aloud and you could smell the cauldron bubbling. She could transform a vocabulary lesson into an exciting quest for new words. She could show you how to decode Harbrace and use it as a road map into the world of communications. And she made a certain four-eyed lad believe people would pay him to write, and then he wouldn't have to work for a living.
>
> Firm? Indeed. But not strong-arm firm. On rare occasions of civil disorder, all Miss Anderson had to do was cut her eyes and stare for a moment—and calm was instantly restored.
>
> I do hope St. Peter has everything in order. If that poor boy is chewing gum when Miss Anderson arrives, or tries to sign her up with green ink, he's gonna wish he had applied for a transfer.

The reporter must write death stories objectively and with dignity. Every effort should be made to resist the temptation to make the reader weep. The language of the story should be simple and precise, avoiding saccharine words and phrases such as "he will be missed by all." A person "dies" instead of "passes away"; he or she is "buried" instead of "interred," no matter what the family and the funeral director say. However, the reporter should learn the practices of the various religions and refer to them properly in the story.

Occasionally, a reporter is faced with a problem in writing a death story about a person whose past was marred by a scandal—a prison term, disbarment or a messy divorce that had made the front pages. If the person was entirely private, many newspapers would elect to leave out such facts, especially if the person had lived down the incident. However, if the person who was once a convict later became a prominent public official, the story must mention the prison term. Because the deceased was a public person and the criminal case was a well-known fact, the newspaper cannot leave it out. Facts of that nature, no matter how unpleasant, are essential to an adequate story.

When a death is announced in the afternoon newspaper, the next day's morning newspaper in the same city generally does not repeat the same lead. It usually features a different angle—the announcement of the funeral services, for example. Even if the funeral arrangements were carried in the original obit, they are the feature of the lead for the second-day story.

FUNERALS

The funeral announcement is the follow-up of a death story, except in the case of more prominent persons whose funerals might attract large numbers of mourners. As in any follow-up, a brief summary of the preceding story must be included, but the lead features the funeral.

Story Content

1. Time
2. Place
3. Whether public or private (open to the public unless otherwise stated)
4. Who will officiate
5. Place of burial
6. Active pallbearers
7. Honorary pallbearers.

Here is a typical funeral story:

> Funeral services for Col. E.B. (Buck) Ewing, 71, who had served as mayor of Hernando for two terms after he retired from the U.S. Army, were held at 11 a.m., Monday, at Calvary Baptist Church. Burial was in Hernando Memorial Cemetery.
>
> The Rev. Charles Louis Griffen, pastor of the church, praised Mr. Ewing for his "dedicated service to the nation and his untiring efforts to make Hernando a better place for all of us to live."
>
> Mr. Ewing, who died Saturday after suffering a heart attack at home, served as mayor from 1973 to 1981. During that time, he brought several industries to the community and established the 911 emergency telephone system.
>
> He did not run for re-election after his second term and later became chairman of the Hernando Park Commission. He helped develop a public park downtown on land donated to the city.

The remainder of the story would include the highlights of his military career, his education, his civic and fraternal memberships, and a list of survivors.

The funeral story of a prominent person would be greatly expanded and reported in the same manner as any other news story of similar importance. It would include excerpts from the minister's eulogy, description of the service, and an account of relatives and prominent friends and members of associations who attended in addition to any other information required to report the funeral adequately to readers.

The New York Times, for example, reported the funeral of Archbishop Fulton J. Sheen, the famous television priest, under the headline "Sheen Rites at St. Patrick's." The story was accompanied by two photographs of the funeral services. The story began this way:

> Behind the high altar of St. Patrick's Cathedral, the ornate bronze doors of the crypt stood open yesterday as Terence Cardinal Cooke said the funeral mass for Archbishop Fulton J. Sheen, who died Sunday at the age of 84.
>
> More than 50 ushers dressed in dark suits helped seat the hundreds who attended and then cordoned off the pews as they became full.
>
> Archbishop Edward T. O'Meara delivered the homily, praising Archbishop Sheen for his work during 63 years in the priesthood, during which time he wrote more than 50 books and gained lasting fame and the affection of millions through his radio and television ministry. . . .

Most newspapers prefer to list the cause of death. However, some families either refuse to give that information or request it be withheld. This is particularly true in the case of certain diseases such as cancer and acquired immune deficiency syndrome (AIDS). Newspapers generally defer to the family's wishes. But increasing numbers of families have consented to have AIDS listed as the cause of death.

A similar situation exists with listing the survivors. Some individuals who have died of AIDS have had long-term relationships with a companion. An increasing number of death stories list that person among the survivors, if that information is provided.

Here is how The Associated Press (AP) reported the memorial services for Canadian AIDS activist David Lewis:

> VANCOUVER, B.C.—AIDS activist David Lewis was surrounded by friends and family when he changed his intravenous drip solution from a harmless saline solution to a "sleeping potion," says a man who was with Lewis when he died Aug. 24.
>
> "David died supremely happy, at first frightened, then peaceful," Roedy Green told 40 people who attended a memorial service Tuesday evening for Lewis.
>
> Lewis attracted international attention in July when he revealed that he helped eight people with AIDS kill themselves during the past nine years.
>
> He said he placed overdoses of their drugs within the AIDS sufferers' reach.
>
> "I think it's immoral and unethical to not help someone die if that's what they want," Lewis, who was 38, said at the time.
>
> His own health then deteriorated from a number of illnesses related to acquired immune deficiency syndrome (AIDS) and he announced last month he would commit suicide rather than endure a painful and undignified death.
>
> "David did not want to die," said Green. "He enjoyed his life immensely, even to the very last second."

Green drew laughter and applause when he told the mourners that Lewis detested British Columbia Premier Bill Vander Zalm right to the end for charging AIDS patients for drugs.

"If possible, David will haunt the premier's theme park, Fantasy Gardens," he said.

Robert Gard, who knew Lewis for almost 20 years, remembers him as an activist even at the age of 19.

"He was on television. He was in the newspaper. He was championing human rights at that point in time. That has been part of his life's work and that's one of the things I'm going to remember about him."

The 10 friends and family members who were with Lewis when he died fulfilled his last request and toasted his life with champagne, Green said.

EXERCISES

1. Study how daily and weekly newspapers in your community handle stories on illnesses and deaths. Interview the city editors of the papers about their policy on obituaries. Write a short report on your findings.

2. Clip a death story and an illness story from any newspaper and make a news analysis of each.

3. Select a prominent woman or man in your community or state whose death would be a significant news story. Make a list of the facts about her or him that you would need to write a story. Then, using all sources available to you (but do not call the person or any immediate relative), collect all the facts for the story. Organize those facts similarly to the form on page 268 and turn it in to your instructor along with the list of sources.

4. In your college or university library locate microfilm copies of a major newspaper such as the Chicago Tribune, the Los Angeles Times or The New York Times. Study the way that newspaper handled the death of any major U.S. or world figure in the past two years. Locate the microfilm of your local newspaper or the major newspaper in your state and compare handling of the same story. Write a brief report on your findings.

5. Write stories from these notes:
   a. Dr. Roberta Rogalata, 55
      Professor of botany at
      Whitewater Community College
      Spending weekend at
      Her Norris Lake cottage
      Became violently ill
      Rushed to St. Mary's Hospital
      In critical condition
      Husband, Armando, said
      She had picked mushrooms
      Cooked them with hamburgers
      She collapsed after eating
      He became ill but recovered
      She is in coma
      "Her situation is grave,"
      Dr. Yuzuru Kondo said

Mushrooms were poisonous,
Dr. Kondo believes
Both meat and mushrooms
Being analyzed in lab
    (Sources: Norris Rescue Squad, Hospital spokeswoman Mary Sharpe, Dr. Kondo, Armando Rogalata)

b. Lee A. Johnson, 59
Assistant police chief
Suffered a broken right ankle
When he fell off a ladder
At his home on Westland Drive
He is in Regional Medical Center
Reported in good condition
Johnson said he was cleaning
Leaves out of the gutters
Around his home
Started down the ladder
Apparently missed a rung
Lost his footing
Fell about 10 feet
Landed on cement patio
Wife, Eula, called 911
Rescue Squad took him
To hospital where
He was admitted
He said he hopes to
Be back to work in two weeks
On crutches
    (Sources: Mrs. Johnson, hospital officials, Police Department public relations office)

c. Wilma Hammond Fry, 48
Director of Human Services
Department for City
Has taken leave of absence
For unspecified period
Has not been in office
More than two weeks
Staff members refused to
Discuss her whereabouts
Mayor said she took leave
"For personal reasons"
Made no further comments
Rumors around city hall
Say she "flipped" and
Is patient at private
Psychiatric hospital
Husand and family
decline to comment
Her department just
Underwent investigation

And audit for mismanagement
Of public funds
City officials decline
To say if investigation results
To be submitted to grand jury
  (Sources: Mayor, Human Services office staff, district attorney's office)

6. Write an obituary using information in the report on the death of Joe Thomas (Red) McCord (see reproduction of report, below).

7. Write a death story using the information in the report in Exercise 6 plus this additional information:

He had played trumpet on Keith Vaudeville Circuit for several years, then formed his own band and became a local tradition playing dances, clubs, parks and fairs. His

---

Death Report

Date __March 17__

Name __Joe Thomas (Red) McCord__   Age __78__

Address __716 Pine Ridge Road__

Place of death __Memorial Medical Center__   Date __March 17 (2:30 a.m.)__

Cause of death __Heart attack__

Date of birth __October 25__   Place of birth __Cleveland, Tennessee__

Parents __Mr. and Mrs. John A. McCord (deceased)__

Education __Cleveland Public Schools, Vanderbilt University AB Music__

Occupation __Professional musician, band leader__

Husband or wife (maiden name) __Sally Marie McCord (deceased)__

Date of marriage __June 16, 1937__   Place __Cleveland, Tennessee__

Residence here since __1946__

Previous residences __Cleveland, Tennessee; Knoxville, Tennessee__

Name of present employer __Retired after leading own band many years__

Previous employer __WSM Radio, Ted Weems Orchestra__

Military record __Captain, U.S. Air Force, 1941–45, military band leader__

Church affiliation __First Baptist Church__

Clubs, fraternal organizations, other affiliations __American Federation of__
Musicians Bluff City Lions Club

Special interest or hobbies __Collecting early sheet music__

Survivors with relationship and address on each __Mrs. Joan Counts, 1421__
Spencer St.; two grandsons, Joe Thomas Counts and Donny Counts

Body at __Woodlawn Funeral Home__

Funeral arrangements __Incomplete__

FUNERAL REPORT: Joe Thomas (Red) McCord

Time _2 p.m., March 19_

Place _First Baptist Church_

Officiating _The Rev. William Robert Scrubbs_

Burial place _Lakeview Cemetery_

Active pallbearers _Representatives of the American Federation of Musi-_
_____cians_

Honorary pallbearers _none_

Remarks _Music for funeral services will be provided by members of Musi-_
cians Union who played in various bands with Mr. McCord. In lieu of flowers,
family requests donations be made to American Heart Association.

---

band was the staff band for WSM radio and backed some of the greatest performers visiting the city when they played concerts in the municipal auditorium or other arenas. Daughter, Joan Counts, said: "Daddy was famous with all of the show people and vaudeville acts because they thought he was the best director in the area, and they all requested that Daddy be their director when they would call to book local musicians. Liberace came and walked into the Municipal Auditorium for rehearsal and saw Daddy on the bandstand and said: 'Everything is gonna be just perfect because Red's here.' " Jay Katz, president of Local 257, American Federation of Musicians, called him "simply the best musician I have ever worked with."

8. Write a story based on the report on funeral for Joe Thomas (Red) McCord received by the newspaper the day after publication of the death story (see reproduction of funeral report).

9. Select a prominent individual in your state or at your college or university and write a death story about him or her. Do not talk to the individual or a member of the family. However, use all other available sources in gathering your biographical information. For example, if you ask the university public information office for material, double check it with such references as Who's Who. Since this will be an "advance" similar to ones prepared by the wire services and major newspapers on prominent individuals, do not list a cause of death or funeral details. At the end of the story list the prominent individuals you would get statements from about the "death" of the person.

10. Using only the facts of your life as they now exist, write an advance death story about yourself. Do not add any imaginary detail.

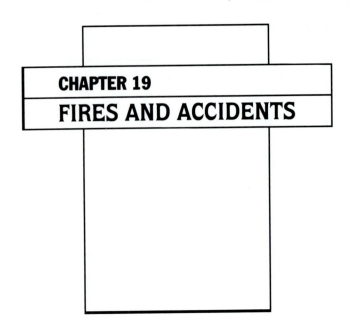

CHAPTER 19
FIRES AND ACCIDENTS

Writing a fire or accident story can present a real challenge to a reporter because much of the information is collected after the event, and often the details of the accident or fire are quite similar to those of almost every fire or accident story.

Except for the most dramatic fires and accidents, facts for the story generally are obtained from records of the police and fire departments. To avoid writing a dull and routine story, an alert reporter will attempt to get additional information by telephone or in person from witnesses—policemen, firemen, spectators and the persons involved, if possible.

Although most stories of this type are picked up as routine on regular beats—police and fire headquarters and hospitals—or from phone calls, the reporter has an obligation to the reader to make stories interesting as well as informative. Here's how Gary Marx of the Chicago Tribune began his story on a house fire that killed three children:

> By all accounts, Raoul Hanford was a good kid living in an area racked by poverty, drugs and violence.
>
> The boy helped his neighbors with chores, helped his friends with their homework and gave the small bits of money he earned from odd jobs to just about anybody in need.
>
> On Saturday, Raoul—called "Ro Ro" by his friends—celebrated his 11th birthday. He died at 1:50 a.m., Sunday, the victim of a house fire that also took the lives of his sister and niece, both 4.
>
> "I bought a GI Joe to give him for his birthday, but I didn't get a chance," said Mark Johnson, 11, Raoul's best friend, who was standing Sunday outside the burned-out two-story row house at 711 N. Montecello Ave., where the Hanfords lived. "He was generous and nice. He would always give me stuff when he had a little."
>
> Sgt. Roger Elmer, of the Chicago Police Department's bomb and arson squad, said the cause of the fire that swept through the first-floor apartment at about 12:45 a.m. remains unknown. Investigators suspect it was started by kids playing with a lighter or matches.

In addition to Raoul, those killed in the fire were Tatiana Hanford, his sister, and Davisha Allen, his niece.

The remainder of the story gave details of other family members who were injured in the fire and quoted residents of the area about the daily tragedies in the neighborhood where alcoholism, drug abuse and poverty touch almost everyone.

In some major cities, newspapers are connected with the fire department's alarm system, and the fire bells ring in the city room as well as at fire headquarters. Most newspapers monitor the police radio so they can dispatch reporters and photographers to accident and fire scenes.

No matter how the information is gathered, certain facts are always required for a complete story. The newspaper reader is eager to know who was killed or injured; the extent and amount of property damage; and the disruption the event caused, such as blocked streets and traffic delays. If, in addition, the drama of major events can be effectively presented, so much the better. But the drama should be implicit in the facts. The reporter shouldn't overwrite for effect.

Here's a fire story lead with an unusual twist by Charles Appleton of the Nashville Banner:

> SHELBYVILLE—One of the few items untouched by a fire that destroyed the 200-year-old Bethel Baptist Church yesterday was a Bible.
> "The good Lord had a hand in it. That's the only way I can explain how that Bible was spared," said Alice Bias Bell, a member of the church that authorities believe was destroyed by arsonists.
> "It was on the commune table. The commune table ain't too badly ruined, but everything else is destroyed," said Bell, 78, who has been a member of the church all her adult life.
> Sheriff Don Edwards said arson investigators have two suspects in the fire, but no charges have been filed.

The rest of the story gave the details of the fire and the community efforts that were already under way to help rebuild the tiny, predominantly black church in the El Bethel community three miles north of the city.

FACTS AND SOURCES

Story and Contents

The following formula indicates the facts and sources usually available in a major fire or accident story. Minor stories use fewer details.

Facts	*Sources*
1. Casualties	1. Police, firemen, hospitals,
a. Name and identification of every person killed and injured	funeral homes; friends and relatives of dead and injured; witnesses; neighbors
b. Manner in which persons killed or injured	

    c. Nature of injuries
    d. Disposition of dead and
       injured
  2. Damages   2. Police, firemen and property
    a. Damages to property   owners
    b. Description of property
    c. Owner of property
    d. Insurance
    e. Other property threatened
  3. Description   3. Police, firemen, persons
    a. Cause   involved, witnesses
    b. Time and duration
    c. Chronological account of
       incidents
    d. Relief work of firemen,
       police or others
    e. Spectators
  4. Escapes   4. Police, firemen, persons
    a. Rescues   involved, witnesses
    b. Experiences of those
       escaping
  5. Legal action   5. Police, firemen, fire marshal,
    a. Investigations   property owners, lawyers
    b. Arrests
    c. Suits
  6. Sidelights (human interest, as
    part of main story or as
    separate story)

In a major fire and accident story the number of persons dead or injured is usually featured. The amount of property damage is commonly featured if there are no injuries or deaths. But involvement of a prominent person, an unusual cause, a dramatic rescue or any one of the five W's may sometimes be featured in the lead.

STORY FORMS

Fire and accident stories can range in form and size from a brief to a lengthy several-feature story. The multiple-casualty story form is often used when such treatment is justified. The following are examples of several fire story leads:

      ANCHORAGE, Alaska (AP)—More than 150 wildfires raced across Alaska's interior, forcing the evacuation of a town of 900 people and blocking the Alaska Highway, the main road into the state.
      Gov. Steve Cowper declared a statewide state of emergency and called on the Alaska National Guard to help fight the 159 fires that raged over

172,500 acres of forest and open tundra. An elite firefighting team from California was being flown into the region later today.

No one was reported injured by Thursday night, officials said. . . .

A five-year-old boy was admitted to University Medical Center today suffering from smoke inhalation following a midday fire in his family's apartment.

Antonio Johnson was reported in critical but stable condition in the pediatric intensive care unit, Medical Center officials said.

The child was pulled by firefighters from a bedroom at 536 Townsend Dr., said Fire Chief Leonard Basler.

Two other children, Stephen Johnson, 4, and Contra Johnson, 3, fled the burning apartment and were uninjured, Basler said. . . .

Frequently a fire story will produce a follow-up that deals with the cause of the fire or the condition of the injured. Here is the lead on a follow-up to a story of a fire in which one child was killed and three others injured:

Every month, Johnetta Crowell and her four children received a $278 Aid for Dependent Children check from the federal government—hardly enough to pay the $250 rent on a new apartment and an electricity deposit.

Crowell couldn't afford the $100 deposit required to turn on the electricity for her duplex, so she relied on candles for light, her aunt, Annie Clack, said.

But things began looking up last weekend when she learned she'd been hired as a housekeeper starting next Monday. With full-time employment, she believed Metro Social Services would provide the deposit, so she set up a Tuesday meeting.

Instead, Tuesday found her and three of her four children critically injured in a fire that badly damaged her apartment and her fourth child, Jerome, 7, dead.

Metro Fire Marshall Bill Hamilton said the fire started when a "candle tipped over and set a bed on fire." . . .

Sometimes fires can lead to criminal charges. Here is a short story about an arrest that grew out of an attempt to burn a house:

A 59-year-old man was charged Friday with trying to set his home on fire.

Police said witnesses reported the man poured gasoline on his front door and porch and a side door Thursday night, and then tried to light it. The witnesses said the man tried two matches, but they didn't work, so he went next door to borrow more.

Police arrived, though, and caught him after a short chase. They charged John Maddox, Jr., 1723 Holman, with attempted aggravated arson.

Accidents often involve injury and death. The leads on stories about them should focus on the human element as in these examples:

BRENTWOOD—One person was killed and at least 14 others were injured this morning in the fireball that erupted after a tractor-trailer rammed a stranded Greyhound bus into another bus on the shoulder of Interstate 65.

Names of the victims were not immediately available, pending notification of families, a Highway Patrol official said.

The Greyhound and the cab of the rig which was loaded with produce burst into flames. . . .

One transient was killed and five others injured outside a downtown Los Angeles homeless mission Saturday when they were struck by a hit-and-run driver whose car collided with a tomato truck and then careened onto the sidewalk.

The names of the three male and two female victims were not released.

The accident occurred at about 8:30 a.m., while the transients were either sleeping or sitting outside the Fred Jordan Mission, 445 Towne Ave., Sgt. Jeff Siggers said. . . .

A 26-year-old Cleveland, Miss., man was critically injured Monday in a two-vehicle accident at Brooks Avenue and South Third Street. He is in intensive care at Mercy Hospital.

James D. Yeager was driving a four-wheel-drive vehicle north on South Third when it struck a tractor-trailer driven by Glenn L. Ricks, 48, of Southhaven, about 7:50 p.m.

Police Lt. J. R. Krepela said Yeager's vehicle struck the right side of the truck which was traveling east on Brooks Avenue.

Ricks was not injured, Krepela said.

Vocabulary and Fact Reporting

In reporting accidents—notably automobile accidents, because of their frequency—the reporter must use words carefully, with an eye to precise meaning. Only moving objects collide, strictly speaking. Therefore, "*struck* a parked car" is better than "*collided with* a parked car." "The accident occurred *when the car in which they were riding*" is awkward, yet "their car" is usually inaccurate. A number of newspapers, however, have come to accept the latter.

Libel actions grow out of inaccurate phrasing, and shortcuts of language should be used with care. Except in reports of storms, earthquakes and other "acts of God," colorful language should always yield to fact reporting. The phrase *completely demolished* (or *destroyed*) is redundant. To *demolish* or *destroy* means completely, so the word *completely* is unnecessary. A statement that a person is *not expected to live* should be reported as *critically injured* unless a direct quote is available from a physician using those exact words.

Factual reporting and careful language will also help the reporter write without expressing an opinion on the person responsible for a fire or accident. The reporter does not attempt to fix that responsibility. Who the guilty person is may seem apparent from the facts, the arrests and the statements of officials as reported in the case; but the reporter makes no effort to point out the guilty party, for that is the job of the courts.

If the facts of a story tend to point the finger of guilt at a person, the ethics of fair play require that the reporter make an effort to get that person's side of the story and report it at the same time. If the reporter is unable to reach the person, then the story should indicate that fact.

COMPLETE REPORTING

Most disasters are treated adequately when presented as straight news, with little interpretation. However, if such events accumulate into a daily threat to the security of life and property, the newspaper may feel compelled to develop a story or series of stories dealing with the problem.

Most communities face the serious continuing problem of automobile accidents. Occasionally there may be a series of fires, and there are epidemics of disease and crime. What causes those disasters? How do they occur? How could they be avoided? Before the community can protect itself or take the proper remedial steps, it must know the facts. That is where the reporter and the newspaper come in. In such cases it is the reporter's job to report not merely the surface events but the underlying causes as well. Often it is the reporter and the newspaper who force reluctant or foot-dragging public officials to undertake programs to correct potentially dangerous situations.

Almost every newspaper, at some time during the year, will print a story or series of stories touched off by a single news event such as an accident or fire. Three school bus accidents in less than a month caused a midwestern newspaper to do a series on how carefully the buses were checked for mechanical failure. The stories forced the school board to institute rigid new inspection policies. Fires in three apartment complexes in a southeastern city sent reporters checking county building codes that turned out to be virtually non-existent. County and state officials quickly promised a new enforcement program.

Some newspapers have used news events to bring about improved traffic enforcement and better sanitary conditions at public housing and sewage treatment plants, for example. In each case, the reporter and the newspaper saw a need to reach the heart of a community problem. Rather than stopping with the initial report, the newspaper assigned the reporter to go beneath the surface of the initial event and through investigation and interpretative analysis present the problem to the public and public officials. Public service awards are won each year by many newspapers that investigate and report on communitywide problems.

EXERCISES

1. Clip a fire story and an accident story from any newspaper available to you and make a news analysis of each.

2. Using a story of a major accident or fire from a newspaper in your community, seek to determine its cost, not only to the persons involved but to the community. Interview the police or fire chief to find out how much it cost in manpower, time and equipment to handle the fire or accident. Talk to an insurance executive to find out what fires and accidents do to local insurance rates. If there were injuries, check with hospital officials to find out what the medical treatment cost. If a major building burned, what impact did it have on tax collections, tenants and the businesses and professionals who occupied the building? Write a report on your findings.

3. Clip a traffic accident story for a daily and a weekly newspaper in your community. Compare the stories and write a brief report on how each newspaper handled its story.

4. Interview the fire and police chiefs in your community. Write a human-interest story on each of the departments.

5. Write stories based on these notes:

a. Linda K. Nicholas, 38, Miller Village
Driving an Olds 98
Lost control of her car
As she entered the parking lot
At Kingstown Shopping Mall
About 12:45 p.m. today
Crossed a grass median
And three low concrete curbs
Hit 1984 Plymouth Reliant
Bounced into a 1978 Volkswagen Rabbit
Hit a 1987 Chevrolet station wagon
Struck a 1989 Toyota Celica
Sideswiped a 1987 Dodge
And rammed the side of a 1990 Mercury
Witnesses said it appeared
She had "floorboarded" her car
Others said it appeared the
Accelerator was stuck
Patrolman Jerry Mowl said
Apparently it wasn't
He said investigation would continue
When Nicholas "settles down"
from all the excitement
She suffered minor bruises
Did not require medical treatment
(Sources: Police report, Patrolman Mowl)

b. William B. Dunne, 59,
Lives in suburban Willow Grove
Driving his 1989 Cadillac
South on Neely Road
About 7:30 p.m. Saturday
He fell out of the El Dorado
Car kept rolling
Crashed into metal mailbox
At 3341 Neely
Crossed a vacant lot next door
Slammed into a 1983 Silverado pickup
Parked in drive at 118 Lawndale
Dunne taken to Methodist Hospital
In critical condition
With leg and chest injuries
He told police the car door opened
He lost control and fell out
While trying to close the door

Police charged him with
Driving while intoxicated
Reckless driving, public intoxication
Refusal to submit
To blood alcohol test
    (Source: Police report, Patrolman Larry Lloyd, hospital officials)

c. State Highway Patrolman John Bailey
Reported two Carrol County residents
Killed in head-on crash
Friday morning on Highway 22
In Weakly County near Gleason
Killed were Robert L. Simms, 40, Melrose
Driver of 1989 Pontiac
And Janie Triplett, 3, Atwood
Passenger in second vehicle
Injured were Betty D. Triplett, 32, Atwood
Driver of a 1973 Dodge
And mother of Janie
Two other Triplett children
Robert, 1 month, Rebecca, 9
Also in car but uninjured
Trooper Bailey said
Simms southbound on Route 22
About one mile south of Gleason
His car crossed into
Northbound lane and
Struck Triplett car head on
Mrs. Triplett's husband, Don
Killed in traffic accident
About a month ago
    (Sources: Patrolman Bailey, police report)

d. Charita T. Mathenia, 9
1608 Michigan Ave.
Daughter of Maxine Mathenia
Ran into path of car
On South Third near Essex
Injured critically when struck
By car driven by Margarito Martinez, 52
3780 Oaklawn in Millington
Child in intensive care unit
LeBonheur Children's Medical Center
Witness told police that
Charita was walking to
A.B. Hill Elementary School
About 7:45 a.m.
Suddenly ran across Third
Into path of Martinez car
No charges placed against driver
    (Source: Pat Rowland, police traffic division secretary)

e. City and county fire departments
   Responded to four-alarm blaze
   At Sunset Dinner Theater
   About 3 a.m., today
   Theater located about three miles
   Outside city limits on
   Northshore Drive near Bluegrass Road
   Building was a former horse barn
   Converted to dinner theater
   About three years ago
   Blaze discovered by
   Carl Parker who was driving
   On Northshore headed for
   Home in suburban Concord
   Six fire units responded
   Took three hours to control fire
   Fire Chief Leonard Basler
   Said 70 percent of building destroyed
   Investigation of fire continuing
   But Basler said it appears
   Faulty wiring in stage lights
   May have caused the blaze
   Freddie Savoy, theater owner
   Estimated damage at more than
   Half million dollars
   Hopes to rebuild and reopen in fall
   Rehearsing for new production
   Of musical review
   Starring all local entertainers
   Will seek temporary quarters
   "Because it's a terrific show
   "People ought to see these
   "Very talented kids perform"
   Traffic blocked on Northshore
   Detoured on to Morrell Road
           (Sources: Chief Basler, Savoy)

f. Four mountain homes destroyed
   Four others damaged
   By forest fire early Saturday
   On hillside at Lake Arrowhead
   Fire officials believe
   Fire deliberately set
   Fire caused estimated $1 million damage
   Blackened 17 acres of forest near houses
   About 150 firefighters
   From six agencies brought
   Blaze under control about
   Three hours after 12:11 a.m.
   Arrowhead Fire District Capt.

Pat O'Kelly said fire started
In house under construction
He said it was "definitely arson"
Gave no other details
He said when firefighters arrived
"The whole hillside was ablaze"
Called it most destructive fire
"In recent memory" at Arrowhead
A dozen families evacuated from
Path of fire to nearby resort hotel
Two of destroyed homes
Appeared to be unoccupied
Vacant lots dot much of hillside
Fire companies nearly saved
Many other homes that were
Threatened by blaze, O'Kelly said
    (Source: O'Kelly, residents in area)

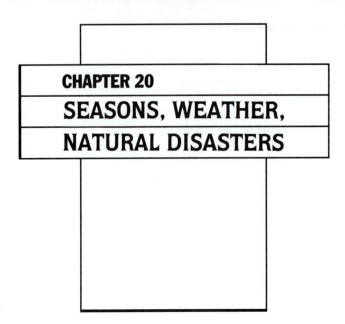

CHAPTER 20
SEASONS, WEATHER, NATURAL DISASTERS

A tornado rips through a Chicago suburb, killing 26 people and injuring 350 others. Damage to homes and business property runs into the hundreds of millions of dollars.

Hurricane Hugo devastates the North and South Carolina coasts, causing more than a billion dollars' damage and leaving 35 dead; 26,000 are left homeless and 224,000 are temporarily out of work.

A 7.1-point earthquake in the mountains near Santa Cruz, in northern California, spreads death and destruction for more than 100 miles in the San Francisco Bay area. Sixty-seven die, 3,000 are injured and 14,000 are left homeless.

Major national disasters of this nature challenge and strain the strengths and talents of a newspaper's staff. But they also often bring out the best in the writers and editors. The impressive results of their individual and team efforts can and do result in national recognition. The San Jose Mercury News, for example, won the 1990 Pulitzer Prize for its coverage of the Santa Cruz earthquake.

But there is an equal challenge in having to write about the weather on a daily basis, especially when the forecast changes little from day to day. Until recently the daily weather story in many newspapers was dumped on the newest or weakest reporter in the newsroom. But not any longer. The continuing popularity of television weather forecasts and the excitement generated when USA TODAY introduced its four-color weather map and detailed regional summaries changed all of that.

Newspapers pay attention to the weather story every day now, not just when there is a blizzard or thunderstorms that send creeks and rivers over their banks. And many newspapers send their reporters to seminars and short courses in meteorology and climatology to help them improve their ability to write about the weather accurately and authoritatively.

WEATHER STORIES

Mark Twain was half right when he said everybody talks about the weather but nobody does anything about it. Everybody does talk about the weather. Newspaper editors know that the weather story is consistently one of the best-read items in the paper every day. Many newspapers carry a regular front-page news story about the forecast. Almost all newspapers carry a detailed weather map, frequently in color, and complete local, regional and national forecasts that are provided by independent weather forecasting services or the National Weather Service. A listing of high and low temperatures in major cities across the nation generally is included.

A reporter assigned to write the weather story is often faced with making the same or nearly the same forecast sound fresh and interesting day after day during extended hot or cold, wet or dry, spells. It's not easy. During a heat wave in Memphis, Tenn., a local restaurant owner gave the writer of the weather story a different angle. Here's the lead on that story:

> Attempting to meet a hot demand, a Memphis restaurant showered its customers with water Friday.
> The Cottage Restaurant at Summer and Holmes perched oscillating lawn sprinklers atop its entrance. So despite a hazy blue sky and temperatures in the 90s, water drops marked the lunch crowd's clothes as they took their seats.
> The Cottage may not have to resort to such tactics this weekend, however. ''The outlook for rain this weekend is the best it's been since July,'' said meteorologist Brad Grant of the National Weather Service.

The remainder of the story gave the complete weather forecast for the area and recapped the daily temperatures for the week. It also included information about school closings.

To avoid a routine story based on the day's forecast only, many editors insist that the reporter look for a human-interest approach. But reporters should avoid trying to be overly cute or clever. Adding imaginary elements or stretching the facts could change or misrepresent the forecast and lead to angry readers. It could also bring a rebuke from federal officials. It is a violation of federal law to falsify a weather forecast.

Hyped up, overly dramatic efforts to give a lead a dramatic impact (such as this example from The Atlanta Constitution) not only fail but can be an embarrassment to the newspaper. This story was compiled from the wire services, but perhaps it should have been credited to the Armageddon Press International:

> Pigs screamed in the heat Wednesday and died on broiling Illinois farms. Chickens keeled over in North Carolina. The sturdy old brick homes of St. Louis turned into deadly ovens for the elderly and sick.
> The heat wave that has oppressed the nation's eastern half for more than a week groaned on and got worse. Temperatures soared from the 90s toward the 100s in much of the torrid zone.
> Across the nation the blistering weather was blamed for at least 29 deaths. Ten died in the St. Louis area alone, where a heat emergency was in force and 50 civic cooling centers were open.

If humans were dying, shouldn't they have been mentioned before the pigs and chickens? And is St. Louis really in the nation's eastern half or more toward the middle?

Frequently the weather figures into other stories. Here are several examples:

> GASSAWAY, W.VA. (AP)—A big-rig truck loaded with a cargo of new automobiles crashed into two cars stopped alongside an interstate during a violent thunderstorm Thursday.
> Seven people in the stopped cars were killed, State Trooper Frank Biggs said.
> The carrier, hauling eight vehicles, came around a curve on Interstate 70 near this central West Virginia town, sideswiped a concrete divider and careened into the cars.

> Winter blasted back into the Chicago metropolitan area Wednesday with a fierce combination of relentless winds and biting snow that left rush hour travelers stranded for hours on snarled roads and expressways.
> Most commuters who worked in Chicago's Loop suffered hours-long delays in traveling home to outlying areas such as Will, McHenry, DuPage and Kane counties. Commutes from suburb to suburb were equally taxing.
>   (Chicago Tribune)

And here's the lead on an animal story with a weather angle from The Commercial Appeal, Memphis, Tenn.:

> The three normally snow-white polar bears at the Memphis Zoo have taken on a distinct green tinge—evidence they have been spending lots of time submerged during the searing summer heat.
> "We bleach the pools and we do everything we can to avoid it," Chuck Brady, the zoo's curator for animals, said Thursday.
> "But once they start turning green, it's almost impossible to stop."
> The culprit is algae.

Special Weather Stories

Often the weather may become the lead story or one of the major stories of the day. A special story is demanded if:

1. The weather results in disasters—floods, hurricanes, tornadoes, droughts, dust storms, blizzards, lightning and other weather quirks that cause deaths or serious damages
2. There are sudden changes—cold waves, early snows, heavy rains or other out-of-the ordinary conditions
3. Records are approached or broken—highs and lows in monthly and annual temperatures or rainfall
4. A special event is affected by the weather—football and baseball games or other major sports events, parades, other outdoor events and even some indoor events.

Readers are interested not merely in data but also in the social and economic effects of unusual weather. The effects of weather on crops in farming areas can be of major local interest and perhaps even have national and international implications. A poor Russian wheat harvest resulting from bad weather eventually affected the price of bread in the American supermarkets, for example.

Such news is obtained from a variety of sources: the hospitals for deaths, injuries, and illnesses; the police for accidents and traffic problems; the fire department for fires and rescues; the charity agencies for suffering of the poor; government offices for relief work; transportation and utility companies for interruptions in service. There is also a variety of reports that come into the newspaper office from eyewitnesses. All are usually bound together in one weather story.

The multiple-casualty story (discussed in Chapter 9) is a popular form to use for weather stories concerning a number of deaths and injuries. Even if there are no casualties, this same form may be used as a convenient method of presenting reports on a wide variety of property damages and other effects, the list of damages in this instance taking the place of the list of dead or injured.

Story Contents

The facts and sources of various weather stories include:

Facts	*Sources*
1. Statistics	1. Weather Service
a. Temperature (high and low)	
b. Precipitation	
c. Visibility	
d. Humidity	
e. Wind velocity	
f. Flood stage (if any)	
2. Forecast warnings	2. Weather Service, police, fire
a. Crop warnings	department, relief workers,
b. Sea or lake warnings	agriculture extension agents
3. Casualties	3. Police, fire department,
a. Names and identification of	hospitals, friends and relatives,
dead and injured	witnesses
b. Cause of deaths and	
injuries	
c. Nature of injuries	
d. Disposition of dead and	
injured	
4. Damages	4. Police, fire department, rescue
a. Damages to property	workers, owners, witnesses
b. Description of property	
c. Cause of damage	
d. Property threatened	

5. Relief   5. Police, fire department,
   a. Relief done   charitable agencies, city
   b. Relief needed   officials, relief workers
6. Escapes   6. Police, fire department, relief
   a. Experiences of those who   workers, witnesses
      escaped
   b. Rescues
7. Legal action   7. Police
   a. Arrests
   b. Investigations
8. Tie-in or tie-back   8. Newspaper file, reference
                                                books

NATURAL DISASTERS

Some natural disasters are so monumental that they dominate the news for weeks and occasionally much longer because of their devastating impacts. The October 17, 1989, earthquake that caused more than $10 billion in damages from Watsonville and Santa Cruz to Oakland and San Francisco in northern California is a classic example.

A year later, it was still making news because many private homes, particularly near the epicenter in the mountains near Santa Cruz, had not been rebuilt. The business district of Santa Cruz remained in shambles and behind a wire fence. For miles, collapsed double-decker freeway running through Oakland was being torn down. Across the bay, miles of its counterpart leading into San Francisco remained closed, causing horrendous traffic jams and a threat to the livelihood of merchants in Chinatown, while city, county and state officials were still debating who would pay for repairs.

Some newspapers are prepared to continue their operation whenever a natural disaster strikes. They have disaster plans that encompass all aspects of their operation, from gathering the news to printing and delivering it. Others, unfortunately, do not.

It was just such a plan that permitted the San Jose Mercury News to publish a complete 104-page newspaper with a 12-page ad-free earthquake wraparound the next morning and to distribute 175,000 extra copies of it. Although the earthquake knocked out power throughout the area, including San Jose, the Mercury News' backup generators provided the power for the editorial and production staff to work through the night. The Mercury News was on the streets by 6:30 a.m.

On succeeding days the paper contained a 16-page earthquake section on October 18; a 12-page section on October 19; and a 16-page commemorative section, "We will never forget," on October 21. For its distinguished coverage of one of the worst natural disasters to hit the United States that year, the Mercury News won a Pulitzer Prize.

The lead of a disaster story should describe the extent of the disaster, focusing on the human element—casualties in particular. Here is the lead on the Mercury News' main earthquake story, written by David Schrieberg:

> The biggest earthquake since 1906—7 on the Richter scale and possibly higher—hit the Bay Area at 5:04 p.m., Tuesday, killing at least 76 people, injuring more than 460, setting off fires in San Francisco and sending buildings, highways and bridges crashing down on people and cars across the region.
>
> The quake, centered in the Santa Cruz Mountains, lasted from 20 to 40 seconds and frightened millions from Ukiah to San Diego. It was as strong as the quake that ravaged much of Soviet Armenia in December.
>
> Damage throughout the Bay Area was staggering, as death and injury reports poured in to disaster centers and rose by the hour. Lt. Gov. Leo McCarthy said the damage could reach $1 billion.
>
> In Oakland, officials feared that up to 200 people may have died when an elevated section of Interstate 880 toppled onto another part of the road. And the Alameda County coronor said the toll was expected to grow.

Writing the first story of a major disaster such as an earthquake or tornado presents a particular challenge because of conflicting reports of the casualties and damages. Officials often are unsure and can only guess, as those in Oakland did, about the total number of people who might have died when the interstate collapsed, and as the Lieutenant Governor did when he underestimated the total damage by about $9 billion. But they are the most reliable sources at the time, and it is important to give the readers those figures. The readers know that they will be adjusted in subsequent stories.

The Mercury News editors just like their counterparts at other papers know that the real story of a natural disaster is in the human element—the people who are killed, those who are rescued, those who rescue them, the homeless, the displaced. That is why one of the prime elements of disaster coverage is the feature or human-interest story focusing on the individuals whose lives were dramatically impacted by the disaster.

Here is the lead on the Mercury News' story of one of the most startling of all the rescues of the quake victims. It was written by Laura Kurtzman, Dan Stober and Philip J. Trounstine.

> OAKLAND—They were dirty, drained and demoralized after a fruitless search for life in the rubble that once was the Cypress Street Viaduct.
>
> Then, unbelievably, a Caltrans engineer in a cherry picker saw a movement—a faint promise—in a 3-1/2-foot-high concrete tomb.
>
> And from the flattest and most hopeless section of I-880, rescue workers on Saturday pulled 220-pound dockworker Buck Helm from his squashed silver Chevrolet Sprint—89 hours after he was buried.
>
> "Thank God, I'm alive," said the 57-year-old Weaverville man, according to one of the rescue workers who cheered and wept as Helm waved weakly from his gurney.

The feature treatment was also given to a follow-up story on the tornadoes in Illinois that killed 26 that appeared in the Los Angeles Times. It was written by Tracy Shryer and Bob Sector.

FIGURE 20–1 The San Jose (Calif.) Mercury News won a Pulitzer Prize for its in-depth coverage of the massive earthquake that brought death and destruction to a four-county area in Northern California in 1989. The newspaper combined five days of stunning photographs and excellent stories into a special earthquake section that drew extensive praise from the public and press colleagues alike. (Courtesy of the San Jose (Calif.) Mercury News.)

CREST HILL, Ill.—Dazed and heartsick, Joann Eads stared absently into space Wednesday as she sat on the curb outside what only the day before had been her trim two-story townhouse on Cedar Drive.

Next to her lay a bottle of blue antacid. Behind her, total devastation.

"You wanna buy a house cheap?" she asked facetiously.

Eads was just one of thousands of people struggling with tears, black humor and hope to piece together their scattered lives and possessions after a series of monster tornadoes unleashed their fury across parts of the southwestern Chicago suburbs Thursday afternoon.

The storms killed at least 26 people, injured 350 more and caused destruction to homes, businesses, schools and churches on a scale not seen in these parts in more than two decades.

"It was like the devil came to visit," said Mike Brewer, who safely rode out the twister in the bathroom of his now-mangled pizza parlor in nearby Plainfield.

SEASONS

Seasonal stories are a staple in most newspapers. They also can become a problem for a reporter. How can he or she make this year's St. Patrick's Day story different from last year's? Is there a new angle to St. Valentine's Day, Mother's Day, the Fourth of July, and the dozens of other holidays and anniversaries newspapers dutifully write about each year? Fortunately, most newspapers handle seasonal stories as features. If a reporter has an active imagination and a flair for words, what might have been a routine story can be turned into a clever, original and highly readable feature.

Chase's Calendar of Annual Events and Appleton's Book of Holidays are two good guides to seasonal and other special events. The accompanying chart points out some of the events and dates that may receive attention by newspapers. Not all of them are reported by any one newspaper, although all are potential stories. Local interest and available space in the newspaper may be the deciding factors.

To this list may be added many seasonal events of local interest only: anniversaries of Revolutionary or Civil war battles, admission of the state into the Union, anniversary of the founding of the city, and various "weeks" (Book Week, National Newspaper Week, and so on) are proclaimed during the year. When it occurs, an astronomical phenomenon such as an eclipse, sun spots or the arrival of a comet is also covered extensively in the newspaper.

January
1—New Year's Day
8—Jackson's Birthday
17—Franklin's Birthday
19—Lee's Birthday

15—Women's Suffrage Day
22—Washington's Birthday
28—Leap Year Day (every four years)

February
2—Groundhog Day
12—Lincoln's Birthday
14—St. Valentine's Day

March
17—St. Patrick's Day
21—Vernal Equinox
Last of month—evidence of

spring, first robin, spring fever, outside activities

Between March 22 and April 25— Easter, first Sunday after full moon following equinox; Good Friday, Friday before Easter

April

1—All Fool's Day

13—Jefferson's Birthday

26—Arbor Day (varies in different states)

May

1—May Day

Second Sunday—Mother's Day

30—Decoration or Memorial Day

June

6—D-Day

14—Flag Day

Third Sunday—Father's Day

22—Summer Solstice

During month—vacations, trips, picnics

July

4—Independence Day

August

During month—height of "dog days"

September

First Monday—Labor Day

17—Constitution Day

23—Autumnal Equinox

During month—school openings, harvest time, fairs

October

12—Columbus Day

Fourth Monday—Veterans Day

30—Halloween

November

First Tuesday after first Monday—Election Day (not every year)

Fourth Thursday—Thanksgiving

During month—beginning of winter, sports, migration of birds

December

First of month—Christmas shopping

22—Winter Solstice

25—Christmas

28—Wilson's Birthday

The handling of some seasonal stories became complicated when Congress passed a law making Monday the day of observance for five federal holidays, no matter which day the holiday actually came on, in order to create three-day weekends. They are Washington's Birthday, Memorial Day, Labor Day, Columbus Day and Veterans Day. Starting in January 1986, the birthday of the late civil rights leader Dr. Martin Luther King Jr. has been observed on the third Monday in January. The matter can get even more confused because on some of those holidays, in some states, only federal offices are closed. State and local officials may elect to keep their offices open. For example, most Southern states do not observe Memorial Day as an official holiday.

Weaving the Story

The key to writing all seasonal or holiday stories is to combine the present and the past—to tell not only how the holiday will be observed but also why it is being observed—and to make the story sound fresh. Something is lacking if a feature on Columbus Day fails to recall highlights of the discovery of America. In addition, the story is really incomplete if it mentions nothing of local residents' plans to observe the holiday.

The sources for seasonal stories is evident. In developing a feature, the reporter has to go to reference books or other sources to obtain facts of the past. But reporters also have to interview informed persons for facts of the present. This information has to be woven into a coherent and interesting story. To give the story timeliness, the reporter often puts emphasis on the present in the lead.

Research is the key. A reporter should not settle for the quickest, easiest reference work—an encyclopedia. Much historical, and sometimes scientific, research is done annually in many areas that might give a reporter a new approach to a holiday. Reports of such research often are listed in the standard periodical indexes available in most libraries. For example, a check of such indexes turned up a scientist who had made a study of Ireland and produced a theory that it was the Ice Age and not St. Patrick that drove the snakes out of Ireland. This gave a fresh touch to a St. Patrick's Day story and brought dozens of responses by mail and phone from staunch supporters of the good saint.

Sometimes the cause of the celebration does not date back to a historical event—the vernal equinox, for example—and the reporter must develop a scientific rather than a historical background. The reporter may assume that many persons will approach a certain day with interest, and it is permissible to predict what will be done as an unplanned observance of that day. Depending on the tenor of the story, the reporter sometimes may make his predictions imaginative as well as factual. However, this approach requires imagination similar to that of an Associated Press (AP) reporter who wrote a personality sketch on a turkey as a Thanksgiving feature. Often an offbeat feature can be developed on one of the lesser known "days," such as Bachelor's Day on February 28.

Seeking information on local celebrations, the reporter naturally will question leaders of clubs and organizations. The American Legion and Veterans of Foreign Wars might be the principal sources for a Veterans Day story if there is no government-sponsored observance planned. The labor unions should provide information for a Labor Day story. Schools observe most anniversaries by class programs. Most other organizations will announce such special programs in advance.

Here are several seasonal story leads:

Fall leaf lovers can expect a normal fall with good color in the Great Smoky Mountains National Park.

The best time to see colorful leaves will be the last two weeks of October, Nancy Gray, park ranger, said.

"Conditions over the summer and the first part of fall have been good as far as determining how colorful the leaves will be," Gray said. "Rainy summers, warm days and fair nights make for the best colors."

(The Knoxville News-Sentinel)

As the Fourth of July approaches, those uninhibited public relations people in Philadelphia are at it again, shamelessly bragging for the third straight year about having "the world's largest birthday cake."

If only it were true; but, alas, the claim seems half-baked.

Once again, the concoction, sponsored by convenience store operator Wawa Inc., will be 80 feet long, 10 feet wide and weigh about 1,800 pounds. On the nation's birthday, an estimated 25,000 people milling around the Liberty Bell will be offered a little taste of freedom, including a portion iced to look like the American flag.

The story, written by Alex John London for The Wall Street Journal, detailed how the Philadelphia claim was disputed by Martin Day, editor for the Guiness Book of World Records in London, who said the world's largest cake—90,000 pounds, 84 feet by 114 feet—was served up in 1986 in Austin, Texas, to celebrate the 150th anniversary of the founding of the Republic of Texas.

Story Contents

The formula for a seasonal story is:

Facts	*Sources*
1. Explanation of seasonal event	1. Reference books or reliable
a. History	persons
b. Past observances	
2. Observance	2. Officials of organizations,
a. Formally by organizations	reasonable predictions of
b. Informally by whole city	reporter

EXERCISES

1. Write a news story for today's morning newspaper using the current weather forecast for your area.

2. In many areas there is a local weather "prophet," someone who predicts the weather by unusual means—the number of frogs, the travels of woolly worms, the length of a billy goat's beard and so forth. Try to locate such a person who may live in your area and write a personality piece on her or him.

3. Using Appleton's Book of Holidays or Chase's Calendar of Annual Events in your college or local library, write a short feature on the unusual holidays celebrated annually across the nation.

4. Pick a timely, upcoming national holiday and write a story on it, focusing on the local angle.

5. Select a timely local event—a winter carnival, a spring flower festival, a holiday parade and so forth—scheduled in the near future. Interview the sponsors of the event and write a story about it. Attend the event when it is held and write a descriptive feature story on it.

6. Write news stories using the following notes:
   a. Forecaster Rich Heller
      Of AccuWeather who
      Provides weather service
      For your newspaper
      Says there is a
      75 percent chance
      For first heavy frost
      In the area tonight
      But only 50-50 chance
      For the city where low

Will be 35 degrees
Surrounding area can
Expect temperatures of
32 or even lower
Frost would be about
Two weeks early
For this area, he said
Cold snap follows
Two days of wind and rain
Area received .16 inches of rain
By midnight Wednesday
Monthly total 2.22
Which is .77 inches above normal
Temperatures in city expected
To be near 70 tomorrow
Which is normal for time period
Heller advises covering
Tender plants left outdoors

b. Jackie Waynick, spokeswoman for
State Division of Air Pollution Control
Says preliminary figures
From air pollution in Hendersonville
Recorded ozone levels above
Federal standards seven times
Between June and August
Monitors in three other mid-state areas
Recorded levels above standards once each
Recordings were worse than last year
But not as bad as two years ago
When federal standards were
Exceeded 20 times, Waynick said
High pollution levels caused by
Gasoline and solvents called
Volatile organic compounds (VOC)
Auto emissions and some industrial processes
Such as dry cleaning produce
VOC which reacts with
Heat and sunlight to send
Ozone levels above standards
Bill Bussee, head of local chapter
American Lung Association
Said figures point to serious
Mid-state pollution problems
"Any time we exceed the standards
We have a problem," Bussee said
"I think it's a good indication
That all the counties in the area
Must get together to solve
This very serious problem."

7. Research the global warming problem in your college or local library. With that information as a background, interview a professor at your college or university who teaches meterology to obtain his or her views on the controversial theory. Also interview the chief forecaster for the National Weather Service in your area. Ask about local weather patterns and solicit his or her views if they are indicative of a warming trend. Write a feature story on the interviews and the research material.

8. Write a hard-news story on the following information about a snow storm that hit your area:

> Severe winter storm
> Brought heavy rains to area
> Early Friday but rain changed
> To heavy snow by midnight
> Five feet of snow recorded
> In local mountains
> Forecasters said higher elevations
> Could get more snow before
> Storm moves eastward
> Storm dropped 2.51 inches of rain
> In 24-hour period
> Years total 5.43 is still
> 10.01 inches below normal
> Police said slick roads
> Played havoc with motorists
> Hundreds of motorists
> Clogged interstates to reach
> Regional ski slopes
> Traffic backed up 15 miles
> Leading to Grandfather Mountain
> Where storm dumped 50 inches of snow
> Up to six feet reported
> At higher elevations
> Some motorists waited
> Two hours in traffic
> State Highway Patrol reported
> Interstate 5 between Birdsong
> And Mountain Views closed
> Because of heavy snow, icy conditions
> Earlier a 40-mile stretch
> Of the interstate closed
> While crews cleared accidents
> One driver killed when
> His Chevrolet station wagon
> Skidded off interstate near
> Canyon Road exit and slammed into
> Concrete highway divider
> He was pronounced dead at scene
> Name withheld till relatives notified
> Storm knocked out power
> To 3,200 homes in Palisades area

For more than three hours
Power also out to 4,000 customers
In Lake Arrowhead area
For about five hours
Other areas in six counties
Had brief power outages
Consolidated Utilities Co. spokesman said
In all some 44,000 customers inconvenienced
For up to an hour or more overnight
Storm dumped two inches of rain
In nearby Hendry County
Causing estimated $24 million
In damages to county's strawberry
Citrus and avocado crops
Butler Davis, county's agricultural agent
Said rain destroyed 15 to 20 percent
Of county's strawberry crop
Daryl Watson, National Weather Service
Said storm area will have
Rain-free skies next two days
Slightly warmer temperatures
And Northwest winds to help
"Dry out the area"

(Sources: Janet Brazeale, spokesperson for utility firm; Cpt. Frank Biggs, State Highway Patrol; Watson)

9. Write a news story using the following notes on a weather-related accident:

Heavy, dense fog shrouded
50-mile stretch of Interstate 40
Between Canton and Newport today
Charles Dockery, spokesman for
National Weather Service, said
Fog moved into area shortly
After 12 o'clock last night
Doesn't expect enough sun today
To burn it off before mid-afternoon
Traffic slowed to crawl
On most major highways in area
State Highway Patrolman Mark Miller
Reported 51 people injured
In 52-vehicle pile-up on Interstate 40
About 10 miles northeast of Newport
Only three people admitted to hospitals
"It's a miracle no one was killed"
Trooper Miller said
Traffic on both sides of interstate
Backed up for 10 miles in each direction
Accident began about 8:10 a.m.
Eastbound 10-wheeled truck
Became disabled when driveshaft

Fell from vehicle which was
Stranded in right lane
Visibility less than 10 feet
Vehicles began colliding
As they approached stalled truck
All collisions within
Quarter-mile stretch near truck
School buses dispatched
To take injured to Haywood Hospital
And Memorial Mission Hospital
Two injured admitted at Haywood
One admitted at Memorial
All in fair condition
48 treated for minor injuries
The accident occurred on section
Of Interstate 40 known for
Fog-caused accidents
Dockery said geography of mountains
Often results in temperature inversions
That trap moisture and smoke
Inside valley, creating heavy fogs
State Department of Transportation
Spent $500,000 to install
High-tech fog-sensing devices
Designed to automatically change
Speed limit signs posted on highway
Depending on density of fog
It was dismantled after four years
Because it was not reliable
Transportation Commissioner Jack Reese said
The section of I-40 where
Collisions occurred today
Has been scene of at least four
Major traffic accidents
In last two years
In which five people were killed
And 25 injured, state police say

10. Suggest newsworthy pictures and write appropriate cutlines on Exercise 8 and 9 in this chapter.

11. Write a 90-second newscast based on Exercise 9.

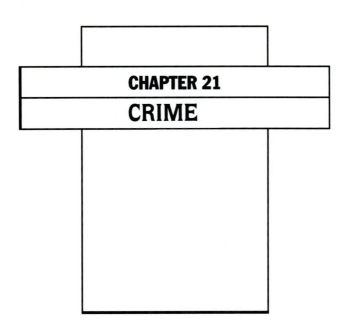

CHAPTER 21
CRIME

An infamous junk-bond king paid $600 million in fines for securities violations.

An insider trader was sentenced to three years in prison for stock manipulation.

Officials of defunct savings and loan associations were standing in line waiting for their trials in one of the largest and most costly financial scandals in the nation's history.

These were among the "stars" of the white-collar crime wave that grabbed the biggest headlines during the late 1980s and early 1990s. But they certainly weren't the only ones arrested, tried and convicted of such non-violent crimes as bank fraud, embezzlement, theft by computer, tax fraud and assorted con games and get-rich-quick schemes designed to separate the gullible and greedy from large sums of money.

Although the sheer magnitude of the amount of money involved in these white-collar crimes captured the attention of the public and press, violent crimes also continued to increase during that same period, the Federal Bureau of Investigation's annual report, "Crime in the United States," shows. The importation and sale of illegal drugs with all their associated crimes—murder, robbery, police bribery among them—tended to dominate the news of violent crimes. In addition to the crime stories traditionally reported—muggings, rapes, robberies, holdups—newspapers also were giving increased coverage to stories about child abuse, incest, child pornography, and cases involving battered wives and husbands.

Critics of the press still mistakenly claim that the reason crimes are reported is to sell newspapers, although most newspapers are pre-sold through home delivery. In response to this criticism, many newspapers have broadened their coverage of criminal activities to focus on their root causes.

As a result, crime stories are no longer exclusively the work of the police or investigative reporters. They turn up on almost every beat, including the religion beat occasionally. Stories about teachers selling drugs to students, computer technicians stealing valuable information from employers and selling it to the competition, and ministers who defraud their flocks and disappear have become almost daily items on every news budget.

The high cost of crime in human as well as financial terms, the shortage of trained police, jail and prison overcrowding, and lack of adequate funding for law enforcement are just a few of the kinds of stories that are reported regularly by most newspapers. Often they are the work of the police reporter, but many are generated by reporters who cover city, county and state governments among other beats.

Occasionally, a "police" story may even touch on fashion, in a manner of speaking, as this story from Portland, Ore., did:

> PORTLAND, Ore. (AP)—Earrings probably won't become de rigueur among the ranks of Portland's finest, but policemen wishing to adorn their ears with dainty pieces of precious metal may now do so.
>
> The city attorney's office has advised the department to allow male officers to wear earrings after a policeman filed a labor grievance recently.
>
> Police officials say they'll follow the city attorney's advice, but they don't have to like it.
>
> "I don't think the public is prepared to see a male police officer wear an earring," said Capt. Wayne Inman.
>
> The grievance challenged rules that specified female officers' earrings must be small and non-dangling, but didn't address the question for male officers.

The city police, the county or parish sheriff's office, state police and other state agencies, and numerous federal agencies are involved in various aspects of law enforcement. Sometimes they enforce identical laws, but each has its separate law-enforcement machinery. For the most part they work closely together and share information.

In most cities, the chief source of crime news is the city police station, but in a major city there may be as many as a dozen agencies, all with law-enforcement powers. A wide variety of important news is reported to the police—murders, robberies and other criminal acts, accidents, fires, missing persons. City police generally enforce state laws on murder, larceny and other crimes in addition to ordinances covering crimes and regulations that apply within the city limits.

The county jail, where the sheriff and other county law-enforcement officers are headquartered, is also an important source of crime news. County officers function chiefly outside the city limits to enforce state and county laws, but they also have authority within the city.

Federal officers make few arrests compared to city and county officers, but even this number is increasing as the incidence of crime in general is soaring. Often stories resulting from federal arrests can be of a more spectacular nature than the crime story growing out of an arrest by a city or county officer. Federal officers enforce laws dealing with kidnaping, counterfeiting, narcotics (smuggling and sale), federal tax evasion, mail fraud, manufacture and sale of illegal beverages, and hijacking of airplanes as well as trucks involved in interstate shipment of goods, interference with civil rights and similar matters.

The states generally maintain state police for highway patrol duty, a state bureau of criminal investigation, fire marshals, tax collectors and investigators, game wardens, forest rangers, and other units of law enforcement that will produce crime and other news stories.

Often the first beat assigned to a new reporter is the police beat, which includes some if not all of the law-enforcement agencies. The police beat is an excellent training ground for beginning reporters because it offers good practice in the fundamentals of reporting, in cultivating news sources, in gathering all the facts needed to write an accurate story (often requiring the checking of several sources) and in writing under the pressure of approaching deadlines. It also presents some serious hazards for the lazy reporter who does not check the facts or the reporter who gets too close to police sources and begins to serve as a police spokesman rather than a fair and accurate reporter.

Reporting crime news can be demanding. At times, if properly done, it is a public service that can be a deterrent to certain types of crime. But, badly handled, it can show how to commit crime successfully. It can give a false impression of the amount of crime, or build sympathy for or glorify criminals. Crime news also can help criminals by informing them of police strategy or hamper justice by "trying the case out of court"—making it difficult to get a fair trial. And, of course, it can turn the spotlight on the law-abiding family of the criminal, adding to their humiliation. Fortunately, over the years, leaders in the news media have come to recognize these problems, and most newspapers today practice considerable restraint in handling crime news. At the same time the news media continue to fight for their First Amendment rights to report freely and fairly all crime news, despite repeated efforts over the years to force controls on them.

CRIMES

Before examining the content of the typical crime story, the reporter should know what is meant by "crime." A breach of law is a crime and may be either a felony or a misdemeanor. A felony is one of the more serious crimes, usually carrying a penalty of long imprisonment and sometimes death. (Although the Supreme Court held in the 1970s that the death penalty was "cruel and unusual punishment," it later reversed that stand and a number of executions have been carried out.) A misdemeanor is a minor breach of law, usually resulting in a fine and no imprisonment, although some misdemeanors provide confinement and penalties. A study of most state laws will show that the following crimes are usually regarded as felonies:

FIGURE 21–1 After a rash of particularly vicious street crimes, including one in which a young visitor was stabbed to death during a robbery on a subway platform, the New York Post devoted its front page to a plea to Mayor David Dinkins to "do something." In a dozen stories and columns, the newspaper cited the city's increasing crime rate and reminded the mayor that he had campaigned on a promise to be "the toughest mayor on crime." (Courtesy of the New York Post.)

Homicide (killing a person)
1. Manslaughter
    a. Voluntary (intentional, in a fit of passion)
    b. Involuntary (unintentional, through negligence)
2. Murder
    a. First degree (with evident premeditation)
    b. Second degree (no premeditation but intent to kill)

Assault
1. Assault with intent to kill or maim
2. Felonious assault
3. Mayhem (maiming)
4. Kidnapping

Violating Property Rights
1. Larceny (illegally taking property)
2. Burglary (entering dwelling to take property, housebreaking)
3. Robbery (larceny with assault, threatened or committed)
4. Embezzlement (larceny through trust)
5. Forgery
6. Arson
7. Receiving stolen property

Obstructing Justice
1. Interfering with an officer
2. Perjury
3. Bribery
4. Contempt of court

Conspiracy in Crime
1. Accessory before fact
2. Accessory after fact

Others
1. Gambling
2. Manufacture, possession or sale of illegal beverages and drugs
3. Disturbing peace (fight, riot)
4. Sexual crimes
5. Criminal libel

Misdemeanors include such violations as public drunkenness, speeding, illegal parking, simple assault and a variety of lesser infractions ranging from littering to public nudity.

In crime stories the reporter must be sure to write only privileged facts gathered from public records, and they must be accurate. Of course, accuracy is important in every news story, but it is vital in crime stories because a libel suit lurks behind every one of them. If a person is arrested and charged with a certain crime, the reporter can say just that. It is a matter of public record. But a detective's chance remark that a certain person committed a crime is not a matter of public record and therefore is not privileged. Its publication may result in a libel suit. Even in cases in which police obtain confessions, the reporter must exercise care. In one case on the records, a man arrested for a crime confessed. During the trial he repudiated his confession and was found not guilty. He then sued the newspaper that had reported his confession and won the libel suit.

A person who is arrested is not necessarily guilty of a crime. No matter how damaging the evidence may appear, the reporter's story should not imply guilt. The story should include the evidence the police have against the person, but it should be fair and accurate and should not draw conclusions.

Reporters should always remember that a person is arrested on "charges" of a certain crime, not for the crime. And reporters should be cautious when reporting the evidence police or prosecutors say they have against a prisoner. The reporter should ask to see the evidence to make certain it exists. At one infamous murder-rape trial in Illinois, a prosecutor claimed he had a pair of the prisoner's blood-stained undershorts, which he even showed in court. During the appeal process in the case, it was proved that the undershorts did not belong to the prisoner and that the "blood" on them was red dye.

If doubt exists that the prisoner gave a correct name, newspapers often write that the person "was booked at the city jail as John Smith" or the prisoner "gave his name as John Smith." If a prisoner refuses to give an address, the reporter should say so or write "address not given." Some newspapers no longer publish the addresses alleged criminals give to police because quite often they are fictitious and create problems for the legitimate residents at those addresses. Instead, the newspaper may print "John Smith, who said he lives in the 1200 block of South Park Street, has been charged. . . ." But before resorting to that, reporters should use telephone books, city directories and other available sources to check on the correct name and address of anyone arrested for a crime. In fact, it is good practice to check all names and addresses automatically, no matter what the arrest record may show. Police have been known to make mistakes.

Stories involving juveniles are particularly sensitive. Some states have laws prohibiting the publication of a juvenile's name in connection with a crime report. Juvenile cases are generally not tried in open courts, and juvenile judges establish the standards for releasing names and information. Most newspapers do not use the name of a juvenile unless it is a major offense—perhaps a son's killing a father—or unless the prosecutor elects to try the juvenile as an adult.

Here's how the Los Angeles Times handled one story involving a juvenile burglary ring:

> A gang of tiny toughs, ages 9 to 14, used a cutting torch to crack safes in seven businesses in Salinas and may have committed up to 50 burglaries during a downtown crime spree, police said Friday.
>
> Thousands of dollars in cash and goods were taken during the series of break-ins over an eight-month period and the little burglars often vandalized the stores they broke into, investigators said.

The case was broken late Thursday when two boys, one 11 and the other 12, were arrested after they allegedly robbed an elderly person in front of a fast-food restaurant, police Lt. Rick Anderson said.

When police questioned the two youngsters they confessed to the burglaries and named four accomplices. Anderson said police had a half-dozen boys—one age 9, one 11, one 12, two 13 and one 14—in custody and were sifting through a mound of burglary reports.

Police Records

Two types of records commonly yield local crime news in most localities: (1) city and county jail "blotters" and (2) complaint sheets or bulletins. The first is an entry or log book of arrested persons maintained at city and county jails; the second is a record of complaints made to police and of investigations by police. The accompanying illustration of this type of record has been condensed to conserve space.

These records give the reporter only a few bare facts about a case. Many cases are so trivial that they either will be a one-line entry in a crime log published in many newspapers or will be ignored. Additional facts about the more interesting cases have to be collected through interviews with the officers and the persons involved in the case.

Here is an example of a major crime story that required the reporters to gather facts from a variety of sources other than the police record alone:

> A prominent San Francisco attorney was shot and killed yesterday in his Market Street office by an assailant who was gunned down just minutes later in an exchange of shots that left two police officers wounded.
>
> The slaying took place shortly before 1 p.m., when the suspect, described as a man with a wooden left leg, shot Garfield Walton Steward, 75, who had offices on the sixth floor of the historic Flood Building at 870 Market Street.
>
> After police responded to an emergency call reporting the shooting, they cornered the armed assailant on the third floor and ordered him to drop his gun, police said. When he refused, he was fatally wounded in an exchange of gunfire. . . .
>
> (San Francisco Chronicle)

In addition to the details of the shooting provided by the police, the reporters interviewed the Police Chief and several other occupants of the building who either saw the gunman or heard the shooting. They also talked to numerous persons who knew the lawyer as well as members of his family.

The San Jose Mercury News handled the story this way:

> SAN FRANCISCO—Police killed a gunman who walked into a busy downtown office building Tuesday, shot a lawyer to death and then wounded two police officers.
>
> The lunchtime gunbattle was fought in the marble hallways on two floors of the James Flood Building at the crowded corner of Powell and Market streets.
>
> The slain lawyer was Garfield Steward, 75, according to the coroner's office. . . .

KNOXVILLE, TN. POLICE DEPARTMENT

EVENT REPORT
FORM PD 370 5/80   PAGE _____ OF _____ PAGES

VICTIM

1. VICTIM/FIRM	SEX	RACE	D.O.B.	5. COMPLAINANT'S NAME	SEX	RACE	D.O.B.	8. COMPLAINT NO.

2. HOME ADDRESS   6. COMPLAINANT'S ADDRESS   9. WHEN REPORTED M D Y T

3. BUSINESS ADDRESS/SCHOOL   4. TEL RES. BUS.   7. BUSINESS ADDRESS   10. TEL RES. BUS.

EVENT

11. CLASSIFICATION   12. OFFENSE/EVENT   13. LOCATION OF EVENT   14. NEAREST CROSS STREET   15. ☐ PUBLIC ☐ PRIVATE   16. BEAT   17. RELATION TO VICTIM

18. TIME OF OCCURRENCE M D Y T   19. TOOLS/WEAPON USED   20. METHOD USED

M.O. INFORMATION

Type of Structure		28. Point of Entry	29. Security Used	32. Impersonated	33. Suspect Actions	
21. Non-Residential	24. Target(s)					

21. Non-Residential
1 ☐ Convenience
2 ☐ Drug
3 ☐ Medical
4 ☐ Financial
5 ☐ Mfg./Const.
6 ☐ Other Retail
7 ☐ Public Bldg.
8 ☐ Restaurant/Bar
9 ☐ Transportation
10 ☐ Wholesale
11 ☐ Fast Food
12 ☐ Other

22. Residential
1 ☐ Apt./Condo.
2 ☐ Duplex
3 ☐ Hotel/Motel
4 ☐ House
5 ☐ Mobile/Camper
6 ☐ Townhouse

23. Type Lock Defeated
1 ☐ Chain/Bolt
2 ☐ Deadbolt
3 ☐ Padlock
4 ☐ Springlatch
5 ☐ Other

24. Target(s)
1 ☐ Cash Register
2 ☐ Display Items
3 ☐ Person
4 ☐ Safe/Box
5 ☐ Sales Area
6 ☐ Vending Machine
7 ☐ Attic
8 ☐ Basement
9 ☐ Bathroom
10 ☐ Bedroom
11 ☐ Den
12 ☐ Family Room
13 ☐ Garage/Carport
14 ☐ Kitchen
15 ☐ Living Room
16 ☐ Storage
17 ☐ Other

25. Weather Conditions
1 ☐ Clear
2 ☐ Cloudy
3 ☐ Fog
4 ☐ Rain
5 ☐ Snow
6 ☐ Other

26. Point of Entry
1 ☐ Unknown
2 ☐ Front
3 ☐ Garage
4 ☐ Rear
5 ☐ Side
6 ☐ Door
7 ☐ Duct/Vent
8 ☐ Roof/Floor
9 ☐ Trunk/Hood
10 ☐ Wall
11 ☐ Window
12 ☐ Other

27. EXIT:

28. Victim/Offender Relationship
1 ☐ Family
2 ☐ Acquaintance
3 ☐ Friend
4 ☐ Co-Offender
5 ☐ Other
6 ☐ None

29. Security Used
1 ☐ Alarm
2 ☐ Bar/Grate
3 ☐ Dog
4 ☐ Ext. Light
5 ☐ Guard
6 ☐ Int. Light
7 ☐ Locked Doors
8 ☐ Locked Windows
9 ☐ Neighbor/Watch
10 ☐ Photo/Camera
11 ☐ Fence
12 ☐ Other

30. Point of Entry Visible From
1 ☐ Adjacent Structure
2 ☐ Alley
3 ☐ Street
4 ☐ Not Visible

31. Lighting Conditions
1 ☐ Dawn
2 ☐ Daylight
3 ☐ Dusk
4 ☐ Dark (street lights off)
5 ☐ Dark (no street lights)
6 ☐ Dark (street lights on)

32. Impersonated
1 ☐ Survey
2 ☐ Customer
3 ☐ Delivery Person
4 ☐ Disabled Motorist
5 ☐ Drunk
6 ☐ Employee/Employer
7 ☐ Friend
8 ☐ Ill/Injured
9 ☐ Use Phone
10 ☐ Police/Law
11 ☐ Renter
12 ☐ Repairman
13 ☐ Salesman
14 ☐ Seeking Assistance
15 ☐ Directions
16 ☐ Relative
17 ☐ Seeking
18 ☐ Selling
19 ☐ Soliciting
20 ☐ Other

33. Suspect Actions
1 ☐ Unknown
2 ☐ Bound Victim
3 ☐ Blindfolded Victim
4 ☐ Child Molest
5 ☐ Demand Cash
6 ☐ Demand Jewelry
7 ☐ Disabled Phone
8 ☐ Ate/Drank
9 ☐ Hideout
10 ☐ Injured Victim
11 ☐ Sex Acts
12 ☐ Ransacked
13 ☐ Raped
14 ☐ Smoked
15 ☐ Took Money
16 ☐ Took Tools
17 ☐ Took TV
18 ☐ Took Stereo
19 ☐ Took Vehicle
20 ☐ Threats
21 ☐ Had Lookout
22 ☐ Demand Note
23 ☐ Forced Entry
24 ☐ Used Matches
25 ☐ Stolen Vehicle
26 ☐ Used Tools
27 ☐ Vandalized
28 ☐ Vehicle Needed To Remove Property
29 ☐ Was Neat
30 ☐ Snatched Purse
31 ☐ Other

34. Place of Attack
1 ☐ Structure
2 ☐ Vehicle
3 ☐ Street/Alley
4 ☐ Lot/Park/Yard
5 ☐ Other

35. Description of Surrounding Area
1 ☐ Residential
2 ☐ Business
3 ☐ Indust./Mfg.
4 ☐ Recreational
5 ☐ Institutional
6 ☐ Open Space
7 ☐ Other

36. IS THERE A SIGNIFICANT M.O. PRESENT? IF YES, DESCRIBE IN NARRATIVE   IF NO PLACE AN X IN BOX A ⟶   A.

37. IS STOLEN PROPERTY TRACEABLE?   IF NO PLACE AN X IN BOX B ⟶   B.

38. PROPERTY CODE   (D) DAMAGED   (V) VEHICLE FROM WHICH THEFT OCCURED   (S) STOLEN   (A) VEHICLE USED BY SUSPECT   39. CONFISCATION NO.
(R) RECOVERED   (L) LOST   (E) EVIDENCE   (F) FOUND   (O) OTHER

PROPERTY/UCR

CD		SER. NO./OP. I.D. NO./DRIVER'S LIC. NO.	COMP. VALUE

YEAR	MAKE	MODEL	COLOR	BODY	TAG/STATE/YEAR	VIN. NO.	TOTAL VALUE

40. IGNITION LOCKED ☐ YES ☐ NO   KEYS IN IGNITION ☐ YES ☐ NO   DOORS LOCKED ☐ YES ☐ NO   41. VEHICLE/PROPERTY INSURED BY   42. IDENTIFYING CHARACTERISTICS   C.

43. CAN SUSPECT VEHICLE BE IDENTIFIED?   IF NO PLACE AN X IN BOX C ⟶

44. TIME SUSPECT VEHICLE INFORMATION BROADCAST.   PLACE TIME IN BOX 44 ⟶   D.

45. IS THERE SIGNIFICANT PHYSICAL EVIDENCE PRESENT? IF YES, DESCRIBE IN NARRATIVE. IF NO PLACE AN X IN BOX D ⟶

46. HAS EVIDENCE TECH WORK BEEN PERFORMED? (BY:) REQUESTED? IF NO PLACE AN X IN BOX E ⟶   E.
TECH WORK PERFORMED/REQUESTED: ☐ PHOTO ☐ FINGERPRINT ☐ COMPOSITE ☐ OTHER _____

47. INVESTIGATOR NOTIFIED   I.D. NO.   48. SUPERVISOR NOTIFIED   I.D. NO.   49. CRIME LAB TECHNICIAN ASSIGNED   I.D. NO.

OFF.

50. REPORTING OFFICER   I.D. NO.   51. SECOND OFFICER   I.D. NO.   52. SUPERVISOR   I.D. NO.

The story also included interviews with police officers who had been at the scene during the gunbattle and three other persons who worked in the building and were present during the shooting.

Access to police records and other public records varies from state to state. By the early 1980s, nearly all states had open records laws requiring police and almost all other records to be open for inspection by the public as well as the press. Every reporter should learn what his or her state's law on open records is.

Many state press associations have published their state's laws in convenient booklets for reporters to use.

As a general rule, law-enforcement officials cooperate with the press. This is not always the case, however. As a result, a number of newspapers resort to court action to force police and other public officials to open public records.

The computerization of public records has presented some problems for the press, but in a number of states with open records laws, the information stored in computers is considered public and must be made available to the public and the press.

A reporter must use extreme care when copying information from a police blotter and especially in the use of complaint sheets. Both of these records frequently contain misspellings of names and incorrect addresses. In addition, complaint sheets often contain misinformation, exaggerations and, from time to time, outright lies. They usually are a form of interoffice correspondence between the complaint desk and the investigating officers. Reporters should verify everything in the complaint sheet with the investigating officers before making use of complaint-sheet information. The reporter also is expected to use good judgment in handling information from police sources if publication would aid a suspect in escaping, prevent a fair trial or cause other difficulties.

Although the record on page 310 pertains to city police, similar records are kept by other types of law-enforcement officers—county, state and federal. Every reporter should know that federal law-enforcement agencies, as a general rule, tend to be far less open than city and state officials in revealing information to the press. Although there is a federal freedom of information law designed to open federal records to the public, the release of certain criminal information is exempt from the law.

The coroner is another public official whose records are often important in crime news, although coroners usually are not considered law-enforcement officials. The coroner, in many states a medical doctor, conducts an inquiry (inquest) into deaths from "unnatural causes"—those in which foul play, violence, suicide or unusual circumstances may be involved.

If the coroner's report shows that the cause of a death points to evidence of crime, arrests by law-enforcement officers may result. However, the coroner's functions are limited to determining the cause of death only. The coroner does not "try" a case against persons who may be accused of causing the death. Any legal action arising from the coroner's report must go through the regular legal system in the usual manner.

Story Contents

The usual information and sources for a crime story might be outlined as follows:

Facts	*Sources*
1. Casualties	1. Police, hospitals, friends and
a. Name and identification of	relatives of dead and injured,
persons	witnesses

       b. How persons were killed or
          injured
       c. Nature of injuries
       d. Disposition of dead and
          injured

2. Damages   2. Police, property owners
       a. Value, property stolen or
          destroyed
       b. Description of property
       c. Owner
       d. Insurance
       e. Other threatened property

3. Description   3. Police, involved persons,
       a. Chronological account   witnesses
       b. Description of involved
          persons

4. Escapes   4. Police, involved persons
       a. Rescues
       b. Experiences of those
          escaping

5. Legal action   5. Police
       a. Investigation, clues,
          evidence
       b. Arrests

6. Tie-backs   6. Library-morgue

The length of a crime story is usually determined by the seriousness of the crime. Other factors that add paragraphs and increase the size of the headline are the prominence of the persons involved, the place of the crime, unusual circumstances and incidents of human interest. Often one of those factors leads a reporter to write a feature lead, or an entire feature story, about the incident instead of a straight-news story. In selecting facts to go into the story and in the treatment of those facts, the reporter must be careful to observe the ethics of the newspaper. How much gory description should be included in the story of a particularly gruesome murder, for example? (A review of newspaper ethics would be appropriate in this connection; see Chapter 5.)

Here are some examples of leads on crime stories:

> A man who stole glass tabletops from an unoccupied Southside apartment was killed by an Atlanta police officer Thursday, investigators said.
> The victim, about 19, died in surgery at Grady Memorial Hospital three hours after the 8:30 p.m. shooting. Police would not release the victim's name.
>
> (The Atlanta Journal and Constitution)

> A woman was burned to death in a three-alarm fire set after she was locked inside a steel-enclosed room in the headquarters of a major Brooklyn crack operations, police said yesterday.

The woman, Valerie Livingstone of Brooklyn, was heard screaming late Thursday night as the blaze engulfed the four-story building at 523 Nostrand Avenue, police said.

(The New York Times)

A man who had just been handcuffed and arrested on suspicion of mail theft fell to his death from the 11th-floor balcony of his room at a Sherman Oaks hotel, Los Angeles police said Saturday.

Darren Mark Gertz, 26, of West Hills fell six floors onto the roof of an adjoining hotel building about 1:30 p.m. Friday, Sgt. Hary Mauk, said. . . .

(Los Angeles Times)

A popular Dunbar High School junior was shot and critically wounded yesterday, the second student from that school to be shot in the last week.

Sadiqa D. Bay, 16, was in critical condition yesterday at Howard University Hospital after being shot at least once in the head, police said. . . .

(The Washington Post)

Two Nashville men were charged Wednesday night with the weekend rape of a 15-year-old girl who apparently was passed out drunk.

The assault allegedly occurred Saturday night in the apartment of one of the suspects, Ronnie Stinnett, 23, of 365 Paragon Mills Road, Sex Abuse Detective Cordelia Maxwell said. . . .

(Nashville Banner)

A man was found fatally shot early yesterday in a 1979 Ford parked near Grove and Divisadero streets, police said.

Neighbors reported shouts around 12:30 a.m. and witnesses said they saw five young men run from the vicinity of the car. The victim was pronounced dead at 4:40 a.m. at San Francisco General Hospital. . . .

(San Francisco Chronicle)

CANTON, Ohio (AP)—An 11-year-old boy was arrested yesterday in the microwave death of a dog owned by a Humane Society worker.

A white Maltese owned by Marlene Stephens was put to sleep after it was found in the microwave oven Thursday. The dog was cooked for an undetermined amount of time, Canton police said. . . .

CHICAGO (AP)—A blind woman identified a 14-year-old boy as the person who raped her in her apartment building's laundry room by smelling his cologne and touching his hands, police said.

The 24-year-old woman, legally blind for three years, immediately recognized the scent of the suspect's cologne and later felt his hands in a lineup at a police station, investigators said. The assailant held his hand over the victim's mouth during the attack.

Occasionally, police can be on the opposite side of the law, as this lead from the Los Angeles Times shows:

SAN DIEGO—Two San Diego police officers were arrested Thursday and charged with kidnaping and robbing three Latino illegal aliens while patrolling the downtown area.

Officers Lloyd J. Hoff, Jr., and Richard P. Schaaf later appeared in San Diego Municipal court where they entered not-guilty pleas for five felony counts each of kidnaping, kidnaping for robbery and robbery. . . .

RAPES

Traditionally newspapers do not print the names of rape victims, even during the course of a trial. However, the issue became a topic of considerable discussion among journalists, lawyers and women's rights advocates in the early 1990s after one victim permitted her name to be used by The Des Moines Register in a five-part series that detailed the emotional pain she experienced after the rape.

This, of course, was not the first time a rape victim's name had been printed. It did not lead to a flood of similar stories, although several did appear in major newspapers such as the San Jose Mercury News. Yet critics of the policy expressed their concern that the Des Moines series and the support it received from a number of journalists as well as women's rights advocates could lead to a wholesale printing of the names of rape victims without the victim's consent. That has not happened. Most newspapers still do not print rape victims' names.

However, in 1991 when a woman charged that she had been raped by William Kennedy Smith (a nephew of Sen. Edward M. Kennedy) on the grounds of the Kennedy family estate in Palm Beach, the National Broadcasting System and The New York Times used her name about a week after the initial news story. Both news organizations were criticized.

The Times drew particular fire from critics because in addition to its basic news stories, it printed a story that detailed the young woman's troubled personal history. That story included information about her mother's divorce and subsequent marriage to a wealthy businessman; it also quoted acquaintances of the women who discussed her alleged "high living" lifestyle in Palm Beach.

Accompanying the story about the woman, The Times printed an explanation of why it elected to use her name. The statement said, in part:

". . . Like many other news organizations, The New York Times ordinarily shields the identities of complainants in sex crimes, while awaiting the courts' judgment about the truth of their accusation."

The Times pointed out that they used her name finally because "NBC's nationwide broadcast took the matter of her privacy out of the hands" of its editors.

"The practice of withholding names became almost unanimous in the 1970's when women argued that it would make rape victims more likely to come forward," The Times story said.

"Many editors said that using names would increase the pain of a traumatic experience. But some editors now believe that failing to identify rape victims perpetuates the idea that rape is a crime that permanently damages a woman's reputation."

Generally speaking, rape stories are relatively brief. They may include:

Facts	*Sources*
Statement of alleged victim	Police
Hospital treatment	Hospital officials, police

Arrest of suspect   Police
Possible statement of suspect   Suspect, suspect's attorney
Possible court action   Police, district attorney

It should be noted, however, that in many rape cases the victim is unable to identify her attacker or the attacker is never caught.

Here is an example of a rape story from the Knoxville Journal:

> A 27-year-old East Knoxville woman reported to police that she was raped at knifepoint Friday night in a car on a parking lot near the intersection of Pershing Street and Atlantic Avenue.
>
> The woman told police that she was walking along Vine Avenue around 8:40 p.m., when a man pulled up in a car and offered her a ride. After she got in the vehicle, she said, the man drove to the lot, placed a knife against her throat and threatened her life if she did not have sex with him.
>
> The man tied the woman's hands behind her back and continued threatening her with the knife during the assault, the woman told police.
>
> She described her assailant as a white male, about 35 years old, 5-10, 240 pounds, with a full beard and mustache, and straight brown, collar-length hair.
>
> The victim was treated and released at St. Mary's Medical Center.

Here is the lead on an Associated Press story about court action in a rape case:

> JOHNSON CITY—A civil court judge has awarded $4 million to a woman who claimed she was sedated and raped by her doctor nearly two years ago.
>
> She may have a tough time collecting, however. The bondsman who posted $100,000 bail for Dr. Mohamed F. Ali and an attorney for the state board of medical examiners say he's left the country.
>
> Washington County Judge Thomas Seeley awarded the woman $1.5 million in compensatory damages and $2.5 million in punitive damages on Wednesday. She had filed a $10 million suit against Ali, an Egyptian native.
>
> Ali, 36, is believed to have fled the country last year before criminal charges of rape and attempted bribery were tried . . .

SUICIDES

In covering a suicide, the reporter must be extremely careful. The official police report, not the reporter's judgment, determines whether a death is a suicide. In many states police can determine if the case is a suicide; in others a final ruling has to await action by a coroner. Even if a man plunges from a 14-story window in front of a large crowd, it may not be a suicide. Even if a woman is found dead on a lonely road with a pistol in her hand and a bullet in her head, there may be no definite evidence that she fired the bullet. Until police or the coroner completes the investigation, the reporter should say only that the person was "found dead," or "plunged," or "fell." If police report they found a suicide note or say that the wound was self-inflicted, the reporter should quote them. But the reporter should not say the case was a suicide without quoting an authority.

It may be possible to discover a motive, after suicide has been clearly established, but the reporter must be careful. Reporters should not piece together certain facts about the person's ill health, financial difficulties or love affairs and then conclude that they were the motives. If there is a definite, authentic statement of motive from a suicide note or a close relative, it is generally safe to use that information in the story. However, if no motive is found, the reporter should say so in the story by quoting an authoritative source.

Even more caution is necessary in reporting attempted suicides. Unless the suicide attempt is evident and backed up by statements of authorities, or unless the person admits the suicide attempt, the reporter must give only the facts. It is wise to be cautious even in cases in which the person admits the attempted suicide. It could be a grandstand play for attention or a fabrication for some other reason.

The method of suicide is usually described only in general terms. Newspapers never give details of methods because that might show others how to commit suicide. For example, the name of a poison or drug is not used in suicide stories. The means of suicide is simply called "a poison" or "a drug." Gory details are nearly always omitted in suicide stories.

Story Contents

The following is a formula for the usual suicide story:

Facts	*Sources*
1. Name and identification	1. Police, coroner or coroner's
a. Disposition of body	report, hospital, relatives,
	friends
2. Method	2. Police, witnesses
a. Cause of death	
b. Circumstances surrounding	
death (when and how	
found)	
3. Motive	3. Police, relatives, friends,
a. Suicide note	physician
b. Statement from relatives,	
physician, friends, business	
associates	

Any of the three principal facts named above may be the feature of the suicide story. An unusual method or motive is usually the feature, unless the person's prominence overshadows that feature. Under no circumstances should the reporter attempt to treat a suicide story in a lighthearted or humorous manner.

Here is an example of a suicide story from The New York Times. The story was given considerably more attention than most suicide stories because of the prominence of the family.

A retired Wisconsin newpaper editor and publisher who had been suffering from cancer shot and critically wounded his wife yesterday and then killed himself in their home on a Rockefeller estate in the Adirondacks, state police said.

Miles J. McMillan, 69 years old, who retired four years ago from "The Capital Times" of Madison, Wis., and his wife, Elsie Rockefeller, 58, were found by her daughter and their son. Both were shot in the head.

The story quoted state police as its authority for McMillan's cancer, saying he had undergone radiation and chemotherapy treatment at the Mayo Clinic in Rochester, Minn. It also said the couple was found on a bed, and a .22 calibre automatic pistol was nearby. But it gave no other details of the shooting.

EXERCISES

1. Interview the editor of your local newspaper about his or her policies on handling crime news. Write a news story based on the interview.

2. Tour the police department or sheriff's headquarters in your city, interview the police chief or sheriff, and write a feature story based on the tour and the interview.

3. Using a copy of the FBI's Annual Crime Report from your college or community library, write a news story comparing the crime statistics for your city with those of similar-size communities.

4. Interview the chief of your campus police about crime on your campus. Ask to see the crime statistics for the past three years. Write a story based on the interview and the statistics detailing how safe your campus is.

5. The following are several crimes reported to police. On a separate sheet of paper explain how you would handle the story on each. For example, explain if you would simply write a story based on the available information or if you would call the persons involved for more information. Would you do a sidebar story or a follow-up?

   a. Ray McCord, 62, 2608 Highland Dr., a retired city detective, was arrested for aggravated assault and for killing an animal. The three teen-agers said they skipped school Wednesday and went to a barn on McCord's property near the Cornelia Fort Airport. McCord found the youths in his barn's hayloft, smoking cigarettes. He was armed with a shotgun. One youth jumped out the window and ran, but McCord put ropes around the necks of the other two to hold them until police arrived. He struck one in the back of the head with the gun. He then shot and killed a 7-month-old puppy belonging to one of the boys.

   b. Robert Allen Grice, 35, told police that two armed men burst through an unlocked door at his home at 7321 Winchester Dr. about 11 last night. One of the men forced his wife, Sherri, 34, into an upstairs bedroom and tied her up with duct tape. He said he arrived home and because he had forgotten his door key, he rang the doorbell. The robbers ran for a side door, only to meet Grice. One of the robbers fled and drove off in a car parked on the street, while the other fired two shots at Grice. Both shots missed. Grice said he lunged at his assailant and the men struggled. Grice was shot once in the chest at close range. The robber then ran away. Grice is in stable condition in the intensive care unit of Memorial Hospital.

   c. State Representative Don Campbell, a Spencer pharmacist, was robbed by two men Saturday at the Warwick Drug Co. He said the men took Schedule II drugs with a street value of about $15,000 and an undetermined amount of cash. The men bound the lawmaker, who is a Democrat seeking re-election, with tape and took the key to a locked drug cabinet. He said the men were out of the store in about three or four minutes. Campbell was found on the floor of the pharmacy minutes later by a customer. He described the two as "clean-cut" white males in their 20s, one with light-colored hair and the other with dark hair. He said they were of average height and weight.

d. George W. Johnson, 70, a Williamson County farmer, spent five hours pinned beneath an overturned tractor he was using to move hay on his farm yesterday. Investigators believe the tractor overturned on Johnson when he was moving round bales of hay in a field off Del Thomas Road just inside the county line. The tractor rolled completely over and all four wheels were up in the air, Dallas Johnson, 40, his son, told police. Members of the Volunteer Rescue Squad responded to a call from the elder Johnson's wife, Bessie, and got the tractor off him. Johnson is in serious condition in Southern Hills Hospital, Nolensville.

6. Write news stories using the following notes:

a. Jeffrey Dee Gray, 29
Convicted of second-degree murder
For killing a bail bondsman
Whose wife offered $20,000
For the slaying two years ago
Superior Court Judge Gordon Baranco
Sentenced Gray to 15 years to life
After sentencing Judge Baranco
Stepped down from the bench
Conducted brief ceremony
Marrying Gray and Karen Vardanian
Friends and relatives took pictures
Gray and Vardanian allowed
To embrace and kiss
Before he was led away to prison

b. David Sublett, 34, Madisonville
Charged with aggravated robbery
Of Dominion Bank branch
At 1171 N. Broadway
He used stick and handkerchief
Pretended they were a gun
While trying to leave
Bank parking lot a red-dye bomb
In money bag he was carrying
Exploded, covering him with dye
A young boy saw Sublett
Get out of car and run
Police tracked him to nearby alley
His hands, face, clothing
Were covered with red dye
He was also charged with
Theft of property
Detective Robert Womack said

Because car he used
Had recently been stolen
From Beaman Pontiac lot
At Broadway and West End Lane
He is being held without bond

c. Body of Marvin F. Mackey, 40
Watertown auto mechanic
Found in back of his pickup today
By passing farmer on Walnut Hill Road
Police say Mackey was murdered
But they aren't sure how
Body found about 1 p.m.
In bed of truck which was
Cluttered with tires, equipment
He was last seen alive two days ago
His mother said he was a hunter
And she thought he had gone hunting
Police said several persons later
Reported seeing the truck
And thought Mackey was
Sleeping in the back of it
Autopsy will be conducted
To determine cause of death
Detective Gary W. Lawson said

d. Jimmy Gladden, 34, Route 6, Columbia
Arrested on aggravated rape
And aggravated sexual battery charges
Involving 12-year-old female niece
Charges placed after he was
Indicted by the County Grand Jury
He is jailed under $50,000 bond
Arraignment set next week
In Circuit Court
Detective J.S. White said
Girl's parents reported
Incident after being told
About it by her younger brother
Who was at Gladden's home
When incident took place

e. Floyd J. Thompson, 31
A Waverly truck driver
Charged with murder of
Joe Luna, 27, of 4508 Iowa Ave.
Outside Silver Dollar Saloon
At 5511 Charlotte Ave.
Thompson being held without bond
Pending a preliminary hearing
Murder Squad Detective Larry Flair
Said possible motive was jealousy

Friends told Flair the Thompsons
Were getting divorced
Suggested he thought she was
Having an affair with Luna
But investigation shows
No relationship between
The two, Flair said

f. Michael R. Glenn, 42
Driver of truck
Hauling U.S. mail
From Chicago to Atlanta
Arrested about 11:30 last night
During routine traffic check
At Harding Place exit off I-24
State police said they found
Amphetamines and what may be cocaine
Along with two sets of scales
And numerous plastic baggies
On front seat of truck
He was taken to Metro jail
Charged with possession
Of controlled substance for resale
And possession of drug paraphernalia
Bond was set at $70,000
He was released after bond posted
A court date will be set later
Samson Bros. Truck Leasing Co.
Owners of the truck
Said Glenn had good record
During four years he worked there
    (Source: Capt. Hugh Eakes, State Police spokesman)

g. Two men in stocking masks
Hijacked airport shuttle bus
Carrying two passengers early today
Took about $200 in cash
Kicked them and driver out of van
Crashed it on nearby Highland Boulevard
Before running away
Van driver Silbert Toms
Told police he was enroute
To airport about 5:45 a.m.
When two men in black-and-white patrol car
Ordered him to stop on I-280
Toms said the masked men
Armed with shotguns
Forced him out of van
Made him lie on highway
While they frisked him
When gunmen turned away
Toms ran to nearby convenience store

    Asked owner to call police
    Hijackers took over van
    Robbed Rev. Edward Stans, 71
    A priest enroute to Chicago
    Of $60 and took $150 from
    Lucretia Bjorklund, 38
    A housewife returning to Dallas
    Forced them out of the van
    Robbers crashed van into guardrail
    About five miles away
    Police said patrol car stolen
    About 3:30 a.m. from Ingleside Station
    It was found on I-280
    Near Geneva Avenue off-ramp
    Neither driver nor passengers injured
        (Sources: Toms, Detective Anthony DePaule)
h. George W. Baxter, 46
    Who lives at 110 Binkley Ave.
    Arrested under state's domestic violence law
    After his girlfriend, Martha White, 39
    Refused to press charges against him
    He went to her house on North Street
    Beat her with fists and a hammer
    Refused to let her out of house
    Police called by neighbors
    Officers Paul Flournoy and Terry Watts
    Forced way into house
    Through back door
    After hearing someone
    Moaning and screaming
    Inside they found couple
    Hiding in bathroom
    She had large cut over left eye
    Told police she had been beaten
    And struck with hammer
    She was treated at General Hospital
    Baxter charged with
    Aggravated assault, kidnapping
    Being held in Metro jail
        (Sources: Officers Flournoy and Watts)
i. Haywood County Sheriff's deputies
    Began rounding up 43 persons
    Indicted Monday on charges
    Involving sale of cocaine and marijuana
    District Attorney Clayburn Peepers said
    Sale of crack cocaine involved
    In 34 of the indictments
    Twenty-two of sales were
    For regular cocaine
    Fifteen were for marijuana

"The amount of crack in county is alarming,"
Peepers said. "Crack is becoming
The drug of choice for those who use cocaine."
Peepers said undercover operation
Began six months ago with help
From Criminal Division of state's
Department of Safety whose agents
Worked with County Sheriff's Department
Most of drug buys were made
By Department of Safety agents
Peepers said he thinks most cocaine
Comes from metropolitan area
In nearby county
"The Interstate is a tremendous drug highway,"
Peepers said, "And it runs right
through our county."
By sundown, 29 persons
Had been arrested
Five had made bail
Ranging from $7,500 to $25,000
Three being held without bail
    (Source: District Attorney Peepers)

7. Write a one-minute newscast from Exercises 5c, 5d, 6b, 6e, and 6i.

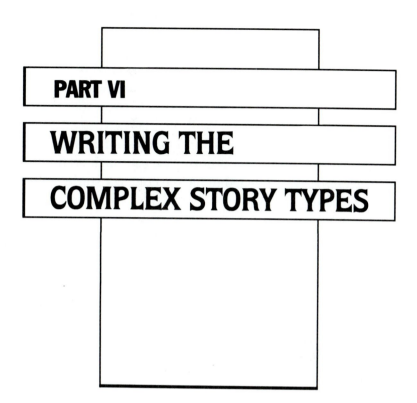

PART VI

WRITING THE

COMPLEX STORY TYPES

Society continues to change, often dramatically, and newspapers continue to change the way they report on it. Few newspapers today simply tell the reader what happened and stop at that. Life is now far too complex for that kind of treatment of the news, and editors are aware that many stories require explanation and interpretation if the reader is to grasp their true significance.

A few editors, however, still prefer to stick to straight-news accounts of what happened, no matter how complex the event. They shy away from interpretation or analysis.

Most editors realize that analysis and interpretation are essential to complete reporting. This is especially true in such areas as law, business, government and politics, among others. Readers often need help to understand complex issues such as environmental concerns.

Here are some of the problems reporters may encounter in covering complex fields:

1. Stories often involve a web of conditions and events stretching into the past, the future and even into related fields.
2. The reader must be told not merely the facts but also the significance of those facts.
3. Because much interpretation is necessary, the reporter needs to develop a knowledge of the field he or she is covering.

4. The reporter might need a technical vocabulary in order to communicate with the specialists he or she is writing about and has to have the ability to translate that technical vocabulary into words the reader can understand.

Many newspapers seek reporters who have professional training in various specialized fields. However, a good reporter can, through study, practice and experience, develop the skills needed to handle complex stories successfully.

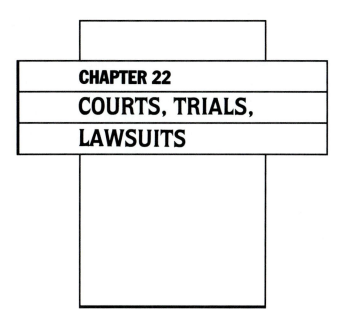

CHAPTER 22
COURTS, TRIALS, LAWSUITS

"If you don't have that fundamental interest in the people who are in the courtroom, what makes that defendant's case different, what makes that lawyer in that case interesting—that's what journalism is—if you don't have that, you are unfortunately going to end up practicing some form of sociology rather than journalism."

Frank Caperton, managing editor of The Indianapolis News, expressed that opinion about court reporting during a Scripps Howard Foundation Seminar on Public Affairs Reporting.

Unfortunately, a lot of sociology is being practiced by reporters covering civil and criminal courts today because they often get bogged down in the court system and ignore the human element, except in the most spectacular of trials. Court stories—whether based on information gathered outside the courtroom or while witnessing the trial—are among the most difficult and demanding stories to report because of the complexity of the legal process.

Lawsuits and court cases are boringly alike, which creates a problem for a reporter who spends much of his or her time sifting through blizzards of legal paperwork in the offices of various court clerks before getting into a trial. In fact, newspaper court reporters spend very little time in courtrooms covering trials. Most of their day is spent going from one clerk's office to another and talking to lawyers about cases pending in court. Not every trial rates on-the-spot coverage, and not every case goes to trial. But that does not mean they aren't worth writing about.

There is an added danger not only from the reporter's point of view but also from that of the principals involved in the case because of the continuing debate about pretrial publicity and its possible influence on the outcome of the case. Strong arguments have been made on both sides. But there still is no conclusive evidence to prove that in most instances pretrial publicity prevents a fair trial. Usually the issue arises only in the most spectacular or sensational cases.

For the most part, stories about criminal court cases, in particular, are concerned with events that have appeared previously in the news. So, in a sense, the court story is a follow-up. The crime, already reported at the time of commission and arrest, will reappear in the news as a trial for murder, larceny, arson or embezzlement. Fires and accidents, already reported, may reappear as lawsuits developing from them. Many business conflicts may result in litigation. And, of course, litigation can and does develop from such areas as medical and legal malpractice, violation of civil rights, unfair labor practices and many other alleged violations of both criminal and civil law.

After evaluating the importance and newsworthiness of a trial or lawsuit, the reporter may ignore it or write a story summarizing it. Often a reporter may never attend such a trial, obtaining information about it from court officers and documents or from the attorneys involved. Usually trials given lengthy coverage have to do with the more controversial or sensational cases.

In previous chapters, the newspaper's right to public judicial proceedings as privileged materials was pointed out. In this chapter, it is important to explain that judges have the power to limit a newspaper's rights and freedoms to some degree where cases in their own courts are concerned. Judges can back up their power by having reporters (as well as attorneys and court personnel) jailed on contempt-of-court charges for refusing to abide by court orders pertaining to the conduct of a case. This is not to say that all judges use this power wantonly, although in some cases judges have gone beyond the bounds of both reason and law.

Reporters have the right to appeal any restrictions placed on news coverage by a judge, and a number of reporters have appealed such restrictions. For the most part, the higher courts have upheld the rights of reporters to cover trials in open court.

The problem from a news point of view is that if a newspaper elects to obey a judge's gag order and then appeal, the coverage of the trial obviously will be inadequate. Disobeying the gag order, on the other hand, could mean time in jail. Reporters involved in contempt-of-court disputes with judges generally do not spend long periods in jail; however, several have been locked up for as much as 50 days before a conflict was resolved.

The conflict grows out of two provisions of the United States Constitution, one guaranteeing freedom of the press and the other guaranteeing an individual a fair and impartial trial. No ethical journalist would want to deny anyone a fair trial, but reporters are aware that judges, lawyers and law-enforcement officers are not necessarily ethical, nor are all trials fair. In such cases, reporters frequently believe that the only way the defendant will receive a fair trial is with the presence of the media. Some reporters feel so strongly about their First Amendment rights that they are willing to risk jail by defying judicial gag orders.

Judges and lawyers generally feel otherwise. If a judge thinks the presence of newspaper reporters, photographers or television cameramen in the court will affect court proceedings to the extent that the rights of the individual in receiving a fair trial may be impaired and justice obstructed, the judge has the power to limit the number of communications representatives in the courtroom. In some cases, judges have even barred reporters and photographers from the court-house itself. Others have issued extensive rules of coverage for the media along with stern lists of instructions to all the lawyers and participants as well as court officers in regard to discussing the case with the media.

Judges in the lower federal courts began in the early 1990s to reconsider allowing photographers for newspapers and television stations into their courtrooms. But not the justices of the U.S. Supreme Court. Photographers generally are not allowed in federal courts. However, all but five states and the District of Columbia permitted photographic coverage of both criminal and civil cases by the start of the final decade of the century.

The practice varies from state to state and, in truth, from court to court in those states. For example, in more celebrated cases some judges will bar photographers but permit artists to sketch courtroom scenes for newspapers and television. Some lawyers, however, have even objected to allowing artists in the courtroom during a trial.

Restrictions on a trial's coverage naturally will depend on the individual judge. In most cases such restraints are really unnecessary because newspapers today generally exercise caution in their coverage. They are interested, of course, in seeing that a fair trial is conducted. But they also want to avoid the embarrassment and loss of credibility with their readers that they might suffer if a conviction were reversed upon appeal due to unfair or sensational publicity. Reporters also would prefer not to be cited for contempt of court by a judge, for that could mean a fine as well as a jail term.

The press does have the right of "fair comment and criticism" on the action of a judge or the court. As a general rule, newspapers will not editorialize while a case is still in court. However, they have that right. To be successful in holding a newspaper in contempt, a judge has to show that its editorial and/or trial coverage presented a "clear and present danger" to the successful completion of the trial.

The judge does have absolute power in the courtroom (subject to review by a higher court), and, to lessen the animosities between judges, lawyers and reporters, a number of state press and bar associations have worked out sets of guidelines for trial coverage acceptable to both groups. In other states, members of press associations have voted against such guidelines, seeing them as an infringement of their First Amendment rights.

Before covering a trial a reporter should:

- Do the homework. Make sure to read the court file. Know as much about the case and the charges as possible.
- Talk to the attorneys involved in the case. Usually, attorneys are willing to explain terms and give background information.
- Find out who the key witnesses in the trial will be.
- Know who the members of the jury are and how to contact them after the trial. It is not uncommon for judges to instruct jurors not to talk to reporters after a trial.

- Summarize each day's events with key quotes from witnesses and attorneys made during the courtroom action.
- Observe the reaction of the people who attend the trial, particularly those who are related to or associated with the principals in the case.

STORY FORMS

No definite forms can be prescribed for reporting trials and lawsuits. But the general principles of good news writing should always apply. The lead of a typical trial story should either summarize the events of the day in the courtroom or emphasize an outstanding feature such as a particular bit of testimony or legal maneuver by the lawyers.

Here is an example of a summary lead:

> SAN FRANCISCO—In opening statements Thursday in the trial of U.S. District Judge Robert P. Aguilar, prosecutors contended that he sought to use his position to sway fellow judges.
>
> Aguilar's lawyer countered with a charge that "reactionary" federal administration targeted him because of his liberal rulings.
>
> Prosecutor Ralph D. Martin said Aguilar, appointed to the federal bench in 1980, engaged in an eight-year "pattern of racketeering."
>
> But defense lawyer Patrick Hallian told jurors that some of Aguilar's rulings, such as his decision that homosexuals could enter the country as immigrants, resulted in the "consternation of prosecutors" who represented a "reactionary administration."
>
> (Los Angeles Times)

This lead emphasizes the most significant testimony given on a particular day of a trial:

> An Eastside student told a King County jury she didn't like the former Juanita High School teacher whom she later accused of rape.
>
> But the student, 19, said she did not have a grudge against him.
>
> The student, calmly speaking in a clear voice, said she thought the teacher was "weird."
>
> "I just thought of him as another teacher I didn't like," she said yesterday at the trial of Thomas Gretz, who is charged with second-degree rape.
>
> (The Seattle Times)

The body of the story should amplify the lead, as in other types of stories. However, it is essential in the case of a trial that continues over several days to include a tie-back (summary of the case so far) high in the story. Some reporters work the tie-back into the second or third paragraph, as in this example from The Knoxville News-Sentinel.

> A Knoxville doctor testified in U.S. District Court Tuesday that he gave $30,000 to his girlfriend to halt a drug investigation. But he said he did not know he was being set up in a bribery scheme.

Dr. Richard Winn Henderson, who operated the East Tennessee Medical Clinic on Washington Pike, is on trial in U.S. District Court, charged with attempting to halt a federal probe of his operation by paying off an assistant U.S. Attorney.

Henderson is accused of making payments totaling $30,000 earlier this year to an undercover FBI agent, who posed as the brother-in-law of Assistant U.S. Attorney Mike Mitchell.

Mitchell was directing the investigation of the clinic, which began after Henderson's girlfriend, Alex Wright, went to authorities following a fight with the doctor last January.

In organizing the story, the reporter should use both direct and indirect quotations with interpretative summaries interspersed. Because trials can be difficult to follow, reporters often will present what happened in court in chronological order.

Much of what happens in trials is window dressing and legal posturing. A reporter must learn to evaluate what is important and what is not. The use of character witnesses at trials is a classic example of window dressing. Many lawyers, especially if they have a weak defense, seek to influence the jury with a parade of witnesses who are willing to testify to the accused's good name and character. Most of the time this testimony would rate not more than a sentence or two in a story.

Unless the information elicited from a witness is startling in nature, most trial stories do not include extensive direct testimony. Quotations from testimony are usually presented either in chronological order or in short question-and-answer form in the body of the story.

A reporter may choose one of two forms in handling questions and answers. Here is a narrative style that is common for brief excerpts of testimony:

Assistant District Attorney Ronald Miller questioned Booth's contention that he was only firing to protect himself.

"You fired 10 times and you didn't mean to hurt them?" Miller asked.

"It was so frightening. I didn't know how many times I fired," Booth said.

The second form is used for extended questions and answers and is used especially when reporting key testimony:

Q—How many times did you fire?

A—I don't know. I was just trying to protect myself.

Q—Isn't it true you fired 10 times?

A—I don't know. I just stuck the gun out the window and started firing. I didn't mean to hurt them.

Q—You fired 10 times and you didn't mean to hurt them?

A—It was so frightening. I don't know how many times I fired.

Quotation marks are not necessary in the Q-and-A form. Before testimony is given in this form, it must be preceded by an explanation such as "Booth's testimony follows."

In addition to noting feature highlights in court proceedings, the reporter should take notes on the background of court actions—descriptions of the crowd, witnesses, jury. Sometimes a lead feature comes from an event not included in regular court procedure. For example, outside the courtroom the attorney's actions could have a direct bearing on the case and provide a far more significant lead than anything that happened in the courtroom that day. Reporters should be particularly observant during trials, for the courtroom is an excellent source of human-interest stories.

Although most court stories are reported as straight news, a considerable amount of interpretation might be necessary to enrich and clarify the significance of facts and procedures.

Background and Interpretation

In addition to having an understanding of the organization of the courts in the state, the reporter assigned to cover any trial must acquire a background of facts and relationships of the particular case. Is the embezzlement of bank funds related to a previous bank failure, to business conditions or to personal problems of the person charged in the case? Is the case a striking parallel of other cases? When, where, how and by whom was a suit filed? The same questions should be answered about the crime itself. Have there been any previous consequences? Are other suits or indictments pending? What consequences will develop from the case? Is there a particularly interesting problem of law, court jurisdiction or other novel feature involved in the case? Only with such a background can the reporter do full justice to the case and write a clear account for the newspaper's readers.

A reporter must have a thorough knowledge of legal terms and procedures to write effectively about a case. In law there is a difference, for example, between "evidence" and "testimony." A reporter must use those and other legal terms properly. In addition, a reporter must be able to translate legal terms clearly for the reader. Court stories should not sound like legal briefs. Many legal terms mean nothing to the average reader.

The reporter should explain legal terms as well as the consequence of legal action. "The grand jury returned a no-true bill against Sidney Westchester . . ." might be understood by a few readers but not the majority; but "The grand jury freed Sidney Westchester of charges . . ." would be clear.

If the case involves the constitutionality or validity of a certain law being tested in the courts, the reporter must explain the consequence of the court ruling. For example, "The State Supreme Court today upheld the constitutionality of the new open-meetings law in the Palm County School Board case" is infinitely more meaningful than "The Palm County School Board was told by the State Supreme Court today that it could not meet behind closed doors anymore." Readers are not expected to be interpreters of court decisions. The newspaper must tell them, in language of the layperson, exactly how a decision affects their life routines.

The following are several examples of court story leads:

State Bureau of Investigations agents said there is no question that Paul Stuart was licensed. Unfortunately, it was as a roofer and not as a doctor.

But Stuart—who pleaded guilty in Federal Court today to one count of knowingly making a false statement—practiced both professions, agents said.

Stuart claimed to be a licensed physician when he hung out his shingle at the former offices of Goodlettsville physician G.S. Chikkannaiah, Jim Taylor, agent-in-charge of the state's Medical Fraud Unit, told Judge George Brown.

However, Stuart, 53, of Madison, did not forget his real trade, Taylor said.

He once convinced a patient she needed a new roof and siding on her house. She gave him almost $10,000 but he didn't complete the work, Taylor said.

Stuart was indicted in February on 13 counts of billing Medicaid for treatment that Taylor said he never rendered to patients.

(Nashville Banner)

EL CAJON—Cyrus Zal, an attorney for Operation Rescue, an anti-abortion group, was sentenced Friday to 90 days in jail and ordered to pay a $10,000 fine for repeatedly ignoring a judge's orders not to discuss abortion at a recent trial where Zal represented six anti-abortion activists convicted of trespass.

Zal, 42, of Folsom said he planned an immediate appeal of El Cajon Municipal Judge Larrie T. Brainard's order.

(Los Angeles Times)

NEW YORK (AP)—John Gotti, reputedly the boss of the nation's most powerful crime family, won his third victory over government prosecutors Friday with an acquittal on charges that he ordered the shooting of a union official.

The dapper Gotti, who favors $1,800 suits and pinky rings, left the Manhattan courthouse without comment after the victory. His supporters applauded loudly as the verdict was read. One man shouted, "Yeah, Johnny!"

One boy smiled, the other burst into tears as the judge handed down his verdict: guilty of first-degree manslaughter in the shooting death of their Kent neighbor, Brett Yolstedt.

"The acts of both of these boys were stupid. Words cannot describe the loss," King County Superior Court Judge Norman Quinn said yesterday at the trial of the two teen-agers. "Neither youth nor stupidity can excuse such an act."

The boys, 14 and 15, were being tried as juveniles. The King County prosecuting attorney's office alleged that Yolstedt, who had been walking his dog in the woods near his home last November, had been killed just for looking at the boys the wrong way.

(The Seattle Times)

Myron Wright, the popular Ripley High School basketball coach, pleaded guilty to drug-selling charges Monday morning just minutes before jury selection was to begin in his second trial for the crime.

A mistrial was declared last November after jurors reported they were "hopelessly deadlocked" on whether Wright had sold 7 grams of cocaine to a government informant on the school grounds.

(The Commercial Appeal)

Recently judges and juries have been called on to deal with moral and ethical issues as these leads show:

> A California mathematician suffering from a brain tumor has gone to court in search of permission to have himself frozen to death.
> Thomas Donaldson, 46, of Sunnyvale, Calif., is a longtime proponent of cryonics, the controversial practice of deep-freezing people after they've died in hopes that someday they can be thawed and revived. But he wants to go one step further and have himself frozen before he is legally dead. Actually, he wants to have his head separated from his body after freezing in hopes that future scientists will discover a way to cure the tumor and attach his head to a healthy body.
> Donaldson's suit, filed Monday in Santa Barbara County Superior Court, contends he has the constitutional right to prevent state and county officials from interfering with his death by freezing.
>
> (Chicago Tribune)

> A 63-year-old woman almost completely paralyzed by Lou Gehrig's disease wiggled her thumb Friday to tell a judge why she wants to be unhooked from her respirator.
> Davidson County Chancellor C. Allen High requested the extraordinary hearing in the woman's home to determine whether she is competent to make the decision to die ''naturally.''
> The Chancery Court lawsuit filed Monday is believed to be the state's first right-to-die case. High is expected to make a ruling early next week.
>
> (Nashville Banner)

THE LAW AND THE COURTS

Two general types of law are recognized: "civil," comprising suits for damages involving two or more persons; and "criminal" under which charges of offenses against society may be brought by a governmental officer or a citizen against one or more persons. The authority for enforcing the two types of law comes from the Constitution ("constitutional law"), the acts of legislative bodies ("statutory law"), and customs and judicial precedents ("common law"). There is another type of law on the federal and state levels, called "administrative law," generated from the powers granted governmental regulatory bodies such as the Federal Trade Commission or (state) Public Utilities Commission to enforce certain rules over particular industries and businesses. The two fundamental types of law are further classified as follows:

1. Civil cases
   a. *Cases in law,* which abide closely by the law
      1. *Contracts*—cases in which the plaintiff (the person bringing the suit) claims the defendant (the person against whom the suit is brought) did not follow the terms of an oral or written contract.
      2. *Torts*—cases that treat private injuries not arising from a breach of contract. For example, it is usually a tort for a person to damage someone or his or her property purposely or negligently.

b. *Cases in equity,* which are distinguished from cases in law rendering "equitable" judgment by not following definite laws. Persons go to an equity court when they can get no relief from the definite writs existing in the regular law courts. This relief often is obtained by compulsory or preventive decrees (mandates and injunctions) issued by the judge. Controversies over property ownership are usually brought to an equity court.

2. Criminal cases
   a. *Misdemeanors*—minor criminal cases usually resulting in fines, sometimes in imprisonment
   b. *Felonies*—major criminal cases usually resulting in imprisonment and sometimes death by execution (see Chapter 21, Crime)

State courts—which also include county and city courts serving by authority of the state—and federal courts deal with these types of law. Local affairs and cases concerning state laws are tried by state courts. Cases concerning federal laws and interstate cases are tried by federal courts. The dual system of courts is outlined in the accompanying chart.

To obtain a better understanding of the chart, and at the same time to learn a few of the most common legal terms, it is necessary to trace the route of a criminal case and a civil case in a state court. (Be sure to learn the meaning of each italicized term.)

ROUTE OF A CRIMINAL CASE

1. In a court of limited jurisdiction (county or city magistrate court):
   a. A warrant is sworn out charging a person with a crime and enabling officers to bring the person before a magistrate (judge).
      (1) If the person has been arrested on a warrant from another state, an extradition order is obtained; this will enable officers from that state to take the prisoner back to that state to stand trial.
      (2) Attorneys who feel their clients are being held illegally may obtain a writ of habeas corpus from a superior court and get an immediate hearing. The arresting officers must prove that the prisoner is being held for a just cause.
   b. The magistrate hears the case.
      (1) If the crime is a *misdemeanor,* the accused may be fined (within prescription of state law).
         (a) Fines may be appealed from this court to a court of general jurisdiction, where such cases are tried anew.
      (2) If the crime is a *felony,* the magistrate may *bind the prisoner over* to the grand jury.
         (a) The prisoner may *waive* the preliminary hearing and be bound over to the grand jury.

STATE SYSTEM   FEDERAL SYSTEM

State Supreme Court

Appellate Court, usually of last resort for state, though some cases may go from here to U.S. Supreme Court if they involve federal questions.

(Criminal and Civil)

U.S. Supreme Court

Appellate Court of Last Resort in the United States.
(Criminal and Civil)

Circuit Court of Appeals

Intermediate Appellate Court, created to relieve Supreme Court.
(Criminal and Civil)

Court of Appeals

Intermediate Appellate Court, created to relieve Supreme Court.
(Civil only)

District Court

The Court of Original Jurisdiction in the federal system. One judge hears cases in *law*, in *equity*, and in *criminal* law. This judge also appoints a Bankruptcy Referee who relieves the district judge of these cases.

Courts of General Jurisdiction

(Where cases are first tried)
In the various states these courts have different names: Circuit, District, Superior, Common Pleas, Chancery. Jurisdiction is in criminal law, law, and equity. Each district court may be divided into units, a separate judge passing on each of the three phases of law named above. Or one judge may have jurisdiction in all three. Petit juries hear many of the cases.

Grand Jury

This body must hear the prosecutor's evidence against anyone and indict that person before he is to be tried in the district court on a *criminal* charge.

Grand Jury

In many states no person may be tried in a court of general jurisdiction on a criminal charge unless indicted by a grand jury.

U.S. Commissioner's Court

This official is appointed by the district judge to give preliminary hearings on criminal cases.

State Courts of Limited Jurisdiction

These inferior courts handle only petty cases. They enforce local laws in addition to state laws. They serve as courts for *preliminary hearings* in major *criminal* cases, and the *civil* cases they handle are *limited* to *stated amounts* (except in probate courts) by the state code or constitution. The most common inferior courts are shown below.

In Criminal Law   In Civil Law
                                      In Law   In Equity

County Justice of the Peace or Magistrate Courts

City or Municipal Courts   Probate Court (Wills)

Juvenile Court   Domestic Relations
                                          (Divorce Court)

(3) In binding the prisoner over, the magistrate *sets the bail bond,* which the prisoner may post in order to be released until trial.

   (a) In some very serious cases, the magistrate may not allow the prisoner freedom from jail but will bind him or her over *without bond.*

2. In the grand jury:

   a. Evidence is given to members of the grand jury *ex parte,* or without the presence of the defendant.

      (1) Only the evidence against the defendant is heard. This is not a trial body. Cases are not heard in public.

   b. If the grand jury feels the evidence against the defendant warrants a trial, it may return an *indictment,* or *true bill,* against the defendant, arraigning him or her for trial in a court of general jurisdiction.

   c. If the grand jury feels the evidence is not sufficient or in order, a *no-true* bill is returned, and the defendant is released.

3. In a court of general jurisdiction (officers of this court usually include the judge, clerk, attorney, jury and bailiff).

   a. The trial opens with charges made against the defendant.

   b. Pleas and motions are made by attorneys. Some of the pleas and motions that could be made are

      (1) "Guilty" or "not guilty."

      (2) Motion for continuance.

      (3) *Demurrer*—challenge the sufficiency of the indictment.

      (4) *Plea in abatement*—contention, among others, that the indictment is illegal.

      (5) *Motion to quash indictment*—contention that indictment is unfair or defective.

      (6) *Nolo contendere*—defendant does not admit guilt but decides not to fight case.

      (7) *Nolle prosequi*—prosecuting attorney decides not to prosecute the case because new evidence indicates the person's innocence or because the prosecutor believes the case against the defendant is weak.

      (8) Plea of insanity—claiming defendant is mentally ill and not responsible.

      (9) *Motion for change of venue*—defense attorney claims it is impossible to get a fair trial in that district and asks to have the case transferred to another legal district.

   c. The judge acts on pleas or motions.

   d. *Petit* (or *trial) jurors* are selected if the case continues.

      (1) The jurors are selected from a *panel of veniremen,* or a list of persons who have been *summoned* for jury service.

      (2) Attorneys on both sides may *challenge* certain prospective jurors and prevent their serving on the jury.

      (3) The judge also excuses from jury service those who show evi-

dence that they might be prejudiced in the case or are disqualified
for other reasons.

e. Opening statements of the prosecutor (in most states) are made to
the jury in which the prosecutor outlines the state's case against the
defendant.

f. Opening statements of the defense attorney are made to the jury.

g. Testimony is given by witnesses who have been subpoenaed to testify
for the prosecution.

  (1) Prosecuting attorney questions witnesses—the direct examination.

  (2) Defense attorney questions same witnesses—the cross-
examination.

  (3) Depositions, usually written sworn statements, from witnesses
who may be forced to be absent or are not present for other
reasons are entered into the trial record.

h. Testimony of witnesses for the defense is heard (same procedure as
for prosecution).

  (1) The trial is concluded with arguments of attorneys to jury.

    (a) The prosecutor speaks first, reviewing what has been
"proved."

    (b) The defense attorney speaks next, attempting to show jury
prosecution did not prove its case against the defendant.

    (c) The prosecutor speaks again.

i. The judge instructs jury on the law in the case.

  (1) Explains what verdicts it can return.

  (2) Explains certain points of law in the case.

j. The jury deliberates in secret.

  (1) If jurors cannot agree unanimously, a mistrial is declared.

  (2) If jurors can agree, they report their verdict to the judge.

k. Motions may be made by the attorney for the defendant who is found
guilty.

  (1) Judge may be asked for a new trial based on the claim that errors
were made in the trial proceedings or that new evidence has
shown up.

  (2) Judge may be asked for an arrest of judgment.

l. The judge can reject all motions and pass sentence if the defendant is
found guilty.

  (1) The judge may send defendant to prison immediately, issuing a
mittimus, a court order of commitment to prison.

  (2) Judge may declare a suspended sentence (in some states), holding up imprisonment. Judge can reserve the right to put the
sentence into effect later or keep it suspended indefinitely, as
long as the defendant gets into no more trouble.

  (3) Judge may (in some states) place the defendant on probation,
which might be called a suspended sentence on good behavior
for a certain period of time.

(4) Judge may fine the defendant (within the limits of the law).

4. In an *appellate court* (appeal made on errors, with a *transcript* or *record* of trial sent to appellate court):

    a. The decision may be *reversed.*

    b. The decision may be *affirmed.*

    c. The case may be *remanded* (and reversed or affirmed) or returned to the court in which it originated and a new trial ordered.

5. After a case has been tried and possibly appealed:

    a. The governor may *commute* (or decrease) the sentence.

    b. The governor may issue a *reprieve,* staying for a time the execution of the sentence.

    c. The governor may *pardon* the prisoner outright.

    d. The prisoner may be put on *parole* and allowed his or her freedom after serving part of the sentence. But the prisoner has to report to parole officers periodically.

ROUTE OF A CIVIL CASE

Because a civil case is in some respects like a criminal case, explanations of similar steps and terms are not repeated.

1. In the court of limited jurisdiction (the case may be heard here if the amount involved is lower than the maximum fixed by law for such courts):

    a. The plaintiff submits a *declaration* or *complaint* that he or she is due relief or compensation.

        (1) If the case involves recovery of property, the magistrate may issue a *replevin,* which is a court order enabling officers to take the property.

        (2) The magistrate may also issue a *writ of attachment,* usually when convinced that the defendant may dispose of certain property involved in the suit. By that writ, the court takes charge of the property until the case is settled.

    b. The defendant is summoned to answer the complaint.

    c. The magistrate hears the case and passes judgment. Either party may appeal the case to higher court, where it is tried anew (*de novo*).

    d. The magistrate may attach the funds of the defendant (if the case is lost) to carry out the judgment. This order may be served on a third party, who may owe or will owe money to the losing party. In other words, the magistrate may *garnishee* the losing party's income if the court's judgment is not paid.

2. In the court of general jurisdiction (cases may originate here, or they may come up from courts of limited jurisdiction; in either case, they are handled similarly):

    a. The plaintiff submits a declaration, which is recorded with the clerk (the declaration sometimes is not necessary in appeals from courts of limited jurisdiction).

  b. The defendant is summoned.

  c. The defendant may submit motions and demurrers attacking the complaint.

  d. The defendant submits an *answer* or *plea*, which is recorded with the clerk.

  e. The plaintiff submits motions and demurrers attacking the answer.

  f. The case is set for trial, which may be held by a judge without a jury.

  g. If the trial is by jury, the jury is selected.

  h. The attorney for plaintiff makes an opening statement (in some states), explaining the case and outlining arguments.

  i. The attorney for defendant makes an opening statement.

  j. The plaintiff presents evidence.

  k. The defendant presents evidence.

  l. The plaintiff may present more evidence in rebuttal.

  m. The defendant may also present more evidence in rebuttal.

  n. The plaintiff's attorney makes a closing argument.

  o. The defendant's attorney makes a closing argument.

  p. The plaintiff's attorney makes a rebuttal.

  q. The judge renders a decision in the case (if tried without a jury) or instructs the jury.

  r. The jury deliberates and returns a verdict if agreed on unanimously.

  s. Motions may be made by the attorney on either side, such as asking for a new trial or arrest of judgment.

  t. The judge renders judgment on any motions.

  u. The judge acts on the verdict.

3. In the appellate court:

  a. The decision may be reversed.

  b. The decision may be affirmed.

  c. The decision may be remanded (and reversed or affirmed) to the lower court and a new trial ordered.

Cases in equity are usually not tried before a jury. The judge (sometimes called a *chancellor* when there is a separate court of equity) hears cases and renders verdicts and judgments.

The *probate court,* named in the accompanying chart, has a limited jurisdiction in the disposition of a deceased person's property. If the person dies *testate* (having written a will), the probate judge has the *executor* named in the will to carry out its provisions. If the person dies *intestate* (without a will), the judge appoints an *administrator* for the property.

Only a small portion of cases will be followed through the full routine outlined in the preceding pages. Still, nearly every step may result in a separate news story if the case is important enough. The outline should be checked against local variations because each state determines its own court procedure.

Here are several leads from stories about civil cases:

First National Bank of Chicago, in a suit filed Wednesday, accused Senior Vice President Jeffrey P. Tassani of hiding his ownership in Wally's First and Streetside restaurants in the bank's Loop Plaza.

The suit, filed in Cook County Circuit Court, seeks to seize the assets of Wally's First Inc. and Streetside Inc. which are registered as being owned by Louis J. Elliott and Mark Elliott of Park Ridge.

The bank also is seeking to have a receiver appointed to operate the restaurants and candy stand owned by the firms.

A federal grand jury is investigating an alleged kickback scheme involving Tassani. . . .

(Chicago Tribune)

CINCINNATI (AP)—A jury concluded Tuesday that two former Cincinnati Bell Telephone Co. installers defamed the company and two managers by claiming they had them perform hundreds of illegal wire taps in the 1970s and 1980s.

The jury's decision meant it did not believe the wiretapping claims of former Bell employees Leonard Gates and Robert Draise, who said they performed 1,200 illegal telephone taps for police and the telephone company.

U.S. District Court Judge Charles Kocoras has denied Mattel Inc.'s request for a retrial and awarded the inventor of the Hot Wheels racing track $71.3 million in damages and interest, attorneys for the inventor said Wednesday.

A spokesman for the toymaker, based in Hawthorne, Calif., said it would appeal.

A jury in Chicago in November found Mattel guilty of infringing on the 1969 flexible racetrack patent of Jerome Lemelson, 66, of Princeton, N.J. Lemelson has patented more inventions than anyone in U.S history except Thomas Edison and Edwin Land, inventor of the Polaroid camera.

(Chicago Tribune)

EXERCISES

1. Draw a chart of both the civil and the criminal court systems that operate in your city and county. Interview judges from a civil and a criminal court and write a story about each.

2. Invite to class a reporter who covers courts for the local newspaper, the local prosecuting attorney and a well-known defense lawyer for a panel discussion of the courts and the press. Write a story on the discussion.

3. Using newspapers available to you, compare the coverage of a criminal trial in your local newspaper with the coverage of the same trial distributed by one of the wire services that was published in another newspaper in your region.

4. Visit the court for traffic violations and minor offenses in your city, and observe a number of cases being tried. Write a feature story on your "day in court."

5. Visit a criminal court in your city on a day a major case is under way, and write a news story on the events that occur there.

6. Write brief news stories from the following notes:

   a. Juvenile Court Judge Gail Palmer
   Ruled today that Donnie Williams, 17
   Must stand trial as an adult
   For the beating death of

Glenda Haynes, 36, 854 Vaughn Dr.
Mother of his girl friend
Jennifer Havens, 14
At home on August 26
Young couple fled to Iowa
Where they were arrested
And returned here 10 days later
Jennifer testified she thought
Williams was only going
"To knock her out" so
The couple could leave house
She said mother objected
To her seeing Williams
Williams did not testify
In statement to police
He said he had been drinking
And someone known as "Joe"
Gave him drugs
Williams also told police
After he struck her mother
Jennifer took the baseball bat
"And hit her three or four times"
Williams is being held in county jail
Jennifer is in juvenile detention home

b. Circuit Court Judge Richard Hollow
Granted Dr. Gordon Rutherford
A Hendersonville physician
A three-month delay in his trial
On three counts of sexual battery
On a 17-year-old male patient
Trial had been scheduled
To begin next Tuesday
Rutherford, 46, was indicted
Earlier this year
After the youth told police
The doctor had fondled him
On three separate occasions
During physical examinations
In the doctor's office
Rutherford denied charges
He had asked court for
Pretrial diversion
But Judge Hollow denied that motion

c. George Graves, 22, Fairfield
Frankie Caffin, 22, Gallatin
Pleaded guilty in Sessions Court
To killing a deer illegally
"They killed a fawn out of season"
Wildlife Agent Bob Parsons said
"The deer they killed is only one

Of many that will be taken by
Poachers this year," Parsons said
Judge Dorothy Briggs ordered
The two men to pay $425 in fines
And court costs and declared
.22-calibre rifles contraband
She also suspended their
Hunting and fishing licenses
For a year and placed them
On probation for a year

d. Former Fairfield County Sheriff
James Butler Yates, 63
Found guilty today of
18 counts of accepting
More than $23,000 in extortion
Payments from two bail bonding companies
By a federal court jury
U.S. District Judge John Mills
Set sentencing for May 31
Yates' attorney Robert Millburn
Said he would seek a new trial
Yates faces up to five years
In prison and $250,000 in fines
He refused to take stand
In his own defense
Refused to comment after trial
Yates' attorney Duke Dillard
Said Yates didn't dispute
He received the money
But he insisted it was
Campaign contributions
He received $19,500 from
One bonding company
And $3,800 from another
Over a two-year period

e. Attorney J. Phillip Hancock
Defending Gary A. Groves, 50
And Bruce Babbett, 39
Both from Tallahassee
Argued the men were too dumb
To carry off their crime
The two were arrested for
Printing $4.6 million in
Counterfeit $20 bills
"What this crime encompassed
Was two men so rash as to ask
At a store for green ink
To match 61,000 sheets
Of linen paper they bought
The kind of paper on which

Currency is printed," Hancock
Told U.S. District Judge Walter Stephens
The men printed 233,090
$20 bills carrying 36 different
Serial numbers, U.S. Secret Service said
They hoped to select the most
Genuine-looking $300,000
To help Groves start a
Construction company
"If they had sat down and
Thought about it, they would
Have realized there was no way
They could have done it,"
Hancock told the judge
Judge Stephens sentenced
Both to 33 months in federal prison

7. Write a story based on the following information:

This assignment involves a trial that is under way in Criminal Court. Joseph M. Ringgold, 31, is charged with the murder of Michael Martin Davis Sr., 48, postmaster in Bedford, a town of about 15,000 in Hancock County. Testimony showed that trouble began three years ago when Ringgold moved in with Davis' next-door neighbor, Johnny Scott. Davis and his two sons, Michael Jr., 19, and Phillip, 16, the testimony showed, had had a number of arguments over loud parties, blocked driveways and other problems. The Davises also objected to two single men living together in a house. They thought "it didn't look good for the neighborhood."

After a series of preliminary witnesses, Michael Davis Jr. was called as a witness. Excerpts from the transcript of the day's trial, during which Davis was questioned by Prosecutor Lee Keck, follows:

Keck:	Please give the court your name and occupation.
Davis:	Michael Martin Davis Jr. I am a freshman at State Tech.
Keck:	Do you know the defendant, Joseph M. Ringgold?
Davis:	I do. He killed my daddy.
Keck:	Just answer my questions, please. Do not volunteer any information. How do you know the defendant?
Davis:	He lives next to us.
Keck:	Please tell the court what happened on September 1 at your home.
Davis:	Well, me and Buddy Webb had been target practicing in a field behind our house. And when we finished we went in and put the guns away and went back out in the backyard.
Keck:	Please go on.
Davis:	Well, we was just standing there talking and I noticed him.
Keck:	You mean the defendant, Joseph Ringgold?
Davis:	Yeah. He was standing there just staring at us for the longest time. So I just said, "What the hell you staring at?" He said "a couple of momma's boys who are trying to act grown up shooting off those guns in a residential neighborhood." Well, I don't like nobody calling me a momma's boy so I started over to where he was. About that time, Daddy came rushing out of the house and walked right past me, headed for him.
Keck:	What happened next?
Davis:	Well, when Daddy got about three feet away, he just pulled out this

revolver and shot him. Daddy fell backwards and we rushed over and picked him up and carried him up on the back porch while my brother called the police. He claims he thought Daddy had a gun, but Daddy didn't have a gun.

Ringgold's attorney, Ethel Johns Rucker, objected strenuously to Davis' comments. Davis yelled back at her: "Well, it's true. He shot my daddy deliberately. He's weird. There's something going on in that house. . . ."

Judge Kevin Wilson rapped his gavel repeatedly and told Davis to be quiet. "Another outburst like that and I'll find you in contempt of court, young man," the judge said.

At that point, Judge Wilson said he would sustain the objection and recess the court "until 9 a.m. tomorrow. That should give everyone a chance to cool off."

8. Write a one-minute newscast using Exercises 6b, 6d, 6e and 7.

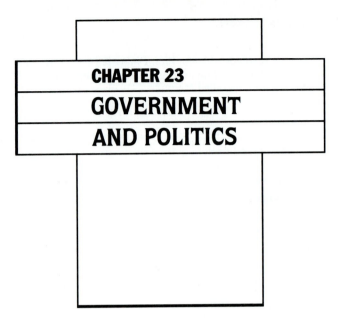

CHAPTER 23
GOVERNMENT
AND POLITICS

A major function of every newspaper should be to keep the public informed about the affairs of government at all levels—local, state and national. Most try. Some do it extremely well. Many others unfortunately become little more than a press agent for public officials by allowing them to set the agenda for what is news about government.

To compound the problem, much of what is written about government is "excruciatingly dull," "boring" and "confusing," as Robert Boyd, veteran Washington bureau chief for Knight-Ridder Newspapers, said in an article in the Bulletin of the American Society of Newspaper Editors.

Writing about government is challenging because most governments are complex, multi-billion-dollar enterprises, often having a penchant for operating in secret. In addition, government activity is so repetitive, a reporter is faced with the decision of how to cover it in ways that would be both informative and interesting for readers.

Although government is the public's business and public officials frequently are in conflict with the mass media, most public officials recognize that the media perform a significant role in our society, even if those same officials are displeased with what is written about them. Ideally, at least for the public officials, only good things would be printed about government. That is one reason there has never been a time since the adoption of the First Amendment to the Constitution that there have not been efforts on every level of government to restrict and control the mass media. The task of telling the people about their own business becomes difficult and occasionally hazardous whenever public officials try to control the news about government.

But the people must be informed if democracy is to work. They provide the money and elect the individuals who run the government. Properly financed and managed, the government's role is to ensure the various benefits of "life, liberty and the pursuit of happiness" for the general public. Improperly operated government may mean insecurity of life and property. At a thousand points, day in and year out, the complex machinery of democracy touches and influences the daily lives of citizens. There is no way of escaping it, even in death. It affects jobs, business, education, health, safety, transportation—all aspects of the public welfare.

Without the press to report regularly on what is happening in city hall, the state house and the Congress, most citizens would have no source of government news, other than the government itself. They would have no broad base with which to evaluate the performance of government.

The press is an important source of information for the government as well. Every day the president gets a news summary culled from dozens of newspapers, television news programs, and news and opinion magazines. The president's office is equipped with television monitors tuned to all the major networks. In every congressional office staff aides clip newspapers from the home district to keep the representatives and senators they work for informed of current events "back home." Government agencies at both the federal and the staff levels frequently subscribe to the wire services in an effort to keep informed. They also monitor the television network news programs. The mass media provide the foundation on which many public officials base their knowledge of current events. Naturally, they supplement this knowledge with information from many other sources.

Government News

What do people want to know and need to know about government? What is meant by "government news" and "political reporting"? Much news that comes from government offices is of one or more of the various types discussed in other chapters. Some of the stories include:

Type of Story	*Sources*
Crimes and accidents, suicides	Police, sheriff, state police
Illness, deaths, accidents	Public hospitals
Fires and accidents	Fire departments
Trials and lawsuits	Courts
Weather	National Weather Service
Meetings	Legislative bodies and boards

In other words, government is a source of virtually all types of news. In reporting such matters the reporter is giving an account to the public of government activities. Over and beyond these reports of daily activities are other important materials that need reporting as government news by a political reporter. They do not constitute a story type; nevertheless, they can be illustrated and studied, and they must be written if the public is to have a complete report on its government.

Several examples of government story leads follow:

Depending upon whose figures you use, the city's new Civic Center made $60,000 or lost $130,000 during its first nine months of operation.

Last summer, former Civic Center director William B. Leal displayed records which showed the center had earned $60,000 during that period.

But a new audit released yesterday concludes the facility lost $130,000 during the same time.

The City Council had good news for property owners Monday night— you'll have 60 additional days to pay your property taxes this year. And you'll even get a break if your taxes are delinquent.

The Haywood County school system won't be able to meet its payroll in July, Superintendent John Gibson told the Haywood County Commission Monday.

OLYMPIA—Spanking in public schools would become a thing of the past under a bill passed by a state Senate panel today.

The measure, which now heads to the Senate floor, is one of several attempts in recent years to ban corporal punishment in Washington classrooms.

Federal regulations are needed to impose a near-zero tolerance for alcohol or drug use by truck drivers because of a high incidence of drug-related highway facilities, the Public Service Commission chairman said yesterday.

The Political Reporter

A political reporter does not cover a political campaign or a political personality only, although much time may be spent following a candidate, listening to the same speech over and over again. Most of a political reporter's time is spent looking at the purely political aspects of government and the men and women who run the government.

Although it is true that on a national level news organizations assign reporters specifically to cover the president, most other political reporters have to cover far more territory. A political reporter covering state government, for example, does not report on the activities of the governor only. There are the members of the cabinet as well as the leaders of the state legislature to write about. In addition, a vast array of department heads and supervisors in state government are potential news sources.

Although the political reporter may not visit state hospitals, inspect highway construction projects, or spend a day in a food stamp office as part of the daily routine, he or she must be in regular contact with the commissioners who run those departments as well as other cabinet officers. Along the way the good reporter also will collect and pass along to the city editor tips for other stories as well as personal items and briefs about the men and women in government.

The good political reporter goes beneath the surface of routine government news and comes up with stories on issues and policies and the broad aspects of government. Routine government news generally is provided in press releases by government press agents. The chief role of the political reporter, therefore, should be to interpret government actions and policies for the reader.

There are specific matters—and others not so specific—that the political reporter should look for and report. The specific items include:

Legislative actions (whether of the state legislature, the city council, the governing body of the county or Congress)

Executive branch actions (whether of the governor or mayor, or department heads)

Judicial decisions (of the Supreme Court usually—not trials and lawsuits, but precedent-making decisions)

Financial and budgeting matters (including bond issues, debt reductions, taxes and tax delinquencies).

Less specific items would include the following matters pertaining to any governmental office whenever they are of sufficient importance to affect policies and trends:

1. Daily records	7. New laws
2. Periodic reports	8. Enforcement of laws
3. Changes in personnel	9. Taxes imposed and paid
4. New projects and programs	10. Publications
5. Speeches	11. Changes in policies
6. Discussions	12. Interviews and features.

The substance of these items can be determined only by the reporter in contact with, and thoroughly informed about, a specific official over a period of time. The political reporter should be so well informed about the activities of a governmental office and its officials that he or she can detect any significant changes that should be reported to the public. The reporter should not have to wait for the changes to be announced by the officials. Often the unannounced changes involve political developments that should be exposed.

A reporter's duties as both a government news and political news reporter require a thorough knowledge of government itself. The following brief analysis of governmental forms and their news potential should prove helpful.

FORMS OF GOVERNMENT

In general, there are four levels of government: city, county, state and federal. Each provides the citizen certain services, paid for ultimately by taxes. Each has a legislative, an executive and a judicial branch. The legislative branch, composed of representatives elected by the voters, enacts the laws that make possible the government's services and imposes the taxes that bring in revenue to support those services. The executive branch, composed of elected and appointed persons, carries out the laws of the legislative branch, performs the services and collects the taxes to pay the bill. The judicial branch, composed of persons either elected or appointed, administers justice, interpreting the laws enacted by the legislative branch as well as common laws and constitutional laws. In addition to the four levels of government, there may be others such as special districts created by legislative act to perform and charge for special services (such as water and sanitation). On a state and federal level there may be regulatory agencies empowered to enforce administrative law governing numerous state and federal agencies such as public utilities commissions and the Federal Trade Commission.

City Government

The accompanying charts show sample forms of city government. The specific form of any particular city can be found in its charter, which is granted (enacted like any other law) by the state legislature. The charter will define the duties and powers of city officials and otherwise outline the corporate structure of the city. A city can change its form of government, but such a change usually requires a popular election and in some cases approval of the new charter by the state legislature.

No reporter should attempt to cover city hall or report on any aspect of city government or political affairs in a city without a complete understanding of that city's charter. The reporter will find that no one else (probably including the mayor and the city law director) is thoroughly acquainted with it. Reporters who know the charter have an advantage because such knowledge will lend strength and authority to their stories.

The city charter (and a chart the reporter should draw from it for personal use) will suggest the many important areas of city government that should be reported. Major issues should be checked with the proper city officials from day to day. The reporter should resist the tendency to rely only on the mayor's office for all information. It is important that the city hall reporter know every department head and most of the subordinates in a department as well as the office staff, visiting them regularly. Every official pronouncement from the mayor's office about any department in the city should be checked with additional sources in that department and outside sources that may have knowledge of it or a vested interest in it.

It is important to keep in close contact with department sources inasmuch as problems change from time to time. One month may find the major public issue to be teachers' salaries. The next month it may be the traffic plan, zoning irregularities or garbage collection. In most cities today, problems tend to fluctuate in importance, so none should be overlooked or ignored.

Knowledge, background and personal acquaintance with city officials and employees are paramount for success in reporting city affairs. But reporters should not become the captives of their sources. They must have independent sources of information to ensure that government sources do not use them as press agents.

FIVE SAMPLE FORMS OF CITY GOVERNMENT

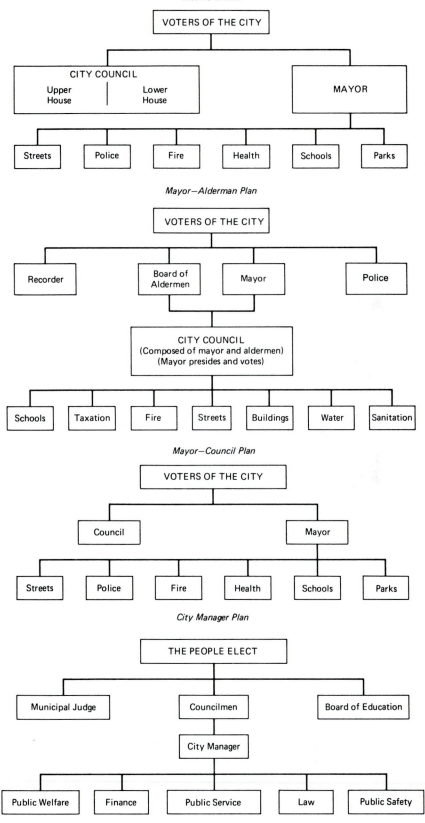

Bicameral Plan

VOTERS OF THE CITY

CITY COUNCIL — Upper House | Lower House

MAYOR

Streets | Police | Fire | Health | Schools | Parks

Mayor—Alderman Plan

VOTERS OF THE CITY

Recorder | Board of Aldermen | Mayor | Police

CITY COUNCIL
(Composed of mayor and aldermen)
(Mayor presides and votes)

Schools | Taxation | Fire | Streets | Buildings | Water | Sanitation

Mayor—Council Plan

VOTERS OF THE CITY

Council | Mayor

Streets | Police | Fire | Health | Schools | Parks

City Manager Plan

THE PEOPLE ELECT

Municipal Judge | Councilmen | Board of Education

City Manager

Public Welfare | Finance | Public Service | Law | Public Safety

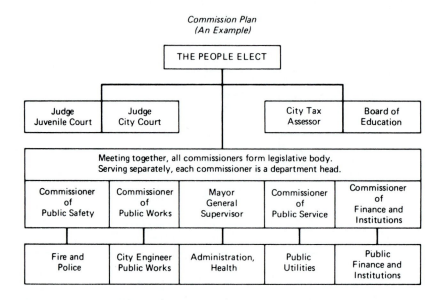

Commission Plan
(An Example)

County Government

Forms of county government (see sample charts) vary from state to state and in some cases even between counties within a state. It is important that the reporter covering county government have a complete knowledge of the local county government structure. Unlike the city, the county has no charter. It derives its forms and powers from acts of the state legislature and from the state constitution, and perhaps from precedent. In many areas, the county government acts as an arm of state government, providing state services such as the sale of auto licenses. The way county governments are formed often makes the task of learning about their structure difficult and may force the reporter to spend time reading old legislative acts in the state code. But it is essential for the reporter to know very specifically how the county's government evolved in order to understand its power and authority.

Without a complete understanding of how county government is structured and what powers it has, a reporter may be unable to recognize the special political interests that may attempt to control government. The reporter may thus become an unwitting press agent for those interests. To get a firm grasp on county government, many reporters draw up a chart listing county officials and their duties and note the specific enabling act under which that department operates. It is essential to keep abreast of new enabling acts, passed by each successive state legislature, that might affect county government.

State Government

A sample of state government structure is shown in the accompanying chart. But state governments differ, and reporters therefore must acquaint themselves with the structure of the state government they are reporting about. Knowledge of the state constitution is an important tool for any reporter. But

THREE FORMS OF COUNTY GOVERNMENT
"Long Ballot" Plan Used by Some Counties

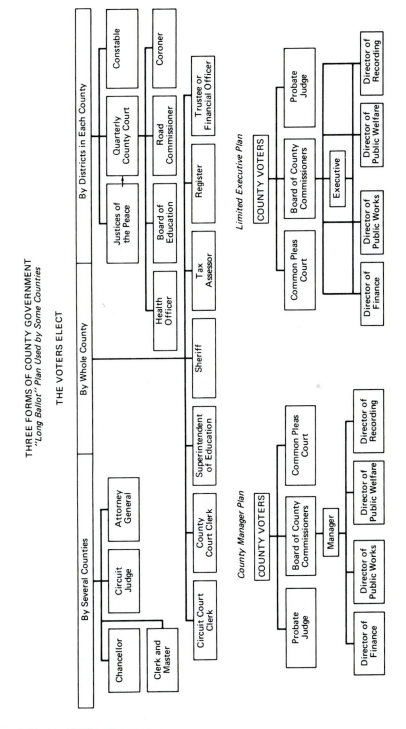

ORGANIZATION OF A SAMPLE STATE GOVERNMENT

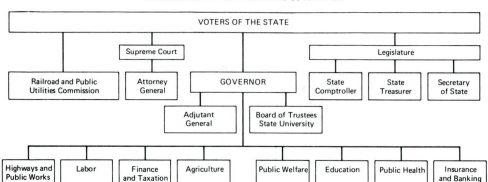

there will be many reorganizational statutes that alter the basic pattern established by the state's constitution, setting up the current organization of government. Every state regularly publishes a "Blue Book," a reference volume of the state's government. Included are the state's constitution as well as descriptive information on all branches of government and biographical data on governmental officials. Every reporter on state government should have a personal copy of this reference book. In addition, many states publish (often through a major state university) a statistical abstract, a reference volume giving statistical data on each county. Such a volume can be an important research tool for a reporter, and an up-to-date copy, if published, should be available in the newspaper office.

Many states have created special agencies to help the smaller cities as well as the counties to operate. These agencies provide legal and technical advice for elected officials who serve only part time in office. These agencies can be an important source of information for the reporter.

SPECIFIC NEWS MATERIALS

All of the story forms previously discussed and diagramed are employed in reporting government and politics. They are used to present the following types of specific story materials.

Legislative

No aspect of the state legislature, city council or governing body of the county should be ignored. Frequently, what happens behind the scenes at committee meetings, occasional secret sessions of public officials and lobbyists, and seemingly routine staff conferences can be more important and significant than what happens at the public sessions of legislative bodies. It is at these private sessions that much of the groundwork of government is done, decisions made and deals struck.

A reporter covering government has to be alert. New laws are important news, but even more important may be proposed laws, proposed changes in zoning, or plans for projects that would commit the taxpayers to enormous

A SUMMARY OF GOVERNMENTAL SERVICES
PROVIDING SOURCES OF NEWS

Services and Activities	City	County	State	Federal*
Protection of person and property	Police Fire Courts Building inspectors	Sheriff Magistrates Deputies Constables Courts	State police, courts, fire marshals, rangers, game wardens, National Guard	Army Navy and Marines Air Force Coast Guard FBI inspectors
Promotion of health	Water supply Health Department Garbage and sewage disposal, Hospitals	Health Department	Health Department	Public health service
Regulation and promotion of agriculture	None	Agricultureal agents and departments	Department of Agriculture	Department of Agriculture and other agencies
Regulation and promotion of business of industry	City ordinances enforced by inspectors	Licensing	Department of Commerce (may have another name)	Department of Commerce and other agencies
Regulation of working conditions	Usually none	Usually none	Department of Labor	Department of Labor and other agencies
Construction and maintenance of public roads	Department of Public Works, Streets	Department of Highways	Department of Highways and Public Works	Bureau of Public Roads and other agencies

Education	School boards Superintendents Libraries	School boards Superintendents Libraries	Department of Education and state institutions	Office of Education and other agencies
Conservation of natural resources	Parks Planning agencies	Agricultural agents Planning agencies	Department of Conservation	Department of Interior, Regional agencies
Regulation, control, and operation of public utilities	City water Power Light	Rural electrification corporations	Utilities and Railroad Commissions	Interstate Commerce Commission
Promotion of general welfare Social Security	Department of Welfare, almshouses Hospitals	Almshouses Hospitals	Department of Welfare, mental hospitals Special schools	Social Security and programs of many other agencies
Other major services		Property and other records	Regulations and controls	Post Office, Department of State (foreign relations)
Administration	Taxes Budgets Regulations Routines	Taxes Budgets Regulations Routines	Taxes Budgets Regulations Routines	Taxes Budgets Regulations Routines

* Federal agencies form too vast a network to permit detailed analysis here. Only standard services are suggested.

public debt. The public record is replete with examples of public officials who, by behind-the-scenes maneuvering, have cost taxpayers billions of dollars through unneeded and occasionally foolhardy projects. The public depends on the reporter for advance information that will help prevent this type of abuse by public officials.

Citizens frequently want the opportunity to be heard. Once alerted, citizens can act to arouse public opinion against unnecessary waste of the tax dollar. The reporter can serve as a watchdog of the public welfare by carefully observing and reporting trends in legislation. It is important not only to cover the action on the floor of legislative bodies but also to follow bills through committee rooms and public hearings. The reporter should poll authoritative opinion and canvass similar legislation in other states and communities to determine whether it has been successful or constructive. Finally, the reporter should tell the reader what the legislation will cost and what specifically the taxpayer will get in return.

Executive

An alert reporter covering government will be aware of the relationship between the executive branch and many new laws. Although officials of the executive branch may insist that they are only the executors of the law, they in fact often are the sponsors of legislation for reasons that may not always be the most honorable. A good reporter will know what government official is behind a law and why. Once a law has been passed, a reporter must be aware of its permanent news potential. If it is a tax law, for example, the reporter should follow its effects, checking with the proper official—perhaps the commissioner of finance or city financial director. What is its yield? Is it easily enforced? And, naturally, the reporter should check with the public to see whether the law is popular and how it directly affects taxpayers.

Aside from its function in the execution and enforcement of new legislative measures, the executive branch of government (governor, mayor, county judge or manager and chief department heads) is a permanent news source. Are the laws being enforced? Too strictly? Not strictly enough? What specific problems arise from day to day? What new policies are in effect? The reporter also must make certain that the executive branch (through the specific departments of government) is providing the proper services to the public as required by law and paid for by tax dollars.

The reporter not only keeps the public informed but also aids the executive branch in educating the public about matters of government. But the reporter must be careful not to become an unquestioning mouthpiece for the executive. The governmental reporter plays a key role. Without the reporter as a news channel, the interaction of government and the people would be difficult.

Judicial

A political reporter must also watch the courts closely. Here the same laws that were enacted and put into operation may come up for adjudication. Trials and lawsuits will usually be covered by other types of reporters, but sessions of the Supreme Court or any court in which decisions fraught with economic and social consequences—in which the constitutionality of laws is involved—will find the political reporter present.

Fiscal

Revenues and expenditures—the budgets of state, county and city—demand careful attention from the political reporter. Bond issues; taxes; delinquent taxes; special assessment; and the entire financial structure, fixed and current, need adequate interpretation to the people. The cost of government increases every day, whereas the quality of governmental services sometimes declines. The reporter must tell the public why this is happening and what can be done about it. Government officials may tell why costs are going up, but usually the explanation is wrapped in technical terms and governmental double-talk. The reporter is responsible for translating all of this into plain language the public can understand.

Public Records and Meetings

To cover government effectively, a reporter must have access to public records and the right to attend meetings. Even in states that have open meetings and open records laws, questions arise over what is and what is not a "public record" or a "public meeting." National and state journalistic organizations continue to conduct crusades charging officials with too much secrecy in government and demanding that all public records and meetings be open to the public and the press, for the press must base its claim for access on the public's right of access. The Tennessee Press Association, for example, sponsored such a campaign with a slogan, "What the People Don't Know WILL Hurt Them," and was able to obtain a state law requiring that all public records be open to the public and the press. It followed with campaigns to protect the confidentiality of news sources and to open all public meetings. Although all three laws have been tested in the courts and upheld, public officials still seek ways to circumvent them and conduct public business in secret.

Of course, there is no quarrel over certain types of public records and meetings, such as property transfers, delinquent tax notices, arrests, periodic fiscal reports, city council meetings and sessions of the state legislature. The disputes have been over certain types of records that officials claim are not open to public inspection, despite the word "all" in the laws, and certain types of meetings (special sessions of the city school board, for example, when personnel matters are being discussed) that officials do not want the press or public to attend even though public business is being conducted. Newspapers have had varying success in opening records and meetings that have been closed for unjustified reasons.

In any event, if there is no open record or open meeting law in a state, the press still can demand the right to see records and to attend meetings that are accessible to anyone other than specific government officials and employees. In addition, the press can insist that final action on a legislative or governing matter (such as action taken by a school board) be taken in open session. In states where open meeting laws exist, the press has successfully sued public bodies, forcing them to rescind action taken in secret meetings. In states where such laws do not exist, the press should bring the pressure of public opinion, legislative action and the courts to force governmental bodies to conduct the public's business in the open.

ELECTIONS

Despite the efforts of the press to inform the public on the issues and the candidates, public apathy is not uncommon in most elections. At all levels of government, increasing numbers of citizens are not voting. A reporter assigned to election coverage has a special responsibility to write accurately and fairly so voters can be fully informed. The complexity of the nation's various election laws complicates the reporter's job. The nation's system of political parties and election practices has grown up by trial and error. Although various state laws have stabilized them somewhat, both primary and general election practices require a broad knowledge and considerable political acumen if they are to be properly interpreted for the public.

PARTY ORGANIZATION AND METHODS OF
CALLING CONVENTIONS
(Democratic and Republican Parties)

National Executive Committee
Composed of representatives from each state and territory chosen by the national convention. In general, manages the national party affairs and issues the call for the national convention.

State Executive Committee
Composed of representatives from each congressional district chosen at biennial primary elections. In general, manages state party affairs and, in response to call of National Executive Committee, issues call to County Executive Committees for the election of delegates to the State Convention.

Congressional District Executive Committee
Composed of the chairman of, or other delegates from, the County Executive Committees of the particular district. Frequently inactive.

County Executive Committee
Created usually by party usage. Its organization is different in each of the political parties and is not uniform in the counties, even in the same party. The committee issues call for county convention or primary election to nominate party's candidates.

STATE PRIMARY ELECTION MACHINERY
(Democratic and Republican Parties)

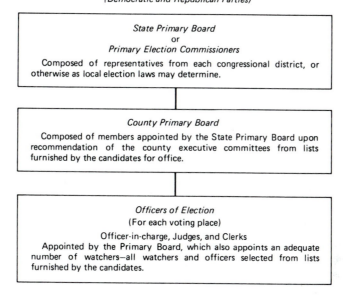

State Primary Board
or
Primary Election Commissioners

Composed of representatives from each congressional district, or otherwise as local election laws may determine.

County Primary Board

Composed of members appointed by the State Primary Board upon recommendation of the county executive committees from lists furnished by the candidates for office.

Officers of Election
(For each voting place)

Officer-in-charge, Judges, and Clerks
Appointed by the Primary Board, which also appoints an adequate number of watchers—all watchers and officers selected from lists furnished by the candidates.

STATE GENERAL ELECTION MACHINERY

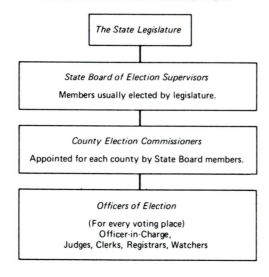

The State Legislature

State Board of Election Supervisors

Members usually elected by legislature.

County Election Commissioners

Appointed for each county by State Board members.

Officers of Election

(For every voting place)
Officer-in-Charge,
Judges, Clerks, Registrars, Watchers

The accompanying charts are simplified pictures of party organization. The national party system is made up basically of two parties, with third-party efforts sometimes emerging in response to the intensity of the issues before the public at a given time. Third-party campaigns are most often launched during a presidential campaign.

Although the organization of the two major parties and their practices are somewhat uniform on the national level, states show considerable variation in their party organizations and practices. The political reporter has to have the same understanding of the state's election laws as of state and local government operations in order to report political campaigns adequately.

The political reporter also is expected to evaluate candidates for readers, and it is therefore essential that not only the election machinery but also the issues and personalities be understood. Without editorializing—unless writing a signed column—the reporter must present a fair and factual evaluation of all candidates. Obviously this takes careful study or long experience and close contact with the politics of the community, state or nation.

During a political campaign, a reporter will interview candidates, write biographical sketches and evaluate the candidate's position on major issues while reporting daily on the candidate's activities. In major political races, often the same reporter will follow a candidate, report on his or her speeches and the audience reaction to them, and be on hand at campaign headquarters on election night to report on the victory or concession speech.

Interpretation of Politics

Covering politics offers endless pitfalls for a reporter. Some reporters become too close to a candidate and find it difficult to write a critical article if the need arises. Some candidates deliberately try to "use" a reporter to plant favorable stories. Even the most routine handout from a candidate must be carefully interpreted to prevent the reporter's innocently advancing one candidate over another.

To cover a political campaign fairly, a good reporter must "know the politics" of the men and women involved. It is important for the reporter to understand the facts behind the so-called news in the political handout, the motives for certain governmental action during a campaign and the behind-the-scenes maneuvering of the political leaders that could have an effect on the outcome of an election.

Many readers depend on newspapers to help guide them in making a political choice. They expect the newspaper to expose the bad and commend the good deeds of candidates as well as public officials. A good reporter will look for motives in everything a candidate for office says or does, and those motives should be explained to the readers.

To represent the newspaper's readers faithfully, the reporter of governmental news must know the men and women who hold public office and all the political, social and economic pressures that influence their actions. Who are their associates in and out of office? Who contributed to their campaigns? Which lobbying groups have access to them? What political debts do they owe? How do they rank with their fellow party members? How do they rank with the opposition party? What is their voting record?

In short, a reporter should know as much as anyone else, if not more, about the people who are currently holding office as well as those seeking office and should know about the political party organizations of both incumbents and candidates. However, reporters should not bargain their rights as reporters to obtain a close working relationship with sources. Reporters should not make deals with sources. Developing a broad knowledge of politics and establishing important sources takes time. That is why the political reporter often is one of the older and better reporters on the staff—a person who has the ability and personality to be an important figure in the political life of the city.

James A. Hogan, a partner in Coopers & Lybrand, one of the top four accounting firms in the world and one doing more municipal auditing than any other firm, made a list of questions that should be asked any politician responsible for making financial decisions. They were presented by Sylvia Porter in her syndicated financial column, "Your Money's Worth." They are

1. What are you doing to retain and gain private-sector businesses and jobs for the area you represent?
2. Have you maintained autonomy by not increasing the city's dependency on the federal government for resources with strings attached?
3. What steps are you taking to assure provisions of only those services which citizens demand and are willing and able to pay for?
4. Are you insisting that proven management methods (zero-based budgeting, for instance) be used to set new priorities for the types and levels of public services to be provided to keep taxes and spending down?
5. Are you making sure that goals and objectives are written into new laws so their effectiveness can be measured and reported to the public?
6. What efforts are you making to find new ways to deliver essential public services more efficiently?
7. What plans are you making to increase the percentage of our government's income that is used to pay for current services instead of general administration—and to pay off old debts and retirement benefits earned in the past?
8. Will you help in publishing a simple annual city report that anyone who usually reads business news can understand?
9. Will you seek improved credibility of financial reports by calling for mandatory audits by a qualified independent firm?
10. Have your bond ratings improved in relation to other governmental units?

Of course, it is important that the government reporter check regularly to make certain the official is doing what was promised in answer to each of those questions.

Reporting politics and government is a year-round job, but at election time most newspapers devote special attention to the campaign and the candidates. The public turns to newspapers for information about the candidates for office, the issues at stake, the political alignments and maneuvers. The reporter must wade through the propaganda being dished out by the candidates and their staffs to tell the voters what they need to know about the issues as well as the men and women seeking office. When the final votes are counted, the reporter must analyze election statistics so that they mean something to the reader.

Frequently newspaper policy (see Chapter 14) is involved in reporting politics and government. This will arise if the newspaper has partisan views on those holding or running for office or if it has a policy relating to governmental affairs. Such policies may range all the way from efforts to consolidate the city and county school systems to a campaign to change the entire form of city government. More than all other communications media, newspapers have taken the lead in crusading for governmental reforms. The public has come to expect the newspaper to be not only a guardian of governmental conduct, but also an adviser on progressive steps needed in governmental organizations. Newspapers rejecting their responsibilities and conducting unreasonable partisan coverage of election campaigns (and some still do) are doing a disservice to the public and their communities. Obviously, candidates seeking endorsement of newspapers may be swayed by the opinions of the press when they set their platforms. It is essential that a reporter recognize this. With such great responsibilities, the reporter who covers government and politics must be one of the most competent members on the staff.

Here are several political story leads:

Marcia Gonzales was fuming when she walked into a Denver voting booth Tuesday.

"All I could think about was new taxes headed my way," said the secretary, a Democrat. "And I'm maddest at President Bush."

As usual, the midterm election was a forum for voters' anxieties and disappointments. Many had the federal deficit reduction plan and its tax hikes on their minds Tuesday, according to analysts and voter interviews.

(USA TODAY)

Election Day dealt a crushing defeat to state GOP candidates, but Tuesday was also a victory for slow but steady efforts to make Georgia a two-party state.

(The Atlanta Journal and Constitution)

WASHINGTON (AP)—Democrats unseated the Republican governor of Florida and won a hard-fought victory in Texas, but the GOP captured the governorship of California, the biggest prize in the 1990 election sweepstakes.

Republicans, who virtually ignored the state's major races to pour their resources into legislative contests, made history in Tennessee by moving within three seats of seizing control in the Senate.

"The plan has worked beyond our wildest dreams," said a jubilant Tommy Hopper, executive director of the state Republican Party. "This is historic."

(Nashville Banner)

POLITICAL POLLS

The increased use of polling to measure the public's attitude toward nearly every aspect of our lives has presented an added problem for the political reporter. Every candidate sponsors polls. So do political parties, citizens' groups and the news media. So much attention has been focused on poll results that the public can easily be misled if the reporter is not careful.

It is the responsibility of the reporter to understand polling techniques and not to misinterpret the results of a poll. Before writing about the results of a poll, it is important for the reporter to know who sponsored the poll; who conducted it (was it a reliable polling organization such as Harris or Gallup, or was it the candidate's own staff?); the wording of the questions (to make certain they weren't biased in favor of one point of view over another); how many persons were questioned; where they were questioned; when they were questioned (was the survey done in a day or over a long period of time?) under what circumstances (at home, by telephone or on the street in person); the characteristics of the persons in the sample (were they all young, old, registered voters, unemployed, etc.?); and the response rate, including the number who said they did not know or did not have an opinion.

When reporting the results of any poll, responsible newspapers will always explain to the reader exactly how the poll was conducted. Some newspapers include the information as a part of the story. However, others carry a separate story giving the reader all the information about the mechanics of conducting the poll.

In an article for the "Washington Journalism Review," Evans Witt, a reporter on politics and polls for The Associated Press (AP), offered these rules for journalists covering polls:

1. Do not overinterpret poll results.
2. Include the results of other polls, even if they cast doubt upon the latest results.
3. Always include and be aware of sampling error.
4. Never forget the base.
5. Look at the exact wording of questions carefully.
6. Do not use non-scientific readings of public opinion for anything except entertainment value.
7. Be very, very careful when writing about polls conducted for candidates, special interest groups or political parties.
8. Never forget that polls give little hint about the depth of people's emotions or commitment.
9. Do not disguise your own interpretations as poll results.
10. Use common sense and do not fall under the spell of numbers.

And the National Council on Public Polling offers these guidelines for public pollsters:

1. State who sponsored the survey.
2. Give the dates of interviewing.
3. Define the method of interviewing.
4. Describe the population interviewed.
5. Reveal the size of the sample.
6. Describe and give the size of any subsamples used in the analysis.
7. Release the wording of all questions.

8. Release the full results of the questions on which the conclusions were based.

9. Do not remain silent if a client publicly releases and misrepresents a poll's results.

Reporters should be leery of any pollster who does not follow those guidelines.

MEETINGS

Every governmental body and local group has meetings that reporters spend a great deal of time covering. The problem with meeting coverage is that it can be repetitive and dull if the reporter does not strive to make every story interesting and informative. Polls of readers have found that many simply do not read local government stories because they are dull and boring.

Fred Palmer, writing in the "Editorially Speaking" section of the Gannetteer, a magazine for Gannett Group people, recommended two initial steps to his fellow editors that he said would make a meeting story readable and, maybe, excellent:

—Convince beat reporters that the newspaper office is a place where they can pick up their mail and see who is trying to get in touch with them. The office is not a place where they work.

—Convince beat reporters that the city hall, the county courthouse or the police station are only starting points on their beats. Warn them that those places are almost as deadly as the newsroom.

Palmer said nothing much really happens at city hall.

People draw maps, apply for grants, gripe about the declining sales-tax revenues and talk to reporters.
All of that is very boring.
It is difficult to take something that is basically very boring and turn it into a story that anyone would want to read.
But if we get away from city hall, we can find people who think their street needs to be fixed, who don't like it when rainwater backs up into their toilets and who worry a lot about an iron deficiency in their oak trees.
These people also will talk to reporters and very often what they have to say has something to do with a meeting.

In that same issue, Kathleen O'Dell, a veteran Gannett reporter, columnist, city editor and editorial writer, said she would tell reporters covering meetings to

• Do your homework. Meeting coverage seems to be 60 percent background work and 40 percent actual meeting. Find out what is expected to happen, and background yourself on those points. Attend the study sessions that often are scheduled days before the regular meetings of school boards and city councils.

• Break the news before the meeting. The days before a meeting offer a good chance to run stories exploring issues that are expected to be raised at the session.

- Background yourself on the names, personalities and special interests of the board members or meeting principals.
- Be sure your quotes are correct. If you miss part of a quote during a meeting, pull the speaker aside later and get it.
- Don't rely on your memory to get answers or quotes or correct name spellings after the meeting. Jot down questions as they occur.
- Immediately alert your city editor by phone or messenger if something unusual happens at the meeting. That will allow time to plan for space needed or to send a photographer.
- If possible arrive at the meeting early. This will allow you to keep an eye on board members and time to interview people about meeting issues.
- Read agendas and meeting handouts carefully, and as much before the meeting as possible.
- Get details, such as the number of people attending, any protest signs that were displayed, applause, heckling and any gestures or mannerisms the speakers made that you can include in your story to add life to it.
- Always keep in mind this question: "How will it affect the readers?" It will prompt you to ask the most important questions for the story and help you write the lead as well as the rest of the story.
- Watch for trends that develop over weeks or months of meetings of the city council, county commission and other governing bodies. Some stories don't happen at meetings but do stem from information that you can pick up there.
- If you decide not to attend a meeting, cover yourself. Arrange for a trustworthy person at the meeting to alert you during it if something important happens and always talk to the person after the meeting to check on what happened.

This example shows that the reporter used imagination in covering a meeting and came up with a bright lead:

> The No. 2 man in Lebanon is now a woman.
> Fourth Ward Councilwoman Jeannie Smith, who in 1985 became the first woman elected to the council, scored another first last night when she was elected mayor pro tem—or vice mayor—by the Lebanon City Council.
> Smith, a 39-year-old homemaker, sees her position as something all women in Lebanon could take pride in.
> The city's No. 1 man, newly elected Mayor Bobby Jewell, said Smith's election was a positive step for equality.

The following lead on a story in The Knoxville News-Sentinel played off on the way announcers wind up each episode of a soap opera with a series of questions:

> Will Stella Brookshire be reinstalled? Will the absent members of the County Housing Authority attend the next meeting? Does Executive Direc-

tor William G. (Bill) Pierce have the power to hire and fire? Will tenants' support of Stella have weight in the authority's decisions?

All those questions and more were left unanswered yesterday when Authority Chairman Cas Walker was the only board member to attend a meeting he had called, presumably to hold a hearing on Mrs. Brookshire's firing by Pierce Jan. 28.

Here is a meeting lead that never should have been written:

City Council members were told last night that because of nearby potential hazards to children, it might be "inadvisable, perhaps even negligent" to site 45 units of public housing designed for low income families on the so-called "Federal Office Building Tract" because of potential dangers from heavy equipment, plating solutions and radioactive materials in that area.

BUDGETS

The budget story often is the most important story a reporter covering government will write in any year. The budget always gives the public a fairly clear understanding of where the administration places its priorities. On a national level, in recent years, the major priority obviously has been defense. In many states, the top priority has been public education (more than half the annual budget in some states is allocated to the public schools). In some cities and counties, law enforcement agencies get the biggest slice of the budget.

Ideally, every reporter covering government should have more than one course in city, county, and state government finance and perhaps a course or two in accounting. In addition, a reporter must know how to read a budget. If a reporter does not know how to read a budget, it is important to seek help. Perhaps the newspaper's own accountant can conduct a quick course in budgets for all the reporters on the staff.

Government budgets usually come with a quick and easy summary at the beginning. Often the summary is prepared to make the official submitting the budget look good. The reporter should not become a captive of the official summary. The real story of the budget is buried deep inside the tables, graphs and charts it contains. A good reporter should be able to dig out the financial picture.

The original budget story often is somewhat routine. It should include the total amount of the new budget for the coming fiscal year; whether that amount represents an increase or a decrease over the preceding year; if an increase, where the money will come from; if a decrease, what services are being cut; what new taxes, if any, the budget calls for; if there is an increase in property taxes; in particular, what this will mean for a typical home owner; any pay increases (or decreases) for public employees; and a review of the departmental allocations, including the largest and the smallest, and any departments that may be marked for dramatic changes.

Here is an example of a good budget story lead from The New York Times:

TRENTON, Jan. 29—Governor Kean will ask the New Jersey Legislature on Monday to approve a $6.8 billion budget with no new taxes but with further increases in tuition at state colleges and in fares for mass transit.

The budget is only $511 million higher than the current one, and 75 percent of the increase involves mandated rises in expenditures for pensions, Social Security and state aid.

Seventeen of the state's 20 departments would be required to keep expenditures the same as in the current fiscal year. . . .

In the next example, the reporter tried to get away from the usual lead that says, "The city council passed a $25 million budget for the coming fiscal year." But one thing is missing—the total amount of the budget.

"There's more going out than coming in," said Mayor Jim Sells somberly at Tuesday night's meeting of the Rogersville Board of Mayor and Aldermen when the budget was tentatively adopted on first reading.

"It is a bare bones budget," he continued, "and we'll have to learn to live with it."

Before the budget will become final it will have two more readings. A number of amendments were added and aldermen were given an amended budget for study and will meet on Tuesday at 5 p.m. at city hall for its final adoption.

Whatever happens to the wobbly budget, its adoption will not require a hike in the property tax rate which has been $2.25 per hundred for the past several years.

Here is an example of a story written in advance of the formal presentation of a state budget to a state legislature. Details of the budget had been given legislators informally several days before its formal presentation:

NASHVILLE (AP)—Gov. Ned McWherter hopes to squeeze expanded help for poor families, including $16 million for welfare support and added Medicaid health care, out of his $8.5 billion budget for next year.

He will outline details of the budget to a joint meeting of the House and Senate this afternoon.

The new budget is up nearly $1 billion from the $7.8 billion it will cost to run state government this year.

The following lead localizes the national budget by emphasizing its impact on federal facilities in the newspaper's circulation area:

WASHINGTON—President Bush's $1.23 trillion budget proposal provided good news for Fort Campbell and Oak Ridge and bad news for the Tennessee Valley Authority.

The president's budget called for continued operations at Fort Campbell near Clarksville and increased spending for cleanup programs at the Department of Energy's Oak Ridge facilities.

The bad news included cuts in environmental, agricultural and economic development programs for the Tennessee Valley Authority.

(Nashville Banner)

Budget-making is a year-round process. Departments usually submit their requests for funds six to eight months before the budget is completed. A series of

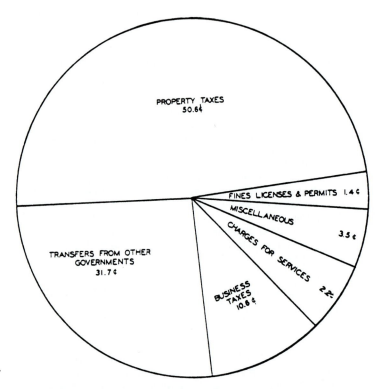

GENERAL FUND SERVICES*

REVENUES

WHERE EACH DOLLAR COMES FROM

* Includes the City's three basic operating
funds-General Fund, Revenue Sharing, and
State Street Aid.   Total Amount $71,810,299

FIGURE 23–1 Budget documents usually contain pie charts that
help the reporter—and the public—understand the overall budget. This one shows the source of revenue for a city.

conferences is held between top officials, budget officers and department heads
before the final budget is completed. A careful reporter keeps track of the budget
as it develops and should be able to predict with some certainty what the final
document will be like, although officials prefer to keep most of the work on the
budget secret until it is officially presented to the legislative body that must act
on it.

At the same time, the reporter must keep track of all revenue sources. It is
important to know if taxes on property, businesses and other specialized areas
are being collected on time. It is important to know if funds from the state and
federal governments have been reduced. In short, is the income meeting the
projections made in the previous budget? If not, what impact might that have on
the upcoming budget?

GENERAL FUND SERVICES*

EXPENDITURES

WHERE EACH DOLLAR IS SPENT

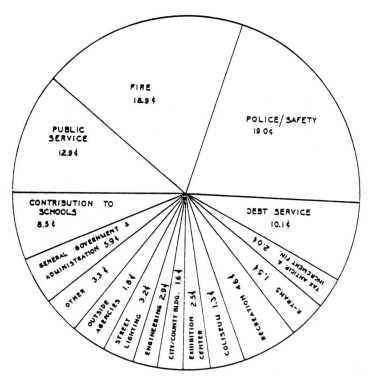

* Includes the City's three basic operating
   funds-General Fund, Revenue Sharing, and
   State Street Aid.   Total Amount $71,810,299

FIGURE 23–2 This pie chart shows where each dollar of the
budget is spent.

In working with a budget, a reporter should never guess at anything. It is
important not to rely solely on the people who wrote the budget for an interpretation. A reporter should have access to several outside sources—an accountant or
perhaps a professor of finance at a local university—to answer questions about a
budget.

EXERCISES

1. Using the charts in this chapter as guides, draw an organization chart for your city,
   county and state governments.

2. Locate a copy of your state's Blue Book in your college library and use it as a source
   of the names of all top state government officials. Enter those names on your state

government chart. Obtain the names of all city and county officials and department heads from the mayor's office and the county executive's office and enter them on your city and county charts.

3. Invite the mayor of your city or the chief executive of your county to class for an interview. Question her or him about current problems facing the local government. Write a news story based on the interview.

4. Attend a regular meeting of your city council or county commission and write a news story on that meeting. Turn the story in to your instructor, with your rough notes, the following morning. Do not copy the story used by the morning newspaper. But you should compare your story to the one in the local paper later.

5. From your city or county government chart, select the head of one of the city or county departments such as legal, financial or street departments, interview the department head and a number of the department's employees. Write a feature story explaining that department to your readers. Turn in your notes with your story.

6. Interview a candidate for a major local or state political office. Question her or him on current problems facing government. Write a story based on the interview and any background material on that person that is available to you. Turn in your notes with the story.

7. Interview the state representative or senator from your district about the major issues confronting the state legislature and state government in general and the district that person represents in particular. Write a story based on the interview. Turn in your notes with the story.

8. Write a news story from each of the following sets of notes:

   a. City Council member Barbara Asbury
   Plans to introduce ordinance
   To make it illegal to possess
   Child pornography material
   "The public is on our side,
   The Lord is on our side
   Now we need the law on our side"
   She told her colleagues
   On the council last night
   Her ordinance, she said,
   Makes it easier to keep
   Young people from materials
   Or performances deemed harmful
   To minors because they involve
   Nudity, sexual activity, excessive violence
   The ordinance would restrict
   Sale of sexual material
   To adults, if, after sale,
   It would likely be
   Viewed by minors
   Asbury, who is up for re-election
   Was featured speaker at rally
   Of Citizens Coalition Against Pornography
   Last Monday night in Civic Auditorium
   Some 4,000 persons attended the rally

Her opponent, Billy Bob Pullen
Called her ordinance
"A desperate move by a desperate
Candidate to try to win re-election"
Joseph Rodgers, chief counsel for
The local chapter of the
American Civil Liberties Union,
Called the ordinance
"Patently unconstitutional" and
Vowed to fight its passage

b. Bill Littleton, director of
City Social Services Department
Announced that six staff members
At the Riverside Home for the Aged,
A city-owned extended-care home
For indigent persons over 65,
Have been "furloughed"
Because of the city's budget crunch
"They include a property guard,
Three persons who worked in the
Kitchen and two from the
Cleaning crew," Littleton said
"No care-givers have been furloughed
And the $85,000 a year we save
Will be used to hire part-time
Temporary group help"
Little added that the layoffs
Did not threaten the quality
Of care given to the residents
City Finance Director Jamie Benson
Said city is facing "tough year"
She said she doesn't expect
The situation to get any better
And it "may even get worse"
If there is a large drop in
Sales tax collections
"We don't have reserve funds
To bail out departments that
Overspend their budgets," she said
Littleton says the unexpected
Increase in food and utilities
Forced the layoffs

c. State Representative Douglas Craft
A Democrat from Grapeview
Introduced a bill today
To increase benefits for
Welfare recipients by 8 percent
During the next fiscal year
And nearly double them by
The end of the decade

Craft says his bill has
Enough bi-partisan support
To pass this year
He says current benefits
Equal only about 56 percent
Of what Department of Social
And Health Services considers
Standard for "basic needs"
Under his plan, benefits
Would rise steadily until
They equal 100 percent of
The standard by the decade's end
"We call this our standard of decency,"
Craft said. Advocates tell us
That the core of the problem is poverty
And our standards have eroded
Currently, a family of three
Receiving Aid to Families with
Dependent Children receives
A maximum of $501 a month
Plus food stamps and medical benefits
That is only $40 more than
A similar family received
Ten years ago, Craft said
Opponents of the plan say
State's welfare benefits
Already among 15 highest
In the nation and that the
State can't afford such
A dramatic increase
Political observers say
Craft's plan has no support
In Republican-controlled Senate

9. Contact the city finance director and ask him or her for a copy of the city budget. Review the budget very carefully and then write a story on the unusual items you find in the budget. These should be items the general public is not readily aware that their tax dollars are being used to finance. Do not include the cost of police and fire protection, for example. However, do include any allocations for unusual items for those and other city departments.

10. Invite the finance director for the city or county to class for a discussion of city finances. Write a news story based on that discussion.

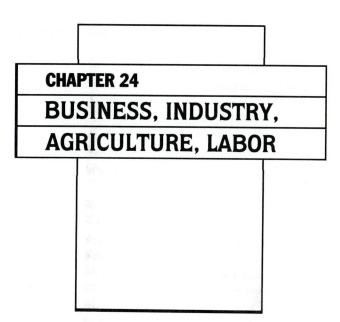

CHAPTER 24
BUSINESS, INDUSTRY, AGRICULTURE, LABOR

Economics—more specifically, the nation's declining economic health—became a major news story in the early 1990s as the nation slipped into a full-blown recession.

Reporters assigned to cover business frequently saw their stories on the front page as banks and savings and loan associations folded, industrial plants closed when parent companies moved their operations overseas, unemployment rates climbed while retail sales declined, and many shops and small businesses went out of business.

The business beat, which had grown in importance during the previous decade, became a glamor assignment for many reporters who once considered it the graveyard of the new business.

The face of American business and industry changed dramatically, largely because of advancing technology and competition from Japan and Germany during the 1980s. Most newspapers attempted to reflect that in their coverage of both local and national business and economic news.

Editors recognized that there is an economic angle to literally every story. A football game that brings 95,000 persons to a city on a Saturday afternoon, for example, has an economic impact on local businesses. A prolonged and harsh winter, normally thought of as just a weather story, will send the cost of heating homes, schools, businesses and industrial plants skyrocketing. It could also lead to plant closings; delay spring planting; and cost local governments large sums of money for repairs to damaged streets, highways and bridges.

The greatest change caused by increased attention to the economy has been in the business pages. Once many editors were content to reprint publicity releases (perhaps rewritten) from local industries or their parent companies, together with the wire service stock quotations, for the business page. Being a business-page reporter then was not a particularly demanding job. Today's business- or financial-page reporter, however, must have more than just a passing knowledge of economics and finance. The reporter must be able to understand what is going on and explain it to readers in a language they will understand.

Several trends have brought this about. Probably the most significant is the changing nature of ownership of American businesses and industries. Millions of small investors now own stock in major corporations, either directly or through pension and retirement plans, and have an interest in their success. In addition, the nation's unprecedented economic expansion during the first three decades after World War II was followed by a dramatic slowdown in the 1980s that sent shockwaves through the public. To report and interpret those developments, the business- or financial-page reporter has had to become something of a specialist in economics and finance.

National and international economic events and trends often have direct influences on local business, industry, agriculture and labor just as national and international political events have. A depression, major unemployment, inflation, a poor wheat crop in Russia, frost damage to the coffee trees in Brazil—all can have a direct effect on the economic life of a community.

It should also be pointed out that the economic health of a community will have an effect on the newspaper. Being a business itself, the newspaper derives its financial support as an advertising medium for the establishments that compose the economic structure of the community. As a general rule, newspapers do not open their news columns to free advertising space just to please advertisers. At the same time, most editors realize that there are many legitimate news items developing within the business community that have strong reader interest.

Even the routine business stories are usually of much local consequence, affecting the pocketbooks, jobs, household budgets and general plans of local citizens. The stereotyped real estate transfers reported in a "column" without benefit of lead will be read by many adult readers. The price paid for the corner building lot may reflect the value of every piece of property in the block. Will a service station be located there? Or perhaps an all-night market or a laundromat? If so, it may be the first sign of decay of a substantial residential neighborhood. Progress or disaster thus might exist below the surface of a routine as well as a major business story. The announcement of the consolidation of two major steel firms in other cities might have a direct bearing on a local steel plant that is a subsidiary of one of the merged firms. Will they phase out the local operation or perhaps expand it, bringing new money into the community and creating new jobs?

Although it is true that handouts, publicity releases and promotional stories may save the business reporter a lot of leg work, a reporter must always question their news value. Is a fashion show, a Santa Claus parade or a Washington's Birthday sale legitimate news or free advertising? The news policy of the individual newspaper will determine how much and in what manner such material will be accepted. Many newspapers join with local merchants in promoting some events. Some national "weeks" and "days" with a commercial tinge may be publicized. Mother's Day, Father's Day, Harvest Moon Sale Days (with special entertainment features provided by the stores) and other worthy though special-interest occasions may find the reporter writing not news but promotion and publicity. In all such cases the safeguard of honest reporting is the ability to distinguish the wolf in sheep's clothing. A Washington's Birthday sale, for example, can be a legitimate news story if traditionally thousands of people start lining up outside stores at midnight to get first crack at the bargains when the doors open in the morning.

Types of Establishments

Establishments and organizations that come within a community's economic complex include

Retail stores
Wholesale distributors
Banks and finance firms
Real estate agencies
Insurance agencies
Transportation firms—passenger and freight—both surface and air
Industries
Communications—telephone, telegraph
Business and industrial organizations—chamber of commerce, Better
     Business Bureau, various trade associations, automobile club
Farms
Agricultural markets
Agricultural organizations and agencies—state, county and federal
Labor—organized and unorganized
Various types of service establishments, some indigenous to the locality.

The extent to which a newspaper will cover each of these activities may depend on local characteristics. If a sizable number of the newspaper's subscribers are engaged in one of these activities, special sections of the newspaper may periodically be devoted to news and timely information published for the benefit of those subscribers and other interested readers. Such sections range from the fairly common farm page used in regions that have substantial agricultural interests to a special section on a new airport, for example.

Many newspapers put out annual business and industry editions or so-called progress editions devoted to the economic growth of the community over the previous year. Whether or not any special sections or pages are printed on a regular basis, stories from all of the listed economic activities are published as the news becomes available. Frequently the story, if of major significance, may appear on the front page. A prolonged drought in an agricultural region is sure to make page 1, just as a strike that idles a large number of the city's work force may be the main story of the day.

Types of Stories

The great variety of stories from business, industry, agriculture and labor will not conform to any simple general type. Some will be reported as meetings, speeches, interviews and publications. Some will appear as trials and lawsuits. Even crimes, accidents, fires, illnesses, deaths and funerals may affect the economic life of the community and require an interpretation of their influence.

The following are some general varieties (rather than special types) of news on economic developments that appear from day to day in the newspapers:

1. *Markets.* Stocks and bonds, livestock, and commodities—mostly tabulations and stereotyped reports, national and local, but accompanied by interpretative stories.
2. *Real estate.* Routine transfers, new additions, large sales, improvements and expansions of buildings, construction permits issued.
3. *Merchandising.* Retail and wholesale stores—expansions and improvements, new corporations and partnerships, mergers, bankruptcies, prices, cost of living.
4. *Financing and banking.* Stockholders' and board meetings, dividends, bond issues, discounts and interest rates, the money market in general, refunding, trends.
5. *Industry.* New industries, new products, improved processes or methods, expansions, removals, bond issues, mergers.
6. *Transportation.* Changes in schedules, rights of way, board meetings, stocks and bonds, refunding, rates.
7. *Labor.* Wages and hours, unemployment, strikes, lockouts, relief, policies.
8. *Business and government.* Taxes, legislative acts and court decisions affecting business, regulations and enforcement.
9. *Agriculture.* Crops, sales, droughts, new methods of farming, regulation by government, new varieties.

For all of these varieties, stories on personnel changes (including human-interest stories on retirements and the like) along with a countless supply of features are available to the imaginative reporter.

Story Forms

Stories about business, industry, agriculture and labor are not limited to a single form. Although the straight-news style is still fundamental, many reporters write human-interest, feature and interpretative stories to help readers understand the often complex issues involved. The Wall Street Journal consistently uses the feature approach to tell business and economic news.

Here is the lead on a Journal article about a small Ohio community, once the home of eight underwear manufacturers, that bills itself as "The Underwear Capital of the World." It was written by Clare Ansberry:

PIQUA, Ohio—Madonna would have felt at home here a week ago. People were walking around town in their underwear.

There was Mary Miller, a bartender at the Best Western, heading down Main Street in red long johns. Visiting New Zealander Peter O'Toole strolled about in a red lace bra (36-C) while singers belted out these words to the tune of the World War I ditty "Over There":

"Underwear. Underwear. Wear it here, wear it there. Everywhere.

"It's a stylish fashion, for work or passion, a far-out treat for those who dare.

"Underwear. Underwear."

The normally inhibited become uninhibited at the two-day event called the Great Outdoor Underwear Festival, which promotes Piqua's newly self-proclaimed position as the underwear capital of the world. Until 1988, the town's big claim to fame was "Home of the Mills Brothers." A granite monument in the town square honors the singers as musical ambassadors who "made the world a better place" with songs like "Glow Worm."

But the rainless summer three years ago caused a drought delay in the town's annual Heritage Festival and sent festival yearing Piquads (yes, Piquads, pronounced PICK-wads) scrambling for a proxy. Bereft of a major crop such as tomatoes or strawberries to anchor the festival, Piqua (population 21,000) picked underwear.

The following sampling of other leads will give some indication of the breadth of coverage found on business-news pages now:

The Tennessee horse industry is in a slump, but the prized Tennessee walking horse is holding its own pretty well, state statistics show.

In the past year, the number of horses in Tennessee plunged to 145,000, a 19 percent drop. The biggest losers were quarter horses, 10,000 fewer than in 1989, and "just plain" crossbred or unknown breed horses, whose numbers were more than halved to 8,000 in 1990.

"Any time you have a slump in the car business, you have a slump in the horse business," says Vic Thompson, horse marketing expert for the Tennessee Department of Agriculture. "When the economy comes back, the horse business will come back, too."

The remainder of the story from the front page of the Nashville Banner's business section gave the readers a detailed look at this business that generates more than a half billion dollars in revenue annually.

From March until October, most of Lexington's cavernous tobacco warehouses are silent and empty.

But during the sales season, which begins today and lasts through February, farmers from throughout Kentucky and tobacco buyers from across the country will generate millions of dollars for Lexington's 17 warehouses and the local economy.

Last season, Lexington's auctioneers sold more than 68 million pounds of tobacco for almost $115 million. That amounts to 16 percent of all burley sold in Kentucky and 12 percent in the nation.

No other city in the eight-state Burley Belt comes close.

The rest of the story focused on the business of growing tobacco and was the cover feature for the Herald-Leader's "Business Monday" tabloid section.

FIGURE 24–1 This front page of the business news section of the Nashville Banner reflects the diversity of stories now being used on the business pages of most newspapers. In the past, a story on prenuptial agreements might have appeared in the "Lifestyle" section, while a story on privately managed prisons would have been considered a government story since prisons are operated by government. (Courtesy of the Nashville Banner.)

ORLANDO, FLA.—Federal officials are discussing proposals that would reverse a decade of deregulation in banking.

The proposals would step up government oversight of financial institutions, require disclosure of more details about bank finances and impose new lending rules aimed at reducing banks' exposure to risky business.

Federal Deposit Insurance Corp. Chairman L. William Seidman said the ideas on the table include hiring several hundred additional banking examiners to permit every bank to be examined every year and assigning full-time government monitors to more than 100 of the nation's biggest banks.

The Washington Post story went on to describe other potentially far-reaching changes in bank regulations Seidman made at a meeting of the annual convention of the American Banking Association.

After nearly 15 weeks of higher gasoline prices, motorists are getting a break just as they hit the road for the Thanksgiving holiday.

The average price of a gallon of self-serve, regular unleaded fell 2.6 cents from last weeks—to $1.359 a gallon—the American Automobile Association said Tuesday. That put prices at their lowest since Oct. 2.

The story, which led the business pages of USA TODAY during the Middle East crisis in 1990, recounted the factors that brought about the decline in oil prices after the threat of war in that region sent prices skyrocketing.

The Atlanta Journal and Constitution introduced a new and unusual business in this feature by Scott Thurston:

The name: Sky Warriors.

The mission: Turn one of the great macho fantasies of American culture into a money-making enterprise.

The target: Anyone who thinks Top Gun was a film classic.

Starting Monday, Atlanta will be the home of the nation's second fighter pilot fantasy camp.

Sky Warriors Aerial Laser Combat, based at Fulton County Airport-Brown Field, will charge customers $490 a pop to fly a vintage T-34 military trainer in aerial combat.

The rest of the story included personal information on the two pilots who founded the firm and explained just what the customers would be getting for the $490.

This Scripps Howard News Service story reported on one of the stranger fashion trends:

SODDY-DAISY, Tenn.—Cal Lugo loaded his 12-gauge shotgun and took aim.

Ker-BLOOM.

The denim jacket jumped, then was still. "Let's see what we did," he said walking over to check what kind of fashion statement he has made. "Aw, shot off the pocket—that one's out. Can't sell them that way."

Yes, it's Tennessee's newest fashion explosion—shotgun washed jeans—the fashion brainchild of Jensen-Smith, Inc., based in Chattanooga.

It's a company that makes perfectly good blue jeans and jean jackets, takes them out to a nearby shooting range, places them on a mound of dirt

FIGURE 24–2 An air fair half a world away was a prime business news story in Seattle, home of Boeing, the area's leading employer and one of the nation's largest manufacturers of commercial airplanes. So was a boycott of Nike, manufacturers of sports footwear, by Operation PUSH. Both Boeing and Nike play a major role in the economy of the area. (Courtesy of The Seattle Times.)

and shoots 'em up with a 12-gauge. Again and again. Then they wash them, fade them, and sell them to stores where dangerously chic people pay 60 to 70 bucks for them.

"It's kinda taking the ripped-jeans look a step farther," said Sheldon Smith, president of the company. "We can't keep them in stock."

INTERPRETING THE NEWS

Interpretation is the key to most stories on business, industry, agriculture and labor—even most of the routine stories. The reader wants to know what happened, why it happened and what it means. The reporter has to be able to tell all this in a language the reader understands. The worlds of business, industry, agriculture and labor have languages—jargon—all their own, and the reporter must not fall into the trap of using this jargon without explaining to the reader what it means.

Statistics seem to be a language common to business and industry, for example, so a reporter should learn to simplify figures for the reader without distorting them. The average reader probably would not take the trouble to analyze "A total of 60,613 of the 147,604 persons in Thomasville own automobiles, according to. . . ." The figures probably will slip right past the reader. But "Two out of every five Thomasville residents own an automobile. . . ." might be more of an attention-grabber.

The significance of statistics should be made clear. Usually a comparison is needed. How do the figures compare with other figures? Are they high or low? How do they compare with figures of past years and other sections of the nation? Most figures are meaningless unless comparisons are made. When the reporter writes that local automobile sales increased 50 percent last month, the reader needs to know how many automobiles were sold last month and the month before if the percentage figure is to have any meaning.

The following list of technical terms used by business, industry, agriculture and labor will emphasize the need for interpretation:

partnership	strikes and lockouts	contracts
corporation	clearinghouse	overhead
articles of	assets and	trustees
incorporation	liabilities	directors
charter	discounts	interlocking boards
bonds	interest	pyramiding
refunding bonds	dividends	holding companies
serial bonds	premiums	public utilities
sinking-fund bonds	exchange	municipality
common stock	liquidation	debt and deficit
preferred stock	credit	"blue sky" laws
bankruptcy	trusts	audits
referee in	monopolies	balance sheet
bankruptcy	receiver	tariff

"bull" and "bear"	Federal Reserve	state capitalism
markets	surplus	parity
collateral	socialism	balance of payments
call loans	communism	gold reserve

In using such terms the reporter should either translate them or use them within a context that enables the reader to understand their meaning.

Some economic terms may require only simple definitions, but others require analyses that are possible only if the reporter knows the language of business and industry. Such documents as an auditor's report, a profit and loss statement, or a market report require special knowledge in economics to be read and translated accurately.

THE REPORTER'S BACKGROUND

A reporter needs an academic foundation in economics, sociology, economic history, economic geography and political economy in order to cover business, industry, agriculture and labor with any degree of success. These subjects generally are studied by journalism students at college, but never make the assumption that those few required economics courses provide a sufficient background for depth reporting on the economic structure of the community. They help, but the college graduate stands at the entrance, not at the exit, of all economic education.

College courses will give a reporter the general theories, principles and history of economics, but a successful business- or financial-page reporter needs more than that. The reporter must learn the specifics of economic activities in the locality where he or she works and be able to tell readers how national and international events and trends affect the local economic community. The reporter should have ready answers to basic questions on the area—population, wealth, chief sources of income, chief occupations, tax rates, school enrollment, bank deposits, labor force, value of properties and other vital facts about the community and the people whose economic life he or she will attempt to interpret. Most of this information is available in standard reference works such as atlases and state statistical surveys. However, the local chamber of commerce will probably be able to provide more up-to-date information on the community.

Even with all of this, the reporter is just starting. To be established as a competent journalist on economic affairs, a reporter needs to acquire additional expertise in each of the four areas of economic coverage.

Business

A thorough knowledge of the business houses and a more than passing acquaintance with the business executives of the city are major requirements for a business-page reporter. Retail and wholesale stores, finance houses, transportation agencies and other firms, particularly the principal officers of those firms, are news sources for the business reporter. The reporter must know about these businesses to get the real news and must be able to separate free advertising and publicity from legitimate news in order to present an accurate picture of the city's economic progress or decline. The reporter should develop a relationship with the major business executives in the city. If the reporter is respected, business executives will be willing to answer penetrating and sometimes distasteful questions, and a number of them will volunteer tips that can lead to important stories. Since business firms are private enterprises and a reporter has no legal right to see their records (in most cases), it is essential to cultivate contacts. An alert reporter with good contacts should be able to anticipate most stories that will develop on the business beat.

Often a business story comes from another beat. Here's one that originated on a court beat:

> Walt Disney Co., in a lawsuit filed Thursday, accused movie executive David Kirkpatrick of trying to raid Disney's film projects and executive ranks in violation of an agreement he signed on leaving the studio to join Paramount Pictures a month ago.

The Los Angeles Times story outlined the charges made in the suit, carried a rebuttal from Kirkpatrick's lawyer and explained that relations between the two studios had often been strained since several Paramount executives left five years earlier to join Disney.

Industry

Most industries have their sales sights on a regional or national rather than a local market. Nevertheless, the people employed by a local industry are local citizens, and their activities as well as the industry's well-being are of interest to all the people of the community. They are vital to the local economy, especially if the number of industries in the community is limited. The reporter covering industries should know them well—the products they manufacture, the number of persons they employ, the distribution of their products, the sources of their raw materials and the people who manage and operate them. As in the case of covering local businesses, the reporter must cultivate and keep alive all news sources in industry.

Federal regulation of industry frequently generates important stories such as this one about the meatpacking industry:

> WASHINGTON—The Labor Department Thursday took a first step toward extending federal regulations of workplace safety to the world of ergonomics in an effort to stem repetitive-motion injuries.
>
> At a press conference here, Labor Secretary Elizabeth Hanford Dole unveiled a set of ''voluntary guidelines'' for guarding against such injuries in the meatpacking industry, an estimated 305 of whose workers are hurt annually.

Agriculture

One does not have to be a farmer to be interested in agricultural news. In fact, what happens on the farms of the nation can and does have a day-to-day effect on the lives of everyone. A prolonged drought that wipes out the corn crop is reflected in the prices on the supermarket shelves. Freezing weather that damages the truck crops can send prices of fresh vegetables skyrocketing. And an extended farm laborer strike might cut the supply of some products completely.

In dozens of ways each day, the news emanating from the nation's farms influences our lives. Well-written, informative farm news should hold the interest of most readers. The local agricultural community can be an important source of news. The county agricultural and home demonstration agents, farm bureaus and other offices of agricultural agencies and associations have long-standing affiliations with hundreds or thousands of individual farm operators, and those offices generally are the primary sources of agricultural news. The reporter must know the officials and the scope of services of those organizations to be effective.

Knowledge of agriculture is also required if the reporter is to explain accurately the how and why of farming to the reader. It is all too easy for a "dude" reporter to make a screamingly funny mistake in writing about planting peas or milking cows. A few such errors will cost a reporter the confidence of both news sources and readers. A reporter from a non-farm background can learn to avoid mistakes through reading and regular visits to farms. A reporter who does not know about farming should not be afraid to ask questions or to look up information. Even reporters with farm experience should refer to books and other publications regularly to keep abreast of the latest developments in the field.

In many areas farm production is seasonal, and the harvesting of a major crop ranks as a major news event. This story on the Tennessee burley tobacco crop, along with a color photograph, was the play story on the front page of the Nashville Banner's business page. It was written by Bob Battle, senior business editor:

> An estimated 85.8 million pounds of Tennessee burley tobacco—the best yield since 1978—starts hitting auction blocks Nov. 19 where it is expected to command higher prices than last year.
> The year yielded a near-record crop for per-acre production, state agriculture statistics show. The average yield was 2,200 pounds an acre, close to the record 2,245 pounds in 1972.

Farm exports and competition from other nations around the world generate important agriculture stories. Here is the lead on a United Press International (UPI) story dealing with European agricultural export subsidies:

> GENEVA, Oct. 11—U.S. farm leaders said today that they cannot accept any agreement at free-trade talks that excludes deep cuts in European Community agricultural export subsidies.
> An EC offer to cut farm export subsidies by 30 percent—if the 12 nations at the talks can agree on even that figure next week—would be "completely unacceptable," said American Farm Bureau Federation President Dean Kleckner.

The remainder of the story explained the American farmer's concern that European agricultural products could be sold at lower prices in America because of the large amount of government support given farmers by European governments at a time when the U.S. government was proposing cutting supports to American farmers by 70 to 75 percent.

Labor

The labor beat can be one of the most significant of a newspaper's beats, especially in a highly industrialized and unionized area. A community's labor force, which constitutes much of the total population, cuts across the areas of business, industry and agriculture. This makes the job of the labor reporter particularly sensitive, especially in times of labor disputes. A strike against a major advertiser, for example, might present serious financial problems for the newspaper if the advertiser did not like the tone of the stories reporting the strike. The struck firm might seek to influence coverage of the strike by threatening to withdraw its advertising from the newspaper. That does happen, but it is the exception rather than the rule.

The labor force can be organized by crafts or industries or not at all. As a result, covering the labor beat involves developing many sources of news. The general run of labor news offers no more than briefs on elections, routine meetings, social events and the like. But when strikes are threatened or in progress, or contracts are up for renewal, such developments may become front-page news. A labor reporter should make every effort to report the labor-management affairs that are settled without strife just as vigorously as those that threaten or result in conflict. News sources cultivated by the handling of routine stories often become quite valuable during periods of labor strife. Moreover, to develop latent reader interest in labor news, the reporter needs to search for stories and features that are not centered on conflict.

A labor reporter should not be a crusader for labor or a spy for management. A careful reporter does not choose sides. It is important to know the pros and cons of both sides of an issue. For example, a good reporter will be well versed in the role of organized labor in the local community, the structure of labor organizations, the extra benefits resulting from labor union membership (such as pension funds), the salary scales of union as well as non-union laborers, and other information important to local workers. It also is important to have a working knowledge of the major labor laws that affect all workers, as well as those laws that have a direct bearing on local industries. The reporter should know and understand the position of business and industry in any labor dispute. This knowledge is essential if a reporter is to give labor stories depth and interpret labor news accurately for readers of the newspaper. Labor stories demand careful balance. When writing of strikes and lockouts, for example, a reporter must be objective, giving the facts but not stacking the deck for one side or the other. Even in violent strikes, the reporter should resist the temptation to write them as if they were military warfare. Strike stories should be factual but not inflammatory.

The following labor story rated the top position on the front page of The Commercial Appeal, Memphis, because of the potential impact of a strike at the plant should workers reject the new labor contract. It was written by Ted Evanoff:

> Nearly 1,200 employees at Mississippi's largest fish processor, Delta Pride Catfish Inc., in Indianola, are scheduled to vote Monday on a new labor contract.
>
> When a three-year pact expired last week, production employees represented by Memphis-based United Food and Commercial Workers Union Local 1529 extended the agreement through midnight Wednesday.
>
> The vote comes as Delta Pride adjusts to a new president and confronts slowing sales throughout the United States. And Indianola merchants hope the workers accept the offer and avoid a strike that could cripple the local economy.

The remainder of the story discusses the issues involved in the labor contract and gives the reader a clear picture of the economic role this particular industry plays in the community and state.

COMPLETE REPORTING

The most important form of interpretation in reporting the economic life of a community is that which reaches below the surface of events and brings forth significance and trend. Stock market figures, commodity prices, car loadings and other financial data are usually not significant in themselves. Compared with what they were a year ago or last month, however, they may have a meaning and be a prophecy of the future. This does not mean that the reporter should become a forecaster; on the contrary, he or she must be cautious about making forecasts on business conditions because serious consequences could result—stock shifts, sales slumps and the like. Nevertheless, the reporter can point up the trends of the past. Although analyses of business conditions may be the prerogative of "business analysts" or special columnists, the reporter cannot afford to restrict questions to the obvious facts.

Is a factory to be established in the community? What, then, will be its effect on the labor situation, unemployment, housing, taxes, and the demands on city utilities and services? No columnist or analyst writing for a feature syndicate can interpret this sort of local story for the citizens. Only the local reporter can provide this service. Complete reporting is expected of the reporter as a public service. Concerning a new city auditorium, a new freeway through the city, a strike at a major industry or the status of retail sales during a recession, the question is not just "What is happening?" but also "What does it mean in the lives of local people?"

EXERCISES

1. The commerce department in most states prepares an annual economic report for the coming year that is often used by the governor in making budget projections. Check

your local library for a copy of that report or call the commerce department and ask for a copy. Review the report and write a news story based on the projects in it.

2. Ask your college librarian if a statewide statistical analysis of business and industry exists. If a copy is available, study it closely and then write a news or feature story on a single industry that is profiled in the statistical analysis.

3. Invite a local stockbroker to class to discuss various aspects of the stock market. Write a news story based on that interview.

4. Using your local county extension agent as a contact, invite a local farmer to class to discuss his or her views of the state of agriculture locally and across the nation. Write a news or feature story based on that interview.

5. Invite a local labor union leader and a representative of management from a local industry to class to discuss labor issues. If there is no unionized industrial plant in your area, invite the head of the local public school teachers' union or organization to class to discuss salaries and working conditions. Write a story based on the interview with the union and management discussion or the teachers' representative.

6. Write stories using the following notes:
   a. Stride Shoe Company
   Negotiating new contract with
   United Food and Commercial Workers and
   Amalgamated Clothing and Textile Workers Union
   Which represents workers at
   Company's 18 factories and
   Distribution centers
   In four southern states
   Company a major regional employer
   Has approximately 2,000 workers
   At five plants in your state
   Proposed a two-year contract
   Three weeks ago but
   Workers rejected it by 70% margin
   Contract negotiations broke off
   Union sent letter to retailers
   Who stock Stride shoes
   Reporting contract vote
   And asking for their support
   Company officials blasted unions
   For sending the letter
   Union officials criticized
   Company for holding small group
   Meetings with workers
   Curtis Pullen, production vice-president
   Charged message could
   "Damage sales potential"
   Joan Sanchez, union vice president
   Said letter wasn't "unusual"
   "Just an effort to alert
   Retail folks," she said
   Unions reported widespread
   Complaints from workers
   Who were asked to attend

Small group meetings with management
To discuss contract talks
Union claims management
Threatening to close plants
"To scare workers to death"
Contract negotiations are
To resume again Tuesday

b. National Tire Wholesale
Announced plans today
To build its second
Tire store in the city
In Fountain Park area
New store will have 12,000
Square feet of space
It will open in three months
Negotiations under way for
A third undisclosed location
For a store to open next spring
Tom Dean, company spokesman
Says Fountain Park store
Will be among the first generation
Of new stores and all future
Stores will be similar to it
"This expansion indicated our
Faith in this city as a marketplace"
Dean told city officials
Attending the groundbreaking
For the Fountain Park store
W.R. Newhouse & Associates is
Contractor for project

c. Fleming & Associates
Local real estate company
Has merged with Carter & Associates
A real estate firm
Based in Chicago to form
Carter/Fleming & Associates
Will handle real estate leasing
Management and brokerage activities
Richard Fleming, who formed
Fleming & Associates three years ago
Will be president of new company here
The Chicago firm developed
Ten Compton Place here
Has been its management
And leasing firm for 10 years
Owns 100 acres near Interstate 5
At Moores Lane in Brentwood
New firm plans to develop area
As commercial and office area
Carter/Fleming will have 16 employees

But plans to expand by fall
Company represents tenants
In five major business complexes
And shopping centers in area

d. Minority Enterprise Development Week
To be observed here
First week in October
Sponsored by Chamber of Commerce
And Minority Business Development Center
At the state university here
Designed as showcase for
Minority businesses and organizations
More than 60 churches to recognize
Minority businessmen and -women in their congregations
Other events include
Exhibit of products produced
By minority businesses at
Civic Coliseum all week
A tour of Urban League headquarters
And an awards dinner at which
Achievement awards will be given
To outstanding minority
Businessmen and -women
Maya Angelou, actress and author,
To be featured speaker at
The achievement dinner
More than 600 people
Expected to attend

7. Write a story from the following notes:
Martin Perlman, president
National Home Builders Association
Speaking at annual meeting of
Mid-State Home Builders Union
Made the following comments:

Overzealous banking regulators are hurting builders. Banking regulations make it very difficult for builders to acquire construction financing because regulators have made lending policies tighter than they were before the latest real estate slump. Even those builders who have contracts from good home buyers find it impossible to get construction loans. Right now the forecast for housing starts has been lowered for the fourth time this year. The count is down from 1.4 million to 1.2 million.

My gut feeling is we'll have to lower it even more. It is the lowest forecast since the 1981-82 recession, when the interest rates were up around 21 percent. By contrast the peak years saw 1.7 million annual housing starts.

I am hopeful that if a recession occurs it will be shallow and 1992 will see starts perk back up to about 1.3 million.

I hope to meet with the president sometime before the end of the year to discuss this problem with him. He needs to know that home builders are being painted with the same brush as the vacant office buildings and that's unfair.

Builders have also faced problems from higher mortgage interest rates as a result of the scrutiny banks and savings and loan associations have faced from banking regulators the past two years.

Because of the downturn in the economy and the difficulty builders face getting financing, it is a buyer's market. People are getting values that they have not seen in a long, long time.

Perlman is a builder from Houston who has built more than 6,000 single-family homes.

8. Using these items taken from press releases sent to the business editor by local firms, write a "Business Briefs" column. Keep each item to one or two paragraphs:

   a. United Parcel Service announced
   Opening of new $1 million
   Package delivery center
   In suburban Beech Grove
   Center is 30,300 square feet
   Space for 28 delivery vehicles
   Plans to expand to space
   For 48 vehicles already under way
   Center had capacity to process
   Approximately 3,000 items an hour
   UPS is world's largest
   Package delivery company

   b. Digital Associates
   Music business service company
   Provides digital audio rentals
   Digital editing, mixing
   Cassette duplication and
   Audio engineering services
   Has acquired Corner Cartage Company
   Music equipment moving
   And storage company
   Renamed the firm
   Music Movers Inc.
   It will remain in its
   Berry Hill location

   c. John Higashi, founder
   President, general manager
   Maintenance Equipment Co.
   Based in suburban Franklin,
   Received the International
   Sanitary Supply Association's
   National Service Award
   For outstanding service
   To the cleaning and
   Maintenance products industry
   Award to be presented in June
   At group's national meeting

   d. Curtis Rajotte, president
   Chief operating officer
   Valley National Bank,

Appointed chairman of annual
U.S. Savings Bond program
For greater metropolitan area
He will work with leaders
In community and businesses
To encourage more people
To buy savings bonds
And join Payroll Savings Plan
Where they work
His goal is for 8,500 people
To become involved in
Savings bond programs

  e. Margaret Ann Long
Owner of a public relations agency
Will speak at annual meeting
Of the Mid-State Business
And Professional Club
On Tuesday in Union Club
For reservations call 293-7233
Meeting is open to public

9. Write a one-minute newscast using the information in Exercises 6a, 6b, 6d and 7.

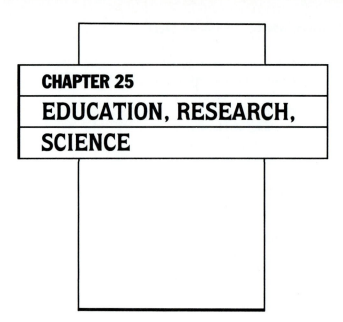

CHAPTER 25
EDUCATION, RESEARCH, SCIENCE

The thunderstorm of complaints about the poor quality of America's public schools that began in the 1980s continued unabated into the 1990s. A new wave of national reports, similar to those in the 1980s, again castigated the education establishment, teacher training, public school boards, teachers' unions, teachers and even parents for the decline and fall of education in America.

The "rising tide of mediocrity" in public education that was cited by the National Commission on Excellence in the 1980s continued to rise. Scholastic test scores declined even further, the national high school dropout rate hovered around 25 percent, and almost daily there were press reports of high school graduates who could not read or write and teachers who could not spell simple words or punctuate a sentence accurately.

Parents, community leaders, business people and politicians called for higher standards and improved quality of instruction in public schools. Several governors campaigned and won strong support for re-election by promising public school reform. Newspaper editorial writers often joined the chorus.

Increasingly, newspapers began to put more emphasis on the education beat. Their efforts paid off with important stories about local schools, not just routine coverage of school board meetings. More and more editors and education writers came to realize that the education beat had a strong built-in interest for readers because it involves two things that most people value highly—their children and their money. The cost of education often is the largest item in any local government's budget. In fact, the cost is of special concern because everyone in a community helps pay for public education, whether he or she attends school or has children who attend, through sales or property taxes.

In addition to their educational role, schools are important news sources because they frequently play a major role in the social life of a community. Moreover, the press has a particular interest in schools because they are producing tomorrow's consumers of newspapers.

The criticism of the public schools has made many newspapers rethink their coverage of education. Enrollment figures, bond issues, faculty changes, and the fortunes or misfortunes of the athletic teams still form the backbone of school-news coverage. But increased emphasis is being placed on stories that try to help the taxpayer understand what is happening not only in local schools but also across the nation.

Problems in school financing, trends in classroom teaching, changes in graduation requirements, increased standards, labor negotiations with teachers and dozens of other significant problems are being reported with renewed vigor. Newspapers are also showing increased interest in church-related and private schools as well as the trade schools that have developed in many areas.

Research and education go together. Persons in the field of education, especially those on the upper levels, seek not only to teach but also, through research, to add new knowledge. Research, of course, is by no means confined to educational institutions. Government agencies, industries, hospitals and clinics, and private laboratories sponsor many research programs. A large percentage of those programs, however, are linked to educational institutions, either through special contracts or through the services of educators as consultants. In any event, educational institutions must train most if not all of the personnel qualified to operate research programs.

Research is conducted in both scientific and non-scientific fields. Studies by researchers in the basic sciences, medical sciences and engineering often result in scientific breakthroughs that become significant news stories. But equally important is the research being conducted in other fields of knowledge. Studies in the humanities and social sciences, for example, also lead to important news stories. Many newspapers now have writers who cover medicine as well as the latest developments in pure science, the humanities and social science.

The education beat cuts across virtually every other subject a newspaper covers: politics, religion, business, courts, sports, race relations, social issues, even lifestyles and fashions. An imaginative reporter can find enterprise stories in all of those areas and more. The list of potential stories beyond routine coverage is endless.

A reporter does not have to be a former schoolteacher or have taken education courses in college to cover education effectively. But he or she must have an understanding of the education system and must keep informed about what is happening in education generally and on the local scene specifically. The education beat cannot be covered from the city room or the school superintendent's office. The education reporter has to be involved daily.

To cover the education beat, the reporter must know the organizational structure of the public and private school systems in the community and the state. Whether it is a single school or a large school system encompassing many schools, the organizational pattern of each will be much the same. At the top is some type of board, elected or appointed, on which membership is generally considered to be a public service. Board members generally serve without pay. The board meets regularly and is responsible for the total operation of the school or the system.

Voters elect or empower the board to employ an individual, usually a professional educator, who serves as the chief administrator (superintendent, president, chancellor, headmaster) of the school or system. Some communities still elect the school superintendent along with school board members, although there is some research that indicates appointed superintendents are more effective than elected ones. From this point on, the functions of the board and the administrator usually are clearly defined.

The board, after consultation with the administrator, normally sets the basic policies for the operation of the school or the system. The board decides on capital-outlay measures and formalizes regulations concerning appointments, retirements, leaves of absence and terminations of faculty and staff. The administrator usually is in complete charge of operating the school or system within the policies set forth by the board and makes recommendations on the appointments, terminations and other matters requiring formal school board action.

Board members are not expected to move into the professionalized area of administration, nor should the administrator extend his or her authority beyond the policies fixed by the board. In actual practice, it does not work that way. Board members often get involved in such matters as teacher assignment, new curricula, student disciplinary matters, and other areas on a day-to-day or individual basis. Many superintendents have been known to "dictate" to boards on a variety of policy issues. The latter is especially true in cities and counties where the superintendent is an elected official. The operation of school systems in such major cities as Baltimore; Boston; Chicago; Minneapolis; Philadelphia; St. Louis; Washington, D.C.; and San Francisco and of those in dozens of smaller cities has been jeopardized because of disputes between board members and superintendents that have grown out of the wide range of difficulties facing the schools—squeezed budgets, rising teacher militancy, increased crime in the schools and, in some areas, race problems.

The top organizational officials, as well as the subordinate ones (supervisors, principals, deans, directors, department heads), are vitally important to the operation of a school or an educational system, but more important is the teacher-student relationship. Everything should be done for the purpose of getting the teacher and the student together, giving them adequate facilities for the learning process, with the hope that the student will absorb the desire for learning as well as the knowledge that the teacher can transmit. Presumably, if the organization is efficient and effective at the top levels, it will achieve those goals at the teacher-student level. It does not always work that way, however, and it is essential that the education reporter be aware of that fact.

Scope of Coverage

The education reporter usually is expected to cover activities at all levels of the school system from the policy-making boards to the teachers in the classrooms. Large or small, the education beat offers the opportunity for many routine stories as well as major news breaks, features and interpretative pieces. Routine stories may be written about subjects such as:

1. Scheduled dates—opening and closing, holidays
2. Enrollments—statistics, comparisons, trends
3. Honors—citations of students and faculty
4. Changes in curricula—courses added and dropped
5. Commencements—speakers, graduating students
6. Personnel changes—appointments, resignations, retirements
7. Board meetings—policies, budgets, capital-outlay plans
8. Activities of affiliated organizations—education associations, parent-teacher chapters, "booster" groups, alumni.

Major stories develop in such areas as teacher strikes, academic freedom of teachers, racial strife, crime in the schools, rejection of bond issues by taxpayers and a long list of other troubles that often beset school systems. Although these are important stories and generally rate the front page, there are numerous other major interpretative and feature articles that can come out of the schools. The alert reporter will be looking for them constantly.

Here are some examples of school stories covering a wide range of subjects:

PHILADELPHIA (AP)—A group of parents is suing a school system over its new program requiring students to perform 60 hours of volunteer work.

"I don't want my son being told what to do," said Thomas Moralis, one of the plaintiffs, whose son David is in the Bethlehem Area School District, which is beginning the program. "I went to school in a free America and I want the same for my children."

Moralis and his wife, Barbara, and two other parents filed suit Wednesday in Federal District Court against the school board which instituted the volunteer plan last spring.

Under the plan, the 60 hours work can be spread over four years. The students choose where they will work from a list of organizations and sites approved by the school board.

Metro School Board members Wednesday night said they're hesitant to ask the public to vote to raise their own property taxes.

But that's the decision they have to make tonight in a special meeting of the board, called after the Metro Council voted against a tax hike.

(Nashville Banner)

NORMAL, Ill.—The Illinois Mathematics and Science Academy has won the large-school division of the state high school math contest for the first time, edging out eight-time winner New Trier.

New Trier finished second and last year's champion, Evanston, was third.

The publicly supported three-year residential high school for gifted students, which graduated its first class in 1989, competed for the second time. The Aurora school placed second last year.

(Chicago Tribune)

Angry Karns High School parents vented frustration Thursday night and demanded an investigation of the U.S. Department of Education's Office of Civil Rights.

"Who are these people that have the right to legislate where we send our kids to school?" parent Ed Mays asked. "Karns High School was the only reason I live here.

''I just want to know, these OCR people, has anyone ever investigated them? Has anyone ever questioned their quotas? What are their hiring practices like? They're wanting us to lay everything on the line. The only thing I am asking you people is to investigate these people.''

Mays was one of about 400 people who met to discuss the Knox County school board's proposed desegregation plan ordered by the Office of Civil Rights.

(The Knoxville News-Sentinel)

WASHINGTON—At a time when urban schools have the reputation of war zones, Shepherd Park Elementary School is an educational demilitarized zone.

Much of the credit for that goes to principal Edith Smith, who has the no-nonsense air of a woman who wouldn't stand for it any other way.

In the northernmost corner of the District of Columbia, where urban blight begins to give way to the clipped lawns of the black middle class, Mrs. Smith is known for prodding and inspiring the best from her students as well as from teachers and parents.

(The Christian Science Monitor)

A problem facing all education reporters involves the cooperation of board members and the school officials with the press. School board members and officials are extremely sensitive to criticism from the media or the community. They are equally sensitive when the press reports (as it should) on major problems such as student unrest. Boards frequently meet in private to conduct "public" business, and school officials sometimes decline to provide information needed for a reporter to write a balanced story.

However, as noted earlier, in almost all states there are open-meetings laws and open-records laws on which reporters can rely to obtain their information if officials are uncooperative and if the newspaper elects to follow that course. Ideally, school officials and the press should cooperate in an effort to inform the public and improve the cause of education.

Story Forms

Education stories range from the one-feature brief to the multi-feature report on a significant board meeting. In between can be found all story forms, including human-interest stories on students and teachers and feature articles on school activities.

COVERING RESEARCH AND SCIENCE

Newspeople are having difficulty keeping up with the new knowledge pouring out of the millions of research projects and studies being conducted by scientists and other scholars. These developments push the boundaries of man's knowledge to new heights almost daily. The public is not always aware of these advancements because the changes are frequently so specialized that it is difficult if not completely impossible for a layperson to understand them. As long as science and scholarship remain enshrined in technical language, society cannot

14   THE CHRISTIAN SCIENCE MONITOR   Monday, September 10, 1990

Hi-Ho, Off to School Wee Ones Go

More prekindergarteners enter school as mothers work and academic pressure mounts

LEARNING

By Laurel Shaper Walters
Staff writer of The Christian Science Monitor

BOSTON

ONCE upon a time children started school at age 5, if they attended kindergarten, or age 6, if they started in first grade. But this fall, millions of three- and four-year-olds will begin their school experiences in public and private preschool programs across the United States.

In the past 25 years, the percentage of three- and four-year-olds attending school in the US has quadrupled. Thirty-nine percent now enroll in school; in 1965, only 10 percent of youngsters that age went to school.

And the number of three- and four-year-olds in school is expected to quadruple again by 1995, according to Samuel G. Sava, executive director of the National Association of Elementary School Principals (NAESP). "Accommodating our youngest children is perhaps the greatest challenge for educators in this decade," according to Dr. Sava.

Fifty-five percent of mothers with preschool-age children now work outside the home, according to the Census Bureau, which expects the percentage to continue growing.

"As more and more women go into the work force, the need for having children cared for outside the home is greater," says David Elkind, professor of child study at Tufts University in Medford, Mass., and author of "Miseducation: Preschoolers at Risk."

At the same time, public recognition of the value of early-childhood education has increased over the past two decades, says Barbara Willer at the National Association for the Education of Young Children.

This is partly attributable to the success of such federal initiatives as Head Start, which has provided preschool education to low-income children for the past 25 years. "The legacy of Head Start is that we've learned that children are capable of learning much more, much sooner than we thought," Ms. Willer says.

The education reform movement, which swept across the US in the 1980s, brought a wave of heightened expectations for academic performance.

"We are living in a time now when we no longer see children as innocent but as competent," Dr. Elkin says. "That could be OK as long as we don't just extend downward the schooling of the elementary school...."

Debate over the type of schooling appropriate for young children is not new. But with the increased enrollment of preschool youngsters, the issue has taken on renewed interest for both parents and educators.

• Pressure from parents and

LITTLE LEARNERS: *Youngsters in Beverly, Mass., gather 'round in Head Start class. The national preschool program has underlined value of early learning.*

educators for early academic achievement.

• Evidence that preschool education is beneficial for children.

Lizzie Parrie, a mother in Covington, La., has had both her children in school since they were 3. "They could stay home with me," says Mrs. Parrie, who does not work outside the home. But she says the group activity they get at preschool is something she could not provide at home. "They have jobs to do at school," Parrie says, adding that while they have jobs at home, they learn to work with others at school.

Parents like Parrie are most concerned about the learning environment a school provides. NAESP recently released a publication outlining the standards for quality early-education programs. "What's happened in a number of cases," Sava says, "is that individual school systems have taken the kindergarten curriculum or the first-grade curriculum and they've watered it down and begun to use the program for three- and four-year-olds."

"I don't think there is a disagreement about ultimate goals here," says Tom Schultz at the National Association of State Boards of Education. "Everybody is interested in children being successful in school...."

The disagreement is over what kind of early experiences lead to

Ready, Set, Learn

"BY the year 2000, all children will start school ready to learn." So states one of the national goals drafted by President Bush and the United States governors in the aftermath of last year's education summit.

In the context of this goal, how do parents, educators, and politicians make sure that young children entering school – more and more of whom are three and four-year-olds – are "ready to learn"?

"If we are serious [about this goal], we must recognize that there are major social changes that have taken place in our society," says Samuel G. Sava, executive director of the National Association of Elementary School Principals. In fact, 3.2 million mothers now work outside the home, according to the US Census Bureau, which predicts that 80 percent of all children under 6 will have mothers working outside the home by 1995.

The effort to provide school readiness is undermined by socioeconomic differences. "Poverty is putting kids behind even before they enter school," says Barbara Willer at the National Association for the Education of Young Children, a 75,000-member organization based in Washington.

Some educators and scholars suggest that the national goal is misguided. "I think readiness is the wrong concept because that sounds like readiness is something in the child," says David Elkind, a professor of child study at Tufts University in Medford, Mass. "Readiness is never the child; readiness is the relationship between the child and the school."

Dr. Elkind and early-education experts call for modification of the schools rather than attempting to change the children. "We should be getting the schools ready for children, not children ready for schools," Elkind says. "It's much easier to change schools than it is to change children."

Part of the "readiness" issue involves addressing basic inequities so that children are able to enter school on an even keel. This involves basic nutrition and other needs.

But the difficulty is in coming up with a standard definition of "school readiness." "We're trying to define something that is fundamentally at odds with childhood development," Ms. Willer says. "Development is individual; it is normal to have a wide variation of abilities."

"The intent of a school is to take a youngster from where he or she is," Dr. Sava says, "identify their needs, and then help them achieve their dreams."

— L. S. W.

Enrollment Rates For US Three- and Four-Year-Olds

Year	Rate
1965	10.0%
1970	20.3%
1975	22.5%
1980	28.9%
1985	30.5%
1990	39.0%

Source: US Department of Commerce, National Center for Educational Statistics

FIGURE 25–1 The Christian Science Monitor devoted its "Learning" pages to an in-depth report on the increasing number of three- and four-year-olds enrolled in public and private preschool programs. The story was timed to coincide with the opening of schools and detailed the social and economic reasons for the dramatic increase in enrollment. (Reprinted by permission of The Christian Science Monitor. Copyright 1990 The Christian Science Monitor Publishing Society. All rights reserved.)

understand them fully. They must be interpreted to the people, reduced to terms laypeople and legislators can comprehend.

Newspapers have become increasingly aware of their responsibility not only to keep the public informed about scientific developments but also to interpret their implications for the public. That is why a number of newspapers have employed reporters specially trained in science and medicine who can communicate with scientists almost as equals and can then translate new developments accurately and clearly for the reader.

The science editor or the reporter covering research has problems and responsibilities that must be understood and mastered. Reporting a research project—giving the public an understandable explanation of research findings—is quite often an assignment unlike any other given a journalist. The reporter often faces three significant challenges: first, the researcher (or researchers); second, the research project; third, writing an accurate and interesting interpretation of the project for the public. Any one of these can become a difficult experience for a reporter.

The Researcher

In interviewing a researcher, the reporter must keep in mind that the subject of the interview may not be eager for, or even mildly interested in, newspaper publicity. Often a researcher prefers to present his or her findings in a scientific publication or at a scientific gathering. Because scientific news has been poorly handled in the past, a researcher may be afraid of both inaccuracies and sensationalism in the newspaper account. Having spent days or months on a carefully worded paragraph, the researcher may be averse to having an article slashed to bits in a three-minute effort by a reporter to emphasize an "interesting" feature.

Dullness, often attached to preciseness, is a researcher's prerogative. Frequently, a researcher does not see and may be indifferent to the utility or human-interest aspects of a project. Consequently, the researcher may have no sympathy whatsoever for the reporter's problem in writing the story for the general public.

A researcher may even be antagonistic toward publicity. A newspaper article on a particular project will mean little if anything to the researcher's professional career. In fact, it might have negative effects. The researcher might be branded as a publicity hound, especially by a fellow scientist who might be nearing a breakthrough in the same area. He or she might be hounded by well-meaning people as well as kooks who phone, write or even come in person seeking help. For that reason medical researchers generally are extremely careful about announcing breakthroughs in the mass media. Usually, they make their reports in a major medical journal. Fortunately, as newspapers have made a serious effort to improve science writing, many leading scientists have become more willing to share their findings with the public. They realize that they have an obligation to do so just as a newspaper has a responsibility to report scientific discoveries carefully and accurately.

Obviously, then, the reporter's first task is to establish a good relationship with the researcher, winning enough confidence for at least a chance to show a sincere desire for accurate interpretation. When handling a scientific story, a reporter should never guess. At the risk of delaying a story, the reporter has the responsibility to make certain that the story is accurate. When in doubt about any

FIGURE 25–2 The number of newspapers devoting special coverage to science, health, technology and research continues to grow. The San Francisco Examiner's "Your Health" section devotes its coverage to health stories its readers will find useful. (Reprinted with permission from the San Francisco Examiner, © 1990 San Francisco Examiner.)

aspect of a story, the reporter must check back with the original source and any additional sources available in the scientific community.

Most major institutions and organizations have men and women on their public relations staffs to assist reporters in their efforts to work with scientists and researchers. Public relations people can be a valuable asset, but the reporter should not rely on them alone for information. The major source always has to be the man or woman who conducted the original research.

The Research Project

A reporter should recognize the two broad types of research: (1) basic or fundamental research and (2) practical or utilitarian research. Further, it is important to understand that a basic research project may be the predecessor of valuable practical research, even though this might not be immediately apparent to the reporter.

Many projects that may have appeared on the surface to be pointless, even frivolous, have proved to have enormous consequence. Sir Alexander Fleming's early experiments with molds eventually led to the wonder drug penicillin. A research project to study aggression in apes provided important data on aggression in humans and helped the National Aeronautics and Space Administration in the selection of astronauts for the space program. If a reporter or the public does not understand the value of a basic research project, that does not make the project any less justified. In most instances, neither the average reporter nor the general public is competent to judge its value.

Many thousands of research projects, basic and practical, are being conducted at considerable cost to the people of the nation through the National Science Foundation and other federal and state agencies. Some will turn out as failures, but others will pay spectacular practical dividends that make the total cost of research look small indeed.

It is fairly easy to report a project dealing with an improvement in the rate of emission of pollutants from automobiles by the use of a new catalytic converter. But what can be done, for example, with a project "concerned with the synthesis and biochemical evaluation of drugs which influence psychological processes through their effects upon the central nervous system"? The answer calls for interpretative skill.

Interpretation of the Research Project

Although dullness is the researcher's prerogative, it is the reporter's enemy. Given the task of writing an interesting story, the reporter must seek to humanize the research project, spelling out for the reader what it means in clear, careful and accurate words. The reporter must find out what the discovery or theory means or may mean eventually to the average person and then provide the details necessary to give the layperson a clear picture of the research.

Early on, a reporter who starts writing research and scientific stories must develop a dictionary of the scientific or professional words used by the researchers in the fields being covered. It is also necessary to work with researchers to develop accurate definitions or synonyms for scientific words that an average reader will understand. Far too many reporters—not only those covering science but also those covering other professional fields—fall into the trap of writing in professional jargon and not in the language of the general reader.

The keys to research projects that are designed to fill specific practical needs are ready-made, but the secrets of many basic projects are not easily unlocked. For basic research the reporter must interpret the nature and findings of the project without stretching facts in an attempt to indicate practical value. The interpretation can perhaps explain that a project reveals knowledge that may contribute to the solution of practical problems, but this must be done with extreme caution. There is a world of difference, for example, in what is being said in the following two paragraphs:

> The reaction of cells to certain acids manufactured by the human body is being studied by Dr. A.B. Count, Southeastern University zoology professor, who hopes his findings will contribute basic knowledge to science's fight against cancer.

> A cure for cancer is being sought by Dr. A.B. Count, Southeastern University zoology professor, in studying the reaction of cells to certain acids manufactured by the human body.

If the first paragraph is accurate, no one can blame Dr. Count for becoming furious with the reporter who takes the liberty of "interpreting" the basic research project as is done in the second paragraph. As a researcher who demands facts and accuracy, he cannot shrug off such "sensationalized" reporting. He considers such extravagant claims as damaging to his professional career, and he remembers this the next time a reporter approaches him for a story.

Every effort should be made—with the researcher's help—to inform readers of any practical use of a research project. However, the reporter must recognize that there are times when no practical angle is available. This may be true in the case of pure basic research being performed solely for the purpose of finding new knowledge. Sometimes that new knowledge or the search for it is itself interesting enough to give the reporter the key to a story. Other times, the subject of the research may be so complicated and so far from public interest that the reporter must abandon the story.

In gathering information to interpret a research story, the reporter must not be afraid to ask questions. The best rule of thumb is: "If you don't know, ask." To write an accurate story, the reporter must have a clear understanding of what he or she is attempting to explain. It is imperative that a reporter check with the researcher before writing the story to make certain that his or her interpretation of the facts is accurate.

One of the major criticisms researchers and scientists have of the press is the tendency of some reporters to want a quick, five-minute explanation of a project that has taken five years to develop. Reporters writing a story on a scientific development or a research project must allow time to conduct a thorough and careful interview so that there can be no misunderstanding of the information collected. Careful, thoughtful, accurate research stories cannot be written in a few minutes. They often require hours, even days, of multiple interviews.

Story Forms

Increasing numbers of newspapers are following the lead of The New York Times, the Boston Globe and other metropolitan dailies and establishing special sections each week devoted to science, research, medicine and technology. In addition, the wire services regularly distribute news stories dealing with major scientific topics, and syndicates distribute to the daily press articles from a number of specialized magazines such as Prevention and Longevity.

A review of these stories will show that all the story forms discussed earlier are used in writing about research. As a general rule, if the research has significant practical value or is the first report of a major breakthrough, the straight-news form is used. As practical value diminishes, reporters tend to use the feature-story form to tell the story.

These leads illustrate the scope of research, scientific and medical stories that appear in newspapers regularly:

> Drinking caffeinated coffee does not appear to increase the risk of heart disease or stroke among men, according to a research report to be published today in the New England Journal of Medicine.
> The findings, the latest in a series of conflicting reports about risks of coffee consumption, appeared to rebut those of earlier, smaller studies that suggested drinking five cups of coffee a day might increase the risk of coronary heart disease twofold or threefold. . . .
>
> (The Washington Post)

> The average U.S. life expectancy may never exceed age 85, even though millions of people will live into their 90s and hundreds of thousands will become centenarians.
> Researchers at the University of Chicago and Argonne National Laboratory arrived at their conclusion by computing how steeply the current death rate would have to decline to achieve average life expectancies of 80, 85, 90 and up.
> The death rate is the number of people per 100,000 who die in a given year.
>
> (USA TODAY)

> In a remarkable advance, researchers have shown that older women who have gone through menopause can easily become pregnant using donated eggs.
> The results, being published today, give women who have been considered hopelessly infertile an unexpected second chance, the researchers said. "It turned their lives around," said Dr. Mark V. Sauer of the University of Southern California, who led the group that conducted the study.
>
> (The New York Times)

> In the '60s, it was protein. In the '70s, Vitamin C. In the '80s, oat bran, of course.
> And this decade's nutrition fad? It could be minerals, particularly one that sounds like it belongs on your car.

Chromium is hot. Researchers are pushing for grants, it's the subject of a popular book and it has underground fan clubs ranging from middle-agers fighting early-stage diabetes to bodybuilders seeking bigger, better bulges.

A review of recent findings turns up promising news of chromium along with a warning: Until more is known, most people probably should get chromium from their diets, not supplements.

(Knight-Ridder Newspapers)

SAN FRANCISCO—A new cancer treatment using genetically engineered molecules has produced major shrinking of tumors in breast-cancer patients who could not be helped by any other therapy, researchers announced Tuesday.

Treatment with monoclonal antibodies resulted in a 50 percent to 75 percent reduction in tumor size in six women with advanced breast cancer that had spread to other parts of their bodies, according to Dr. Sally DeNardo and her team of researchers at the University of California-Davis School of Medicine.

(San Francisco Chronicle)

When the research project or medical advance is conducted by local researchers or scientists, the story often becomes front-page news in the local daily. This story by Bill Snyder rated a top spot on the front page of the Nashville Banner (Fort Campbell is about 50 miles from Nashville):

Soldiers infected with the AIDS virus show minor but significant intellectual impairments compared to their uninfected peers, a new study shows.

The study of soldiers at Fort Benning and Fort Stewart in Georgia and Fort Campbell, Ky., raises new questions about what occupational limits—if any—should be placed on people who are infected with AIDS virus but have not yet developed symptoms of acquired immune deficiency syndrome.

"Should HIV-positive pilots, knowing they may demonstrate cognitive or motor impairment, be limited?" said Col. Stephen N. Xenakis, medical commander of the Blanchfield Army Community Hospital at Fort Campbell.

HIV—the human immunodeficiency virus—causes AIDS.

"The Army will have to come up with a policy," said Xenakis, a co-author of the study. "Society will too."

"What about surgeons?"

The study was reported Sunday during the annual scientific assembly of the Southern Medical Association.

MEDICINE

Most newspapers dramatically increased their coverage of medical news during the 1980s and 1990s. No medical/scientific issue in recent memory created as much anguish and debate in newspaper city rooms as the acquired immune deficiency syndrome (AIDS) epidemic. The complex medical, ethical and legal aspects of AIDS stories presented challenges to editors and reporters unlike any they had faced in decades.

Because AIDS was originally labeled the "gay" disease, many newspapers shied away from coverage, except for an occasional wire story. However, that

FIGURE 25–3 The Los Angeles Times devoted this front page of its "Science/Medicine" section to research on the immune system of sharks that could lead to a better understanding of the various immune-system disorders in humans. (Copyright 1990, Los Angeles Times. Reprinted by permission.)

changed as more was learned about AIDS and it spread to other groups, in particular intravenous drug users. Most newspapers performed an admirable public service with their open and detailed discussion of how AIDS is transmitted.

Although many AIDS sufferers and their families have cooperated with newspapers in an effort to give the public a better understanding of the fatal illness, editors still have to struggle with a host of ethical questions such as:

- Do we use the person's name? How will that affect the family?
- Do we use the name of the employer, especially if the person is working in a public service job such as in a restaurant or a hospital?
- Do we use the person's address, knowing that the fear of AIDS may make the apartment or building or house unrentable?
- How do we handle the implication of homosexuality or drug addiction?
- Do we print the story if the family asks us not to?
- In the obituary, do we list AIDS as the cause of death? Do we list the person's companion among the survivors?
- How do we avoid lawsuits that a story of such a personal nature could generate?

Most newspapers tend to treat each case individually, and they often seek the advice of their lawyers before running a story about a local AIDS sufferer, even when the person and family members willingly cooperate.

As a result of the coverage in newspapers and other media of the scientific as well as the human side of AIDS, the public has a far better understanding of the disease and its impact than it has of many others.

EXERCISES

1. Invite the education reporter from the local newspaper to your class to discuss the state of public school education in your community. Write a story on that discussion.

2. Organize a panel composed of a parent of a public school student, a teacher from a public school and the superintendent of schools for a class discussion of the quality of public education in your community.

3. Interview the president of your college or university about the problems currently facing your institution. Write a story based on that interview.

4. Arrange through the local school superintendent to spend one day in a school where the students score the highest on standard achievement tests and a school where the students score the lowest on those tests. Write a story comparing the two schools.

5. Using the following notes, write news stories for the next day's newspaper:
   a. State Board of Education
      Recently approved program
      "Young Educators of Tomorrow"
      To attract more young people
      Into teaching profession

Fulton County high school students
To begin program this spring
First school system in state
To put plan in effect
Students will take credit course
On teaching methods
Similar to college teaching course
Then will spend one quarter
Teaching at nearby elementary school
Or in their own high school
Superintendent James H. Fox said
He was "confident we can help reverse
The teacher shortage through this
Cadet teaching program in our schools"
Allowing the course to be taught
Is turnaround for state board
Earlier it had cut off state funds
When Fulton schools offered
A similar education course
But board said schools would
Lose funds if students just
Served as tutors or
Teachers' aides during class

b. Four Stockton teachers
Honored yesterday for risking
Their lives to save children
From a madman's gunfire
On school playground last year
Certificates of valor
Were presented to
Cleveland Elementary teachers
Janet Geng, Mary Haas,
McGanister Graham, Eugene Cronk
By state Attorney General
John Van de Kamp, who said
"Without a doubt, their actions
Saved the lives of many
Cleveland Elementary students"
Geng was wounded, along with
29 children, during the attack
On the school by Patrick Purdy
Five children were killed
Purdy shot himself to death
With attack rifle before
Police arrived on the scene
Geng and Cronk were supervising
Children on playground
When Purdy opened fire
Although wounded, Geng
Herded children to safety

Cronk directed other children
To safety in nearest building
While bullets struck around them
Haas and Graham both in classrooms
Haas opened classroom door
To let children in and
Ran to playground and pulled
Fatally wounded child into room
Graham ran to playground
Pulled child inside and
Gave child first aid
Until help arrived
The child died
Teachers were nominated
For the awards by
Stockton school police

c. Sue Hurd, business manager
Loudon County School System,
Told school board last night
Rising cost of oil and projected
Loss of state aid next year
Will force cuts in next year's budget
"The worst in more than a decade"
Other officials were predicting
The 14,500-student system's
Class size, athletics and
Gifted and talented students
Programs would be affected
Lack of funds could set back
Spending on academic programs
Hurd and others told board
Loudon schools need at least
$11 million more in local taxes
Next year to maintain programs
And services in the current
$95 million budget
That doesn't include funds
For pay raises, officials said
Loudon system expects to lose
$4 to $5 million in state aid
For last four years
Spending has increased
Approximately 10 percent annually
School officials are reviewing
15 areas that could be cut
To save $7.2 million
They include elementary art,
Music, driver education, athletics
Gifted and Talented program
Physical education and others

School board member Barbara B. Beghtol
Said system may have to increase
Class sizes and charge book rent
Kay Franklin, president of
Teachers Association, told board
"Teachers' salaries must continue
To improve. Teachers can't be asked
To forgo their own economic well-being
For the good of the county."

6. Write a story on the following set of notes. Background: Seventy-seven small school systems in the state have sued the state, charging that the state's education funding system discriminates against the poorer school districts in favor of the richer ones. Schools financed through local property taxes and sales taxes. State provides 44.9 percent of school funding, 45.4 comes from local funding and 9.7 from the federal government. Because richer districts can raise more taxes, some are able to spend 2-1/2 times as much for each pupil as the poorer districts. Poorer districts are seeking a larger share of the state funds. Kern Alexander, former president of Western Kentucky University and an expert on education, testified today in Chancery Court on behalf of the small school systems. Here are the highlights of his testimony:

> The state's school funding system makes already large disparities between rich and poor districts worse. In addition, a "regressive" tax structure contributes to ranking the state as one of the worst in the nation in the amount put into funding education. The state's support for public schools does not correspond to its financial ability even though this is not a rich state.
> The state ranks 35th in personal income available for each student but ranks 50th in per capita spending per student and 48th in the amount spent as a percentage of personal income.
> The state's tax system tends to rely too heavily on property taxes and sales taxes, which tend to be regressive. The result is the state taxes the poor at a higher rate than it taxes the affluent. A person making $100,000 in income would pay approximately 5.8 percent in local taxes, while someone making $20,000 would pay 8 percent.
> Differences in sales tax revenue, which reflects the ability of a school district to fund education, can vary by as much as 30 to one between the richest and poorest school districts. Some richer school districts are able to spend 2-1/2 times as much per pupil as poorer districts.

Alexander's testimony is expected to continue through much of the week. The trial is in its second week.

7. Write a news story on the following notes:

Dr. John Montgomery
Talbott County health director
Proposed last month that
County school nurses be allowed
To distribute contraceptives
To students of both sexes
Who request them
Without getting parents' approval
But only after students are
Counseled on their choices

Including abstinence
Proposal has divided community
School board holding hearings
On Montgomery's proposal
Which he calls "disease control"
But opponents say it will lead
To promiscuity among students
Opponents also question board's
Role in issues of morality and ethics
Supporters of program claim
It will reduce spread of
Sexually transmitted diseases
Including AIDS
Program endorsed by county PTA
Chairman of county's AIDS task force
Opposed by school board president
Several local ministers
"Most people think it's a moral issue
And something the school system
Shouldn't be involved in," School Board
President Laura Harrison, a nurse, said
School system has two high schools
With a total of 1,014 students
Two students have tested
Positive for HIV this year
Board expected to act on issue

8. Attend a meeting of your local city or county school board. Write a story about the meeting and turn it in the next morning with your notes.

9. Write a news story based on the following information provided by Dr. Louisa Chapman, an epidemiologist at the Center for Disease Control in Atlanta.

Last season was the worst flu season in 10 years. Flu contributed to 25,725 deaths in 121 U.S. cities between October and May. Nearly all flu sufferers last season caught the severe A-Shanghai flu strain.

This year we think there will be less mortality because flu strains from different "families" should develop. Usually after a year of high flu deaths, two or three years of lesser flu infections follow. We don't expect the upcoming flu season to be as bad as last year's.

But we can't be sure so we are recommending those at high risk be vaccinated as soon as possible. It usually takes two to four weeks to develop immunity.

Flu symptoms include fever, chills, sore throat, headache, muscle aches and pains, dry cough and malaise. Symptoms typically last five to seven days, but can continue for several weeks.

Flu season usually begins in mid-November and lasts until March or April and one of the reasons death rates can be high is that many people in the high-risk group refuse to get shots. In fact, fewer than one-third get shots which are recommended for persons older than 50 in particular as well as persons who work in contact with large numbers of persons in closed areas, such as school teachers.

Some people actually think they can get flu from shots and others think having the flu once protects them for the rest of the season. It doesn't. People who are at risk ought to get the flu vaccine every year and not rely on their own immune responses to protect them. Any symptoms they get from the vaccine are insignificant compared to the protection they get. About 25 percent get a sore arm or mild 24-hour fever.

10. Using any research journal available to you in your college library, select an article containing research results that you think would be of widespread interest to readers and write a news story based on it.

11. If your local daily has a reporter assigned full-time as a science writer, invite him or her to class to discuss techniques used in covering science, medicine and research.

12. Write a 90-second newscast based on Exercises 5a, 5c, 7 and 8.

CHAPTER 26

RELIGION AND PHILANTHROPY

More space is being devoted to news of religion today than at any time in the past two decades, although some critics still claim unfairly that most newspapers have room for only two words a year about religion.

While it is true that some newspapers still relegate news of religion to the regular Friday or Saturday "Church" page, a systematic review of many others would show that religion has nearly equal news status with education, business, health—occasionally sports. And why not? After all, more people are in church on any given Sunday than attend all sports events put together during a whole month.

News of religion is placed throughout the paper as the individual stories merit. Often such stories merit being on the front page as leaders of religious denominations and their followers engage in spirited and occasionally violent debate over nuclear arms and chemical warfare, abortion and euthanasia, genetic tinkering and even American foreign policy in Latin America and the Middle East.

More and more, newspapers are analyzing trends and movements ranging from the rise in popularity of Eastern religions in the West and the continuing battle over women's becoming priests to debate over ordination of homosexuals in several denominations. Those stories might complete successfully for front-page space because they often involve conflict. That conflict is the news peg, but, more than that, it sharpens the issues and makes visible the important underlying questions and issues.

This example, by George W. Cornell, The Associated Press' religion writer, is the type of story given prominent display in the news sections of many papers:

WASHINGTON—In adopting their first comprehensive guidelines on human sexuality, U.S. Roman Catholic bishops call it a "divine gift" that should be carefully nurtured.

"We do not fear sexuality, we embrace it," the bishops said both in lauding that universal human endowment and reaffirming traditional church restraints in expressing it.

> In the 185-page assessment of sexuality, approved Wednesday to guide education on the subject, the National Conference of Catholic Bishops added: . . .

Of course, a general circulation newspaper should advocate no religion but should be a channel of communications for all religions. Freedom of religion, like freedom of the press, is protected by the Bill of Rights of the United States Constitution, and the press must recognize both the place of religion and the right of religious choice in its columns.

Although the proportion will vary from community to community, a conservative estimate is that substantially more than half the people served by a newspaper are members of a church or synagogue. News of religion, then, should have many potential readers. Even though religious institutions have a large total membership, the news interest of an individual member is, first, in his or her own church; second, in the denomination; then, to a milder degree, in other churches. Sometimes churches are competitive to the point that publicity given to one may stir up envy in the members of others—even of the same denomination. Religion news must therefore be broad enough in denominations, diverse enough in the same denominations, and selective enough in the newsworthiness of materials that readers will recognize the stories on religious activities as solid news rather than puffery or press agentry in favor of a particular minister, church or denomination.

As noted earlier, many newspapers publish a weekly page or special section devoted largely to news of religion in the community, appearing generally on Friday or Saturday. A member of the staff may hold the title of religion editor or church editor (often in addition to other duties), and it is his or her job to gather and write the material for this page or section. Much of the material comes by the way of press releases or telephone calls from ministers or persons acting in a public relations capacity for a church or religious organization. As a general rule, the news stories appearing on this page or in this section would not be classified as major news stories dealing with religion.

A hotly contested pastor-vs.-a-faction-of-the-congregation controversy, however, may be reported on the front page. A split in a major congregation, especially if it lands in the courts; the filing for divorce by a popular minister; or the leaving of the church by a local priest or nun to get married are stories that almost surely will get front-page play. News sources cultivated by the religion editor in handling routine stories often prove valuable in gathering information when such special stories develop.

The religion reporter must learn the organizational patterns of the churches covered, for the sources of news on religion include church-governing officials as well as local churches. But the reporter must have outside sources as well. Church leaders frequently are unwilling to discuss controversial issues with the press. Church organization varies widely among the different denominations. Some are completely independent, selecting their own ministers and setting up their own programs. At the other extreme, some local churches are under the strong control of a central governing body that assigns ministers to the various churches and also has a strong influence on the local program of each church.

The program of a church encompasses many activities in addition to worship services and Sunday schools. It may also include the sponsorship of such projects as foreign or domestic missionary work, local relief projects, kindergartens, grade and high schools, and colleges and universities. It is not uncommon for religious leaders and their congregations to be involved in very controversial moral, social and political issues in a planned and organized way. Such activities always make news, whether they are in the "Religion" section, in the "Education" section, or on the front page or other sections for special news stories.

THE "RELIGION" SECTION OR "CHURCH" PAGE

Newspapers that carry a regular page or section on religion should use a systematic plan of compiling news for that section. Church officials should be informed that they must submit materials for the section by a specific deadline; this puts the burden of getting publicity on the churches and at the same time protects the religion editor from the criticism of members whose churches are not mentioned in the news. Some highly newsworthy stories can often be developed from materials submitted by the churches, but for the most part these handouts must be condensed into one- or two-paragraph stories, if used at all. On the other hand, the reporter might have to get additional information to develop the potentially better stories that are submitted.

A religion editor or reporter takes pride in the assignment and considers the news on religion to be as important as much of the other news in a given edition. If the "Religion" section reflects accurately the community's religious or moral tone, it can be a strong influence on the life of the community. To do an effective job, the religion reporter must make the page or section more than just a bulletin board compiled from church press releases.

Like many other sections of a newspaper, the religion pages have to be planned in advance. The seasonal stories are obvious—Christmas, Easter, and the like—but a good reporter will develop significant news and feature stories on the most important trends in the religious life of the community as well as on the most newsworthy national and international developments and how they affect local churches. That is why it is important for the religion reporter, like the reporter in any other specialized field, to be constantly aware of what is happening in the field of religion. Current trends or controversies frequently can be localized into significant stories.

The following are some subjects and types of stories that the reporter may develop from materials submitted by the churches and from other sources:

1. Regular worship services (some newspapers publish a weekly listing of church services)
2. Sermons—if unusual
3. New buildings or other facilities
4. Changes in church personnel

5. Special events and campaigns—evangelistic efforts, fund-raising drives for worthy causes, attendance promotions
6. New policies of local church or denominational groups
7. Meetings of denominational groups, ministerial associations and lay groups
8. Human-interest and feature stories—on unusual church members, historical anniversaries, retiring pastors, interesting projects of Sunday school classes, work of missionaries.

The following examples are typical of stories often found on religion pages in newspapers:

> After 7-1/2 years of leading Bethel Temple Assembly of God to new heights both spiritually and physically, the Rev. Steve Allen has resigned as pastor of the church to shepherd a flock near Nashville.

> Highland Park Baptist Church will celebrate its 100th anniversary on Sunday with State Rep. David Copeland and Judge Steve Bevil as special guests.
> Dr. J.R. Faulkner, pastor, will speak on "Where Do We Go From Here?" during the 10:50 a.m. service.

> Each United Methodist Church in the nation has been asked to read a pastoral letter from the Council of Bishops Sunday. The letter seeks to have each church member join the bishops in fasting, in prayer and in helping the denomination become more vital.
> In part, the letter seeks to end the denomination's self-termed "spiritual malaise" and reverse a 22-year decline in membership.

> Each Sunday at 11 a.m., prime time for U.S. Christian church services, a handful of Vietnamese Buddhists begin their weekly chanting in a house near Grant Park.
> In Vietnam, services are held three times a month on a lunar calendar, said Phong V. Le, a temple secretary. "That's hard to do here."
> By scheduling the traditional Buddhist worship at the Chua Quang-Minh Temple according to American custom, its leaders are preserving the culture of the old country while adapting to life in the new.

Here are the leads on several stories that deal with broader topics involving religion that do not fit the routine church-story category and were used in the regular news sections of papers:

> On a warm Saturday evening, 17 gays and lesbians sit in a small chapel in Westwood and sing a Catholic hymn called "Be Not Afraid." The lyrics tell of "crossing a barren desert" and "wicked men who insult and hate you."
> There is a deliberate poignancy here, as the song and voices echo off the rafters.
> In the eyes of the Roman Catholic Church, these men and women are infidels—spurned because their active gay lifestyle is regarded as a sin. Although they have not been excommunicated, they pray alone, without a priest to lead them. Except for the grace of another religion's pastor, they would not even have a place to worship.
> In 1989, Archbishop Roger M. Mahony ordered priests in the vast Los Angeles Archdiocese to stop saying Mass for members of Dignity/Westside

and two other local chapters of the 21-year-old national organization for gay Catholics.

Mahony's decision was a major defeat for the beleaguered Dignity, with 84 chapters and 4,200 members nationwide, for the decision signaled agreement with most other U.S. bishops.

The remainder of the story, which was written by Hank Stuever for the Los Angeles Times, described the service and the struggle gay Catholics have with recognition and acceptance from their church.

NEW YORK (AP)—Moslems, long isolated from America's religious mainstream, have started edging into it.

An initial step into working collaboration with Christians and Jews came last week as national Islamic representatives joined a major interfaith operation, Religion in American Life.

Dawud Assad, president of the Council of Mosques of the United States, said that in taking the step, "we look forward to some good cooperation in the future" with "our brothers and sisters."

Unexplained phenomena of a religious nature often are used in the regular news section of a paper because of the attention they have generated. Here is an example from the AP that was printed in hundreds of papers:

NEW YORK—Thousands of people are flocking to a Greek Orthodox church to see an icon that they believe began shedding tears last month after a special prayer session for peace in the Middle East.

The icon of St. Irene, patron saint of peace, has drawn Christians of many denominations and smaller numbers of Moslems, Jews and the curious to the St. Irene Chrysovalantou Cathedral, church officials say.

Visitors have come from as far away as France, Japan and India, according to Maria Galiatsatos, assistant secretary at the church in a largely Greek neighborhood in Astoria in Queens.

She says she receives up to 500 calls a day.

"We have had more than 100,000 people visit here since she began crying," Galiatsatos said. "One Sunday we didn't close the church until 4 a.m. and we reopened at 6 o'clock in the morning."

The church's Bishop Vikentios of Avlon says he believes the icon of St. Irene—whose name means "peace" in Greek—is weeping for the Persian Gulf.

Occasionally, a story about religion can have a humorous twist, although a reporter should never deliberately attempt to treat religion humorously:

A Texas woman was arrested for singing off key for several months, but a parish attorney bailed her out of jail the day of her arrest, according to Catholic News Service.

Eulogia Macias, 34, a member of Our Lady of Sorrows Roman Catholic parish in San Antonio for two years, is a former member of the church choir.

"She sings the same songs as the choir, but she doesn't always match up and she's very off key," said Monsignor Alexander C. Wangler, pastor of the parish.

The parish had obtained a restraining order against the woman, but she failed to attend a hearing on the order.

Interpreting Religious Terminology

It is essential that any reporter writing about religion make a serious effort to learn the technical words and phrases commonly used by the various denominations. Not every minister, for example, is called "reverend" or "pastor." "Father," "rabbi," "elder" and "brother" are just a few of the formal and informal titles used for ministers by various denominations. The reporter should know which is applicable within the denomination being covered.

Reporters should also learn and correctly use the terms associated directly with the various worship services of denominations. Many groups have prepared a glossary of the terms and phrases that are used in their churches. They usually are available through the headquarters of the denomination. If one doesn't exist, a reporter should prepare one for his or her use. In the interest of accuracy, most ministers would be willing to help prepare a glossary.

In covering religion, a reporters should be thorough and objective, applying the same standards of accuracy that are required elsewhere in the paper. A reporter doesn't have to be religious to cover religion effectively, but he or she needs to be knowledgeable. Knowing which terms and titles are used in each denomination is just as vital as understanding the issues and trends.

PHILANTHROPY

The basic meaning of "philanthropy" is "love of mankind." However, a secondary and more general meaning has developed that involves the expression of such love and concern for others in terms of hard cash. By the start of the 1990s, Americans were contributing more than $100 billion in hard cash annually to philanthropic causes. In addition, they contribute billions of hours of volunteer time to thousands of organizations devoted to the health, welfare and betterment of individuals as well as the community as a whole.

Philanthropy includes a wide diversity of activities. Among them are projects designed to promote and support religious and educational institutions and programs, the cultural arts (music, drama, art), character-building youth groups, welfare agencies, senior citizens' organizations, Christmas charities, disaster relief, hospitals, community civic projects, historical observances, recreational facilities, the treatment of and research for the cure of diseases and disabilities, and other promotions requiring the raising of funds.

Not all philanthropic movements ask for money, however. Some solicit a person's time; a pint of blood; housing accommodations for visitors or the needy in an emergency; old clothes and newspapers; or a pledge to drive safely or to eliminate fire hazards. Whether for money, time or blood, all these movements are in the public interest—the service of humankind—and, as such, are associated with philanthropy. All of them can generate not only promotional stories but also special stories of major significance to the community.

Often individuals take on philanthropic projects of their own. Here is an AP story about one individual committed to feeding the poor:

BOSTON—A dilapidated truck and its near-bankrupt owner parked outside a church in one of the city's poorest neighborhoods yesterday and out stepped Nancy Jamison, on her daily rounds to feed the less fortunate.

"Millions of pounds of food, darlin', are dumped everyday while people are starving," she said. "Mayonnaise sandwiches are a reality, my dear."

Jamison, 40, a former fashion designer, is a one-woman food program, delivering vegetables and bread to the city's neediest people. Her truck, running perpetually in second gear because the transmission is shot, is always met at the Pilgrim Congregational Church in the city's Dorchester section by hungry people.

Sponsors of philanthropic movements are many times more numerous than the types of movements. Included are the Community Chest or United Fund organizations; Red Cross; Salvation Army; the YMCA and YWCA, along with their youth counterparts in other religions such as the YMHA; Boy Scouts and Girl Scouts; all types of civic and service clubs and fraternal groups; drama, music, and art societies; recreation organizations; health associations, such as those serving in the areas of tuberculosis and heart disease; societies to assist the blind, deaf, and physically handicapped; and churches, schools, colleges, hospitals and similar institutions. Newspapers also sponsor their own philanthropic promotions. Some of the various philanthropic movements are short-term drives; others are long-term continuing efforts, generally on an annual basis.

The newspaper, a public service institution itself, is by its very nature interested in philanthropic programs and promotions. Much space, as well as the time of reporters and editors, will be contributed to the success of worthy causes. In these cases the newspaper often will make an exception to its regular demands for stories based strictly on newsworthiness, and it will accept material that is more promotional than informative.

One of the paradoxes of the newspaper profession is that its critics frequently cite the "negative" or allegedly "sensational" content of newspapers while rarely mentioning the thousands of column-inches of free space given to community promotion and philanthropic drives. A study might reveal that there is indeed a much better balance between "good" news and "bad" news than critics would have the public believe.

Problems in Publicizing Philanthropy

Handling news of philanthropy poses some special problems for a newspaper. Often an editor must take the responsibility for deciding whether the publicity being sought is intended to promote the self-interest of an individual or organization rather than a charitable or other social goal. If a newspaper uses all of the publicity that certain groups wish, it risks loss of reader interest and consequently of circulation. On the other hand, if it restricts such publicity sharply, the newspaper risks loss of the good will of the groups involved.

The number of different philanthropies has increased to the point that the public has insisted on the consolidation of some of the fund-raising campaigns under a Community Chest or United Fund plan. Even though such plans have combined many campaigns—in some cities 50 or more charitable or welfare-type agencies receive funds from such plans—some social service and charitable groups still elect to carry on their own local and national campaigns with special weeks or months set aside for fund drives. Newspapers generally bear a heavy portion of the promotional work for such plans as United Fund and Community Chest. Occasionally an editor may decline to support a campaign that he or she believes should be part of a united drive. However, most editors find it difficult not to give space to any legitimate cause. As a result, most newspapers spend considerable time and money in writing about these various public-service activities.

Promoting Philanthropic Movements and Civic Projects

Newspapers serve as the principal channel of communication for most of the promotional efforts of philanthropic and civic projects. However, various media are used in the campaigns and drives—letters, brochures, meetings, radio, television, billboards.

Despite all the publicity in newspapers and other news media, the most effective method of soliciting funds is the person-to-person approach—the volunteer workers who visit prospective donors. Many employers arrange a plan for monthly deductions from donors' paychecks, which contributes greatly to the success of such fund drives. Solicitation by mail and other means is used when the number of prospective donors is so great that direct contact is impractical. Numerous professional fund-raising organizations have come into existence to conduct local as well as nationwide campaigns for a fee. Like the amateur fund-raiser, they rely on the newspaper for publicity.

How does the newspaper fit into these approaches? Publicity given a project in the press will "set the stage" and help develop a climate of generosity among prospective donors. And, of course, the recognition afforded by publicity stories is important in obtaining and encouraging volunteer workers. However, the sponsors of the project will be greatly disappointed in expecting such publicity to do the whole job. While many people may be inclined to give to a worthy cause publicized in the press, very few remember to respond to their inclinations unless a solicitor visits them or a letter reminds them. There are things that the reporter and the campaign sponsor should keep in mind, or they may expect too much from newspaper publicity.

A newspaper can publish many promotional stories for philanthropic movements and projects. The following is a listing of some of the developments that could be reported:

1. Initial announcement of campaign or project
2. Appointment of persons in charge of project
3. Appointment of personnel or committees who will assist
4. Various meetings of campaign workers—goals, campaign plans, time schedules

5. Series of straight-news stories, features and human-interest stories reporting recent benefits of the project
6. Special stories on large donations
7. Progress reports on campaign
8. Stories on conclusion of campaign and its achievements.

Here are several examples of leads on stories reporting philanthropic activities:

> The United Way of Greater Knoxville has broken its $5.8 million goal, its campaign chairman announced Friday.
> "We made $5,802,452, which is 6.6 percent over last year," Sam Furrow said at a press conference. "It is about $360,000 more than we raised last year . . . It shows what a caring and loving community we are, and that we take care of our own."
> The United Way funds 48 non-profit agencies and community organizations.
>
> (The Knoxville News-Sentinel)

> When Nashville's inner-city Boy Scout troops collected cans for the Second Harvest Food Bank, Scout leaders said they were also gathering food for thought.
> Boys in Troop 2000 were among the 15,000 Middle Tennessee Scouts who went door to door collecting food for the needy Saturday. They hoped to bring in 360,000 cans this year to top last year's 350,000 total.
> Troop 2000, which is for inner-city youth, played a special role in the collection because many come from homes that are not financially well off, said Chuck Simmons, spokesman for the Middle Tennessee Council—Boy Scouts of America.
> "What makes it so important to these Scouts is that most of them have very little, yet they're going out asking the community to feed those who have even less than they have," Simmons said.
> "There's a great lesson for them and for us," he said. "You can always help others, regardless of your situation in life."
>
> (Nashville Banner)

Philanthropy is not always for the obviously needy, as this Washington Post story indicates:

> WASHINGTON—Friends of Dan and Marilyn Quayle raised $340,000 in tax-deductible funds from nearly 200 contributors around the country to add children's bedrooms on the third floor of the vice president's residence, his office says.
> Of that amount, about $140,000 was spent on improvements, supplementing $200,000 in money appropriated by Congress last year in response to an indirect appeal by Marilyn Quayle.

EXERCISES

1. Contact the executive director of an umbrella organization such as the National Conference of Christians and Jews or the local council of churches. Interview her or him about the role of the organization and its programs promoting religious tolerance and racial harmony in your community. Write a story based on that interview.

2. Invite the religion editor of your local newspaper to class to discuss coverage of religious news in your community. Write a story on that discussion.

3. Interview several ministers in your community to find out how their churches provide for the religious needs of special groups like the hearing-impaired or the physically handicapped. Write a story based on those interviews.

4. Locate the largest church in your community and the smallest. Interview the ministers and a number of members of both churches and write a feature story contrasting the two.

5. Interview a woman minister at a church in your community or a nearby city and write a personality profile on her.

6. Write stories from the following notes:
   a. Calvary Independent Baptist Church
      27145 Brooks Road
      Recently organized
      Romanian Relief Ministry
      Will send its first shipment
      Of Bibles and other material
      To Romania next week
      Church has 40-foot trailer
      Loaded with 15,000 Bibles
      20,000 Bible study lessons
      25,000 "Source of Light" lesson booklets
      Over 1 million gospel tracts
      In Romanian and Russian
      3,000 Romanian and 3,000
      Russian Christian books
      Also, 7,000 pounds of vitamins
      $2,400 worth of building materials
      More than 1,000 pounds of
      Flour, sugar, cooking oil
      And boxes of clothing
      The Rev. Elbert Hooker said
      Donations came from all over
      He said the church plans
      To make similar shipments
      At least four times a year
   b. Gary Ealy, pulpit minister
      At Brownsville Road
      Church of Christ, Lexington
      For past eight years
      Appointed pulpit minister
      Of Farragut Church of Christ
      4010 Farlow Drive here
      He was graduated from
      David Lipscomb University
      And has a master's degree
      In Christian apologetics
      From Harding Graduate School of Religion

He was a campus minister
At the University of North Texas
And Texas Women's University
For seven years before moving
To the Lexington church
Married to former Mary Croft
A registered dietitian
Has two children
Angela, 14, Nathan, 11
Will preach his first sermon
At the church next Sunday

c. Church Street United Methodist Church
To present 20th annual
Madrigal Dinner Dec. 4 and 6
Dinner set in time
Of King Henry VIII
Dinner is Elizabethan feast
Celebrating coming of Christmas
The madrigal is a 16th century
Choral composition
Dinner at 6:30 p.m.
Preceded by music program
By the Brass Wind
Professional instrumental group
Master Arts Madrigal Singers
Will perform during and after
Prime rib dinner
Tickets are $23 a person
Reservations required
Call 876-9854 for reservations
And more information

7. Write a "Church Briefs" column from the following information. Keep each announcement to two sentences.

   a. Rev. Charles Thompson
   West Covena evangelist
   Will conduct revival services
   At Grace Fellowship Church
   Highway 95, Lenoir City
   At 7 p.m. Wednesday, Thursday

   b. Chordsmen, gospel radio, TV
   And recording artists
   Appearing in concert
   At Greenway Baptist Church
   On Greenway Road
   At 7 p.m. Sunday
   Public is invited

   c. Rev. C.W. Martin senior minister
   New Hope Presbyterian Church
   Celebrates 34th anniversary

As a minister Sunday
A special service planned
At 3:30 p.m. at church
To be followed by social hour
In church social rooms

   d. Resurrection Lutheran Church
   To present video program
   "What It Means to Be a Christian"
   At 11 a.m. Sunday
   Sunday School is at 9:45 a.m.

   e. St. Martin's Episcopal Church
   Will celebrate Holy Eucharist
   During 8 and 10:30 a.m. services
   Church school begins at 9:15
   A covered-dish lunch to be served
   After 10:30 services Sunday

   f. Evangelist Billy Mayor
   Lead revival services
   Valley Church of God
   At 10 a.m., 7 p.m. Friday
   7 p.m. Saturday, Sunday
   Mayor former vocalist
   Drummer with rock group
   Calls rock music today
   "A tool of Satan"

8. Interview the director of the local Salvation Army about his or her organization's work with the homeless and street people. Write a feature story based on that interview.

9 Interview the head of the local Shrine Club or other organization that conducts fund drives for charitable purposes. Write a story about the group's work.

10. Ask the director of your college's alumni office for the name of a person who has consistently contributed at the college, perhaps the person who has contributed longer than any other. Interview him or her and write a story based on the interview.

11. Assume your newspaper has decided to set up a fund drive to help the needy. It can be a special fund to buy food and gifts for the needy at Christmas, a special fund to buy fresh milk for underprivileged children, or a fund to provide coats and winter clothing for the homeless. Outline the number and type of stories and photographs you would want to develop for your campaign to solicit funds from the public. Assume the campaign will last approximately one month.

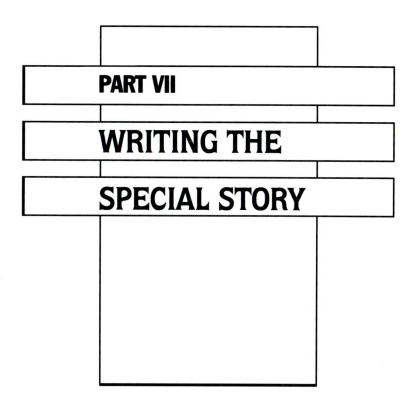

PART VII

WRITING THE

SPECIAL STORY

Straight-news stories make up only part of the content of a newspaper. Readers want more. That's why a good newspaper is a careful mix of hard news and special stories.

Special stories appear in the sports pages; the section devoted to family, foods, fashion and social events; and the reviews or criticisms of television, movies, music, books and the fine arts. In addition, many newspapers have regular sections on developments in science, medicine and technology. These special areas usually are operated as separate departments with their own editors and staffs, who are responsible to the managing editor.

Even though the departments are specialized, the principles used in gathering and writing straight-news stories apply to special stories as well. News is always paramount. However, special stories often employ writing devices not commonly used in straight-news stories. It is essential that every reporter learn the techniques needed to handle special stories because most reporters are required to write them from time to time.

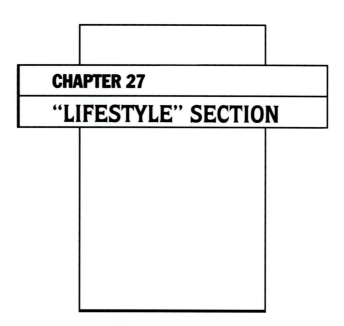

CHAPTER 27
"LIFESTYLE" SECTION

When Kent W. Cockson, then executive editor of the Pensacola (Fla.) News-Journal, was asked what a "Lifestyle" section should do, he replied "Everything. And anything." He said if he had to write The Lifestyles Law, it would say that a typical "Lifestyle" section is:

Entertaining

Helpful

Informative

Lively

Personal

Reflective

Septic (as opposed to antiseptic)

Topical

Trendy

Useful

Versatile

Well-planned

It should convey a sense of community, with no less impact than a ton of feathers.

Most "Lifestyle" sections, whether they are called "Focus" or "Tempo" or "Living" or "Style," try to be all of that and sometimes even more to their readers. As a result, some of the best writing in today's newspapers can be found in them.

Unlike the women's pages of a decade or two ago, today's "Lifestyles" sections report the issues, problems and solutions that affect the readers and their families, homes and communities. Most still carry the traditional engagement, wedding, fashion, food and social notes in some form. But those subjects often are secondary to stories about every phase of living known to woman and man. Stories dealing with the environment, the economy, personal finances, family nurturing and loving, personal values, leisure activity, personal relationships and parenting dominate the pages.

While the sections often deal with such issues as the woman alcoholic, the woman shoplifter, the unwed mother, the problems of a single mother and the runaway mother, they also tackle such topics as the househusband, the single father, the male rape victim, the impact of AIDS and other provocative stories. These dramatic changes have caused some critics to complain that the once proud, but prissy "Women's Page" has been neutered. Others see the broad sweep of most "Lifestyle" sections as a reflection of the diversity of interests of men as well as women.

Today's better "Lifestyle" sections are a pleasing blend of substance and fun. For the most part they are a showcase for quality reporting, quality writing, quality editing, quality packaging and quality graphics, as Ruth D'Arcy, who directed the J.C. Penny-University of Missouri Awards Program for many years, said in an article in The Bulletin of the American Society of Newspaper Editors.

Many newspapers follow a regular pattern in their "Lifestyles" sections, perhaps using general features on Monday and Tuesday, food stories on Wednesday, fashions on Thursday, entertainment on Friday, family-oriented features on Saturday and a cover story on a major social or moral issue on Sunday. The pattern varies from paper to paper. This arrangement allows for a vast range of stories generated by staff writers or provided by the wire services or feature syndicates. In many cases, a lifestyles writer will seek to localize a wire or syndicate story or will write a separate local story as a sidebar to the major story.

A survey of "Lifestyles" sections of several dozen newspapers will show that many regularly use cover stories dealing with significant social, political, moral and ethical issues: "The Extra Marital Affair," "Lust or Trust," "How to Protect Your Child From a Molester," "Incest: A Family Affair," "How to Tell If You Are Becoming an Alcoholic," "The Great Abortion Debate," "Date Rape" and dozens of other topics that 20 years ago might not have even made the newspaper.

Generally, the traditional lifestyles news is given secondary play. However, some newspapers do reserve special days for printing engagements and weddings, columns covering local social events, syndicated features, club announcements and service features such as special sections for senior citizens.

In addition, many newspapers have developed specialists in consumer news who write stories designed to help the reader cope with the problems often associated with making major or even minor purchases of every possible product or service. A story might be about something as simple as how to tell if your butcher is cheating you or how to cope with a doctor who will not give you adequate time to discuss your medical problems. Often these stories have enough reader interest to be used as the cover story in the section.

The following are some leads from stories that have become commonplace in the "Lifestyles" sections of many newspapers:

> A vacationing couple fears the popcorn they bought at a gas station is contaminated.
> A woman panics when an employee sneezes while scooping her ice cream.
> A man wonders if he could be infected by shaking hands.
> Some worry about using public restrooms or hot tubs or being bitten by mosquitoes.
> More than 3,000 times every day people with concerns like these call the toll-free National AIDS Hotline. The world's largest health-information telephone service, the hotline has fielded nearly 5 million calls since 1987.
> Hotline staff members say that many of the callers are panicked and seek reassurance and information about whether the disease that has killed more than 100,000 Americans since 1981 can be casually transmitted.
>
> (Washington Post)

> Susan holds up the hand mirror and studies her eyelashes. Jane shakes her head to test the bangs of her newly-cut wig. Gayle's quick smile is evidence enough that she likes her change in lipstick color.
> Pretty not only is as pretty does. For these cancer patients, pretty is as pretty feels.
> "Look Good . . . Feel Better: Caring for Yourself Inside and Out" is a new program developed by the Cosmetic, Toiletry and Fragrance Association Foundation, the National Cosmetology Association and the American Cancer Society specifically for cancer patients undergoing chemotherapy or radiation treatments.
> The program has given Gayle Lauer a new lease on life. . . .
>
> (The Knoxville News-Sentinel)

> They live by the numbers: two careers with a combined six-figure income, at least one child in a top-ranked private school, one nanny, a house in a socially accepted ZIP code.
> They pace their frantic lives by the clock: leave home early, come home late, carve out "quality time" for their children.
> The payoff for these "fast-track" parents is achievement—commonly measured in earnings that provide for the house, the cars, the nanny, the school tuition and the endless array of lessons and things that keep the household up to speed.
> But what does this mean for their children?
> That's what experts are asking. . . .
>
> (Los Angeles Times)

The "Lifestyles" section of most newspapers is under the supervision of a special editor. On larger newspapers, the editor may have one or more assistants. Writers assigned to this section generally operate independently of the city editor. They are responsible for gathering and writing news and feature stories for the "Lifestyles" section only. However, it is not uncommon for their stories to appear in the news section, depending on the news value they possess. The copy editing, rewriting, headline writing and makeup are often handled within the section but coordinated with the copy desk and the graphics department.

One of the major changes in "Lifestyles" sections in the past 20 years has been the change in staff. The sections are no longer exclusively a "woman's

FIGURE 27–1 "Living" sections no longer limit themselves to stories of interest to female readers alone as they once did. This front page of The Knoxville News-Sentinel's section is representative of the in-depth reporting that often characterizes "Living" section cover pages. (Courtesy of The Knoxville (Tenn.) News-Sentinel.)

world." Many have men as writers, columnists, copy editors and graphic designers. At a number of larger newspapers the "Lifestyles" editor is a man.

TRADITIONAL SOCIAL NEWS

Most "Lifestyles" sections still carry traditional social news—engagements, weddings, personal items, club notes and the like. The personal items might be collected in a column, or they might be used as individual stories with headlines of their own. Their reader appeal may be measured by the various news values (Chapter 15), but their largest single value is prominence. The prominence of persons involved in the stories determines the importance and therefore the length of social news stories. Prominence in this sense must be understood as local and relative rather than national. The smallest and most unsophisticated community will have its socially prominent persons, usually based on wealth or professional position. In fact, the first "Society" pages were originated by New York City newspapers in the last half of the nineteenth century to report the purely social activities of the wealthy and socially prominent.

Initially only the social activities of the so-called elite were reported. However, this began to change gradually, and in the period immediately after World War II most newspapers broadened their concept of "society" and began to cover the social activities of a broader range of individuals in the community. Although the banker's daughter generally got the biggest picture and story when she announced her engagement, no longer was the engagement of the baker's daughter ignored. In more recent years, many newspapers have sought to standardize the coverage of engagements and weddings by using the same size of picture and story for everyone, regardless of social standing in the community.

Nevertheless, prominence is still a major news value. Most newspapers still base their general policy on the principle that names, especially the widely known names in the community, make news. But they recognize that all names make news if they are involved in certain types of activities suitable for the "Lifestyles" section.

In addition to engagements and weddings, which are not given the same prominence in many newspapers as they once were, basic social-news stories that appear in the "Lifestyles" section include:

- Personals and briefs not carried elsewhere in the newspaper
- Births, if not published elsewhere
- Receptions, teas, parties, dances, luncheons, showers, dinners
- Women's clubs and organizations: routing meetings, programs, speeches and special activities such as benefits, bazaars, recitals and charity events
- Social columns or social notes that sometimes are gossipy and include editorialized comments by the writer about the local social scene
- Stories and columns on fashions, food, child care, interior decorating, family relationships, home and beauty tips
- Stories and columns on local women and men in the business and professional world, if they are not carried elsewhere in the newspaper.

News Sources

The editors and writers who handle social news generally become personally acquainted with the individuals in the community who are principal news sources. This is particularly true in smaller communities. Clubs and organizations usually have someone in charge of publicity who seeks out coverage for their events. Often tips on significant events can come from florists, caterers and others whose services have been engaged by the family or organization sponsoring the event. Far from having to seek social news, the editor is generally under pressure for more space to use everything that comes in by mail or phone or is delivered in person. Although a great amount of news is unsolicited, to have a well-rounded section, the "Lifestyles" staff has to seek other sources of timely stories and features.

Writers for "Lifestyles" sections often become specialists in such fields as foods and nutrition, family relations, child development, textiles and clothing, interior decorating, fashion and other subjects and write by-lined columns in addition to news and feature stories about their specialized areas. But it is important for any writer to be versatile and be able to write about engagements, weddings, clubs and other social events with care and accuracy.

PROBLEMS OF SOCIAL-NEWS SECTIONS

One of the most serious problems facing the reporter handling social news is the lack of story substance. Social-news stories do not have the impact of hard news, although they are an important ingredient in a well-balanced newspaper. Social events not only are categorized but also tend to be stereotyped. Yet the reporter must strive for freshness and variety. The monotonous, stereotyped story forms must be avoided.

A second and very definite responsibility of the social-news reporter is to spell all names correctly. To misspell a name or use the wrong initial of a person is to strike at the heart of social (or, for that matter, any kind of) news. There can be no acceptable excuse for carelessness. Also, great care must be exercised by the reporter and editor in checking sources of announcements of engagements and weddings to ensure validity. Many a practical joker has sent a phony engagement announcement to the newspaper "to get a laugh on a friend," and some of those announcements have unfortunately been printed.

Lead Features

One of the most critical problems for the reporter in avoiding stereotyped forms and writing more effectively is the selection of the proper feature or features for the story lead. Any social function or occasion will produce the following subject matter, in which the feature may be sought.

1. The occasion itself may be defined. Perhaps it is an anniversary or the hundredth anniversary of an event. Perhaps it is devoted to a "cause," or it might have other special features or a theme.

2. The place itself might be significant—an ancestral home, a national shrine or the site of a local historical event.

3. In general, the persons present at the function offer the most obvious feature. Hosts and guests, honorees, distinguished visitors, those in the receiving line, those who "poured," committee members, famous names —all are available features.

4. Decorations and color schemes might be features—or costumes, gowns or jewelry.

5. Refreshments and music or other forms of entertainment may also be featured.

Here are several examples of leads on social-event stories. Most come from community newspapers. However, larger newspapers often include personal items of this nature in a personal or social column that appears once or twice a week.

Three pink and blue showers honored Mrs. Terry Dale Mantooth, the former Crystal Gregg. The events on three consecutive Fridays this month were held in the Gold Medallion Room at the Newport Beach Hotel.

The turkey was off the hook for the Thanksgiving hunt at Thomas and Kelsey Nelson's farm in Strawberry Plains. It was the fox that led the chase.
The farm was the site of the second annual Green Valley Hunt Club fox hunt that officially opened the 1990 season.

It was a happy 90th birthday that Asa Bundy celebrated Sunday with a party given by his daughter, Bonnie Sue Jochaim, and her husband, Joe. Autumn flowers, balloons and a collage of memorable photographs were used in the decorations.

A beans and wieners dinner, lots of children's activities and prizes will proceed the Del Or Woman's Club annual charity auction Saturday in the Community Center.

Frequently items like this one will appear in a column of social notes in larger newspapers:

The City Symphony League's annual gala holiday ball on Saturday evening at the Cherokee Country Club promises to be a fashionable event. Lucky Schwartz, League President, is wearing a black, burgundy and gold gown . . . Freddie Tubbs is going with black and gold, too—black velvet skirt with black and gold silk top . . . Muffin McVey is wearing ivory silk charmeuse encrusted with pearls and sequins.

WRITING STYLE

Writers of social news should strive to overcome the stereotyped story without straining for effect. Even in standardized columns, announcements may become monotonous if every story begins "Mr. and Mrs. James VanSycle Howard Brewer announced the engagement of their daughter Lotty. . . ." In describing social events, the writer has the freedom to use a few more adjectives than are used in news stories. However, the story should be accurate and avoid puffy or gushy language. Not all luncheons are "delicious," nor are all brides automatically "pretty" or "lovely." And certainly not all parties or dances are the "biggest social event of the season." Such expressions as "everyone is cordially invited" and "a good time was had by all" should not be used. Restraint should be the guide when writing social news.

ENGAGEMENTS AND WEDDINGS

Although many newspapers have standardized their engagement and wedding stories, in many smaller newspapers they are given considerably more space with larger photographs. Newspapers rely on families to provide the basic information for both engagement and wedding stories and pictures. To ensure accurate information, newspapers have detailed questionnaires for prospective brides to complete. They call for the names and addresses of those participating; descriptions of gowns, flowers, ribbons, etc.; themes; and all other essential information about the event and the couple and their families. In most cases, the story is written directly from the form, although a reporter might call the prospective bride or her mother for additional details if needed. In every case, engagement and wedding announcements brought to the newspaper or mailed in should be verified to avoid a hoax.

Here are several examples of engagment announcements and wedding story leads:

An Engagement Announcement Lead

A summer supper Saturday at the home of Roberta and Walter McIntire celebrated the announcement of the engagement of their daughter, Mildred, to Beau Lolly. An August 31 wedding is planned at the Church of the Immaculate Conception.

Newspapers that have standardized their engagement announcements generally use this type of lead:

Mr. and Mrs. Walter McIntire, Blackberry Farms, announce the engagement of their daughter, Mildred, to Beau Lolly, son of Mr. and Mrs. Buford Lolly.

A Wedding Story Lead

The chapel of First United Methodist Church was the candle-light setting for the nuptials of Patricia Dagmar Motte and Anderson Kurt Huffman.

In a standardized announcement, the lead generally is more direct:

Patricia Dagmar Motte and Anderson Kurt Huffman were married June 2 at First United Methodist Church.

Both styles of engagement and wedding announcements have merit. The danger of the first type of story is that the writer may get a bit too flowery. The problem with the standardized version is that it is colorless and boring, especially when 16 to 20 wedding stories, reading exactly alike except for the names, are displayed on a single page.

Here is an example of an unusual wedding story from The Knoxville News-Sentinel:

> Miss Terry Nell Morris, artist and illustrator, hand-lettered the invitations for her wedding to David Allan Quimby, which took place at 2 p.m. Sunday at the home of the bride's parents, Dr. and Mrs. Robert W. Morris Jr., Duncan Road.
>
> Parents of the bridegroom are Mr. and Mrs. Henry H. Quimby, 944 Brantley Drive.
>
> Dr. R. Frank Porter, retired Methodist minister, officiated at the ceremony.
>
> The bride chose a gown of ivory lace and cotton trimmed in ivory satin ribbon and pearl buttons. She made her veil of rose-patterned lace and carried a bouquet of white roses and baby's breath.
>
> Rosanne Morris, sister of the bride, was maid of honor, and LeAnne Quimby, sister of the groom, was bridesmaid. They wore ivory lace Gibson Girl dresses and carried long-stemmed roses with baby's breath.
>
> The bridegroom had his father as best man. Robert W. Morris III, brother of the bride, Steven K. Minor and Michael Tuller were ushers.
>
> Ring bearer was the bride's black Labrador Retriever, whose full name is Barney De Witt Morris. Barney's wedding attire was an old-fashioned white collar with white tie.
>
> The bride made the wedding cake and her mother catered the other refreshments for the reception at the Morris home.
>
> After a trip to Disney World, the newlyweds will be at home on Canberra Drive. The bride, a graduate of Webb School and the University of Tennessee, attended Parsons School of Design, New York. Two of her books for children are soon to be published by Random House.

MISCELLANEOUS STORIES

In smaller newspapers the largest group of strictly social stories are provided by receptions, teas, parties, dances, luncheons and dinners. The prominence of the persons involved and the magnitude of the occasion often determine the amount of space allotted to the stories. In some cities, even large ones, there still is a formal social season and debutantes are introduced at a banquet and dance. Newspapers cover them in depth, sometimes devoting the front page of the "Lifestyles" section to a single event. But for the most part, individual events might be confined to no more than three or four paragraphs.

Another large group of stories appearing in "Lifestyles" sections includes the reports of churches and club activities, which might be largely social yet also have significant substance such as a charity auction or a scholarship fund-raising banquet. The following examples demonstrate the variety of miscellaneous stories that appear in "Lifestyles" sections:

Parties

The American Cancer Society will have a "plaid shirt affair for the black tie crowd" Tuesday evening at the home of Goldie and Nelson Barnes.

The barbecue will honor Billy Baldwin, Dr. Walter Frickel and Bootsy Bartlett, veteran Cancer Society volunteers. Entertainment will be by the Sundowners Trio.

Clubs

The Middle Tennessee Reading Association will meet at 6 p.m. Tuesday at John Trotwood Moore Middle School, 4425 Granny White Pike. This year's theme is "Literacy Links the World."

Ruth Ann Leach, Nashville Banner columnist, will speak on motivation. Admission is free and open to the public. Call 262-6685 or 333-5170 for more information.

Baked goods, plants, crafts and antiques will be available to the highest bidders at the annual auction of the Neartsease Garden Club at 7 p.m. Monday in the Cosby Civic Center.

The club uses funds raised at the auction for its city-wide beautification programs. Last year the club planted more than 1,000 flower plants in city parks.

Trips. The "Lifestyles" sections of community newspapers often carry announcements of trips local people make to visit friends or relatives or for vacations. Similar items are used in larger newspapers if they have a column of social news. Usually the names used in the larger papers are of the city's more prominent citizens. The following are common examples:

Mrs. Edwina Maples has returned from Savannah, Ga., where she visited her son and family, Stephen, Susan and Scott Maples. She also visited her brother, Sam Craig, and helped him celebrate his 92nd birthday.

Mary Ruth Emrick and her husband-to-be Floyd Ginger drove to Hooker's Point Saturday evening where they were honored at a dinner party given by Mr. and Mrs. Elbert Hooker at the Okeechobee Country Club. Mrs. Hooker is Mary Ruth's sister.

Kitty Sue Crumpton has just returned from a 15-day tour of the Southwest by Greyhound. She visited Texas, Oklahoma, New Mexico and Arizona.

Guests. Hosts and hostesses with out-of-town guests frequently ask newspapers to report the fact not only to honor the visitor but also to inform other friends who might wish to entertain them. Here are several examples:

Misty and Roland Greenberg of Dallas are spending two weeks with her mother, Mrs. Irene Jacobe, 4718 Greenbriar Lane, so their first son, Jason, who is just three months old, will get to know his grandmother.

Ingrid and Ryan Dauphin of What Cheer, Iowa, have joined her parents, Bobbie Joe and Elmer Scott, at their condo in the Smokey Mountains for two weeks. Ryan was manager of the Free Service Tire Store here for five years before being transferred to Iowa.

Births.   Some newspapers, especially in smaller communities, regularly carry birth announcements. They may be used as individual stories, grouped in a column or simply printed under hospital notes. The stories usually give the names and addresses of the parents; time and place of birth; weight and sex of the infant; name, if one has been chosen; and the names of grandparents. Here are two examples:

> Robin and Mitch Coakley are the parents of a daughter born Nov. 1 at Cocke County Baptist Hospital.
> Mara Paige weighed seven pounds, five ounces. She is the couple's first child.
> Her grandparents are Evelyn Webb and Wayne Fine and Holland and Beverly Coakley.

> Barron Mark Suggs, born yesterday at Greeneville Memorial Hospital, has been named in honor of his uncle who is president of the First National Bank, Wartburg. He is the first son of Mr. and Mrs. Randy Suggs of London, Ky., formerly of Wartburg.

CONSUMER NEWS

A number of newspapers continue to devote special pages to consumer news, which gained considerable attention in daily newspaper in the 1960s and 1970s. However, many other newspapers use consumer news as a part of their offerings in their "Lifestyles" sections, arguing that it should not be singled out for special treatment. They oppose reporters' playing the role of advocate, as do newspaper advertising managers.

Although the so-called action-line columns to help the average reader who might be having difficulty with the local store or a government agency are not as popular as they once were, some newspapers still have them and display them prominently. Some editors say their action-line column is one of the most popular features in their newspaper.

The more aggressive consumer reporters launched a wide range of investigations that produced front-page news stories and often brought about reform or spurred legislation to protect the consumer. Dozens of reporters investigated such things as the shabby workmanship and exorbitant prices of local television and auto repair shops or the unsavory practices of used car dealers. Others tested the often exaggerated claims of advertisements. Banks, funeral homes and other institutions that had been considered untouchable were being investigated in the name of consumer advocacy. Several newspapers established buyer panels of citizens who tested products and reported their findings to readers. The comparison-shopping story, in which a reporter compared the price of the same brand-name product at a number of retail outlets and reported the findings, became commonplace.

Although there has been considerable business backlash, most papers that established consumer reporting continue to engage in some form of it. They cover newsworthy consumer events, write about product safety, cover changes in laws affecting consumers, provide shopping guides for products and services, and make critical assessments of everything from food to colleges.

Those newspapers without consumer reporters of their own often run consumer-oriented stories from the wire services or a syndicated consumer column. Consumers Union syndicates material from its magazine Consumer Reports, for example. And many newspaper chains have a consumer reporter whose work appears in all of the papers in the chain. Ann McFetters, the consumer reporter for Scripps-Howard Newspapers, did a consistently good job of reporting consumer affairs from Washington for a number of years.

After an initial flurry of consumer-news reporters and even some consumer newspapers, a number of dailies began incorporating consumer news in their "Family Living" and "Lifestyle" sections. The rationale behind this decision was that consumer news is not unlike the reports on foods, fashions, home furnishings, and other family and home-oriented articles that have become the staple of this type of section. The New York Times, for example, has a "Living" section on Wednesdays and reports on weddings and engagements separately in its Sunday edition. The St. Louis Post-Dispatch combines fashions, decor, wine and food in its "Lifestyle" section on Sunday. The Washington Post mixes fashions, food, culture, entertainment, and even books and health in its "Style" section.

Many smaller dailies and weeklies also have developed family and living sections that include social news as well as consumer-oriented stories, food, fashions and entertainment. The Montgomery Journal, an award-winning newspaper from Chevy Chase, Md., calls its section "Tempo." The Jackson Sun in western Tennessee includes a broad range of consumer stories in its "Living" section and tends to downplay the traditional engagement, wedding and social-event types of stories.

No matter where the consumer story appears, it requires particular care. It is a form of business reporting, but the emphasis is placed on the role of the buyer or user rather than the producer. As such, it is frequently critical of the producer or seller. This type of story can damage a person or a business and can bring a libel suit.

In most newspapers, consumer news is broadly defined. While it could be a story on a sales fraud or misleading solicitations for charity, it also could be a story to help readers cope with a particular problem. The following examples will demonstrate the range of consumer stories. The first, from a special section called "fortysomething—Creative Planning for the Years Ahead" in the San Francisco Chronicle, is a story on how to ensure that your parents are provided for:

> Many of the dilemmas of caring for an elderly or infirm parent can be minimized by planning ahead, yet adult children often don't have all the information they need to help. . . .
> Many seniors think that as long as they've drafted wills that's all that they need to do. Others are afraid that their children will take advantage of them. Still others may find it a relief to talk to children about their concerns.

FIGURE 27–2 "Food" pages are generally well read by both men and women. Most newspapers no longer rely on handouts from food companies for their cover stories. Bernie Arnold, food editor of the Nashville Banner, often features local and area cooks in her weekly cover stories. (Courtesy of the Nashville Banner.)

FIGURE 27–3 The Los Angeles Times editors and graphic designers created this colorful cover page for its "Food" section, devoted to favorite American foods. (Copyright 1990, Los Angeles Times. Reprinted by permission.)

Here's how experts suggest meeting your parents' needs without threatening their independence and dignity, and preserving the financial and emotional resources of both generations.

Skidding across the ice into the guardrail was bad enough. The $3,000 repair bill was worse. But perhaps the biggest shock of all came when his insurance company declared his 1978 car a "total loss" because the cost of repairs exceeded its value. This gave Bob Garfield's budget a terrific beating.

Rather than pay for $3,000 worth of repairs, the insurance company paid him $2,500 for the "totalled" car—its current market or book value. This was less than he still owed on his auto loan. Then came the real sting—Garfield had to pay $8,200 for the 1982 model of the same car.

(Palm Beach Post)

The story went on to detail a new type of auto protection called "replacement cost auto insurance" being offered by major insurance companies.

EXERCISES

1. Read several issues of the "Lifestyles" sections of both a daily and a weekly newspaper in your area. Then invite the editors of both sections to class for a discussion of their approach to their pages. Write a story based on that discussion.

2. Contact local businesses, industries and government agencies in your area for the names of women holding non-traditional jobs such as construction workers, coal miners and telephone installers, and interview a number of them for a story on how they are accepted by their co-workers or persons they supervise.

3. Contact the public affairs office at any military base in your area, including National Guard and Military Reserve units, and ask for the names of women whose military specialty is traditionally thought of as a man's job—a jet crew chief, for example. Interview several of them and write a feature story about their role in the military.

4. Ask local social service agencies or churches for the names of several men who are raising their children alone. Interview them and write a feature story about them.

5. Contact the head of your state consumer protection agency and interview her or him about the complaints they receive and the various scams tried by unscrupulous individuals and businesses on the elderly residents in the state.

6. Do a comparison price survey on several products that do not normally fluctuate greatly in price—light bulbs, toothpaste, deodorants, among others—that are sold at major supermarkets, large discount stores and several convenience markets in your community. Make certain the products are not being offered as a leader item that week or are not on sale. Write a story on your findings.

7. Interview the head cook in your college dormitory dining room. Ask his or her responses to the most common complaints students have about the food. Write a feature story on the interview.

8. Write a story comparing the food served in your college dorm and that served at the athletic training table.

9. Interview at least a dozen of your fellow students about their preference in food and their eating habits. Write a story on your findings.

10. Ask at least six fellow students what types of problems they have experienced dealing with the bureaucracy at your college or university. Then contact the official responsible for each of those areas and ask him or her why the problem exists and how students can avoid a hassle in the future. Write an action-line-type column based on the questions and answers you obtain.

11. Write short stories from the following notes:
    a. Natalie Ann Harris
       Food, Lodging, Tourism major
       At State Technical University
       Manager of Guest Services
       Grove Park Inn
       Daughter of Mr. and Mrs. James Holt
       They announced her engagement
       To Sonny Vaughn, son of
       Mr. and Mrs. Delbert Vaughn
       Who live in Charlottesville, Va.
       Couple met at Grove Park Inn
       He is food service director there
       Wedding will be in December
       In Dutch Bottoms Baptist Church
    b. Sandra Elane Hartford
       Daughter of Mrs. Mervin Hartford
       And late Mervin Hartford
       Married John D. Gale Jr.
       Son of Mr. and Mrs. John Gale
       In ceremony at 6 p.m. Saturday
       In the Church in the Valley
       The Rev. C.J. Maze officiated
       Bride escorted to altar
       By brother, Kim Hartford
       Cousin Judi Cureton sang
       "You Are So Beautiful"
       Bride wore designer gown
       Of white lace and satin
       Accented with seed pearls and sequins
       Rosemarie Grimes, sister of groom
       Was matron of honor
       She wore blue satin tea-length dress
       With white sheer ruffled collar
       Bride carried white Bible
       And pink sweetheart roses
       Matron of honor carried
       White magnolia blossoms
       Accented with greenery, pearls
       Col. Calvin L. Gale, USA, brother
       Of bridegroom, was best man
       Reception followed ceremony
       At the Holiday Inn
       Couple will live in Miami
       Where both are employed
       A delayed wedding trip
       Is planned next summer
    c. Eighth annual Symphony Ball
       Scheduled Saturday evening
       In grand ballroom at Meadow Gold Country Club

Theme is "Grand Traditions"
Decorations will reflect
Victorian era
Evening begins with
Cocktails at 6:30 p.m.
Followed by silent auction
Banquet begins at 8
Guests will dine on salad
Of hearts of palm and artichokes
Filet of Beef Rossini
Dauphine potatoes, spinach Maria
And a secret dessert
Open auction begins at 9:30
Vintage wines, furs, jewelry
Original works of art
To be auctioned to raise
Funds for City Symphony Orchestra
Dancing follows auction
Music by Bill Britt Orchestra
Buddy Morrow Combo
Patron tickets are $500 a pair
Regular tickets $100 a person
For information and reservations
Call symphony office, 458-9740

12. Write a photo caption from the following information:

Daughters of American Revolution
Presented annual Good Citizen Award
To Shane Vickors, guidance counselor
Mayfield Senior High School
Cited for his efforts to keep
Students from dropping out of school
Award presented by Janette Franklin
DAR Award Chairwoman
During assembly at school

13. Write short stories based on the following notes:
   a. Blintzes and borscht
   Prepared by Effie Finebaum
   Who was born in Russia
   Will be featured Sunday
   At Heska Amuna Synagogue's
   Annual Harvest Bazaar
   Hours from 10 a.m. to 9 p.m.
   Gift shops, fine art, rummage
   And white elephant booths
   Also will be featured
   Admission is free
   b. Maryville Women's Center
   To offer mini-course
   On women's health

Three sessions to cover
Osteoporosis, women's cancers
Treatment of PMS
Classes meet 6:30–8:30 p.m.
Three Tuesdays in a row
Beginning next Tuesday
Course fee is $25
Dr. Donna Creech, internist
Will conduct course
For more information
Call Center at 691-8850

c. Fort Dickson Chapter
American Business Women
To meet at 6 p.m. Tuesday
At Brandy's Restaurant
Michael Brill, trust officer
First National Bank
Will speak on "Women and Money"
For reservations call 552-1324

d. Seymour Extension Homemakers Club
To sponsor canning workshop
From 10:30 a.m. to 1:30 p.m. Tuesday
At Utility Board Test Kitchen
Winnie Bowman, nutritionist
For Utility Board will
Demonstrate safe canning techniques
Advance registration required
Call 543-4569 to register
No charge for workshop

e. Concord Hills Women's Club
To sponsor 11th annual
Luncheon and fashion show
At 11:30 a.m. at
Dean Hill Country Club
A coffee hour and cards
Will begin at 9:30
In the club's recreation room

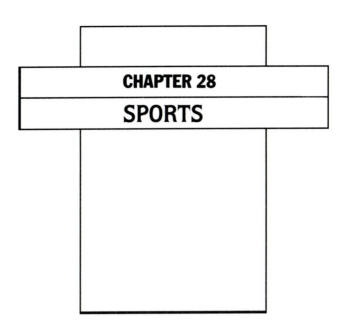

CHAPTER 28
SPORTS

"The world of sports, from pee wees to pros, provides more daily conflict and resolution, competition, trial and tribulation, heroes and heroines and just plain human drama than any other section of the newspaper," Steve Hannah, managing editor of the Milwaukee Journal, wrote in an article for APME (Associated Press Managing Editors) News. He was defending the sports section and sports writers from the often-heard criticism that sports coverage isn't a serious business and sports reporters mainly cover boys and overpriced jocks in short pants and sneakers who play games.

To prove his point, Hannah said that sports writers expend a lot of time and energy covering complex contract negotiations and the migration of multi-million-dollar sports franchises with their effects on a community's economics, mental health, drug problems, gambling scams and alcohol rehabilitation. In many ways, he said, sports news is not much different from the news in the rest of the newspaper.

Although the content of sports pages has changed dramatically in the past two decades, game coverage remains the lifeblood of most sports pages. Readers want national sports news, but they also want very localized sports coverage. They want to know who played, what they did or did not do on the field or the court, who won and who lost and why. Readers of the sports sections know they will automatically get an analysis of why the Oakland A's folded in the World Series, so they expect a similar analysis when their favorite Central High Bobcats are eliminated in the first round of Triple A football playoffs.

Hannah said sports stories are "some of the best written and most interesting" in any newspaper, on any given day. He's right. But some of the worst-written stories in any newspaper on any given day appear in the sports section also. To a talented writer, the sports page offers an unlimited challenge because sports reporting allows far greater freedom of expression than straight news.

A number of writers—Grantland Rice, Damon Runyon, Paul Gallico, Red Smith, Jim Murray and others—made sports writing an art form. All, of course, had several things in common: discipline; a thorough knowledge of sports; imagination; and, most important, a command of the language. This lead on a famous Notre Dame football team by Grantland Rice remains a sports writing classic:

> Against the gray October sky, the Four Horsemen rode again in legendary lore. Their names are Death, Pestilence, Hunger and Fire. These are only aliases. Their real names are Stuhldreyer, Crowley, Miller and Layden.

Unfortunately, too many sports writers, lacking imagination or a flare for the language, produce leads like this statistic-laden one from a large daily:

> BIRMINGHAM, Ala.—A freshman, Bo Jackson, ended a 67-yard drive with a 1-yard plunge with 2:26 left to give the Tangerine Bowl-bound Alabama a 23-22 triumph today over Georgia.

But many sports writers, like Gene Wojciechowski of the Los Angeles Times, repeatedly grab readers with outstanding story-telling leads. Here's an example:

> BIRMINGHAM, Ala.—Seven years after his death, the legend of Paul (Bear) Bryant still comes equipped with a hounds-tooth halo.
> Memories usually fade, but here in Alabama, where college football is the center of all things, Bryant's aura never dims. People won't let it.
> At last count, the University of Alabama had named four buildings and one street in his honor. Visit any local mall and you'll discover an entire cottage industry based on this state's obsession with preserving Bryant's glittering 25-year career. Bryant postcards sell for a quarter, Bryant wall clocks go for $19.95, "limited edition" plaques are priced at $130 and lithographs of him grandly surveying a Crimson Tide practice start at $1,750.
> This is what happens when the present can't compete with the past. Bryant won 232 games, a handful of national championships and 13 Southeastern Conference titles at Alabama. His successors—Ray Perkins and Bill Curry—could manage only a single SEC championship (a three-way tie, at that) in their combined seven years. . . .

The sports reporter's field is broad and interesting enough to test the finest talent. Each sport has rules and records. Each has its gallery of personalities and hall of fame. Perhaps in no other field of reporting is the opportunity greater for a writer to hone his or her talents.

World of Sports

Although it shouldn't be, at most newspapers the sports section is a world unto itself. Generally, on larger newspapers, it is operated as an independent department, often isolated from the news department, and has little contact with other writers and editors. The sports editor and staff are responsible for all phases of gathering, writing and editing. This freedom often results in sports pages that feature flamboyant graphic design with large headlines, large photographs and imaginative graphic illustration.

Some readers may see a curious misconception of news values at a newspaper that prints a three-paragraph story with a one-column headline about a $1 million cancer-research grant in its general news section and a 20-paragraph story with an eight-column headline and three photographs on the sports page about a high school or college football game on the same day.

Most newspapers respond to criticism of too much sports coverage by pointing out the high readership of the sports section. They also note that the countless hours devoted to coverage of sports by television have simply whetted the reader's appetite for more sports coverage. Several studies indicate the many sports fans who watch a game on television automatically read the newspaper's story about the game. That has forced sports writers to use greater care and accuracy in reporting. No longer can sports writers take too much license with what happened on the field, as their counterparts in radio used to do in those days when former President Ronald Reagan was a radio sportscaster.

NEWS VALUES OF SPORTS

The whole scale of news values characterizes sports news. Clustered around conflict as the pivotal appeal are prominence, progress, disaster, human interest and—in the sports sense—consequence. Moreover, the reader is a "fan," highly conditioned for ready response, at once appreciative and critical. The sports reporter—usually a by-lined writer—acquires a "public" that may become a valuable career asset. Thus there is something over and beyond news values— something of camaraderie and clan esprit—that enhances reader interest in the sports page. Men particularly, but also women and children, look at the sports section for news on their favorite teams and frequently to see what their favorite writer had to say about a game or a team.

Qualifications of a Sports Writer

The sports reporter has certain responsibilities that are perhaps not different from, but merely more obvious than, those in less specialized reporting. Two of them have been mentioned—background and judgment gained from either experience or extensive reading.

Background can be acquired. One does not have to be a former football player to write about football, but a detailed knowledge of the fine points of the game is certainly essential. Many sports reporters are "addicted" to one or more sports and have been since childhood. Although this can be a help, it also can be a hindrance, especially if their "addiction" clouds their judgment.

Some sports may have to be mastered vicariously. Story backgrounds should be historical as well as technical. A fire, an accident or an occasion may be reported adequately from within the event. Too frequently, also, sports reporting confines itself in the same manner. But the richness of reporting from a full background outside the event should be evident in the story. The Kentucky Derby winner has to be compared with Derby winners of all time and of all

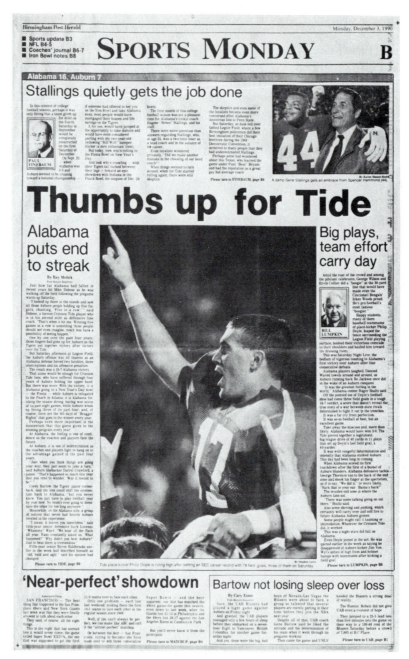

FIGURE 28–1 Large headlines and pictures distinguish the front page of many sports sections, as in this example. (Courtesy of the Birmingham (Ala.) Post-Herald.)

tracks. The reader should be told if the "sire" and "dam" are of distinguished ancestry. Many—perhaps even most—readers will have partial knowledge of this background. They want not only to be told what they already know (and it had better be correct), but also to have their knowledge expanded. They want the whole significance of the event, and they look to the sports reporter as interpreter and final authority. They demand that the reporter have an adequate

FIGURE 28–2 When the San Francisco 49ers won the Super Bowl for the fourth time, the San Jose Mercury News produced a special souvenir Super Bowl section for the team's loyal fans. It featured large pictures, large headlines and a variety of graphics to tell the story of that team's successful season. (Courtesy of the San Jose Mercury News.)

background. If the background of the reader is deeper than that of the writer, the writer is faced with a serious credibility gap.

To some extent, also, the sports reporter can acquire good judgment if aided by adequate knowledge. Familiarity and experience with various sports will acquaint the reporter with the standards used to measure the merits and demerits of plays and players. Ultimately, though, the reporter will succeed or fail because of the accuracy or inaccuracy of his or her independent judgment. A reporter's ability to see beyond the surface and the statistics is a tremendous asset. It is insight, too, and not background, that must detect the cause of weakness or the source of strength of a team or of an individual player. (Some call it a "gut" feeling.) Nor can a sports reporter take comfort in the thought that, if he or she fails to detect and report an error or an achievement, no one will be the wiser. Unlike other reporters, the sports reporter writes for a public, some or many of whom have observed the same event in person or on television with a highly critical eye. A positive requirement for success is sound judgment.

A third desirable qualification of the sports reporter is perspective, or detachment, which should be the result of sufficient knowledge plus good judgment. Being a fan of a particular game or a team does not always make one the best of sports reporters. Thumping the drums for the local team with brass and bias is not detached reporting. The reporter's responsibility is to the public and not to the local team. Although the fans are quick to resent any lack of unrestrained support for local heroes, they will, in the long run, respect the sports reporter's honesty, accuracy and detachment.

The sports reporter is a judge as well as a reporter. But the good one avoids the arrogance of trying to usurp the coach's authority and run the team through the newspaper's columns. There is a difference between good critical judgment and second-guessing, and every sports reporter should learn this early.

Scope of Sports Writing

Sports writing ranges from straight-news reporting through all degrees of interpretative and feature writing and the editorialized column. A sports event may be treated in any one of those degrees or in all of them combined. The general practice is to treat the important event as straight news, utilizing any of the lead and story forms already discussed, with sufficient interpretation to enrich the report with background. Separate stories, features and columns devoted to the sidelights supplement the straight-news account. Many newspapers permit sports writers to use a highly informal style, often with few restrictions on editorializing, even in a story handled as straight news. Careful reporters keep their editorial comments to a minimum in their straight-news account of a sports event.

For important sports events, "buildup," or advance, stories and articles sometimes are used for days, even weeks, before the event. The event is thoroughly covered when it occurs, and "post-mortem" stories may be used for days afterward in commenting on what took place.

Here are several examples of free-wheeling leads on sports stories:

NEW YORK—Sassy and flashy and psyched to the max, Andre Agassi put on a show of blast-away tennis to set up a fiery Saturday match against Boris Becker in the U.S. Open semifinals.

(The Associated Press)

It's that time of the year again, the time when normally sane people start wearing deflated basketballs on their heads and their hearts on their T-shirts.

(Chicago Tribune)

News Sources

Local and regional schools and colleges, recreation departments, professional teams of all types, sponsors of all kinds of sports leagues (such as Little League groups, bowling leagues and country clubs) and other local organizations that promote or conduct events in the sports world are all covered by the sports staff. The editor has, on the one hand, to avoid overlooking some activities deserving space, and on the other, to avoid giving too much space to some teams and groups having very active publicity directors or chairpersons.

A sports staff could not begin to cover all events deserving space, but with the proper encouragement and instructions a sports writer can get valuable assistance in gathering news from many of the people engaged in the various sports. Many newspapers arrange with high school and even junior high students to phone in results of games the newspapers are unable to staff. Little League coaches or their spouses, interested parents, bowling lane owners and tennis and golf club professionals generally are willing to call in the results of an event.

A word of caution is needed on sports news sources. Gambling on sporting events seems to be a national pastime, but the sports staff should be cautious about quoting gambling odds on sports events, although the practice has become more commonplace today in reporting on upcoming professional sporting events. (Gambling is illegal in most states.)

Style in Sports Writing

Good sports writing should be vigorous, virile and audacious. It should not be hackneyed or so exaggerated that it strains the boundaries of believability. It should not be dull. Each reporter must develop a style of writing that is bright and readable but that does not violate the principles of standard English rhetoric. The basic rules of English grammar apply to sports writing as well as to all other newspaper writing.

A sports reporter's objective is to bring the event to the reader with all of the impact that event had on the spectators. Twisting, straining and mangling the language should not be used to accomplish this. The informality of writing on most sports pages may tempt a weak writer to fall back on cliches and hackneyed expressions.

The most effective and vivid sports writing is achieved through the use of active rather than passive verbs and the judicious use of precise adjectives. There is a great difference between carefully selected, precise verbs and adjectives and worn-out cliches such as "banged the apple" and "smacked the pill."

It is important for the sports reporter to remember that the story should be written for the reader-spectator and not the athlete and the coach. The language must not be so technical that the general public will not understand it. At the same time, however, the reporter must be aware that the coach and the players will be reading the story. If the writing reveals an ignorance of techniques and misuses the language of the sport, those involved in playing the sport are not likely to respect the writer and may not be willing to cooperate on future stories.

SPORTS STORY LEADS

The sports page contains stories on a wide variety of events. Most space is devoted to such major sports as football, baseball, basketball, golf and tennis, but other sports that may be written about include swimming, hunting, fishing, automobile and horse racing, track, volleyball, trapshooting, bowling, boxing, wrestling and gymnastics. Depending on the season, and perhaps the section of the country, skiing, hockey, soccer, polo, rowing, rodeos, hiking and a variety of other sports might get even more space than some of the major spectator sports. In an effort to be complete, most sports pages try to carry stories on all major events in all sports. In many cases these include horse shows, dog shows and other events that might not be classified as true sports.

Sports stories are usually reported in a news fashion. Although allowed more freedom in the use of language, the sports reporter usually follows the regular news principles in building the story. The five W's are generally in the lead of the straight news account of the event, and the features usually are summarized at the beginning and elaborated in the body of the story. The general principles of the single-feature and the several-feature lead also apply to straight-sports writing. However, many sports stories, particularly the second-day story or a sidebar story, take a strong feature approach.

No matter what type of sports event is being covered, the reporter may look for one or more of the following elements to provide features for the story:

1. The score of the game or the outcome of the event (The final score may be subordinate to other features, but it should be in the lead or no later than the opening sentence of the second paragraph.)
2. Spectacular plays
3. Scoring plays or sequence of plays
4. Individual stars
5. The significance of the game—championship or effect on record
6. General comparison of teams or opponents
7. Background of game—weather, crowd, special occasion.

These leads illustrate the use of various features of an event:

The Score or Outcome

SAN FRANCISCO (AP)—The San Francisco 49ers defeated the stubborn Cleveland Browns 20-17 on Mike Cofer's 45-yard field goal with five seconds remaining today. It was the 49ers' 15th consecutive victory.

West High's Rebels defeated Rule 21-6 in a 3-AA game last night in a rain storm that turned the West field into a mud hole.

"It was more like mud wrestling than football," West quarterback Dan Walsh said.

Individual Performance

INDIANAPOLIS—Back home in Indiana, Dave Duerson scored the first touchdown of his eight-year career to seal the New York Giants' 24-7 victory over the Indianapolis Colts Monday night.

"Maybe I've been playing for the wrong team all these years," Duerson said.

(Chicago Tribune)

CHICAGO—Bobby Thigpen doesn't stomp around the mound like Al Harbosky, or glare down at hitters like Goose Gossage. Never will the Chicago White Sox right-hander be seen pumping his fist and exhorting the crowd, like Tug McGraw.

Unlike many renowned relievers, Thigpen has no gimmicks, no act, just a darting fastball, nasty slider and an outstanding changeup that have brought him within three saves of the major league record of 46 set in 1986 by Dave Righetti of the New York Yankees.

(Los Angeles Times)

Significance of the Game

SAN FRANCISCO (AP)—San Francisco's 18-game winning streak ended Sunday, one short of the all time record, as the 49ers committed six turnovers in a 28-17 loss to the Los Angeles Rams.

NEW ORLEANS—The offense that once bragged of living on the edge has teetered over the brink. The passing game once described as high octane is running on empty. The quarterback thought to be on the verge of stardom now speaks defensively about unnamed outside forces he claims are trying to "rip his team apart."

And an Atlanta Falcon club that just four weeks ago was with 12-1/2 minutes of the .500 mark is once again assured of a non-winning season for the eighth year in a row.

"I guess," said New Orleans Saints linebacker Rickey Jackson after his club's 10-7 victory over the Falcons on Sunday, "that the more things change, the more they really do stay the same, huh?"

(The Atlanta Constitution)

Comparison of Teams

Vanderbilt University's football team is giving up 44 points a game and has been roughed up for an average of 50 points in its last four games.

Still Ole Miss football coach Billy Brewer says he's worried . . . about Vandy's defense. . . .

"They have changed their defensive philosophy," Brewer said. "We don't know what to expect from them."

(Nashville Banner)

Feature Leads

The use of feature leads on sports stories is more popular than ever since they were introduced by writers on afternoon newspapers as a way of gaining a fresh look on a game that was already 24 hours old. This type of lead may be based on a quote, an after-the-game visit to the locker room, or perhaps an analysis of a player's or team's style. Some writers also use descriptive leads effectively.

Sometimes a good quote tells the story of a sports event better than the score alone. One of the better quote leads of all times didn't get into print because the sports editor thought it would offend the readers. Here it is:

> Reporter: What happened, coach?
> Coach: They beat the hell out of us!
>   That's how Rebel coach Buster Jones explained his team's humiliating 56-0 defeat to the Western Raiders last night.

Reporters who elect to use feature leads often collect most of their material after the game, talking to the coach and players in the locker room, interviewing happy or disappointed fans, observing crowd reaction as the game draws to a close. That is the material television often misses.

Here are several examples of feature leads:

> A few things got fixed Saturday for the University of Tennessee football team. A few more need to be in the next week.
>   The view to the rear as the Vols trotted into Neyland Stadium on a brilliant fall afternoon was a confidence-shaking, perspective-adjusting loss to Alabama.
>   Looking ahead, you could almost see the Four Horsemen and one Rocket of Notre Dame rolling in over the ridges from the North.
>   The here and now was Temple.
>   With a crowd of 93,898—including some legendary Vols in town for the "100 Years of Volunteers" weekend—looking on, No. 11 Tennessee dispatched the Owls rather methodically, 41-20.
>   (The Knoxville News-Sentinel)

> NEW YORK—If Stefan Edberg were a baseball player, he would either hit a home run or strike out. If he played golf, he would either make a hole in one or dunk his tee short into the water.
>   But Edberg is a tennis player, full of his own baffling contradictions.
>   On a muggy Thursday morning at the U.S. Open, he proved he can be No. 1 in the world, win Wimbledon and still lose in the first round of a Grand Slam event.
>   Edberg celebrated his second week as the top-ranked tennis player in the world with a shocking straight-set loss to 52nd-ranked Alexander Volkov of the Soviet Union, 6-3, 7-6 (7-3), 6-2.
>   Edberg's explanation was simple: "I didn't play a very good match."
>   (Los Angeles Times)

Feature leads generally are used on sports-personality pieces like this one by Doug Segrest of the Nashville Banner on Notre Dame football star Raghib Ismail—the Rocket.

> What price fame?
>   They won't leave Raghib Ismail alone. He changes his telephone number, and people still track him down. Ring, ring, ring goes the phone, day and night.
>   Sorry, mom. If you want to reach the Rocket, leave a message.
>   "I'm still scared to answer the phone," says Ismail, Notre Dame's latest Heisman Trophy candidate. "It got real bad after last season. It was every day. 'Why don't you come to this banquet? Why don't you come to that?'

"I was spreading myself too thin too much of the time, and not concentrating on what's important. I didn't want to say no because I didn't want to come off cocky."

Hell may have been wrought in the dorm room. But that's only justice.

Since he first fielded a Michigan kickoff three seasons ago, Ismail has made life miserable for coaches from Los Angeles to Mount Nittany.

LAS VEGAS, Nev.—Even without the imminent arrival of Andre Agassi in an ultimate driving machine, there is already more than enough here to meet the eye.

The sun is bright and molten, attempting to burn a hole in the desert, but one can't actually say that Las Vegas is waking up. Thanks to its endless canopy of neon and manic casinos that clang night and day like competing belfries, this, and not Sinatra's New York, is the city that never sleeps.

Veneer is what turns heads, excess is what charms. Only sunglasses spare the eyes from a surfeit of Americana at its gladdest and gaudiest on the shiny strip where Agassi, a favorite son, has picked up right where Liberace left off.

It hardly comes as a surprise that Vegas is where Agassi, the enigmatic tennis-playing entertainer on the cusp of showing his country whether he will be a true champion or a tinselly chump, calls home.

(The New York Times)

The sports world transcends the playing field and the court. Sports writers frequently produce excellent feature stories about other aspects of the field. This feature for The Charlotte Observer is a good example:

A knee is an injury waiting to happen.

There is not a more complicated or vulnerable joint in the human body.

It also is misunderstood. If people really were meant to play games and run races, the knee would have been built with greater durability. It is not suited for the running, jumping and cutting involved in basketball or marathons, or the knocks that come with soccer or football.

"We've done more with the knee," says Charlotte orthopedist Dr. Joseph Estwanik, "than Mother Nature had in mind."

Here's how the Chicago Tribune's Paul Sullivan began this story on rapidly escalating baseball players' salaries:

Seventy-six years ago in Baltimore, Babe Ruth experienced what he later would describe as his greatest "thrill" in baseball.

In February of 1914, according to Ruth's autobiography, Baltimore Orioles boss Jack Dunn ventured to the St. Mary's orphanage and convinced the 19-year-old Ruth to sign a contract with the minor-league Orioles for the princely sum of $600 a year. . . .

Times do change.

Pascual Perez, who pitched 198 innings while finishing 9-13 with Montreal last year, signed a $5.7 million, three-year contract with the New York Yankees during the off season. If the newly pin-striped Perez pitches the same amount of innings this year (if there is a this year) at a salary of $1.9 million, he will receive $3,198.65 for every out he records.

Most newspapers have one or more sports columnists. Some of them are not very good. Others are tremendously talented. One of the best is Jim Murray of the Los Angeles Times. He is often witty and not afraid to poke a little fun at sports and sports figures. The following is an example of one of his column leads:

> Wait just a darn minute here! Hold it! Time out!
>
> What's going on in the United States of America?
>
> Let me ask you something: didn't we used to win international athletic events with monotonous regularity? Didn't the rest of the world have trouble keeping up with us? Didn't we used to win Wimbledon, U.S. Opens, golf and tennis, British Opens, French Opens, auto races, foot races, Olympic games? Like clockwork?
>
> The rest of the world got sick of hearing "The Star Spangled Banner," right?
>
> Well, take a look around you. What's happening here?
>
> A guy whose name you can't pronounce without a mouthful of marbles, Jose Maria Olazabal, has just won the World Series of Golf, our World Series of Golf, by—hear this!—12 shots.
>
> That wouldn't be so bad—but a Briton won our Masters tournament this year. An Aussie won our PGA.
>
> A Swede won Wimbledon and will probably win the U.S. Tennis Open. Unless, of course, a Czech or German does.

The rest of the column catalogued other events American athletes once won but haven't won lately, including the Little League World Series.

THE BODY OF THE STORY

The body of the sports story must, of course, complete the development of the lead. If the lead is a summary, the body may proceed in the logical development of the various features as presented in the summary lead. If the lead is an outstanding feature, it must be followed by a summary of the features and by the subsequent development of each feature. These are the general principles of lead and body development that have been observed from the beginning of our text as applying to all types of stories.

In many sports stories, however, two types of body development must be utilized: (1) the general interpretation and (2) the running story. The general interpretation is essential. It is merely the development of the lead or lead block. The reporter must narrate and explain (interpret) the highlights (features) of the event. This is the logical body development that is used in other types of stories. The running (chronological) story (play-by-play, inning-by-inning, round-by-round) sometimes appears after the general interpretation or is printed separately under its own headline. Play-by-play or blow-by-blow accounts of sports events are used only infrequently by some newspapers and not at all by others, particularly when radio or television covers the major event.

EXERCISES

1. Invite the coach of a major male or female athletic team at your college or university to class for an interview. Write a story based on the interview.

2. Contact a star high school athlete in your area who is considered a top prospect for college recruiters. Interview him or her about the various techniques athletic recruiters use to convince him or her to sign a letter of intent. Write a story on the interview.

3. Contact the university official who is in charge of maintaining the football stadium or basketball arena at your college or university. Interview him or her and write a feature story on the strange items found in the stadium or arena after a sporting event.

4. Most colleges and universities have an athletic council that is supposed to establish policies for the intercollegiate athletic teams. Often a faculty member serves on that board. Obtain the name of the faculty representative from your university who serves on that board and interview him or her. Write a story based on that interview.

5. If your college has both male and female intercollegiate athletic teams, interview both the men's and women's athletic directors about their budgets and write a story comparing those budgets.

6. Most colleges and universities have large intramural programs. Interview the individual who is responsible for that program as well as a number of students who participate. Write a story describing the scope of the program and the views of the male and female students who participate in it.

7. Invite the sports editor from the local newspaper to class for a discussion of sports coverage in his or her newspaper. Write a story on that interview.

8. Interview university officials as well as officials of the local chamber of commerce, hotel and motel association, restaurant association, and other businessmen and -women to determine the economic impact of a major sports event such as the annual homecoming game in your community. Write a story using the information you collected.

9. Interview coaches and athletes from a major and minor sport on your campus—the football or basketball team and the track or tennis team—and write a story describing the difference in the support provided the teams, including such things as athletic scholarships, special dorms, travel arrangements and the like.

10. Many newspapers have female sports writers covering major sports teams. Contact one of them who is working at a paper in your area and interview her. Write a feature story on her experiences covering male athletes.

11. Write short stories from the following notes:

    a. Mark Gudlin, coordinator
       Small game division
       State Wildlife Division
       Said state's hunting season
       On rabbits and quail
       Opens at 7 a.m. Saturday
       Daily limits set at
       5 rabbits, 10 quail
       Gudlin said he is very optimistic
       "It will be a good season"
       He said he had seen
       "A lot of quail and rabbits
       In good habitat" and "the
       Early frost will help hunters."

    b. DuPont National Clay Court
       Tennis Tournament in Phoenix
       State University women's
       Tennis team competing

Yesterday Mandy Barnette
Advanced to second round
Of women's qualifying play
Defeated Micki Ireland
Of Temple 6-2, 6-0
Plays Melba Ricks-Chapman
Of University of Illinois
This morning
Her team mates Michele Martin
Dawn Schwartz extended
Main-draw invitations
Begin play Friday
State's Val Drabeck
Ranked 28th in preseason poll
Received at-large bid
Into 32-player field
Begins play Friday

c. College basketball recruiters
Signed five Morgan County High
Girls' basketball players
To scholarships today
First day for early signing
All-stater Betty Emrick
A 5-11 post player will play
For South Carolina
Point guard Terry Simpson
Will play at Furman
Jennifer Chavez, a guard
Goes to Seaton Hall
Sheryl Bartlett, a post player
Will play for Mercer
Forward Christine Chapman
Will play for Western Carolina
This is the first time
Five members from one team
Have been signed on same day
Their team ranked 10th nationally

d. Robin Brentwood, football player
At Clewston Senior High
To undergo more surgery today
To repair damaged muscles
He was wounded in both legs
When felled by shotgun blast
Outside a party Saturday
In suburban Belle Glade
Police called it a drive-by shooting
They have no suspects
He underwent emergency surgery
Following the shooting at

Clewiston General Hospital
His mother, Denise Johnson
Said his condition was stable
Coach Elrod Wesley said
He was concerned about the
Gunfire at games this year
Brentwood is a sophomore
Punt and kick-off returner
Wesley said Brentwood was
"An innocent bystander in
The wrong place at the wrong time"
He played in first
Eight games of the season
Coach said he didn't think
Brentwood is out of
Playing football forever.

12. Attend a major sports event on your campus or in your community and write a straight-news story about it.

13. Using the information collected for the first story (Exercise 12) plus other information you collected through interviews with coaches and players, write a feature story on the same game.

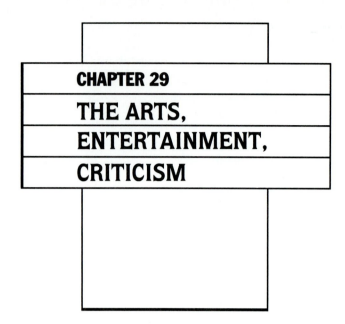

CHAPTER 29
THE ARTS, ENTERTAINMENT, CRITICISM

"No statue has ever been put up to a critic," composer Jean Sibelius once wrote. But that lack of being singularly honored certainly has not slowed the flow of criticism of the arts, music, literature, films and popular entertainment appearing daily in newspapers and other publications.

Newspapers, in particular, are devoting more space than ever before to the arts and entertainment. And nearly every young journalist seems to harbor a desire to be a critic or a reviewer, even though he or she may be tone deaf, admire paintings done on black velvet and rank Barbara Cartland's romance novels as great literature.

Critics and reviewers often are not well liked by the artists and performers they write about. Throughout the history of modern journalism there have been some monumental feuds between critics and performers. The contention between the two stems from the fact that there are no absolute standards in the arts. "There is no final authority," Pauline Kael, movie critic for The New Yorker, has written. "There is only fallible judgment." Unfortunately, some critics and reviewers write as if their judgment is infallible. Whenever they move on, there are countless others waiting in line who also believe their judgment is, indeed, the final authority.

John Crosby, television critic, syndicated columnist and author, has lamented that the job of the critic is to be "literate about the illiterate, witty about the witless and coherent about the incoherent." As grim as that might sound, the job of the critic or reviewer often is the most coveted one at the newspaper. Being a reviewer or critic is much more than simply saying, "I know what I like, so I can write about it." Some background, knowledge and understanding about such areas as drama, literature, film, music and fine arts are essential to write with authority about those fields.

In writing about cultural subjects, the reporter has far more latitude than that offered in almost any other area. Unlike the straight-news story, much of what is written about entertainment or fine arts is appraisal and evaluation for the reader. Obviously, hard-news stories do come out of these fields, and they often have a news peg—a new book or play, a concert, an art show or a performance by a musical group or drama company that leads to the coverage by the newspaper. But for the most part, the prime purpose of a review or critique is to help readers enjoy, understand and appreciate the performance or work of art.

REVIEWING VS. CRITICISM

The difference between reviewing and criticism might be mainly one of definition. In practice, at most of today's newspapers and magazines, the terms are almost synonymous. Yet there is a distinction.

A reviewer, who is not competent by way of background and knowledge, should not criticize the performance or work of another. A review should present facts without editorializing. For example, a reviewer assigned to cover a popular music performance should tell the reader who performed, mention where and when the concert took place, give a summary of the performance and describe the reaction of the audience. A reviewer should tell the reader what the performance was like without attempting a critical evaluation of the performer's musicianship. Of course, in a number of newspapers, reviewers are allowed to engage in various degrees of criticism in their reviews.

Pure criticism, on the other hand, requires expert judgment. Usually a newspaper will not engage in criticism unless it has a qualified staff member to handle the assignment. Many smaller newspapers buy columns from syndicates and feature services written in such areas as theater and music. At times, however, a newspaper may assign its most qualified reporter or employ an outside specialist (musician, artist, author) to write criticisms of public performances.

The good critic uses his or her knowledge and understanding of a particular field to evaluate the performance or work of art. Critics should know the respective standards of each art form and be able to measure fairly the success or failure of the work or performance in attaining those standards. The work or performance should be compared with others in its class, and the ability of the artists, performers, or musicians to present it successfully should be carefully evaluated.

A critic must make certain that his or her judgment is not clouded by a particular bias against a composer, a style of art or music, or an individual performer. Criticism can be clever, sarcastic, even cutting, but it should also be insightful. For example, this clever line by drama critic John Mason Brown remains a classic today: "Tallulah Bankhead barged down the Nile last night as Cleopatra and sank." But criticism should never be mean-spirited.

Entertainment, literature and the fine arts that are the subjects of review or criticism in newspapers include:

1. Books and articles

2. Dramatic performances
3. Concerts and other musical performances (classical and popular)
4. Recordings
5. Films
6. Radio and television programs
7. Lectures
8. Art—painting, sculpture
9. Architecture
10. Professional dancing
11. Photography
12. Nightclub performances.

PRINCIPLES OF CRITICISM

The person assigned to write a review or a critical piece should remember that the standards of good writing always apply. Far too many critics write more in the jargon of the particular field they are covering than in the language the typical reader of a mass publication can understand. This is particularly true in such a field as abstract art.

The following are important points anyone writing a review or critical article should consider.

1. It is important to give readers a view of the woods before pointing out individual trees. The reader is interested in knowing what to expect in the book, play or performance. What is the nature of the work? Is it sensational, intellectual, calm or boisterous? Is it worthwhile and in what way?

2. The work should be criticized in the light of its intentions and within its genre. A detective story or mystery play should not be compared to a classic drama. Amateurs have a right to compete with other amateurs without being judged by professional standards. However, amateurs should not be praised lavishly if they do not deserve it. It is generally wise to report the amateur performances fairly, emphasizing audience reaction.

3. The contents of books or plays should be outlined only to the extent needed for readers to determine whether they are interested and not so fully as to give away the plot. One purpose of the critic is to promote popular interest, not to discourage it.

4. The criticism should be interesting in itself. Readers will not read dull criticism any more readily than they will read dull news. Good criticism may rise to the heights of literature itself.

5. The critic is addressing lay readers who do not possess technical vocabularies. Some of them cannot be expected to know the difference between crisis and climax or protagonist and antagonist, for example, and they may not be familiar with Aristotle's theory of catharsis. So the critic

should write a language the reader will understand and not attempt to "show off" his or her literary prowess.

6. The significance of the work should be suggested. Is it extraordinary, distinguished, superior, mediocre, below standard? Does it have social or economic implications?

7. If the critic likes or dislikes what is being evaluated, he or she should explain why. It is not enough merely to praise or to condemn a literary or artistic production. Critical comment should be supported with examples.

8. The critic must stay within ethical and legal bounds (see Chapter 5). In using copyrighted material, he or she may quote a reasonable amount with no fear of violating the law. A reasonable amount might be interpreted as "a taste but not a full swallow" of the quality of the material. In other words, the critic cannot present the full impact of a reviewed work's quality under the guise of a critical review.

9. Above all, the critic must keep in mind that his or her major responsibility is to the reader, not to the authors, performers or painters. It is important to tell readers whether the production is worth seeing or hearing and why. A critic must be honest with the reader and fair to the artist. A critic should never become a public agent for a performer or production.

Writing Style of Criticism

Some newspapers use a set form to give essential data at the beginning of a critical review. It generally is set off in a box and often is in bold type. Here is an example of the style used by The New York Times for films, television, opera and musical performances:

Roger Corman's
Frankenstein Unbound
Directed by Roger Corman; written by Mr. Corman, F.X. Feeney and Ed Neumeier; director of photography, Armando Nannuzzi; production designer, Enrico Tovaglieri; produced by Mr. Corman, Thom Mount and Kobi Jaeger; released by Warner Brothers. Running time: 96 minutes. This film is rated R.

Dr. Joseph Buchanan .... John Hurt
Dr. Victor Frankenstein .... Raul Julia
Mary Godwin .... Bridget Fonda
The Monster .... Nick Brimble
Byron .... Jason Patrick
Shelley .... Michael Hutchence

Other papers do not have an established pattern for presenting these details. The reviewer or critic will work most of them into the article, which often takes the form of an essay. First-person is permitted because the critic or reviewer is expressing a personal opinion, and the story will carry a by-line.

Most small newspapers do not offer many opportunities for beginning reporters to develop their critical faculties. Even many medium-size newspapers purchase their critical reviews of the arts and entertainment from syndicates or use those distributed by the wire services.

A reporter interested in developing as a reviewer or critic should read the writings of other critics, especially the good ones, and analyze all the devices and techniques they use. But the beginner should not copy the writing style of other critics. It is important for anyone writing criticism to develop a personal writing style.

SUBJECTS OF CRITICISM

Books and Articles

Most metropolitan dailies have book-review columns or pages. They often are a part of the Sunday or weekend edition. Many newspapers use reviews written by members of the staff as well as reviews from the wire services and syndicates.

The public frequently looks to the reviewer or critic for guidance in selecting books, and often the critic can help mold public taste. The better critics do not limit themselves to writing about new books. Often they write about literary trends as well as the business and economics of the publishing industry.

In judging a book, the critic must not lean too heavily on the publisher's publicity release announcing the book. Nor should a critic write a review from the notes on the dust jacket, a practice many authors insist is commonplace. Publicity releases and dust-jacket notes can be used as aids, and some critics may find that they agree with their assessment of the work, but publicity material should not influence the critic's own appraisal.

These examples will illustrate the range of writing style in book reviews:

FRIDAY NIGHT LIGHTS: A TOWN, A TEAM, AND A DREAM
By H.G. Bissinger. (Addison-Wesley, $19.95)
Notre Dame's football coach Louis Holtz, when asked if winning the game his team would play the next day ''was a matter of life and death,'' quipped ''Oh no! It's much more important than that.''
In west Texas, high school football is no less important.
''Friday Night Lights'' records the staggering effect of sports on American life when a community cannot distinguish between good schooling and a winning football team. It pits the American passion for football against the need for schools in the United States to prepare the next generation for a global economy. . . .
(Jim Bencivenga, The Christian Science Monitor)

ANOTHER KIND OF AUTUMN
By Loren Eisley (Scribner's $8.95)
Harriet Van Horne said it best: A friend I never knew died last weekend. Let me paraphrase it: A friend I met only once died a few weeks ago. There is a large hole where he vanished. One can only hope that as with those problematic black holes in space, there is a compensating white hole in some far part of the universe where his energies are a source of never-ending wonder.
Loren Eisley is the name of the friend met only once, a shy man, seemingly unaware of his genius. His new and last book of poetry is properly

titled ''Another Kind of Autumn.'' Autumn was always in his work, as was poetry. His earliest essays, 30 years ago in Harper's, struck an awe into me that never stopped, but went on from article to article, prose-poem to prose-poem and finally to his poetry itself, the poems with brightness in them, but with autumn narrowing the light. . . .

(Ray Bradbury, Los Angeles Times)

IF I EVER GET BACK TO GEORGIA, I'M GONNA NAIL MY FEET TO THE GROUND
By Lewis Grizzard (Villard Books $17.95)

As Lewis Grizzard explains in the first paragraph of his new book, ''If I Ever Get Back to Georgia, I'm Gonna Nail My Feet to the Ground,'' long before he was a syndicated columnist he was a newspaper man.

One of the best.

This is his 13th book.

One of his best.

Grizzard, whose column appears regularly in the Nashville Banner, is one of the best known columnists in the country and is a top rated humorist who has made a number of comedy albums and often performs live shows.

If anyone was destined to live his life up to his elbows in printer's ink, it was Grizzard. . . .

(Mark McGee, Nashville Banner)

Movies

For the young writer, movies present one of the best opportunities to develop as a critic or reviewer. Students interested in this type of writing would benefit greatly from some of the film courses now being offered at many colleges and universities. They should also study the works of a wide range of critics writing for major newspapers and magazines as well as the many collections of movie reviews in book form. The collected reviews of James Agee, for example, are excellent for style, form and critical judgment. And the works of Pauline Kael, film critic for The New Yorker, should not be overlooked.

A movie reviewer or critic should prepare for the job by studying the works of the great critics while making every effort to keep current on the economic as well as artistic trends in the film industry. Too often newspaper writers who report on films content themselves with simple reviewing when they have an opportunity for conscientious criticism in the manner of Agee and Kael. The critic has an opportunity to do more than create audiences for films. The critic can exert much influence on the medium and can help bring about a higher type of entertainment. In the final analysis, the moviegoer is the one who really determines the fare offered. However, an effective critic can do much to refine the moviegoer's taste.

Although the temptation might be great, a reviewer or critic should resist seeking personal attention through snide and devastating comments. A review or critique should be an honest and fair evaluation of the work. Criticism is not synonymous with slurs. A fair critic—one who gains the respect and even the admiration of readers—is not constantly negative; neither does he or she forever praise every film. Few works are entirely good or entirely bad. A reader who has been misled by a reviewer or critic generally ceases to be a reader.

The following are leads from several movie reviews:

Allan Moyle could have come up with a better title for his new film about a pirate radio station taking over the airwaves in a small Arizona town. While "Pump Up the Volume" is about teenagers, funky music, and a sentimental romance, it is also a realistic look at life in the '90s for the under-20 crowd.

Teenage films such as "Footloose" and "Pretty in Pink" tend to portray teens as simple people searching for simple solutions to their problems. "Pump Up the Volume" tries, fairly successfully, to show life as a bit more complicated and a lot more painful.

(Suzanne MacLachlan, The Christian Science Monitor)

Like "Lassie," "Baxter" is a movie about a dog, but, unlike the mannerly collie of the children's classic, Baxter is a rude, questioning mind inhabiting the stocky, dirty-white body of a bull terrier.

Though he looks as if he should have a monocle painted around one eye, Baxter is anything but comic. Not for him to shepherd dim-witted sheep, save the lives of weak bratty babies or cock his head to listen to the voice of just any master.

Baxter is his own master, even if he'd rather not be. He is scarily logical. In the world he inhabits he is right to be suspicious of humans. . . .

"Baxter," which opens today in New York, is a very good, appropriately vulgar and disorienting first feature directed by Jerome Bolvin. . . .

(Vincent Canby, The New York Times)

Compared to most Stephen King movies, "Misery" is a winner. This story of a writer (James Caan) held captive by a woman who calls herself his "number one fan" delivers the goods in terms of suspense and jolts of horror. It is, however, a bit of a disappointment compared to some of the other works of director Rob Reiner ("When Harry Met Sally . . .") and Oscar-winning writer William Goldman ("Marathon Man").

(Harper Jones, St. Louis Post-Dispatch)

You may have heard that Sylvester Stallone actually considered killing off his cinematic alter ego in "Rocky V" but was persuaded by United Artists management to let the hero live.

You can't kill off a cherished figure, Stallone was told.

But after taking an exclusive peek at Stallone's original script, dated July 24, 1989, one can only conclude that the actor-writer was right.

(Gene Siskel, Chicago Tribune)

Television, Radio, Recordings

The television industry produced major news stories almost daily. The decrease in audience shares of the major networks, the shabby treatment of a beloved morning news/entertainment program hostess, the networks' fight with the rating services, the astronomical cost of advertising during the Superbowl, the multi-million-dollar contracts of news anchors and dozens of other news stories often make the news sections of most newspapers because television plays a major role in the daily lives of millions of persons.

Major daily newspapers have staff writers and columnists who cover television both as a business and as an entertainment medium. Often they write about radio as well. In addition, the wire services and most feature syndicates distribute news stories, special columns and features on television and radio.

The same basic standards that apply to all news and critical writing apply to writing about television and radio. The news stories should be complete, fair, accurate and balanced. The critical reviews should be informed, fair and just. Flippant reviews can be amusing, but they serve no useful purpose in most cases. Television, in particular, has far too great a social, cultural and economic impact to be treated lightly. It should be written about as the serious social phenomenon it is.

Here are several examples of news stories about the industry and a review of a major television drama:

> NEW YORK—ABC, CBS and NBC ended the important November ratings sweeps with an all-time low 63 percent share of the viewing audience, apparently because the young abandoned Bill Cosby for Bart Simpson and the old fled CBS for cable.
>
> NBC won the sweeps, one of four held each year to set advertising rates for affiliates, for the sixth consecutive time. But its ratings for all programs were down 13.1 from 15.1 last November, while it maintained a 22 share.
>
> ABC held second place, with a 12.8 rating and a 21 share, and CBS came in third, at 12.1 with a 20 share. . . .
>
> (A single national C.C. Nielsen rating point represents 931,000 homes with television sets. A share is the percentage of television sets in use that are tuned to a given program. A local point equals 31,000 homes.)
>
> (Kenneth R. Clark, Chicago Tribune)

> WASHINGTON—Legislation to regulate the cable television industry, considered all but dead when it was blocked on the Senate floor two weeks ago, may be resurrected with a last-minute deal reached today.
>
> Late this afternoon, Senator Albert Gore Jr., Democrat of Tennessee and a primary sponsor of the measure, said he had reached an agreement with Senator Timothy E. Wirth, Democrat of Colorado, who had blocked consideration of the bill on Sept. 28.
>
> Mr. Gore said today that he hoped to bring the bill back for consideration on the floor before the Senate adjourns this month.
>
> A similar measure has been passed by the House. But President Bush has indicated he might veto the legislation, contending that it would impose too many regulations rather than increase competition.
>
> (Edmund L. Andrews, The New York Times)

> Quick—name the most popular performer on TV.
>
> Bill Cosby, easy. But No. 2 is a little tougher. Marketing Evaluations TVQ ratings, which measure performers' recognition factor and likability, say the honor goes to 4-year-olds Mary Kate and Ashley Fuller Olsen of ABC's "Full House."
>
> Mary Kate and Ashley are the twins who play Michelle on the hit sitcom.
>
> The girls started on the show when they were 9 months old. Some say watching their progress is part of the show's success.
>
> (Jefferson Graham, Gannett News Service)

> There is nothing like James Garner to brighten a television set. An actor whose talent threatens to burst from the small screen, Garner is great in "Decoration Day" (8 p.m., Sunday WMAQ Ch. 5) a Hallmark Hall of Fame presentation. He is perfectly capable of holding the firm middle ground of what is a crafty and subtly constructed tornado of human emotions, pains and joy.
>
> He's a retired Southern judge, recently widowed and spending his days fishing and not much else. He has gone, says the longtime housekeeper (Ruby Dee, in a dazzling performance), "from bein' no nonsense to just plain nasty" and one can easily see him drifting off into dull dotage. . . .

> Garner, for whom the Hallmark Hall of Fame has been a near-perfect mate—he previously shone in "The Promise" and "My Name is Bill W."—brings great depth to his character, showing us his pain at past neglect and his resolve to embrace not only old friends but new. Cranky, yet compassionate, his character is real and touching in every way.
>
> (Herman Kogan, Chicago Tribune)

> The Muppet master's legacy lives on in "Jim Henson's Mother Goose Stories," a captivating new half-hour series for young children premiering Saturday at 8:30 a.m. on the Disney Channel.
> Adapted from L. Frank Baum's "Mother Goose in Prose" and directed by Henson's son, Brian, the series tells whimsical stories based on familiar nursery rhymes, using real children, storybook settings and new visual delights from Jim Henson's Creature Shop.
>
> (Lynne Heffley, Los Angeles Times)

The growth of cable television resulted in television writers' and critics' focusing more attention on its offerings. Here is the lead on a story about cable programming written by Mike Hughes for Gannett News Service:

> What a strange world those cable-TV boxes lure into our living rooms and our minds.
> Tonight, cable ranges from cartoon goofiness to a cartoon effort to save the world. It ranges from a well-crafted lesbian drama to Patty Duke as a reformed spider.
> Even without cable, Thursdays are overloaded.

Radio

Radio's local programming formats and its declining influence as a national entertainment medium, except in music and sports, has caused many newspapers to limit their coverage to an occasional important news story and a limited listing of programs. However, some newspapers continue to carry a locally written radio column and report on such activities as changes in format by local stations, ownership changes, and the arrival or departure of radio personalities. When a popular morning radio personality is pulled off the air during sticky contract negotiations with the station, it's an important local news story. Many newspapers also supplement their coverage of radio with wire service stories and syndicated columns.

The next story, from the Los Angeles Times, was the outgrowth of a national story about an Irish singer who refused to have the U.S. national anthem played before her concert in New Jersey. It was written by Phil West.

> A San Bernadino radio station has joined several East Coast radio stations in banning Sinead O'Connor from its airwaves.
> The action by KGGI-FM (99.1) is part of a growing protest over the Irish singer's refusal to have the U.S. national anthem played at her concert last Friday at the Garden State Arts Center in Holmsel, N.J.

Recordings and Music Videos

The recording industry in the late 1980s and early 1990s was the source for two major news stories—one as a result of technology and the other of duplicity. The introduction of compact discs that offered clearer sound literally revolution-

FIGURE 29–1 Graphic artists at The Knoxville News-Sentinel created this impressive cover for its Sunday "Showtime" entertainment tabloid section. (Courtesy of The Knoxville (Tenn.) News-Sentinel.)

ized the record industry and brought an end to the era of long-playing vinyl record albums. In addition, the candid admission that an immensely popular and award-winning singing duo had not sung a single note on their best-selling album shocked the public and the music business much the same way as the 1950s payola, drugs and sex scandals had damaged the credibility of the industry.

Although these hard-news stories capture the public's attention briefly, it is the columns, reviews, critiques and feature stories about recording artists written by the music writers and critics that readers rely on for information and a fair evaluation of recorded performances. Most larger newspapers have assigned staff writers with some musical training to cover the recording industry. But many smaller papers purchase columns and features about music and musicians from feature syndicates. At some newspapers, the critic or reviewer who covers live musical performances also writes about recordings.

The stars of the musical field—especially the popular music performers—are national and international heroes to their fans, and a reporter who attempts to write about them and their work must be knowledgeable or risk the wrath of legions of irate followers. A performer's work should not be dismissed or degraded simply because it does not please the taste of the reviewer.

In addition to evaluating performances, the reporter writing about recordings also has a responsibility to keep the public informed, not only about new releases, but about the many fads, trends and other changes in the field, especially the technological changes that continue to reshape the industry. One of the most significant changes came about with the advent of the music video, which revived the sagging rock music industry through MTV, a cable network devoted entirely to music videos. It became the hottest basic operation in the history of cable. It's popularity spilled over from rock music into other popular music as well as country music. Music videos became a staple in all fields except classical. And newspapers across the country began reviewing them just as they do records.

These leads from record and music-video reviews illustrate the style of writing commonly used by writers. Often the reviews are limited to three or four paragraphs, and many newspapers group them in a column under a single headline.

"MY FUNNY VALENTINE": Frederica von Stade sings Rodgers and Hart (EMI Angel)

This is the album Frederica von Stade was born to record.

We already knew from her splendid work on EMI's best-selling "Show Boat" recording that the American mezzo-soprano has an instinctive flair for Rodger's lilting melodies, their subtle rhythmic inflections perfectly wedded to often bittersweet emotions expressed by Hart's lyrics. But in this collection of 17 Broadway and Hollywood show tunes (including the title tune from "Babes in Arms"), also conducted by John McGlinn, she tops previous work.

There isn't a dud in the lot.

(John von Rhein, Chicago Tribune)

"Miles in Paris" (Warner Reprise Video)

On this hour-long video, Miles Davis performs his powered-up music of recent vintage with a spatial economy that recalls his appealing "Kind of Blue" sound of the late '50s. Culled from a Paris Jazz Festival concert of last November, the video captures America's most dynamic jazz man sculpting his sleek, angular sound with an unexpectedly talented ensemble of young musicians. . . .

Director Frank Casenti floats his cameramen around the stage to profile the ensemble from various angles. The several brief interview passages that he inserts—with Miles talking about his hiatus from music, South Africa and various musical ideas—seem poignant and undisruptive. The editing moves nicely with the music, and the few behind-the-camera flourishes—mostly dissolves and freeze frames—achieve their desired effects.

(Paul A. Harris, Los Angeles Times)

Occasionally, a music video, like other performances, is so controversial it becomes a news story. That was the case when singer Madonna released her video "Justify My Love," which was rejected by MTV. Here is the lead on USA TODAY's story, the top news on the front page of the newspaper's "Life" section. It was written by Edna Gundersen.

NEW YORK—Madonna's "Justify My Love" video, a carnal carnival of voyeurism and leather-and-lace sex, brims with so much hanky-panky that even cleavage-inclined MTV refuses to air it.

The grainy black-and-white video by Jean Baptiste Mondino, who also directed Madonna's peep-show exhibitionism in "Open Your Heart," is an eye-popping sexcapade set in a Paris hotel room. . . .

The first Madonna video ever refused by MTV, "Justify" strikes a few poses the channel's standards and practices division could not abide.

Declining to specify what was deemed objectionable, MTV spokeswoman Carole Robinson says, "The (video) is just not for us."

Home Videos

The video cassette recorder became a technological sensation in the late 1980s and changed the way millions of Americans watched television and movies. Renting or buying videotapes of major motion pictures became a multibillion-dollar business and cut into the audience share of network television. Video rental stores popped up like convenience markets. Some cities passed ordinances to control the types of videos that were being sold or rented when it became apparent that so-called X-rated films on tape were in great demand.

Newspapers quickly introduced columns announcing the latest releases and providing readers with brief reviews. Larger newspapers assigned the task to staff writers, while smaller publications used reviews provided by the wire services and feature syndicates.

The following are the leads from several movie videos:

"Another 48 HRS." (R) Paramount. R. 102 min. 1990.

This film has Eddie Murphy once again being released from prison to help his old cop buddy, Nick Nolte, tackle a dangerous case. This time Nolte is close on the trail of the Iceman, the Bay Area drug kingpin. Murphy may be able to help—especially after Nolte's gun and badge are lifted by his superiors in one obligatory scene of most modern cop movies. The action is confusing, the plot is murky, and Nolte and Murphy don't have much to say to one another; the movie is violent chewing-gum for the brain.

(The Tennessean, Nashville)

"Stanley and Iris" (PG-13) MGM/UA Home Video. 100 min. 1990.

Jane Fonda just can't get enough blue-collar pathos. She's happiest when she's got her little muck rake out, scraping the American landscape for causes. Here, she plays a new widow with a dead-end job in a bakery, a pregnant teenager, an abused sister, a grieving son and a beau who can't read so much as a street sign. All this trouble is borrowed, relished and ballooned in "Stanley and Iris," an oh-woe-is-me romance that co-stars Robert De Niro, who took the part even though he doesn't get to fatten up, or suffer half as much as Fonda. Iris realizes that Stanley, a bachelor fry-cook, is illiterate, gets him fired, then tries to make amends by teaching him to read.

(Rita Kempley, The Washington Post)

Live Performances—Music, Drama, Dance

Newspapers cover a wide range of live performances—popular singers and musical groups, plays, classical music concerts by individual artists as well as orchestras, nightclub performers, outdoor dramas, dance companies, jazz singers and instrumentalists, among others. Good critics/reviewers are careful observers as well as listeners. They do not simply label a performance "good" or "bad," "adequate" or "inadequate," because that does not tell the reader much. Rather, they use verbal images that help the reader visualize what they saw on the stage or platform.

Although writing reviews and critiques of live performances certainly is not as restrictive as writing hard-news stories, the same principles of fairness and accuracy certainly are called for. Although it is true that the review or criticism is the personal opinion of the writer, the principles of criticism (pages 458–460) should still apply.

The critic of a live performance should always describe and evaluate a performance for the reader. But he or she may have to make certain allowances for unexpected or unpleasant conditions (which should be pointed out in the review) that might affect the performance. The critic should not pounce or dwell on a minor defect if the performance as a whole is excellent. But if the orchestra was so loud that the audience had difficulty hearing the singers, it should be pointed out. If the costumes were shabby, the reader should be told. If the sets were poorly executed and the lighting ineffective, the reviewer should say so because sets, lights and costumes are all part of the performance.

When reviewing the performance of a star who appears both in concert or in plays and in the movies, the critic should avoid scathing comparisons. Most performers who appear in films are helped immeasurably by a film editor who can save most performances with careful editing. Live performance can be a minefield for even the most seasoned performers. On the other hand, a performer is expected to act like a professional, and the critic has an obligation to give an honest appraisal of a live appearance. If the performance is shoddy and unprofessional, the critic should say so. Readers who may be planning to attend should be told what to expect.

In the case of a stage play, especially a new one, the critics should evaluate how well the author succeeded in the writing as well as how successful the actors were in presenting it. The same applies to performances of new musical compositions or a newly created dance. If a widely known work is being performed, comparisons can be made with interpretations by other performers.

Performances by amateurs should not be judged by rigid professional standards. They should neither be lavishly praised out of a sense of loyalty nor be viciously attacked. A critic can and should be as encouraging as critical to amateurs.

Many critics or reviewers try to develop a personalized style in their writing. Since first-person is acceptable in reviewing, critics often write highly personal reactions to performances. But not all criticism should be written in that style.

The following leads from reviews of live performances illustrate the range of coverage given performing artists by newspapers:

> Stephanie Haynes is one very appealing singer.
> She has a marvelous voice, a warm, personable alto that's distinctively her own. She chooses terrific tunes which she performs terrifically, remaining true to the songs' emotional intentions and musical constructs, yet not reluctant to nudge them this way or that to suit her feel-free-to-fool-around jazz-based rhythmic concepts. She enunciates clearly, so you can hear every word and she's got a dandy ear that keeps the pitch right on target and handles a modulation from A flat to G with nary a slip.
> Friday in a cozy back room of Giorgio's Place (located at the base of the Arco Towers in Long Beach, where singers and trios have been appearing for a few months), Haynes brought along all the above qualities and, backed by her regular accompanists—pianist Larry Flahive and bassist Jack Prather—gave listeners there an aural treat. . . .
> Haynes is a rare vocalist in an area that is known for its fine singers. She should be heard more often.
>
> (Zan Stewart, Los Angeles Times)

> NEW YORK—Russia's greatest orchestra, the Leningrad Philharmonic, is touring the USA for the first time since 1973, and it's in marvelously imperious form.
> In the Monday performance of its four-concert run at Carnegie Hall, the orchestra was clearly among the world's most distinctive symphonic groups—and not because it has a clean, silk sound like U.S. orchestras. The Leningraders sound darker—coarser and more imposing.
> Rehearsed down to the tiniest nuance, it's able to scale itself down to a filligree strand of barely audible sound. When in full cry, it's electrifying, and the sound touches something elemental inside you. . . .
> This is music-making with a depth and individuality that's rare these days. . . .
>
> (David Patrick Stearns, USA TODAY)

> It was a pleasure to see the San Francisco Ballet back at the Kennedy Center Opera House Tuesday night after a two-year hiatus, launching a week's engagement in typically gracious and spirited form.
> Having passed a half a decade under the artistic direction of Helgi Tomasson, the troupe has reaffirmed and palpably bolstered its position as one of the nation's outstanding classical ensembles. Even a less than prepossessing opening night program, surprisingly devoid of a single major choreographic opus, couldn't seriously dampen the gratification of watching this splendid band of dancers in action.
>
> (Alan M. Kriegsman, Washington Post)

> In the 26 years since it was first produced on Broadway, "Fiddler on the Roof" has become a universally cherished folk musical. With countless versions performed throughout the world, it is part of our musical heritage, just as the Sholom Aleichem stories on which the show is based derive from an Earlier European literary heritage.
> As the revival that opened last night at the Gershwin Theater proves, "Fiddler on the Roof" has not lost an ounce of its charm or its emotional power.
> From the Chagall-inspired settings by the late Boris Aronson to Topol's performance as Tevye the dairyman, this is a heartwarming production. . . .
>
> (Mel Gussow, The New York Times)

FIGURE 29-2 The "Arts & Leisure" section of The Cincinnati Enquirer often uses large photographs and imaginative headline displays to attract readers to its cover story. (Courtesy of The Cincinnati Enquirer.)

Art—Paintings, Sculptures, Photographs

The "I know what I like and this isn't it" school of criticism is of little value to any reader and often reveals the shallowness of the critic. This is especially true in reviewing art, where it is essential for the critic to have a broad knowledge of the different art forms and various interpretations of them.

Like all other critics, the arts writer must not let personal prejudice for or against a particular art form or style influence the critical assessment of the work. To be effective, a critic must have some understanding of what the artists sought to do before being able to evaluate the work fairly.

A writer hoping for a career as an art critic should at least study art history and read the works of major art critics. Colleges and universities offer numerous art courses that will give a writer a solid foundation for art criticism.

Here are several leads of art stories and reviews:

WASHINGTON—The Kasimir Malevich retrospective that opened Sunday at the National Gallery of Art is more than a landmark exhibition. It is an exceptionally moving event. For the first time the American public is being given a thorough look at the greatest 20th-century Soviet painter, one of the select few who helped shape the modernist imagination.

(The New York Times)

LONDON—The painter Georges Braque once wrote: "Nobility comes from contained emotions. I love the rule which corrects emotion." A classical credo. It might also be the motto for an exhibition here called "On Classic Ground."

At the Tate Gallery (through Sept. 21), this show explores a period of art when "classicism"—once the academic, traditionalist bedrock of painting and sculpture—became for a decade the language of the "avant-garde" itself. . . .

. . . Perhaps the Tate exhibition tried a little too self-consciously to argue that our history of the 20th century avant-garde is a distortion, which we should see more correctly through today's eyes.

(Christine Andreae, The Christian Science Monitor)

Art in its many forms can become news, not only when collectors pay $50 million or more for a painting, but also when controversy over art becomes a constitutional issue involving free speech, as it did in the 1990 furor over the funding of art exhibits and presentations by performance artists by the National Endowment for the Arts (NEA). After a controversial exhibit of photographs by the late Robert Mapplethorpe that included seven sexually explicit pictures brought congressional threats to its funding, the NEA instituted a policy of asking persons who receive its grants to sign an anti-obscenity pledge. Many artists and musical and theater groups refused. Here is the lead on one of the many stories that controversy generated. It was written by Allan Parachii and Greg Braxton for the Los Angeles Times.

The Los Angeles Festival, saying even its cash woes could not justify signing a National Endowment for the Arts anti-obscenity certification, rejected a $30,000 federal grant Thursday, but said private donations are expected to make up the shortfall—starting with a $1,000 personal check from Mayor Tom Bradley.

Rejection of the NEA money was apparently the first concrete result of a decision by endowment chairman John E. Frohnmayer to spurn a recommendation from the NEA's advisory National Council of the Arts that Frohnmayer eliminate the controversial obscenity certification.

FIGURE 29–3 The Los Angeles Times combines entertainment, the arts and television listings in its Friday "Calendar" section to give the readers a broad overview of what is available to them in theater, music, art and entertainment in the week ahead. (Copyright 1990, Los Angeles Times. Reprinted by permission.)

EXERCISES

1. Invite to class the persons who write movie, popular music and classical music reviews for the local newspapers for a panel discussion about their work. Write a story based on that discussion.

2. Invite to class a director and an actor from the drama department at your college or university or a local theater company for an interview on what they think of critics in general and the local critics in particular. Write a story based on that interview.

3. Locate a local writer, artist or musician who has received a grant from the state arts council or the National Endowment for the Arts. Interview her or him about the impact of that sponsorship on her or his creativity. Write a story based on that interview.

4. Check out a copy of the book "Agee on Film" by James Agee from a library. Compare the reviews of several movies he wrote when he was a critic for Time magazine and The Nation at the same time. Study how they differ in form and in style.

5. Interview a group of popular musicians, preferably students who play for dances and concerts in the area while attending college, and write a feature story about them.

6. Interview your university's chief architect about the various styles of architecture of campus buildings. Ask her or him to tour the campus with you to discuss the buildings and their style. Write a critical review of the design of campus buildings.

7. Attend one or more of the following (as assigned by the instructor) and write a review:
   a. a motion picture
   b. an art show
   c. a live pop or classical musical performance
   d. a live dramatic performance
   e. a photographic exhibit

8. Watch a new television program or musical video or listen to a new record album and write a review. Compare your review to one appearing in a major daily newspaper or magazine such as Time or Newsweek.

9. Most colleges and universities sponsor concert programs. Arrange to interview the next nationally known performer who comes to your campus. Write a story based on that interview.

10. Write a review of a current book you have read. After completing your review, locate a copy of Book Review Digest in your college or community library and compare your review with one in the Digest. Analyze your own writing style as well as that of the critic.

11. Check the catalog of your college or community library for books that are collections of criticisms of movies, art, architecture, music and so forth. Study each reviewer's writing style and compare it to the style used in reviews that appear in the newspapers in your area. Write an essay comparing the styles.

12. Teaching, it has been said, is performing. Write a review of the classroom "performance" of one of your instructors this semester, but not necessarily the instructor of this course.

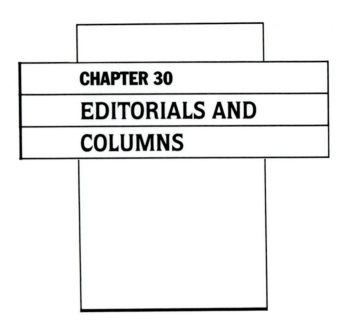

CHAPTER 30
EDITORIALS AND
COLUMNS

Paul Neely, managing editor of The Chattanooga (Tenn.) Times, once suggested, quite seriously, that newspapers "get rid of editorials." But not the editorial page. He argued that editorials are outdated, sound arrogant, color how the newspaper is perceived and undermine the credibility of the rest of the paper.

Neely, who had been an editorial writer before he became a managing editor, suggested that in place of writing institutional editorials that were supposed to represent the collective views of the newspaper, editorial writers be allowed to present their provocative personal opinions as their own. He advised hiring local opinion writers the way syndicated columnists are often selected, for variety rather than conformity and for originality rather than repetition. He also recommended newspapers actively solicit opinion from knowledgeable outsiders and develop such a mix of opinion that readers could not guess how the owners or management of the newspaper stood on any given subject. He wrote:

> Let's publish opinion pages of such excellence and such diversity that readers believe there is no concerted effort to sway their thoughts in our direction.
> Then maybe they'll start to believe the same thing about the news columns.[1]

Neely's suggestions did not exactly sweep the industry; newspapers still have editorial pages. However, many of them are making a concerted effort to solicit diverse opinion—both local and national—that is published as commentary on the editorial page or its companion "Op-Ed" page, which also features local and syndicated columnists.

[1] The Bulletin of the American Society of Newspaper Editors (June 1985), pp. 16–17.

The editorial page represents journalism as practiced in its early days, the so-called days of personal journalism, when the editor interpreted current events as he saw them (there were few female editors or editorial writers then) and when readers were about as familiar with the name of the editor as they were with the name of the newspaper. In that era, the policies and opinions of the editor for or against a public issue or candidate were known by the readers and often influenced the editor's presentation of the news.

In the coverage of the presidential campaign that followed the Civil War, for example, there could be no doubt where the editor of the Chicago Times stood on General Ulysses Grant's candidacy. Here is part of his scathing editorial after Grant received the Republican nomination:

> Hiram Ulysses Grant, did you resign your commission in the army in 1853, for fear that you would be court-martialed for conduct unbecoming an officer and a gentleman? Did you scandalously foul a soup tureen? Was it your habit frequently to get into a state of beastly intoxication when you were living on a farm of your father-in-law, General Dent, near St. Louis? In Galena, were you supported by charity of your father and brother, although you were then in good health? Were you intoxicated on the day of the battle of Belmont? Were you intoxicated on the day of the battle of Shiloh? . . . Is it true as charged by . . . prominent members of the Republican party that you "cannot stand before a bottle of whisky without falling down?" . . . Did you get into a controversy with President Johnson in which was mixed a question of veracity and did you come out of that controversy branded a liar and as a man who was guilty of an act of inexpressible meanness and dishonor?

Perhaps it is because most editorial writers refrain from such direct, slashing attacks that they are branded as timid by media critics. As modern journalism evolved from those early personalized newspapers, the news was presented in a more objective (and, presumably, more accurate) manner by reporters. The editor, however, retained the right to express opinions and state policies on the editorial page. The by-lined opinion column developed early in the 20th century as an adjunct to the editorial page.

A major criticism through the years has been that the editorial page is a closed shop, that only the editor's opinion is expressed and that editors print only columnists who reflect their own points of view. That may have been a valid criticism once, but no longer. Most newspapers now present a diverse set of opinions to the public through the use of conservative, middle-of-the-road and liberal columnists. In addition, most newspapers have expanded their use of "Letters to the Editor" in which the newspaper and the editor may be criticized for a particular stand on an issue.

One of the most successful ways editorial pages have been opened up is through the "Op-Ed" or commentary page pioneered by The New York Times. Editors of these pages regularly seek the view of persons who differ with the newspaper's stand on public issues. Political, social, religious and academic leaders are asked to write for the page. Some newspapers present, side by side, the views of two persons who differ on an issue. In its editorials, on the opposite page, the newspaper's editorial writers may present still another point of view.

The commentary page is also an outgrowth of the concept that on the modern editorial page readers have a right to express their opinions and that they may "talk back" to editors and columnists. They do this in "Letters to the Editor," which are used in increasing numbers by both daily and weekly newspapers. Some newspapers, USA TODAY among them, often solicit the opinions of readers on a particular topic with survey forms printed in the paper or special telephone numbers for readers to call. Often these form the basis for a front-page news story. On several occasions newspapers have used letters and survey responses to cover a front page: these letters and responses then were continued on several inside pages.

Only bona fide, signed letters are generally used, and the editors reserve the right to reject a letter or to reduce its length to meet space limitations or to conform to ethical codes or the laws of libel. In a sense, each of these letters is an editorial, but it is an expression of the opinion of a reader instead of an editor.

With by-lined columns, however, the situation is different. Although these often appear on the editorial page or the "Op-Ed" page, the editor does not necessarily agree with the views expressed by the writer. It is not uncommon for a newspaper's own editorial opinion to differ with that of the by-lined columnist. Some editors have on occasion either edited offending material from a column or withheld the column completely, for which they have usually faced a storm of accusations about stifling free speech.

But for the most part, publishers and editors today believe tbat a newspaper has a social responsibility to seek out and publish the opinions of writers who effectively represent all points of view. Both the editorial and the by-lined column represent personal journalism and have some things in common; chiefly, they are an expression of personal opinion. But in writing style and form they often are radically different.

EDITORIALS

It is essential for the writer to recognize that there is no formula for writing editorials. They will vary widely, depending on the writing style of the editor. But a good editorial is always a carefully constructed analytical essay in which the writer explains, interprets and appraises an event or public issue. It shouldn't be simply a restatement of an issue with a few lines of criticism or comment tacked on at the end. The following are some generalized statements about the attributes, purposes, value and content of editorials that can serve as guidelines for editorial writers.

Attributes of Editorials

To comment on current events, editorials should be timely. Readers are more interested in news than in history, unless there is a historical tie-in to the day's news. What happened today affects readers today, and they are open to suggestions and opinions on such matters. This factor dovetails with the second essential attribute—consequence. Minor news stories rarely make interesting editorials. The editorial writer usually may choose from a large selection of important events—events that attract and affect a large number of readers. The current issues and problems arising from events, rather than the events themselves, often form the subject matter for editorials.

Value of Editorials

The editorial is valuable to both the newspaper and the reader. It gives the newspaper a chance to present its policies and beliefs without coloring the regular news stories with biased statements. If the newspaper believes taxes are high, it can carry on a campaign to get them lowered, using every timely opportunity that arises to present its arguments. The newspaper's appraisal of local, state, national and international events can be offered effectively in this manner.

On the other hand, readers benefit from the expert interpretations and opinions on current events offered by the well-informed editorial writer. The key word here is "expert." To be believed and respected, the editorial writer must be a trained thinker, a keen student of society and a skilled interpreter.

Editorial writing requires knowledge in many fields as well as patience and aptitude for careful research. The average reader who spends somewhere between 30 and 45 minutes a day reading a newspaper has neither the time nor the ability to unravel the complexities of major political and social events. The typical reader does not have the general background or knowledge to know if the city really will benefit from a proposed new eight-lane highway through the heart of a residential district. The editorial has a responsibility to research the proposal and tell the reader if it is worthwhile and why.

Types of Editorials

The ultimate purpose of most editorials is to convince, whether or not the writer hopes to stir the readers to immediate action. An analogy can be made between an editorial writer and an attorney speaking to a jury. "Here is the evidence," the attorney declares. "With these facts before you, the verdict should be as I have indicated."

Just how far the writer goes in trying to influence the reader varies from editorial to editorial. It depends on what the writer wants to accomplish. In one editorial the writer may merely interpret an event and offer no specific recommendations of reader action. This type of editorial should add dimension to the reader's knowledge and understanding of an issue. In another type of editorial, the writer may suggest, outright or subtly, one or more courses of action. And in a third, the writer may demand action on the part of public officials or exhort readers to take immediate action because of the gravity of the issue. Of course, a writer who shouts "Wolf!" too often without sufficient cause or evidence to support the cry will quickly go unheeded.

Still another type of editorial is the short, humorous kind intended to lighten the seriousness of the editorial section and to inject an element of

FIGURE 30–1 The San Jose Mercury News devoted the front page of this Sunday's "Perspective" section to a combination of local and international issues. (Courtesy of the San Jose (Calif.) Mercury News.)

amusement or lightheartedness into the day's events, although it also can be a humorous jab at a serious subject. No matter what type of editorial it is, the writer should keep it reasonably short. Some experts recommend 1,000 words as the outer limit of length.

Contents of Editorials

Editorials usually have a news peg, an introductory statement explaining the subject, followed by the writer's interpretation and appraisal of the topic. The two parts should be tied together in a unified essay. The facts and the arguments for or against should be organized in a logical pattern to bring the reader around to the writer's point of view. (Courses in argumentation and debate or participation in college debating can give a writer an excellent background for preparing editorials.)

The reader must understand the question being written about before he or she can understand comments on it. The editorial writer often has to assume that the reader knows little or nothing about the event under consideration. The writer must prepare the reader by briefly reporting the news that has prompted the editorial. That part of the editorial is similar to the tie-back in a follow-up story. After setting the scene, the editorial writer then presents an interpretation of the event and recommends a course of action.

No standard form or style, except that of effective newspaper English, is used in writing editorials. The writer is free to use any dramatic device—open letters, mock reviews of documents (as of the city budget), question-and-answer, and even verse—that will effectively enhance the arguments presented. In style, however, the editorial should be as polished as anything in the newspaper. Editorial effectiveness is a blend of sound thinking and good writing, and the two are often indistinguishable. A catchy headline and opening will be helpful for any editorial, no matter what subject is discussed. The concluding paragraph also deserves special care in the writing, for it is the last chance the writer has to impress the reader on the points being made in the editorial.

Jenkin Lloyd Jones, editor and publisher of the Tulsa Tribune, says the editorial writer's trick is "to be both right and positive . . . we must catch their eye, intrigue them and entertain them. We must leave them with the impression that we know whereof we speak and that our suggestions are associated with their own self-interest. . . . A good editorial is not a battle-ax. It is a rapier. It doesn't smash. It thrusts, parries and drives its point home."

Here are several examples of editorials dealing with national and local issues. The first was written by Randy Schultz, associate editor of the editorial page of The Palm Beach Post.

> BUSH PRIORITIES ASKEW
> Strategy overlooks other enemies in drug war
>
> This week President Bush, the nation's principal, went on television at noontime and boldly declared to millions of American schoolchildren that refusing to use illegal drugs would not make any of them a "nerd." The week

earlier, he had gone on television in the evening to tell those children's parents the less colloquial facts of his plan to fight drug abuse.

Even some of the children who listened were skeptical as to how effective the speech would be. The grown-ups should have simply scoffed. Despite his many words, Mr. Bush has offered little more than the well-meaning but simplistic Reagan message: "Just say no." He would like to think that he has mobilized the nation. Sadly, the fighting force he has asembled poses as much of a threat to international drug trafficking as a pee wee football team would to the Miami Dolphins—even this season.

Presidents do set national priorities, but they do so with more than words. When the Soviets fired off Sputnik in 1957, President Dwight D. Eisenhower declared it a national crisis. The space program was begun. The nation's schools were told to train engineers. President John F. Kennedy raised the stakes with the moon program. No amount of money was too much. We were told that space exploration was a national quest.

When Lyndon B. Johnson took office, civil rights was the cause. Not only were laws passed, all government agencies that could help enforce them were drafted. Later, LBJ's obsession was Vietnam, even as the money he printed to fight the war kicked the U.S. into a cycle of inflation that lasted more than a decade. Under President Ronald Reagan's administration, as inflation ebbed, the national motto became Get Yours. Government's job was to stay out of the way.

Now comes Mr. Bush, saying, "All of us agree that the gravest domestic threat facing our nation today is drugs," and, "Our weapons in this strategy are: the law and criminal justice system; our foreign policy; our treatment systems; and our schools and drug prevention programs. So the basic weapons we need are the ones we already have."

Hardly. Has Mr. Bush put any pressure on the nation's banks to halt redlining, the practice of deliberately refusing to make loans in poor areas, those where crack cocaine money talks the loudest because no other voice is heard? Has Mr. Bush mobilized the Justice Department and the Treasury to investigate laundering of drug money in the nation's financial washing machines? Has Mr. Bush proposed any relief for families in which both parents must work, leaving children alone too long?

The president, a sincere but cautious man, hopes mightily that drug abuse can be stopped. So do we. But the problem is far more complex than can be summed up in a message to schoolchildren. It represents the greatest threat to our domestic security since World War II. It won't be beaten by a "nerd" speech.

Mr. Bush said, "Those who judge our strategy only by its price tag simply don't understand the problem." True, drug abuse must be fought with more than money. But numbers do make for interesting comparisons. And they do show that Mr. Bush has his priorities. To struggling families, he offered a $1,000 child care tax credit for children under 4. To the nation's drug fighters, he proposed giving $8 billion. And the savings and loans that were in trouble because of their own bad judgments got $150 billion.

Thanks to Mr. Bush's priorities, the sick thrifts will get better and the drug dealers will stay healthy. Which may be appropriate. Now that they're back in business, those savings and loans will be looking for new deposits.

Dan Coleman, editor of the "Forum" page in the Nashville Banner, campaigned against a re-zoning request that he felt would destroy the integrity of a historic section of the city in this editorial:

Reject this 21-story intrusion

The row of Victorian Era warehouses along Second Avenue is one of Nashville's most valuable architectural jewels. The buildings there are recognized nationally. They comprise the longest remaining row of such structures anywhere outside the East Coast, and the most outstanding collection of 19th century commercial buildings in the Southeast.

Now a developer from Montgomery, Ala., wants to put a 21-story office building on a block where three historical warehouses were destroyed by fire last year. In order to do so the developer, the Algernon Blair Services Corp., needs a variance from the Metro Board of Zoning Appeals.

The variance should not be granted. The Board of Zoning Appeals should firmly reject this plan.

A 21-story building in an area of historic warehouses six to nine stories tall would have a jarring visual impact. It would represent a needless intrusion into a district that has come to represent Nashville's best effort in preservation. For while the individual buildings on Second Avenue are significant, it is the sum of the parts that makes such a noteworthy whole.

That is not to say that no building at all should be constructed in that area. Widely accepted national guidelines for building in preservation areas call for compatibility, or blending, in matters such as height, setback, materials, texture, and pattern of windows and doors. A contemporary development that blended in those ways with the buildings that remain could be an asset.

But a historic district is not the place for a 21-story office building. There are plenty of other sites in Nashville where one could be put without such damaging effects.

This is not the first time the Algernon Blair enterprise has shown its contempt for the city's values. Last year metro officials were hopeful that the company would preserve the facades of the three old buildings—the Goodies, Carriage Building, and Phillips and Buttorff warehouses—that it owned and that had mysteriously burned. But the company, acting with great haste, tore the facades down. It refused to make any gesture that could have preserved what little was left to be incorporated in a new structure.

The Board of Zoning Appeals should take the company's past actions into consideration Thursday when it considers the request for a variance. Then it should answer with a loud "no." And the Metro Council should enact conservation zoning for Second Avenue that would give the city a way to make sure any future development plans blend in with the buildings that are there.

In defense of free speech, The Courier-Journal, Louisville, Ky., made this response to a U.S. Supreme Court action or lack of action:

THE RIGHT TO BEG

An important tenet of civilized life—basic human decency—was obscured Monday when the U.S. Supreme Court refused to review a lower court's ruling that permits a ban on begging in the New York City subways. Regrettably, instead of standing up for the rights of beggars, the Court turned a deaf ear to them.

The issue the court bypassed bore on the fundamental right to free speech in a public forum. The government should not have the right to prohibit people who may be dirty, unattractive and smelly from asking passersby for money if it places no such restrictions upon socially acceptable solicitors—rosy-cheeked Santas or Salvation Army bell ringers.

Unfortunately, those who govern New York's subway don't see it that way. They don't even believe rights to free specch are at stake in their ban. It was unrelated to the panhandlers' spoken message, they said. Rather, the ban was an effort to eliminate conduct "injurious to the transit system and its passengers."

A test of our commitment to constitutional principles is the extent to which we recognize the rights of those in our midst who require us to confront their pain and hunger. The Court failed.

COLUMNS

An opinion column is closely related to an editorial. But the two differ in a number of ways. While a columnist often makes editorial comments on a public issue or subject, the column represents the views or opinions of the writer alone. An editorial, on the other hand, speaks for the newspaper. The writing styles of the two are quite different. Some columnists choose to write in first-person because the column carries a by-line. Editorials are rarely signed and even more rarely written in first-person.

Columns usually reflect the personality of the writer who seeks to develop such a rapport with readers that they will turn to the page on which the column regularly appears to see what the writer has to say. Many columnists, both local and syndicated, have large followings who turn to them before reading anything else in the paper. Columnists who do not maintain significant numbers of readers usually are dropped by newspapers.

Essential Qualities of Columns

How does the column writer cultivate box-office appeal? First and foremost, by having something to say. And then by having the knowledge and resources to qualify as a commentator on a given subject. Trying to write a political column, for example, without a broad knowledge of politics and politicians and the resources needed to obtain information would be pointless.

Next, the columnist must be interesting. The most erudite individual may fail as a columnist if he or she is unable to write in a readable, interesting style. Having something to say and saying it with style and grace are absolute requirements for a successful columnist.

Some columnists fail to attract broad readership because they are too heavy-handed, too pedantic. On the other hand, many influential columnists writing on the national political scene frequently depart from a more serious tone to present a subject in a witty and entertaining manner.

The acid test of a columnist is durability. Successful columnists maintain high quality day after day and week after week. The one who runs out of something to say or falls into the trap of saying everything exactly the same way loses box-office appeal and risks being cancelled.

Types of Columns

There are several broad types of by-lined opinion columns. The largest group, one that includes a wide variety of offshoots, is the public affairs or straight-editorial type, in which the writer comments on current issues and events. This type dominates the editorial pages of most newspapers. Tom

Wicker, James J. Kilpatrick, David Broder and George Will are a few of the dozens of writers whose columns are syndicated in American newspapers. A number of other columnists, however, have made a reputation for their light-hearted approach to some of the more serious topics of the day. Many newspapers now include at least one such columnist on their editorial or "Op-Ed" pages. Perhaps the most successful practitioner of the "art" is Russell Baker of The New York Times.

Here is a lead from a classic Baker column:

> The idea behind the MX missile system is sound enough. Place bomb-bearing missiles on wheels and keep them moving constantly through thousands of miles of desert so enemy bombers will not have a fixed target. To confuse things further, move decoy missiles over the same routes so the enemy cannot distinguish between false missiles and the real thing.
>
> As my strategic thinkers immediately pointed out, however, the MX missile system makes very little sense unless matched by an MX Pentagon system. What is the point, they asked, of installing a highly mobile missile system if this command center, the Pentagon, remains anchored like a moose with four broken legs on the bank of the Potomac River?
>
> This is why we propose building 250 moveable structures so precisely like the Pentagon that no one can tell our fake Pentagons from the real thing and to keep all of them, plus the real Pentagon, in constant motion through the country.

Among the other types of columns prominent in most newspapers are sports, humor, advice and social. There are columns covering almost every topic imaginable from pets to stamp collecting. Most newspapers use their own staff members to write sports and social columns that deal with local personalities and buy columns from syndicates dealing with national sports, entertainment and other public personalities.

Most of the columns dealing with the national scene are used in the section or on the page of the paper most closely related to their subject. However, they can be used anywhere in the newspaper.

EXERCISES

1. Invite the editor of your local newspaper to class for an interview. Discuss with him or her the newspaper's editorial stand on an important local issue. Write a story based on that interview.

2. Interview the news director of a local or area television station about that station's policies on airing editorial comments. Write a story on that interview.

3. Using any newspaper available to you, select three news stories on local issues that you believe worthy of editorial comment. Write an editorial on each of them. Make one editorial interpretative, another an editorial recommending a course of action to solve a particular problem, and the third a humorous comment on a particular event or situation.

4. Select the most serious problem facing students at your college or university and write an editorial offering suggestions for solving that problem.

5. Write a "Letter to the Editor" expressing your views on a particular local or national issue. Submit the letter to a local newspaper for possible publication.

6. Invite a local editorial columnist to class for a group interview to discuss his or her work, with emphasis on how column writing differs from editorial writing. Using the information from the interview, write a feature story on that person.

7. Write a 650-word column on any topic of your choosing. It can be an editorial column or one dealing with any other subject—sports, music, drama, humor—and submit it to the campus newspaper for possible publication.

8. Study the editorial and "Op-Ed" pages in three daily newspapers in your state. Analyze the editorials, cartoons and local editorial columns as well as all syndicated columns and letters to the editor to determine if the content of the pages is balanced or biased. Write a report on your findings.

PART VIII

EDITING THE NEWS

Newspaper stories pass through an editing process before they appear in print. It is essential that a reporter know and completely understand that process. This section deals with what happens to a story after it has been written.

Once a story has been completed and before it appears in print, it is handled by several other individuals. Generally, a story will pass through all or most of the following stages:

1. It may need to be rewritten.
2. It must be copy edited
3. It must have a headline written on it
4. It must be set in type
5. It must be proofread
6. It must be assigned a place in the newspaper by the makeup editor
7. It must be printed
8. The newspaper must be delivered to homes or newsstands or mailed.

Only the first, second, third and sixth steps are the responsibility of the editorial department. They will be discussed in detail in this section.

It is essential that a reporter learn these steps. On smaller newspapers, reporters frequently edit their own stories and write headlines on them. Understanding the copy editing process will help a reporter prepare clean, clear copy that requires minimum corrections. Many reporters serve as copy editors from time to time. Copy editing, even for a limited time, invariably strengthens a reporter's grasp of his or her work as a writer.

CHAPTER 31
REWRITING FAULTY STORIES

The language of newspapers is replete with multipurpose words. One of the more frequently used is "rewrite." It has at least three meanings in most newsrooms, depending on the particular circumstances.

In Chapter 11, "Rewrites and Follow-ups," two of those meanings were discussed: rewrites of stories appearing in competitive newspapers and stories written in the office from facts phoned in by a beat reporter or a reporter at the scene of an event in an effort to meet a deadline.

The third use of the word is in connection with stories that have to be rewritten by the reporter, if time allows, or by someone assigned "rewrite" duties by the city desk because the original has serious flaws in construction, organization or perhaps tone. Occasionally, copy editors may be called on to rewrite a story. However, most newspapers prefer to have the reporter who wrote the original story do the rewrite after consulting with his or her editor.

SERIOUS ERRORS

Few reporters turn out completely errorless copy. That's why newspapers have backup systems—the city or section desk and the copy desk. Many errors in news stories—such as those involving grammar, style, spelling and punctuation —can be corrected by a copy editor if they slip past the city or section editor. However, some errors are so serious they require that the story be rewritten. Whenever the original writer of the story is not available and the story is being pushed because of an upcoming deadline, the story is turned over to another writer who is assigned rewrite duties. Often larger newspapers have a group of women and men assigned full-time to rewrite. They handle all three kinds of rewrites. Frequently they are among the newspaper's most experienced staff members and write with skill, grace and speed.

What are those "serious" errors that would require a story to be completely rewritten?

The Main Feature Might Not Be Stressed in the Lead.   The choice of the news hook of any story generally is a matter of opinion. Generally, the most important point of the story is obvious. The reporter's sense of news values is usually an excellent guide in selecting the facts to feature in the lead when there are several to choose from. However, reporters sometimes overlook what is undoubtedly the oustanding feature and may bury it deep in the story. For example, suppose a reporter wrote a lead about a fire in a nursing home, using two or three paragraphs to describe the scene and mentioning for the first time in the fourth or fifth paragraph that 11 persons died in the fire. The story, or at least the lead, probably would be rewritten at most newspapers to emphasize the 11 deaths in the opening paragraph, if not the opening sentence.

A rewrite might also be called for if the story doesn't get to the point quickly enough. Here is an example of that type:

> AIKEN, S.C.—In a milestone on the road to cleaning up the residue of 40 years of atomic bomb making, the Department of Energy dedicated a $1.3 billion plant today to deal with its most hazardous wastes: millions of gallons of highly radioactive sludges and liquids in decaying steel tanks.
>
> The department said the plant, the largest of its kind in the nation, would be treated for two years with non-radioactive wastes and would begin operating in 1992.
>
> More than half the radioactivity from the nation's military waste is held in 51 underground tanks at the Savannah River Site here, each with 750,000 to 1.3 million gallons of waste. The wastes will be dangerously radioactive for thousands of years, but the tanks were never intended for long-term storage, and some have leaked. Throughout the cold war, production took priority over finding a way to handle the wastes.
>
> "All we've done with waste for 40 years is store it," said W. Henson Moore, Deputy Secretary of Energy, in an interview. "Thank God, we haven't had any major accidents." Stabilizing the wastes, in glass and steel canisters or in concrete, will be "a heck of a lot safer," he said.
>
> The wastes produce explosive chemicals, and for years outside experts have warned that radiation could be spread by an explosion or earthquake. The new plant, the Defense Waste Processing Facility, will not reduce the amount of radioactivity and will increase, not decrease, the waste's volume. But it will leave the most radioactive material encased in logs of strong glass, wrapped in steel, sharply reducing the chance of leaks into streams or underground supplies.
>
> "We don't understand the chemistry of the tanks," Mr. Moore said. "We understand the chemistry and the physics of the glass logs."

The remainder of the story described the process of encasing the radioactive wastes in steel-wrapped glass logs, the environmental impact of radioactive waste and the dispute over this new process, which was pioneered by the French.

The basic flaw in this story is that the reader has to wade through several hundred words before becoming aware of what the milestone on the road to cleaning up the residue of 40 years of atomic bomb-making actually is—storing the waste in glass logs encased in steel. The milestone certainly should have been spelled out in the second paragraph, if not the first. But the writer kept the reader in the dark for four or five paragraphs.

The Story Might Be Poorly Organized.   In some stories the main feature may be handled properly in the lead, but the body of the story may be jumbled and confusing. Or the reporter might not support the lead with information until five or six paragraphs into the story. In other stories, it may be that the reporter jumps too quickly into a chronological account of the event, forgetting to summarize all features before relating details. Sometimes only a few paragraphs need to be changed, and this might be done by an editor or the copy desk by simply rearranging the paragraphs on the video-display-terminal (VDT) screen. But other times a completely new and rewritten version of the story might be needed.

The Story Might Be the Wrong Type.   Deciding just how to handle a story properly can present a problem for some reporters. Obviously, some stories should be handled as a feature, but the reporter—especially one not accustomed to writing features—will ignore that approach and produce a lackluster hard-news story. If the lead is what journalist/author Tom Wolfe calls "said-yesterday-that" stories—"Police Chief John Bailey said yesterday that . . ."—

At other times, the reporter may try to write a feature about an event that should be handled as straight news. The results often appear strained, and that may be obvious to the reader. The switch from straight news to feature or feature to straight news usually requires a complete rewriting of the story. Generally, a major rewrite can be avoided if the reporter discusses the story with the editor before starting to write it.

Rewriting should not be done capriciously, and the rewritten version of the story should always be better than the original. If the reporter cannot handle the rewrite, the person assigned to do it should first read the story carefully to get a clear picture of what the story is about and how it is organized. During the rewriting process, the reporter should be consulted to make certain the new version is an accurate representation of what took place. Special care must be taken during the rewriting process not to make errors of fact. The person doing the rewriting should never assume anything and never guess. When in doubt, questions should be asked and facts checked. If a fact cannot be verified, it should not be used.

Persons assigned to rewrite and copy editors often are assigned to combine several stories into a single one. Although some try to blend the stories by moving paragraphs around, the most effective way to handle this type of assignment is simply to rewrite the facts from the stories into a single new one. Trying to blend two or more stories into one can lead to awkward transitions, missing facts or incomplete names.

EXERCISES

1. Interview the city editor of your local daily newspaper about the paper's method of handling rewrites. Write a short report based on your interview. In your report, include several examples of stories that had been rewritten and explain why the changes were made.

2. Read the following short story carefully. Make a list of any flaws you find in how the story is written. If you believe the story is acceptable, explain why:

> Blue Ash Police are hoping for a closer look at a bank robber than the fuzzy pictures caught by the surveillance camera.
>
> The suspect was snapped in action when he walked into People's Savings Association on Hunt Road in Blue Ash about 2:32 p.m., Nov. 13 and walked out with cash that didn't belong to him.
>
> The man, described as about 40 years old, entered the S&L alone and handed a teller a note. The message was, "This is a hold up," said Blue Ash police Sgt. Robert Lilley. "It also said, 'I have a gun. Don't use a dye pack,' " Lilley said.
>
> A dye pack is made up to look like a bundle of money but triggered to spray brightly colored bye on anyone holding it.
>
> The teller, one of two on duty, gave the man money. Lilley would not say how much.
>
> The robber did not threaten the tellers.
>
> The man was described as white, 6 feet tall and stocky. He had brown, over-the-collar length hair and was wearing glasses with thick lenses.
>
> He wore a green, thigh-length Army-style fatigue jacket and a dark baseball-type had with the letters "BT" in script.
>
> Police are asking anybody who can identify the suspect to call Blue Ash police at 745-8555

3. Using any newspapers available to you, clip at least four examples of short straight-news stories that could be made more lively if given a feature treatment. Rewrite the stories as features, and hand in both the clipping and your version of the story.

4. Using the following information, write a short feature story:

> Thirteen Polk County elementary schools will take part in a two-year study on the effect of sugarless gum on teeth.
>
> Approximately 4,000 students will take part in the study which begins next week. They will be required to chew gum for 10 minutes each day in school, as well as at home.
>
> For participating, students will receive toothbrushes and annual dental checkups at no cost to parents.
>
> Study being directed by Dr. Anthony J. Conti, a professor of dentistry at the State University Medical and Dental School.
>
> University will donate $325,000 to the schools and the school district's scholarship fund for participating, Conti said.
>
> Conti said the students are good test subjects because drinking water in this part of the state is not fluorinated and fluorides also prevent cavities.
>
> He said research shows that sugarless gum prevents tooth decay in children by reducing plaque. His study will compare two sugar substitutes used in gum, sorbitol and xylitol.
>
> "We're certainly not going to have to fight to get the kids to do this," Stephen White, principal of Hillcrest Elementary School, said.
>
> Teachers, who generally force students to spit out their chewing gum, agreed to the study after Dr. Conti presented his proposal to them at a recent meeting.

5. Rewrite the following feature lead into a hard-news lead:

> BIRMINGHAM, Ala.—George Hodges once gave his friend, multimillionaire Ralph Waldo Besson, a pair of corduroys. After Besson told him how much he enjoyed them, Hodges gave him another pair.
>
> But, as Hodges now recalls, "He would not accept them because he already had one pair, and he said that was enough."
>
> Besson, who made his money in insurance, practiced frugality all his life and spent sparingly.
>
> "Two or three years ago, he gave his yard man about $10 and sent him to buy groceries, and the man came back with three or four dollars in change," said Thomas Corts, president of Stamford University in Birmingham. "He asked the man for the rest of the change and he said that was all there was. 'Well, good gracious, you must have bought enough groceries to last a month.'"
>
> Besson died Oct. 15 at age 89 and left more than $80 million to schools and his church.
>
> The bulk goes to Stamford University, to which he had already given $14.4 million over the years, and to Asbury Theological Seminary in Wilmore, Ky.
>
> Each will get $38.8 million.

6. Rewrite the following stories to make them more lively and interesting:

> **a.**   Federal officials in El Paso last week showed off the $2 million the government confiscated nine months ago after concluding that its owner, Salvadore Reale, had not reported his gambling winnings to the IRS.
>
> Reale, now serving a 10-year federal sentence for labor racketeering, was carrying $3.79 million and the equivalent of $98,000 in Swiss francs when he was stopped at a border checkpoint Feb. 6.
>
> "He claims he had gambled in several states in the United States . . . over a period of 25 years," said U.S. Attorney Ron Ederer.
>
> The money, Ederer said, is the "fruits of his labor. Of course, he forgot to take care of some of the IRS procedures that applied."
>
> Still, Reale gets to keep about $1.7 million of his earnings.
>
> And the Swiss francs.
>
> **b.**   Ria Katz is known as the Cat Lady of Reno.
>
> The 62-year-old casino hostess said after her husband died 10 years ago she went to work as a volunteer at the city's animal-control office. Unable to bear the thought of cats—particularly kittens—being euthanized, she began taking some home.
>
> In addition to the hundreds she has granted reprieves over the years, and eventually found new homes for, dozens more have been temporary house guests whose owners are hospitalized, in a local shelter for abused woman or in prison.
>
> How many does she have in residence now?
>
> Well some are sprawled on her carpet. Others perch on the shredded remains of her stereo speakers and a few lounge on the couch.
>
> But if you really want to see some cats, Rita says, "just watch this."
>
> As her electric opener whirs through a can of Friskies at least 40 cats bound into the kitchen—white ones, black ones, orange ones, striped ones, big ones, little ones—leaping, squirming and jostling for space on the counter top, dishwasher and refrigerator.
>
> And that's why she's called the Cat Lady of Reno.

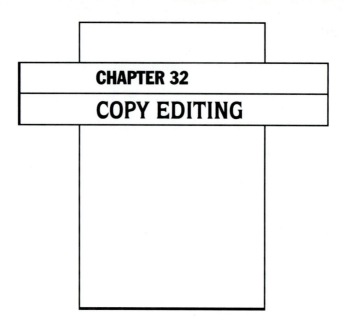

CHAPTER 32

COPY EDITING

In one of his periodic fulminations about the verbal sins of newspaper writers and editors, James J. Kilpatrick, syndicated columnist and author of The Writer's Art, demanded to know: "Doesn't Anyone Edit Copy Anymore?" To prove his point, he proceeded to cite dozens of examples of what he called "slovenly writing" that he had collected in a four-month period from large and small newspapers: "peak" for "peek"; "foreward" for "forward"; "whose" for "who's"; "your" for "you're"; "its" for "it's"; "bazaar" for "bizarre"; "peels for peals" and others.

"In today's hushed and antiseptic newsrooms, the path from the video display terminal seems to run straight to the waiting press. . . . My gut feeling is that on too many papers the indispensable function of a venerable copy editor has been dispensed with," Kilpatrick wrote in the Washington Journalism Review.

Kilpatrick's concern about the quality of writing and editing in American newspapers has been echoed by dozens of others. And they reinforce the vital role of the copy editor. Comparatively few stories, when they have been completed by the reporter, are perfect. Most writers need some careful checking and expert editing. After all, good editing helps make good writing.

The copy editor's main function is to read the story carefully, eliminate mistakes, improve the language and write the headline. As the last person to check the story before it is set in type, the copy editor must be the watchdog for the newspaper and something of a guardian for the reporter, although reporters often do not see it that way. Often reporters accuse copy editors of butchering stories and destroying creativity, while copy editors believe reporters need to be reminded that they do not have a license to kill the English language. Despite their differences, reporters and copy editors have one thing in common: the readers of their newspaper.

Copy editing is one of the most important and painstaking jobs on a newspaper because the number of possible errors in a news story is great. Many of the most common ones that need to be corrected are a result of carelessness on the part of the reporter. Other errors are far more complicated. That is why a copy editor must have a commitment to accuracy, a knowledge of and respect for the English language; the ability to grasp not only what a story says, but also what it fails to say; and enough sense to know the difference between good, tight, creative editing and butchering.

The copy editor

1. *Checks the story for accuracy.* A careful and well-informed reader of the newspaper, the copy editor should know the background of most news events or where background information can be found. Doubtful statements should be checked automatically. In addition to familiarity with the city—its streets, buildings, leading citizens and officials—such standard references as the city directory, dictionary, atlas, encyclopedia, clippings and other information should be readily available. Personal knowledge and reference material help the copy editor catch most errors unless the error has to do with a fact that can be verified only on the scene or at the source of the story.
2. *Makes corrections of grammar.* Haste and carelessness on the part of the writer often result in grammatical errors. The copy editor makes certain that standards of good English are observed in all newspaper stories.
3. *Eliminates verbosity in newspaper copy.* Newspaper writing style should be lean and crisp. The copy editor, by killing one word or even a complete paragraph, can often make a dull, wooden story come alive.
4. *Eliminates libelous statements.* Potentially libelous statements should be toned down or eliminated. "When in doubt, leave it out" is an excellent guideline if a statement in a story could be interpreted as libelous. Of course, no copy editor can catch libelous statements resulting from erroneous reporting.
5. *Simplifies the story.* All confusing or ambiguous statements and all words that will not be understood by the layperson are eliminated. Technical terms or professional jargon is replaced or defined.
6. *Eliminates editorialized matter in news stories.* Editorial opinion should not be included in news stories. If a story is by-lined, however, a certain amount of editorial expression is sometimes permitted when the writer is relating a first-hand account.
7. *Checks all stories for adequacy.* If the reporter evidently has omitted certain essential facts, the copy editor often returns the story to the city desk. The story might be given back to the reporter or to a person on the rewrite desk for completion.
8. *Sometimes trims or shortens a story.* If the story is longer than the news editor desires, the copy editor might be instructed to cut it down to a certain length by eliminating the least essential paragraphs.

9. *Makes the story conform to the newspaper's style.* Each newspaper has certain rules covering optional forms of punctuation, abbreviation, capitalization and spelling, and the copy editor sees that every story observes those rules.

10. *Attempts to polish and improve the story.* Generally, copy editors should not completely rewrite a reporter's story unless it is hopeless. However, they should try to transform every story into a smooth and lively account by inserting or deleting certain words and phrases or by rearranging paragraphs and sentences.

11. *Writes identifying labels and instructional notes.* For each story, certain codes, labels and instructions must be provided to expedite processing through the computer in the mechanical department. They include identifying labels for each story, codes for typesetting and instructions for type face and size of the headlines to be used on the story. Some newspapers include the section and page number where the story will appear. Each paper, however, has its own set of codes and instructions. While they might be similar in a number of ways, each has its own particular way of handling stories sent from the copy editor to the composing room.

At most newspapers, the copy editors work at video-display terminals (VDTs) grouped in one section of the newsroom, still referred to as the "copy desk." Copy editors generally handle all stories for the paper. However, at larger newspapers some special sections such as "Sports" and "Lifestyles" may have their own copy desks. Some newspapers have been experimenting with assigning copy editors to other sections of the paper as well. In those cases, the copy editor would work at a VDT next to the section editor. When the editing and headline process has been complete, the copy editor sends the story from that section directly to the composing room, where it is set in type.

ELECTRONIC EDITING

Computers dominate the newsrooms of American newspapers. Reporters write their stories on VDTs and store them in the computer's memory bank. City editors and section editors use VDTs to call the story up from storage for review and preliminary editing. Copy editors use them for the final editing and headline writing.

The so-called front-end system will vary from newspaper to newspaper, depending on the particular equipment purchased. However, most computers are quite similar and once a reporter or copy editor has learned one system, using a different one requires very little adjustment.

The VDT is considered a blessing by some copy editors. Others still are not sure. There is no question that a VDT is more flexible than a typewriter. A copy editor can perform the following functions on a VDT:

1. Delete characters, words, lines and paragraphs as well as move entire blocks of copy within a single story
2. Delete the entire story
3. Add new text at any location in the story being displayed on the VDT screen
4. Instruct the computerized typesetting machine how wide to set the copy and what type size and typeface to use for a particular story
5. Write the headline for the story.

A wide range of electronic editing systems are available, and they are being refined and made more sophisticated every year. The functions that can be performed depend entirely on how sophisticated the equipment is. Some, for example, have split-screen capabilities that allow two stories to be shown at the same time should a copy editor want to compare or possibly combine the stories.

It is important to remember that the VDT is the central device for the system. The codes a reporter and copy editor must learn will vary from newspaper to newspaper, and the keyboard on the VDT may vary slightly. However, all systems are essentially the same.

The early 1990s also saw the introduction of the personal computer (PC) in the newsroom. Graphic artists at many papers used them for a number of years before they began being used as a supplement to the front-end system. In fact, in some places they have supplanted the front-end system. For example, The Miami Herald added PCs to an existing front-end system. The Houston Chronicle, the Chicago Tribune and many smaller papers installed complete systems based on PC technology.

USA TODAY is a leader in the industry in the use of personal computers. They operate in the editorial art department, the photo department, the library and the sports department to produce some of the agate sports results listings. Plans call for them to be used for reporters to tap into outside data bases and for developing their own data bases.

A number of newspapers have named "systems editors" whose responsibility is to know everything there is to know about the particular computer equipment used in the newsroom and other editorial departments. The systems editor serves as a troubleshooter for the editorial staff when glitches develop in the computer system.

Wire News

Most copy coming into newspaper offices from wire services like The Associated Press (AP) and United Press International (UPI) now is fed directly into the newspaper's computer, eliminating the need for clattering teletype machines and reams of paper copy. Copy editors retrieve the wire stories from the computer on their VDTs and complete the editing and headline writing process before sending the story to the composing room to be set in type.

Generally speaking, newspapers follow the style set in the AP Stylebook, so wire stories may not require extensive editing to make them conform to the style

```
(DBO:) DESK1: HOSTAGE STORIES;6   11-DEC-90  09:05:10                  PAGE: 1


  1    <7927 CHARS, 3089 POINTS, 561.6 AGATE, 42.9 INCHES, 282 LINES>
  2
  3    *b48*[p47.4v49.4][c41]/]
  4    Ex-hostages relate/]
  5    frightful ordeals/]
  6    /]
  7    /]
  8    *m24*[c11.7]Man, dog hid/]
  9    in air duct/]
 10    for 23 days/]
 11    /]
 12    /]
 13    *9*[c11.7]/]
 14    *bl*By Pat Leisener@Associated Press@/mTAMPA, Fla. .. A Florida
 15    man trapped in Kuwait by Iraqi
 16    invaders hid for 23 days with his
 17    dog in a tiny crawl space, eating
 18    only uncooked spaghetti. </P>
 19    A New Mexico man defended
 20    his hide-out with a machete, kil<L-
 21    >ing an intruder. </P>
 22    A freed Baltimore man told of
 23    watching a Kuwaiti man gunned
 24    down by a platoon of Iraqi sol<D-
 25    >diers. </P>
 26    The family of a Missouri man
 27    who endured four months in hid<L-
 28    >ing plans to burn his passport so
 29    he can't leave the United States
 30    again. </P>
 31    Tales of captivity ranged from
 32    those who cringed inside dark<L-
 33    ened apartments in terror to a
 34    hostage held in Kuwaiti royal
 35    palace who ate off fine china and
 36    drank from gold-rimmed crystal
 37    goblets. </P>
 38    Tom Kreuzman of Holiday,
 39    Fla., hid with his Yorkshire ter<L-
 40    >rier, Chu Chu, in an apartment
 41    air-conditioning duct about 8 feet ...
```

FIGURE 32–1 An Associated Press story after it was edited and a headline was written for it by a copy editor at the Nashville Banner. All the codes, symbols and typesetting instructions were entered on the VDT by the copy editor.

in such matters as spelling, grammar, punctuation, use of titles and the like. However, a number of newspapers have their own style, which may differ from AP style. In such cases, the copy editor follows the newspaper's style.

Copy editors often have to shorten wire copy, rewrite stories to emphasize a local angle, or combine several wire stories into one. Here is an example from the Detroit Free Press Editing Workbook of how that newspaper's copy desk handled the editing of a wire story:

The Version Before Editing

VATICAN CITY (AP)—Vatican and Italian security officials cleared half of St. Peter's Square of pilgrims and tourists Saturday to let a motorcade for First Lady Nancy Reagan pass through an arch preceding her 30-minute audience with Pope John Paul II.

After her meeting with the pontiff, Mrs. Reagan toured the Sistine and Pauline chapels for 20 minutes. She flew back to Bonn at 3:15 p.m. from Rome's Cimpino military airport to rejoin President Reagan in his state visit to West Germany.

Mrs. Reagan discussed her anti-drug campaign with the 64-year-old pontiff, who opened the meeting by handing Mrs. Reagan a three-page speech in English in which he deplored the "tragic and debilitating" effects of drug abuse and lauded her "participation in the fight against drug abuse and in the rehabilitation of those whose lives have been affected by this evil."

The Edited Version That Appeared in the Newspaper

VATICAN CITY (AP)—First lady Nancy Reagan brought her anti-drug campaign to the Vatican Saturday in a 30-minute audience with Pope John Paul II, who deplored the "tragic and debilitating" effects of drug abuse.

After her meeting with the pope, Mrs. Reagan flew back to Bonn to rejoin President Reagan in his state visit to West Germany.

The Vatican and Italian security officials cleared half of St. Peter's Square of pilgrims and tourists to let Mrs. Reagan's motorcade pass through an arch.

At the start of the meeting, the 64-year-old pontiff handed Mrs. Reagan a three-page speech in English in which he lauded her "participation in the fight against drug abuse and in the rehabilitation of those whose lives have been affected by this social evil."

It should be noted that some reporters do use AP hard copy, and a number of AP features are mailed to newspapers. This material generally is entered into the computer by a local staff member and edited on the VDT screen like other wire copy.

A few newspapers and some special publications, newsletters and journals are still edited by pencil rather than on a VDT screen. For the convenience of persons who edit by pencil, a set of standard copy editing symbols appears in the Appendix.

EXERCISES

1. Invite the chief of the copy desk of your local daily newspaper to class to discuss the role the copy editor plays in producing the paper. Write a story based on that discussion.

2. The following leads are based on real news events, but each has one or more problems that can be corrected by careful editing and revision. Revise each to emphasize the news and improve clarity.

   a. WASHINGTON—Soda bottles, motor oil, hotel rooms, insurance policies and hundreds of other goods and services are being taxed by states in an effort to raise badly needed cash, a study released to day by the National Association of Governors shows.

   All states raised taxes this year, with New Jersey and New York ranking first and second in the size of the hike. New Jersey increased its taxes by $2.6 billion while New York added $1.67 billion to its coffers.

The study by the National Association of Governors said no other state approached New York for the variety of tax code changes. Much of New Jersey's tax increases came through raising income and sales tax rates while New York taxed soda bottles, motor oil, hotel rooms, and insurance policies, the study said.

The survey also found New York will be one of only four states to end the year with a negative cash balance.

b. NASHVILLE—On Thursday, Gov. McWherter said he supported a state income tax but said political necessity jay lead to another route for raising taxes for education this coming year.

"We've got to get people to understand the need to lower a tax on sales they accept and raise on income that they don't accept," the governor said. "We've got to tell that story."

The governor said his first and foremost priority remains the launching of an education reform movement and "we'll give it our best shot" in the next legislative session.

He said he had made no decision on how to seek first-year funding of the educational reform package, pegged at $344 million by the State Board of Education.

That is partly because he recognizes that a substantial number of legislators—though not a majority—are absolutely opposed to voting for an income tax, the governor said.

Noting that some legislators have called for him to "get in front of the parade," McWherter said, "I'm willing to do that. I just can't find the parade."

c. WASHINGTON—People who have too much money to qualify for welfare food stamps or other housing assistance qualified as homeless under a federal program intended for the poor, The Fort Worth Star Telegraph reported Sunday.

The program was designed to provide temporary shelter to the nation's homeless poor and has helped some of them, but has also resulted in abuses, the paper said.

Under the program, the Department of Housing and Urban Development makes available up to 10 percent of 50,000 foreclosed houses that the government owns nationwide. HUD-approved sponsors lease the housed for ont year to those who qualify for assistance. The sponsors are given additional two-year options to buy the houses at a price 10 percent below market value.

A homeless person is defined by HUD as virtually anyone without a permanent home, regardless of income. And there is no limit on size and value of homes covered by the program, the paper said.

It gave these examples of abuses:

—Roy Gray, a businessman and part-time street minister from Keller, rents a $92,500 home in the Dallas suburb of Rowlett for $1 a year.

—The net worth of Bill Robinson's nonprofit company will soon exceed $1 million, but the businessman and Baptist minister has moved into a two-story house in Arlington appraised at $92,500.

—Robert Holton, a construction contractor, pays $348 in monthly rent for a four-bedroom, $85,500 house that he "thought would be adequate to house our furniture."

3. Copy edit the following stories using the standard symbols in the Appendix. Note: To avoid mutilating the text, make a copy of the stories on a copying machine for class use.

a. Jones

Drugs

All County Sheriff's department jailers were searched Thursday night when they arrived at work after authorities received a tip that one of them would smuggle drugs into the jail.

No drugs, however, were found, Sheriff's spokesman Dan Hicks says.

"Everyone who cam eon duty was searched," Hicks said. "We didn't find nothing."

This is not the first time the Sheriff's Office has received a tip that drugs would be smuggled in to inmates by a jailer, Sheriff Tom Hutchinson said.

b. Marks
Reporter
CORPUS CHRISTI, Texas (AP)—A Texas judge Thursday ordered a newspaper reporter jailed because she refused to reveal all that she and a murder defendant discussed during interviews.

Prosecutors want to enter as trial evidence articles written last month by Libby Aceryt, 26, about Jermarr Arnold, accused in the 1983 slaying of a jewelry store clerk. But the reporter and her paper—The Corpus Christi Caller-Times—maintain that anything unpublished is protected under the First Amendment.

State District Judge Eric Brown held Aceryt in contempt and said she'll be jailed until she answers questions about the interviews. Jorge Rangel, the newspaper's lawyer, said he planned to appeal to the Texas Court of Criminal Appeals.

c. David
Bull
A stray Pit Bull terrier that had been chased through a neighborhood for 2 days was gunned down when it lunged at a lawman who had come to the rescue of an animal control officer.

Now local law enforcement authorities want to know who owned the pit bull and why it was allowed to run free in the East State Street area.

Officer Alvin Baird responded to a call form animal control officer Tommy Busey who had tried to catch the dog with a pole and noose. When the dog lunged at Baird, he killed it with a shotgun blast.

The dog had a red collar but no identification and police Friday were still trying to find out who owned it.

4. Retype the following sentences as they appear in the text and then edit them to conform to AP style.

a. Registration for all Freshmen class members begins at nine o'clock this morning in reese auditorium.

b. He grew up in Bay City, michigan, before moving to California.

c. Spring vacation will begin at Noon on Wed., March 13th.

d. He was a member of the Y.M.C.A. board of directors and a former republican state senator for Bean Blossom

e. Bleacher tickets to the Madonna concert at Legion field will cost $25.00 in advance and $32.50 at the door.

f. He has lived in the US for 5 years and became a US citizen last month.

g. She has an eleven year old daughter and a son who attends state University of New York at Buffalo, New York.

h. More than 18% of all Sophomores flunk American lit courses, dean Albert Sidney Johnson said.

i. 7 members of the local chapter of Hells' Angels motorcycle club were arrest for loitering about 9:30 pm last night in front of Googie's salon on Cumberland Ave.

j. Fire destroyed a $350,000 home at 1421 Whitower Avenue at dawn today, fire chief Leonard Basler said.

CHAPTER 33
PROOFREADING

Error-free newspapers simply do not exist, unfortunately. Despite the concentrated efforts of writers, editors and proofreaders, errors still appear in every issue of every newspaper.

Critics, both inside and outside the newspaper profession, insist that the advent of computerization has resulted in the elimination of "backshop" proofreaders who generally make the final check on a story after it has been set in type and just before the pages are made up. There is some evidence that the critics may be right. At a large daily in the South, section editors do the final checking for errors, not a proofreader working in the composing room. Most smaller dailies and weeklies have always had reporters proofread their own stories as well as those written by others.

The object of proofreading is to eliminate any errors made during the editing and typesetting process. Although proofreading and copy editing are similar in that their chief purpose is to catch errors, the responsibility of the proofreader is to see that the proof follows the original copy—that no words, sentences or paragraphs are jumbled or omitted—and that there are no typographical errors. However, proofreaders generally correct misspelled words, incorrect English and other blunders that might have slipped past reporters and copy editors.

USING PROOFREADING SYMBOLS

Many proofreading symbols are similar to copy editing symbols, but there is an important difference in their use. The copy editor uses symbols within the body of the story, making changes at the point in the text at which the error occurs. The proofreader places all of the proofreading symbols in the margin of the proofs, indicating at which point changes are needed in the story. This speeds the process of correcting errors after the story is in type. The person correcting the mistakes need only scan the margins, not read the entire story word for word.

Two methods are used by proofreaders to indicate that corrections are needed:

1. The correction is noted in the margin directly to the right or left of the line in which the error appears, with an additional symbol within the line pointing out the error. The correction should appear in the margin closest to the error.

```
A 33-year-old Brooklyn woman was accused of killing her          #
husband. . . .
```

If the line contains several errors, the correction symbols are placed in sequence and are separated by slanting lines.

```
A 33-year-old Brooklyn Woman was accused of killing her          lc /tr
husband. . . .
```

2. The correction is noted in the margin with the correct symbol marking the point of error.

```
A 33-year-old Brooklyn woman was accused of killing her          tr
husband. . . .
```

Corrections requiring words and short phrases usually can be handled in the margin by either of the two methods just illustrated. However, if a complete line of copy has been omitted or jumbled, the proofreader may mark "See copy" in the margin and return the original copy with the corrected proof. The proofreader must indicate exactly where the words and phrases are to be changed or added. For example:

```
A 33-year-old Brooklyn woman was accused of/her husband. . . .   killing
```

If the error is only a single letter, the correction can be made this way:

```
A 33-year-old Brooklyn woman was accused of killing /er          h
husband. . . .
```

As an additional duty, the proofreader must check the method of dividing words between lines and correct the words that are not divided between syllables according to accepted usage. A dictionary is usually the best guide for this purpose. Split-word corrections are made as follows:

```
    suit filed in State Sup-
  reme Court in Manhattan.
```

The more common proofreaders' symbols are shown in the accompanying chart.

EXERCISES

1. Using any newspaper available to you, make a collection of errors you find in stories, headlines and photo captions that slipped past the proofreader. Clip and paste them on sheets of paper and, using standard proofreading symbols, make the necessary corrections.

2. Here are several newspaper stories as written by reporters, and below each is a galley proof of that story. Proofread each galley proof. To avoid defacing the text, make a copy of the galley proof and use it to complete the exercise.

   a. Women are twice as likely as men to suffer depression, says a study sponsored by the American Psychological Association.

       Depression hits 1 of every 4 women vs. 1 in 8 men. Other findings: biological factors (other than infertility) are not significant cause of depression in women. Abuse early in life, unhappy marriages and poverty are important factors.

       Depression goes untreated in most women or is misdiagnosed 30% to 50% of the time, the study says.

   > Women are twice as likely as men to suffer depression, says a study sponsored by the american Psychological Association.
   >
   >   Depression hits one of every 4 women vs. 1 in 8 men. Other findings: biological factors (ohter than infertility) are not significant cause of depresion in women. Abuse early in life, unhappy marriages and poverty are important factors.
   >
   >   Depression goes untreated in most women or is misdiagnosed 30 percent to 50 percent of the stime, the study says.

   b. The State Supreme Court today upheld a 1951 law making it a misdemeanor for groups such as the Ku Klux Klan to wear masks in public.

       The 6-1 decision oveturns a lower court judge's ruling to drop charges against Klan member Shade Miller Jr. The high court ruled that the law prevents violence and intimidation by mask-wearers, and does not violate free speech.

   > The State Suprmem Court today upheld a 1951 law making it a misdemeanor for

Symbol	Definition	Example of Use
Rom ++++	Use Roman type	cause it amounts to a deprivation of natural liberty without any
Ital —	Use italics	compensating benefits to the public at large.
(:)	Insert colon	James C. Carter, in his "Origin and Function of Law," says,
]or[	Move to right or left, as indicated	"It is the function] of government to define the limits or sphere
↑or[	Move down or up, as indicated	in which the individual may act as a member of
eq# ∨∨	Equalize spacing	the social state, without at the same time encroach-ing upon' the' freedom of others.
∨∨	Insert quotation marks	It follows, there-fore, that to live under
spell out O	Spell out circled word	civil (gov) is to surrender a portion of our natural
∨'	Insert apostrophe	liberty for the public good, in order that that which remains to us may be the better safeguarded
⌣	Push down slug that prints	by the strong arm of the law. But liberty may be destroyed by law. The Romans furnish a con-crete example, The pre-vailing ethos or national spirit of the Romans
!/	Insert exclamation mark	
ℓ.f. ⌢⌢⌢	Use boldface type	was law. Did not law regulate everything, A citizen could not fix a
?/	Insert question mark	price upon his own goods. It was the oppression of
=/	Insert hyphen	law which cheap-ened the desire for life.

Symbol	Definition	Example of Use
X	A defective letter	Civil liberty is freedom from restraint by any law, save that which
ϑ	Delete material	conduces in a greater or less degree to the gen-eral welfare.
ϑ	Letter is inverted	To do what I will is natural liberty. To do what I will, consistently
#	Insert space	with equal rights of others, is civil liberty,
w.f.	Wrong font	the only liberty possible in a state of civilized society.
stet...	Do not make change. Let copy stand as it is.	If I wish to act, in every instance, in ac-cordance with my own un-restrained will, I am made to reflect that all
(;)	Insert semicolon	others may do the same, in which case I shall meet with so many checks and obstructions to my
⌢	Close up space	own will my that liberty and happiness will be far
tr. ⌣	Transpose	less than if I, with the rest of the community
∧	Insert comma	were subject to the re-straints of reasonable
⊙	Insert period	laws applying to all,
¶	New paragraph	So it is, that proper and adequate laws are essen-tial to the well-being and good order of
cap ≡	Capital letter	civil society. but legal restraint, for no other
ℓ.c. /	Lowercase letter	Reason than mere re-straint, is certainly unphilosophical, and in-herently wrong, be-

groups such as the Ku Klux Klan to wear masks in public.

The 6-1 decision overturns a lower cour judge's ruling to drop charges against kaln member Shade Miller, Jr. The high court ruled that the law prevents violence and intimidation by mask-wearers, and does not violat free speech.

c. A commuter plane carrying eight passengers landed safely yesterday after it apparently was hit by lightning on a flight from Springfield to Municipal Airport here, airport officials said.

No one aboard the Midwest Express turboprop plane was injured. However, the plane sustained slight damage to one of its propellers, Dennis Rosenbrough, a spokesman for Municipal Airport, said.

The pilot and co-pilot landed the craft without incident about 9:30 a.m., and taxied it to the gate without assistance.

Midwest operates three daily flights between Springfield and Municipal Airport, Rosenbrough said.

Allan Miller, a public relations executive coming here for a professional meeting, said "the whole thing was a bit frightening."

A commuter plane carrying 8 passengers landed safely yesterday after it apparenlty was hit by lightning on a flight from Springfield to Municipal Airport here, airport officials said.

No one aboard the Midwest Express turboprop plane was injured. However, the plane sustained slight damage to one of its propellers, Dennis Rosenbrough, a spokesman for Municipal airport, said.

The pilot and co-pilot landed the craft without incident about 9:30 a.m., and taxied it to the gate without assistance.

Midwest operates three daily flights between Springfield and Municipal Airport, Rosenbrough said.

Allen Miller, a public relations executive coming her for a professional meeting, said "the whole thing was a bit frightning."

d. A motorist was killed and two others suffered minor injuries when a tractor-trailer truck and a car collided on the Golden State Freeway in Sun Valley Friday night, the Highway Patrol reported.

The truck landed on top of the car in the northbound lane near Hollywood Way shortly after 8 p.m., Trooper Dean Malsono said.

A Corvette "lost control and spun out in front of the semi-tractor-trailer carrying a load of bricks," Malsono said.

The Corvette hit the center divider and caught fire, then the truck hit the divider and ran up over the car. The driver of the Corvette was killed, but his passenger and the driver of the truck suffered only minor injuries.

The name of the Corvette driver has not been released, pending notification of next of kin. The passenger, Ron Wright, 23, of Newport, and the truck driver, Jose Martines, 51, were treated at Sun Valley Memorial Hospital and released.

A motorists was killed and two others suffered minor injuries when a tractor-trailer truck and a car collided on the Golden State Freeway in Sun Valley Friday night, the Highway Patrol reported.

The truck landed on top of the car in the northbound lane hear hollywood way shortly after 8 p.m., Trooper Dean Malsono said.

A Corvette "lost control and spun out in fron of the semitractor trailer carrying a load of bricks, Malsano said.

The Corvette hit the center divider and caught fire, then the truck hti the divider and ran up over the car. The driver of the corvette was killed, but his passenger and the driver of the truck suffered only minor inuries.

The name of the Corvette driver hasnot been released, pending notification of the next of kin. The passenger, Ron Wright, 23, of Newport, and the truck driver, Jose Matines, 51, were treated at Sun Valley Memorial Hospital and released.

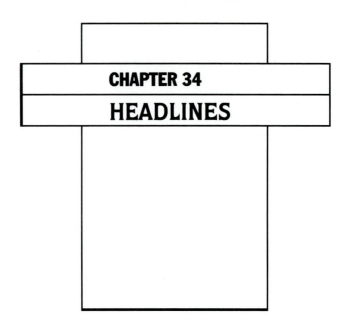

CHAPTER 34
HEADLINES

Writing headlines, it has been said, is easy. All you have to do is make them accurate, fair, clear, precise, punchy, thoughtful, inviting, relevant, urgent and readable and do it in half a dozen words, often in three or four minutes. Obviously, that's stretching the point. The truth is, headline writing is often the most difficult and demanding part of a copy editor's job. What a reporter said in 30 words or more in a lead, a headline writer might have to say in six words or less. But it can be done. It requires skill and a comand of the language. Most of all, it requires imagination.

The following is quite an imaginative headline on a story about a September baby boom from the Star Tribune, Minneapolis. It was written by Sue Loth:

Maybe that's why Labor Day falls in September

Headlines are, in a sense, an advertisement for the story. A good headline will reach out and grab the reader. When it is bright, informative, clear and accurate, the readers are hooked. They read on, and that's the whole object.

In addition to grabbing the reader's attention, a headline should:

- Summarize the story so a hurried reader can get the gist of the story at a glance.
- Help the reader evaluate the news.
- Help make the newspaper attractive and interesting to the reader.

All of this must be done clearly and intelligently in a small amount of space, within the additional restrictions placed on the headline writer by the required type size.

Generally, the headline on most straight-news stories should be drawn

from the lead. The headline should be the lead translated into sharp, punchy, dramatic words. Material from the body of the story is used in the secondary head, or deck, if the newspaper's headline style permits decks. If a headline writer has to go into the body of the story for the headline on a straight-news story, chances are the lead needs to be rewritten.

Some headline writers are intimidated by the limited space they have to work with. They tend to think first of something to fit the space rather than the idea they want to convey. As a result, their headlines often are dull, little more than vague labels.

Advice on how to write good headlines abounds. Some suggest that you get what you want to say down on paper first without worrying about headline count, then refine and polish those words. One copy editor suggests: Write the headline, then imagine swinging open a barroom door and shouting it. Depending on how many heads turn, either set it or forget it.

A good headline does not require translation. The reader should understand it immediately, unlike the following example (that was actually used):

BN VP at BS

It translates "Boys Nation Vice President at Boys State." Although that is an extreme example, many headlines are almost as difficult to grasp because they are vague, such as:

Trip needs volunteers

What trip? Where? How many volunteers? Actually, it referred to a trade mission to Ireland. But you'd never know from that vague headline. Some copy editors read their headlines aloud to make certain they "read" smoothly. If the copy editor stumbles over his or her own headline, then the reader will almost certainly do the same.

Reading the following headlines aloud could have spared the writer and the newspaper some embarrassment. They are from Columbia Journalism Review's "The Lower Case" page:

Lawmaker backs train through Iowa

Another body found missing

Most newspapers have a list of guidelines for writing headlines. Although they often are quite similar, some vary according to the particular views of the editor and copy desk chief. Here are the rules followed by the Bellingham Herald, Bellingham, Wash., which were included in a special section on better headline writing in the Gannatteer:

1. Make the headline say something; don't write non-heads.
2. No headline may start with a verb.
3. Conjunctions, prepositions and modifiers in headlines may not be placed at the end of the line.
4. Commas or semi-colons may be used at the end of a line in multi-deck heads. Single-line heads may have commas or semi-colons, but they should be used sparingly.
5. Do not pile modifiers one after another.
6. Do not split the parts of verbs from one line to another.
7. Do not use pronouns alone and unidentified.
8. It is NOT always necessary to use a verb in a headline. But when you do not, the omission must help make a better headline.
9. Do not use "hit" or "flay" or "rap" or "score" or "blast" or anything in that category of verbs, unless the word means precisely what it says.
10. Fill out the lines in your head.

The paper then tells its copy editors to "break the rules" if it will help make a better headline. Substance outranks form.

Copy editors are given considerably more freedom in writing straight-news heads now than they were in the past. For example, the Clarksville (Tenn.) Leaf-Chronicle used this well-written headline on a straight-news story about television evangelist Jim Bakker and his friends:

Airwave apostles have had a devil of a time

The Cincinnati Enquirer brightened its front-page story on the controversial prediction of an earthquake along the New Madrid fault in Missouri with this headline:

It's shake up or shut up time
Some take predictions seriously; others say wait and see

The "wait and see" crowd won. The earthquake did not happen on the hour or the day climatologist Iben Browing predicted it would.

Copy editors have always had greater freedom in writing headlines for feature stories than they had for straight-news stories. That doesn't mean they can take an "anything goes" approach. After all, the feature head should reflect the tone of the story, and it should not necessarily summarize the facts as a straight-news head would. Moreover, feature heads should not divulge a story's surprise ending or unusual twist.

The Santa Rosa (Calif.) Press Democrat used this clever head on a feature about a "Dear John" letter written to author Ernest Hemingway by a nurse. The headline was written by Sophie Jense:

Nurse's Farewell to Hemingway's Arms

The Wall Street Journal used this lively headline on a front-page feature about scientists' prediction of man's future:

Good News: You Can't Live Forever; Bad News: No Sex

It's the Far Edge of Robotics As one Scientist Asks: What's a Body to DO?

TRENDS IN HEADLINES

In modern typography the trend is toward simplicity. This means shorter main heads and fewer, if any, secondary headlines. Some newspapers have eliminated decks completely. Others still use them. And some mix them up. Many others have introduced a variety of headline techniques, often similar to those used in magazine makeup and even advertising.

The flush-left headline is still the most common in modern newspaper typography because it is based on the instinctive pattern in which the reading eye moves in Western cultures—from left to right. The following are several examples of flush-left headlines:

New York sets record with 2,000 murders

Iraq says All Soviet experts may leave

Many newspapers, however, use a variation on the flush-left theme. Here are some of them:

1. *Inverted pyramid*—two or three lines, each one indented one character more than the previous one.

Secret payments made by coal firm suit says

2. *Drop or stepped lines*—two or three lines, each approximately the same length. The top one is flush left, the second line is indented one space, and the third line is indented two and is flush right.

'91 budget deficit
will set a record,
Congress is told

3. *Hanging indentation*—two, three or four lines, the first line longer than other lines and flush left. Other lines are equal and are indented an identical number of spaces at the left.

Weak regulations, greed
blamed as investors,
home owners lose out

4. *Crossline or barline*—a single line, centered.

Waitress Bags Suspect

The variety of headlines used by newspapers is endless. Four- and even five-line heads are showing up frequently. Decks and banks are making a comeback. Headlines in all capital letters are used more often now than they were 20 years ago, even though they are considered more difficult to read than those written in capital and lowercase letters.

Kickers and reverse kickers are popular at some newspapers. The kicker usually is about one-third the width of the main headline and should be approximately one-half the type size of the main head. A 60-point headline should have a 30-point kicker. Kickers most often are used on multicolumn headlines, although they can be used on one-column heads if they are kept short. With a kicker, the main head should have no more than two lines, as a general rule, and a deck should not be used. The main head under a kicker should be indented several spaces but the kicker is set flush left or centered over the main head. The combination of the kicker and the indention of the main head creates white space around the mass of type in the head, and white space tends to attract the reader's eye.

The use of the kicker led to the introduction of a reverse kicker, also called a hammer. In this style, the headline writer simply reverses the size of the main head and the kicker. The reverse kicker usually is twice the size of the main headline and it is set flush left. It should be no wider than half of the headline space, which means it should not be attempted too often in two columns of space and never in one. The main head under a reverse kicker also is indented to help balance the area of white space at the right created by the kicker.

Here are examples of kicker and reverse-kicker headlines:

<u>Libel</u> <u>Suit</u> <u>Filed</u>

Newspaper Fights Order Prohibiting Editorials

BARGAIN SOURCE

. . . Postal Service auctions packages that can't be delivered, returned

Kickers and reverse kickers allow the headline writer to expand the ideas to be conveyed in the headlines. However, they are difficult to write and unless done with care can be pointless. Even when excellent kickers are written, the reader should be able to get an accurate message from the main headline alone. If a kicker, using a qualifying word or phrase for the main head, is accidentally left off, the main head might end up to be more of an editorial comment than a straight headline.

One of the more popular headline styles is called "down" style. Only the first letter of the first word in the headline and any proper names are capitalized.

Here are just a few examples of headline styles selected at random from daily newspapers across the nation:

A Stolen Bird Sings So a Thief Is Caught

US SET TO VACATE EMBASSY IN KUWAIT

<u>Spring for a day</u>

Record high temperatures draw flowers into bloom, people outside

Pointless precision Skilled pianist Ivo Pogorelch just can't find the feeling

Shocked pilot
He didn't know engine fell off
Until emergency landing

Airport
runway
finished
New strip to boost
facility's standing

Surgeon's death spurs AIDS test offer

Twin bites off more than
he can chew: officer's ear
But which brother did the dastardly deed?

Counting Heads

Headlines can be either all caps or caps and lowercase. The choice will make a difference in the number of units of space in the headline, depending on the size of the type—the smaller the type, the more letters and spaces. The headline writer must compose a headline that will fit into that limited space allotted for the headline. However, it is possible on most video-display terminals (VDTs) to "squeeze" in extra letters by very slightly reducing the headline's point size. Some newspapers do not allow squeezing headlines in that fashion. At others, substance outranks form.

Although the headline count will vary from newspaper to newspaper depending on the type family used, the following is a typical schedule. For heads set in capital and small letters, use this unit count:

One-half Unit

Small i and l, capital I, numeral 1
Punctuation marks (except dash and question mark)
Spaces between words

One Unit

All small letters except i, l, m and w

All figures except 1
Dash and question mark

One and One-half Units

Small m and w
All capitals except M and W (and I, which is 1/2)

Two Units

Capital M and W

For all-capital heads the following applies:

One-half Unit

I, numeral 1
Punctuation marks (except dash and question mark)

One Unit

All letters except I, M and W
All figures except 1
Spaces between words
Dash and question mark

One and One-half Units

M and W

If, for example, a headline writer is told to write a three-column, one-line, 30 point head, caps and lower case, he would count it this way:

```
1½  ½  1  1½ 1½  ½  1  1½ 1½  1   1   1   1   ½  1½  1   ½  1   1   1  1½ 1½  1   1   1   1 -1½  1        1
F  i  r  e  H  i  t  s  L  a  u  r  e  l  H  e  i  g  h  t  s  A  p  a  r  t  m  e  n  t  s
```

This is the accepted method of counting in headlines, but headline writers on some staffs do not follow the system carefully. Writing heads on a typewriter, they count each letter and space as one unit, depending upon the compositor or pasteup person to space the lines correctly. In most cases such headlines will fit the space, but sometimes they must be rewritten because they are too long. Most VDTs are now programmed to "count" headlines and signal the writer if they are too long.

Writing good headlines requires a mastery of the language, an affinity for words, a lively imagination and a bag full of tricks. The good headline writer always remembers that she or he has only a few milliseconds to grab the reader's attention. A headline that may be perfectly clear to the writer because he or she has read the lead, the first three paragraphs or the whole story may be confusing, even meaningless, to the reader who knows nothing about the story.

SELECTING THE HEADLINE

The practice will vary from newspaper to newspaper, but the responsibility for evaluating news stories and deciding what size headline should be written for each is the job of the news editor, often in conjunction with the makeup or graphics editor. They may be the same person at a smaller newspaper.

How does an editor determine what headline should go on a story? In general, the importance of the story or the local interest in it dictates the size of the headline on the story. The position the story will occupy on the page also influences the headline size. Longer stories frequently get larger headlines, partly out of reader interest, but also because a large head on a long story generally makes the page more attractive. Stories compete with each other, not only for length and headline size but also for position in the paper. A short news story may be the most significant that given day and may end up with a large headline, prominently displayed on the page. So length does not automatically ensure a large headline.

News is inconsistent. A fairly interesting story may get a rather large headline on a day when outstanding stories are scarce. On other days, several leading stories might be of equal importance, but the editor cannot use the same type and size of headline for all of them. In such a case, the editor attempts to make all of them approximately equal but uses a variety of typefaces and headline combinations to signify to the reader their relative importance.

The importance of the story should always dictate the approximate size of the headline. Although planning is necessary, stories should not be greatly overplayed or underplayed to meet space requirements or a predetermined page design.

Here are a few suggestions for selecting heads:

- Nearly every page will need a few large heads with one more dominant than the others.
- Double-column and other multicolumn heads improve the appearance of the newspaper's pages.
- Both Roman and italic typefaces are available and should be used. Italic type is generally used to break the monotony of the darker Roman type often used for headlines on hard-news stories.

PRINCIPLES OF HEADLINE WRITING

Good headline writing is an art practiced under the pressure of deadlines. Every headline writer will develop individual techniques, but a study of headlines, good and bad, will show that there are some general principles usually practiced at all newspapers.

1. The headline should tell the story's essentials and tell them accurately. It should be based on the lead in the case of news stories and should give as many of the five W's as necessary, playing up the proper W. Each head should be a complete sentence with unnecessary words omitted:

Poor

Man Sustains A Fatal Injury

Better

Guard Killed In Gun Fight

2. The symmetry of line length required by the style of a particular headline should be achieved. The lines must not appear to be too crowded with type or too empty. They should not appear grossly unbalanced:

Poor

McDonald to Head FBI Office

Better

McDonald Named FBI Agent Here

Poor

Mayor Urges Crackdown

Better

Mayor Urges Crackdown

3. If a headline is made up of several different forms, each part should be a full statement and should stand alone:

Poor

Huge Oil Slick 100 Miles Long

Reported by Coast Guard

Better

Huge Oil Slick Threat to Coast

Covers 100 Miles Reports Guard

4. A thought should not be repeated. Each deck or bank should advance the story with additional information:

Poor

Heavy Truck Bill Postponed

Truck Weight Increase Sought

Better

Heavy Truck Bill Postponed

Public Hearings Planned for Fall

5. Involved, confusing or ambiguous heads should be avoided:

Poor

Aged Fight Pension Plans for Future

Better

Aged Group Fights New Pension Plans

6. Feature stories should have feature headlines:

Poor

Dog Is Favorite White House Pet

Better

'Dogging' It at the White House

Poor

Patrons Borrow Free Umbrellas Permanently

Better

Free Umbrella Idea
Picked up Quickly

7. Each headline should contain a verb in order not to appear as a mere label. The verb should be in the first line if possible, but the headline should not start with a verb.

Poor

College Mall

—

Urge Milk Fund
For City's Needy

Better

College Mall Opens

—

Milk Fund Urged
For City's Needy

8. Headlines generally should be written in the active voice, not the passive, for impact:

Poor

Strikers Warned
by Mayor

Better

Mayor Warns
Rail Strikers

9. Headlines should be written in the historical present tense (or future). However, some newspapers permit past tense in headlines:

Poor

Penal Farm Inmate
Escaped Into Woods

Better

Penal Farm Inmate
Escapes Into Woods

10. The headline should use vivid, fresh language; avoid dull and trite words:

Poor

Congress Studies
Gun Control Again

Better

Congress Takes Aim
At Gun Control Again

11. Words should not be repeated in the headline:

Poor

Strike Conference Ends
Steelworkers Strike

Better

Mediation Session Ends
Steelworkers Strike

12. Headlines should be specific. Try to find the exact word to convey a thought:

Poor	*Better*
# Youth Injured # In Knife Battle	# Youth Slashed # In Knife Fight

13. Provincial slang expressions should be avoided:

Poor	*Better*
# Stockers Sales # Cut in Half	# Local Cattle Sales # Drop 50 Per Cent

14. The headline writer cannot use simplified spelling (such as "tho") unless it is the style of the newspaper:

Poor

Rain to Continue
Thru Another Day

Better

Rain to Continue
Through Tomorrow

15. Single quotation marks should be used in headlines.

Poor	*Better*
Kidnaped Boy **"Buried Alive"**	**Kidnaped Boy** **'Buried Alive'**

16. Abbreviations should not be used unless standard, conventional and generally understood, such as U.S., FBI:

Poor	*Better*
500 of ASE **At Meeting Here**	**500 Engineers** **Convene Here**

17. Words, phrases consisting of nouns and adjective modifiers, prepositional phrases and verb phrases should not be split between lines:

Poor	*Better*
Council Passes Sales **Tax Despite Protest**	**Sales Tax Passes** **Despite Protest**

18. Opinion headlines should be attributed or qualified:

Poor	*Better*
Taxes Too High **On Businesses**	**Taxes Too High** **Say Businessmen**

19. Articles and other unnecessary words should not be used, except with names of books and other proper titles:

Poor	*Better*
Fireman Saves **A Little Puppy**	**Fireman Saves** **Dog from Blaze**

20. "Half truths" must be avoided. Sometimes such heads can be libelous or misleading.

Poor	*Better*
Pastor Sought In Larceny Case	**Pastor Sought As Eyewitness**

Subheads

Subheads are boldface lines of type used to break up the body type used in long news stories. They are a typographical device to relieve the grayness of long columns of type. As a general rule, they start after the first three paragraphs of a story and are placed evenly three or four paragraphs apart throughout the story. The last one generally is placed three paragraphs before the story ends. Some newspapers set their subheads in all caps, boldface type slightly larger than body type. Others use boldface-cap and lowercase subheads. The general principles of headline writing apply to subheads. They should not fill the entire line, nor should they be too short.

A number of newspapers have eliminated subheads in favor of other devices to break up the monotony of large masses of solid body type. One is to boldface whole paragraphs, parts of paragraphs, or even parts of sentences—the first four words of a sentence, for example. Others take sentences or paragraphs right out of the story, set them in larger type and insert them into the body of the story with ample white space around them.

Trends in newspaper headlines come and go just as they do in the overall design of newspapers. But the principles of headline writing remain the same. Good headlines say something.

EXERCISES

1. Invite the copy desk chief from the local daily newspaper to class for an interview. Write a story based on the interview.

2. Using newspapers available to you on the newsstands or in your college library, compare the stories covering the same major news event in two competing dailies. Compare those stories to coverage of the same story by The New York Times, USA TODAY or other major dailies with national circulation. Compare the headlines on the stories in each paper for content, size and style. Write a brief report on your findings.

3. Using any daily newspaper available to you, rewrite all of the headlines on the front page. Try to improve them. Do not change the type size or column width of the original headlines. Turn in the originals with your rewritten versions.

4. Select one story from any newspaper front page and using the headline schedule presented at the end of Chapter 35, write the following size headlines on that story: No. 8, No. 7a, No. 5, No. 3a, No. 2, No. 1.

5. Assume you are the news editor of your daily newspaper and you have the following stories available for the front page. Read the list carefully, then rank the stories in importance of their news value. You can use no more than six stories. Indicate the headline size you would use on each story:

   a. Helicopter crash kills two pilots on night-training mission near local Air Force Base. (15 inches long)

   b. Temperature will drop to freezing tonight, as cold wave sweeps the state. (12 inches long)

   c. FBI director to visit city next week for meeting with community leaders. (12 inches long)

   d. Police, Sheriff's deputies, State Highway Patrol issued 443 citations and made three drunken driving arrests in four days of saturation patrols to crack down on drunk drivers. (10 inches long)

   e. Fire leaves three local families homeless. (8 inches long)

   f. Local woman charged with killing ex-husband. (8 inches long)

   g. Price of heating oil going up, local suppliers say. (10 inches long)

   h. State Supreme Court rules that legislators violated the state constitution when they voted last year to raise their salaries in the middle of their terms. (12 inches long)

   i. Killer of four women given nine life terms. (15 inches long)

   j. Three-year-old boy killed in car accident. (5 inches long)

   k. Three policemen cleared of gambling charges by internal investigation. (6 inches long)

   l. Audit shows $40,000 stolen from city clerk's office. (7 inches long)

6. Write a one-column, two-line, flush-left headline for each of the following leads. Use capitals and lower case with 15 to 16 units in each line:

   a. A 48-year-old man accused of vehicular homicide in the death of a jogger he hit with his car sentenced to five years in prison.

   b. Grand jury indicts Charlotte Johnson, 48, and her daughter, Karen Arington, 25, on first-degree murder charges in the killing of the daughter's boyfriend.

   c. Two local policemen were suspended today for allegedly using excessive force during a drug arrest. They will receive no pay during the five days they are off duty.

   d. Two men seriously injured in a two-car collision in front of Civic Coliseum. Both hospitalized, in critical condition.

   e. Body of a 27-year-old man who had been fatally stabbed was found in his 15th-floor room at the Downtown Hilton today.

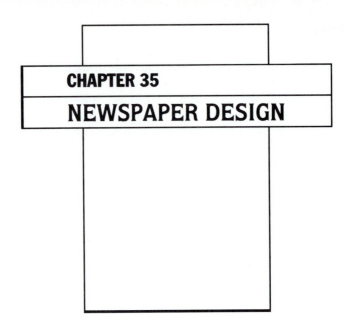

CHAPTER 35
NEWSPAPER DESIGN

"Newspaper trends come and go," Tim Harrower, assistant graphics editor of the Portland Oregonian, says in his book, The Newspaper Designer's Handbook.

"What's hip today will probably look hopelessly out-of-date in a decade or two. Tastes change; newsroom philosophies change, too. The same goes for theories of page design," Harrower says.

"Remember this: Readers will look where you want them to look. If you know what you're doing, you can create a page that's logical, legible and fun to read—you can guide the reader's eye wherever you choose."

The appearance of American newspapers has drawn considerable criticism. Chief among the complaints is that they all look alike. There is some validity to that charge. However, the advent of personal computers, especially the Apple Macintosh®, in the newsroom has had a positive impact on the way some newspapers look because they give the graphic designer a tremendous amount of flexibility and speed.

Designers are using Macintoshes, in particular, to do their layouts rather than drawing them on paper grid sheets. Newspapers from Newsday, on Long Island, to The Seattle Times have found them indispensable. Designer Dan Van Bemtjiusem of Newsday says the Macintosh has "revolutionized things. I compare this to what type did for editors."

The arrival of USA TODAY in the mid-1980s, with its non-traditional makeup, splashy use of color, information graphics, short stories and columns of news summaries, not only grabbed a lot of attention but had an important influence on a number of other newspapers. Its use of information graphics and its large colorful weather map quickly became the models for countless other newspapers. Many also have introduced more news summary columns.

There have been other influences on newspaper appearance as well. A major one has been the visual competition offered by television. But for the most part, the apearance of a newspaper still is a reflection of its owner and the women and men who run it.

One of the key players in most newsrooms today is the graphics editor. Working with other key editors, he or she helps to decide what each day's edition is going to look like. Graphics editors take part in daily editorial conferences in which the city, state, wire, sports, business, lifestyles and other departmental editors meet with the managing editor to plan the paper. Each presents a list of major stories, and as a group they discuss which stories will go on page 1, the section fronts and the inside pages. After the stories have been selected and ranked according to their importance, the graphics editor and staff do their layouts either by personal computers such as the Macintosh or by hand.

On smaller newspapers, the news or managing editor might serve as the designer. And at many newspapers, sections such as "sports" and "lifestyles" do their own design.

CHANGES IN DESIGN

One of the more popular phrases heard around newspapers in the early part of the 1990s was "reader friendly." All newspapers were seeking a way to hold on to readers and win new ones as daily newspaper circulation decreased. One of the most talked about efforts was the splashy makeover of the Boca Raton News, a Knight-Ridder Inc. daily, in Boca Raton, Fla.

The redesign of the Boca Raton News was aimed specifically at attracting the so-called baby boom readers whose ages ranged from 25 to 43. It was an attempt to bring reader-friendly journalism to new levels.

The new design borrows heavily from the innovations of USA TODAY. It features information graphics and bright colors to highlight stories baby-boomer readers have told researchers interest them most: the environment, divorce, personal finance, housing trends and the workplace. A front-page column carries readers' gripes on things like the "inconsiderate boobs" who talk on portable phones in local restaurants. Editorials end with what the paper calls "empowerment boxes" that give names and phone numbers, so readers can take action. The editor has said the News will continue to print tough and long stories but cut dull pieces on government and bureaucracy in favor of community growth, environment and housing stories.

Other newspapers have made a lot of changes, but most continue to display their stories horizontally rather than vertically. There are a few exceptions to that rule, like the Wall Street Journal's front page. In most of the new designs, headlines are multicolumn rather than one-column. Pictures are often large and more horizontal than vertical. Charts, graphs, maps and information graphics, frequently in color, are used with stories and sometimes even stand alone. News-summary columns are commonplace now.

Many newspapers continue to place the main story in the top right corner of the front page, as was the practice when the eight-column banner (a page-wide headline in very large type) was the standard headline on the most important story of the day. However, now the headline on that story might be only two or three columns wide. Some newspapers place their main story in the upper left-hand corner, where it catches the reader's eye. Then, they display a story or photograph of almost equal importance in the upper right of the page. A variety of other combinations are used, depending on the length of the stories, their importance, and the photos or illustrations available for the page.

One of the early proponents of modern newspaper typography, Edmund Arnold, cited the following principles of makeup. They are just as sound today as they were when he introduced them:

1. Good typography should be the packaging of content, and content should determine what the package looks like. You must first know what you are packaging. A good layout of any kind must be organic, must grow from what it has to work with—the content, the day's news.
2. The newspaper design should present a lot of different news in a minimum of space.
3. A good newspaper page must be functional. Every element—every line of type—must communicate with the reader, must transmit information.
4. Good typographic layout of any kind must be invisible. It should not overpower the message.

Some design traditionalists argue that the design of USA TODAY tends to overpower the message. However, its circulation figures indicate that a lot of readers don't agree. USA TODAY has one of the largest circulations of any newspaper in the nation.

DESIGN PROCEDURE

In designing a standard-size page—the front page or an inside page—the first step most designers take is to place a strong attention-getter in the upper left-hand corner of the page. That's where the reader's eyes normally "enter" the page. If there is nothing in that spot, the reader's eyes are likely to go on to something else, perhaps less important in basic news value. One of the functions of design is to help the reader "grade" or "evaluate" the news by its placement on the page and the size of its headline.

The attention-getter should be a strong headline, a large picture or an unusual story placed in a box, or a graphic. Whatever is used, it should rivet the reader's attention to the top part of the page, where the most important story of the day is traditionally placed. The attention-getter should be counterbalanced by an equally important item, often the major news story that day. The object is to keep the reader's eyes moving across the page from left to right.

After placing stories and other elements at the top of the page, the designer should plan the center, by using a strong display element. Finally, the lower part of the page is designed, also with strong headlines or other display elements so it does not fade away.

The way the entire top third of the page looks is influenced by where the newspaper's flag (nameplate) is placed. Many papers display their flag at the top of the page and never move it. Some use a strip of promotion boxes above the flag (see Figure 35–2). Other newspapers use three- or four-column flags, as USA TODAY does (see Figure 35–1). Still other newspapers float the flag and place stories above or beside it.

Another factor that influences the display of stories on the front page is summary or other columns in a permanent position on the front page. For example, the Nashville Banner places its promotion boxes in the first column on the left side of the page. USA TODAY places a two-column news summary down the left side of its front page.

It is important for the designer to achieve a sense of balance on the front page. The top should not totally dominate the bottom of the page. There should be some strong display elements in the center as well as on the bottom third of the page. Some designers anchor the bottom corners with stories in boxes or the index. Display elements can be a photograph, a graphic or a strong multicolumn headline. The display elements used in the center and lower third of the page should not be larger than those used on the top third of the page.

One of the marks of an attractive front page is the lack of crowding. (The same goes for inside pages.) The use of white space is a significant design tool in attaining a balanced look. It can be used around the flag or art, above headlines, between lines of heads, between the head and the by-line, between the by-line and the credit line, between the credit line and the lead, modestly between paragraphs, between the photo and the caption, and between the ads and the editorial matter.

Many designers attempt to place the headlines so they are not tombstoned (placed side by side) or armpitted (a narrow head placed immediately under a wider one with no body type between them). The separation of heads by lighter body type makes the page more attractive and much easier to read, and it creates contrast. Some newspapers, however, ignore that concept. USA TODAY and The Wall Street Journal are two examples.

Contrast also is important in the selection of headlines. A range of headline sizes should be used on a page. A variety of sizes provides contrast and also helps the reader grade the value of the stories. The large headline is a signal to the reader that the story has greater news value than the one with a smaller headline.

Although the practice varies widely, it is a generally accepted design principle that the front page should be organized into horizontal blocks, not unlike the page of a book. Research shows that type in horizontal blocks tends to appear to have a smaller mass. Besides, readers are more willing to dive into a shorter story. In some tests, a 15-inch story displayed horizontally attracted more attention and was said to be easier to read than a 15-inch story displayed vertically. This is a signal to reporters, editors and designers that some readers, perhaps even large numbers of readers, may not complete a long story.

The practice of jumping long stories from the front page to an inside page varies from newspaper to newspaper. Research repeatedly has shown that half the readers never turn to the part of the story jumped to the inside page unless it is an unusually compelling one.

Here are some generally accepted guidelines about jumping stories, ignored from time to time by any number of newspapers:

1. Avoid jumping too many stories from page 1. Some newspapers limit the jumps to three. Others allow none. Still others, like The New York Times, jump almost every story.
2. Do not jump short news stories. Make room on the page by careful editing. Short jumps are not only unattractive but also difficult for the reader to find.
3. Avoid jumping a story within the first two or three paragraphs. A sufficient number of paragraphs should be placed beneath the headline to balance the size of the headline and prevent it from appearing to overpower the small amount of body type.
4. Do not jump stories from one inside page to another, if possible. Unless there is enough space on an inside page to accommodate the entire story, it should not be placed on that page.

Related Stories

Sometimes a graphics editor will have several stories related to a single event or incident. Generally, these stories should be grouped. A common method is to put one large headline on the most important story and smaller, separate headlines on the secondary stories that are placed adjacent to the larger story. Often the most important story is placed on the front page with a box indicating that related stories are on an inside page. If the front-page story jumps, it is usually jumped to the same page with the related stories.

FRONT-PAGE DESIGN

Most newspapers strive for an attractive, readable, well-balanced front page. Every element on the page performs an essential function. Most newspaper designers strive to make their pages clean and uncluttered. Column rules, cutoff rules and multiple decks have been eliminated from most newspapers.

A full-size page will vary slightly, depending on the size of the newsprint roll. Some pages are approximately 15 by 22 inches. Others are approximately 13-½ by 22 inches. The standard format is six columns. However, computerization has enabled newspapers to vary the column width considerably. For example, some newspapers mix column widths, setting some stories in the standard width and others a column and a half or two columns, depending on the desired design effect.

Every year, a number of suggestions are floated about professional meetings and gatherings of graphic designers for changing and "improving" the appearance of newspapers. Some include turning the front page into a "super" news summary or capsulization of the day's news into down-sized pages with larger body type. Until that day arrives, these hints for designing page 1 can be helpful:

1. Do not design a page first and then force the news to fit it. That will destroy or distort the news value of the stories and undermine one of the prime purposes of design—to help grade the news.
2. Put the most important story or display items at the top of the page.
3. Avoid placing large multicolumn heads in adjoining columns at the top of the page. Use a picture or graphic to separate them.
4. Avoid tombstoning headlines. Use display devices such as pictures, boxes, graphics, even white space, to separate heads, especially if the heads are the same size.
5. Place at least one strong multicolumn headline in each quarter of the page and the center, if possible.
6. Use pictures generously. If a picture looks good as a two-column, it will look even better as a three-column most of the time. Crop pictures artfully. Do not waste space.
7. Put big pictures toward the top of the page, but do not be afraid to use a big picture at the bottom as well. Just make certain the one at the top is larger.
8. Use multicolumn headlines at the bottom of the page, even a banner. Be certain the banner's type size is not larger than that of the main headline at the top of the page.
9. Don't be afraid to float the flag to give some variety in makeup, but always keep it close to the top of the page.
10. Don't let subjects in photographs based in outside columns look off the page, which destroys unity.
11. Run stories horizontally rather than vertically whenever possible. Attempt to keep major stories 15 to 20 inches on page 1. If they run longer, either jump them or make two stories out of one.
12. Run related stories in the same area on the page.
13. Vary the size of body type and the width in which some stories are set. But don't overdo it.
14. Limit the number of one-column headlines on the page.
15. Use a variety of headline sizes to give the page contrast.
16. Do not let the story run out from under the headline.
17. Vary your page design from page to page.
18. Try a few surprises by ignoring these hints from time to time.

TYPES OF INSIDE-PAGE DESIGN

The inside pages, unlike the front page, carry advertising—at least most of them do—and this factor presents some special problems in design. The graphics editor usually receives from the advertising department page dummies with the advertisements drawn in. The task then is to make a page as attractive as possible within the framework of the stories and display elements that will fit on the page with the advertisements. Some newspapers automatically leave certain inside pages exclusively for editorial matter. Others keep advertisements to a minimum for the first several pages. Some put no advertisements at all on the front page of a section.

No matter what the custom of ad placement, the designer planning an inside page should remember that the reader's habits do not change automatically when reading the inside pages of a newspaper. The eyes still move from left to right. The upper left-hand corner of the page is still the first place the eyes touch down.

The same basic principles of display that apply to the front page should apply to the inside pages. But obviously the placement of the advertisements on the page will limit the designer's freedom. Advertisements can be pyramided from the right or from the left. They also can be placed up each side of the page, forming a well in the center. They can all be grouped across the lower part of the page, leaving the upper part open. Ideally, pyramiding to the right is most effective because it opens the upper left-hand corner for a display of editorial matter and permits the designer to take advantage of the reader's normal eye movements. The best ad pyramid is one that leaves at least four or five inches of space at the top of the page. This creates a more usable space in the upper-left corner.

Here are some handy guidelines to consider in making up an inside page:

1. Put a strong (multicolumn) headline or a reasonably large picture in the upper left-hand corner of the page at the point of initial eye contact.
2. Use a careful combination of multicolumn and single-column headlines on the page.
3. Restrict the use of banner heads on inside pages. If a banner head is used, do not use another on the adjacent page.
4. Do not tombstone heads. Also avoid butting headlines, especially heads that are exactly the same size.
5. Include a picture (or pictures), cartoon, chart, map or some other graphic device on each page, if possible, except on pages containing advertisements with large photographs.
6. Keep pictures toward the top of the page. Avoid putting a picture right on top of an advertisement or adjacent to an advertisement.
7. Whenever possible, try to make the headline wide enough to cover all the body type.
8. Do not run the headline for a story across the top of an advertisement. Make certain there are at least one to two inches of body type separating the headliner from the advertisement.
9. Use a variety of headline type sizes and widths to give the page some contrast.
10. Avoid the cluttered look. Do not use too many stories, and leave generous white space.

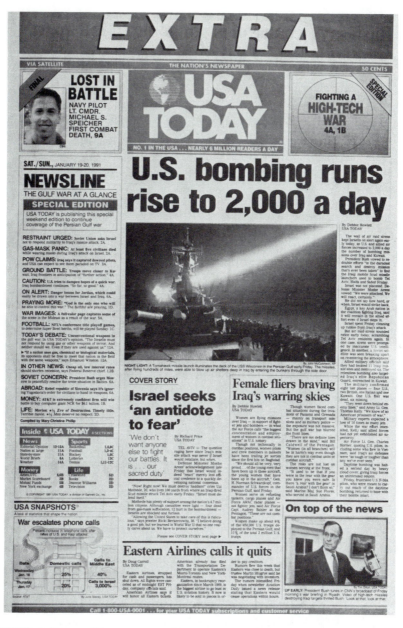

FIGURE 35–1 Extra editions are rare. However, when the war in the Persian Gulf began, USA TODAY published this "extra" to continue its coverage of the war over the weekend. The newspaper normally publishes only five issues a week. (Copyright 1991, USA TODAY. Reprinted with permission.)

FIGURE 35–2 The San Francisco Chronicle's front page is a strong mix of local and state news and national and international stories. (Copyright San Francisco Chronicle. Reprinted by permission.)

FIGURE 35–3 The St. Louis Post-Dispatch uses bold headlines, large photographs and information graphics to create interesting and readable front pages. (Courtesy of the St. Louis Post-Dispatch.)

FIGURE 35—4 The Boca Raton (Fla.) News underwent a complete redesign to create a newspaper that was more "reader friendly." Its graphic design owes much to USA TODAY. (Courtesy of The News, Boca Raton, Fla.)

FIGURE 35–5 The Christian Science Monitor did not adopt the traditional tabloid front-page makeup, which features giant headlines and pictures, when it converted from a broadsheet. Its front pages are clean, uncluttered and subdued compared to those of other tabloids (see Figure 21–1). (Reprinted by permission of The Christian Science Monitor. Copyright 1990 The Christian Science Publishing Society. All rights reserved.)

FIGURE 35–6 The Houston Chronicle, like many other newspapers, offers its readers a second front page devoted exclusively to local and area news. (Courtesy of the Houston Chronicle.)

FIGURE 35−7 The "Metro & State" news section front page from The Atlanta Journal and The Atlanta Constitution. The newspaper's front page and first section is traditionally devoted almost exclusively to national and international news. (Courtesy of The Atlanta Journal and Constitution.)

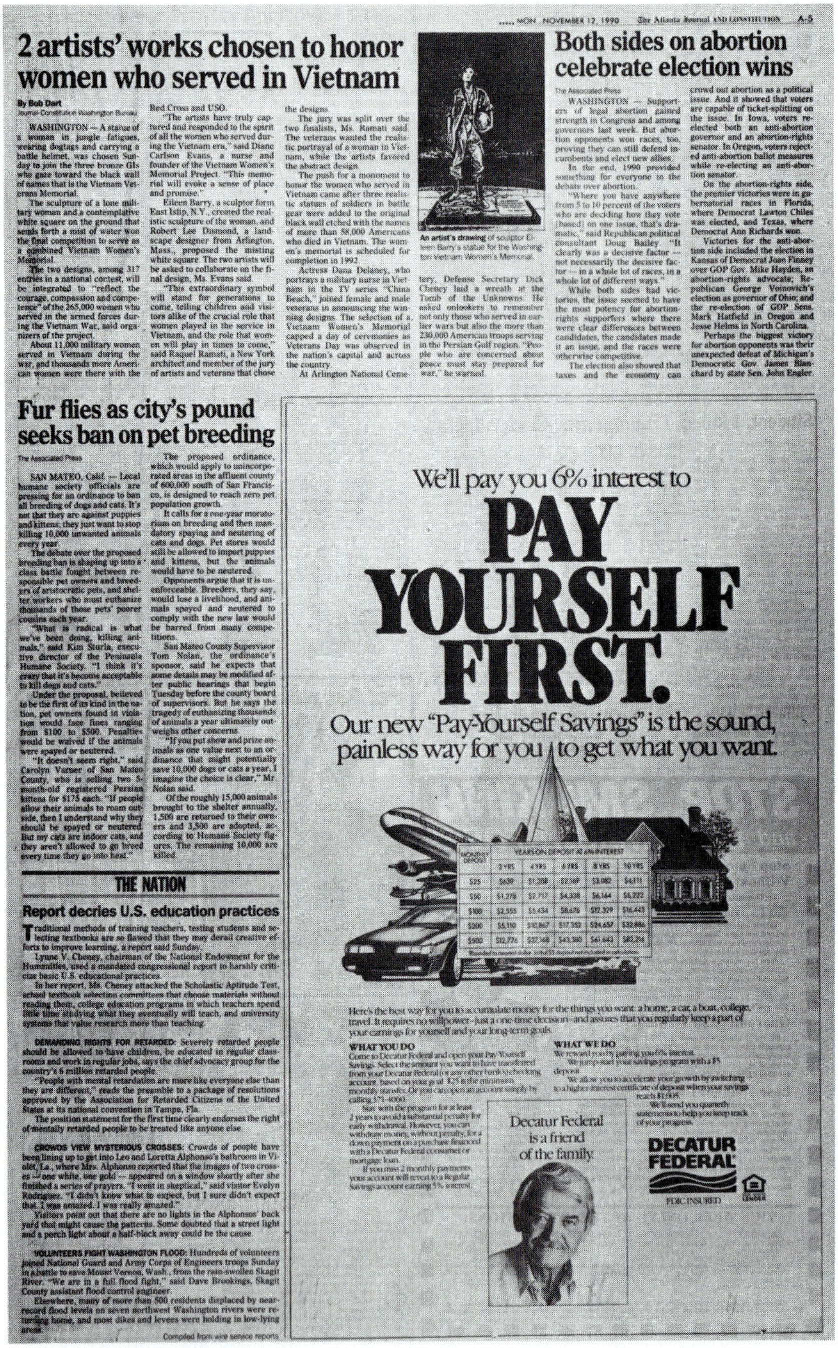

MON. NOVEMBER 12, 1990 The Atlanta Journal AND CONSTITUTION A-5

2 artists' works chosen to honor women who served in Vietnam

By Bob Dart
Journal-Constitution Washington Bureau

WASHINGTON — A statue of a woman in jungle fatigues, wearing dogtags and carrying a battle helmet, was chosen Sunday to join the three bronze GIs who gaze toward the black wall of names that is the Vietnam Veterans Memorial.

The sculpture of a lone military woman and a contemplative white square on the ground that sends forth a mist of water won the final competition to serve as a combined Vietnam Women's Memorial.

The two designs, among 317 entries in a national contest, will be integrated to "reflect the courage, compassion and competence" of the 265,000 women who served in the armed forces during the Vietnam War, said organizers of the project.

About 11,000 military women served in Vietnam during the war, and thousands more American women were there with the Red Cross and USO.

"The artists have truly captured and responded to the spirit of all the women who served during the Vietnam era," said Diane Carlson Evans, a nurse and founder of the Vietnam Women's Memorial Project. "This memorial will evoke a sense of place and promise."

Eileen Barry, a sculptor form East Islip, N.Y., created the realistic sculpture of the woman, and Robert Lee Dismond, a landscape designer from Arlington, Mass., proposed the misting white square. The two artists will be asked to collaborate on the final design, Ms. Evans said.

"This extraordinary symbol will stand for generations to come, telling children and visitors alike of the crucial role that women played in the service in Vietnam, and the role that women will play in times to come," said Raquel Ramati, a New York architect and member of the jury of artists and veterans that chose the designs.

The jury was split over the two finalists, Ms. Ramati said. The veterans wanted the realistic portrayal of a woman in Vietnam, while the artists favored the abstract design.

The push for a monument to honor the women who served in Vietnam came after three realistic statues of soldiers in battle gear were added to the original black wall etched with the names of more than 58,000 Americans who died in Vietnam. The women's memorial is scheduled for completion in 1992.

Actress Dana Delaney, who portrays a military nurse in Vietnam in the TV series "China Beach," joined female and male veterans in announcing the winning designs. The selection of a Vietnam Women's Memorial capped a day of ceremonies as Veterans Day was observed in the nation's capital and across the country.

At Arlington National Cemetery, Defense Secretary Dick Cheney laid a wreath at the Tomb of the Unknowns. He asked onlookers to remember not only those who served in earlier wars but also the more than 230,000 American troops serving in the Persian Gulf region. "People who are concerned about peace must stay prepared for war," he warned.

An artist's drawing of sculptor Eileen Barry's statue for the Washington Vietnam Women's Memorial.

Both sides on abortion celebrate election wins

The Associated Press

WASHINGTON — Supporters of legal abortion gained strength in Congress and among governors last week. But abortion opponents won races, too, proving they can still defend incumbents and elect new allies.

In the end, 1990 provided something for everyone in the debate over abortion.

"Where you have anywhere from 5 to 10 percent of the voters who are deciding how they vote [based] on one issue, that's dramatic," said Republican political consultant Doug Bailey. "It clearly was a decisive factor — not necessarily the decisive factor — in a whole lot of races, in a whole lot of different ways."

While both sides had victories, the issue seemed to have the most potency for abortion-rights supporters where there were clear differences between candidates, the candidates made it an issue, and the races were otherwise competitive.

The election also showed that taxes and the economy can crowd out abortion as a political issue. And it showed that voters are capable of ticket-splitting on the issue. In Iowa, voters re-elected both an anti-abortion governor and an abortion-rights senator. In Oregon, voters rejected anti-abortion ballot measures while re-electing an anti-abortion senator.

On the abortion-rights side, the premier victories were in gubernatorial races in Florida, where Democrat Lawton Chiles was elected, and Texas, where Democrat Ann Richards won.

Victories for the anti-abortion side included the election in Kansas of Democrat Joan Finney over GOP Gov. Mike Hayden, an abortion-rights advocate; Republican George Voinovich's election as governor of Ohio; and the re-election of GOP Sens. Mark Hatfield in Oregon and Jesse Helms in North Carolina.

Perhaps the biggest victory for abortion opponents was their unexpected defeat of Michigan's Democratic Gov. James Blanchard by state Sen. John Engler.

Fur flies as city's pound seeks ban on pet breeding

The Associated Press

SAN MATEO, Calif. — Local humane society officials are pressing for an ordinance to ban all breeding of dogs and cats. It's not that they are against puppies and kittens; they just want to stop killing 10,000 unwanted animals every year.

The debate over the proposed breeding ban is shaping up into a class battle fought between responsible pet owners and breeders of aristocratic pets, and shelter workers who must euthanize thousands of those pets' poorer cousins each year.

"What is radical is what we've been doing, killing animals," said Kim Sturla, executive director of the Peninsula Humane Society. "I think it's crazy that it's become acceptable to kill dogs and cats."

Under the proposal, believed to be the first of its kind in the nation, pet owners found in violation would face fines ranging from $100 to $500. Penalties would be waived if the animals were spayed or neutered.

"It doesn't seem right," said Carolyn Varner of San Mateo County, who is selling two 5-month-old registered Persian kittens for $175 each. "If people allow their animals to roam outside, then I understand why they should be spayed or neutered. But my cats are indoor cats, and they aren't allowed to go breed every time they go into heat."

The proposed ordinance, which would apply to unincorporated areas in the affluent county of 600,000 south of San Francisco, is designed to reach zero pet population growth.

It calls for a one-year moratorium on breeding and then mandatory spaying and neutering of cats and dogs. Pet stores would still be allowed to import puppies and kittens, but the animals would have to be neutered.

Opponents argue that it is unenforceable. Breeders, they say, would lose a livelihood, and animals spayed and neutered to comply with the new law would be barred from many competitions.

San Mateo County Supervisor Tom Nolan, the ordinance's sponsor, said he expects that some details may be modified after public hearings that begin Tuesday before the county board of supervisors. But he says the tragedy of euthanizing thousands of animals a year ultimately outweighs other concerns.

"If you put show and prize animals as one value next to an ordinance that might potentially save 10,000 dogs or cats a year, I imagine the choice is clear," Mr. Nolan said.

Of the roughly 15,000 animals brought to the shelter annually, 1,500 are returned to their owners and 3,500 are adopted, according to Humane Society figures. The remaining 10,000 are killed.

THE NATION

Report decries U.S. education practices

Traditional methods of training teachers, testing students and selecting textbooks are so flawed that they may derail creative efforts to improve learning, a report said Sunday.

Lynne V. Cheney, chairman of the National Endowment for the Humanities, used a mandated congressional report to harshly criticize basic U.S. educational practices.

In her report, Ms. Cheney attacked the Scholastic Aptitude Test, school textbook selection committees that choose materials without reading them, college education programs in which teachers spend little time studying what they eventually will teach, and university systems that value research more than teaching.

DEMANDING RIGHTS FOR RETARDED: Severely retarded people should be allowed to have children, be educated in regular classrooms and work in regular jobs, says the chief advocacy group for the country's 6 million retarded people.

"People with mental retardation are more like everyone else than they are different," reads the preamble to a package of resolutions approved by the Association for Retarded Citizens of the United States at its national convention in Tampa, Fla.

The position statement for the first time clearly endorses the right of mentally retarded people to be treated like anyone else.

CROWDS VIEW MYSTERIOUS CROSSES: Crowds of people have been lining up to get into Leo and Loretta Alphonso's bathroom in Violet, La., where Mrs. Alphonso reported that the images of two crosses — one white, one gold — appeared on a window shortly after she finished a series of prayers. "I went in skeptical," said visitor Evelyn Rodriguez. "I didn't know what to expect, but I sure didn't expect that. I was amazed. I was really amazed."

Visitors point out that there are no lights in the Alphonsos' back yard that might cause the patterns. Some doubted that a street light and a porch light about a half-block away could be the cause.

VOLUNTEERS FIGHT WASHINGTON FLOOD: Hundreds of volunteers joined National Guard and Army Corps of Engineers troops Sunday in a battle to save Mount Vernon, Wash., from the rain-swollen Skagit River. "We are in a full flood fight," said Dave Brookings, Skagit County assistant flood control engineer.

Elsewhere, many of more than 500 residents displaced by near-record flood levels on seven northwest Washington rivers were returning home, and most dikes and levees were holding in low-lying areas.

Compiled from wire service reports

We'll pay you 6% interest to

PAY YOURSELF FIRST.

Our new "Pay-Yourself Savings" is the sound, painless way for you to get what you want.

MONTHLY DEPOSIT	YEARS ON DEPOSIT AT 6% INTEREST				
	2 YRS	4 YRS	6 YRS	8 YRS	10 YRS
$25	$639	$1,358	$2,169	$3,082	$4,111
$50	$1,278	$2,717	$4,338	$6,164	$8,222
$100	$2,555	$5,434	$8,676	$12,329	$16,443
$200	$5,110	$10,867	$17,352	$24,657	$32,886
$500	$12,776	$27,168	$43,380	$61,643	$82,216

Here's the best way for you to accumulate money for the things you want: a home, a car, a boat, college, travel. It requires no willpower–just a one-time decision–and assures that you regularly keep a part of your earnings for yourself and your long-term goals.

WHAT YOU DO
Come to Decatur Federal and open your Pay-Yourself Savings. Select the amount you want to have transferred from your Decatur Federal (or any other bank's) checking account, based on your goal. $25 is the minimum monthly transfer. Or you can open an account simply by calling 571-4060.

Stay with the program for at least 2 years to avoid a substantial penalty for early withdrawal. However, you can withdraw money, without penalty, for a down payment on a purchase financed with a Decatur Federal consumer or mortgage loan.

If you miss 2 monthly payments, your account will revert to a Regular Savings account earning 5% interest.

WHAT WE DO
We reward you by paying you 6% interest.

We jump-start your savings program with a $5 deposit.

We allow you to accelerate your growth by switching to a higher-interest certificate of deposit when your savings reach $1,005.

We'll send you quarterly statements to help you keep track of your progress.

Decatur Federal is a friend of the family.

DECATUR FEDERAL

FDIC INSURED

FIGURE 35–8 Most newspaper designers strive to make the inside pages as attractive and as easy to read as the front page. Here is an excellent example of inside-page makeup. (Courtesy of The Atlanta Journal and Constitution.)

FIGURE 35–9 Examples of tombstoned headlines. Most graphic designers try to avoid displaying stories in this fashion because they make the page look cluttered and often are difficult to read.

Tabloid Makeup

At one time in our modern history, tabloid-size newspapers were almost the exclusive property of metropolitan areas. Several of the nation's largest newspapers—the New York Daily News, Newsday on Long Island and the Chicago Sun-Times—are tabloids. However, increasing numbers of newspapers are turning to this smaller format. A tabloid page is approximately one-half a full page turned horizontally. The page is usually 10-1/2 by 14 inches, but the dimensions can vary by as much as two inches.

There are two basic kinds of makeup for the tabloid front page. The typical kind used in most metropolitan tabloids is called "poster." It will consist of a large photo (or several photos) and several large headlines. There generally are no stories, just headlines and photos on metro tabloid front pages. The headlines are keyed to stories on an inside page. As a general rule, the lead story appears on page three along with the story for the other front-page heads.

The poster technique, to be effective, requires excellent photos and stories with major impact. For that reason and others, another format for tabloid-size pages has developed. It is referred to as "compact." Although the term has not been widely accepted, the style of makeup has. The compact makeup uses the same techniques used for a full-size page, only with fewer stories, slightly smaller photos and smaller headlines.

Most of the general rules of good page makeup for a full-size page apply to the tabloid page. However, special effort should be made to avoid overcrowding tabloid pages with large masses of body type and large headlines. Pages should be designed horizontally with a minimum number of vertical items (stories with one-column heads and vertical photos).

Many tabloids leave four or more pages at the front of the issue free of advertisements to give the news department ample space to create attractively displayed news pages. Frequently several pages at the start of each special

FIGURE 35–10 The Los Angeles Times produces a special Spanish/English section to reach the large Spanish-speaking population in its circulation area. (Copyright 1991, Los Angeles Times. Reprinted by permission.)

section such as the sports section also are left free of advertisements to allow for a more dramatic display of news.

In making up a tabloid page containing advertisements, the general principles used in making up full-size pages should be followed.

EXERCISES

1. Invite the graphics or design editor of your local daily newspaper to class for a discussion of his or her work. Write a story on that discussion.

2. If your college or university has a graphics laboratory, invite the newspaper's graphics editor to demonstrate on a personal computer or Macintosh how the equipment is used in the design of the newspaper.

3. Make a study of the front-page and inside-page design of the four largest newspapers in your state. They should be available in your college or university library. Write a brief report on how they are similar and how they differ. Pick days when a major news event took place so you can compare the way each of the papers handled the story.

4. Redesign the front page of any newspaper available to you. Use all the same stories, photographs and other display elements—charts, information graphics and maps. It is permissible in this assignment to change the type size and column width of headlines. But do not add any additional stories. Use of a different-size masthead also is permissible for the exercise.

5. Adding the following national and international stories to the ones in Exercise 5, Chapter 34, select the stories you would place on the front page, using as many as needed for an attractive layout. Draw a front-page dummy of your layout. Specify which story goes in each position on the page and give the size of headline you would use:

   a. MIAMI BEACH, Fla.—Local school board has signed a contract with Education Alternatives, a Minneapolis firm, to operate a new public elementary school here for the next five years. First of its kind in the state.

   b. BOLOGNA, Italy—A burning military jet crashed into a classroom at a suburban high school today, killing 12 students, officials said. Many survivors jumped from windows, engulfed in heavy smoke. The pilot of the Italian Air Force jet had been trying to land his burning plane in a field near the school.

   c. ATLANTA, Ga.—The homicide rate among black men from the ages of 15 to 24 rose by two-thirds in the last five years, the Federal Centers for Disease Control reported. More than 95 percent of the increase grew out of a rise in the rate at which these young men were being killed by guns.

   d. JERUSALEM—One Israeli and one Palestinian were killed during a bus attack near Tel Aviv yesterday, as the Palestinian uprising made a rare stab into Israel's heartland.

   e. WARSAW, Poland—Poland's Roman Catholic bishops will for the first time issue a pastoral letter attacking the anti-Semitism that has darkened the country's name for centuries. The letter is the most explicit statement on Catholic-Jewish relations ever issued by the Polish church.

   f. ALBA IULIA, Romania—About 100,000 people gathered for the first post-Communist National Day on Saturday and President Ion Iliescu expressed hope for the return of Moldavia after 50 years under Soviet control.

   g. WASHINGTON—The unemployment insurance systems, the main government

program meant to ease the pain of recession, is much less effective than it used to
be, largely because the federal government and the states have let it wither rather
than raise taxes to sustain it, a report says.

h. SALEM, Ore.—Convicted child molester Richard Bateman, sent to prison after
refusing to post signs labeling him a sex offender, was freed on parole Thursday
after serving 32 months of a ten-year sentence.

i. NEW YORK—A teen-age boy who didn't want his mother to know he'd been hit by a
train walked home while police searched the tracks for a body. The 15-year-old boy
was hospitalized in good condition with a puncture and abrasion on his thigh and a
possible broken arm.

j. ANKARA, Turkey—Forty-eight thousand mine workers walked off the job today in
the largest strike since Turkey granted unions the right to strike in 1963.

GENERAL EXERCISES IN HEADLINING AND MAKEUP

On the following pages are two general exercises on editing, including selecting and
writing headlines and makeup. Each exercise contains a list of all the stories and pictures
available for use in making up one front page. Instructions for handling stories in each
exercise are as follows:

1. Sort the stories in order of their importance to the reader. While doing this, try to
visualize where you might place each story on your page. After the stories have been
sorted, use the accompanying headline schedule (samples of different headlines) to
determine what size of head each story deserves. This headline schedule includes all
sizes and types of heads you may use. Each head has been given an arbitrary number
(to expedite these assignments), and the maximum unit count per line is designated.
Keep in mind that all of these (and only these) stories are available for the front page of
your newspaper.

2. Write all headlines.

3. Make up a dummy front page using the headlines you have written. Page-size dummies,
marked off in two-inch columns (or whatever size column width the newspaper uses),
are usually available at nearby newspapers, or they can be made from a large art pad
available at bookstores. (Or, if the instructor so chooses, it will be satisfactory to line
off an unruled 8-1/2 by 11 sheet of writing paper, which will be half-scale, every inch
equal to two inches on the page-size dummy.) The page should be made up as follows:

a. Clip a flag or nameplate from a newspaper, and paste it in the proper place on the
dummy. (Students may design their own flags if they choose.)

b. Determine the appropriate place on the page for each story and picture in accor-
dance with the way you ranked them by their importance to the reader. Before the
actual front-page dummy is completed, you might want to practice arranging the
stories to determine the best display. An excellent way to do this is to clip headlines
similar to those in the headline schedule of this exercise and lay them on the
dummy page in various positions to give a clear picture of the appearance of the
page.

c. When a final decision is reached on the position of a story, print the story's headline
(which you have written) on the dummy in the space reserved for the head. (Make
certain to allow enough room for the heads on the dummy. To do this, measure the
size of the type in the headline schedule and then double or triple that amount,

depending on the number of lines in your headline. Allow at least one-eighth of an inch between lines and at the top and bottom of the head.) The size and style of the hand-printed letters should resemble as much as possible the size and style of letters in the headline schedule for this exercise.

d. In the column or columns below each head (where the story would appear if printed), measure and mark the amount of space necessary for the story. If a story is to be continued on another page, mark the length of the part jumped at the end of the story on page 1 (e.g., "5 inches jumped"). In the column space reserved for the story, write the key word (the slug) the reporter has used to identify the story on the original copy.

HEADLINE SCHEDULE

Notes: The schedule on pages 542–544 offers the instructor and the student considerable flexibility not only in selection of head sizes but also in style of headlines. It is flexible enough to permit the instructor to assign only one headline style if he or she chooses. On the other hand, it allows for considerable freedom on the part of the student who might want to experiment with various combinations of headlines such as the reverse kicker (see Chapter 34).

Kickers may be ordered for any of the multiple-column headlines in this schedule. They should be in a type size approximately one-half the size of the main headline and should not be more than half the width of the main head. (See Chapter 34). If kickers are ordered, write the main headline at least one count short to allow more white space around the head and to avoid a cluttered look.

Number of Head	Sample Letter and Description of Head	Size of Type	Maximum Count per Line in One Column (2¼ inches wide)
1	**S** Streamer—one line deep. Roman type, caps and lower case. Six, seven, or eight columns wide.	96	4 units
1a	**V** Streamer—one line deep. Roman type, caps and lowercase. Five, six, seven or eight columns. Also can be scheduled two lines deep.	84	4½ units
1b	**C** Streamer—one line deep. Roman type, caps and lowercase. Five, six, seven or eight columns. Also can be scheduled two lines deep.	72	5½ units
2	**F** Streamer—one line deep. Roman type, caps and lowercase. Five, six, seven or eight columns. Also can be scheduled two lines deep.	60	6½ units
2a	*F* Streamer—one line deep. Italic type, caps and lowercase. Five, six, seven or eight columns.	60	7½ units
3	**D** Two-column head, three lines deep. Roman type, caps and lowercase.	48	8 units
3a	*D* Three-column head, two lines deep, Italic type, caps and lower-case.	48	9 units
4	**R** Two-column head, two lines deep. Roman type, caps and lowercase	48	8 units
4a	*R* Two-column head, two lines deep. Italic type, caps and lower-case.	48	9 units

Number of Head		Sample Letter and Description of Head	Size of Type	Maximum Count per Line in One Column (2¼ inches wide)
5b	**M**	One-column head, three lines deep. Roman type, caps and lowercase.	36	9½ units
5a	**R**	Two-column head, two lines deep. Roman type, caps and lowercase.	36	9½ units
5	**V**	Three-column head, one line deep. Roman type, caps and lowercase.	36	9½ units
6	**H**	Two-column head, two lines deep. Roman type, caps and lowercase.	30	11½ units
6a	**O**	One-column head, three lines deep. Roman type, caps and lowercase.	30	11½ units
7	**N**	Two-column head, two lines deep. Roman type, caps and lowercase.	24	13½ units
7a	**E**	One-column head, two lines deep. Roman type, caps, and lowercase. Also can be scheduled three lines deep.	24	13½ units
7b	*C*	One-column head, two lines deep. Italic type, caps and lowercase. Also can be scheduled three lines deep.	24	14½ units
8	**T**	One-column head, two lines deep. Roman type, caps and lowercase. Also can be scheduled three lines deep.	18	18 units
8a	*P*	One-column head, two lines deep, Italic type, caps and lowercase. Also can be scheduled three lines deep.	18	19 units

(continued on page 544)

(continued from page 543)

Number of Head		Sample Letter and Description of Head	Size of Type	Maximum Count per Line in One Column (2¼ inches wide)
9	**H**	One-column, two lines deep. Roman type, caps and lowercase. Also can be scheduled three lines deep.	14	23 units
9a	*H*	One-column head, two lines deep. Italic type, caps and lower-case. Also can be scheduled three lines deep.	14	24 units

EXERCISES

1. Story notes appearing at the end of each preceding chapter of The Complete Reporter will be used for these two exercises. Because copy editing and rewriting are not involved, it is not necessary to have the stories written as they would appear in the newspaper. Select and write suitable headlines after a review of each set of notes.

　　The stories listed below by chapter and exercise number have been chosen as those "available" for the front page of one edition. Not all of the listed stories can be used. A slug (guideline) is designated for each story. The length of the story is also listed.

Chapter and Exercise Number	Page Numbers	Guideline	Length in Column Inches
Ch. 6, Ex. 3c	97	Crash	8
Ch. 6, Ex. 3e	98	Fire	9
Ch. 7, Ex. 2f	111	Suicide	12
Ch. 8, Ex. 5b	126	Scroggins	11
Ch. 9, Ex. 7	146	Bus	16
Ch. 10, Ex. 8c	166	Bees	7
Ch. 16, Ex. 6	247	Vaughn	14
Ch. 17, Ex. 8	259	Rehab	13
Ch. 18, Ex. 5a	274	Mushrooms	9
Ch. 19, Ex. 5f	286	Arrowhead	11
Ch. 20, Ex. 6b	299	Pollution	15
Ch. 20, Ex. 8	300	Winter	18
Ch. 21, Ex. 6g	320	Hijack	7
Ch. 22, Ex. 6d	341	Yates	8
Ch. 23, Ex. 8a	368	Budget	12

Pictures available for use, if desired, with preceding stories:

1. Three columns, 5 inches deep, fire at Broadway Cafe
2. Two columns, 4 inches deep, Dockery at podium
3. Two columns, 5 inches deep, Scroggins in ruined apartment
4. Three columns, 5 inches deep, couple with bee-infested house
5. Four columns, 6 inches deep, aerial shot of forest fires
6. Five columns, 6 inches deep, snow storm blankets city
7. One column, 3 inches deep, Yates

Instructions: Indicate placement of pictures on the dummy by putting a piece of colored construction paper over the space covered by each picture or by drawing in the representative size of the picture and marking a large "X" through it. Make certain to indicate the exact picture size and to indicate a space below each picture for the cutline.

Note: It will be impossible to use all of these stories on one page. Pick only the most significant ones.

2. Follow the same instructions as for Exercise 1.

Chapter and Exercise Number	Page Numbers	Guideline	Length in Column Inches
Ch. 6, Ex. 4b	99	Gunmen	6
Ch. 7, Ex. 2b	110	Chase	9
Ch. 8, Ex. 5a	125	Food stamps	5
Ch. 9, Ex. 9b	149	Testing	10
Ch. 9, Ex. 9c	150	Explode	8
Ch. 10, Ex. 4	164	Rusty	13
Ch. 16, Ex. 7	248	Cholesterol	12
Ch. 18, Ex. 5b	275	Johnson	5
Ch. 19, Ex. 5a	284	Crash	9
Ch. 19, Ex. 5e	286	Sunset	12
Ch. 20, Ex. 9	301	Fog	20
Ch. 21, Ex. 6f	320	Drugs	15
Ch. 22, Ex. 7	342	Ringgold	14
Ch. 23, Ex. 8b	369	Layoffs	10
Ch. 23, Ex. 8c	369	Welfare	9

Pictures available for use, if desired with preceding stories:

1. Two columns, 4 inches deep, store clerk who was robbed by gunmen
2. Three columns, 5 inches deep, Rusty, the beer-drinking pig
3. Two columns, 5 inches deep, Asst. Fire Chief Johnson nursing injured leg
4. Three columns, 5 inches deep, drug suspects being taken to police station
5. One column, 3 inches deep, Human Services director

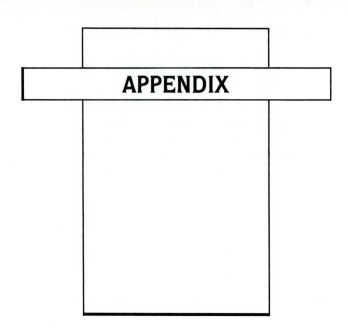

APPENDIX

PREPARING COPY

Most newspaper reporters write their stories on video-display terminals (VDTs) and follow a set of guidelines for preparing their copy that have been developed for that particular newspaper. In many ways they are quite similar to the instructions for preparing a piece of copy on a typewriter; however, more codes generally are used. (See example in Chapter 32.)

For those writers who still use typewriters, here is how your copy should be prepared:

1. Prepare all copy with a typewriter.
2. Begin every story on a new sheet of paper (copy paper is generally 8-1/2 by 11 inches in size).
3. Place your name at the upper left-hand corner of every page.
4. Write the guideline or slug for the story in the same line with your name or in the line below it. This line is a brief identification of the story, such as "fire" for a fire story or "city council" for a report of a city council meeting.
5. Number every page at the top, following the slug.
6. On the first page, leave ample space between the slug and the first paragraph—from one-fourth to one-third of the page.
7. Leave margins of at least one inch on both sides.
8. Double-space all copy.
9. Type on one side of the paper only.
10. Indent five spaces to begin a paragraph.
11. Do not underline.

12. Four-line paragraphs are optimum.
13. Do not split a word at the end of a line.
14. Do not split sentences between pages, and avoid splitting paragraphs between pages.
15. Write "more" or draw a short down-pointed arrow in the center at the end of each page when the story continues on another page.
16. Place an end mark (# or 30) in the center of the page at the end of the story.

COPYREADING SYMBOLS

Copy editors use a standard set of symbols that in most instances allows them to indicate changes without using words. Following is a list:

Symbol	Definition	Example
⊗ or ⊙	Period mark	He was there⊗ He was there◯
∧	Comma	Therefore∧ he will . . .
∨	Apostrophe	Ill let you know . . .
∨″	Quotation marks	I'll let you know . . .
≡ or ⟋	Make capital letter	later that monday . . .
/	Make lowercase letter	Later in The day . . .
◯	Abbreviate or spell out word or number	Doctor Smith said . . . . Dr. Wm. Smith said . . . The 2 men were . . . The twelve men were . . .
⌊ or ⌋ or ¢	Start new paragraph	⌊The end of the . . . ⌋The end of the . . . ¢ The end of the . . .
no ¢	Do not make this a new paragraph	no ¢ The end of . . .

Symbol	Definition	Example
] or [	Indent on left or right	This symbol may be used on either side of the page or on both sides. If used on both sides, it indicates that the material should be centered.
/	Separate letters	Some of our students . . .
⌒	Bring letters together or close space	So me of the students . . . Some of the students . . .
Line from one word to the beginning of the following word.	Bring copy together or join paragraphs	Four men who were found were found adrift near . . .
⊜	Delete letter, word, or phrase	Saailing on . . . Sailing on on toward . . .
∧ or ⌄	Insert letter, word, or phrase	Sailing on . . . Sailing on the . . .
⁓	Transpose letters, words, or phrases	Salifing on . . . Sailing to on the . . .
Stet	Restore original text	Four of the men . . .
∿	Set in boldface text	New residents here . . .
_____	Set in italics	The habeas corpus case

CORRECTING COPY

Although stories written on VDTs are corrected electronically, it is still useful for reporters to learn the standard copy editing symbols. The following are examples of the symbols that are used universally whenever written material is corrected by hand.

Delete letters:

Two men were in the car. . . . .

Delete word or words:

Two men were were in the car behind us with. . . . .

Transpose letters or words:

Two men in were the car with. . . .

Spell out or abbreviate (same symbol in both cases):

②men were in the car with Mister Jones.

Insert word or words:

were
Two men in the car with Mr. Jones.

Capitalize letter:

two men were in the car with. . . .

Make letter lowercase:

Two Men were in the car. . . .

Period mark (either of two symbols):

Two men were in the car with Mr. Jones⊗

Separate letters with space:

Two men were in the car. . . .

Bring letters together:

Two men we re in the car. . . .

Restore copy that has been marked out:

stet
Two men were in the car with Mr. Jones.

In deleting copy on more than one line, mark out all the deleted material and draw a heavy line directly from the beginning to the end of the deleted material:

Located in the center of the little island is a log cabin, built perhaps 100 years ago though no one knows for sure and there is no way of finding out and back of the cabin is the site of the old Indian village.

In correcting misspelled words that have only one or two letters wrong, mark out each misused letter and place the correct letter above it. If a word is badly misspelled, mark out the whole word and write it correctly above:

The b~~o~~y walked ~~nonchalontly~~ into the room.

The reporter should use symbols whenever possible in correcting copy because they are time-saving devices. However, if a phrase (or word) is split between two lines, the simplest procedure is to mark through all or part of the phrase and rewrite it correctly between the lines.

JOURNALISTIC TERMS

Ad. Advertisement.

Add. Copy to be added to a story already written.

Advance. A preliminary story concerning a future event.

Agate. Type 5-1/2 points in depth (72 points to the inch).

A.M. Morning paper.

Angle. The aspect emphasized in a story.

A.P. or AP. The Associated Press, press service.

Art. All newspaper illustrations.

Assignment. Reporter's task.

Bank. (1) Part of headline (also called "deck"); (2) table on which type is set.

Banner. A page-wide headline (also called "streamer").

Barline. A one-line headline.

Beat. (1) The reporter's regular run; (2) an exclusive story.

B.F. or bf. Boldface or black type.

Blind interview. Interview that does not give name of person interviewed.

Blurb. A short statement used to promote the sale of a new book or publication.

Body type. Small type in which most of paper is set.

Boil down. Reduce in size.

Border. Metal or paper strips of type used to box stories, ads, etc.

Box. An enclosure of line rules or borders.

Break. (1) The point at which a story is continued to another column or page; (2) as a verb, refers to the time a story is available for publication.

Bromide. A trite expression.

Bulletin. A brief, last-minute news item on an important event.

By-line. The author's name at the start of a story—"By John Smith."

C. and L.C. or clc. Capital and lowercase letters.

Canned copy. Publicity material.

Caps. Capital letters.

Caption. See Cutlines.

City editor. Person in charge of local news; also called "Metropolitan editor" at some papers.

Clip. Newspaper clipping.

Code. Key words or letters on VDT to assign functions or routines.

Col. Column.

Condensed type. Type that is narrower than regular width.

Copy. All typewritten material.

Copy desk. Where stories are edited and headlines written.

Copy editor. One who edits and headlines news stories.

Correspondent. Out-of-town reporter.

Cover. To get the facts of a story.

Credit line. Line acknowledging source of a story or picture.

CRT. System of editing using a cathode-ray tube and computer or memory bank that produces paper or electronic tape used in composing machines to produce "type"; also see VDT.

Crusade. Campaign of a newspaper for a certain reform.

Cub. A beginning reporter.

Cut. (1) A newspaper engraving; (2) to reduce the length of a story.

Cutlines. Explanatory lines describing a picture or illustration, usually under the picture; also called "captions."

Dateline. Line at the beginning of a story that includes both date and place of origin of story: "NEW YORK, Jan. 1—."

Deadline. The time all copy must be completed in order to make an edition.

Deck. Part of a multibank headline.

Desk. The copy desk.

Double truck. Two adjoining pages made as one.

Down style. A newspaper headline style calling for a minimum of capitalization.

Dummy: Diagram of a page for use in making up a page.

Dump. Changing stored material from one computer unit to another.

Ear. Small box in the upper corners of the nameplate (flag).

Edition. Issue for one press run, as "mail edition," "home edition," "extra edition."

Editorialize. To include opinion of the writer in copy.

Embargo. A restriction, such as the precise date and time, placed on the release of news.

Filler. Short news or informational items used to fill small spaces in a page.

Flag. Name of paper appearing on first page.

Flash. A short message briefly summarizing a news event.

Fold. Place where paper is folded.

Folio. Page or page number.

Follow or Follow-up. Story giving later developments of an event already written up.

Follow copy. Instructions on copy to set story or word exactly as written, used often to indicate that word is purposely misspelled or that spelling is unorthodox.

Folo. Short for "follow."

Font. Type face of one size and style.

Fotog. Short for photographer.

Future file. File in which stories coming up at later date are kept.

FYI. For your information.

Galley. Metal tray for holding type. In offset, the columns of type to be pasted down also are called galleys.

Galley proof. Proof made of a galley of type.

Graf. Short for "paragraph."

Guideline. A slug line, giving title of the story for convenience of makeup editor and compositors.

Halftone. A cut made from a photograph.

Hammer. See Kicker.

Head. Short for "headline."

Headline schedule. All of the headline combinations used by a newspaper.

Hold for release. Instructions to hold copy until editor orders it printed.

HTK or HTC. Instructions on copy of a "head to come."

Insert. Copy that is to be inserted in a story already sent to the compositor.

Interface. Hardware (the VDT's backup machines) "talking to each other."

Itals. Italics.

Jump. To continue a story from one page to another.

Jump head. Headline above a continued story.

Jump lines. Lines such as "Continued on page 6" or "Continued from page 1" to identify a continued story.

Kicker. A short one-line head, sometimes underlined, either centered above or slightly to the left of main head, usually in type about one-half type size of main head; also called "hammer."

Kill. To delete or exclude copy.

Layout. (1) Diagram of page (see Dummy), showing where stories and ads are to be placed; (2) arrangement of pictures on picture page.

L.C. or lc. Lowercase type.

Lead(lĕd). (1) As noun, metal pieces placed between lines of type for spacing; (2) as verb, to space out page with these metal pieces in hot-metal typesetting operations.

Lead (leed). The first paragraph of a news story.

Leg man. Reporter who gathers news, phoning it in instead of going to newspaper office to write it.

Letterpress printing. Process of printing that uses metal type or other raised surfaces that make a direct impression on paper.

Library. Newspaper morgue or files of clippings, photographs, prepared obituaries, biographies, etc.

Localize. To emphasize the local angle in a story.

Log. City editor's assignment book.

Make-over. Rearrangement of stories on page to provide for new copy or to change the position of stories.

Makeup. Arranging stories, pictures, ads, etc., on a page.

Masthead. Editorial page heading that gives information about the newspaper.

Matrix or Mat. A matrix or papier-mâché impression of a cut or of type.

Minion. Seven-point type.

Modem. Portable device that allows reporters in field to write stories and feed them by telephone to computer at the newspaper.

More. Used at end of a page of copy to indicate story is continued on another page.

Morgue. Files for depositing clippings, pictures, etc. (also called "library").

Mug shot. Head-and-shoulders photograph of an individual.

Must. Instructions that story must be used on that day without fail.

Nameplate. Name of paper on page 1 (also called "flag").

Newsprint. The grade of paper used in printing newspapers.

Nonpareil. Six-point type.

Obit. Obituary.

Offset printing. Process of printing that uses a rubber roller that takes the impression from a metal plate and transfers it to the paper.

Op-Ed. Page opposite the editorial page featuring comment, cartoons and other editorial matter.

Overline. Caption above a cut. Also another word for kicker.

Overset. Type in addition to that needed to fill a paper.

Pad. To make longer.

Pasteup. Method of making up a page for the camera in the offset process—pasting in proofs of headlines, body type, line drawings, etc.

Pica. Twelve-point type; also unit of measurement, one-sixth of an inch.

Pick up. Instructions to use material already set in type.

Pix. Picture.

Plate. A stereotyped page of type, ready to lock in press.

Play up. To emphasize.

P.M. Afternoon paper.

Point. A depth measurement of type approximately 1/72 inch.

Policy story. A story showing directly or indirectly the newspaper's stand on an issue.

Precede. Material to precede the copy already set in type.

Proof. An imprint of set type used in correcting errors.

Proofreader. Person who reads proof to correct errors.

Puff. Editorialized, complimentary statements in a news story.

Purge. Eliminate data from the system.

Q and A. Question-and-answer copy, printed verbatim.

Quad. A type character or space equal in width and height.

Query. Question on an event sent by a correspondent to a paper or by a paper to a correspondent.

Queue. Order of priority in scheduling; each schedule is known as a "queue."

Quote. Quotation.

Railroad. To rush copy through to be typeset without careful editing.

Release. Instructions on the time to publish a story, as "Release after 3 p.m. Feb. 6."

Rewrite. (1) To write a story again to improve; (2) to write a story that already has been reported in a competing newspaper; (3) to write a story from facts given by another reporter (sometimes from a leg man over the telephone).

Roll up/down. Commands moving story on a terminal screen.

Rule. Metal strip or paper tape used in separating columns, making borders, etc.

Run. A press run (edition).

Run in. Instructions to make a series of sentences, names, etc., into one paragraph, if each one of the series has been set up as a separate short paragraph or line.

Running story. Story sent to compositor in sections. Also a story reported over several days or weeks.

Runover. Part of a story that is continued on another page.

Sacred cow. News or promotional

material that the publisher or editor demands be printed in a special manner.

Scanner. Optical character reader (also known as OCR), which converts typewritten material to electronic impulses and transmits them to a tape punch or computer.

Schedule. List of assignments.

Scoop. An exclusive story.

Second front. The first page of a second section.

Sked. Schedule.

Slant. To emphasize a certain phase of a news event.

Slot. The place occupied by the head of the copy desk (on the inside of horseshoe-shaped desks). Slot man is also called "copy desk chief."

Slug. (1) The guideline at the beginning of the story, to make it easy to identify (see Guideline); (2) a strip of metal, less than type height and used to space between lines; (3) a line of type cast by the typesetting machine.

Sort. Arranging material in a specific sequence.

Squib. A brief story.

Stet. Restore text of copy that has been marked out. (This is a copyreaders' and proofreaders' sign.)

Streamer. Headline stretching completely across a page (also called "banner").

String. Newspaper clippings pasted together.

Subhead. Small, one-line headline used in the body of a story.

System. The computer and computer programs used in a newsroom.

Take. A section of a running story.

Terminal. Common name for VDT used by reporters and editors.

Thirty. The end of a story (numeral usually used).

Tie-back or Tie-in. That part of the story which reiterates past events to remind the reader or to give background for the latest developments.

Time copy. Copy that might be held over and used when needed.

Top heads. Headline at top of a column.

Tr. Transpose or change the position of.

Trim. Reduce length of story.

U.C. and L.C. Uppercase and lowercase type.

U.P.I. or UPI. United Press International, press service.

VDT. Short for "video display terminal," which looks like a typewriter with a small television set sitting on top of it. Stories may be composed or corrected on these units and stored in a computer for later use or may be punched into paper tape for use in photocomposition machines.

Wrong font or W.F. Wrong style or size of type.

SELECTED BIBLIOGRAPHY

General References on Journalistic Writing

Berner, R. Thomas. *Language Skills for Journalists.* Boston: Houghton Mifflin, 1979.

Bernstein, Theodore M. *Watch Your Language.* Manhasset. N.Y.: Channel Press, 1958.

Callihan, E. R. *Grammar for Journalists.* Radnor, Pa.: Chilton Book Co., 1979.

Cutlip, Scott M., and Allen H. Center. *Effective Public Relations.* 5th ed. Englewood Cliffs, N.J.: Prentice-Hall, 1982.

Kilpatrick, James J. *The Writer's Art.* Kansas City: Andrews, McMeel & Parker, Inc., 1984.

MacDougall, Curtis D. *Interpretative Reporting.* 8th ed. New York: Macmillan, 1982.

Metzler, Ken. *Creative Interviewing.* Englewood Cliffs, N.J.: Prentice-Hall, 1977.

Meyer, Philip. *Precision Journalism: A Reporter's Introduction to Social Science Methods.* Bloomington, Ind.: Indiana State University Press, 1975.

Mollenhoff, Clark R. *Investigative Reporting.* New York: Macmillan, 1981.

Rivers, William L. *Finding Facts.* Englewood Cliffs, N.J.: Prentice-Hall, 1975.

————. *Writing: Craft and Art.* Englewood Cliffs, N.J.: Prentice-Hall, 1975.

Schulte, Henry H. *Reporting Public Affairs.* New York: Macmillan, 1981.

Shertzer, Margaret. *The Elements of Grammar.* New York: Collier Books Macmillan, 1986.

Stonecipher, Harry W. *Editorial and Persuasive Writing.* New York: Hastings House, 1979.

Strunk, William, Jr., and E. B. White. *The Elements of Style.* 3rd ed. New York: Macmillan, 1979.

Zinsser, William. *On Writing Well.* 2nd ed. New York: Harper & Row, 1980.

Journalism and Society

(Freedom of the press, journalistic ethics, legal aspects of journalism, public opinion and propaganda)

DeFleur, Melvin L., and Everett C. Dennis. *Understanding Mass Communications.* Boston: Houghton Mifflin, 1981.

Dennis, Everett C., and John C. Merrill. *Basic Issues in Mass Communication.* New York: Macmillan, 1984.

Gilmore, Donald M., and Jerome A. Barron. *Mass Communications Law Cases and Commentary.* St. Paul, Minn.: West Publishing Co., 1984.

Huiteng, John, and Roy Paul Nelson. *The Fourth Estate.* New York: Harper & Row, 1983.

Pember, Don R. *Mass Media in America.* 6th ed. New York: Macmillan, 1992.

————. *Mass Media Law.* 3rd ed. Dubuque, Ia.: Wm C. Brown Co., 1984.

References on Special Types of Journalistic Writing

Blundell, William E. *The Wall Street Journal: Storytelling Step by Step.* New York: Dow Jones & Company Inc., 1986.

Hunt, Todd. *Reviewing for the Mass Media.* Radnor, Pa.: Chilton Book Co., 1972.

Kelly, Jerome E. *Magazine Article Writing Today.* Cincinnati, Ohio: Writer's Digest Books, 1978.

Kohlmeier, Louis M. Jr., Jon G. Udell, and Laird B. Anderson. *Reporting on Business and the Economy.* Englewood Cliffs, N.J.: Prentice-Hall, 1981.

Ruehlmann, William. *Stalking the Feature Story.* New York: Vintage Books, 1979.

Ullmann, John, and Steve Honeyman, eds. *The Reporter's Handbook: An Investigator's Guide to Documents and Techniques.* New York: St. Martin's Press, 1983.

The Journalistic Profession

(History of journalism, biographies of famous journalists, journalism as a profession)

Berger, Meyer. *The Story of the New York Times.* New York: Simon and Schuster, 1951.

Berges, Marshall. *The Life and Times of the Los Angeles Times: A Newspaper, a Family and a City.* New York: Atheneum, 1984.

Brucker, Herbert. *Communication is Power: Unchanging Ideas in Changing Journalism.* New York: Oxford University Press, 1973.

———. *Eyewitness to History.* New York: Macmillan, 1962.

Buranelli, V., ed. *The Trial of Peter Zenger.* New York: New York University Press, 1957.

Canham, E. D. *Commitment to Freedom: The Story of the Christian Science Monitor.* Boston: Houghton Mifflin, 1958.

Carlson, O. *The Man Who Made News: James Gordon Bennett.* New York: Duell, Sloan & Pearce, 1942.

Deakin, James. *Straight Stuff: The Reporters, the White House and the Truth.* New York: William Morrow & Co., Inc., 1984.

Emery, Edwin, and Michael Emery. *The Press in America.* 5th ed. Englewood Cliffs, N.J.: Prentice-Hall, 1984.

Fowler, Gene. *Timber Line: A Story of Bonfils and Tammen.* Garden City, N.Y.: Halcyon House, 1943.

Gramling, O. *AP: The Story of News.* New York: Farrar, 1940.

Johnson, G. W. *An Honorable Titan: A Biographical Study of Adolph S. Ochs.* New York: Harper, 1946.

Johnson, Michael L. *The New Journalism.* Lawrence, Kan.: University of Kansas Press, 1971.

Kaltenborn, H. V. *Fifty Fabulous Years. 1900–1950.* New York: Putnam, 1950.

Kelly, Tom. *The Imperial Post.* New York: William Morrow & Co., Inc., 1983.

Kluger, Richard. *The Paper: The Life and Death of the New York Herald Tribune.* New York: Alfred A. Knopf, 1986.

Knight, Oliver, ed. *I Protest: Selected Disquisitions of E. W. Scripps.* Madison, Wis.: University of Wisconsin Press, 1969.

McNulty, John B. *Older Than the Nation: The Story of the Hartford Courant.* Stonington, Conn.: Pequot Press, 1964.

Miller, Lee. *The Story of Ernie Pyle.* New York: Viking Press, 1950.

Morris, J. A. *Deadline Every Minute.* Garden City, N.Y.: Doubleday, 1957.

Mott, F. L. *American Journalism: A History of Newspapers in the United States Through 270 Years, 1690–1960.* New York, Macmillan, 1962.

———. *Jefferson and the Press.* Baton Rouge, La.: Louisiana State University Press, 1943.

Nixon, R. B. *Henry W. Grady: Spokesman of the New South.* New York: Knopf, 1943.

Pilat, Oliver. *Drew Pearson: An Unauthorized Biography.* New York: Harpers Magazine Press, 1973.

Robertson, Charles L. *The International Herald Tribune: The First 100 Years.* New York: Columbia University Press, 1987.

Ross, I. *Ladies of the Press.* New York: Harper, 1936.

Rucker, Bryce W. *Twentieth Century Reporting at Its Best.* Ames, Iowa: Iowa State University Press, 1965.

Salisbury, Harrison E. *Without Fear or Favor: An Uncompromising Look at The New York Times.* New York: Ballantine Books, 1981.

Seitz, Don Carlos. *Horace Greeley: Founder of the New York Tribune.* New York: AMS Press, 1970.

Starr, L. M. *Bohemian Brigade: Civil War Newsmen in Action.* New York: Knopf, 1954.

Stone, C. *Dana and the Sun.* New York: Dodd, Mead, 1938.

Swanberg, W. A. *Citizen Hearst.* New York: Charles Scribner's Sons, 1961.

———. *Pulitzer.* Charles Scribner's Sons, 1967.

Talese, Gay. *The Kingdom and the Power.* New York: World Publishing Co., 1969.

Williamson, Samuel T. *Frank Gannett: A Biography.* New York: Duell, Sloan & Pearce, 1940.

References on News Editing and Design

American Press Institute. *Newspaper Design: 2000 and Beyond.* Reston, Va.: American Press Institute, 1989.

Baskette, Floyd K., Jack Z. Sissors, and Brian S. Brooks. *The Art of Editing.* 3rd ed. New York: Macmillan, 1982.

Craig, James. *Designing with Type: A Basic Course in Typography.* New York: Watson-Guptill Publications, 1971.

Garcia, Mario. *Contemporary Newspaper Design.* Englewood Cliffs, N.J.: Prentice-Hall, 1981.

Gerst, Robert E., and Theodore M. Bernstein. *Headlines and Deadlines.* 4th ed. New York: Columbia University Press, 1982.

Harrow, Tim. *The Newspaper Designer's Handbook.* Portland, Ore.: Oregonian Publishing Co., 1989.

Hollstein, Milton, and Larry Kurtz. *Editing with Understanding.* New York: Macmillan, 1981.

Nelson, Roy Paul. *Publications Design.* 3rd ed. Dubuque, Iowa: Wm. C. Brown Co., 1983.

Plotnik, Arthur. *The Elements of Editing: A Modern Guide for Editors and Journalists.* New York: Macmillan, 1982.

Stovall, James G., Charles C. Self, and L. Edward Mullins. *On Line Editing.* Englewood Cliffs, N.J.: Prentice-Hall, 1984.

Westley, Bruce H. *News Editing.* 3rd ed. Boston: Houghton Mifflin, 1980.

INDEX